London
for Children

www.timeout.com

Time Out Guides Limited
Universal House
251 Tottenham Court Road
London W1T 7AB
Tel + 44 (0)20 7813 3000
Fax + 44 (0)20 7813 6001
Email guides@timeout.com
www.timeout.com

Editorial
Editor Ronnie Haydon
Deputy Editor Ros Sales
Sub Editor Jan Fuscoe
Researchers Jill Emeny, Cathy Limb, Patrick Welch
Proofreader Sylvia Tombesi-Walton
Indexer Anna Raikes

Editorial/Managing Director Peter Fiennes
Series Editor Sarah Guy
Deputy Series Editor Cath Phillips
Business Manager Gareth Garner
Guides Co-ordinator Holly Pick
Accountant Kemi Olufuwa

Design
Art Director Scott Moore
Art Editor Pinelope Kourmouzoglou
Senior Designer Josephine Spencer
Graphic Designer Henry Elphick
Digital Imaging Dan Conway
Ad Make-up Jenni Prichard

Picture Desk
Picture Editor Jael Marschner
Deputy Picture Editor Tracey Kerrigan
Picture Researcher Helen McFarland

Advertising
Sales Director/Sponsorship Mark Phillips
Sales Manager Alison Wallen
Advertising Sales Ben Holt, Ali Lowry, Jason Trotman
Copy Controller Amy Nelson
Advertising Assistant Kate Staddon

Marketing
Marketing Manager Yvonne Poon
Marketing & Publicity Manager, US Rosella Albanese
Marketing Designer Anthony Huggins

Production
Production Manager Brendan McKeown
Production Co-ordinator Caroline Bradford

Time Out Group
Chairman Tony Elliott
Managing Director Mike Hardwick
Financial Director Richard Waterlow
TO Magazine Ltd MD David Pepper
Group General Manager/Director Nichola Coulthard
TO Communications Ltd MD David Pepper
Production Director Mark Lamond
Group Marketing Director John Luck
Group Art Director John Oakey
Group IT Director Simon Chappell

Contributors
Introduction Ronnie Haydon. **The Story of London** Fiona Cumberpatch. **Festivals & Events** Jill Emeny, Ros Sales. **Around Town** Introduction Ronnie Haydon; South Bank & Bankside Kathryn Miller (A Wholesome Proposition Ronnie Haydon); The City Kelley Knox; Holborn & Clerkenwell Jill Emeny; Bloomsbury & Fitzrovia Cathy Limb; Marylebone Ronnie Haydon; West End Joe Bindloss; Covent Garden & St Giles's Chloë Lola Riess; Westminster Kathryn Miller; Kensington & Chelsea Kathryn Miller; North London Ronnie Haydon, Zoë Munro (The greening of King's Cross Joe Bindloss); East London Sue Webster; South-east London Ronnie Haydon, Cyrus Shahrad; South-west London Arwa Haider; West London Cyrus Shahrad (Please look after this bear Andrew Staffell). **Eating** Ronnie Haydon and contributors to Time Out Eating & Drinking guide. **Shopping** Ronnie Haydon (Push the button Fiona Cumberpatch, Bought the T-shirt? Cathy Limb, 'I bought it on eBay Kelley Knox); Art & Entertainment Arwa Haider (Dance, then, whoever you may be Kelley Knox). **Parties** Cathy Limb, Ronnie Haydon. **Sport & Leisure** Andrew Shields (Grinding on Kelley Knox). **Days Out** Ronnie Haydon (Sea views Cyrus Shahrad). **Directory** Ronnie Haydon, Ros Sales.

The Editor would like to thank Oliver Basciano at Kew, our models Anthony, Charlotte, Esme, Jane, Oliver, Sebastian, plus Naomi Cooper, Anna Fiennes, Jane, Bruce, John and Rick Jones, and all contributors to previous editions of Time Out London for Children, whose work forms the basis for parts of this book.

Maps JS Graphics (john@jsgraphics.co.uk).

Cover and page 3 photography Adrian Myers, taken at Climbers and Creepers, Kew Gardens (020 8332 5655; www.kew.org/ climbersandcreepers; see page 148).

Photography pages 5, 7, 33, 38, 41, 68, 69, 85, 86, 91, 107, 114, 126, 129, 136, 139, 143, 151, 158, 161, 175, 180, 181, 183, 187, 197, 229, 241, 289 Tricia de Courcy Ling; page 8 Geoff Langan; page 9 Random House; page 11 (top) Private Collection/Bridgeman Art Library; page 11 (bottom) Getty Images; page 12 Mary Evans Picture Library; page 15 Yale Centre for British Art, Paul Mellon Collection/Bridgeman Art Library; page 16 Topfoto.co.uk; page 17 G. Macdominic/Lebrecht; page 18 Lebrecht Music & Arts; page 19 Adrian Dennis/AFP/Getty Images; pages 25, 123, 150, 168, 169, 179 Heloise Bergman; pages 27, 237, 287 Alys Tomlinson; pages 29, 43, 47, 49, 55, 56, 59, 60, 61, 62, 71, 72, 75, 79, 83, 95, 97, 98, 101, 102, 132, 146, 154, 163, 190, 191, 199, 210, 213, 224, 232, 235, 244, 260, 261, 262, 275, 281 Andrew Brackenbury; page 37 Aine Donovan; page 53, 65, 78, 93 Jonathan Perugia; page 109 Piers Allardyce; page 193 Nichole Rees; page 204 Cathy Limb; page 223 EPO; page 249 Stephen Novy; page 251 London 2012; page 254 www.thedavidbeckhamacademy.com; page 271 (top left) Amanda C Edwards; page 271 Mockford & Bonetti.
The following images were provided by the featured establishment/artist: pages 22, 28, 52, 99, 110, 120, 138, 144, 145, 148, 149, 160, 185, 207, 215, 267.

Colour reprographics Wyndeham Icon, 3 & 4 Maverton Road, London, E3 2JE.
Printed and bound Cayfosa-Quebecor, Ctra. de Caldes km3, 08130 Sta. Perpetua de Mogoda, Barcelona, Spain.

ISBN: until 31 January 2006   1 905 042 051
        after 1 January 2007   9781 9050 42050

Distributed by Seymour Ltd (020 7936 8000).

Distributed in USA by Publishers Group West.

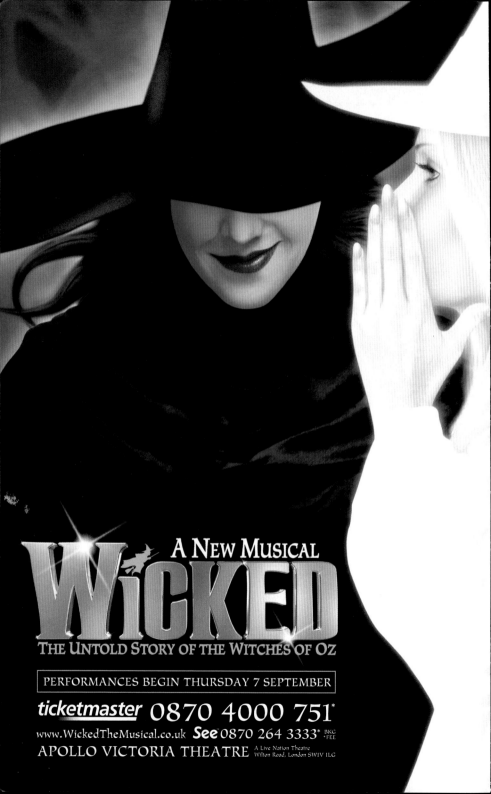

Contents

Introduction

London is one of the world's major business, political and cultural centres, as well as one of its oldest. And youngest. The city dates back 2,000 years, but nearly a quarter of its population haven't yet celebrated their 18th birthday. For these young people, London can be a confusing and bad-tempered city. Indeed, any grown-up who has experienced a rush-hour tube journey would dispute any notion of London distinguishing itself as a child-friendly place. Yet that is exactly what London must be, says the Mayor of London, Ken Livingstone. He has a vested interest; he's bringing up two children in this city. Part of his child-friendly mission was to set up the Children and Young People's Unit at City Hall a couple of years ago.

With or without Ken, London has, over the last five years, become a better place to explore with kids. More museums are free; they're all more entertaining. More parks are well maintained and safe to play in. Few restaurants these days would turn away family groups, and the number of eating places that sell themselves on the minor dining experience grows year by year. There are frequent parades and festivals that reclaim the city's streets for its people. Best of all, improving public transport is a big issue for Mayor Ken. He's made travel on the underground free for under-11s, and bus travel free for under-16s, so getting out to explore all of this metropolis is much more affordable. And fun – which is where this exceedingly child-friendly guide comes in.

TIME OUT LONDON FOR CHILDREN GUIDE

This is the sixth edition of the *Time Out London for Children Guide*, produced by the people behind the successful listings magazines and travel guide series. It is written by resident experts to provide you with all the information you'll need to explore the city, whether you're a local or a first-time visitor.

THE LOWDOWN ON THE LISTINGS

Addresses, phone numbers, websites, transport information, opening times, admission prices and credit card details are included in the listings.

Details of facilities, services and events were all checked and correct as we went to press. Before you go out of your way, however, we'd advise you to phone and check opening times, ticket prices and other particulars. While every effort has been made to ensure the accuracy of the information contained in this guide, the publishers cannot accept any responsibility for any errors it may contain.

FAMILY-FRIENDLY INFORMATION

Having visited all the places with our children, we've added essential information for families. Where we think it's important, we've stated whether a building can accommodate pushchairs ('buggy access'), or if there's a place to change a nappy ('nappy-changing facilities'). We've also listed the nearest picnic place.

Attractions are required to provide reasonable facilities for disabled visitors, although it's always best to check accessibility before setting out.

Disabled visitors requiring information about getting around the city can call GLAD (Greater London Action on Disability) on 7022 1890 or check the website www.glad.org.uk.

PRICES AND PAYMENT

We have noted where venues accept the following credit cards: American Express (AmEx), Diners Club (DC), MasterCard (MC) and Visa (V).

THE LIE OF THE LAND

Map references are included for each venue that falls on our street maps (starting on p310), but we recommend that you follow the example of the locals and invest in a standard A-Z map of the city.

PHONE NUMBERS

The area code for London is 020. All phone numbers given in this guide take this code unless otherwise stated, so add 020 if calling from outside London; otherwise, simply dial the number as written. The international dialling code for the UK is 44.

In Context

Jacqueline Wilson

The Children's Laureate has a busy year ahead.

As far as children are concerned, Jacqueline Wilson had earned her laurels as a national hero years before she was named Children's Laureate in 2005. Her affability is legendary. Back in March 2004, when she turned up to sign books in a Bournemouth bookshop she attracted a queue of about 3,000 besotted children. She stayed eight hours so that she could meet each child. Emily, who queued for several hours to get her copy of *Best Friends* signed, admitted it was a tiring wait, but a massive thrill to meet her 'favourite ever author' Wilson, who signed and smiled until nearly midnight. It was, it's generally agreed, the longest book-signing ever.

Jacqueline Wilson doesn't like to let people down, least of all her fans, which is why this most accessible of laureates finds herself frantically busy. Her gruelling schedule of openings, appearances and special events has become even more high profile thanks to her new role, but she's never too busy to promote a cause that's close to her heart: encouraging a love of books in children.

Awarded the OBE in 2002 for services to children's literature, Wilson spends a lot of time in libraries, which is apt, since she deposed Catherine Cookson as the most borrowed author in the nation's libraries for two years running. 'I opened a new library on Whitechapel Road [the Idea Store, opened 2005]. I'm also very excited about a special event that I recently took part in in the British Library. It was organised by the Fostering Network, who take care of real-life Tracy Beakers.' Tracy Beaker, Wilson's most popular character, lives in a foster home. 'It was an event to promote reading and address the educational needs of looked-after children.'

'I'm glad the post of Children's Laureate is two years because it gives you the chance to get projects up and running. If it was one year you'd spend all your time rushing about trying to see things through.'

Jacqueline Wilson was planning a trip to London to visit the Queen when we spoke to her. The Children's Party in the Palace (25 June 2006), was Her Majesty's beanfeast to celebrate children's literature in its many forms. Jacqueline's diary, however, was choc-a-bloc with reading-related shindigs, right up until her laureate job comes to an end in May 2007.

'I am very busy. I'm one of the judges for the Orange Prize. I'm judging a writing competition at Shakespeare's Globe, taking part in The Word children's literature event at the Polka Theatre. In the autumn I shall be at Downing Street, then at a conference at Congress House in Great Russell Street. Then I'm doing a tour in the first three weeks of October for my new book *Starring Tracy Beaker*.'

Jacqueline Wilson's message as laureate is that reading is 'cool and enjoyable' – whatever your age. In May 2006 she published a book, *Great Books to Read Aloud*, recommending 70 books for reading to your children, not just the little ones who can't read for themselves, but older kids too.

Jacqueline Wilson's books, renowned for their unsugared depictions of modern family life, are great for reading aloud. Wilson's heroines (they're usually young girls) may have experience of divorce, domestic violence or homelessness, but the stories are more optimistic and funny than grim and gritty, and children can't get enough of them. So many of her fan letters begin with 'I don't usually like reading but I LOVE your books…'

The independent spirit of her characters is recognisable in Wilson's own story. As a teenager, she travelled to Scotland to work for publishing company DC Thomson, which later launched a girls' magazine, called *Jackie* after their young recruit. That spirit also saw her through a period as a young writer in the London of the swinging sixties.

'I loved it. I was working for a publisher on Bedford Street. I used to visit the **National Gallery** a lot. Sometimes I'd meet friends from school. We'd have lunch in a café in Leicester Square called the Golden Egg – we'd have

Jacqueline Wilson's capital treats

In Jacqueline Wilson's *The Illustrated Mum* and *Lola Rose*, London is a big treat place, where children are lavished with trips to the London Aquarium, the British Airways London Eye and Hamley's. So what are her big treats in London?

Around Town

As far as big tourist sites are concerned, the **Tower of London** (*see p53*) is a big thrill. I was delighted to be taken around the Crown Jewels – heaven for someone like me who's wedded to flashy jewellery.

I've been on the **British Airways London Eye** (*see p33*) several times and the views are just wonderful. I love the **National Portrait Gallery** (*see p81*), and not just because there was a portrait of me in a recent exhibition called Icons & Idols! And I like to wander through the **National Gallery** (*see p81*).

I must say that the tourist site I'm most impressed with is the **Battersea Park Children's Zoo** (*see p141*). It's under new management and the owners really seem to understand both animals and children. I love all the little details in it, like the plastic viewing bubbles in the meerkats' enclosure. I like the way they place the various species – the barn owl's in an enclosure done up to look like a barn. The animals look really perky. It's a good-value venue too. I must say just talking about it now makes me want to go back!

I adore the lovely Victorian hotel **Hotel Russell**, (Russell Square, WC1) with all its Bloomsbury connections. It's a hoot there, with its Virginia Wolf burgers and what not, but there is also an antiquarian book fair there once a month.

Eating

If I'm meeting someone in London I often choose the restaurant in the **Royal Academy of Arts** (*see p73*), where there's lots of choice and no one minds if you sit there for a long time. If I'm in a hurry I pop into a Prêt a Manger. **Liberty** (Regent Street, W1) is a wonderful shop and has one of my favourite places for lunch in it, the Art Bar Café.

Shopping

I love bookshops in London. My favourites are Richmond's **Lion & Unicorn** (*see p186*) and the **Children's Bookshop** in Muswell Hill (*see p189*). One of the most impressive looking bookshops in town is **Daunt Books** in Marylebone Lane (*see p189*). I like to browse in the collection of second-hand and antiquarian bookshops in **Cecil Court** (off Charing Cross Road, WC2).

Arts & Entertainment

I enjoy going to the theatre in London. I've sat very happily in all kinds of theatre, large or small. I very much liked the **Peacock Theatre** in Bloomsbury (Portugal Street, WC2), where an adaptation of my book *Midnight* was staged. I think it's wonderful that the **Unicorn Theatre for Children** (*see p225*) was able to raise the funds to move into its new premises. It would be brilliant if the **Polka,** in Wimbledon (*see p225*) could be given some funding too. All these places need money. If only someone could raise a magic wand to help them out financially.

Sport & Leisure

All the major parks are delightful. London is a wonderful place for walking. I like to go to **Hampstead Heath** (*see p96*), or a little more local for me, **Richmond Park** (*see p147*). One thing I keep meaning to do is visit one of the Lidos, such as **Tooting Bec** (*see p269*) or **Brockwell** (*see p268*). I should wait for a really hot day this summer.

macaroni cheese and be terribly sophisticated! It was wonderful being in London.'

Since those heady days this bestselling author has written 86 books, and sold millions of copies. Based in Kingston, where she was brought up, Jacqueline Wilson has one grown-up daughter. Jacqueline writes every day with a pencil and a notebook, which means she can write wherever she is, which these days is often on a train, and often travelling into the capital, which she delights in.

'There are so many brilliant places to go in London. It's a tremendously exciting place, both to grow up in and to visit. And it needn't be expensive to get the most out of the city; there's loads to do, so much of it completely free. Once you're in London, if you've brought your own sandwiches you needn't spend anything at all. Another thing I love about this city are the street markets. All those opportunities for people-watching! I think London is the most amazing place.'

In Context

The Story of London

From marsh by the stream to seething metropolis.

In Context

This amazing city's size and continuous expansion have long fascinated visitors and inhabitants, but London's origins are less than grand. Celtic tribes lived in scattered communities along the banks of the Thames before the Romans arrived in Britain, but no evidence suggests there was a settlement on the site of the future metropolis before the invasion of the Roman Emperor Claudius in AD 43.

The Latin name Londinium could have any number of ancient origins. 'Llyn-don', for example, means town ('don') by the stream ('llyn'); 'lunnd' means marsh; 'Laindon', long hill; while the adjective 'londos' translates as fierce. Whoever was the first to stake their claim, we still have the Romans to thank for our ancient city wall (built in AD 200), remnants of which survive in the City of London today. The first bridge across the Thames, which crossed at roughly the point of the present-day London Bridge, was also a Roman achievement. It was built after the British outpost of the Empire was sacked by Boudicca, who led her armies against the soldiers who had seized her lands and raped her daughters. The settlement was almost destroyed, but the Romans rebuilt and surrounded their town with a defensive wall in an attempt to keep out rebellions. Another 200 years passed with the Romans in charge, but with the eventual decline of the Empire, the last troops were withdrawn in 410 and London was left to Angles and Saxons.

LONDON BRIDGE IS FALLING DOWN

Much of what happened in London after the Romans left is stuff of legend, rather than history. Saxon settlers crossed the North Sea to set up homes and farms in eastern and southern England during the fifth and sixth centuries. Lundenwic, 'wic' meaning marketplace, stood about where Covent Garden is today. What is now Trafalgar Square was the site of farm buildings. The Strand is so called because it used to be just that, a strand, or beach for grounding ships. London's first bishop, Mellitus, was a missionary sent by the Pope. He converted the East Saxon King Sebert to Christianity and, in 604, founded a wooden cathedral, dedicated to St Paul, inside the old city walls. Although his people turned back to paganism after Sebert's death, later generations of Christians rebuilt St Paul's. In the ninth century another wave of invaders arrived: the Vikings. They crossed the North Sea to ransack London, forcing the king of the time, Alfred of Wessex, to reoccupy the old Roman town. In 1013, London Bridge was burned down by King Ethelred in an attempt to divide the invading forces. This episode reputedly inspired the well-known nursery rhyme.

As the Saxon city prospered, harassment from the Vikings continued until the 11th century when a Danish king – Cnut (Canute) took power. During this time London replaced Winchester as the capital. Edward the Confessor, an English king, gained the throne in 1042 and set to building Westminster Abbey. He died a week after his abbey was consecrated in December 1065.

Edward's death was a pivotal moment in history. His cousin William, Duke of Normandy, swore that his kinsman had promised him the crown. But Edward's brother-in-law Harold was a solid favourite with the English people. Their armies tried to settle the mattter at Hastings. On 14 October 1066 William defeated Harold and marched to London. He was crowned in Westminster Abbey on Christmas Day.

TALKING SHOP

William knew he had to keep things sweet with the wealthy merchants in the City of London, so he gave them independent trading rights in return for taxes. The charter stating these terms is kept at the Guildhall. But the king was still bothered by the possibly rebellious population, so he ordered strongholds to be built along the city wall. One of these is the White Tower, the tallest building in the Tower of London.

The city became a hotbed of political struggle. Fighting for supremacy were three powerful bodies: the king and aristocracy; the Church; and the lord mayor and city guilds. In the early Middle Ages, the king made all the laws in the country, aided by lords and bishops. During the 14th and 15th centuries, the Palace of Westminster became the seat of law and government, and the king's meetings with the noblemen and clergy – called Parliaments – became increasingly important. As

London Bridge then.

London Bridge now.

In Context

Sir Francis Bacon: Guiding star

Today's child geniuses don't seem to fare as well as those of old. Newspapers are littered with the tragic tales of girls and boys who take A levels at six or enter university before they've hit their teens, then stall, or stagger off into insignificance. No such fate for Sir Francis Bacon, the man who is now regarded as the father of modern science, as well as a famed philosopher, writer and poet, who was up at Cambridge by the time he was 12.

Francis was born during Queen Elizabeth I's reign in January 1561, the second son of Sir Nicholas and Lady Anne Bacon. His father was Lord Keeper of the Great Seal of England, and his mother was one of the most highly educated women of her day. The daughter of a scholar, Anne was fluent in Latin, Greek and Italian, skills she passed on to her son, whom she adored.

The Bacon household in York House, Charing Cross, which adjoined the Queen's Palace of Whitehall, was ramped to the rafters with culture and politics. Not only was his father central to state business, Francis's uncle Sir William Cecil, was also Secretary of State.

Francis's childhood days began with family prayers. He was coached by a procession of the best tutors, as well as his mother, a strong, religious personality who also liked to read him morality tales. The family were often present at court events. On one such occasion the Queen noted the boy's intelligence, and she called him her 'young Lord Keeper' and 'Baby Solomon'.

Francis was only 12 when he started at Trinity College, Cambridge, together with his brother Anthony. The pair were already fluent in spoken and written Latin, Greek, French, Italian and Spanish. The Bacon boys lodged in rooms at the house of Sir John Whitgift, the Master of Trinity and also their tutor.

At 15, Francis followed in his father's footsteps and entered Gray's Inn to study and practise law. He was diverted for three years, when he went to France to be attaché to the ambassador, but this was the start of a career trajectory.

Although Queen Elizabeth cold-shouldered him after he opposed her tax programme, he was trusted by King James after her death in 1603. He was knighted, and appointed to a number of key posts, finally achieving the position of Keeper of the Great Seal, just like his dad. There was a blip in 1621, when he pleaded guilty to accepting bribes, but his enforced retirement allowed him to focus on his writing.

Bacon's brilliance has shrouded his reputation in mystery. While we know that he established the principles of evidence-based science, other rumours of his influence abound, though academics give them little credence. Was he the real author of some of William Shakespeare's plays? Certainly he was a gifted poet, naturalist, lawyer, essayist and linguist. When life touches you with so many talents, anything is possible.

the number of advisors to the king grew, Parliament divided into two groups, the House of Lords (populated by nobles and members of the clergy chosen by the king) and the House of Commons (powerful people elected by rich merchants and landowners). Trade with Europe grew. Imports of spices, cloth, furs, precious metals and wine filled the wharves by London Bridge. The City's markets, already established, drew produce from miles around. The street markets, or 'cheaps', around Westcheap (now Cheapside) were crammed with goods. Foreign traders and craftsmen settled around the port of London. The population rocketed from about 18,000 in 1100 to more than 50,000 in the 1340s.

THE PESTILENTIAL CITY

Overcrowding brought hygiene problems. The water supply, which came more or less directly from the Thames, was limited and polluted. In the east, Houndsditch gained its name because people threw dead dogs into the boundary ditch. At Smithfield meat market, meanwhile, butchers dumped animal guts willy-nilly. Such conditions led to the greatest catastrophe of the Middle Ages: the Black Death of 1348 and 1349. The plague came to London from Europe, carried by rats on ships. In this period about 30 per cent of the population died of disease. The epidemic recurred in London on several occasions over the next three centuries, each time devastating the population.

In Context

After all that **Time Out** how about some **Time In with** NICKELODEON®

nick.co.uk

With plague killing so many, London was left with a labour shortage, resulting in unrest among the overworked peasants. A poll tax – a charge of a shilling a head – was introduced, which prompted the poor to revolt. In 1381 thousands of them, led by Wat Tyler from Kent and Jack Straw from Essex, marched on London. In the rioting and looting that followed, the Savoy Palace on the Strand was destoyed, the Archbishop of Canterbury was murdered and hundreds of prisoners were set free. Eventually a 14-year-old King Richard II rode out to face the angry mob at Smithfield, but the Lord Mayor William Walworth, angered by Tyler's belligerence, stabbed the rebel leader to death. This stopped the rioting, and the ringleaders were hanged.

HEADS ROLL

The city blossomed under the Tudors and Stuarts. Buoyed up by trade from newly discovered lands, London became one of the largest cities in Europe. Henry VII left his mark on London by commissioning the building of the Henry VII Chapel in Westminster Abbey, where he and his queen are buried. His successor was, of course, the notorious wife collector (and dispatcher) Henry VIII. His first marriage to Catherine of Aragon failed to produce an heir, so the king, in 1527, decided (in defiance of the Catholic Church) that the union should be annulled. Demanding to be recognised as Supreme Head of the Church of England, Henry ordered the execution of anyone who refused to comply (including his chancellor Sir Thomas More). So England began its transition to Protestantism. The subsequent dissolution of catholic monasteries changed the face of London: the land sold off was given over to streets. Henry also founded the Royal Dockyards at Woolwich. The land he kept for hunting became the Royal Parks (Hyde, Regent's, Greenwich and Richmond). Henry's daughter Queen Mary's five-year reign saw a brief Catholic revival. She was dubbed 'Bloody Mary' following her order to burn at the stake nearly 300 Protestants.

Mary's half-sister Elizabeth I oversaw a huge upsurge in commerce: the Royal Exchange was founded by Sir Thomas Gresham in 1566, and London became Europe's leading commercial centre. With Drake, Raleigh and Hawkins sailing to America and beyond, new trading enterprises were developed. By 1600 there were 200,000 people living in London, 12,000 of whom were beggars. Conditions were overcrowded and rat-infested, so plague was a constant threat.

London was a cultural centre, however, as well as a death trap. Two theatres, the Rose (1587) and the Globe (1599), were built on the south bank of the Thames, and the plays of William Shakespeare and Christopher Marlowe first performed. Earthier dramas took place on the street. At Bankside, people visited taverns and brothels, and engaged in bear-baiting and cockfighting.

London was a violent place. Elizabeth's successor, the Stuart James I, narrowly escaped being blown up. The Gunpowder Plot was instigated by a group of Catholics led by Guy Fawkes, who planned to protest at their persecution by dynamiting the Palace of Westminster from the cellar. Unfortunately for Fawkes, one of his co-conspirators warned his brother-in-law not to attend Parliament on 5 November – prompting a thorough search and the foiling of the scheme. Four plotters were killed while resisting arrest, while the remainder of the gang were dragged through the streets and executed, their heads displayed on spikes.

James I had escaped death, but his son Charles I wasn't so lucky. He stirred up trouble by throwing his weight around in the House of Commons, threatening the City of London's tax-free status and sparking a civil war: Charles and his Royalists were the losers. The king was tried for treason and beheaded outside the Banqueting House in Whitehall in 1649. Oliver Cromwell's Puritans declared Britain a Commonwealth, and theatres and gambling dens were closed down.

The exiled Charles II was restored to the throne in 1660, and Londoners were relieved. But there was trouble ahead: the 1664-5 bubonic plague killed nearly 100,000 Londoners. At the height of the epidemic, 10,000 people were dying each week. When plague was diagnosed in a house, the occupants were locked inside for 40 days, while watchmen outside ensured no one escaped. London reeked of death. The following year, an oven in Farriner's bakery in Pudding Lane started a fire that lasted three days and destroyed four-fifths of the City. Rumours of a Popish plot were everywhere, and Frenchman Robert Hubert was forced to confess to starting the fire and hanged. Today Christopher Wren's Monument marks a spot near where the fire broke out. London was rebuilt in brick and stone. As well as completing his greatest work, the new St Paul's Cathedral, Wren oversaw the rebuilding of 51 city churches.

London was a veritable hotbed of dissent between 1680 and the early 19th century; there was a riot almost every weekend, as Professor Clive Bloom, author of *Violent London: 2000 years of Riots, Rebels and Revolts*, writes. The worst example of such disorganised violence in London was the 1780 Gordon Riots, an outpouring of anti-Catholic rage that lasted a week and left hundreds dead.

In Context

Around this time George III was on the throne and the Whig Party, led by Sir Robert Walpole, was in power. Walpole was the first prime minister and was given 10 Downing Street as an official home. This address has been occupied by the serving prime minister ever since. More crossings over the river were built: Westminster Bridge (built 1750) and Blackfriars Bridge (1763) joined London Bridge, which until then had been the only bridge to span the river. While the well-to-do enjoyed their Georgian homes, life for the poor was squalid. Living in slums, ruined by plentiful gin, people turned to street crime. Gangs emerged, who enjoyed near immunity from arrest. The Gregory Gang, one of many that preyed on travellers, included highwayman Dick Turpin.

In 1751 the writer Henry Fielding and his brother John established a volunteer force of 'thief takers' to help the parish constables catch these criminals. This force, originally known as the Bow Street Runners, eventually became the Metropolitan Police (established 1829).

The rich had never had it so good when Victoria was crowned in 1837. Progress was impressive: five more bridges spanned the Thames and the city's first railway line (London Bridge to Greenwich) had been laid. Yet this city, the administrative and financial capital of the British Empire, had a dark underbelly. Crammed into slums, the urban masses led a miserable – and malodorous – life. The summer of 1858 smelled particularly bad: the 'Great Stink' meant that politicians in the Houses of Parliament could not work with their windows open. The stink so got up the noses of MPs that Benjamin Disraeli, the Chancellor of the Exchequor was able to rush through a bill allocating some £3 million to construct a new sewerage system in London.

In Context

The **Great Fire** of 1666 ravaged London.

DEVASTATED BY WAR

The new century started merrily enough, with Edward VII taking the throne in 1901, but the gaiety wouldn't last. World War I saw the first bomb to be dropped on London. It came from a Zeppelin and landed near the Guildhall. Terrifying nightly raids continued throughout the Great War, killing 650 people.

When it was finally over, those soldiers who had survived were promised 'homes for heroes' on their return. Yet few homes materialised and the nation's mood was bleak. Political change was set in motion. In 1924 David Lloyd George's Liberal Party was deposed in favour of a promised fresh start with the Labour Party, under Ramsay MacDonald. While the upper classes partied their way through the Roaring Twenties, the working classes were in the grip of mass unemployment. Dissatisfaction was expressed when all the workers downed tools to support the striking miners. The General Strike of 1926 lasted for nine days: the army distributed food and students drove buses. After nine days of chaos the strike was called off by the Trades Union Congress. Unemployment continued to rise. The New York Stock Exchange crash of 1929 had a knock-on effect; the British economic situation was grim.

The London County Council worked to improve conditions for its people. As the city's population grew (8.7 million in 1939), so did its sprawl. Suburbia expanded, and with it the Tube lines. The main entertainment for people was the radio, until 1936, when the first television broadcast went out live from the British Broadcasting Corporation (BBC) at Alexandra Palace studios.

On 3 September 1939 Britain declared war on Germany. Londoners dug air-raid shelters and sent children and pregnant women to the countryside. In fact, the air raids did not begin until almost a year later. In September 1940, 600 German bombers devastated east London and the docks. The raids continued for 57 nights in a row. Nearly 30,000 bombs were dropped on the city; around 15,000 people were killed and 3.5 million houses destroyed or damaged. People sheltered in the Tube stations. They were safe unless the stations were hit. This happened at Marble Arch, Bank and Balham.

In 1944 a new type of bomb began flattening Londoners' homes – the fearsome V1 flying bomb, or doodlebug. These caused widespread destruction, as did their successor, the more powerful V2 rocket. By the end of the war, about a third of the city was in ruins.

New arrivals. *See p18.*

Jacqueline du Pré: Shooting star

By the age of six, Jacqueline du Pre was already a pupil at the London Cello School. She had first heard the sound of a cello playing on the radio when she was four, and told her mother: 'Mummy, I want to make that sound!'

This child prodigy, born in 1945, and recognised as one of the world's greatest cellists, was a product of nature and nurture. Her mother, Iris Geep, was a talented professional pianist and composer in her own right. Crucially, Iris was also a talented teacher, who filled the family home with music and singing. It was no coincidence that her eldest daughter, Hilary, was also a brilliant musician. The sisters had a close, intense relationship, preferring their own company to that of friends, and they were by turns competitive and supportive of each other's gifts.

On the night of Jacqueline's fifth birthday, her mother put a cello by the little girl's bed. It was love at first sight. Jacqueline quickly outgrew her first school. When she was eight, her mother decided that the time was right for a greater challenge. Jacqueline began studying under William Pleeth, of the Guildhall School of Music and Drama. Pleeth had been a child prodigy too, and he formed a strong rapport with his young pupil. The pair formed such a strong bond that she would call him 'my cello Daddy'.

In 1956, William Pleeth recommended Jacqueline for the international music world's most prestigious scholarships, the Suggia Gift. When Jacqueline played before the panel of famous judges, William Pleeth described her performance thus: '…you knew that there was a vast talent that could flower at a tremendous speed once it was awakened. There was nothing flashy about her. No fireworks. It was just a case of opening a few doors.'

Jacqueline's quiet brilliance meant that she took the prize. But the earning the scholarship demanded everything from her. Practice was a minimum of four hours a day. Jacqueline was 11, and by now, she was no longer a normal schoolgirl, but a fully fledged genius-in-progress.

Her family moved to London from Surrey in 1958. Their flat in Portland Place was perfectly positioned for the capital's concert halls, where Jacqueline would soon be launched to worldwide acclaim. In 1961, aged 16, she made her professional debut in Wigmore Hall. She was playing the Elgar *Concerto for Violoncello in E minor* on a Stradivarius, which had been generously donated to her by an anonymous admirer. Her subsequent recording of the concerto in 1965 remains one of EMI's bestselling records of all times.

Jacqueline's du Pre's star shone brightly until she was in her late 20s. Then the tingling that she'd been feeling in her fingers for years became worse. She was diagnosed with multiple sclerosis in 1973. The disease slowly robbed her of the feeling in her fingers and arms. The magic cello was silenced, but Jacqueline's reputation for passion, emotion and sheer technical brilliance still beams as brightly as ever.

In Context

In the General Election that took place soon after VE Day, Churchill was defeated by the Labour Party under Clement Attlee. The National Health Service was founded in 1948; public transport and communications were overhauled. But life in the city still seemed drab and austere. For Londoners facing a housing shortage there were ambitious initiatives. Some of the buildings whisked up – prefabricated bungalows – were supposed to be temporary, but many are still inhabited more than 60 years later. Many new high-rise estates were shoddy and many have since been pulled down.

It was not all doom for Londoners, though. The city hosted the Olympic Games in 1948 and, in 1951, the Festival of Britain, which celebrated all that was great about British technology and design. The festival took place on derelict land on the south bank of the river, which eventually became the site of the South Bank Centre arts complex. During the 1950s Britain enjoyed a gradual return to relative prosperity. Families were inspired to move to new towns away from the city, where air pollution was a problem. The Clean Air Acts, the first introduced in 1956 as a result of the Great Smog four years earlier, finally ensured the reduction of noxious gas emissions. Inner London was also facing a labour shortage. Workers from the country's former colonies, particularly the West Indies, were recruited for London Transport and in the hospitals. Many immigrants faced an unfriendly reception from indigenous Londoners: matters came to a head in the Notting Hill race riots of 1958. Some parts of

London were more tolerant; Soho, with its jazz joints and clubs, for one. The 1960s saw London – fashion capital of the world – swing.

To find out where the gigs were, people bought a weekly guide to London called *Time Out*; the first issue came out in August 1968. People flocked to Abbey Road, NW8, because of the Beatles album of the same name. Hyde Park was the place to be in the summer of '69 when the Rolling Stones played for half a million fans.

In the 1970s the lights went out, often literally, on London's glamour. Inflation, unemployment, strikes, IRA bombs and an increasingly fractured

Wolfgang Amadeus Mozart: Mega star

When you're arguably the greatest musical genius the world has ever seen, the signs are likely to be there when you're barely out of nappies. So it was for Wolfgang Amadeus Mozart who was born 250 years ago in Salzburg, Austria. Wolfgang started playing the keyboard aged three. He composed his first piano piece at five and had a symphony to his name by nine.

This towering talent didn't come completely out of the blue. Mozart's father Leopold was a court musician to the archbishop of Salzburg, and a composer. He was an educated man, who home-schooled his son and his daughter, Nannerl, in musical theory, as well as maths, French, Latin, Italian and piano. Nannerl was gifted, too, and she and Wolfgang became such excellent pianists that their proud parents decided to show off their children's extraordinary skills on a tour of the European courts.

Word spread and people thronged to see the two little musical prodigies. Invitations besieged the Mozarts, and Leopold crammed in as many concerts as he could manage into an already- hectic schedule.

The plaudits – and the cash – came rolling in. Wolfgang grew fond of the attention lavished on him by the kings and queens of Europe, and the privileged position he'd earned through his performances. He was a seven-year-old superstar.

In 1764, shortly after Wolfgang published his first two works (harpsichord sonatas), Leopold decided to take his family to London. There was a market to be tapped, and money to be made.

Shortly after their arrival, the family had an audience with King George III and Queen Charlotte at Buckingham Palace. A few days later, while walking in St James's Park, the Mozarts were astonished when the royal carriage stopped and the King saluted them. They were soon playing again at the royal palace. Between performances, Wolgang was taken for instruction to Johann Christian Bach, who was resident in the capital at the time. But it was the concert circuit that dominated. At one event, Leopold took 100 guineas in three hours. It was only when illness felled him that Leopold left the children to their own devices. Wolfgang used the time to compose, while Nannerl helped to copy out his work.

But fame has always been a fickle business, and the Mozarts were no longer a novelty in high society. Leopold was reduced to staging concerts in a local inn, before realising that it was time to move back to mainland Europe.

He retained a strong influence on his son throughout Wolfgang's teens and early 20s. The boy worked for the archbishop of Salzburg between the ages of 12 and 25. The inevitable rebellion happened later than most. Wolfgang quit Salzburg in 1781, moved to Vienna, and married.

Life was never exactly easy after that. Wolfgang and his wife had a taste for good living that stretched the resources of a freelance composer to the limit. By the time he died, aged 35, despite a vast body of work, the wunderkind had barely a penny to his name.

Labour government all contributed to an air of gloom. The rebellious punk explosion made a few sparks fly, but that was shortlived. Margaret Thatcher came to power in 1979, and the 1980s are regarded as her decade. Her Conservative government made sweeping changes, and stood up for 'market forces'. This was the era of the yuppie (Young Urban Professional), who cashed in on the Conservatives' monetarist policies and the arrival of the global economy. It did not take long for the city's underdogs to snarl and riot, first in Brixton, in 1981, and four years later in Tottenham, north London.

One lasting legacy of the Thatcher era in London is the Docklands redevelopment. Set up in 1981 to create a business centre in the docks to the east of the City, the scheme was slow to take shape, but to this day businesses and residents continue to move into buildings around the Isle of Dogs, and the area exudes prosperity. But this is a prominent area of London with a split personality, because little of the wealth from the banks and businesses is filtering through to the community. In 1986 the Greater London Council, with its anti-Thatcher outlook, was abolished, and County Hall was sold to a Japanese corporation. But history has a way of turning on you – the GLC's former leader, 'Red' Ken Livingstone, bided his time and, in 2000, was voted mayor with authority over all the city.

LABOUR'S DAYS

London in the early 1990s hit the buffers. A slump in house prices saw the reign of the yuppies come to an end. The last straw for beleaguered Londoners was the poll tax. Demonstrations led to riots in Trafalgar Square. It marked the loosening of Thatcher's grip, leading to her replacement by John Major in 1990. The recession continued. The numbers of rough sleepers rose in London as people lost their homes through unemployment and mortgage–rate rises. The IRA stepped up its campaign against the mainland, bombing the City in 1992 (destroying the medieval church of St Ethelburga-the-Virgin) and Docklands in 1996. Many cheered up when Tony Blair's New Labour ousted the Tories in May 1997, but went into shock when, later that year, Princess Diana was killed. The gates of Kensington Palace were the focus for the nation's tears and bouquets.

Fireworks for the new millennium weren't confined to the celebratory kind. Labour continued with the Conservative-conceived Millennium Dome project. But the spectacular tent on the once-derelict Greenwich Peninsula failed to capture the zeitgeist, and angry voices were raised about the massive sums of money swallowed up by the enterprise. After many

Olympics euphoria on 6 July 2005.

false starts, the Dome has been renamed the O_2 and is finally being transformed into a 20,000-seat sports and entertainment complex. And London still has problems. Housing is both expensive and in short supply, leading some to campaign for a reintroduction of tower blocks. Transport is taking a long time to improve, but much new work is now under way in preparation for the 2012 Olympics. When London was named as the venue, mass euphoria broke out in Trafalgar Square and all over the proud city. The happiness was shortlived, given the tragedy that wounded London not 24 hours later. But the city continues to develop, as a number of inner-city regeneration schemes swings into action, with a now-Olympian urgency behind a will to make our sporting and transport facilities the best in the world. Meanwhile the tourists will keep coming, and Londoners will carry on delighting in their cool, colossal, chaotic, capital.

Key events

1240 First Parliament sits at Westminster.
1294 First recorded mention of Hammersmith.
1348-9 The Black Death ravages London.
1357 The first Sanitary Act passed in London.
1381 Wat Tyler leads the Peasants' Revolt.
1388 Tyburn, near Marble Arch, becomes the principal place of execution.
1397 Richard (Dick) Whittington becomes Lord Mayor.
1497 The first image of London published in a 'Chroncyle of Englonde'.
1513 Henry VIII founds Woolwich Royal Dockyard.
1534 Henry VIII breaks from the Catholic Church.
1554 300 Protestant martyrs burned at Smithfield.
1571 The first permanent gallows set up at Tyburn.
1599 The Globe Theatre is built on Bankside.
1605 Guy Fawkes's Gunpowder Plot is discovered.
1635 London's first public postal service established.
1642 The Puritans defeat the Royalists at Turnham Green.
1649 Charles I is tried for treason and beheaded.
1664-5 The Great Plague kills thousands.
1666 The Great Fire destroys London.
1675 Building starts on a new St Paul's.
1680 Downing Street built.
1686 The first May Fair takes place at Mayfair.
1694 The Bank of England opens at Cheapside.
1711 St Paul's is completed.
1742 Thomas Coram founds his orphanage.
1750 Westminster Bridge is built.
1769 Blackfriars Bridge opens.
1803 The first railway opens.

c66 BC Ludgate built by King Lud (legendary).
AD 43 The Roman invasion. Londinium is founded.
61 Boudicca sacks the city.
122 Emperor Hadrian visits Londinium.
200 Rebuilt Londinium is protected by a city wall.
410 The last Roman troops leave Britain.
c600 Saxon London is built to the west.
604 The first St Paul's Cathedral is built.
841 First Viking raid.
c871 The Danes occupy London.
886 King Alfred retakes London.
1013 The Danes take London.
1042 King Edward builds Westminster Abbey.
1066 William, Duke of Normandy, defeats Harold.
1067 Work begins on the Tower of London.
1099 First recorded flood in London.
1123 St Bartholomew's Hospital founded.
1197 Henry Fitzailwyn becomes the first mayor.

Illustrations by Warwick Johnson Cadwell

In Context

1820 Regent's Canal opens.
1824 National Gallery founded.
1827 Regent's Park Zoo opens.
1829 Metropolitan Police founded.
1833 The London Fire Brigade is established.
1835 Madame Tussaud's opens.
1843 Trafalgate Square is laid out.
1851 The Great Exhibition.
1858 The Great Stink permeates London.
1863 World's first underground railway opens.
1866 Sanitation Act is passed.
1868 Last public execution in Newgate Prison.
1869 J Sainsbury grocery opens in Drury Lane.
1884 Greenwich Mean Time is established.
1888 Jack the Ripper haunts East End women.
1890 First electric underground railway opens.
1897 Motorised buses introduced.
1898 The first escalator installed in London.
1915-18 Zeppelins bomb London.
1916 Horse-drawn buses disappear.
1940-4 Blitz devastates much of London.

1948 Olympic Games held in London.
1951 The Festival of Britain takes place.
1952 The last of the city's 'pea-soupers'.
1953 Queen Elizabeth II is crowned.
1966 England win the World Cup at Wembley.
1975 Work begins on the Thames Barrier.
1982 The last of London's docks close.
1986 The Greater London Council is abolished.
1990 Poll Tax protestors riot.
1992 Canary Wharf opens.
1997 A Labour government is elected; Britain mourns Princess Diana.
2000 Ken Livingstone elected Mayor.
2001 The Labour Government is re-elected.
2002 Queen Mother dies aged 101.
2003 A massive public demonstration – against the war on Iraq – is the biggest ever seen in London.
2004 Mayor Ken is re-elected.
2005 A euphoric London wins bid to host the 2012 Olympics. One day later four suicide bombers kill 52 people. England cricket team wins the Ashes for the first time since 1987.
2006 The Queen celebrates her 80th birthday.

In Context

Festivals & Events

This city just wants to have fun. Join in!

Intent art action at the **Coin Street Festival**.

As well as the many year-round entertainments featured elsewhere in this guide, London has all sorts of annual shindigs that appeal to the younger generation. Check *Time Out* magazine every week for the news, and for details of fairs and circuses coming to a park near you. Zippo's, London's largest traditional touring circus, has a new show every year. See www.zipposcircus.co.uk for the new acts, plus venues and dates for 2007.

Summer

Coin Street Festival

Bernie Spain Gardens (next to Oxo Tower Wharf), SE1 9PH (7401 2255/www.coinstreet.org). Southwark tube/Waterloo tube/rail. **Date** June-Aug 2006. **Map** p318 N7.
Not one but a series of eight or so culturally themed weekday and weekend events celebrating different communities in the capital. Festivities take place on the South Bank and include music, dance and performance events for all ages, with craft and refreshment stalls and workshops for families at each one. This year's internationally themed events include *Carnival de Cuba* (10-11 June) and *Turkish Fest*(15-16 July). Check the website for further details of festivities near the time.

Beating Retreat

Horse Guards Parade, Whitehall, Westminster, SW1A 2AX (booking 7414 2271). Westminster tube/Charing Cross tube/rail. **Date** 7-8 June 2006. **Map** p317 K8.
This patriotic ceremony begins at 7pm, with the 'Retreat' beaten on drums by the Mounted Bands of the Household Cavalry and the Massed Bands of the Guards Division.

Trooping the Colour

Horse Guards Parade, Whitehall, Westminster, SW1A 2AX (7414 2271). Westminster tube/Charing Cross tube/rail. **Date** 17 June 2006. **Map** p317 K8.
Though the Queen was born on 21 April, this is her official birthday celebration. At 10.45am she makes the journey from Buckingham Palace to Horse Guards Parade, then scurries back home to watch a noon Royal Air Force flypast and receive a formal gun salute from Green Park.

In Context

London Garden Squares Weekend

Various venues across London (www.opensquares.org).
Date 10-11 June 2006.
Ever wondered what it's like in those enchanting little private parks dotted around the wealthy parts of town? For one weekend only, the London Parks & Gardens Trust opens many of them to the public. Maps are available to guide you to the gardens, which vary from Japanese-style retreats to secret 'children-only' play areas.

London Youth Games

Various venues in London (8778 0131/www.youth games.org.uk). **Dates** 10-11 June, 17-18 June, 1-2 July, 8-9 July 2006.
This mini-Olympics, now in its 29th year, sees 12,000 sporting hopefuls, all of them under 17, represent the 33 London boroughs in 30 different sports. The teams are selected locally, and activities include archery, fencing, canoeing, football, tennis, athletics and show jumping. Check the website for a programme. The finals on 8-9 July are held at Crystal Palace Sports Ground, where various entertainments including DJs, street sports, graffiti art and dance demonstrations compliment the main event.

Royal National Theatre Summer Festival

South Bank, SE1 9PX (7452 3400/www.national theatre.org.uk). Waterloo tube/rail. **Date** 7 July-2 September 2006. **Map** p318 M7.
Watch This Space is a free outdoor festival of entertainment in Theatre Square, with top-class shows across its ten weeks showcasing the best street theatre,circus, cinema, music, art and dance from all over the world. Special events include a family day on 5 Aug (1-7pm).

City of London Festival

Venues across the City, EC2-EC4 (7377 0540/www.colf.org). Bank tube/DLR, Blackfriars, Cannon Street, Moorgate or Farringdon tube/rail; St Paul's tube/. **Date** 26 June-13 July 2006.
Now in its 44th year, the City of London Festival takes place in some of the finest buildings in the Square Mile, among them the Guildhall and St Paul's. The programme is wide-ranging, with music, visual art, drama and film screenings, alongside architecture walks, talks and other outdoor events. This year takes a Japanese theme; in addition to a number of concerts, there will be a family fun day at Hampstead Heath (24 June) with kite-making and origami workshops and demonstrations.

Wimbledon Lawn Tennis Championships

All England Lawn Tennis Club, PO Box 98, Church Road, Wimbledon, SW19 5AE (8944 1066/info 8946 2244/www.wimbledon.org). Southfields tube/Wimbledon tube/rail. **Date** 26 June-9 July 2006.
Plan ahead for this prestigious tennis tournament. For Centre and Number One court seats, you'd have had to request an application form from the All England Lawn Tennis Club between August and the end of November the year before; this form gives you access to the public ticket ballot. If you queue on the day, you should gain entry to the outside courts. In the afternoon, returned show-court tickets are available from the booth opposite Court One, so it may be worth hanging about to see stars in action.

Henley Royal Regatta

Henley Reach, Henley-on-Thames, Oxon RG9 2LY (01491 572 153/www.hrr.co.uk). Henley-on-Thames rail. **Date** 28 June-2 July 2006; 4-8 July 2007.
First held in 1839, Henley is now a five-day affair. Boat races range from open events for men and women through club and student crews to junior boys.

Greenwich & Docklands International Festival (GDIF)

Various venues in Greenwich & Docklands (8305 1818/www.festival.org). **Date** 22-25 June 2006.
A mix of free theatrical, musical and site-specific outdoor events, this family-friendly festival will be celebrating its tenth anniversary this year. Look out for human mobiles suspended from cranes, stilt artists, plenty of pyrotechnics and the 'birthday party' finale on the last day.

Soho Festival

St Anne's Gardens & St Anne's Community Centre, Soho, W1D 6AE (7439 4303/www.thesohosociety. org.uk). Tottenham Court Road tube. **Date** 9 July 2006. **Map** p315 K6.
Stalls of crafts, books and face-painting, plus music, local artists' displays, competitions and food and drink are all in store for this year's annual event in aid of the Soho Society. The festival starts at midday and entrance is 50p.

Lambeth Country Show

Brockwell Park, SE24 0NG (7926 9000/www. ubiqueleisure.co.uk). Brixton tube/rail, then 2, 3, 68, 196 bus/Herne Hill rail. **Date** 15-16 July 2006.
This annual urban country show fills the rolling hills of Brockwell Park with a mix of farmyard and domestic animal attractions (horse show, dog show, farm animals on display and birds of prey on the wing). Aside from meeting and greeting the beasts, children can have fun on the numerous bouncy castles and fairground rides, and there are also international food and craft stalls, and a whole lot of music and dancing.

Summer in the Square

Trafalgar Square, Westminster, WC2 (7983 4100/www.london.gov.uk). Embankment tube/Charing Cross tube/rail. **Date** June-Sep 2006. **Map** p317 K7.
An annual programme of free (and usually fun) live cultural performances for all ages, Summer in the Square is keenly supported by the Mayor of London.

Young Pavement Artists Competition

Tate Britain, Millbank, SW1P 4RG (01304 611428/www.youngpavementartists.co.uk). Pimlico tube/77A, 88, C10, bus. **Date** Exhibition 1.30-5.50pm 14-16 July 2006. **Map** p316 H10.
This year's competition has a 'rainforest' theme. It's usually organised by schools, local councils or youth organisations as a fun day to raise money for the Duchenne muscular dystrophy charity. Children aged four to 18 can compete, with pitches costing around £1 per entrant. Photographs of the day's winners are then entered into the national competition, judged by Tate Britain and members of the Royal Academy of Arts. Guidelines for organising your own event are detailed on the website.

In Context

BBC Sir Henry Wood Promenade Concerts

Royal Albert Hall, Kensington Gore, South Kensington, SW7 2AP (box office 7589 8212/www.bbc.co.uk/ proms). Knightsbridge or South Kensington tube/9, 10, 52 bus. **Date** *14 July-19 Sept 2006.* **Map** *p313 D9.*
This annual event brings together an eclectic range of mainly classical concerts over the course of two months. Most are televised, but there's nothing like seeing them in person. If you choose carefully, you should able to find something in the grown-up Proms programme that the children will enjoy. The '5 BBC Music Intro' concerts can be seen for £5 per family member, and as usual all under 16s can get half-price tickets to every Prom across the season (apart from the Last Night). Otherwise, check the website for details of the Blue Peter Proms (22 & 23 July).

Fruitstock

Gloucester Green, north-east corner of Regent's Park, NW1 (8600 3939/www.fruitstock.com). Baker Street or Regent's Park tube. **Date** *5-6 Aug 2006.* **Map** *p314 G3.*
The Innocent fruit smoothies drink company's free summer bash has proved extremely popular in past years – 110,000 punters enjoyed the 2005 fest. This year will no doubt build on this success, with plenty of live music, a dance tent, food stalls, a farmers' market, activities for children and, pure and simple, the chance to laze on the grass.

Notting Hill Carnival

Notting Hill, W10, W11 (0870 059 1111/www. lnhc.org.uk). Ladbroke Grove, Notting Hill Gate & Westbourne Park tube. **Date** *27-28 Aug 2006.*
Europe's biggest street party sees thousands of revellers show up each year to drink warm beer and wander about in posh Notting Hill. There is occasional live music and relentless and unavoidable sound systems (loaded on to trucks, followed by unglamorous dancers in T-shirts). There's also a glittering costume parade, but all too often you miss it because of the crowds. Sunday is traditionally children's day, and the best day of the lot.

Autumn

Regent Street Festival

Regent Street, W1 (7287 9601/www.regentstreet online.com). Oxford Circus or Piccadilly Circus tube. **Date** *3 Sept 2006.* **Map** *p316 J7.*
An annual celebration in one of the capital's smartest streets, which closes to traffic for the day to make room for fairground rides, theatre, street entertainers, storytelling, a variety of live music and, of course, shopping.

Trafalgar Great River Race

Thames, from Ham House, Richmond, Surrey, to Island Gardens, Greenwich, E14 (8398 9057/ www.greatriverrace.co.uk). **Date** *16 Sept 2006.*
More than 260 'traditional' boats, from Chinese dragon boats to Viking longboats, vie in the UK traditional boat championship over a 35-kilometre (22mile) course. The race begins at 9.30am and reaches the finish at around 12.45pm. The best viewing point is riverside at Richmond Bridge, or along the South Bank, on the Millennium and Hungerford bridges. Or, for a special treat, take a trip on the passenger boat and watch the action up close (£25; £10 concessions, free under-6s).

Mayor's Thames Festival

Between Westminster & Blackfriars Bridges (7983 4100/www.thamesfestival.org). Blackfriars or Waterloo tube/rail. **Date** *16-17 Sept 2006.*
Always fun and occasionally spectacular, this waterfest runs from noon to 10pm all weekend and is highlighted by an atmospheric lantern procession and noisy firework finale on Sunday evening. Before the pyrotechnics kick off, there are riverside market stalls, various environmental activities and creative workshops, and a lively assortment of dance and music performances.

Horseman's Sunday

Church of St John's Hyde Park, Hyde Park Crescent, W2 2QD (7262 1732/www.stjohns-hydepark.com/ horsemans). Edgware Road or Lancaster Gate tube/Paddington tube/rail. **Date** *17 Sept 2006.* **Map** *p313 E6.*
Hyde Park has long been a popular spot for riding. This ceremony dates back to 1969, when local stables, threatened with closure, held an outdoor service to protest. At noon, after morning service, the vicar of St John's rides out to bless and present rosettes to a procession of horses and riders, and delivers a short service with hymns and occasional guest speakers. There will also be games, face painting and other fun laid on for kids in a special area next to the church.

City Farms Festival

Capel Manor Gardens, Bullsmoor Lane, Enfield, Middx BN1 4RQ (8366 4442/www.capel.ac.uk). Turkey Street rail (Mon-Sat only)/217, 310 bus. **Date** *23 Sept 2006.*
The urban farms we all love have a pleasant day out in the leafy acres of Enfield for this agricultural extravaganza. Events include a farm-animal show and arena events, such as milking and shearing demonstrations, vegetable and plant sales, displays by craftspeople, food stalls, and all sorts of fun and games for children.

Children's Book Week

Booktrust, 45 East Hill, SW18 2QZ (8516 2977/ www.booktrust.org.uk). **Date** *2-8 Oct 2006.*
This annual event dedicated to children's literacy is run by Booktrust, the independent national charity that encourages people of all ages and cultures to discover and enjoy reading to enjoy reading. Booktrust also administers the Children's Laureate award, sponsored by Ottakar's. (Jacqueline Wilson is the current laureate). The country-wide schedule of activities includes hands-on events and author visits. Libraries and schools will have details of local events, otherwise contact visitthe Booktrust website.

Pearly Kings & Queens Harvest Festival

St Martin-in-the-Fields, Trafalgar Square, Westminster, WC2N 4JJ (7766 1100/www.pearly society.co.uk). Leicester Square tube/Charing Cross tube/rail. **Date** *2 Oct 2006.* **Map** *p317 L7.*
Pearly kings and queens – so called because of the shiny white buttons sewn in elaborate designs on their dark suits – have their origins in the 'aristocracy' of London's early Victorian costermongers, who elected their own royalty to safeguard their interests. Now charity representatives, today's pearly monarchs gather for this 3pm thanksgiving service in their traditional 'flash boy' outfits.

Chinese New Year Festival. *See p27.*

Punch & Judy Festival

Covent Garden Piazza, Covent Garden, WC2 (0870 780 5001/www.coventgardenmarket.co.uk). Covent Garden tube. **Date** 1 Oct 2006. **Map** p315 L6.
More domestic incidents involving the crocodile, a policeman and Mr Punch giving Judy a few slaps (and vice versa). Performances take place around the market building. Puppetry means prizes, and there's also puppet-related merchandise for sale.

The Baby Show

Earl's Court Exhibition Centre, SW5 9TA (booking line 0870 122 1313/www.thebabyshow.co.uk). Earl's Court tube. **Date** 20-22 Oct 2006; (ExCeI) 9-11 Mar 2007.
Anything you need to know about babies or toddlers, you can find out here – and buy an obscene amount of paraphernalia into the bargain. To try to list what's there would be an exercise in futility; for best results, consult the website and search for yourself.

Tutankhamun & the Golden Age of the Pharaohs

O2 Centre, Drawdock Road, SE10 0BB (01753 565656/www.kingtut.org). North Greenwich tube. **Date** Nov 2007.
Older parents may remember the thrill (and the queues) of a visit to the Tutankhamun exhibition in 1972. Now, 35 years later, the staggering treasures from the boy king's tomb (including his gold crown) will be on display in London again, this time in the centre formerly known as the Dome. Treasures from other royal graves in the Valley of the Kings – such as the intact tomb of Tutankhamun's great-grandparents Yuya and Tuyu – will also be part of the exhibition. Fill out the online registration form to guarantee yourself a ticket when they go on sale.

Trafalgar Day Parade

Trafalgar Square, Westminster, WC2 (7928 8978/ www.ms-sc.org). Charing Cross tube/rail. **Date** 22 Oct 2006. **Map** p401 K7.
More than 500 sea cadets parade with marching bands and musical performances. Events culminate in the laying of a wreath at the foot of Nelson's Column.

Bonfire Night

Date 5 Nov 2006.
Most public displays of pyrotechnics to commemorate the Gunpowder Plot are held on the weekend nearest 5 November; among the best in London are those at Battersea Park, Alexandra Palace and Crystal Palace. Alternatively, try to book a late ride on the relevant nights on the British Airways London Eye (*see p33*).

London to Brighton Veteran Car Run

From Serpentine Road, Hyde Park, W2 (01280 841 062/www.lbvcr.com). Hyde Park Corner tube. **Date** 5 Nov 2006. **Map** p311 F8.
Get up at the crack of dawn to catch this parade of around 500 vintage motors, none of which exceeds 32 kmh (20mph), setting off on the long run from Hyde Park between 7.30am and 9am, aiming to reach Brighton before 4pm. Otherwise, join the crowds lining the rest of the route. The handsome, buffed-up vehicles are on display the previous day in Regent Street (10am-4pm).

Lord Mayor's Show

Various streets in the City (7332 3456/www.lord mayorsshow.org). **Date** 11 Nov 2006.
This is the day when, under the conditions of the Magna Carta, the newly elected Lord Mayor is presented to the monarch, or his or her justices, for approval. Amid a procession of around 140 floats, the Lord Mayor leaves the Mansion House at 11am and travels through the City to the Royal Courts of Justice on the Strand, where he makes some vows before returning to Mansion House. The procession will take around an hour and a quarter to pass you, wherever you stand. The event is rounded off by a fireworks display from a barge moored on the Thames between Waterloo and Battersea bridges.

Discover Dogs

Earl's Court 2 (entrance on Lillie Road), SW5 9TA (7518 1012/www.the-kennel-club.org.uk). West Brompton tube. **Date** 11-12 Nov 2006. **Map** p312 A11.
This canine extravaganza continues to go from strength to strength. It's far less formal than Crufts: you can meet more than 180 dogs, discuss pedigrees with breeders, and gather info on all matters of the mutt. There are competitions in categories as wide-ranging as 'dog that looks most like a celebrity' to OAP (over seven years old). The Good Citizen Dog Scheme offers discipline and agility courses, and you can also meet husky teams and watch police-dog agility demonstrations and Heelwork to Music displays.

State Opening of Parliament

House of Lords, Palace of Westminster, Westminster, SW1A 0PW (7219 4272/www.parliament.uk). Westminster tube. **Date** Nov 2006 (call for details & changes). **Map** p317 L9.
In a ceremony that has changed little since the 16th century, the Queen reopens Parliament after its summer recess. You can see what goes on inside only on telly, but if you join the throngs on the streets, you can watch Her Maj arrive and depart in her Irish or Australian State Coach, attended by the Household Cavalry.

Children's Film Festival

Main venue: Barbican Centre, Silk Street EC2Y 8DS (Barbican box office 7638 8891/www.londonchildren film.org.uk). **Date** 18-26 Nov 2006. **Map** p318 P5.
Following the resounding success of the first festival last year, the second is planned with the same principles in mind: to attract children from all backgrounds with films from all corners of the globe. Few of the films screened would finsd a multiplex slot, but if the encouraging outcome of last year's festival is anything to go by, that isn't because children only respond to blockbusters: the First Light Young Juries scheme, in which children aged seven to 11 and 12 to 16 are invited to be film critics and vote for their favourites, came up with two clear and surprising winners, both from the world-cinema category with subtitles. Last year's costume and make-up workshops – many of which were free – were so popular that a range of activities to complement the screenings is again planned for this year. Organisers aim to keep ticket prices low (last year they were just £2 if you booked in advance).

Christmas Lights & Tree

Covent Garden (0870 780 5001/www.coventgarden market.co.uk); Oxford Street (7976 1123/www.oxford street.co.uk); Regent Street (7152 5853/www.regent-

In Context

street.co.uk); Bond Street (www.bondstreet association.com); Trafalgar Square (7983 4234/ www.london.gov.uk). **Date** Nov-Dec 2006.
Much of the childhood wonder still remains in the glittering lights on St Christopher's Place, Marylebone High Street, Bond Street and Kensington High Street. The giant fir tree in Trafalgar Square each year is a gift from the Norwegian people, in gratitude for Britain's role in liberating their country from the Nazis.

Winter

The London International Horse Show

Olympia, Hammersmith Road, Kensington, W14 8UX (01753 847 900/www.olympiahorseshow.com). Kensington (Olympia) tube/rail. **Date** 12-18 Dec 2006.
This annual extravaganza for equestrian enthusiasts has dressage, showjumping and more frivolous events, such as the Shetland Pony Grand National, mounted police displays and dog agility contests. There are more than 100 trade stands, so you can do some Christmas shopping.

Frost Fair

Bankside Riverwalk, by Shakespeare's Globe, SE1 9DT (details from Tourism Unit, Southwark Council, 7525 1139). London Bridge tube/rail. **Date** mid Dec 2006.
This tradition started in the winter of 1564, when the Thames froze over and Londoners set up their stalls of mulled wine, roast meats and other popular goodies of the day on the ice, which must have been mighty thick. Sadly,

no ice can be expected these warm wet modern winters (although the ice slide outside Tate Modern was a blast last year), but the event has a wonderful community feel, with crafts, food and wine stalls, children's shows and musical attractions set up on Bankside. It all makes for a good week's entertainment in the run-up to Christmas.

Chinese New Year Festival

Around Gerrard Street, Chinatown, W1, Leicester Square, WC2, & Trafalgar Square, WC2 (7851 6686/ www.chinatownchinese.com). Leicester Square or Piccadilly Circus tube. **Date** 18 Feb 2007 (phone to confirm date). **Map** p317 K7.
Kung hei fat choi! (this translates as 'congratulations and be prosperous') is the traditional greeting for the new Year celebrations. This is the most important of the Chinese festivals, so expect quite a bunfight around London's Chinatown. Celebrations for the Chinese Year of the Pig begin at 11am with a children's parade from Leicester Square gardens to Trafalgar Square, where the lion and dragon dance teams perform traditional dances. And there are, of course, firework displays (at lunchtime and at 5pm).

London International Mime Festival

Various venues across London (7637 5661/ www.mimefest.co.uk). **Date** 12-28 Jan 2007.
Surely the quietest festival the city has to offer, LIMF will invite 20 companies from the UK and abroad to perform a variety of shows for all ages. This year's highlight is the French outfit Compagnie 111, which will perform a slapstick show at the South Bank's Queen Elizabeth Hall. Free brochures are available via phone or website.

London's Irish delight in the **St Patrick's Day Parade & Festival**. *See p28.*

National Storytelling Week

Various theatres, bookshops, libraries, schools & pubs around London (contact Del Reid 8866 4232/www.sfs. org.uk). **Date** 27 Jan-3 Feb 2007.

This annual storytelling week sees venues across the country hosting events for tellers and listeners. The event is held by the Society for Storytelling, an organisation that aims to increase public awareness of the art, practice and value of oral storytelling and the narrative traditions of the peoples and cultures of the world. In 2006 more than 800 nationwide storytelling events and performances were organised, in theatres, bookshops, libraries, schools, museums and arts centres all over the UK. Details of the 2007 programme were unavailable as we went to press (check the website nearer the time), but there are usually storytelling events to suit all tastes and ages.

Spring

Great Spitalfields Pancake Day Race

Dray Walk, Old Truman Brewery, 91 Brick Lane, E1 6QL (7375 0441/www.alternativearts.co.uk). Liverpool Street tube/rail. **Date** 5 Feb 2007. **Map** p319 S5.

The action starts at 12.30pm, with teams of four tossing pancakes as they run, all for a good cause, of course. Phone in advance if you want to take part, or just show up if all you're after is seeing pancakes hit the pavement. Competitors should phone the organisers a few days in advance to avoid batter recriminations.

St Patrick's Day Parade & Festival

Trafalgar Square, Leicester Square & Covent Garden (7983 4100/www.london.gov.uk). **Date** Mar 2007 (check website for date). **Map** p317 K7.

This fun, colourful and noisy parade departs from Hyde Park Corner at noon and continues to romp through the streets until 6pm. Expect lots of Irish music, dancing, crafts and various other activities for all ages.

London Marathon

Greenwich Park to the Mall via the Isle of Dogs, Victoria Embankment & St James's Park (7902 0200/ www.london-marathon.co.uk). Charing Cross tube/rail/Maze Hill rail. **Date** 22 Apr 2007 (check website to confirm date).

One of the world's biggest metropolitan marathons, the London Marathon started in 1981 and nowadays attracts 35,000 starters (many more apply), many in outrageous costumes. Spectators are advised to arrive early; the front runners reach the 13-mile mark near the Tower of London at around 10am. If you think you're fit enough, runners' applications must be in by the October before the race. The 2007 entry system, opening on 1 August 2006, is via an entry form in a free magazine called *Marathon News*, available from all major high street sports stores

London Harness Horse Parade

Phone for venue details (01737 646 132). **Date** 9 Apr 2007. **Map** p313 F13.

A must for pony-mad children, this equine parade takes place on Easter Monday. More than 300 working horses, donkeys and mules with various commercial and private carriages assemble for the main parade (noon-1pm). At the time of press, the 2007 venue was yet to be decided.

The **Canalway Cavalcade** hots up.

Canalway Cavalcade

Little Venice, W9 (British Waterways London 7286 6101). Warwick Avenue tube. **Date** May bank hol weekend 2007.

The Inland Waterways see to it that this bank-holiday boat rally transforms the pool of Little Venice into an assembly of more than 100 colourful narrowboats, all decked out in bunting and flowers. Events include craft, trade and food stalls; kids' activities; music and boat trips. The beautiful lantern-lit boat procession is a must-see – pray for fine weather. Phone to confirm dates.

May Fayre & Puppet Festival

St Paul's Church Garden, Bedford Street, Covent Garden, WC2E 9ED (7375 0441/www.alternative arts.co.uk). Covent Garden tube. **Date** 13 May 2007. **Map** p317 L7.

Celebrating the first recorded sighting of Mr Punch in England (by Pepys, in 1662), this free event offers puppetry galore from 10.30am to 5.30pm. A grand brass-band procession around Covent Garden is followed by a service held in St Paul's (*see p52*), with Mr Punch in the pulpit. Then there are puppet shows, booths and stalls, as well as workshops for puppet-making and dressing up.

Around Town

Introduction

London up close.

In the Around Town pages we provide full listings for all of London's picture-postcard sights as well as great parks, museums, city farms and galleries off the tourist track. Do ring to check that a listed establishment is open before you visit.

London's sheer size can make it overwhelming to the novice. The Tube may be the quickest way to get around (see p290), but if you're not in a hurry, the bus is the most picturesque. Some good routes for stringing the sights together are the 7, 8, 11 and 12 (all double deckers) and the RV1, a single decker plying the river circuit.

Most Routemaster buses have been taken off Transport for London's commuter roster for good, but two of them at least – numbers 9 and 15 – are up and running again as Heritage Routes, operating between Trafalgar Square and Tower Hill (15) and the Royal Albert Hall and Aldwych. Normal fares apply; for more details check www.routemaster.org.uk.

USEFUL INFORMATION

If your sightseeing programme includes expensive places, such as **London Zoo** (see p67) and the **Tower of London** (see p53), a London Pass (0870 242 9988, www.londonpass.com), which gives you pre-paid access to more than 50 attractions, may be of interest. Phone or check the website for prices.

The initials 'LP' before the admission price in our listings means your London Pass grants free admission. 'EH' means English Heritage members, and their kids, get in free. 'NT' means National Trust family members get free admission.

Trips and tours

On the buses

Big Bus Company 48 Buckingham Palace Road, Victoria, SW1W 0RN (0800 169 1365/7233 9533/www.bigbustours.com). **Departures** every 10-15 mins. Summer 8.30am-6pm daily. Winter 8.30am-4.30pm daily. **Pick-up** Green Park (near the Ritz); Marble Arch (Speakers' Corner); Victoria (outside Thistle Victoria Hotel, 48 Buckingham Palace Road, SW1W 0RN). **Fares** £20 (£18 if booked online); £10 5-15s; free under-5s. Tickets valid for 24hrs, interchangeable between routes. **Credit** AmEx, DC, MC, V.

Open-top buses, with commentary, stop at various sights, where customers can hop on and off at will (tickets are valid for 24 hours). Big Bus also runs cruises and walking tours.

Original London Sightseeing Tour 8877 1722/ www.theoriginaltour.com. **Departures** Summer 9am-6pm daily. Winter 9am-5pm daily. **Pick-up** Grosvenor Gardens; Marble Arch (Speakers' Corner); Baker Street tube (forecourt); Coventry Street; Embankment tube; Trafalgar Square. **Fares** £18; £12 5-15s; free under-5s. £1.50 discount if booked online. **Credit** AmEx (not internet), MC, V.
Kids' Club tours include a specially designed commentary and an activity pack.

Pedal power

London Bicycle Tour Company 7928 6838/ www.londonbicycle.com. **Fares** £3 per hr; £16 1st 24hrs, £8 thereafter; £48 per week.
In addition to bicycles, kids' trailers are also available.

London Pedicabs 7093 3155/www.london pedicabs.com. **Fares** from £3 per person (per mile). Rickshaws based around Covent Garden and Soho.

Take a walk

Original London Walks 7624 3978/www.walks. com. **Tours** £6; £4.50 concessions; 1 free under-15 per adult.

Waterways

City Cruises 7740 0400/www.citycruises.com. City Cruises organises sightseeing tours and sells Rail & River Rover tickets. See also p292.

London Duck Tours 55 York Road, SE1 7NJ (7928 3132/www.londonducktours.co.uk). **Tours** Check website for departure details. **Fares** £17.50; £14 concessions, 13-15s; £12 under-12s; £53 family ticket (2+2). **Credit** MC, V,
Tours are conducted in a DUKW (an amphibious vehicle developed during World War II). Tours comprise a 75-minute road and river trip.

London RIB Voyages Kiosk, British Airways London Eye, Milliennium Pier, SE1 7PB (7401 8834/ www.londonribvoyages.com). **Tours** Check website for departure details. **Fares** £25; £15 under-12s. 10% discount for families (2+2). **Credit** MC, V.
Rigid Inflatable Boats, with a guide on board to give a commentary, skim speedily along the Thames on an hour-long river tour.

London Waterbus Company 7482 2660/ www.londonwaterbus.com. **Tours** Check website for departure details. **Fares** Single £5.80; £4 3-15s. Return £7.50, £5 children. **No credit cards.**
Cruises along the Regent's Canal via Camden Lock and Little Venice.

Staying over?

if you're on a budget, the **Youth Hostel Association** (www.yha.org.uk) can help. To request a brochure call 0870 770 8868. Hostels in the City, Rotherhithe, Hampstead and King's Cross all have family rooms that sleep up to six.

The London branches of international chains also offer good deals for families. At **Novotel** (see www.novotel.com) two children under 16 can share your room free. **Premier Travel Inn** (www.premier travelinn.com) have family rooms with a double bed and two sofabeds; cots available on request.

For extras like an indoor pool or spa, look to **Marriott** hotels (www.marriott.com). Cheaper, if plainer, are **Holiday Inns** (www.holiday-inn.com). Several offshoots offer 'kids eat free' deals.

If you prefer self-catering, consider a **Citadines** apartment (www.citadines.com). Studios, which sleep up to six people, have a kitchenette and baby facilities. You can even bring the family pet.

Here are our ten favourite, affordable, centrally located, family friendly, guesthouses and hotels.

Amsterdam Hotel

7 Trebovir Road, Earl's Court, SW5 9LS (0800 279 9132/fax 7244 7608/www.amsterdam-hotel.com). Earl's Court tube. **Rates** *£80-£86 single; £90-£100 double; £132-£148 family.* **Credit** *AmEx, DC, MC, V.* **Map** *p312 B11.*
Comfortable, modern and jolly, with high chairs, cots and buggies available on request.

Arran House Hotel

77-79 Gower Street, Bloomsbury, WC1E 6HJ (7636 2186/fax 7436 5328/www.london-hotel.co.uk). Goodge Street or Tottenham Court Road tube. **Rates** *£45-£55 single; £72-£95 double; £90-£113 triple; £96-£117 quad; £105-£130 quint.* **Credit** *MC, V.* **Map** *p315 K4.*
A lovely Georgian townhouse near the British Museum. The proprietors welcome children.

Baden-Powell House

65-67 Queen's Gate, South Kensington, SW7 5JS (7590 6900/fax 75906902/www.scoutbase. org.uk). South Kensington tube. **Rates** *(public prices) £72.50-£76 single; £49.50-£52 (extra pull-out bed £17.50-18.50) double; £35-£37 per adult, £22-£23 per child under 18 for family rooms.* **Credit** *AmEx, MC, V.* **Map** *p313 D10.*
The Chief Scout's Memorial Hostel. See p84.

Garden Court Hotel

30-31 Kensington Gardens Square, Bayswater, W2 4BG (7229 2553/fax 77272749/www.gardencourt hotel.co.uk). Bayswater or Queensway tube. **Rates** *£42-£64 single; £66-£92 double; £90-£120 triple; £100-£140 quad.* **Credit** *MC, V.* **Map** *p310 B6.*
Cheery rooms and a walled garden. Look out for the giant Beefeater statue.

Knightsbridge Green Hotel

159 Knightsbridge, SW1X 7PD (7584 6274/ fax 7225 1635/www.thekghotel.co.uk). Knightsbridge tube. **Rates** *(breakfast not incl) £105-£120 single; £140-£160 double; £160-£185 (plus £25 for each sofabed) suite.* **Credit** *AmEx, DC, MC, V.* **Map** *p316 G9.*
Not so cheap, but perfectly positioned for the big Kensington museums, Knightsbridge Green in family-run and friendly.

Morgan House

120 Ebury Street, Westminster, SW1W 9QQ (7730 2384/fax 7730 8442/www. morganhouse.co.uk). Sloane Square tube/ Victoria tube/rail. **Rates** *£46-£76 single; £66-£86 double; £86-£110 triple; £122 quad.* **Credit** *MC, V.* **Map** *p316 H10.*
The family room on the top floor sleeps four in bunk beds; there's also a patio garden.

New Linden

59 Leinster Square, Bayswater, W2 4PS (7221 4321/www.mayflower-group.co.uk). Bayswater tube. **Rates** *£50-£65 single; £59-£110 double; £80-£140 triple; £99-£200 quad.* **Credit** *AmEx, MC, V.* **Map** *p310 B6.*
An attractive budget hotel. The split-level family room retains elaborate period pillars and cornicing.

Swiss House Hotel

171 Old Brompton Road, South Kensington, SW5 0AN (7373 2769/www.swiss-hh.demon.co.uk). Gloucester Road or South Kensington tube. **Rates** *£60-£75 single; £95-£120 double; £135 triple; £145 quad.* **Credit** *AmEx, MC, V.* **Map** *p313 D11.*
A family-friendly hotel with a fleet of high chairs and family rooms.

22 York Street

22 York Street, Marylebone, W1U 6PX (7224 2990/fax 7224 1990/www.22yorkstreet.co.uk). Baker Street tube. **Rates** *£89 single; £100-£120 double; £120-£188 family.* **Credit** *AmEx, DC, MC, V.* **Map** *p311 F5.*
Right near Regent's Park, this isn't really a budget option, but it is a friendly, tasteful and unpretentious B&B with free internet access.

Windermere Hotel

142-144 Warwick Way, Pimlico, SW1V 4JE (7834 5163/fax 7630 8831/www.windermere-hotel. co.uk). Victoria tube/rail. **Rates** *£89-£99 single; £114-£139 double; £135-£149 family.* **Credit** *AmEx, MC, V.* **Map** *p316 H11.*
Rooms have recently been refurbished and bathrooms are clean and modern. There's a good on-site restaurant.

Around Town

South Bank & Bankside

Take a riverside walk to see how the dark side of the Thames came good.

The pedestrian-friendly South Bank has become a favourite Sunday-walk destination for families with young children and accompanying buggies, bikes, scooters and rollerskates. But the marshy south side of the Thames hasn't always been so salubrious. For centuries it was popular for all the wrong reasons: bear-baiting, brothels and hard drinking, to name a few. Even when the Festival of Britain was held here in 1951, the South Bank was still a rather grim proposition. It took the run-up to the Millennium festivities in the late 1990s to really effect the transformation of the area. The river may look a bit murky, but the Environment Agency say that the brown appearance is merely caused by the silt stirred up by the tide. According to the Agency, the Thames is the cleanest metropolitan river in Europe.

The **British Airways London Eye**, designed by architects Marks Barfield, and the magnificent **Tate Modern** are symbols of the success of the South Bank's regeneration. The elegant Millennium and Hungerford footbridges continue the theme. Add to these the dramatic, drum-shaped IMAX cinema (see p216 for screenings), the reconstructed **Shakespeare's Globe**, the **Design Museum** and the most recently regenerated patch, More London Riverside, incorporating the Unicorn Theatre (see p225) and you can see why the South Bank and Bankside area is now the arts and entertainment showpiece of the capital. Incidentally, if it's raining or you don't want to walk from Waterloo to Tower Bridge, the eco-friendly RV1 bus stops on Belvedere Road on the opposite side of the National Theatre and at both ends of Tower Bridge (alight on the north side for the Tower of London), passing Borough Market en route.

The **Tourist Information Centre** (7357 9168, www.visitsouthwark.com, open 10am-6pm Tue-Sat; noon-4pm Sun), remains in its temporary home in Vinopolis wine museum (1 Bank End, SE1 9BU) until at least September 2006, and is a good place to start your tour. Parents fond of a tipple should note that the Vinopolis tasting tour is, for children, the least interesting Bankside attraction.

South Bank

Along the riverside from Lambeth Bridge to Festival Pier you'll find something to suit all tastes. The **Museum of Garden History** celebrates John Tradescant, who brought back exotic plants from the tropics in the 16th century. Pineapples were among his discoveries, which is why this fruit is set in stone on Lambeth Bridge.

Continuing eastwards will reward you with spectacular views of the Houses of Parliament and Big Ben, which sit opposite St Thomas's Hospital, where you'll find the **Florence Nightingale Museum** and the new £60-million Evelina Children's Hospital, which opened on its new site at St Thomas's in October 2005. The original Evelina was founded in 1869 by Baron Ferdinand de Rothschild following the death of his wife in childbirth. Its new state-of-the-art home is a glass-fronted seven-storey building that was specially designed to be welcoming and friendly to its young patients. The hospital provides specialist care on floors with themes like 'Ocean' and 'Savannah'. There's also a performance space, art gallery, school and a 5-metre (17-foot) helter skelter. Jubilee Gardens, adjacent to the British Airways London Eye, is being re-landscaped. Design team West 8 plans to transform the flat, grassy area into a space with 'softly undulating hills', with trees and pathways; work should be completed by summer 2007. Nearby, County Hall – once the home of the Greater London Council – houses the **Dalí Universe**, noisy **Namco Station** and the **London Aquarium**.

The £91-million redevelopment to improve the Royal Festival Hall continues (see p214); the building is due to reopen in June 2007. The transformation of the National Film Theatre (www.bfi.org.uk) into a National Film Centre on the South Bank is in progress and will provide a research and study area as well as a space for education events. The work is due to be finished in autumn 2006, and the cinemas will remain open throughout (see p216). Outside the NFT under Waterloo Bridge you'll find the Riverside Walk

Market, where second-hand books are sold from trestle tables. The rumblings and thuds nearby emanate from skateboarders and rollerbladers, who practise their ollies, grinds and slides in the concrete space under Queen Elizabeth Hall.

The handsome Oxo Tower Wharf, with its deco tower advertising the stock-cube company, was saved from demolition in the 1970s by the Coin Street Community Builders, which is also responsible for the high-spirited Coin Street Festival every summer. Gabriel's Wharf is another Coin Street enterprise. For more information about what to look out for when you're walking in this area, download the PDFs of the popular Walk This Way guides from the website (www.southbanklondon.com).

British Airways London Eye

Riverside Building (next to County Hall), Westminster Bridge Road, SE1 7PB (booking line 0870 500 0600/ customer services 0870 990 8883/www.ba-londoneye. com). Westminster tube/Waterloo tube/rail. **Open** *Oct-May,* 10am-8pm daily. *June-Sept* 10am-9pm daily. **Admission** £13; £6.50 5-15s; £10 concessions (not applicable weekends or in July or Aug); free under-5s. **Credit** AmEx, MC, V. **Map** p317 M8.
Voted the world's favourite tourist attraction in 2005, the Eye attracts long queues on fine days, but the wait is rarely more than 30 minutes. Or you can pre-book online to get a 10% discount, and take a gamble with the weather. The views are brilliant, both by day and at night, when the outlook is twinklier. The Eye gets fairy lit at Christmas, and there are usually seasonal specials for half-term holidays (Hallowe'en, Christmas, Easter). A guide to the landmarks, and photos of your trip (£3.95 are on sale).

There are various packages available; you may also choose to combine your flight with a 40-minute river cruise, for instance, or a meal deal at a restaurant (visit the website or call 0870 500 0600 for details). *See also p43* **Eye eye**. *Buggy access. Café. Disabled access: toilets. Nappy-changing facilities. Nearest picnic place: Jubilee Gardens. Shop.*

Dalí Universe

County Hall (riverfront entrance), Riverside Building, Queen's Walk, SE1 7PB (7620 2720/www.dali universe.com). Westminster tube/Waterloo tube/rail. **Open** 10am-7pm daily (last entry 6pm). **Tours** phone for details. **Admission** *Oct-Apr* £11; £9.50 concessions; £6.50 8-16s; £5 4-7s; free under-4s; £28 family (2+2). *May-Sept* £12; £10 concessions; £8 8-16s; £6 4-7s; free under-4s; £30 family (2+2). **Credit** AmEx, DC, MC, V. **Map** p317 M8.
The main exhibition, curated by long-term Dali friend Benjamin Levi, includes wall-mounted quotes by, and (silent) videos and photographs of, this eccentric artist. There are sculptures, watercolours, rare etchings and lithographs. Many of the works seem like artistic comedy: melting clocks, long-legged elephants, crutches, lobsters, ants and stretched buttocks casting shadows over dreamy sunny plains. The gallery also shows work by new artists. *Buggy access. Disabled access: lift, ramp, toilets. Nearest picnic place: Jubilee Gardens. Shop.*

Florence Nightingale Museum

St Thomas's Hospital, 2 Lambeth Palace Road, SE1 7EW (7620 0374/www.florence-nightingale.co.uk). Westminster tube/Waterloo tube/rail. **Open** 10am-5pm Mon-Fri; 10am-4.30pm Sat, Sun (last entry 1hr before closing). **Admission** (LP) £5.80; £4.80 5-18s, concessions; free under-5s; £16 family (2+5). **Credit** AmEx, MC, V. **Map** p317 M9.

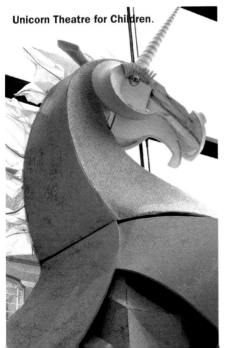

Unicorn Theatre for Children.

Around Town

Such is Florence's celebrity status on Key Stage 1 and 2 of the National Curriculum that you often hear parents being instructed by six-year-olds on the finer points of the lamp lady's remarkable life. Any gaps in their formidable knowledge can be filled by the information provided in this museum. Mementoes and tableaux depict the harshness of the field hospitals of Scutari, where Nurse Nightingale first came to public attention, but details of her privileged life before this, and the studious one thereafter, are just as interesting. A 20-minute film tells Florence's story, with Anna Massey giving her voice. Other displays include clothing, furniture, books, letters and portraits. Florence's pet owl, Athena (now stuffed), is also on display. A temporary exhibition at the museum celebrates another Crimean war hero, Mary Seacole, recently voted the greatest black Briton.

Free trails for children aged five to seven (I Spy Worksheet), seven to ten (Find Out About Flo!) and ten and over (Find Out About the Museum) are available at all times. Family activities are held on the second weekend of every month and during half-term and the Easter holidays. Events may include craft work, such as making your own lamp, poetry and performance sessions with actors playing the parts of nurses Nightingale and Seacole, or object handling and dressing up. Check the website for details. *Buggy access. Disabled access: toilets. Nearest picnic place: benches by hospital entrance/Archbishop's Park. Shop. (In hospital: Café. Nappy-changing facilities. Restaurant.)*

Hayward Gallery

Belvedere Road, SE1 8XX (7960 5226/box office 0870 169 1000/www.hayward.org.uk). Embankment tube/Waterloo tube/rail. **Open** *During exhibitions* 10am-6pm Mon, Thur, Sat, Sun; 10am-8pm Tue, Wed; 10am-9pm Fri. **Admission** £7.50; £4-£7 concessions; £3 12-16s; free under-12s. Prices may vary, phone to check. **Credit** AmEx, MC, V. **Map** p318 M8.

Inside the light, bright pavilion, designed by Daniel Graham, casual visitors can watch cartoons on touch screens or just wander around the visually confusing space created by curved, two-way mirrors. The neon tower on the gallery roof was commissioned by the Arts Council in 1970. Its yellow, red, green and blue tubes are controlled by changes in the direction and strength of the wind. Until 30 July 2006 the temporary exhibition is Undercover Surrealism, with works by Dali, Picasso and others; from 7 September to 19 November 2006 it is Sixty Years of the Arts Council Collection. Family activities linked to the exhibitions might include poetry workshops or puppet-making sessions; consult the gallery's website for details. *Buggy access. Café. Disabled access: lift. Nappy-changing facilities. Nearest picnic place: Jubilee Gardens/riverside benches. Shop.*

London Aquarium

County Hall (riverfront entrance), Riverside Building, Westminster Bridge Road, SE1 7PB (7967 8000/tours 7967 8007/www.londonaquarium.co.uk). Westminster tube/Waterloo tube/rail. **Open** 10am-6pm daily (last entry 5pm). Phone for late opening during holidays. Closed 25 Dec. **Tours** (groups of 10 or more) phone for details. **Admission** (LP) *Apr-3 Sept, 14-29 Oct, 16-31 Dec 2006* £11.75; £9.50 concessions, disabled; £8.25 3-14s; free under-3s; £36 family (2+2); all prices rise by £1 during school holidays. *4 Sept-13 Oct, 30 Oct-15 Dec* £1 reduction from prices above; £32 family (2+2). **Credit** AmEx, MC, V. **Map** p317 M9.

To grown-ups, London's Aquarium might lack a certain wow factor, but youngsters make a beeline for the impressive one-million-litre Pacific tank as soon as they are through the doors. Most children are obsessed with the sharks, who can give you a bit of a turn when they glide past your nose. There are brown, sandtiger, nurse and zebra sharks to examine before attention can be given to other aquatic species. The aquarium's 14 zones cover freshwater stream to coral reef to rainforest, and contain some 350 species of marine life that occupy 50 tanks on two floors beneath County Hall. Steer your shoal to the tropical tanks, which are aglow with seahorses, angelfish, pufferfish and that celebrity species, the clownfish. An interesting display about the tidal River Thames may well seem a little provincial among the more exotic environments recreated in the Pacific, Atlantic, Mangrove, Rainforest and Coral tanks. The touch pool attracts large crowds of children keen to stroke the long-suffering rays as they skim along the surface. Feeding times are fun for children: every day you can watch the rays being fed (11.30am) and listen to a talk about coral (3.30pm); on Monday, Wednesday and Friday divers feed the Atlantic tank inhabitants (rays, dogfish) at noon; on Tuesday, Thursday and Saturday the sharks are fed at 2.30pm, and there are daily shark talks at 2pm and 4pm. Conservation and breeding programmes are part of the Aquarium's brief, and visitors are directed towards the work of campaigning organisations, such as the Shark Trust, London Wildlife Trust, Seawatch Foundation and Marine Conservation Society. Children pick up an activity sheet and trail as they go in, and the education department runs regular popular activities for children during school holidays – badge-making is always a popular one; check the website for details. Queues are long during wet and cold school holidays and at weekends; book online for fast-track advance tickets. *Buggy access. Café. Disabled access: lift, ramp, toilets. Nappy-changing facilities. Nearest picnic place: Jubilee Gardens. Shop.*

London Fire Brigade Museum

94A Southwark Bridge Road, SE1 0EG (7587 2894/ www.london-fire.gov.uk). Borough tube/Southwark tube/rail/344 bus. **Tours** by appointment only 10.30am, 2pm Mon-Fri. Closed bank hols. **Admission** £3; £2 7-14s, concessions; free under-7s, school groups. **Credit** MC, V. **Map** p318 O9.

This friendly museum, housed in eight small rooms within the London Fire Brigade Training Centre, is packed with firefighting memorabilia, photographs, paintings and equipment. Access is by booked guided tour only. Tours last roughly an hour and present an entertaining, potted history of firefighting since the Great Fire in 1666. Exhibits include uniforms dating from the early 20th century when breathing apparatus was first introduced, a 17th-century manual firefighting pump and paintings by firemen and firewomen who recorded their Blitz experiences. There's also one of only three George Crosses that have been awarded to firefighters. Tours take in the appliance bay, where pumps dating back to 1708 stand in tribute to blazes past. Small children are given colouring pencils and encouraged to draw any of the 20 fire engines, ranging from a horse-drawn, hand-pumped 1830s model to shiny red and brass vehicles from the early 20th century, and today's more streamlined heavyweights. Sadly, climbing on the vehicles is not allowed, but trying on uniforms is. *Buggy access. Disabled access: toilets. Nappy-changing facilities. Nearest picnic place: Mint Street Park. Shop.*

Museum of Garden History

Church of St Mary-at-Lambeth, Lambeth Palace Road, SE1 7LB (7401 8865/www.museumgardenhistory.org). Waterloo tube/rail then 507 bus/Lambeth North rail/ 77, C10 bus. **Open** *10.30am-5pm daily. Closed 24 Dec-2 Jan.* **Admission** *free; suggested donation £3 (£2.50 concessions).* **Credit** *Shop (over £10) AmEx, MC, V.* **Map** *p317 L10.*

The world's first museum dedicated to gardening is contained within the deconsecrated and refurbished church of St Mary's. The Tradescants, a pioneering family of gardeners and botanists, and Captain William Bligh, of *Bounty* fame, along with half a dozen archbishops of Canterbury, are entombed in the graveyard. A replica of a 17th-century knot garden is a living memorial to the Tradescants. Look out for the Pedlar's Window, a stained-glass window illustrating a man and his dog. History has it that an early 16th-century pedlar came into an acre of land (now the site of County Hall) and donated it to the church on condition that an image of him be preserved in glass. The current window is the fourth, made in 1956 after its predecessor was destroyed in 1941.

In March 2006, thanks to a £40,000 Heritage Lottery Fund grant, the museum opened a multimedia local history display all about the borough of Lambeth over the past 1,000 years. Permanent exhibitions about ancient horticultural practices and garden tools are joined by temporary ones: Tradescant Inspiration: A Botanical Exploration of 17th-Century Plants (14 July-30 Aug), and Repatriating the Ark, which tells the Tradescant story (3 July-29 Oct). Free garden-themed activities for children take place during the school holidays (every Wed in Aug and also on 25 Oct 2006); check the website for details. *Buggy access. Café. Disabled access: ramps, toilets. Nappy-changing facilities. Nearest picnic place: Archbishop's Park. Shop.*

Namco Station

County Hall (riverfront entrance), Riverside Building Westminster Bridge Road, SE1 7PB (7967 1066/www.namcoexperience.com). Westminster tube/Waterloo tube/rail. **Open** *10am-midnight daily.* **Admission** *(LP) free; games prices vary.* **Map** *p317 M9.*

A noisy, cavernous hideaway beloved of kids with more pocket money than sense, Namco has more than 200 types of video game on which to waste your 'Nams' (the unit of currency used here). Bumper cars, Techno Bowling, computerised dance machines and pool tables lurk downstairs (as do many over-18s, who inhabit a bar tuned to the Sports Channel). This pleasure dome shares its entrance with McDonald's: talk about teen paradise. *Bar. Buggy access. Disabled access: lift, toilets. Nappy-changing facilities. Nearest picnic place: Jubilee Gardens.*

Around Town

A wholesome proposition

Traffic-light warning labels on packaged food and celebrity beetroot endorsements are all very well, but as a nation we're still getting fatter on fast food and fizzy pop. It would be a different story if everyone had a **Borough Market** on their doorstep. The ancient market, which has occupied this Southwark site since 1756, reinvented itself as a quality-food retailer six years ago, became beloved of high-profile chefs and foodies, and is now established as a top tourist destination.

But it's not all about purveying speciality olives and venison sausages to the elite. Borough doesn't want to be a niche market. The board of trustees believes that locally produced vegetables and fruit should be available to all. Which is why many of the traders are keen to engage local people, especially those who wouldn't ordinarily buy quality raw materials when a supermarket can sell them with three pizzas for the price of half an organic chicken breast. Market traders host barbecues for residents of the local Peabody Trust estate; some of the traders also speak at schools, two of them, Silfield Farm and Furness Fish, have for some years hosted trainee chefs (previously unemployed youngsters) from Jamie Oliver's Fifteen restaurant.

The next big thing for the board of trustees is more ambitious and far reaching. The Borough Market Food Centre of Excellence will build on the market's charitable status and its work in the field of community education and health. The Centre will use the market as a teaching tool to promote healthy eating, food and nutrition education and become a catalyst for other local and national food-related programmes and initiatives. At the heart of the project will be an education centre, the Borough Market Food School, at 1 Cathedral Street, a building owned by the market. The school is scheduled to open in early 2007; visit the website for information.

The trustees have brought together a board of people with different food specialities. The Centre plans to capitalise on their knowledge and share it with a wider audience, providing an educational facility within the market itself. Indoors, at the Food School, there'll be a more conventional classroom, and a kitchen where children and adults can take part in cookery workshops and demonstrations, using food from the market. They'll learn about where their dinner comes from, the importance of using seasonal produce and how farmers and growers produce and distribute food. Courses for people with special dietary needs, workshops on preparing family meals on a budget and an introduction to careers in food production and catering are also planned.

The project has already attracted interest from parties ranging from the Prince's Trust to Southwark Council. Everyone can see that there's never been a better time to take an interest in food, and that there is no better place than Borough Market to do just that. The Centre of Excellence won't exist for profit, kids' educational activities will be offered for little or no charge and should pay huge dividends if they help raise a generation that can whizz up a vat of vegetable soup for the price of a packet of chicken nuggets.

Royal National Theatre

South Bank, SE1 9PX (info 7452 3400/box office 7452 3000/www.nationaltheatre.org.uk). Waterloo tube/rail. **Open** 10am-11pm Mon-Sat. *Box office* 10am-8pm Mon-Sat. Closed 24, 25 Dec, Good Friday. **Tickets** *Olivier & Lyttelton* £10-£37.50. *Cottesloe* £10-£28. *Standby* £10, £18. *Backstage tours* £5; £4 concessions, under-18s. **Credit** AmEx, DC, MC, V. **Map** p318 M8.

The outdoor space – Theatre Square – has done much to draw families' attention towards Sir Denys Lasdun's landmark concrete theatre complex. It's the home of the terrific Watch This Space season every summer (7 July- 2 Sept 2006), which includes daily street theatre and comic performances suitable for a family audience at lunchtimes and in the early evening. Indoors, the National is full of bright ideas to secure tomorrow's audiences. Around the ground-floor refreshment area, free exhibitions and music events take place throughout the year. You can catch free concerts from Monday to Friday in the early evenings before the plays begin. The NT runs a range of educational activity programmes, from half-term shows by visiting theatre companies to school-based initiatives (call 7452 3388 or visit the website for details). Backstage tours (not suitable for under-sevens) take place three times a day, last an hour and may be booked at the information desk (£5, £4 under-18s). Tours take in the rehearsal rooms, workshops where costumes and props are made, dressing rooms and stages. *Café. Disabled access: lift, toilets. Nappy-changing facilities. Nearest picnic place: Bernie Spain Gardens. Restaurants. Shop.*

Bankside

The entire riverside stretch between London Bridge and Blackfriars Bridge, once the epicentre of bawdy Southwark, is rightfully popular with tourists and Londoners, who come for the history and culture. It's a far cry from the Bankside that was presided over by various bishops of Winchester, who made money fining the women of easy virtue who used to ply their trade here. All that remains of the Palace of Winchester, home of successive bishops, is the rose window of the Great Hall on Clink Street, just around the corner from the fun-filled **Golden Hinde**.

The parish church during Shakespeare's time was St Saviour's, known since 1905 as **Southwark Cathedral**, which sits modestly away from the river. The **Millennium Bridge** in front of Tate Modern provides a pedestrian carriageway to the puffed-up other cathedral across the water, namely **St Paul's** (*see p52*). The wonkily ancient terrace of houses between Tate Modern and the Globe is owned by Southwark Cathedral; Sir Christopher Wren is reputed to have stayed in one of them during the building of St Paul's in 1680.

Borough Market, hard by Southwark Cathedral, is positively bursting to the brim with foodie visitors at weekends. This area south of the river had terrible associations for Charles Dickens,

High culture under the **QEH**. *See p32.*

whose debtor father was imprisoned in Marshalsea Prison, which once stood near Borough High Street, but was destroyed long ago.

Bramah Museum of Tea & Coffee

40 Southwark Street, SE1 1UN (7403 5650/ www.bramahmuseum.co.uk). London Bridge tube/ rail. **Open** 10am-6pm daily. Closed 25-26 Dec. **Admission** £4; £3.50 concessions; £10 family (2+4). **Credit** AmEx, MC, V. **Map** p317 P8.

A restorative museum set up and run by Edward Bramah, who knows a thing or tea about brewing the perfect cuppa (one of his coffee machines is displayed in the Science Museum). The displays and exhibitions constitute an informative tribute to the history of top hot beverages, with all sorts of forgotten tales about the tea trade's power to influence the course of history. Enjoy a pot of tea or a cup of coffee – plus scones, muffins and cakes if you're peckish – in the old fashioned tea rooms (you don't have to visit the museum), in which a pianist is usually tinkling away and where the walls are adorned with vintage posters advertising the two great brews. *Buggy access. Café. Disabled access: toilets. Nearest picnic place: Southwark Cathedral Gardens. Shop.*

Clink Prison Museum

1 Clink Street, SE1 9DG (7403 0900/www.clink.co.uk). London Bridge tube/rail. **Open** *June-Sept* 10am-9pm daily. *Oct-May* 10am-6pm daily. **Tours** hourly when available. **Admission** £5; £3.50 5-15s, concessions; free under-5s; £12 family (2+2). *Tours* £2. **Credit** MC, V. **Map** p318 P8.

Like its close neighbour the London Dungeon, the Clink Prison Museum informs visitors of the hideous practices that were dished out to wrongdoers of London past, but there the similarity ends. The Clink might not employ actors or use gimmicky special effects to act out the dastardly deeds of yore, but is nonetheless fascinating.

Around Town

The **Millennium Bridge**. *See p37.*

main gun deck can't be more than 0.9metres (3-foot) high. The five levels, recreated in minute detail, are fascinating. Hugely popular with families and school groups, all of whom have to book ahead to live the Tudor life at sea, 'are the Living History' overnighters (Apr-Sept). These take place on Saturdays (£40 per child or adult, costumes and entertainment provided – bring a sleeping bag). The best time to visit is during the school holidays, when there are frequent storytelling sessions, guided tours and family workshops; details are posted on the website.
Nearest picnic place: Southwark Cathedral Gardens/ riverside benches. Shop.

London Dungeon

28-34 Tooley Street, SE1 2SZ (7403 7221/www.the dungeons.com). London Bridge tube/rail. **Open** *Sept-June 9.30am-5.30pm daily. July, Aug 9.30am-7.30pm daily.* **Admission** £15.95; £12.50 OAPs, students; £11 5-15s; £2 reduction for wheelchair users; free carers, under-5s. **Credit** AmEx, MC, V. **Map** p319 Q8.
The popularity of the Dungeon doesn't appear to be waning, even after more than 30 years of scaring the general public witless, judging from the length of the weekend queues outside the Victorian railway arches that form its home (you can purchase fast-track tickets online to avoid queueing). Your visit begins in the pungent Great Plague Exhibition, a walk-through set with a medley of corpses, boils, projectile vomiting, worm-filled skulls and scuttling rats. From here, visitors are escorted back in time to revisit a variety of gruesome eras of horrible London history, including the Great Fire, from which you escape through a rotating dry-ice-filled drum. In the Traitor Boat Ride to Hell visitors play the part of condemned prisoners (death sentence guaranteed). Then there's a gruesome section devoted to Jack the Ripper and, in this year's new addition, Sweeney Todd, the demonic 18th-century barber. Costumed actors aren't averse to picking on visitors to take part, for instance, in demonstrating torture implements, standing in the dock as part of a mock court case or as a model for the finer points of the bubonic plague (tall dads are prime targets). The dungeons are wreathed in dry-ice fog and echo with blood-curdling screeches, and as you ogle scenes of torture, death and disease, actors lurk, ready to jump out on you – it's all in good humour, of course, and doesn't seem to bother younger visitors who relish the chance to be spooked out of their wits for the duration of the hour and a half that the tour takes.
Guaranteed to generate a scream or two is Labyrinth of the Lost, a horror mirror maze, the largest scary mirror labyrinth in the world. The shop sells, naturally, all kinds of spooky toys and gags. Little horrors can also have a birthday party here. The price (from £17 per head for the basic package) includes a tour, an hour in the café's games centre, a themed photograph and a well-filled party bag.
Buggy access. Café. Disabled access; toilets. Nappy-changing facilities. Picnic place: Hay's Galleria. Shop.

Much of the material is on wall panels that are generally well presented if unsettling. A few waxwork models and props, like old beds with straw mattresses, are used to bring scenes to life. There isn't too much gore, apart from a number of unsavoury devices, such as a medieval scold's bridle (used by husbands to keep their wives in check) and a few 'hands on' execution blocks, fetters and foot crushers, thumb screws and chains, 70 per cent of which are original. The prison, which was owned by the Bishop of Winchester, was in operation from 1247 until 1780, the year it burned down during the anti-Catholic Gordon Riots. This museum is on the site of the original Clink (so called, it's said, because the inmates clanked their chains). It was where thieves, prostitutes, debtors and priests served their sentences – some of them had hideously long incarcerations and suffered unimaginable tortures. The museum is a useful resource for students at Key Stage 3 who are learning Tudor and medieval history, particularly as it deals with issues such as the power of the Church and the role of the monarchy.
Buggy access. Nearest picnic place: Southwark Cathedral Gardens. Shop.

Golden Hinde

St Mary Overie Dock, Cathedral Street, SE1 9DE (0870 011 8700/www.goldenhinde.co.uk). Monument tube/London Bridge tube/rail. **Open** *10am-5.30pm daily but times may vary; phone for details. Tours phone for times.* **Admission** £4.50; £4 concessions; £3.50 4-13s; free under-4s; £12.50 family (2+2). **Credit** MC, V. **Map** p319 P8.
Children love this replica of Sir Francis Drake's 16th-century flagship, which has altered its remit within the past year to focus on education rather than all-out fun, which sadly means there will no longer be children's birthday parties here. It's still child-friendly, though. The ship was built in 1973 to commemorate the admiral-pirate's 400th birthday, after which it sailed to San Francisco. The

Old Operating Theatre, Museum & Herb Garret

9A St Thomas's Street, SE1 9RY (7188 2679/ www.thegarret.org.uk). London Bridge tube/rail. **Open** *10.30am-5pm daily (last entry 4.45pm). Closed 15 Dec-5 Jan.* **Admission** (LP) £4.95; £3.95 concessions; £2.95 6-16s; free under-6s; £12 family (2+4). **No credit cards. Map** p319 Q8.
Ascend the spiral stairs of the medieval church of St Thomas to find an ancient treasure: a 300-year-old herb

A 75 minute adventure tour of the City of Westminster by road and river on board an amphibious 'Duck', including a live commentary.

London Ducktours offers more than just a sightseeing tour - it's an exciting road and river adventure appealing to visitors of all ages taking in some of London's most famous landmarks.

Ask about our personalised tours for weddings, children's parties, hospitality, educational tours, special events etc!

www.londonducktours.co.uk 020 7928 3132

garret and Britain's only surviving 19th-century operating theatre, the oldest surviving part of St Thomas's Hospital. The operating theatre was used in the first half of the 19th century, largely for amputations and treatment of superficial wounds, before being boarded up and forgotten about until 1956. The hospital was built around the church, and when the need arose for a new theatre, the roof was the obvious choice: there was plenty of light and enough room for students to view the proceedings. The rest of the museum displays hideous-looking surgical instruments and images of early surgical procedures alongside bunches of dried herbs in the atmospheric attic. Check the website for details of weekend and school-holiday events, which include Speed Surgery demonstrations, hands-on pill- and poultice-making or object-handling sessions. Free trails and worksheets are available for children. *Nearest picnic place: Southwark Cathedral Gardens. Shop.*

Shakespeare's Globe

21 New Globe Walk, Bankside, SE1 9DT (7401 9919/ tours 7902 1500/www.shakespeares-globe.org). Mansion House tube/London Bridge tube/rail. **Open** *Box office* (theatre bookings, 5 May-8 Oct 2006) 10am-6pm Mon-Sat; 10am-5pm Sun. **Tours** 10am-5pm daily. From May-Sept, afternoon tours visit only the Rose Theatre, not the Globe. **Tickets** £5-£31. *Tours* £9; £7.50 concessions; £6.50 5-15s; free under-5s; £25 family (2+3). **Credit** AmEx, MC, V. **Map** p318 O7. This reconstruction of the Bard's own theatre, built 100 yards from where the original stood, was the brainchild of actor Sam Wanamaker, who died before it was finished. Tours of the theatre take place all year round, but the historically authentic performances in the 'wooden O' (*The Comedy of Errors, Antony and Cleopatra, Titus Andronicus* and *Coriolanus* will play in rep during the 2006 season) run from May to October. The Globe runs workshops and events for students of all ages, including drama sessions for eight- to 11-year-olds during the summer theatre season; consult the website or ring 7902 1433 for further details. The remains of the Rose Theatre, where many of Shakespeare's early works were originally staged, lie around the corner in the basement of an office block (for details, check www.rosetheatre.org.uk). *Café. Disabled access: lift, toilet. Nappy-changing facilities. Restaurant. Shop.*

Southwark Cathedral

London Bridge, SE1 9DA (7367 6700/tours 7367 6734/www.dswark.org/cathedral). London Bridge tube/rail. **Open** from 8.45am daily (closing times vary). *Restaurant* 10am-5pm daily. Closed 25 Dec, Good Friday, Easter Sunday, 24 Dec. *Services* 8am, 8.15am, 12.30pm, 12.45pm, 5.30pm Mon-Fri; 9am, 9.15am, 4pm Sat; 8.45am, 9am, 11am, 3pm, 6.30pm Sun. **Admission** free (LP) *Audio tour* £3; £2.50 OAPs; £1.50 under-16s, students. Donations appreciated. **Credit** MC, V. **Map** p319 P8. The oldest Gothic building in London, this small but handsome cathedral was one of the few places south of the river that Charles Dickens had a kind word for. He, like us, found it inspirational, despite the fact it was (and still is) hemmed in by buildings and the screeching railway.

Dating from the 13th century, Southwark Cathedral was originally known as St Saviour's church. It fell into disrepair after the Reformation, and parts of it were used as a bakery and a pigsty. In 1905 it was reclaimed as a cathedral. It has an education centre, a shop and a refectory. As well as more recent memorials – including one for the 51 victims of the 1989 Marchioness riverboat tragedy – there are tributes to Shakespeare (whose brother Edmund is buried here), John Gower and John Harvard, benefactor of Harvard University. Children are drawn to the scary tomb topped by a stone carving of an emaciated body in a shroud, which is in the chancel. The windows contain images of Chaucer, who set off to Canterbury from a pub in Borough High Street, and John Bunyan, who preached locally. Every year families enjoy the Christmas Eve crib service (4pm), and there's anEaster egg hunt on Easter Sunday after the morning service.

The cathedral choir is one of the best in the country, its success in no small measure down to the dedication of the boys and girls who attend three practices a week before weekday Evensong and Sunday services. Joining the choir gives children a fantastic musical education, and the lads have a useful footie team too. Ring the above number for details of audition dates. *Buggy access. Disabled access: lifts, ramps, toilets. Nappy-changing facilities. Nearest picnic place: gardens. Restaurant. Shop.*

Tate Modern

Bankside, SE1 9TG (7887 8000/www.tate.org.uk). St Paul's tube/Blackfriars tube/rail. **Open** 10am-6pm Mon-Thur, Sun; 10am-10pm Fri, Sat (last entry 45mins before closing). **Admission** free (charge for special exhibitions). **Map** p318 O7. This former power station opened in 2000 as a gigantic gallery for modern art. Just trotting round this awesome space is an event in itself. The architects who converted it left relics of the building's industrial days – the original gantries and lifting gear in the vast Turbine Hall, where the Unilever Series of large-scale commissions is displayed, changing every autumn. The gallery holds several temporary exhibitions throughout the year. The summer show for 2006 is on the paintings of Kandinsky (22 June-1 Oct), then there's work by the American abstract sculptor David Smith (1 Nov 2006-14 Jan 2007). For the first time since it opened, all 48 galleries displaying the permanent collection have been rehung. Tate Modern's new look, which was revealed in May 2006, has a new concept: the curators have organised four wings on Levels 3 and 5 into themes of Cubism, Futurism and Vorticism; Surrealism and Surrealist tendencies; Abstract Expressionism and European Informal Art; and Minimalism.

Family activities are mostly available from Level 3. A pack called Start, which contains puzzles, art materials and an architectural trail, is available every Sunday (11am-5pm) and in school holidays. Start is intended to help over-fives explore the collection. There's also a children's audio tour. Since the rehang, two new activity zones aimed at children and their families have opened. On Level 3 you'll find the UBS Openings: Family Zone, which introduces youngsters to the materials and meanings of modern art. Here you can pick up a Tate Teaser paper trail, play art-related games, or browse books in the library. On Level 5, Bloomberg Learning Zone holds a collection of interactive activities and one of a series of free paper trails. Healthy meals are prepared for children in the café. Signing up for the email bulletin via the website is a good way of finding out about holiday workshops for families with young children, as well as short courses for teens. *Buggy access. Café. Disabled access: lifts, toilets. Nappy-changing facilities. Nearest picnic place: grounds. Restaurant. Shops.*

The angelic choir of **Southwark Cathedral**.

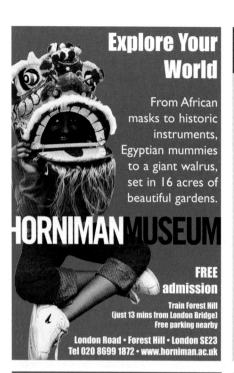

Eye, eye

Despite a shaky beginning (it missed the Millennium, with the inaugural flight delayed until February 2000 because of technical problems), the **British Airways London Eye** shows no signs of waning in popularity. The South Bank has been transformed since the big wheel started rolling and local businesses have boomed.

The Eye is one of London's tallest structures, dwarfed only by the three Canary Wharf towers, the BT Tower and Tower 42. Parents might worry that energetic offspring won't take to standing in a confined space for half an hour. But far from finding it dull, most kids are in such awe of the Eye's giant size that they can't wait to climb aboard for their 'flight'. Indeed, youngsters seem so amazed at how the vast metropolis is reduced to the proportions of a model village that they often beg for another spin – something most parents will draw the line at, considering the cost of tickets. But costs have done little to diminish the Eye's attractiveness. It won two golds at the 2005 Visit London Awards: one in the Tour London category for its schools programme; the second Best Day Out For Londoners (for the London Eye and River Cruise Experience).

For grown-ups, a flight on the Eye offers new insight into the position of London's attractions in relation to one another and to the river; kids gain more from the experience if they've seen the main sights from ground level beforehand. Pack a camera as views from the top are spectacular:

eastwards is Tower Bridge, Tate Modern, the Oxo Tower and St Paul's. Further out, in Greenwich, ask the kids to spot the O_2 (formerly the Dome) and the Thames Barrier (you won't see that one until your pod reaches the top of the wheel). To the north you can see the green roof of the British Museum and beyond that Hampstead Heath. Eyes west for Nelson's Column, Buckingham Palace and Battersea Power Station. On a clear day you can see one of the Queen's other residences, Windsor Castle, 40 kilometres (25 miles) away. You'll have a different perspective on the Houses of Parliament – as you look for MPs on the terrace ask observant youngsters if they can spot the difference between the bridges on either side of the Palace of Westminster (Westminster Bridge is coloured green for the Commons, Lambeth Bridge is red, for the Lords).

The Eye's original five-year lease was extended in 2003 and again this year, securing its future for many years to come and ensuring that generations more can enjoy the ride.

Eye say, did you know that?

● The Eye has 32 capsules. Each holds 25 people, so there's a maximum of 800 people per revolution.
● It carries an average of 10,000 people each day, totalling some 20 million visitors since its inaugural flight in 2000.
● It is 135 metres (450ft) high – the sixth-largest structure in London – and is taller than the Statue of Liberty in New York.
● It is the world's largest observation wheel.
● It cost £75 million to build, including the landscaping costs for the surrounding area.
● The wheel turns 8,000 rotations per year.
● The wheel is 200 times larger than your average bicycle wheel.
● There are 18 maintenance technicians who are responsible for keeping the great wheel turning smoothly.
● The Eye weighs 1,700 tonnes, which is heavier that 250 double-decker buses or 280 adult African elephants.
● Architects David Marks and Julia Barfield were responsible for the design; it took seven years to turn their dream into reality.

Around Town

Winston Churchill's Britain at War Experience

64-66 Tooley Street, SE1 2TF (7403 3171/www. britainatwar.co.uk). London Bridge tube/rail. **Open** *Apr-Sept* 10am-6pm daily. *Oct-Mar* 10am-5pm daily. (last entry 1hr before closing). Closed 24-26 Dec. **Admission** £9.50; £5.75 concessions; £4.85 5-16s; free under-5s; £25 family (2+2). **Credit** AmEx, MC, V. **Map** p319 Q8.
Enter via an original London Underground lift into a reconstructed Blitz-era Underground air-raid shelter –

where the walk-through set – which gives the impression the place is still in use – includes bunks, a temporary kitchen and library, original posters and newsreel clips from the time. Other displays explain the roles of women at war and the life of evacuated children. Set pieces take in a BBC broadcasting room and visitors can experience (with wartime sound-effects) Morrison and Andersen bomb shelters. The visit culminates in a full-size street scene where a bomb has recently exploded. Children can try on a variety of wartime regalia in the dressing-up corner. *Buggy access. Disabled access: toilets. Nearest picnic place: Southwark Cathedral Gardens. Shop.*

✕ LUNCH BOX

For recommended restaurants and cafés in the area, see p162-84.

Amano *Victor Wharf, Clink Street, SE1 9DG (7234 0000).*
Auberge *35 Tooley Street, SE1 2PJ (7407 5267).*
Azzuro *1 Sutton Walk, SE1 7ND (7620 1300).*
Café Rouge *Hay's Galleria, SE1 2HD (7378 0097).*
Doggett's (pub*) 1 Blackfriars Bridge Road, SE1 9UD (7633 9081).*
EAT *Oxo Tower Wharf, Bargehouse Street, SE1 9PH (7928 8179); Royal Festival Hall, Riverside level, SE1 8XX (7401 2989).*
Festival Square Café *Ground Floor, Royal Festival Hall, South Bank Centre, SE1 8XX (7928 2228).*
Film Café *Charlie Chaplin Walk, South Bank, SE1 8XR (7960 3118).*
Founders' Arms (pub*) 52 Hopton Street, SE1 9JH (7928 1899).*
Giraffe *Royal Festival Hall, Riverside level, SE1 8XX (7928 2004).*
House of Crêpes *56 Upper Ground, SE1 9PP (7401 9816).*
McDonald's *St Thomas's Street, SE1 9RT (7378 6758).*
Ned's Noodle Bar *County Hall, Belvedere Road, SE1 7GQ (7593 0077).*
Pizza Express *4 Borough High Street, SE1 9QQ (7407 2995); 24 New Globe Walk, SE1 9DS (7401 3977); The Cardamon Building, 31 Shad Thames, SE1 2YR (7403 8484); The White House, Belvedere Road, SE1 8YP (7928 4091).*
Southwark Cathedral Refectory *Southwark Cathedral, Montague Close, SE1 9DA (7407 5740).*
Starbucks *Winchester Wharf, Clink Street, SE1 9DG (7403 0951).*
Strada *Royal Festival Hall, Riverside level, SE1 8XX (7401 9126).*
Studio Six *56 Upper Ground, SE1 9PP (7928 6243).*
Tate Modern Restaurant *2nd Floor, Tate Modern, SE1 9TG (7401 5014).*
Wagamama *Royal Festival Hall, Riverside level, SE1 8XX (7021 0877).*

Tower Bridge & Bermondsey

The fascinating area through which the Thames Path takes you, from London Bridge towards Tower Bridge is known as the Pool of London. A useful resource for those visiting the area with children is the website www.pooloflondon. co.uk/familyfriendly, from which you can download free self-guiding family trails and find out about events in the area. Walking along the riverside from London Bridge will take you through Hay's Galleria, a rather odd touristy enclave, where there's a sparkly year-round Christmas shop, stalls selling leather goods and London souvenirs, and an often-deserted Café Rouge, and past **HMS Belfast**, the floating wing of the Imperial War Museum. Continue along the Thames Path towards Tower Bridge, and you come to the riverside's most recent development known as More London, one of many business and leisure projects for architects Foster and Partners. You can cool your feet in the fountains inset in the piazza on a hot summer's day and enjoy a picnic or pick up a snack from one of the nearby shops. There are also great views of the towering buildings of the City from this stretch of the riverside. The area's main landmark is City Hall, the unusually shaped glass-sided headquarters of Mayor Ken Livingstone, the London Assembly and the Greater London Authority. The structure leans rather drunkenly away from the river so as not to cast unwelcome shade on the walkers below. The ground floors are open to the public and have changing exhibitions and a café. Outside, The Scoop is a sunken amphitheatre that seats several hundred people and stages a number of free events throughout the year, from film screenings and theatre performances to outdoor art; check www.morelondon.com for forthcoming events. A more exciting landmark is the new £13-million **Unicorn Theatre** (www.unicorn theatre.com), which opened in December 2005. The Unicorn is the first specially designed theatre for children in central London, *see also p225.*

Nearby is Tower Bridge; a noticeboard announces when the bridge will next open for tall ships to pass through (it does so about 500 times a year). This is what a wealthy American developer allegedly thought he was buying when he invested in the old London Bridge, (it was replaced in 1967), and had it shipped, stone by stone, to Arizona. We've still got Tower Bridge, which you can cross to reach the Tower of London (*see p53*). Until 30 June 2006, the south side of the Thames by Tower Bridge will be home to a gigantic ice structure, Ice Space, a frozen touring show; details of this and other Ice Space locations are on www.icespace.net.

Further east, on Shad Thames, the main thoroughfare behind the wharves, is the **Design Museum**. Years ago dockworkers unloaded tea, coffee and spices to be stored in the warehouses round here. Now listed buildings, those warehouses have been converted into upmarket apartments, offices and the restaurants of Butler's Wharf. The term Shad Thames comes from the area's orginal name, St John at Thames, as it was called under the Knights Templar.

Up past the Design Museum, across Jamaica Road and down Tanner Street, is historic Bermondsey Street. Nearby, St Saviour's Dock was a place of execution for pirates. Once, this part of Bermondsey was all slimy tidal ditches surrounding a nasty neighbourhood called Jacob's Island. Charles Dickens, appalled by conditions here, chose it as the place for Bill Sykes to meet his end in *Oliver Twist*. Bermondsey antiques market on the corner of Bermondsey Street and Long Lane, (4am-2pm Fri), has been around for about 60 years. Nearby Bermondsey Square is undergoing redevelopment; a hotel, apartments, shops and an outdoor cinema are due to be completed in spring 2008. For decades Bermondsey was know as Biscuit Town, because of the preponderance of confectionery factories in this part of Southwark. Sadly for Jammy Dodger fans, the last biscuit factory, Peek Freans, closed in 1989.

Design Museum

28 Shad Thames, SE1 2YD (7403 6933/ www.designmuseum.org). Tower Hill tube/London Bridge tube/rail/47, 100, 188 bus. **Open** 10am-5.45pm daily. **Admission** £7; £4 concessions; free under-12s. **Credit** AmEx, MC, V. **Map** p319 S9.

Design in all its forms is celebrated inside this stylish white main building, while outside, in the riverside Design Museum Tank, is a little outdoor gallery of constantly changing installations by leading contemporary designers; and a taster of exhibitions within the museum. Upcoming temporary exhibitions include Formula One (1 July-29 Oct 2006), work by British graphic designer Alan Fletcher (11 Nov-18 Feb 2007) and Italian designer Bruno Munari (13 Jan-6 May 2007). The annual Designer of the Year exhibition runs from March to June 2007.

Every child visiting the Design Museum is given a free Design Action Pack with observation and creativity exercises, including treasure trails of exhibits and a 'Spot the Building' game to identify the architectural landmarks visible from the riverfront terrace (including quirkier edifices, such as Foster's 'Gherkin' and Rogers's Lloyd's Building). The museum's acclaimed programme of children's creativity workshops – design-and-make sessions for those aged six to 12 – are free for all except 12-year-olds, who pay £4. They take place on weekend afternoons and are always well worth attending. In June 2006 the theme is making a modern home; July is racing cars; August is surfing; September takes a flying theme; October is taken up with 1960s Pop graphics; it's fashion and accessories in November, and December is designing Christmas. Booking is essential, either by phone (7940 8782) or by email at education@designmuseum.org. *Buggy access. Café. Disabled access: lift, toilets. Nappy-changing facilities. Nearest picnic place: Butler's Wharf riverside benches. Shop.*

Fashion & Textile Museum

83 Bermondsey Street, SE1 3XF (7407 8664/ www.ftmlondon.org). London Bridge tube/rail. **Open** *June-Sept* 11am-5.45pm Tue-Sun. *Oct-May* 10am-4.45pm Tue-Sun (last entry 30mins before closing). **Admission** Workshop prices vary; phone for details. **Credit** MC, V. **Map** p319 Q8.

This pink and orange museum stands out like a beacon in grubby Bermondsey. However, at the time this guide went to press its permanent galleries were closed. Educational events and workshops will go ahead as planned and will allow participants to view a selection of the core collection of 3,000 garments, which were donated by Zandra Rhodes, along with her archive collection and sketchbooks, garments and videos. Check the website for details of workshops, children's fashion-illustration courses and special courses for 14- to 17-year-olds. *Buggy access. Café. Disabled access: lift, toilet. Nearest picnic space: Bermondsey Playground/Leathermarket Gardens. Shop.*

HMS Belfast

Morgan's Lane, Tooley Street, SE1 2JH (7940 6300/ www.iwm.org.uk). Tower Hill tube/London Bridge tube/rail. **Open** *Mar-Oct* 10am-6pm daily. *Nov-Feb* 10am-5pm daily. Last entry 45mins before closing. **Admission** (LP) £8.50; £5.25 concessions; £3 disabled; free under-16s (must be accompanied by an adult). **Credit** MC, V. **Map** p319 R8.

This 11,500-ton World War II battlecruiser has been enjoying a peaceful retirement on the Thames, her only distraction being the hordes of children that clamber over her decks at weekends and school holidays. Guided tours take in all nine decks, from the bridge to the boiler room, visiting the galley, sick bay, dentist, NAAFI (Navy, Army & Air Force Institutes) canteen and mess deck. There's even an operating theatre on board. The permanent exhibition, *HMS Belfast* in War and Peace, tells the battleship's story, from launch in 1938 through her wartime service to her retirement in 1971, when the decision was made to turn her into a museum. The guns that destroyed the German battleship *Scharnhorst* on Boxing Day in 1943 and supported the D-Day landing a year later are, literally, a big attraction. There's usually a queue to climb into the port deck Bofors gun, which enthusiasts can swivel, elevate and aim. From September 2006 visitors can take an audio tour – available in adult, children or family versions and in English, French, German or Spanish – that features testimonies from *HMS Belfast* veterans as well as historical and technical information about the ship.

The Kip in a Ship experience is for groups of up to 50 children (schools and youth groups usually book these), who get to sleep in the original sailors' bunks for up to three days – Scouts and Guides can earn their Community Badge while taking part. Accompanying adults take the officers' cabins. On the last weekend of every month there are free drop-in family events (11am-1pm, 2-4pm) that might involve art, craft, music or dance activities, or handling sessions about life on board ship, where children can examine artefacts and equipment. Check the website for a full calendar of exciting holiday activities; scheduled for 2006 are Flagdeck Weekends (24-25 June, 29-30 July), Communications Weekend (26-27 Aug), Navy Games (30 Sept-1 Oct) and A Cook's Life Weekend (14-15 Oct). *HMS Belfast* gets spooky and becomes a ghost ship for Hallowe'en (28-29 Oct), and in the run-up to Christmas local schools sing carols on the quarterdeck (11-15 Dec; to get involved, phone 7940 6323/6336/6348). Children can even have a birthday party on board; see the website or phone 7940 6320 for information. Although children's buggies can be left on the quarterdeck, this attraction is most suited to over-fives. *Café. Disabled access; lift, toilets (check website for limitations). Nappy-changing facilities. Nearest picnic place: Potters Field. Shop.*

Around Town

The City

The capital's flashy cash stash is guarded by silver dragons.

The confident, prosperous City has survived many trials throughout history, and it bears the marks of its tribulations. Established by the Romans, ransacked by Boudicca, the home of royalty, and the tomb of national heroes – there are stories to enthrall children here. Conveniently, one of the best places to hear them, the **Museum of London**, is right at its centre.

Until the end of the 18th century almost all of London was contained within this square mile, the boundaries of which are marked by silver griffins (*see p55*). Development began in earnest after 1066, when the Normans started building the Tower of London. In 1397 Dick Whittington was persuaded to become Lord Mayor. This medieval period was marked by massive accumulation of wealth by traders and merchants, and by the foundation of many of the institutions that still control the City today.

As shipping on the Thames decreased, London turned its attention from trade goods to the money markets that now form the backbone of City business. Banks and insurance buildings replaced housing, the middle classes moved to new suburbs like Brixton, the well off moved to the West End and the poor to the East.

From a peak population of around 200,000 in the 17th century, the City is now home to only about 7,500. It would be much less if it were not for the **Barbican Centre** complex, built in 1981. Over 300,000 commuters invade the square mile from Monday to Friday but leave the streets gloriously crowd-free for the rest of the time, which makes the City perfect for weekend family visits.

The City's history has shaped its governance. It is the only local authority in London that isn't run on a party political basis and has its own police force. The Corporation of London dates from the ninth century, making it older than Parliament, and its administration still retains elements of the feudal system it developed from. Centuries ago residents essentially paid off the monarchs in return for a measure of independence and self-governance. The Corporation is also unique in that it benefits from the wealth generated from the rental of the many company buildings erected on its common land. This enormous private income is known as 'City's Cash'.

A walk through the City takes you past some of London's most imposing monuments, old and new. Modern landmarks like the Lloyds Building and the Swiss ReTower (the Gherkin) are now as recognisable a part of the skyline as **St Paul's Cathedral** and **Tower Bridge**. Historic churches swell the numbers of ancient buildings. Tiny St Ethelburga's was flattened by an IRA bomb but rose from the ruins as a centre for peace and reconciliation. It stands bravely on Bishopsgate, the mighty Gherkin looming over it. Many peaceful pockets among the concrete and glass exist because of tragedies that scarred the City – Bunhill Gardens is a former plague pit, and other smaller public gardens were created from spaces left by the Blitz.

The City is a fascinating place to walk round after dark; indeed, it is the venue for one of the most popular peregrinations organised by London Walks (7624 3978, www.walks.com). Even a child with no particular appetite for history and a positive distaste for walking can be lured on to a tour with talk of ghosts, ghouls and the shadowy possibility of seeing something spooky after dark, which is why 'Ghosts of the Old City' (choose the Saturday evening one, when the storyteller dresses up) is a hit with the younger generation.

Bank of England Museum

Entrance on Bartholomew Lane, EC2R 8AH (7601 5491/cinema bookings 7601 3985/www.bankofengland. co.uk/museum). Bank tube/DLR. **Open** 10am-5pm Mon-Fri. Closed bank hols. **Admission** free; £1 audio guide. **Credit** *Shop* MC, V. **Map** p319 Q6.
The Bank's story, told here, also covers the evolution of the British economy. There's a re-creation of an 18th-century banking hall (with bewigged and bestockinged mannequins); displays of old and modern notes and coins; early handwritten cheques; a million-pound note and many ponderously impressive documents. Most exhibits are static, but there is an introductory film describing the Bank's origins, and an interactive foreign exchange-dealing desk to test the skills of budding entrepreneurs. Dummies move and speak as you pass, and a touch screen explains the origin of different features of British banknotes. Activity sheets are available for kids, and there are plenty of special events throughout the year. Calligraphy lessons take place on the first Tuesday of each month, and from 1 May there is a large display of unusual money boxes as part of an exhibition on the history of currency. Lord Mayor's Day sees face painters in the museum, and right through to November for 'Hooked-on Money' kids can decorate their

own '£' sign, designed to be hung on their bedroom door. For the Big Draw event kids will be designing a money-box to enter into a competition. Consistently popular, though, is the gold bar insert a hand into a perspex case and try to lift the bar encased within. Its value fluctuates daily (roughly £115,000 as we went to press), but its weight 12.7kg (28lb) – is shocking to anyone who has ever fantasised about running off with a load of bullion. *Buggy access. Disabled: ramp, toilet. Nappy-changing facilities. Nearest picnic place: St Paul's Cathedral Garden. Shop.*

Barbican Centre

Silk Street, EC2Y 8DS (7638 4141/box office 7638 8891/www.barbican.org.uk). Barbican tube/Moorgate tube/rail. **Open** *Box office 9am-8pm Mon-Sat; noon-8pm Sun.* **Admission** *free; phone for details of ticket prices for events.* **Credit** AmEx, MC, V. **Map** p318 P5.
Study the maps and follow the notices on the walkways carefully and you need not get lost in this rather complex arts complex. The centre also contains 6,500 handsome flats and is a very desirable pace to live. There are also some pockets of pleasant calm for everyone to enjoy: the fountains in the inner courtyard; the Waterside Café, with its children's menu; the exotic plants and lazy koi carp in the conservatory (open to the public on Sunday afternoons); and the library, with its extensive children's section. You can still see remains of the Roman walls on which the Barbican (originally a fortified watch tower) was built. The building's £12.5-million scheme to improve the foyers and entrances is scheduled for completion this year, with the dramatic 22m (72ft) light-wall installation for the main foyer ready in September 2006.
The Barbican's range of cultural offerings is certainly big. The best child-related reason to visit the Barbican is the Saturday morning Family Film Club (*see p214*). The Barbican Art Gallery has family workshops alongside some exhibitions and the resident London Symphony Orchestra (LSO) is another draw – family ticket holders can take part in special pre-concert events held once a term. Important diary dates will generally include a related family event: summer 2006 sees a family singing workshop as part of celebrations for Mozart's anniversary, and March 2007 will have a family event in conjunction with festivities marking the Barbican's 25th year. The annual two-week London Children's Film Festival in November is also a must. To join the Family News mailing list and find out more about the festival, as well as LSO and Barbican projects for children, call 7382 2333.
Bars. Buggy access. Cafés. Disabled access: lift, toilet. Nappy-changing facilities. Nearest picnic place: Barbican Lakeside Terrace. Restaurants. Shops.

Broadgate Arena

Broadgate Circle, EC2A 2BQ (7505 4068/www. broadgateice.co.uk). Liverpool Street tube/rail. **Open** *Mid Oct-early Apr noon-2.30pm, 3.30-5.30pm Mon-Thur; noon-2.30pm, 3.30-6pm, 7-9pm Fri; 11am-1pm, 2-4pm, 5-7pm Sat, Sun. Early Apr-mid Oct phone for details.* **Admission** *£8; £5 under-16s (incl skate hire).* **No credit cards.** **Map** p319 Q5.
The smallest and least expensive of London's selection of outdoor winter skating rinks is also open for longer than the others, until April. The rink has a circular form, enclosed by a sort of amphitheatre of offices and shops in Broadgate Circle. If you're prepared to support the kids in their first, clinging experience of the ice, skates available

St Ethelburga, pursued by Gherkin.

here range from child's size six; otherwise, why not consider skating lessons from Jacqueline Harbord? From April to October the arena is used for corporate events, outdoor drama and music – phone for details.
Buggy access. Cafés. Disabled access: lift, ramp, toilet. Nappy-changing facilities. Nearest picnic place: Finsbury Circus. Shops.

College of Arms

Queen Victoria Street, EC4V 4BT (7248 2762/ www.college-of-arms.gov.uk). Mansion House tube/ Blackfriars tube/rail. **Open** *10am-4pm Mon-Fri. Closed bank hols.* **Tours** *by arrangement 6.30pm Mon-Fri; prices vary.* **Admission** *free.* **Map** p318 O7.
This beautiful 17th-century house with heraldic gates in red, black and gold can be seen as you wander over the Thames across the Millennium footbridge. The college occasionally holds temporary exhibitions, and pre-booked group tours can be arranged. The main business carried on here is the granting of arms by royal heralds to modern knights and the tracing of family lineages. The college was responsible for creating a new coat of arms for Camilla, Duchess of Cornwall, granted by the queen to signify her new position as wife to Prince Charles. Unfortunately not all of us are eligible – you must either have a coat of arms formally granted to you or be descended in the legitimate male line from someone to whom arms were granted in the past. However, you can get help with your family tree by making an appointment, to which you should bring along as much genealogical information as possible; a fee is charged for the work according to how long it is expected to take. Note that the College of Arms doesn't deal with information on clans – that's an entirely Scottish affair.
Buggy access. Nearest picnic place: St Paul's Cathedral garden. Shop.

Around Town

Dr Johnson's House

*17 Gough Square, off Fleet Street, EC4A 3DE
(7353 3745/www.drjohnsonshouse.org). Chancery
Lane or Temple tube/Blackfriars tube/rail.* **Open**
May-Sept 11am-5.30pm Mon-Sat. *Oct-Apr* 11am-5pm
Mon-Sat. Closed 1 Jan, 24-26 Dec, bank hols. **Tours**
by arrangement; groups of 10 or more only.
Admission £4.50; £1.50 under-18s; £3.50 concessions;
free under-10s; £10 family (2+unlimited children).
Tours free. *Evening tours* by appointment only.
No credit cards. Map p318 N6.
The main points of interest in this faithfully restored
Georgian house are the pictures of Dr Johnson and his
eclectic social circle, about which plenty of background
information is provided. A 20-minute film gives you a
decent introduction to the famous lexicographer's life.
Johnson had to leave university before completing his
degree due to financial difficulties. and he came to London
with the equally impecunious David Garrick to seek his
fortune. Garrick achieved phenomenal success as an actor
and theatre manager, and Dr Johnson, much later, received
an advance to compile his *Dictionary of the English
Language*, the first ever English dictionary and the task
with which he made his name. It was published in 1755, a
replica first edition is on display in the library upstairs.
Dr Johnson's House primarily appeals to grown-ups, as
does the historic public house at which he used to wet his
whistle, Ye Olde Cheshire Cheese, down the road at 145
Fleet Street. The addition of some replica Georgian
dressing-up clothes and accessories for children on the top
floor of the house can turn a visit into a family event. Most
children's activities organised by the museum are for
school groups only, but there are occasional family workshops at the house; one is always scheduled for the summer holidays. Previous topics have included
communicating in code with a fan, as ladies used to do in
order to converse with their lovers right under the noses
of their chaperones.
Nearest picnic place: Lincoln's Inn Fields. Shop.

Guildhall

*Gresham Street, EC2P 2UJ (7606 3030/tours 7606
3030 ext 1463/www.corpoflondon.gov.uk). St Paul's
tube/Bank tube/DLR/Moorgate tube/rail.* **Open** *May-
Sept* 9.30am-5pm daily. *Oct-Apr* 9.30am-5pm Mon-Sat.
Last entry 4.30pm. Closes for functions; phone ahead to
check. **Tours** by arrangement; groups of 10 or more
only. **Admission** free. **Map** p318 P6.
The Guildhall survived both the Great Fire of London and
the Blitz, making it one of the few structures in the City to
date to before 1666. Now it's the seat of local government;
the Court of Common Council meets at 1pm on various
Thursdays each month, in the cathedral-like 15th-
century Great Hall (visitors are welcome; phone for dates).
  You can also visit the Hall when it is not being used for
official business. The impressive space has a vaulted
ceiling, marble monuments, and banners and shields of 100
livery companies on the walls. Every Lord Mayor since
1189 gets a namecheck on the windows. Two large
wooden statues of Gog and Magog stand in the West
Gallery. These giants represent the mythical conflict
between Britons and Trojan invaders; the result of this
struggle was the founding of Albion's capital city, New
Troy, on whose site London is said to stand. On the north
wall hangs a fascinating list of notable trials and grisly
executions. Visits to the Guildhall's enormous medieval
crypt are allowed only in the context of group tours.

Of more immediate appeal is a room beyond the library
devoted to a collection of watches, clocks and marine
chronometers belonging to the Worshipful Company of
Clockmakers. This small museum contains a range of time-
pieces dating back to the 14th century, including important pieces by John Harrison and the watch Edmund
Hillary wore to the top of Everest. The 700 exhibits include
a silver skull watch said to have belonged to Mary Queen
of Scots (though more likely to be of 19th-century vintage),
a 14th-century cast-iron clock and tiny, highly detailed
watch keys. Many of the watches and clocks are exquisite,
and the museum does a good job of explaining historical
developments in the watchmaker's art.
*Buggy access. Disabled access: lift, ramp, toilet. Nappy-
changing facilities. Nearest picnic place: grassy area
by London Wall. Shop.*

Guildhall Art Gallery

*Guildhall Yard, off Gresham Street, EC2P 2EJ
(7332 3700/www.guildhall-art-gallery.org.uk). Mansion
House or St Paul's tube/Bank tube/DLR/Moorgate
tube/rail/8, 25, 242 bus.* **Open** 10am-5pm Mon-Sat
(last entry 4.30pm); noon-4pm Sun (last entry 3.30pm).
Admission £2.50; £1 concessions; free under-16s.
Free to all after 3.30pm daily, all day Fri. **Credit**
(over £5) MC, V. **Map** p318 P6.
This gallery was opened in 1999 after a break of over 50
years; its predecessor was destroyed by World War II
bombing. Upstairs, the Main Gallery is decorated chiefly
with stuffy portraits of dead politicians, paintings and
marble busts of kings and queens and various dignitaries
connected to London. Mrs Thatcher's statue (repaired after
having its head lopped off by a visitor in 2002) is on loan
here. The centrepiece is the vast Siege of Gibraltar by John
Copley – the largest painting in Britain
  The Ground Floor Gallery is rather more interesting for
kids, hosting temporary exhibitions and, below, the
Victorian Galleries. There is an activity sheet for the latter
and the works here are dramatic and recognisable. A full-
sized marble Hamlet, modelled on famous 19th-century
actor Henry Irving, dominates the Undercroft Gallery, and
Topham's vivid painting of a child's escape from a locked
plague house is another treasure. Among the many paintings of children in the Gassiot Room are Millais's *My First
Sermon* and *My Second Sermon* (by which time the young
sitter, his daughter, has nodded off). Dotted around are art
materials and tables and chairs for children's use. In
October the gallery takes part in the annual nationwide
Big Draw, and there are family workshops during half-
terms. Upcoming exhibitions include Spanning the
Thames, artists' views of bridges over the river. Check
nearer the time for accompanying kids' activities.
  Down in the basement lie the scant remains of London's
only amphitheatre. It was known from written accounts
that there was one somewhere in the city, but its location
was a mystery until Roman masonry was unearthed during the rebuilding of the gallery. Despite only the founda-
tions of the walls and entrance surviving, the slick
presentation of the site does an excellent job of suggesting
how the amphitheatre would have looked, with the stag-
gered seats printed on a screen along with dynamic illustrations of gladiators and sound effects to boot.
  There is no café in the Guildhall, but packed lunches are
permitted in the cloakroom area, which has lots of seats,
and a water cooler, but no tables.
*Buggy access. Disabled access: lift, toilet. Nappy-
changing facilities. Nearest picnic place: grassy area
by London Wall. Shop.*

An eyeful of London

When people want a great view of London, it's usually the London Eye that springs to mind, but there are other fab vantage points around the city. For river views you can't beat Tower Bridge (*see p53*), where – from up high on the walkways – you get a great sense of the Thames's breadth. The bridge is relatively new for the City of London – its steel skeleton was clad in stone to match its neighbour, the Tower, but is not of the same era – there are some 800 years between them.

By the 19th century there was a pressing need for a crossing at this point in the Thames to relieve congestion on London Bridge. more than 100,000 people were using the crossing some days. Prior to Tower Bridge's construction there was a tunnel wide enough for trams under the river, close to where the bridge stands now. When the tram venture failed to make a profit the tunnel was converted to a foot passage, which closed when Tower Bridge was completed in 1894. The Thames has low banks, and any proposed design had to provide a crossing that would not prevent the passage of tall ships. Bascule bridges were already in existence, but none had been attempted on this scale. The bridge performed admirably from the start and was opening a few times a day at the sound of a horn. Nowadays, as London is no longer a busy port, it is only opened with 24 hours' notice.

The high walkways were created so that pedestrians could cross uninterrupted when the bascules were raised, but with the whole process of opening, letting a ship through and closing only taking five minutes, it seemed those on foot preferred to watch the spectacle and then resume their path across with the road traffic.

The old engine rooms are no longer needed now that electric hydraulics are used instead of steam, but they remain on show to marvel at. In its day this drawbridge was a triumph of Victorian engineering. The science is explained as simply as possible and illustrated with interactive models. It's fascinating stuff for all ages, and children love hoisting the model bridge in a wind tunnel to compare the difference in force required to lift it on a still and windy day. Calculation of the effects of different wind speeds was essential in the construction of Tower Bridge; in 1879 the Tay Bridge in Scotland was brought down in a storm with the loss of 75 lives.

By combining a trip to Tower Bridge with the Monument, you save money and get double the views. A combined child's ticket is £3.50 and an adult's is £6.50. From Monument you get a bird's eye view of the bridge and from the bridge you can easily pick out Monument, with its flaming urn of copper, representing the great fire, that crowns it. The two are only a short walk apart.

The Monument

Monument Street, EC3R 8AH (7626 2717/www.city oflondon.gov.uk). Monument tube. **Open** *Oct-Mar* 10am-5pm daily. *Apr-Sept* 9.30am-5.30pm daily. Last entry 1hr before closing. **Admission** £2; £1 5-15s; free under-5s. **No credit cards. Map** p319 Q7.
This monument to the Great Fire of London – 61metre (202ft) tall, and 61 metres (202ft) from the exact spot of the bakery in Pudding Lane where the fire broke out in 1666

– is the tallest isolated stone column in the world. It was built by Sir Christopher Wren and, despite the many skyscrapers being built nearby, it still stands out thanks to the golden urn of flames on top. Children who make it up the 311 stairs can expect two treats: the view from the top and a certificate, given out at the bottom, to commemorate their climbing feat. The attraction is closing from 30 September 2006 for 18 months for refurbishment. *Nearest picnic place: riverside by London Bridge.*

Around Town

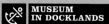

Museum of London

150 London Wall, EC2Y 5HN (0870 444 3852/ www.museumoflondon.org.uk). Barbican or St Paul's tube/Moorgate tube/rail. **Open** 10am-5.50pm Mon-Sat; noon-5.50pm Sun (last admission 5.30pm). **Admission** free. *Exhibitions* £5; £3 concessions. **Credit** *Shop* AmEx, MC, V. **Map** p318 P5.

A visit to the Museum of London is always a busy one. The sheer volume of exhibits on show can seem overwhelming, however, the chronological layout makes navigation easy, leading you through prehistoric times to the 21st century. New cartoon captions on the exhibits make light work of the explanations, and there is plenty of hands-on action as you follow the route – try out Roman weights and measures or, in the Medieval gallery, learn how a longbow is made. Free activity bags cover ages four to 11.

Every Sunday there is a kids' event, which is almost always free. Half-term and holidays see extra events, and throughout the day announcements are made to let you know that a particular activity is about to start. You could learn how to make a feather quill, find yourself in a dressing-up competition or learn about Victorian sanitation. Actors in character, including a Victorian street seller and a Roman merchant's wife, really bring the different eras to life; check the website for dates. Specific periods in history are illustrated with reconstructions of household rooms for fascinating comparisons with modern times. The Roman kitchen even has an original mosaic floor. The Medieval gallery, opened in November 2005, is full of fascinating objects, such as fashion shoes and loaded dice. A short film narrated with first-person accounts relates the devastation of the Black Death. As well as all the above there are temporary exhibitions. Satirical London and Belonging: Refugees in London are scheduled for 2006-7.

The museum café is pretty good, but those looking to save cash will find a picnic area is open at weekends and school holidays. A major refurbishment starting in February 2007 sees the entire lower level closed off until 2009; the exhibits here will be shown in temporary exhibitions. The refurbishment will bring the museum's coverage right up to the present day as well as doubling the number of objects on display. A new learning centre with family area is planned, and there'll be an e-suite where all the museum's objects can be viewed online. *Buggy access. Café. Disabled access: lift, toilet. Nappy-changing facilities. Nearest picnic place: Barber Surgeons' Garden. Shop.*

Museum of Methodism & John Wesley's House

Wesley's Chapel, 49 City Road, EC1Y 1AU (7253 2262/www.wesleyschapel.org.uk). Moorgate or Old Street (exit 4) tube/rail. **Open** 10am-4pm Mon-Sat. Closed bank hols. **Tours** ad hoc arrangements on arrival; groups of 10 or more must phone ahead. **Admission** free; £4 donation requested. *Tours* free. **Credit** *Shop* MC, V. **Map** p319 Q4.

This lovely chapel, with its deep, gated courtyard ringed by Georgian buildings, is a haven from the thunderous traffic of City Road. Known to Methodists worldwide as 'the cathedral of world Methodism', it was built by John Wesley in 1778, and his description of it – 'perfectly neat but not fine' – sums up the architecture. Museum displays in the crypt allude to Methodism's beginnings. Hogarthian prints portray the effects of poverty, alcoholism and moral degradation in 18th-century England. John Wesley experienced a moment of grace that persuaded him to devote his life to serving God and helping the poor, and his rigorous and methodical programme of prayer, fasting and lifestyle led to him being dubbed a 'Methodist'. Artefacts on show in the preacher's house may be examined as part of the ad hoc tours given by stewards. The house has been sympathetically restored and shows a kitchen with a range and no running water, and a bedroom with a tiny four-poster bed. In the study is a 'chamber horse' – if Wesley's foreign preaching tours did not offer enough equestrian exercise, this bouncing chair was supposed to simulate a good gallop.

Through the windows you can see Bunhill Fields, once set aside for victims of the Great Plague. Because it remained unconsecrated, it became a dissenters' graveyard. Cross the road to wander through this secret garden, with its mossy graves tilted at odd angles and its memorials to nonconformists such as William Blake, Daniel Defoe and members of Oliver Cromwell's family. *Buggy access. Disabled access: lift, toilet. Nappy-changing facilities. Nearest picnic places: enclosed courtyard at entrance; Barber Surgeons' Garden; Bunhill Field Cemetery. Shop.*

Postman's Park

Between King Edward Street & Aldersgate Street, EC1R 4JR (7374 4127/www.cityoflondon.gov.uk). St Paul's tube. **Open** 8am-dusk daily. **Admission** free. **Map** p318 O6.

Named after its proximity to a large sorting office (long since demolished), this green space is most famous for its Heroes' Wall, a canopy-covered expanse of ceramic plaques, inscribed in florid Victorian style, that pay tribute to ordinary people who died trying to save others.

LUNCH BOX

For more recommended restaurants and cafés in the area, see pp182-84.
Auberge *56 Mark Lane, EC3R 7NE (7480 6789).*
Barcelona Tapas *1A Bell Lane, E1 7LA (7247 7014); 1 Beaufort House, St Botolph Street, EC3A 7DT (7377 5111).*
Browns *8 Old Jewry, EC2R 8DN (7606 6677).*
Chez Gerard *64 Bishopsgate, EC2N 4AJ (7588 1200).*
Crypt Café *St Paul's Cathedral, Ludgate Hill, EC4M 8AD (7236 4128).*
Gaucho Grill *1 Bell Inn Yard, EC3V 0BL (7626 5180).*
Just the Bridge *1 Paul's Walk, EC4V 3QQ (7236 0000).*
McDonald's *41 London Wall, EC2M 5TE (7638 7787).*
Pizza Express *125 Alban Gate, London Wall, EC2Y 5AS (7600 8880); 20-22 Leadenhall Market, EC3V 1LR (7283 5113); 7 St Bride Street, EC4A 4AS (7583 5126).*
S&M Café *48 Brushfield Street, E1 6AG (7247 2252).*
Tokyo City *46 Gresham Street, EC2V 7AY (7726 0308).*
Wagamama *1A Ropemaker Street, EC2V 0HR (7588 2688).*

Around Town

Museum of London. *See p51.*

'Frederick Alfred Croft, Inspector, aged 31,' begins one typical thumbnail drama. 'Saved a Lunatic Woman from Suicide at Woolwich Arsenal Station, But was Himself Run Over by the Train, Jan 11, 1878.' Many of the dead heroes were children who tried to rescue drowning companions; their fates offer gruesome morals for their modern peers. *Buggy access.*

St Bartholomew's Hospital Museum

West Smithfield, EC1A 7BE (7601 8152). Barbican or St Paul's tube. **Open** 10am-4pm Tue-Fri. Closed for Easter, Christmas, bank hols. **Tours** 2pm Fri. **Admission** free. *Tours* £5; £4 concessions; accompanied children free. **No credit cards**. **Map** p318 O6.

One of London's medieval hospitals, St Bart's was built in 1123 by Rahere, a courtier of Henry I, after a near-death brush with malaria. The museum recalls the hospital's origins as a refuge for the chronically sick hoping for a miraculous cure. Leather 'lunatic restraints', a wooden head used by medical students to practise their head-drilling techniques (but also, apparently, as a football) and photographs documenting the slow progress of nurses from drudges to career women make mildly edifying exhibits. Don't miss the huge painting by William Hogarth, through the museum and up the stairs. Hogarth was born in Bartholomew's Close and offered his services free when he heard the hospital governors were about to commission a Venetian artist. His paintings of the Good Samaritan et al illustrate a fascinating range of skin and venereal diseases – quite a talking point.
Buggy access (ramp by arrangement). Café (in hospital). Nearest picnic place: hospital grounds. Shop.

St Paul's Cathedral

Ludgate Hill, EC4M 8AD (7236 4128/www.stpauls. co.uk). St Paul's tube. **Open** 8.30am-4pm Mon-Sat. *Galleries, crypt & ambulatory* 9.30am-4pm Mon-Sat. Closed for special services, sometimes at short notice. *Tours* 11am, 11.30am, 1.30pm, 2pm Mon-Sat. **Admission** (LP) *Cathedral, crypt & gallery* £9; £3.50 6-16s; £8 concessions; free under-6s; £21 family (2+2). *Tours* £3; £1 6-16s; £2.50 concessions; free under-6s. *Audio guide* £3.50; £3 concessions. **Credit** MC, V. **Map** p318 O6.

St Paul's is not the first place that comes to mind for a family day out but it is more fun than you would expect. The cathedral in isolation can wear on young minds within a few short minutes and in this case the audio guide does a grand job in bringing the place to life. Youngsters are entertained with quirky facts about everything from the organ pipes (some big enough to crawl through) to the problem of getting Nelson's body back to England for burial. During Christmas and Easter holidays there are trails with a small prize at the end, and parents wanting some help for a self-guided tour around the Cathedral can check out the downloadable activity sheets for schools.

Perhaps the most fun of all is the Whispering Gallery, where the acoustics simply have to be tested. From there it is a few more steps up to the Stone Gallery for an amazing 360-degree view of London, one of the best vantage points in the city. If you have the energy to make it further up to the Golden Gallery, try to go early, otherwise you could find yourself sandwiched between boisterous teen tourists jostling for space on the cramped balcony.

Down in the airy crypt there isn't a great deal to excite youngsters, though the tombs of historical figures are here, including Nelson, Wellington and Wren. Florence Nightingale and Lawrence of Arabia are honoured with memorials. At the back is the shop and Crypt Café.

If you want to experience the true spirit of St Paul's, evensong is every day at 5pm and, at only an hour long, isn't too difficult for youngsters to sit through, with lessons and psalms beautifully sung by the all-male choir.
Buggy access. Café. Disabled access: lifts, ramps,toilet. Nappy-changing facilities. Nearest picnic space: garden. Restaurant. Shops.

St Swithin's Garden

Oxford Court, off Cannon Street, EC4N 5AD (no phone). Monument tube/Bank tube/DLR. **Open** 24hrs daily. **Admission** free. **Map** p319 Q7.

This small, carefully tended walled garden (down a small alley that leads behind an O₂ mobile-phone shop) is the burial place of Catrin Glendwr and two of her children. Catrin was the daughter of Owain Glendwr, the Welsh hero whose uprising ended bloodily in 1413. A memorial sculpture is dedicated not only to her, but to the suffering of all women and children in war.
Buggy access.

Tower Bridge Exhibition

Tower Bridge, SE1 2UP (7403 3761/www.tower bridge.org.uk). Tower Hill tube/Tower Gateway DLR. **Open** *Apr-Oct* 10am-6.30pm daily (last entry 5.30pm). *Nov-Mar* 9.30am-6pm daily (last entry 5pm). **Admission** £5.50; £3 5-15s; £4.25 concessions; free under-5s; £14 family (2+2). **Credit** AmEx, MC, V. **Map** p319 R8.

One of London's most popular sites, a visit to Tower Bridge has something of a slick corporate feel. No sooner have you stepped through the entrance than you and yours are whisked on to a stage to have your photo taken. The finished product is ready to pick up on your departure, if you wish, at a rather pricey £10 (for a pack).

A lift transports you to the walkway foyer, where there are models of the alternative designs put forward for the bridge and a video re-enacting Victorian opposition to its construction. Visitors have to pass through both walkways to catch the east and west views. Large aerial photographs mark famous landmarks, and there are photo points where you can slide open the windows to get an uninterrupted shot. Over the summer holidays the walkways host Victorian children's games, including hop scotch and hula hoop, and over weekends in December a costumed story-teller will be in the North tower lounge.

From the walkways it's a short walk to the South tower and the newly refurbished engine rooms for a more thorough explanation of hydraulics. From May bank holiday onwards, visitors can try a new interactive experience called Lifting the Bridge. This, after all, is what every visitor would like to see for real: it happens most often in summer (sometimes several times a day). To find out when the next opening is taking place, call 7940 3984.

Buggy access. Disabled access: lift, toilet. Nappy-changing facilities. Nearest picnic place: Potters Field/ Tower of London Gardens. Shop.

Tower of London

Tower Hill, EC3N 4AB (info 0870 756 6060/ booking line 0870 756 7070/www.hrp.org.uk). Tower Hill tube/Tower Gateway DLR/Fenchurch Street rail. **Open** *Mar-Oct* 10am-6pm Mon, Sun; 9am-6pm Tue-Sat (last entry 5pm). *Nov-Feb* 10am-5pm Mon, Sun; 9am-5pm Tue-Sat (last entry 4pm). **Tours** *Beefeater tours* (outside only, weather permitting) every 30mins, all day. **Admission** (LP) £15; £9.50 5-15s; £12 concessions; free under-5s; £43 family (2+3). *Audio guide £3. Tours* free. **Credit** AmEx, MC, V. **Map** p319 R7.

Visitors mob this fortress daily, but there's so much to see that most people are prepared to put up with the crowds. There are so many parts to the Tower of London (which is made up of several towers – Bloody, Beauchamp, Bell and White, to name but four) that the best, and most entertaining way, to make sense of it all is to follow a Beefeater. These Yeoman Warders, photogenic in their black and red finery, are genial hosts, and the tales they tell are fascinating: they're a mine of information about the history of the Tower, which has served as a fortress, a palace, a prison and a royal execution site over its 900-year existence. Stories of treason, torture and execution keep audiences spellbound during the free 40-minute tour. Special events punctuate the day so be sure to check the programme. Throughout August 2006 there will be sword fights around the tower, and October to December sees storytelling by costumed actors in the Medieval Palace. A Christmas feast runs from 27 December to early New Year.

The crown jewels are the Tower's biggest draw, and the Martin Tower's permanent exhibition, Crowns and Diamonds, is also a must for lovers of sparkle and glitter. It includes a model of the uncut, fist-sized Cullinan, the world's largest diamond, and a display of how it was cut into nine stunning cut diamonds – the two largest are now part of the crown jewels. The 2m-wide Grand Punch Bowl gives new meaning to the phrase 'family silver'.

The Medieval Palace, where kings and queens stayed until the reign of Elizabeth I, has just been restored and uses smell and sound effects to whisk you back in time. In Beauchamp Tower families can read the elaborate graffiti carved by the (mainly) VIP inmates. Outside, on Tower Green, stands the spot where royals were beheaded, including Anne Boleyn and Lady Jane Grey. Battle fans love the armoury in the White Tower, and there is usually a half-term event centred on the collection. The Torture at the Tower exhibition has an even more gruesome appeal.

Buggy access (Jewel House). Café. Nappy-changing facilities. Nearest picnic place: riverside benches; Trinity Square Memorial Gardens. Shops.

Early trading at the **Tower of London**.

Around Town

Holborn

The heartland of the British justice system is legal, regal and eccentric.

Charles Dickens may have been contemptuous of Holborn's many law institutions in his novel *Bleak House*, but he acknowledged that the area has its charms: 'There are still worse places than the Temple, on a sultry day, for basking in the sun, or resting idly in the shade,' he wrote in *Barnaby Rudge*. Dickens was right. The **Inner Temple Gardens** (open 12.20-3pm Mon-Fri) is a lovely spot for a picnic.

The Inner and Middle Temples were named after the Knights Templar, who owned the site for 150 years, and the maze of courtyards and fine buildings makes for some interesting wandering. It is also worth seeking out the **Temple Church** (Kings Bench Walk, 7353 8559, www.temple church.com); consecrated in 1185, it is the last remaining round church in London. Its most recent claim to fame is as a setting for some of the action in *The Da Vinci Code*.

On the Strand, **Temple Bar** marks the boundary between the borough of Westminster and the City of London; it's guarded by a bronze griffin mounted here in 1878 to replace Wren's archway. Nearby the **Royal Courts of Justice** are open to the public, of course, but only children over 14 are allowed in. While London's judicial heart are the Royal Courts of Justice, its veins and arteries spread over all the area – as well as the inns of court, there are the legal wig shops on Chancery Lane, not to mention the pubs that have refreshed lawyers for centuries.

The architecturally contentious **'Roman' Baths** (5 Strand Lane, reached via Surrey Street, 7641 5264, www.nationaltrust.org.uk) were another spot frequented by Dickens (he liked to take a cold plunge). They can be viewed only through a window, unless you've made a prior appointment with Westminster City Council.

In Fleet Street **St Dunstan in the West** (No. 186A, 7405 1929, www.stdunstaninthewest.org) – was once next door to the shop of the murderous barber- surgeon Sweeney Todd.

Those interested in the history of surgery should visit the **Hunterian Museum** on London's largest garden square, **Lincoln's Inn Fields**. Based at the Royal College of Surgeons' headquarters, the museum houses an impressive,

wide-ranging collection of medical specimens in shiny, nose-marked glass cabinets (*see p56* **Body building**). **Lincoln's Inn** (7405 1393, www.lincolnsinn.org.uk) is the most impressive of the four inns of court. Its Old Hall dates back to 1422 and its buildings are a blend of various styles – Gothic, Tudor and Palladian.

Whatever the time of year, **Somerset House** offers a variety of family-orientated activities and workshops inspired by its three galleries: the **Gilbert Collection**, **Hermitage Rooms** and **Courtauld Institute**. The latter is home to such works as Van Gogh's instantly recognisable *Self-Portrait with Bandaged Ear* and Manet's *A Bar at the Folies Bergère*. A few churches of note in the area include **St Clement Danes**, restored after the Blitz, and St Mary le Strand (free lunchtime recitals, Wed-Fri).

Going towards Clerkenwell, the **Museum & Library of the Order of St John** has an ancient crypt that pre-dates even the 13th-century example at nearby **St Ethelreda's** on Ely Place. There is also a gatehouse from the original priory of St John of Jerusalem, dating to 1504.

Further towards Clerkenwell and Farringdon, there are echoes of the area's long tradition of arts and crafts: the **Clerkenwell Green Association** provides studios for tradespeople in the area in St John's Square and Clerkenwell Green. Elsewhere in Clerkenwell, Hatton Garden is the centre of the British diamond trade (look out for some some striking display windows). Nearby Leather Lane market – a good place for bargain hunters – is a vivid contrast.

Courtauld Institute Gallery

Somerset House, Strand, WC2R ORN (7848 2777/ recorded information/Learning Centre 7420 9406/www.courtauld.ac.uk/gallery). Covent Garden or Temple tube (closed Sun)/Charing Cross tube/rail. **Open** 10am-6pm daily (last entry 5.15pm). *Tours* phone for details. **Admission** £5; £4 concessions; free under-18s, UK students, registered unwaged. Free to all 10am-2pm Mon (not bank hols). **Credit** MC, V. **Map** p317 M7. Among the exhibitions at Somerset House (*see p58*), the Courtauld offers a fabulous permanent collection. In residence is a huge corpus of Impressionist and post-Impressionist paintings (including a major group of paintings by Cézanne), works by Renaissance artists and

The present-day **Temple Bar**, where Holborn gives way to the City.

a 20th-century section including Matisse and Kandinsky. While this seems light years away from poster paint and sticky tape, the Learning Centre brings exhibits across all three galleries at Somerset House (the Courtauld Institute, the Gilbert Collection and the Hermitage Rooms) to life , with Saturday workshops for children aged six to 12: themes from 2006 see kids making Byzantium treasures, 'night and day' mobiles and bird models inspired by exhibits in the Gilbert Collection (*see right*). There are also monthly Art Start workshops for under-fives. Phone the Learning Centre for more information.
Buggy access. Café. Disabled access: lift, toilet. Nappy-changing facilities. Shop.

The Gilbert Collection

Somerset House, Strand, WC2R ORN (7420 9400/ www.gilbert-collection.org.uk). Covent Garden or Temple tube (closed Sun)/Charing Cross tube/rail. **Open** 10am-6pm daily (last entry 5.15pm). *Tours* phone for details. **Admission** £5; £4 concessions; free under-18s, UK students, registered unwaged. **Credit** AmEx, MC, V. **Map** p317 M7.

These extensive displays from the collection of the late British-born property magnate Sir Arthur Gilbert were given to the nation in 1996. The jewelled curios, gleaming silverware and decorative boxes are so resplendent that families would do well to don sunglasses before entering.

Around Town

Body building

Since its facelift in 2005, the **Hunterian Museum** – a collection of the Royal College of Surgeons – has been more focused than ever on encouraging interest in all things anatomical. The inspiration behind the museum and its fascinating collection of medical artefacts was surgeon and naturalist John Hunter (1728-1793). During his lifetime he studied the science of the human form and developed innovative methods of surgery.

As you enter the museum, you are greeted by a gallery of sparkling cabinets holding a staggering 3,000 labelled glass jars filled with a menagerie of human and animal specimens, many dating back to the 18th century. Hunter's good friend and fellow naturalist Joseph Banks often gave him specimens from his world tours with Captain Cook; he was responsible for bringing the first kangaroo to Britain. The royal family also contributed to Hunter's collection by allowing him to work on the bodies of any animals that died naturally in the zoo at the Tower of London. In return he gave a full set of anatomical specimens to the royal household to aid the royal children's education.

Sadly, many of the original zoo skeletons were destroyed during the Blitz. However some bones are still on display, including a few examples from extinct animals: there are giant mammoth teeth and the skull of a Tasmanian wolf.

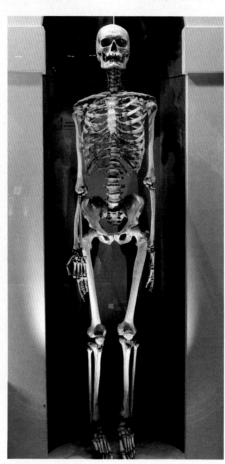

Until the mid 18th century, barber-surgeons had been the first port of call for those in need of surgical assistance. If you have ever wondered about the symbolism behind the red and white cylinder found outside barber's shops, it represented the stick gripped by patients during treatment. Back in Hunter's day, surgery was such a risky business that survivors often kept trophies of bladder-stone operations in small silver boxes, sometimes engraved with the name of the surgeon. The museum runs a regular actor-based workshop with a medieval barber-surgeon – and his leech – where children can admire the tools of the trade and hear some grisly true tales of their use.

On display in pull-out drawers and cabinets are a large number of professional surgeon's tools, many of which are early examples dating from well before the discovery of anaesthetic. Upstairs, the Science of Surgery Gallery may be of more interest to older children who can test themselves on the interactive keyhole surgery game (a doddle for fingers adept at PlayStation, it seems).

If you enjoyed the fascinating exhibits at the Hunterian, you may be interested in some of the other specialist museums of health and medicine to be found in central London: the **Alexander Fleming Laboratory Museum** based at St Mary's Hospital (7886 6528,www.stmarys. nhs.uk/open 10am-1pm Mon-Thur); the **Florence Nightingale Museum** at St Thomas' Hospital (7620 0374, www.florence-nightingale.co.uk, open 10am-5pm Mon-Fri, 10am-4.30pm Sat, Sun); **St Bartholomew's Hospital Archives & Museum** (7601 8152, www.bartsand thelondon.nhs.uk, open 10am-4pm Tue-Fri); and the **Old Operating Theatre** and 300-year-old **Herb Garret** (7188 2679, www.thegarret.org.uk, both closed for repairs at the time of writing). Finally, the brave may wish to visit the **BDA Dental Museum** (7563 4549, www.bda.org/museum, open 1-4pm Tue, Thur; also by appointment).

Hands-on activities designed to open up the collection to little ones include the design and creation of everything from mock jewellery to elaborate mosaics, with workshops taking place every Saturday (daily during school holidays) tailored to illuminate current temporary exhibitions. *Buggy access. Café. Disabled access: lift, toilets. Nappy-changing facilities. Shop.*

The Hermitage Rooms

Somerset House, Strand, WC2R 0RN (7845 4630/ www.hermitagerooms.co.uk). Covent Garden or Temple tube (closed Sun)/Charing Cross tube/rail. **Open** 10am-6pm daily (last entry 5.15pm). **Admission** £5; £4 concessions; free under-18s, UK students, registered unwaged. **Credit** MC, V. **Map** p317 M7.

A window into one of the world's greatest museums – St Petersburg's State Hermitage Museum – the Hermitage Rooms exhibit a selection of work from the Old Master, Impressionist and post-Impressionist collection of its Russian progenitor. A range of regular weekend and holiday workshops for children is themed according to the current exhibition: until September 2006, The Road to Byzantium will explore the classical heritage of Greece, and there will be workshops with storytelling and treasure-making based around the ancient relief carvings and cameos on display. *Buggy access. Café. Disabled: lift. Nappy-changing facilities. Shop.*

Hunterian Museum

Royal College of Surgeons of England, 35-43 Lincoln's Inn Fields, WC2A 3PE (7869 6560/www. rceng.ac.uk). Holborn tube. **Open** 10am-5pm Tue-Sat. **Admission** free; donations appreciated. **Credit** *Shop* MC, V. **Map** p318 M6.

Reopened after renovation in early 2005, the Hunterian Museum in Lincoln's Inn Fields has gone from a labyrinthine collection of chaotically labelled artefacts to a sleek, modernised museum with a broad educational agenda, and it's family-friendly to boot. The sheer volume of preserved specimen jars is fascinating. Among the quirkier exhibits are Winston Churchill's false teeth, the freakish skeleton of 'Irish Giant' Charles Byrne, who reached 2.2m (7ft 7in) in his socks. Children can create drawings using the art materials on site, peruse the concise library of books at hand or perhaps try on the skeleton suit and test their knowledge of the human anatomy with the textile body-part game. A programme of workshops aimed at school groups and families is set to expand in the next year with the introduction of more actor-based events, such as the already popular Barber Surgeon, with his grim array of real-life tools of the trade (*see p56* **Body building**). Tours take place every Wednesday at 1pm, often led by a knowledgeable retired surgeon. *Buggy access. Lift. Nearest picnic place: Lincoln's Inn Fields. Shop.*

Museum & Library of the Order of St John

St John's Gate, St John's Lane, EC1M 4DA (7324 4070/www.sja.org.uk/museum). Farringdon tube/rail/ 63, 55, 243 bus. **Open** 10am-5pm Mon-Fri; 10am-4pm Sat. Closed 24 Dec-2 Jan, bank hol weekends (phone to check). *Tours* 11am, 2.30pm Tue, Fri, Sat. **Admission** free; suggested donations for tours £5; £4 concessions. **Credit** MC, V. **Map** p318 O4.

These days the Order of St John is associated with those nice folk who revive the swooners at sweaty stadium gigs, but the order began with the crusaders in 11th-century Jerusalem. It has been dealing with disease and pestilence ever since, and this museum gives an insight into the history of both the order and medicine. Exhibits are divided between a static collection of antiques (from holy relics to full suits of armour) and a brighter, more interactive room that showcases the order's medical history. Here surgical models and tools of the trade (some of them satisfyingly gruesome) are displayed, as well as a primitive wooden ambulance (essentially a wheelbarrow). The museum is set beside St John's Gate, an evocative Tudor stone edifice and part of the original priory. If you take the grand tour, you'll see the extant 12th-century crypt. There's an annual roster of temporary exhibitions, as well as year-round activity trails for younger groups. Meanwhile, those wanting to get some hands-on experience can become a member (depending on their age) of the Little Badgers or Cadets – membership is free (you only pay for the uniform), and the young lifesavers receive first-aid training. There's also a new online resource for anyone interested in finding out about life on the home front in World War II(www.caringonthehomefront.org.uk). Related sessions, involving handling some of the museum's collections, can be organised for school groups. *Buggy access (not tours). Shop.*

Prince Henry's Room

17 Fleet Street, EC4Y 1AA (www.cityoflondon.gov.uk). Blackfriars tube/rail/11, 15, 172 bus. **Open** closed for refurbishment; due to reopen summer 2006. **Admission** free; donations appreciated. **Map** p318 N6.

Closed for refurbishment at the time of writing (due to reopen in summer 2006, check the website for details), this ornate, oak-panelled room is one of few in central London to have survived the Great Fire of 1666. The original Jacobean plaster ceiling is immaculately preserved, and a popular subject for sketches by architecture students. Originally used by lawyers for Prince Henry, eldest son of King James I, the room was built in 1610 – the same year that the 14-year-old Henry became Prince of Wales. Four years later he died of typhoid, and it was his brother who succeeded to the throne as Charles I. The rest of the building – now an office – was once a tavern called the Prince's Arms, which happened to be a favoured haunt of the diarist Samuel Pepys. So it is that the cases in Prince Henry's Room actually display a range of Pepys memorabilia, including original portraits, newspaper clippings and – of course – extracts from his chronicle of 17th-century life. Children already predisposed towards this particular portion of history will enjoy it, but don't expect the place to inflame younger imaginations.

St Clement Danes

Strand, WC2R 1DH (7242 8282). Temple tube (closed Sun)/1, 171, 172 bus. **Open** 9am-4pm Mon-Fri; 9am-3pm Sat, Sun. Closed bank hols. **Admission** free; donations appreciated. **Map** p318 M6.

No longer believed to be the church namechecked in the popular nursery rhyme 'Oranges and Lemons', St Clement's nonetheless does have bells – they ring four times daily (9am, noon, 3pm, 6pm) as well as in an annual ceremony that involves children from the local primary school choosing from a mountain of citrus fruit. They were silenced when the church, rebuilt by Christopher Wren (a fourth incarnation since it was

⚔ LUNCH BOX

For more recommended restaurants and cafés in the area, see pp162-84.

Al's Bar 11-13 Exmouth Market, EC1R 4QD (7837 4821).
Bank Aldwych 1 Kingsway, WC2B 6XF (7379 9797).
Bierodrome 67 Kingsway, WC2B 6TD (7242 7469).
Fryer's Delight 19 Theobald's Road, WC1X 8SL (7405 4114).
Gallery Café basement of the Courtauld Institute Gallery, Somerset House, Strand, WC2R 1LA (7848 2526).
McDonald's 152-153 Fleet Street, EC4A 2DQ (7353 0543).
Pizza Express 99 High Holborn, WC1V 6LF (7831 5305).
Spaghetti House 20 Sicilian Avenue, WC1A 2QD (7405 5215).
Strada 8-10 Exmouth Market, EC1R 4YA (7278 0800).
Terrace Restaurant Lincoln's Inn Fields, WC2A 3LJ (7430 1234).
Wagamama 109 Fleet Street, EC4A 2AB (7583 7889).
Yo! Sushi 95 Farringdon Road, EC1R 3BT (7841 0785).

founded in the ninth century), was gutted by air raids in 1941. After the war, the Royal Air Force campaigned for its restoration, and on 19 October 1958 St Clement's was reconsecrated as the Central Church of the RAF. Spitfires may not get your pulses racing as they did 60 years ago, but there is a wealth of RAF memorabilia on display. The statue of Arthur 'Bomber' Harris, the man behind the RAF's brutal raids on Dresden, arouses mixed feelings. *Buggy access.*

St Ethelreda's

14 Ely Place, EC1N 6RY (7405 1061). Chancery Lane tube/Farringdon tube/rail. **Open** 8.30am-7pm daily; phone to check. **Admission** free; donations appreciated. **Map** p318 N5.
Despite its postcode, Ely Place is, through a quirk of legal history, under the jurisdiction of Cambridgeshire. Much like the Vatican, it is even subject to its own laws and precedents. Built by Bishop Luda of Ely in the 13th century, it's the oldest Catholic church in Britain and serves as London's only standing example of Gothic architecture from that period. It survived the Great Fire of London thanks to a change in the wind. These days the upper church – rebuilt after damage caused by the Blitz – is used for services. The crypt is dark and atmospheric, untouched by the noise of nearby traffic.
Ely Place is where David Copperfield meets Agnes Wakefield in the Dickens novel. The strawberries grown in the church gardens receive commendation in Shakespeare's *Richard III*. In recognition of this, Ely Place stages an annual Strawberrie Fayre festival, which in 2006 will take place on 25 June, with plenty of traditional fun and games and all proceeds going to charity.
Buggy access. Café (noon-2pm Mon-Fri).

Sir John Soane's Museum

13 Lincoln's Inn Fields, WC2A 3BP (7405 2107/ education officer 7440 4247/www.soane.org). Holborn tube. **Open** 10am-5pm Tue-Sat; 10am-5pm, 6-9pm 1st Tue of mth. Closed bank hol weekends. *Tours* 2.30pm Sat. **Admission** free; donations appreciated. *Tours* £3; free concessions, under-16s. **Credit** *Shop* AmEx, MC, V. **Map** p315 M5.
The son of a bricklayer, John Soane was able to indulge his passion for collecting unusual artefacts only after he married into money. But it was a passion he then indulged relentlessly and without prejudice. Far from confining himself to relics of a specific period, he filled his home with everything from an Ancient Egyptian sarcophagus to paintings by his near-contemporary, renowned satirist William Hogarth. The latter's *Rake's Progress* is on display in a room that also contains several of Soane's own architectural plans, all nestled together in an elaborate and utterly charming series of folding doors and walls. It is such touches of ingenuity that elevate this museum from a mere cabinet of (admittedly extraordinary) curiosities to something altogether more beguiling.
The museum is currently being extended into the house next door. When the work is completed in 2007 it will have a floor fully devoted to educational workshops for families and children. In the meantime, there are regular free Saturday courses held in the Dragon Hall Community Centre (Stukeley Street) that tie neatly into a range of architectural practices. All workshops must be booked in advance (7440 4247) and are mainly aimed at children aged seven to 13 (under-sevens may join with an adult). On the first Tuesday of every month, you can visit in the evening (6-9pm) when the house is candlelit after dark.
Nearest picnic place: Lincoln's Inn Fields. Shop.

Somerset House

Strand, WC2R ORN (7845 4600/www.somerset-house.org.uk). Covent Garden or Temple tube (closed Sun)/Charing Cross tube/rail. **Open** 10am-6pm daily (last entry 5.15pm). *Courtyard & River Terrace* Apr-Sept 8am-6pm daily (extended hours apply for restaurant). **Tours** 1.30pm, 2.30pm, 3.45pm 1st Sat of mth; free. **Admission** *Parts of South Building, Courtyard & River Terrace* free. *Exhibitions* prices vary; phone for details. **Credit** MC, V. **Map** p317 M7.
One small step into the courtyard of Somerset House is one giant leap into the 18th century, with the elaborate stone edifices that surround the courtyard shutting out all but a whisper of traffic from the Strand. Erected on the site of a long-demolished Tudor palace, this grand exercise in neo-classical architecture – originally designed to house public offices – is home to three of the UK's finest galleries: the Courtauld Institute Gallery, the Gilbert Collection and the Hermitage Rooms (*see pp54-7*). Somerset House is a family destination in and of itself, most notably throughout December and January, when the courtyard becomes an attractive ice rink that, vast crowds notwithstanding, is idyllic at Christmas. Equally inspired is the big square fountain in the centre, which entertains with waterjets that dance in formation. On hot summer days, children love running down the brief corridors of water – even more so when the corridors collapse and everyone gets a soaking. The courtyard also provides a stage for events during the summer holidays, and the Family Free Time Festival takes place in July.
Buggy access. Cafés. Disabled; lift, toilet. Nappy-changing facilities. Restaurant. Shops.

Bloomsbury & Fitzrovia

Civilisation as we know it.

The Great Court at the **British Museum** is roundly admired. *See p61*.

It may be forever associated with the Bloomsbury Group – that celebrated band of writers and artists who colonised the area's lofty townhouses, but **Bloomsbury** hasn't always been so high-minded. Way back in the 11th century, it was known as a pig-breeding area. As far as modern visitors are concerned, however, Bloomsbury and Fitzrovia remain fascinating to visit, with a wealth of period architecture, unexpected green spaces and world-class museums.

Literature students can spend hours spotting blue plaques on the former residences of Virginia Woolf, WB Yeats, Edgar Allan Poe, Anthony Trollope and so on. One of Charles Dickens's homes there is now a museum (*see p62*).

Everyone is enthralled by the **British Museum**'s treasures; the Egyptian mummies are an irresistible draw for younger visitors. During half-terms and holidays, Egyptology-related activities are often organised, both here and at the **Petrie Museum of Egyptian Archaeology**.

The Petrie is one of half a dozen small venues of cultural interest in the area. Most appealing is the **Foundling Museum**, a memorial to London's abandoned children, which opened in 2004 and was nominated for the Gulbenkian Prize for Museum of the Year. Its location is child-friendly, too: adjacent to the extensive inner-city park **Coram's Fields** (named after benefactor Thomas Coram). And just a stone's throw from the British Museum you'll find the **Cartoon Museum**, dedicated to collecting and preserving British cartoons, caricatures, comics and animations.

Other prominent names in local history are those of the fourth Earl of Southampton, who built **Bloomsbury Square** around his house in the

1660s (none of this architecture remains), and the Russells – or Dukes of Bedford – who intermarried with the Southamptons and developed this rural area into one of London's first planned suburbs. It was during the 18th and 19th centuries that the lovely Georgian squares and elegant terraces here were built in an easy-to-navigate grid style.

In stark contrast, opposite Russell Square tube is the **Brunswick Centre**. Hailed as the future of community living when it was built in the 1960s, this concrete complex of high-density housing is undergoing refurbishment as befitting its Grade II-listed building status. It provokes strong feelings: denounced by some as Bloomsbury's carbuncle, it's loved by fans of Modernism.

Fitzrovia is less well defined than Bloomsbury. Its highlight, Fitzroy Square, is disappointingly paved over, although its main visitor attraction, **Pollock's Toy Museum**, is a gem for collectors, and has a wonderful shop.

An eclectic mix of transitory students, hospital staff and happily entrenched locals populate the streets to the east of Tottenham Court Road, home to London University and various medical buildings. At their heart is **Senate House**, Malet Street's towering and forbidding monolith, which inspired George Orwell's Ministry of Truth in *1984* and housed the Ministry of Information during World War II. It was a particular favourite of Adolf Hitler: he had planned to make his headquarters there if Germany had won the war.

British Library

96 Euston Road, NW1 2DB (7412 7332/Learning 7412 7797/www.bl.uk). Euston or King's Cross tube/rail. **Open** 9.30am-6pm Mon, Wed-Fri; 9.30am-8pm Tue; 9.30am-5pm Sat; 11am-5pm Sun, bank hols. **Admission** free; donations appreciated. **Credit** *Shop* MC, V. **Map** p317 K3.

Each year the library receives a copy of everything that is published in the UK and Ireland, including maps, newspapers, magazines, prints and drawings. Once part of the British Museum but rehoused in these state-of-the-art premises in 1997, the Library's ever-growing collection of 150 million items is staggering – spread over 388 miles (625km) of shelves in 112,000sq m (1.2m sq ft) of space. This collection is strictly for serious researchers but visitors can glimpse the King's Library: the 60,000 volume collection of George III, given to the nation in 1823 and housed in a six-storey, glass-walled tower as the centrepiece of the building. The British Library's most popular space is the John Ritblat Gallery, where treasures (under glass) include the Magna Carta of 1215, Leonardo da Vinci's notebook and the Lindisfarne Gospels of AD 721.

One of the frustrations associated with paper conservation is subdued lighting: the whole of the British Library is gloomily lit by necessity. However, Turning The Pages digital kiosks let you virtually explore displayed treasures, including the original manuscript of *Alice In Wonderland*. Children may enjoy listening to items from the National Sound Archive on jukebox headphones – Kalahari bushmen performing a healing dance, Bob Geldof at LiveAid or the quavery voice of Florence Nightingale recorded in 1890. Other items of interest include The Beatles' scribbled lyrics alongside recordings of their songs. The long wall flanking the ground floor café holds the philatelic collection – over 80,000 stamps from around the world on view in pull-out cases.

Happy days in **Coram's Fields**. *See p63.*

The two major exhibitions for 2006 are London In Maps: Life Story of a City (until March 2007) and The Front Page (25 May-8 October), which celebrates the last century in British newspapers,. The latter features an interactive newsroom with computers where junior journalists can become the editor of their own newspaper and make up a front page on screen. Free 'Breaking Stories' workshops are planned; call the Learning team for details.

During the summer months the Library stages a variety of events in its open-air piazza area – a haven from the thunderous thoroughfare that is the Euston Road. At other times there are regular free demonstrations of bookbinding, printing and calligraphy for children. During holidays, workshops, activities and storytelling sessions are organised for children aged five to 11 and their families . To join the free Learning mailing list, write to the address above, call 7412 7797 or check the website. (For dates and details of all events, call the information line on 7412 7332.) *Buggy access. Café. Disabled access: lift, toilet. Nappy-changing facilities. Nearest picnic place: St James' Gardens. Restaurant. Shop.*

British Museum

Great Russell Street, WC1B 3DG (7636 1555/recorded information 7323 8783/Learning and Information 7412 7797/www.thebritishmuseum.ac.uk). Holborn, Russell Square or Tottenham Court Road tube. **Open** *Galleries* 10am-5.30pm Mon-Wed, Sat, Sun; 10am-8.30pm Thur, Fri. *Great Court* 9am-6pm Mon-Wed, Sun; 9am-11pm Thur-Sat. **Tours** *Highlights* 10.30am, 1pm, 3pm daily; phone to check. *EyeOpener* frequently; phone to check. **Admission** (LP) free; donations appreciated. *Temporary exhibitions* prices vary; phone for details. *Highlights tours* £8; £5 under-11s, concessions. *EyeOpener tours* free. **Credit** *Shop* AmEx, DC, MC, V. **Map** p317 K5.

Founded in 1753, an embodiment of the Enlightenment concept of all of the arts and sciences being interconnected, the British Museum houses world-famous collections best appreciated in bite-sized chunks. The Great Court, London's largest covered public square, makes an impressive starting point for exploring the Egyptian antiquities (the Rosetta Stone, imposing statues, mummies) and ancient Greek treasures, including the Elgin Marbles, but do make time (or plan a return visit) for its less famous prehistoric, ethnographic, Asian and European collections. Here are artefacts as diverse as Japanese suits of armour, Mexican Day of the Dead papier-mâché figures and the Lindow Man, garotted in 300 BC Britain and preserved in peat ever since.The restored King's Library was built in the 1820s, and its Grade I-listed interior is widely considered to be the finest neo-classical space in London. It has a splendid permanent exhibition, Enlightenment: Rethinking the World in the 18th Century, a 5,000-strong collection examining that formative period of the museum.

Planned temporary exhibitions include Power and Taboo: Sacred Objects from the Pacific (21 September 2006-January 2007), focusing on Polynesian religious practice in the 18th and early 19th century. This promises a wide variety of exhibits: intricate tiki pendants from New Zealand, colourful feather god heads and cloaks from Hawaii, and wooden sculptures from the Society Islands.

The museum offers sampler tours of its top treasures (starting from the information desk) and EyeOpener tours, which concentrate on specific aspects of the collection, such as Africa, the Americas or the classical world. They're not aimed specifically at children, but the volunteer guides are happy for families to dip in and out of them as they like. Check the website for details of free special family EyeOpeners, run twice daily during half-terms and irregularly through the school holidays (book at the information desk), or pick up a family backpack (deposit required) from the Reading Room to navigate the galleries

Around Town

independently. The Roman Britain, Mexico, Africa, Greece and Egypt trails contain hands-on activities. Young Friends of the British Museum (£20 per year for children aged eight to 15) receive a welcome pack, 10% discount in the shop and magazines three times a year. Lasting childhood memories are sure to result from a museum sleepover with the mummies (£27.50), available only to Young Friends. Membership also entitles children to all sorts of half-term activities.

Buggy access. Cafés. Disabled access: lift, toilet. Nappy-changing facilities. Nearest picnic place: Russell Square. Restaurant. Shops.

Cartoon Museum

35 Little Russell Street, WC1A 2HH (7580 8155/ www.cartoonmuseum.org). Holborn or Tottenham Court Road tube. **Open** 10.30am-5pm Tue-Sat. **Admission** £2.50; £1.50 concessions; free under-18s, students. **Credit** *Shop* MC, V. **Map** p315 L5.

Housed in a former dairy, this museum is dedicated to collecting and preserving the best of British cartoons, caricatures, comics and animations. The ground-floor displays are arranged chronologically, with Hogarths and Gillrays leading on to well-known World War II political cartoons, Thelwell's playful countryside images, and satirical works by revolutionary artists Ralph Steadman and Gerald Scarfe. Both the permanant displays and temporary exhibitions rotate every three months or so. The first- floor gallery is the most engaging for children, detailing the history of British comics and cartoon strips from 1884. Here you'll see favourite childhood characters close up: 1920s Rupert, Desperate Dan from the 1940s, Dennis the Menace, Dick Tracy, Tank Girl and Judge Dredd. It's early days , and many activities (dependent on funding) have yet to be finalised, but the museum's email or postal information service is worth signing up to in order to find out about plans for family fun days and activities like making themed comic strips. There are also plans for Claymation and time-lapse photography workshops (£20-£25, for children aged eight to 14), and everyone is encouraged to create their own art for the Young Cartoonists Gallery.

The Cartoon Art Trust also runs the Young Cartoonist of the Year competition, awards for which are presented at the Cartoon Awards each year (check the website for this year's closing date for entries).

Buggy access (ground floor). Nearest picnic place: Russell Square. Shop.

Charles Dickens Museum

48 Doughty Street, WC1N 2LX (7405 2127/www.dickensmuseum.com). Russell Square tube. **Open** 10am-5pm Mon-Sat; 11am-5pm Sun. **Admission** £5; £4 concessions; £3 5-15s; free under-5s; £14 family (2+3). **Credit** AmEx, DC, MC, V. **Map** p317 M4.

Charles Dickens's miserable childhood – his father was sent to Marshalsea Prison for debt and, at 12, Charles had to leave school and work in a shoe-polish factory – shaped his personality and literary career. After the publication and success of *The Pickwick Papers* in 1836, Dickens left his poverty-stricken past and cramped chambers in Holborn and moved to Doughty Street, at that time a private street sealed at both ends with gates and manned by porters. *Oliver Twist* and *Nicholas Nickleby* were written here. This is the author's only surviving London residence, but he lived here only for three years. The museum on these premises is filled with memorabilia and artefacts; its passageways are decorated with paintings of Dickens characters, among them Little Nell, Uriah Heep and Little Dorrit. Dickens's personal effects are all over the place. Displays include personal letters, original manuscripts and the desk on which he wrote *Oliver Twist*. In the basement,

Petrie Museum of Egyptian Archaeology.
See p64.

Body Count

It's amazing how many corpses you come across on a tour around Bloomsbury's great institutions. Here's five of our favourites.

Ginger

You'll find this red-haired cadaver in Room 64 of the British Museum (*see p61*). A naturally-preserved, pre-dynastic mummy, Ginger (check out the hair) is surrounded by burial goods, including pottery vessels that were filled with food to accompany him to the afterlife.

Lindow Man

Stay in the British Musem to meet this dried-out individual. His 2,000-year-old body was discovered near Manchester in 1984 and is now exhibited in a quiet spot in the Celts Gallery.

One unlucky bull

The Ancient Egyptians mummified animals as well as people, and this bull calf, on display in Room 62 of the British Museum, happened to be in the wrong place at the wrong time. This little chap was sacrificed to one of the many gods who had the bull as their special symbol, possibly Ptah, who was thought to occasionally disguise himself as a bull with a white triangle on its forehead. Lucky white-faced bulls would be looked after by priests in a temple at Thebes.

Jeremy Bentham

The moral philosopher (1748-1832) eccentrically requested in his will that his body be preserved and stored in a cabinet at University College London (Gower Street, WC1E 6BT, 7679 2000). It attends official functions so that Bentham's presence can live on. The body has a wax head, as the real one was damaged when the body was preserved. For some years Bentham's real head was displayed in this case, but too many students were mucking about with it so it was locked away.

Minnie

Once you've found the atmospheric Petrie Museum of Egyptian Archeology (*see p63*), trot along to Room 2 to say hello to Minnie. That's the name given by staff to the coiffured head of a mummy, whose eyebrows and lashes are still divertingly intact.

visitors can see a 25-minute film on Dickens's life in London. Children's handling sessions, in which kids get to grips with quill pens, first editions and Dickens family photographs, are held most Tuesdays and Wednesdays (11am-4pm, call ahead as these are volunteer-run).

Special events include readings by costumed actors on Wednesday evenings (6.30pm , May-Sept; tickets £16); this may be more suited to adults and older children, though. There are two mini-trails for children, using Dickens's best-known stories such as *Oliver Twist* and *A Christmas Carol*. Trails for primary-school children are picture-based; older kids get a multiple-choice questionnaire. Check the website for details of occasional Victorian craft workshops. *Buggy access (ground floor). Disabled access: ramp (ground floor only). Nearest picnic place: Coram's Fields/Russell Square. Shop.*

Coram's Fields

93 Guilford Street, WC1N 1DN (7837 6138). Russell Square tube. **Open** *May-Aug* 9am-8pm daily. *Sept-Apr* 9am-dusk daily. **Admission** free. **Map** p317 L4.
Famous long before it became one of young Londoners' favourite parks, this site dates back to 1747, the year Thomas Coram established the Foundling Hospital for abandoned children (site of the Foundling Museum, *see right*). After the orphanage was demolished in the 1920s, a campaign to turn the site into a children's play area kept the developers at bay; the park finally opened in 1936. There are spacious lawns, sandpits and slides, a paddling pool, an AstroTurf football pitch, a basketball court, a wooden climbing tower, swings, a helter-skelter chute and an assault-course pulley. There's also a city farm, with goats, geese, a duck pond, rabbits, guinea pigs and an aviary. Occasionally during the summer bands and circus performers entertain picnicking families; under-fives fun days are often held. For the last three years, there have been two weeks of trapeze activities offered in August; call the office to check if they're running in 2006. A small veggie café in the colonades (closed Mon in winter) provides healthy fuel for all that active play .

Parents love the park because it's safe. It's permanently staffed, and adults are admitted only if accompanied by children. Sports such as football, basketball, aerobics and trampolining are all available free (call for details). In the Band Room and play centre a range of classes are offered; call for details. A youth centre has free IT courses for 13- to 19-year-olds. There are toilets and shower rooms in the sports area (including facilities for wheelchair-users) and a drop-in playgroup (7837 6611). The nursery, after-school and holiday play centres are run by Camden Council (7837 0255). All activities are dependent on funding, so do make a donation or spend some money in the café. *Buggy access. Café. Disabled access: toilet. Nappy-changing facilities.*

Foundling Museum

40 Brunswick Square, WC1N 1AZ (78413600/www. foundlingmuseum.org.uk). Russell Square tube. **Open** 10am-6pm Tue-Sat; noon-6pm Sun. **Tours** by arrangement. **Admission** £5; £4 concessions; free under-16s. **Credit** AmEx, MC, V. **Map** p317 L4.
Up to a thousand babies a year were abandoned in early 18th-century London. Horrified at the common sight of unwanted infants left to die on the streets, retired sea captain Thomas Coram spent 17 years relentlessly campaigning to improve their lot. He established his Hospital for the Maintenance and Education of Exposed and Deserted Children in 1739, the first foundlings being admitted in 1741. During the life of the hospital (it finally closed in 1953), more than 27,000 abandoned infants were taken in and cared for until they were of apprentice age. The Foundling Museum, which stands in a beautifully

Around Town

restored building adjacent to the original site of the hospital, tells the story of those children – and the adults who campaigned for them. Most prominent of these were William Hogarth, whose support and gifts of paintings caused the Foundling Hospital to become established as Britain's first public art gallery, and George Frederic Handel, whose manuscripts and ephemera are displayed on the top floor of the museum. Handel was a Governor and benefactor of the Foundling Hospital, and annual performances of his Messiah provided a sources of income for the institution.

More poignant, however, is the array of humble items left by mothers as a keepsake for their children – a key, buttons, a piece of shell engraved with the child's name and date of birth, a scrap of poetry: 'Go gentle babe.../And all thy life be happiness and love'. Sadly, to keep the mother's identity anonymous, the foundlings were never given these tokens. Children and families can explore the museum through activity packs, audio games, story books and special events throughout the year. These include artistic workshops, drop-in family fun days, concerts and author visits. Call ahead or check the website for details of other regular events.

Buggy access. Café. Disabled access: lift. Nappy-changing facilities. Nearest picnic place: Brunswick Square/Coram's Fields. Shop.

 LUNCH BOX

For recommended restaurants and cafés in the area, see *pp162-84.*

Apostrophe 216 Tottenham Court Road, W1T 7PT (7436 6688).
Busaba Eathai 22 Store Street, WC1E 7DF (7299 7900).
Ciao Bella 86-90 Lamb's Conduit Street, WC1N 3LZ (7242 4119).
Cigala 54 Lamb's Conduit Street, WC1N 3LW (7405 1717).
Coram's Fields Café Coram's Fields WC1N 1DN (7837 6138).
Court Café British Museum, Great Russell Street, WC1B 3DG (7636 1555).
Fryer's Delight 19 Theobald's Road, WC1X 8SL (7405 4114).
Goodfellas 50 Lamb's Conduit Street, WC1N 3LH (7405 7088).
Lino's Café 21A Store Street, WC1E 7DH (7636 9133).
Navarro's 67 Charlotte Street, W1T 4PH (7637 7713).
Pizza Express 30 Coptic Street, WC1A 1NS (7636 3232).
Sheng's Tea House 68 Millman Street, WC1N 3EF (7405 3697).
Spaghetti House 20 Sicilian Avenue, WC1A 2QD (7405 5215).
Wagamama 4A Streatham Street, WC1A 1JB (7323 9223).
Wagamama 14A Irving Street, WC2H 7AF (7839 2323).
Yo! Sushi myhotel, 11-13 Bayley Street, WC1B 3HD (7636 0076).

Petrie Museum of Egyptian Archaeology

University College London, entrance through DMS Watson Library, Malet Place, WC1E 6BT (7679 2884/www.petrie.ucl.ac.uk). Goodge Street or Warren Street tube/29, 73, 134 bus. **Open** 1-5pm Tue-Fri; 10am-1pm Sat. Closed Easter hols; 24 Dec-2 Jan. **Admission** free; donations appreciated. **Map** p317 K4.
If the British Museum has all the big showstoppers, the Petrie Museum of Egyptian Archaeology contains the pieces that made up the minutiae of Egyptian life: cosmetic pots, the remains of a child's rag doll, beautifully painted tile fragments and, most famously, the world's oldest piece of clothing (a dress worn by a teenager in 2800 BC). Some of the collection might be rather heavy-going for young children (the first room, filled with broken pots, is a bit off-putting), but items in the second gallery might rouse more interest: a collection of ancient toys, jewellery, painted coffin cases, a rat trap and a mummy head, with eyelashes and eyebrows still intact. The maze-like journey to this tucked-away museum (there are plans to rehouse the collections in purpose-built galleries in 2009) and its gloomy surroundings give the place a wonderfully spooky, *Indiana Jones*-like atmosphere. Pick up a free torch from reception and explore the dusty aisles and the thousands of item crammed into the dimly lit cases. Children can work through the Rock Trail worksheet, a themed journey around the collection. There's also a Petrie Family Pack archaeology kit, with free postcards and replica objects or painted papyrus (depending on availability). Activities and events crop up regularly; call the Education Officer on 7679 2151 to see what's on over the holidays, or encourage your kids' teachers to visit the website and order packs aimed at seven- to 11-year-olds. Activities (in conjunction with a museum tour (school visits 10am-1pm Tue, Wed; free).
Buggy access. Disabled access: lift, toilet. Nearest picnic place: Gordon Square. Shop.

Pollock's Toy Museum

1 Scala Street (entrance on Whitfield Street), W1T 2HL (7636 3452/www.pollockstoymuseum.com). Goodge Street tube. **Open** 10am-5pm Mon-Sat. **Admission** £3; £2 concessions; £1.50 3-16s; free under-3s. **Credit** MC, V.
Formed from two adjacent houses (one dates from the 1780s, the other a century later), and named after Benjamin Pollock, the last of the Victorian toy theatre printers, this appealingly ramshackle museum is run by the founder's grandson and has been on this site for over 35 years. The upper floor consists of a warren of atmospheric rooms, with creaking floorboards, period fireplaces and sloping walls. These rooms house treasures gathered from nurseries across the world. The oldest item is a 4,000-year-old Egyptian clay toy mouse; among the other curiosities are well-loved teddy bears, dolls, Chinese shadow puppets and 19th-century magic lanterns. The first-floor toy theatre room houses English and European examples; look for photographs of Mr Pollock (in his Hoxton shop, bombed in 1944) in the alcove. Adults are more likely to appreciate the nostalgia value of old board games and playthings; they won't mean much to kids – but there's hands-on fun to be had in the museum shop: reproduction cardboard theatres, wind-up music boxes, animal masks and tin robots are sold alongside modern items such as tubs of fluorescent, maggotty green slime, and jumping spiders.
Nearest picnic place: Crabtree Fields, off Colville Place. Shop.

Marylebone

The former village of St Mary by the Bourne is urbanely idyllic.

London Zoo, 178 years old and still wildly popular. *See p67.*

It's a sobering thought that this chic area, with its attractive high street and quiet squares, was once a violent place. In the 14th century the two ancient manors, Lileston and Tyburn (named after a stream, or bourne, that flowed into the Thames) from which Marylebone takes its name, were best known for their criminal population. Tyburn in fact, was the site of a gallows. The first execution recorded at Tyburn took place in 1196 in a place next to the stream, but in 1571 the 'Tyburn Tree' was erected near Marble Arch. The 'Tree' was a form of gallows supported by three legs, from which felons could be hanged at once. On 23 June, 1649, as many as 24 prisoners were hanged simultaneously. The word Tyburn came to be synonymous with executions – 'dancing the Tyburn jig' was the act of being hanged.

The last public execution took place at Tyburn in 1783, and as the gruesome associations passed into history, so the area became more genteel. The northern half of the village that grew up around the parish church of St Mary by the Bourne was used as a royal hunting ground (now **Regent's Park**), and the southern section was bought up by the Portman family, who developed the land into a series of elegant streets and squares, lending it a dignified air, which it retains today.

Marylebone High Street is today famed for its selection of independent shops, which earns it many plaudits in magazine consumer pages and the devotion of both Londoners and tourists. The squares leading off the high street are serene places to walk. Treasures to admire round here are the glorious gilded **Wallace Collection**, whose appearance belies a most accommodating attitude to children, who busy themselves with weekend sketching and half-termly armour appreciation. The Gothic Roman Catholic church of St James, Spanish Place (22 George Street, 7935 0943), aglow with votive candles, is another inspiring place for a sit-down. Keep strolling in a northerly direction for busy Marylebone Road, which you have to negotiate if you want to manhandle celebs in top tourist destination, **Madame Tussauds**.

Around Town

MADAME TUSSAUDS CALLS YOU TO THE DIARY ROOM

Visit the Diary Room at Madame Tussauds, talk to Big Brother and meet Davina McCall. Book in advance to avoid the queues, call 0870 400 3000 or visit madame-tussauds.com

MADAME
TUSSAUDS

London Central Mosque

*146 Park Road, NW8 7RG (7724 3363/www.iccuk.org).
Baker Street tube/13, 82, 133 bus.* **Open** *9.30am-6pm
daily.* **Admission** *free.*
The complex is much bigger than the dome and minaret
imply. Offices around a large courtyard accommodate
London's most important Islamic Cultural Centre; inside
the reception are a bookshop and an information booth.
Men and boys enter the prayer hall via doors on the ground
floor; women and girls pass through the 'toilets and *wudhu'*
(washing facilities) to head upstairs to a screened-off balcony. Inside the dome is a huge chandelier encircled by
Arabic tiles. All visitors must remove their shoes; women
should wear a headscarf for entry.
*Buggy access. Café. Disabled access: ramp, toilet. Nappy-
changing facilities. Nearest picnic place: Regent's Park.
Shop.*

London Zoo

*Regent's Park, NW1 4RY (7722 3333/www.zsl.org).
Baker Street or Camden Town tube, then 274 or C2
bus.* **Open** *Mar-late Oct* 10am-5.30pm daily. *Late Oct-
Feb* 10am-4pm daily. Check website for any changes.
Admission £14.50; £12 .70 concessions; £11.50 3-15s;
free under-3s; £47 family (2+2 or 1+3). **Credit** AmEx,
MC, V. **Map** p314 G2.
Our favourite route to the zoo is via the London Waterbus
Company from Camden Lock (*see p30*), which takes you
directly to the action (not far from the giraffe house). Plenty
of activities are laid on for families, especially during the
school holidays, although those parents old enough to
remember camel rides and chimps' tea parties will be
sorely disappointed. This venerable institution continues
to trumpet a conservation and captive-breeding message
(talking of trumpets, there are no elephants and the hippos
are of the pygmy variety). There are lions and tigers, which
make you feel a little sad, but they've got their mates with
them, so they're not as gloomy as the solitary tapir and
Komodo dragon, both of which seemed lonely and out of
sorts on our visit. The giraffes' outdoor enclosure now has
a viewing platform for people to get closer to the business
end of these lofty creatures. The best bits in our book are
the new, steamy butterfly sanctuary made out of a large
inflatable caterpillar, and BUGS (the biodiversity
centre with its fascinating ant empire and cockroach
quarters). Do get your paws on a map and find out the
events timetable before you wander round getting footsore
and missing great stuff, such as the Animals in Action talk
in the theatre and feeding time for the penguins (they're
South African ones, in a new enclosure near the shop, as
the famous listed Lubetkin one doesn't suit them). The
meerkats, the otters, the wonderful children's zoo and the
Activity Centre, where you can make a badge or brass rubbing for 50p, are much loved by small visitors. Make a note
in your diary to check out the new gorilla island in 2007.
There are pretty good eating places all over the park, but
many people bring a picnic to save money. Which brings
us to our grumble. This is an expensive, if extensive attraction. There's lots to do, so why put bouncy castles and a
roundabout, (£1 for a few minutes' gratification), bang in
the middle? Small children are distracted from the business in hand by these temptations, and look to their
beleaguered parents, who have just parted company with
£47 for a family ticket, to cough up the cash. 'Snot fair!
*Buggy access. Café. Disabled access: ramps, toilet.
Nappy-changing facilities. Nearest picnic space: zoo
grounds. Restaurant. Shop.*

Madame Tussauds

*Marylebone Road, NW1 5LR (0870 400 3000/
www.madame-tussauds.co.uk). Baker Street tube/
13, 27, 74, 113, 159 bus.* **Open** *9.30am-6pm daily
(last entry 5.30pm).* Times vary during holiday periods.
Admission *9.30am-5pm Mon-Fri, 9.30am-6pm Sat,
Sun* £23.99; £20.99 concessions; £19.99 5-15s.
5-5.30pm daily £15; £13 concessions; £10 5-15s.
Internet booking only for family tickets. **Credit**
AmEx, MC, V. **Map** p314 G4.
It's farewell to the projected stars, planets and black holes
and *Hello!* to much dimmer starry exhibits – yes, there'll
be even more more grinning celebrities now that Madame
Tussauds has done away with the Planetarium that used
to be a joint attraction here. The domed ceiling of that
building is currently being used for a new projected show
by Aardman Animation, with a whole cast of
characters created especially for it. The show was still
under wraps as we went to press, but we're promised a
'smart, surprising new film experience'.
The Aardman show comes at the end of a trip through
celebsville, courtesy of the world famous wax effigies. In
fact the new stars have all been made with silicone – caress
Brad Pitt's cheeks and you'll find them baby soft. Robbie
Williams has been so ravaged by amorous admirers he had
to have extensive repairs in 2005. Robbie and Brad can be
found in Blush!, a live and interactive attraction starring
the celebs of the moment – including Andy and Lou from
Little Britain, as well as Jamie Oliver with his rumbly tum.
The *Big Brother* Experience is suitably vacuous, with a
replica of the series seven Diary Room and a meeting with
a chatty silicone Davina. Premiere Night lets you deliver
your own Oscar acceptance speech alongside movie stars

LUNCH BOX

For recommended restaurants and cafés in the
area, *see reviews pp162-84.*

Caffè Caldesi 118 Marylebone Lane, W1U 2QF
(7935 1144).
Carluccio's Caffè St Christopher's Place,
W1U 1AY (7935 5927); 8 Market Place, W1W
8AG (7636 2228).
Eat & Two Veg 50 Marylebone High Street,
W1U 5HN (7258 8595).
Garden Café Inner Circle, Regents Park, NW1
4NU (7935 5729).
Golden Hind 73 Marylebone Lane, W1U 2PN
(7486 3644).
Honest Sausage Broadwalk, off Chester Road,
Regent's Park, NW1 4NU (7224 3872).
La Spighetta 43 Blandford Street, W1U 7HF
(7486 7340).
Le Pain Quotidien 7275 Marylebone High
Street, W1U 5JW (7486 6154).
Oasis Café London Zoo, Regent's Park, NW1
4RY (7722 3333).
Pâtisserie Valerie at Sagne 105 Marylebone
High Street, W1U 4RS (7935 6240).
Paul 115 Marylebone High Street, W1U 4SB
(7224 5615).
Tootsies Grill 35 James Street, W1M 5HX
(7486 1611).

Around Town

Wallace Collection.

such as Marilyn Monroe and Arnold Schwarzenegger. You can also be dwarfed by the Incredible Hulk, share a press conference with Tony Blair and George Bush or see how small the Queen really is (blimey! She could fit on a stamp!). If it's not too busy, small children can be left with f riendly staff while brave older ones go into the horrible Chamber of Horrors, where an appalling zombie (played by an actor) practically made us wet our pants last visit. Do not let little ones go in there. For the 2006/7 season, Tussauds' promise there'll be more serial killers on the loose in the Chamber's maze than ever before. Yikes. Children are very fond of the time-travel ride, The Spirit of London, which takes you through 400 years of London life in a London taxi pod.

Café. Disabled access: lift, toilet. Nappy-changing facilities. Nearest picnic place: Regent's Park. Shop.

Regent's Park

The Store Yard, Inner Circle, Regent's Park, NW1 4NR (7486 7905/www.royalparks.gov.uk). Baker Street, Camden Town, Great Portland Street, or Regent's Park tube. **Open** 5am-30mins before dusk daily. **Admission** free. **Map** p314 G3.

Used by Henry VIII for hunting and landscaped in 1811 for the Prince Regent, Regent's Park opened its gates to the great unwashed only in 1845, during the reign of Queen Victoria, even then, it was only for two days a week. Today, however, we're allowed in, 365 days a year, to admire the planting schemes in the flower beds, the heronry on the lake, the wonderful café (*see p178*) and the open-air theatre (*see p225*) and the free concerts in the bandstand.

Sporty types appreciate the park for the Hub, the name given to the biggest outdoor sports facility in central London, with tennis and netball courts, an athletics track, football and hockey pitches and a new sports pavilion. Check the website for an energetic programme of school holidays sports courses and events – session that may include cricket, footie, TAG rugby and rounders cost just 50p each and are suitable for ages six to 13.

There are four well maintained playgrounds, each with a sandpit and toilets; one is close to the golden domed London Central Mosque (*see p67*) and the boating lake; there's another by Marylebone Road, north of Portland Place; the third is by the Camden Town entrance; and the last lies at the foot of Primrose Hill. The shallow boating lake is one of the nicest places to spend a summer's afternoon, with rowing boats available for hire by the hour (£6 for adults, £4 for children), but there is also a small, circular lake for children who want to mess about in pedalos. These cost £3 for 20mins and the youngsters must pass a height test to use them.

Buggy access. Cafés. Disabled access: toilets. Nappy-changing facilities.

Sherlock Holmes Museum

221B Baker Street, NW1 6XE (7935 8866/ www.sherlock-holmes.co.uk). Baker Street tube/74, 139, 189 bus. **Open** 9.30am-6pm daily (last entry 5.30pm). **Admission** £6; £4 6-16s; free under-6s. **Credit** AmEx, MC, V. **Map** p311 F4.

Children look a bit bewildered when you explain that this is the home of Britain's most famous detective, who in fact never existed. Such is the blurring between fact and fiction that pilgrims visiting this, Sherlock Holmes's faithfully constructed home, often ask where the great man was buried. When the famous books were written, No.221 was a fictional address: Baker Street didn't extend that far. Now, however, it does, and by some bizarre coincidence, the building on the real 221 Baker Street is being developed into luxury flats by a company called Baskerville Estates. Fans of the books delight in the care with which fictional detail has been faithfully reproduced. The house is set up as if the master detective and associate are in situ, complete with affable housekeeper Mrs Hudson, who can tell you all you need to know about the detective, whose chair you can keep warm in his study. Upstairs is the room belonging to his sidekick Watson. The third-floor exhibit rooms contain a new arrangement of wax models of scenes from the stories. Sherlock Holmes and Professor Moriarty can be seen in the same room. The lumber room in the attic, where the lodgers used to store their trunks and luggage, is also open to visitors, who then rush downstairs to browse the extensive range of Sherlockian merchandise in the shop.

Nearest picnic place: Regent's Park. Shop.

Wallace Collection

Hertford House, Manchester Square, W1U 3BN (7935 0687/www.wallacecollection.org). Bond Street tube/ 2, 10, 12, 30, 74, 113 bus. **Open** 10am-5pm daily. Closed 1 Jan, Good Fri, 1 May, 24-26 Dec. **Admission** free. **Credit** *Shop* MC, V. **Map** p314 G5.

An elegant hall of breathtaking gorgeousness awaits inside this gracious monument to 18th-century aristocratic life. Mount the creaking staircase to discover beautiful rooms full of priceless paintings, furniture, and, of most interest to children, armour, swords and daggers. Other rooms are crammed with gilded clocks, mirrors, snuff boxes and porcelain. The largest part of the collection was amassed by the Fourth Marquess of Hertford, a great Francophile who had bought it for safekeeping from the ravages of the French Revolution. Visitors' facilities include a lecture theatre and a dedicated education room for schools. Café Bagatelle in the central courtyard is far posher than your average museum catering, but it's a splendid place for a light lunch, and they do have a children's menu. In May 2006 the newly refurbished Study and Oval Drawing Rooms were unveiled. They're recreated in the style of Marie Antoinette's Versailles boudoir and include objects once housed in her royal palaces.

Prize paintings in the main collections include Frans Hals's *Laughing Cavalier* and Fragonard's *The Swing.* The first Sunday of every month there is 'The Little Draw,' during which families can pick up art materials and a drawing board and get sketching with help from the gallery's in-house artist. The regular armour workshops (check the website for the next one) have a hands-on approach, helpingkids discover how heavy the armour and weapons are, letting them handle items like 3,000-year-old bronze swords and oriental dagers decorated with jade and gold.

Free general guided tours of the collection are usually given on weekdays at 1pm, Wednesdays and Saturdays at 11.30pm or 3pm and Sundays at 1pm, although these are sometimes replaced by specialist gallery talks covering aspects of the Wallace Collection in more detail; check the website for daily events.

Buggy access. Disabled access: lift, toilet. Nappy-changing facilities. Nearest picnic place: grounds. Restaurant. Shop.

St John's Wood

Walking up from Baker Street, keeping Regent's Park to your right, you pass Dorset Square, which bears a plaque marking it out as the birthplace of Marylebone Cricket Club (Thomas Lord staged his first MCC match here in 1787). A new rural ground, formerly a duck pond, was found for the MCC in 1814 and Lord's Cricket Ground has been there ever since. In 1999 it gained a futuristic media centre, which members have learned to love now it's part of the scenery. The area round here is upmarket and residential. The grounds of St John's Wood Church (Lord's Roundabout, NW8 7NE, 7586 3864, www.stjohnswoodchurch.org), with its picnic tables, wildlife walk, meadow ground and play area, are a useful stopping-off point before or after visiting the cricket museum at Lord's. St John's Wood High Street is well thought of for its high-class traditional purveyors of organic and free-range foods, a variety of smart children's and women's boutiques and a pleasant, villagey atmosphere.

Further north is **Abbey Road**, home of the recording studios and immortalised on the cover of the Beatles album of the same name. Tourists can often be seen risking life and limb on the zebra crossing as they attempt to re-enact said cover.

Lord's Cricket Ground & MCC Museum

St John's Wood Road, NW8 8QN (7432 1033/ www.lords.org). St John's Wood tube/13, 46, 82, 113, 274 bus. **Open** *Tour Oct-Mar* noon, 2pm daily. *Apr-Sept* 10am, noon, 2pm daily. Closed 1 Jan, 25, 26 Dec, all major matches & preparation days; phone to check. **Admission** £8; £6 concessions; £5 5-15s; free under-5s; £22 family (2+2). **Credit** MC, V.

It all seems so long ago now, but when England regained the Ashes in 2005, the event heralded a record-breaking year for this particular sporting attraction. The win sparked so much cricket interest that more guides had to be recruited for tours of Lord's, the 'home of cricket' and the game's spiritual headquarters.

Tours of Lord's let visitors go behind the scenes at MCC's historic ground, taking in the Long Room, in the heart of the Pavilion, which is both a cricket-watching room and a cricket art gallery, then on to the MCC Museum, where paintings, photographs and artefacts, covering 400 years of cricket history, reveal the game's development. Eccentric exhibits include a stuffed sparrow and cricket ball (the bird was killed by the ball in 1936 – a truly freak cricketing accident). The Museum's most precious exhibits include the Wisden Trophy and the delicate Ashes urn. Other attractions include the Tennis Court, where Real Tennis, (one of King Henry VIII's favourite pastimes) is still played, and the MCC Indoor Cricket School with their 100mph bowling machines. A range of cricket kit and equipment for children and adults is available for purchase.

Buggy access. Disabled access: toilets. Lifts. Nappy-changing facilities. Nearest picnic place: St John's churchyard playground. Shop.

West End

Where bigwigs live and the rest of us shop.

Oxford Street, Regent Street & Soho

Shopping is the life blood of the West End, and children are not exempt. Many of the huge emporiums on Oxford Street and Regent Street are deliberately set up to tease money from the wallets of exhausted parents. This is consumerism at its most mercenary, and it takes a brave parent to walk out of the Disney Store empty-handed.

Oxford Street on Saturday afternoon often resembles the annual migration of wildebeest across the Serengeti. Hands must be held at all times, and frayed tempers from exhaustion are par for the course. Getting around is easy by tube but less tiring by bus; kids will have something to look at and the crowds seem much less stressful from the top floor of a double-decker. South of Oxford Street is Soho, with a red-light district and gay neighbourhood that may provoke some challenging questions from intrigued infants.

Running south to Piccadilly Circus, Regent Street was designed to separate the working class population from the royals at St James's Park. The Portland stone arcades were designed by John Nash, but children are likely to be more impressed by Hamleys (*see p208*). On the popular Family Day (3 September 2006), the whole of Regent Street is closed off for a Victorian-style funfair.

There may be some mileage in the West End's small Chinatown, settled in the 1970s by migrants from Hong Kong. Pedestrianised Gerrard Street has gaudy street decorations, shops selling exotic Asian produce, and great Chinese New Year celebrations (*see p27*).

The **Trocadero**, a former theatre converted into a giant amusement arcade, is generally loathed by big people and loved by little ones.

Handel House Museum

25 Brook Street (entrance at rear), W1K 4HB (7495 1685/www.handelhouse.org). Bond Street tube. **Open** 10am-6pm Tue, Wed, Fri, Sat; 10am-8pm Thur; noon-6pm Sun. **Admission** £5; £2 6-16s; £4.50 concessions; free under-6s. **Credit** MC, V. **Map** p316 H6.
George Frideric Handel lived next door to Jimi Hendrix – though not at the same time, of course. The great German composer lived in the Georgian townhouse at 25 Brook Street from 1723 to his death in 1759, while the iconic American axeman lived at No. 23 from 1968 to 1969. Handel's old home now contains a thoroughly modern museum with a firm agenda of spreading enjoyment of classical music to the next generation. As well as recitals of baroque music every Thursday, the museum has a busy programme of weekend concerts and Talking Music events. Saturday is the busiest day for families, with story-telling, live music and the chance to strum, honk, bang and blow down a range of instruments from around the globe. There are also drop-in sessions every Saturday afternoon for under-16s, with Georgian costumes, art and music activities and afternoon tea for parents. The main exhibition space has displays on the life and music of Handel, including original letters and scores and a reproduction of Handel's harpsichord. The child-friendly ethos extends to numerous trails, quizzes and activities to go with the displays.The current temporary exhibition on Handel and the castrati runs until 1 October 2006.
Buggy access. Disabled access: lift, toilet. Nappy-changing facilities. Nearest picnic place: Hanover Square. Shop.

Trocadero

Coventry Street, W1D 7DH (7439 1791/www. londontrocadero.com). Piccadilly Circus tube. **Open** 10am-midnight Mon-Thur, Sun; 10am-1am Fri, Sat. **Admission** free; individual attractions vary. **Credit** varies. **Map** p317 K7.
As the only attraction in the West End specifically designed for children, the Trocadero attracts praise and condemnation in equal measures. Most of the interior is given over to Funland – a vast arcade of coin-in-the-slot

LUNCH BOX

For recommended restaurants and cafés in the area, *see pp162-84*.
Chocolate Society 32-34 Shepherd Market, W1J 7QN (7495 0302).
McDonald's There are seven along Oxford Street from Tottenham Court Road to Marble Arch.
Miso 66 Haymarket, SW1Y 4RF (7930 4800).
Pâtisserie Valerie 44 Old Compton Street, W1D 4TY (7437 3466).
Pizza Express 29 Wardour Street, W1D 6PS (7437 7215); 10 Dean Street, W1D 5RW (7437 9595); 20 Greek Street, W1D 4DU (7734 7430).
Satsuma 56 Wardour Street, W1D 4JG (7437 8338).
Sofra 18 Shepherd Street, W1Y 7HU (7493 3320).
Spiga 84-86 Wardour Street, W1D 0TA (7734 3444).
Zoomslide Café The Photographers' Gallery, 5 Great Newport Street, WC2H 7HY (7831 1772).

video games that eat money faster than the purple people-eater eats people; the noise and disorientating lights are a fast track to tantrums and migraines.

There's a seven-screen cinema on the first floor. Other facilities include a dodgem track, a ten-lane bowling alley, fast-food outlets and a sports bar – adults only. The Trocadero used to host some interesting educational exhibitions but the exhibition space is now being redeveloped as the Academy of Sex and Relationships, a theme park exploring sex and sexual health. Quite how this fits into the Trocadero's role as a children's entertainment venue has never been fully explained.

Buggy access. Cafés. Disabled access: lift, toilet. Nappy-changing facilities. Nearest picnic place: Leicester Square; Trafalgar Square. Restaurants. Shops.

Piccadilly & Mayfair

Piccadilly Circus is the geographical centre of the West End, but the neon billboards are a pale imitation of New York's Times Square. Just east of Piccadilly Circus is Leicester Square, where the latest movie blockbusters have their UK premières. Hollywood stars sometimes put in an appearance if they have a film to promote; there's a small walk of fame with stars' handprints.

Piccadilly is lined with exclusive shops catering mostly for the well-heeled – **La Maison Du Chocolat** (45-46 Piccadilly, 7287 8500) may attract with its chocolaty smells and glorious **Fortnum & Mason** (*see p196*) is generally very appealing. Designed to protect shoppers from the mud of horse-drawn Victorian London, Burlington Arcade is apparently patrolled by beadles in top hats and tails who ensure that nobody breaks the centuries-old ban on 'singing, humming or hurrying' in the arcade.

Piccadilly continues along the top of Green Park to Hyde Park Corner, with a cluster of memorials to heroes of the British Empire. On the far side of Green Park is St James's Park and **Buckingham Palace**, the most touristy place in London.

Mayfair was first developed by the Grosvenor and Berkley families in the 1700s, and most of the townhouses are set aside for diplomats and the English gentry. Children may want to pay their respects at the Animals at War memorial on Park Lane, commemorating the donkeys, horses, dogs, camels, elephants, carrier pigeons and canaries that died during World War I and World War II.

The Faraday Museum at the Royal Institution on Albemarle Street is closed until December 2007 for refurbishment. It will re-open with interactive displays on the miracle of electricity and a programme of science-based lectures and events for families and school groups. Contact the Royal Institute (7409 2992/ www.rigb.org) for the latest developments.

On the trail of the Iron Duke at **Apsley House**.

Apsley House: The Wellington Museum

149 Piccadilly, Hyde Park Corner, W1J 7NT (7499 5676/www.english-heritage.org.uk). Hyde Park Corner tube. **Open** *Apr-Oct* 10am-5pm Tue-Sun. *Nov-Mar* 10am-4pm Tue-Sun. Also opens Mon bank hols all year. **Tours** by arrangement. **Admission** £5.10 (includes audio guide if available); £2.70 5-16s; £3.90 concessions; free under-5s. *Joint ticket with admission to Wellington Arch* £6.50 adults; £3.30 children; £4.90 concessions; £16.30 family (2+3). *Tours* phone for details. **Credit** MC, V. **Map** p316 G8.

This stately Portland stone mansion was the family home of Arthur Wellesley, the first Duke of Wellington, who helped crush Napoleon at Waterloo. Today it contains a museum about Wellington, his campaigns and his extravagant taste in tableware. The address of Apsley House used to be No.1 London, this being the first house seen after passing through the Knightsbridge tollgate. Considering who lived here, it seems quite appropriate.

The state rooms are full of eye-watering Regency details and several display the duke's table settings, used for formal dinners with heads of state. The extravagant porcelain and silverware makes you wonder at the lavish nature of these meals. Ask someone to demonstrate the crafty mirrors in the scarlet and gilt picture gallery, where a fine Velázquez and Correggio hang near Goya's portrait of the Iron Duke after he defeated the French in 1812 (X-rays revealed that Wellington's head had been brushed over that of Joseph Bonaparte, Napoleon's brother). Down in the basement is a room containing Wellington's medals, death mask and Wellington's boots – so named after the duke's victory at Waterloo.

Families can pick up a 'Wellington Boot' pack with activity sheets and puzzles for children aged five to 11. Special talks and storytelling sessions for children take place on Thursdays throughout the year. Probably the most exciting time to visit is during the Waterloo Weekend in June (check the website for 2007 dates) when activities are laid on for the Waterloo memorial celebrations.

Buggy access. Lift. Nearest picnic place: Hyde Park. Shop.

Around Town

In a flap about St James's Park

Diplomats have a reputation for eccentricity, so nobody was entirely surprised when the Russian ambassador donated two live pelicans to King Charles II as a gesture of Anglo-Russian friendship in 1662. Pelicans have lived in St James's Park ever since, and their daily feeding on Duck Island is probably the most child-friendly spectacle in the West End – certainly less stressful than the tourist magnet that is the Changing of the Guard at Buckingham Palace.

The current pelicans come from Eastern Europe and America and they loiter about on an artificial skerry in St James's Park Lake until 3pm, when it's feeding time at the shingled, *Hansel and Gretel*-style Duck Island Cottage. Pelican feeding is a frenetic experience, full of grunts and squawks and the clackety clack of pelican beaks. The bag-throated birds wolf down an impressive 13 kilos of whiting every day. At certain times of year, park staff run guided tours of the island, with visits to nests and roosts – once dates are confirmed, they go on the park website (www.royalparks.gov.uk).

If you can't time your visit to coincide with pelicans' tea, you can feed more familiar birds at stations dotted around the shore of the lake. The range of birds includes dozens of varieties of ducks, geese and seagulls, black and white swans, coots, moorhens, teals, grebes, smews... You name it, St James's has it. Probably the most interesting birds for kids are the noisy geese and swans and the daffy tufted ducks – certainly the models for the Warner Bros cartoon character. The honking, quacking cacophony has to be heard to be believed. Don't overlook the park squirrels – they're tame enough to take food from your hand.

Duck Island is the headquarters of the London Historic Parks & Gardens Trust (7839 3969/www.londongardenstrust.org), which aims to promote and enhance London's parks and green spaces for families and young people. All the feeding stations at St James's have picture boards to help children identify the different species of bird, and the park staff run an interesting programme of free guided tours and offbeat events such as Love a Duck – where members of the public are invited to sponsor a partner for single and lonely exotic ducks.

If it all gets too much, or you run out of bread, you can retire to the unexpected elegance of the turf-roofed Inn the Park (*see p178*), designed by Michael Hopkins. There are more child-friendly attractions all around St James's Park. To the west is Buckingham Palace, to the south is the Guards Museum, to the east is Horse Guards, and to the north is St James's Palace, with its uniformed Grenadier Guards. Further down the Mall is a monument to the nursery rhyme hero, Frederick, Duke of York, of 10,000 men fame.

Buckingham Palace & Royal Mews

SW1A 1AA (7766 7300/www.royalcollection.org.uk). Green Park or St James's Park tube/Victoria tube/rail. **Open** State Rooms 26 July-24 Sept 2006 9.45am-3.45pm daily. Royal Mews Mar-Oct 11am-3.15pm Mon-Thur, Sat, Sun (last entry 4.15pm when palace is open); 26 July-24 Sept 10am-5pm daily (last entry 4.15pm). Queen's Gallery 10am-4.30pm daily. Closed during Ascot & state occasions. **Admission** (LP) £14; £8 5-16s; £12.50 concessions; free under-5s; £36 family (2+3). Royal Mews £6.50; £4 5-16s; £5.50 concessions; free under-5s; £17.50 family (2+3). Queen's Gallery £7.50; £4 5-16s; £6 OAPs, students; free under-5s; £19 family (2+3). **Credit** AmEx, MC, V. **Map** p316 H9.

As the seat of the British monarchy, Buckingham Palace is one of the showpieces of the London tourism industry, pulling in millions of visitors a year. The royal stables and the state rooms are thrown open in the summer, when the Queen retires to her Scottish castle at Balmoral. Buckingham Palace has belonged to the royal family since 1762 but it became the official royal residence in 1837. It used to be smaller, but Queen Victoria moved the Marble Arch to the end of Park Lane to make way for extensions. The famous balcony, so beloved of waving royals and Fathers 4 Justice campaigners, was added in 1913.

The Queen's Gallery, open year round, has collections by Rembrandt, Canaletto, Dürer, Rubens and Van Dyck as well as some exquisite Fabergé eggs and the diamond-studded diadem worn by HM on British postage stamps and coins. In 2006 the State Rooms will display a collection of the Queen's evening dresses and personal jewellery.

There's a nature trail for children in the gardens and a family activity room, open throughout August. At the Royal Mews, children can watch horses being groomed, fed and exercised and examine the ostentatious Gold State Coach, last used for the 2002 Golden Jubilee. *Buggy access (baby slings supplied in State Rooms, Royal Mews). Disabled access: lift, toilet (Buckingham Palace). Nappy-changing facilities (Buckingham Palace). Nearest picnic place: Green Park. Shop.*

The Guards Museum

Birdcage Walk, SW1E 6HQ (7414 3430). Victoria tube/rail. **Open** 10am-4pm daily (last entry 3.30pm) **Admission** £3; £2 OAPs; £1 ex-military; free under-16s. **Map** p316 J9.

Displays in these small museum include all sorts of military relics – flags, medals, uniforms, drums and weapons – covering every major campaign fought by the Scots, Irish, Welsh, Grenadier and Coldstream Guards. Children will get the most out of it as a follow-up to seeing the Changing of the Guard at nearby Buckingham Palace (*see p72*). There are some extremely rare and important pieces in here and the cabinets are carefully arranged so that plenty of exhibits are visible to children.

Worksheets (aimed at eight- to 14-year-olds) help children get the most out of their visit. Highlights on display include Wellington's funeral book, rare examples of 18th-century soldiers' tunics, the bearskin belonging to the 'Grand Old Duke of York', who had commanded while there was no battles to be fought hence the nickname and nursery rhyme, a ball outfit worn by Wellington on the night before the Battle of Waterloo and a display of World War I items. It's not all gung-ho, however: other notable items at the museum include Florence Nightingale's cup, a scarf knitted by Queen Victoria for a soldier, and military tunics worn by a 16-year-old Queen Elizabeth II. More unusual items displayed include medical instruments used by Victorian military surgeons and the mounted head of Jacob, the pet goose of the Coldstream Guards, who was rescued from a fox during exercises in Canada. Staff let kids try on the 'one-size-fits-all' bearskin hats and regimental tunics they keep hidden behind the counter – they can have their photo taken for £5. The museum shop's impressive collection of toy soldiers covers just about every campaign in British military history (the toys were originally made out of lead, but these days, they're cast from metal for safety reasons).
Buggy access. Disabled access: lift, ramps. Nearest picnic place: St James's Park. Shop (closed Fri).

Royal Academy of Arts

Burlington House, Piccadilly, W1J 0BD (7300 8000/ www.royalacademy.org.uk). Green Park or Piccadilly Circus tube. **Open** *Temporary exhibitions* 10am-6pm Mon-Thur, Sat, Sun; 10am-10pm Fri. *John Madejski Fine Rooms* 1-4.30pm Tue-Fri; 10am-6pm Sat, Sun. Opening times can vary for exhibitions. **Admission** *Fine Rooms* free. *Exhibitions* vary; free under-7s. **Credit** AmEx, DC, MC, V. **Map** p316 J7.

Housed in a fabulous 17th-century mansion, with gorgeously ornate rooms, the Royal Academy was Britain's first art school, attracting such luminaries as Constable, Reynolds and Gainsborough. Works by Constable, Reynolds, Degas and others are drawn from the Royal Academy's holdings and are on permanent display – free to view – in the John Madejski Fine Rooms. The main focus is on extravagant temporary exhibitions, however. The schedule for 2006 includes the Dutch landscape painter Jacob van Ruisdael, Modigliani and the sculptor Rodin. Most popular is the annual Summer Exhibition (12 June-20 Aug 2006). For more than two centuries this exhibition has drawn from works entered by the public – anyone can submit work to the show. Some 12,000 pieces are submitted each year by hopefuls (about ten per cent make it past the judges). Next to the Sackler Wing of Galleries is the famous stone plaque the *Virgin and Child with the Infant St John* by Michelangelo.

Talks and activities for school groups accompany most exhibitions; activity sheets for 'art detectives' are available at reception. Interactive family workshops and gallery talks are part of the Summer Exhibition. This year, there are two extra workshops during the autumn half-term to go with the Rodin exhibition.
Buggy access. Café. Disabled: lift, ramp, toilets. Nappy-changing facilities. Nearest picnic place: Green Park; St James's Square. Restaurant. Shop.

St James's Church Piccadilly

197 Piccadilly, W1J 9LL (7734 4511/www.st-james-piccadilly.org). Piccadilly Circus tube. **Open** 8am-6.30pm daily (phone for details of evening events). **Admission** free. **Map** p316 J7.

A rare piece of medieval history, St James's Church has quite a pedigree. It was designed by Christopher Wren, Grinling Gibbons carved most of the details, and Haydn, Handel and Mendelssohn were all resident organists. An unusual outdoor pulpit was added in 1902 so that rectors could preach to the crowds of shoppers. There's a programme of evening choral performances – call for the latest schedule. From Tuesday to Saturday, there's a small but colourful market in the courtyard. Tuesday is set aside for antiques, while the rest of the week is dominated by Covent Garden-style bric-a-brac.
Buggy access. Café. Disabled: ramp. Nearest picnic place: St James's Square; church gardens.

St James's Park

SW1A 2JB (7930 1793/www.royalparks.org.uk). St James's Park tube/3, 11, 12, 24, 53, 211 bus. **Open** 5am-midnight daily. **Map** p317 K8.

This Royal Park is a delightful central London spot, with a good playground and plenty of space for an impromptu picnic. Best of all, however, is the range of feathered friends. *See p72* **In a flap about St James's Park**.
Buggy access. Disabled access: toilet. Kiosk. Nappy-changing facilities. Restaurant.

Wellington Arch

Hyde Park Corner, W1J 7JZ (7930 2726/www.english-heritage.org.uk). Hyde Park Corner tube. **Open** *Apr-Oct* 10am-5pm Wed-Sun. *Nov-Mar* 10am-4pm Wed-Sun. **Admission** £3.10; £1.60 5-16s; £2.30 concessions; free under-5s. *Joint ticket with admission to Apsley House* £6.50 adults; £4.90 concessions; £3.30 children; £16.30 family (2+3). **Credit** MC, V. **Map** p316 G8.

Built in 1828 to honour the Duke of Wellington, the monument was originally topped by a bronze statue of the duke on horseback but it was taken down and replaced by the more aesthetically pleasing Quadriga, a bronze triumphal chariot. The arch used to stand by the northwest corner of the roundabout but was moved in 1883 to reduce horse-drawn traffic congestion. The main lure for kids is the chance to get up on to the viewing deck for views out over Hyde Park Corner and the surrounding area. There's also an interesting photographic display on arches around the world that puts the monument into context. On the lower floors are displays on the casting of the Quadriga, some delightful satirical cartoons about the ill-fated first statue, and a room where children can nominate various contemporary public figures for a commemorative blue plaque. The best way to visit is on a joint ticket with the Apsley House Museum (*see p71*).
Buggy access. Lift. Nearest picnic place: Hyde Park. Shop.

Covent Garden & St Giles

Bumptious, brash and always entertaining.

A beautiful and bustling part of London, Covent Garden breathes history and culture. As one of London's biggest tourist attractions, it throngs with crowds, but that's no deterrent – with its central piazza and several pedestrianised streets, it is one of the most pleasantly navigable parts of the capital. Strolling around the central market on a bright day can bring to mind European piazzas – no coincidence, as the central square's original design was based on the classical Italian style.

The name Covent Garden is most likely drawn from the 'convent garden' surrounding the historic abbey on the original site. The land that belonged to the Convent of St Peter at Westminster was handed over by the Crown to John Russell, the first earl of Bedford following the dissolution of the monasteries. In the 1630s, the earl commissioned master architect Inigo Jones to design a series of Palladian arcades. These tall terraces, opening on to a central courtyard, constituted the first public square in the country and proved popular with wealthy tenants, until the fruit and vegetable market expanded on to their patch. This forced the well-to-do to move further west, in search of more fragrant lodgings, and the market came to dominate the main square. Covent Garden soon became a hangout for less fussy artists, literary and theatrical folk. It was only in 1973 – when the vegetable market moved south to Vauxhall – that the piazza was reclaimed by the shops, cafés, bars and licensed street artists. Performers book weeks in advance to act in front of the portico of St Paul's, but on any given day you'll find mime artists and musicians scattered about the square. Every summer there are open-air operatics courtesy of the Royal Opera House. The area's oldest theatre is the Theatre Royal Drury Lane (Catherine Street, WC2B 5JF, 7494 5000); its largest is the Coliseum (St Martin's Lane, WC2N 4ES, 7632 8300), home to the English National Opera. For an interactive look at the area's theatrical history, visit the **Theatre Museum**.

Covent Garden, especially around Neal Street, is dominated by pricey boutiques. Yet more fashion can be found in the trendy Thomas Neal Centre, (which also houses an airy downstairs café, plus on-site toilets with nappy-changing facilities – see security for the key). The nearby alternative enclave of Neal's Yard is integral to the area. A lively clutter of veggie cafés, New Age crystal shops, herbalists and skate-wear emporia, the Yard is a testament to the sit-ins and demonstrations that saved the area from corporate redevelopment in the 1970s, and it remains blissfully, colourfully unaltered.

Up the road, St Giles's is less renowned as a tourist attraction, and its reputation is seedier than that of Covent Garden. Reviled by Charles Dickens and immortalised in Hogarth's *Gin Lane*, this area was rife with crime and prostitution until the Irish slums were levelled in 1847 to make way for New Oxford Street. Only the church of St Giles-in-the-Fields (60 St Giles High Street, WC2H 8LG, 7240 2532, www.stgilesonline.org) remained. Named after the patron saint of outcasts, the church originated as the chapel of a leper colony, founded in 1011; the first victims of the plague of 1665 were discovered in this dirty neighbourhood. Nowadays, the churchyard gardens provide a family-friendly spot offering lunchtime classical recitals on Fridays at 1.10pm. Otherwise, a rich musical heritage (still manifest in its guitar and music shops) makes Denmark Street – 'Tin Pan Alley' – rock. At the end of the street, Charing Cross Road is famous for bookshops – Foyles, Blackwell's, Borders – and independents selling remaindered stock. Heading towards Leicester Square (*see p71*), more specialist bookshops and a comic shop can be found around Cecil Court.

London's Transport Museum

Covent Garden Piazza, WC2E 7BB (7379 6344/ www.ltmuseum.co.uk). Covent Garden tube.
Map p317 L7.
The LTM closed in August 2005 for an £18m refurbishment, and the original reopening date for November 2006 has now been put back to spring 2007.

In the meantime, these renovations don't entirely eliminate LTM's public presence: events are planned at its depot in Acton Town (118-120 Gunnersbury Lane, W3) throughout the year. There's a special open weekend for

Theatre Museum. *See p77.*

families, focusing on transport safety issues, running 22-23 October 2006, plus many other monthly events; check the website for details of all other activities and online exhibitions. The LTM's wonderful gift shop has, until the museum's reopening, relocated to No.26 in the nearby Covent Garden Market.
Buggy storage. Disabled access: lift, ramp, toilets. Nappy-changing facilities. Shop.

Phoenix Garden

21 Stacey Street (entrance on St Giles Passage), WC2H 8DG (7379 3187). Tottenham Court Road tube. **Open** dawn-dusk daily. **Admission** free; donations appreciated. **Map** p315 K6.
This Phoenix rose from the site of a car park, proving that all is not lost in the war against urban decay. Finding the garden's scrabble of crooked pathways, trellises and

fragmented statues is a delightful surprise and, once you know it's there (tucked away behind the Odeon cinema on Shaftesbury Avenue – rather handily, its entrance is right next to the playground in the garden of St Giles-in-the-Fields), it's a grand spot for an urban picnic. The garden's planting is designed to encourage wildlife and children love the nature sanctuary in the recently extended back area of the garden. The area already includes new plants and flowers, boxes for birds and insects, plus benches for visitors.

The garden and staff rely on volunteers, call for details of how you can help or visit on Wednesdays from 11am for the 'Clean Sweep Group' to help with duties such as weeding. In 2006 there are also plans to take part in the London Open Garden Squares weekend and to hold a Midsummer Night Members Party. Support the garden and receive invitations to activities by signing up for the quarterly newsletter. Membership forms can be picked up at the garden. The annual membership fee is £18 per household (£12 individuals, £5 concessions) and will give you advance notice of events organised for children around Hallowe'en, Bonfire Night and Christmas.
Buggy access. Kiosk.

Royal Opera House

Bow Street, WC2E 9DD (7240 1200/box office 7304 4000/www.royaloperahouse.org). Covent Garden tube. **Open** *Box office* 10am-8pm Mon-Sat. *Tours* 10.30am, 12.30pm, 2.30pm Mon-Sat (times may vary, book in advance). **Tickets** *Tours* £9; £7 9-16s, students, OAPs. **Credit** AmEx, DC, MC, V. **Map** p317 L6.

✖️🍴 LUNCH BOX

For recommended restaurants and cafés in the area, *see reviews pp162-84.*

Café Pasta 2-4 Garrick Street, WC2E 9BH (7497 2779).
Café Rouge 34 Wellington Street, WC2E 7BD (7836 0998).
Christopher's 18 Wellington Street, WC2E 7DD (7240 4222).
Great American Bagel Factory 18 Endell Street, WC2H 9BD (7497 1115).
Papageno 29-31 Wellington Street, WC2E 7DB (7836 4444).
Pizza Express 9 Bow Street, WC2E 7AH (7240 3443); 147 Strand, WC2R 1JA (7836 7716).
Pizza Paradiso 31 Catherine Street, WC2B 5JS (7836 3609).
Ponti's Central Market Buildings, Covent Garden Market, WC2E 8RA (7836 0272)
Spaghetti House 24 Cranbourn Street, WC2H 7AB (7836 8168).
Strada 6 Great Queen Street, WC2B 5DH (7405 6293).
12 Bar Club 22-23 Denmark Place, WC2H 8NL (7240 2120).
Wagamama 1 Tavistock Street, WC2E 7PG (7836 3330).
West Cornwall Pasty Company 1 The Market, WC2E 8RA (7836 8336).
World Food Café 1st Floor, 14 Neal's Yard, WC2H 9DP (7379 0298)

Opera isn't renowned for appealing to the shorter attention span, and it is usually considered too 'civilised' for the stereotypical modern kid. But the ROH is anything but stuffy: its great glass ceilings make it a bright and airy space; regular free recital tasters are given (1-2pm Mon, pick up a ticket from the box office from 10am on the day), and the upstairs café offers terraced seating with fantastic views over the thronging crowds and street entertainments in Covent Garden. Families hoping to take in a show can attend pre-performance workshops explaining the nuances of this highly stylised medium, but there are several annual productions that are less likely to go over younger heads (such as the recent *La Fille Mal Gardée*). Previous hits have included *Wind in the Willows*, *Clockwork*, based on Philip Pullman's short story and, most recently, *Pinocchio*. Children's commissions for 2006 included *Gentle Giant*, a touring opera. No further programme details were released at time of press, but child-friendly Christmas shows are also planned for the 2006/7 festive season. Guided tours (no under-eights) allow curious kids a glimpse into working dressing rooms and rehearsal halls. Over-16s keen to rack up some invaluable hands-on stage experience and administration skills should apply to the ROH's education department, which runs an unpaid work–experience scheme.
Buggy access. Disabled access: lift, toilets. Nappy-changing facilities. Nearest picnic place: Covent Garden Piazza/St Paul's churchyard. Restaurants. Shop.

St Paul's Covent Garden

Bedford Street, WC2E 9ED (7836 5221/ www.actorschurch.org). Covent Garden tube. **Open** 9am-4.30pm Mon-Fri; 9am-12.30pm Sun. *Services* 1.10pm Wed; 11am Sun. *Choral evensong* 4pm 2nd Sun of mth. Closed 1 Jan, bank hols. **Admission** free; donations appreciated. **Map** p317 L6.

Dominating the west side of the Piazza, St Paul's is the last extant section of Inigo Jones's original Palladian squares, and its peaceful interior offers respite from the carnival of tourists outside. It's far from emotionally detached from the theatrical heritage of its surroundings, though: the consecrated 'Actors Church' has walls adorned with plaques commemorating the legends of screen and stage, including Charlie Chaplin, Noel Coward and Vivien Leigh. The first known victim of the plague, Margaret Ponteous, is buried in the churchyard The church has served as a backdrop for several cameos in the history of theatre: on 9 May 1662 Samuel Pepys described being 'mighty pleased' after witnessing the first recorded Punch and Judy show here, an event marked by the annual May Fayre & Puppet Festival (held on the second Sunday in May; *see pxx*), and George Bernard Shaw set the opening to *Pygmalion* under the ornate portico. That same portico is most notable today as a performance site for street entertainers. Well worth a watch, these appearance slots are booked up weeks in advance, and wannabes are auditioned by the Covent Garden Market Committee before receiving permission to perform. At 11am on the first Sunday of each month, Junior Church meets; under-10s can try storytelling, drama and art activities, then rejoin their parents after the service. The church also hosts regular concerts, and productions from the Mountview Academy of Theatre Arts with a musical planned for 2006. A harvest festival is also set for October 2006. This event will be visited by pearly kings and queens. Moving on to Christmas, each year more than 30 carol services are held at the church, so it's all very festive.
Buggy access. Disabled access: ramp. Nearest picnic place: churchyard.

Theatre Museum

Russell Street, WC2E 7PR (7943 4700/group bookings 7943 4806/www.theatremuseum.org). Covent Garden tube. **Open** 10am-6pm Tue-Sun (last entry 5.30pm). Closed bank hols. *Tours* noon daily. Phone for school hols tour times. **Admission** free. **Credit** *Shop* AmEx, MC, V. **Map** p317 L6.

Britain's national museum of performing arts, celebrating the history of live entertainment, had a shadow hanging over it as we went to press. The Victoria & Albert Museum, whose theatrical wing this is, was considering either moving the Theatre Museum's collection and activities to the V&A in South Kensington, where it would have a permanent display space, major exhibitions, educational activities and a touring programme, or continuing exploratory talks with the Royal Opera House, which may be interested in using the Theatre Museum site to extend its educational activities and events. Meanwhile the Theatre Museum sits uneasily in Covent Garden.

The maze-like basement galleries (reached via a corridor decorated with actors' handprints and signatures) reveals glass-encased curios and displays. The regular make-up demonstrations (four times daily on week-days, one at 4.30pm at weekends; observe or be a model) and costume workshops (one at 2pm on weekdays, twice daily on Saturdays) are very popular. On Saturdays, three- to 14-year-olds can get stuck into Stage Truck's range of creative activities (1.30-5pm; also Thur in school holidays). Then there are storytelling sessions inspired by museum exhibits held from 1.30-2pm on the first Saturday of the month, plus Wednesdays and Fridays during school holidays. The Kids West End Club, a joint venture with the Society of London Theatres based on West End shows, is a drama workshop for eight- to 12-year-olds to play games and try out performing with theatre professionals. Times are 2-4pm daily in school holidays (£5 charge); booking is essential. Under-sevenss can participate in Mini Musicals during holidays (11-11.45am for two-and-a-half to four-year olds, and 1.15-2.15pm for five to seven year olds, £3). New museum exhibitions include, at ground level, A Great Night Out, a history of theatre launching 12 March 2006, which features a snakes-and-ladders game of theatrical fortunes. Drama birthday parties can also be held in the museum (£200, maximum 15 children, aged 5-12 years). *Buggy access. Disabled access: ramp, toilets. Nappy-changing facilities. Nearest picnic place: Covent Garden Piazza/St Paul's churchyard. Shop.*

The Strand & Embankment

In the 14th century, the Strand was a residential street, whose waterside homes were rather desirable residences. All this changed when the overflow from Covent Garden threatened to overwhelm this hitherto narrow strip. By 1600 the wealthy folk had run away, and the Strand held a reputation for poverty and bawdiness, rather like Bankside across the river. It was at this time that Sir Christopher Wren suggested the creation of a reclaimed embankment to ease congestion and house the main sewer.

Today, there's little among its collection of overbearing office blocks and underwhelming restaurants to really fire the imagination. Richard D'Oyly Carte's Savoy Theatre, however, which pre-dates the famous hotel by eight years, gives some indication of how the area's fortunes began to change once again after the reinforced concrete Embankment was completed.

The Embankment can be approached down Villiers Street. Cut down Embankment Place to Craven Street, where, at No.36, Benjamin Franklin lived from 1757 to 1775. Continuing down to the river you reach the embarkation point for a number of riverboat tours with on-board entertainment. Embankment Gardens is a tranquil park with an annual programme of free summer music played out on its small public stage. Near the gardens stands Cleopatra's Needle. This stone obelisk was first erected in Egypt under Pharaoh Tothmes III c1500 BC, and underwent truly epic adventures (not least of which was its being abandoned and then rescued after a storm in the Bay of Biscay in 1877) before being repositioned on the Thames in 1878.

Benjamin Franklin House

36 Craven Street, Covent Garden, WC2N 5NF (information 7930 9121/bookings 7930 6601/ www.benjaminfranklinhouse.org). Embankment tube or Charing Cross tube/rail. **Open** *Oct-May* 9.45am-5pm Wed-Sun. *June-Sept* 9.45am-5pm Mon, Wed-Sun. **Admission** £8; £5 4-16s, OAPs, students; free under-4s. *Tours* every 45mins. Pre-booking essential (meet at the box office at the New Players Theatre, The Arches, Villiers Street, WC2). **Credit** MC, V. Map p317 L7.

Who said 'Fish and visitors stink after three days' and 'Early to bed and early to rise makes a man healthy, wealthy and wise'? That's right, Benjamin Franklin, scientist, diplomat, philosopher, inventor, Founding Father of the United States and resident of this restored house from 1757 to 1775. The world's only remaining home of Benjamin Franklin was opened on 17 January 2006, Ben Franklin's 300th birthday, as a museum and educational facility. Independent visitors and school parties can go on the Historical Experience, which uses the rooms where so much took place as staging for a drama. This 'museum as theatre' approach is highly entertaining, taking as its main character Polly Hewson, the daughter of Franklin's landlady. Polly speaks to her guests assuming they are there to see Franklin before he sets off back to America as the War of Independence looms.

In the Student Science Centre (for school groups only), students can replicate some of Franklin's famous experiments. The activities here are designed to support elements of the National Curriculum and stimulate inquisitiveness, creativity and critical thought through enjoyable play-based workshops. The house incorporates the Medical History Room, where the emphasis is on the medical research work of William Hewson, Polly's husband, who operated an anatomy school at 36 Craven Street. In the Discovery Room, children are challenged to identify various objects or artefacts (originals, facsimiles, and present-day items), to explain their function and to suggest how they are used and work. Items are set in both a historical and scientific context. *Café (at New Players Theatre). Nearest picnic place: Victoria Gardens, Embankment.*

Around Town

Westminster

London dressed to impress.

Ask any tourist to name a famous London image and chances are that the **Houses of Parliament**, Westminster Abbey or Trafalgar Square will crop up – these iconic attractions are all within a short distance of each other in the borough of Westminster. But famed as it is for such historic pin-ups, the area has plenty of other places of interest within walking distance to warrant spending at least a day or two exploring Westminster. Ever since the times of Edward the Confessor, 1,000 years ago, this neighbourhood has been at the hub of British politics and religion – Edward was the founder of West Minster, which stood on the site that **Westminster Abbey** now occupies. Today, the Abbey competes with Charles Barry's neo-Gothic Palace of Westminster for prominence on Parliament Square. Nowhere in Westminster is more likely to instil a sense of the area's attachment to nobility than Westminster Abbey: the list of those buried here reads like a *Who's Who* of British history (Chaucer, Darwin, Newton – not to mention virtually every royal to have died in the last 500 years). A short stroll along Victoria Street will lead you to Westminster Cathedral, whose viewing gallery at the top of the 83-metre (273-foot) Campanile Bell Tower is a must. Don't overlook a visit to the oft-neglected **Jewel Tower** – a rare fragment of the original medieval palace – where a permanent exhibition is dedicated to the development of Parliament. A walk along Whitehall will take you past the Cenotaph and towards the steely eyed Horse Guards, whom youngsters can try (and fail) to stare out, but they can always pop into the nearby Guards Museum (*see p73*) for a more in-depth look at these most dashing of royal recruits. The government departments along Whitehall, and even Downing Street itself, hold little interest for children, but the excellent **Cabinet War Rooms** and **Churchill Museum** certainly do.

You'll not be short of places to take eager young artists. Sitting on one corner of Trafalgar Square, St Martin-in-the-Fields is renowned for free lunchtime concerts and a Brass Rubbing Centre. And there are excellent and imaginative children's workshops at the world-class trio of treasure troves: the Tate Britain, the National Gallery and the National Portrait Gallery.

Behind many of the grand buildings there are numerous secluded spaces to discover among the hubbub. Within walking distance of Parliament Square is St James's Park (*see p73*), Westminster Abbey College Garden and the less well-known Victoria Tower Gardens (off Millbank), whose small playground occupies a riverside space next to Parliament. For the full Westminster experience, however, it has to be sandwiches in the public arts forum that is Trafalgar Square. Children clamber gleefully over the lions guarding the 52-metre (170-foot) testament to Britain's most celebrated military commander, Lord Nelson, but outlawing of pigeon feeding by Mayor Ken in 2001 has meant a steady decline in the number of fat feathered Londoners in the square. This is good news for the recently made-over Nelson – the droppings are said to be playing havoc with his

chiselled jawline – but a shame for young ones who'll never know the hysterical pleasure of having a fat pigeon sit on their head and peck seed from their scalp. The Fourth Plinth project sees one piece of contemporary sculpture every other year to occupy the empty plinth on the north-west corner of the square (the others are fairly starchy bronze busts). The current winner (Marc Quinn's gentle *Alison Lapper Pregnant*) will be replaced by German artist Thomas Schütte's refractive Perspex colourscape, *Hotel for the Birds*, in summer 2006. The Summer in the Square festival of outdoor performances, dance and music runs every year and is organised by the office of the Mayor of London; visit www.london.gov.uk for more information, or phone 7983 4100.

Banqueting House

Whitehall, SW1A 2ER (7930 4179/www.hrp.org.uk). Westminster tube/Charing Cross tube/rail. **Open** 10am-5pm Mon-Sat (last entry 4.30pm). Sometimes closes at short notice; phone to check. Closed bank hols. **Admission** (LP) £4.50; £3.50 concessions; £3 5-15s; free under-5s. **Credit** MC, V. **Map** p317 L8.
Designed by Inigo Jones for James I, the Hall was intended to be used for state and ceremonial occasions. Its opening in 1622 was marked by a traditional Twelfth Night masque. But such jollities were a distant memory when, in 1649,

James's son Charles I was found guilty of treason by Cromwell's revolutionary forces and beheaded outside. These rich historical associations pull in today's tourists (the Sealed Knot Civil War Re-enactment Society plays out the execution one Sunday each January), although Jones's architecture is magnificent on its own: from the grand main hall to the cryptic undercroft (conceived as a drinking den for James I). Rubens's original ceilings are still in place, despite extensive fire damage in 1698 and removal for their own safety during World War II. Audioguides (included in the ticket price) bring the scene to life for children. The Hall is also a venue for regular Monday lunchtime classical concerts throughout the year. These are primarily aimed at adults, but there's a lighter Christmas concert in December (call or check the website for the precise date).
Buggy storage. Disabled access: toilets. Nearest picnic place: St James's Park. Shop.

Churchill Museum & Cabinet War Rooms

Clive Steps, King Charles Street, SW1A 2AQ (7930 6961/www.iwm.org.uk). St James's Park or Westminster tube/3, 12, 24, 53, 159 bus. **Open** 9.30am-6pm daily (last entry 5pm). **Admission** £11; £8.50 concessions; £6 unemployed; £5.50 disabled & carers; free under-16s (prices incl audio guides). **Credit** MC, V. **Map** p317 K9.
Churchill's secret underground HQ in World War II, the Cabinet War Rooms resembles a time capsule, sealed against the intervening years. From these halls – a subterranean maze of tunnels and secret rooms – Britain's

London's best room – **Trafalgar Square.**

Around Town

military minds steered the war effort. The rooms have been maintained as a testament to those dark hours. The same maps chart progress on the same walls; the same steel beams – hurriedly put up to reinforce the building against bombs – still line the low ceilings. It's an atmospheric and effective installation guaranteed to bring the period to life for kids, who can take advantage of a number of activities, including a free activity sheet for under-11s (pick up at the information desk) and audioguides (there are separate versions for adults and children), with an expanded programme of family workshops in the school holidays. Family events in 2006, for example, include Life in the 1940s (14-25 Aug), giving visitors the chance to see what their life might have been like during wartime; Churchill and Pets (23-27 Oct); and, until September 2006, an exhibition comparing life in Westminster during 1945 with life in the area today. There are also talks on life in wartime Britain – some of them from actors dressed in period costume – and various online resources in the cutting-edge Clore Educational Centre.

The expansive Churchill Museum opened in February 2005 to commemorate the 40th anniversary of Churchill's death. The centrepiece of the display is an enormous digital Lifeline (essentially a flat-screen monitor the length and breadth of a banquet hall table), in which is stored, chronologically, thousands of Churchill-related documents and images, many of them brought to life with pyrotechnic animations. There's also an intriguing wooden mock-up of his family home in Chatsworth, Kent. Every Saturday (10.30am-5pm, until 30 Dec 2006), children can attend the Cabinet Kids Club.

Buggy access. Café. Disabled access: lift, toilets. Nappy-changing facilities. Nearest picnic place: St James's Park. Shop.

Houses of Parliament

Parliament Square, SW1A 0AA (Commons info 7219 4272/Lords info 7219 3107/tours 7219 4206/ www.parliament.uk). Westminster tube. **Open** (when in session) *House of Commons Visitors' Gallery* 2.30-10.30pm Mon, Tue; 11.30am-7.30pm Wed; 10.30am-6.30pm Thur; 9.30am-3pm Fri. Closed bank hols. *House of Lords Visitors' Gallery* from 2.30pm Mon, Tue; from 3pm Wed; from 11am Thur, Fri. *Tours* summer recess only; phone for details for other times. **Admission** *Visitors' Gallery* free. *Tours* £7; £5 concessions, 5-16s; free under-5s, disabled; £22 family (2+2). **Credit** *Tours* MC, V. **Map** p317 L9.

Little Treasures

The **National Gallery** tops many an artlover's itinerary, but art lovers garlanded with anklebiters might hesitate to enter its hallowed portals. Don't worry. Our national treasure is very kiddie-friendly: pushing a buggy through its spacious galleries is a breeze; lifts whisk you from floor to floor; and you'll not be short of baby change facilities. More importantly, there's plenty here to amuse and inspire restless children. The gallery organises plenty of workshops and storytelling sessions, but if you haven't got time on this visit, there are ways to keep children interested. It will help if you are armed with pencils or crayons and paper; if you forget, you can always buy supplies at one of the gallery shops.

Resist the temptation to dash through every room – this will not endear accompanying children to art, or do anything for your stress levels. Instead, concentrate on a few choice pieces you can enjoy together. There's also an excellent online search facility, so you can look up the pictures before, or after, your visit.

If you have a buggy to push, enter via the impressive Getty Entrance for step-free access from Trafalgar Square. Pick up a free plan at the info desk opposite the door and make for the Impressionists (room 45), where you'll find a wall of Van Goghs. Get the kids to look for his famous *Sunflowers* and the striking bright-red *Two Crabs*. There's also an atmospheric Monet, *London at Westminster*, painted in 1871; amuse older kids by telling them about the old port of London and that big ships used to sail up the Thames right into the heart of the city, and ask younger ones to guess which city is depicted in the painting. The unmissable *Bathers at Asnières* by Seurat

is in the next room. The famed *Execution of Lady Jane Grey* is in room 41 – if you're educationally inclined, you could use it as the focus for a brief history tutorial. Lady Jane, who was queen for only nine days in 1553, was beheaded at just 17 years old at the Tower of London. Take a seat in the long gallery (room 34) while you admire several treasures: Stubbs's fabulous painting of the stallion *Whistlejacket* hangs opposite Constable's *Hay Wain* and Turner's *The Fighting Temeraire*. Look out for the *Rokeby Venus*, works by Flemish master Rubens and Willem Kalf's *Still Life with Drinking Horn* (room 25) whose vibrantly-coloured lobster and lemon look so fresh they could have been painted yesterday. Young ones after something gory will like room 24, where there's the impressive *Two Followers of Cadmus Devoured by a Dragon* by Cornelis van Haarlem.

The Sainsbury Wing galleries tend to be much quieter. They are filled with pictures dating 1250-1500. An image of David holding the head of Goliath (room 62) might spook the sensitive, but in front of Paolo Uccello's *Saint George and the Dragon* you can tell them about the patron Saint of England. Exit via the Portico Entrance, which was recently cleaned to reveal the original ceiling that had been painted over by the Victorians.

Now for a cup of tea and a piece of cake. The Espresso Bar sells fruit and snacks and has computer terminals on which you can explore the collection online while you refuel. There are toilets here too. Obviously, if the weather permits, trot outside to the top picnic spot of Trafalgar Square; otherwise the bright and airy gallery café sells tasty dishes, or there are two Pret a Manger sandwich shops on Trafalgar Square.

The Palace of Westminster became a permanent home for Parliament in 1532, when Henry VIII relocated to Whitehall. These days the only parts of the original palace still standing are Westminster Hall, where the Queen Mother's body lay in state before her funeral in 2002, and the Jewel Tower (*see below*); the rest was destroyed by fire in 1834. The building we see today was rebuilt by Charles Barry and Augustus Pugin. Children are usually satisfied by the mere proximity of the big old bell known as Big Ben (the tower is St Stephen's). The various stories behind its name certainly make for more interesting listening than sessions of the Commons or Lords, which are open daily to families with children old enough to sign their name. The wait can stretch into hours. Prime Minister's Questions (every Wednesday) has to be booked with your local MP, who can also arrange a tour of the building.
Buggy access. Disabled access: lifts, toilets. Nappy-changing facilities. Nearest picnic place: Victoria Tower Gardens. Shop.

Jewel Tower

Abingdon Street, SW1P 3JY (7222 2219/www. english-heritage.org.uk). Westminster tube. **Open** *Apr-Oct* 10am-5pm daily. *Nov-Mar* 10am-4pm daily. (last entry 30mins before closing). **Admission** (EH/LP) £2.70; £2 concessions; £1.40 5-16s; free under-5s. Phone to check prices for special events. **Credit** MC, V. **Map** p317 L9.
One of the two parts of medieval Westminster Palace still standing, the fragmentary Jewel Towe,r or 'King's Privy Wardrobe', originally marked the south-western corner of the palace grounds. The tower was built in 1365 to house the private treasures of Edward III. A moat (now filled) was channelled from the Thames – primarily to protect the royal loot, although it had the added advantage of bringing fresh fish to the kitchen door. Since being built, the tower has served as a repository for parliamentary records and a Board of Trade testing centre for weights and measures, but these days English Heritage keeps it open to the public – winding staircases, unrestored ribbed vault and all. A Parliament Past and Present exhibition looks at the development of today's parliamentary structure. Take the kids to see the ancient sword on display in the on-site shop. It dates back to around AD 800 and looks like something on loan from Middle Earth.
Nearest picnic place: surrounding green. Shop.

National Gallery

Trafalgar Square, WC2N 5DN (information line 7747 2885/www.nationalgallery.org.uk). Charing Cross tube/rail/24, 29, 176 bus. **Open** 10am-6pm Mon, Tue, Thur-Sun; 10am-9pm Wed. *Tours* 11.30am, 2.30pm Mon, Tue, Thur, Fri, Sun; 11.30am, 2.30pm, 6pm, 6.30pm Wed; 11.30am, 12.30pm, 2.30pm, 3.30pm Sat. **Admission** (LP) free. *Temporary exhibitions* prices vary. *Tours* free. **Credit** *Shop* MC, V. **Map** p317 K7.
A national treasure, with one of the finest collections of classic western European paintings in the world (Van Gogh, da Vinci, Ingres, Rembrandt to name a few), and it makes certain that its younger guests have a lot of fun discovering them. There are listening posts offering headphone commentaries on more than 1,000 pieces from the collection, and the excellent ArtStart computer terminals in the Espresso Bar on Level 0 allow visitors to personalise and print out their own themed tour, free. Incidentally, the National's online facilities are an excellent resource for use in the gallery, or when you get home to look up the

history of a favourite painting. There are also audio tours and paper trails (Monster Hunt, for example). Best of all, though, are the laid-back children's workshops, including the Magic Carpet storytelling sessions, aimed at under-fives, whichrun on weekdays during school holidays, and the Second Weekend workshops, led by a contemporary artist. All materials are provided, and the hour-long sessions take place at 11.30am on Saturdays and Sundays (repeated at 2.30pm). The remaining three weekends of the month bring staff talks, starting at 11.30am. Check the gallery website for details of holiday workshops for families and teenagers; so far workshops are planned for the following dates in 2006: 1-26 August, 24-28 October and 27-30 December. Check also the website for details of the free practical art workshops the gallery runs in holiday times for 12- to 17-year-olds. Forthcoming exhibitions include one on rebellious 19th-century artists such as Van Gogh, Gauguin, Manet and Degas (28 June-28 Aug 2006), Cezanne (4 Oct-7 Jan 2007) and Velazquez (18 Oct 2006-14 Jan 2007). *See also p80* **Little Treasures**.
Buggy access. Café. Disabled access: lift, toilets. Nappy-changing facilities. Nearest picnic place: Leicester Square/Trafalgar Square. Restaurant. Shop.

National Portrait Gallery

2 St Martin's Place, WC2H 0HE (7306 0055/ tours 7312 2483/www.npg.org.uk). Leicester Square tube/Charing Cross tube/rail/24, 29, 176 bus. **Open** 10am-6pm Mon-Wed, Sat, Sun; 10am-9pm Thur, Fri. *Tours* times vary, phone for details. **Admission** free. *Temporary exhibitions* prices vary. *Audio guide* £2. *Tours* free. **Credit** AmEx, MC, V. **Map** p317 K7.
What makes the NPG so unique is its philosophy: the collections are concerned with history, not art, gathering together a pantheon of those who have contributed to creating British society. A short wander around its halls will turn up faces as far removed as William Shakespeare and Benny Hill, captured in a variety of media (paintings, photographs, sculptures) by artists ranging from medieval illuminators to celebrity snappers like Mario Testino. The permanent collection is organised by period, so you can select an area, such as the Elizabethans, Victorian portrait photography or British portraits from 1990, to peruse. Upcoming exhibitions include the BP Portrait and Travel Award (15 June-17 Sept 2006), paintings and photographs by David Hockney (12 Oct 2006-21 Jan 2007) and surrealist images and famous faces snapped by British photographer Angus McBain (5 July-22 Oct 2006). To help children fathom the exhibitions, there are family rucksacks – lent on a first-come, first-served basis, which correspond to one of three galleries – Tudor, Victorian and 20th Century. Each rucksack is stuffed with activities (for three- to 12-year-olds) from jigsaws and dressing-up items to paper trails. There are also regular holiday workshops. Free trails are available from the information desk. Monthly Are You Sitting Comfortably storytelling sessions are for under-fives and Small Faces art activities for over-fives are usually held on the third Saturday of each month, but check before visiting. In the summer holidays (31 July-11 Aug 2006) activities on the theme of the BP Portrait and Travel Award will include creative writing and art sessions for over-fives. The October half-term will see Hockney-related events. The smart top-floor restaurant boasts magnificent views over London.
Buggy access. Café. Disabled access (Orange Street entrance): lifts, ramps, toilets. Nappy-changing facilities. Nearest picnic place: Leicester Square/Trafalgar Square. Restaurant. Shops.

Around Town

St Martin-in-the-Fields

Trafalgar Square, WC2N 4JJ (7766 1100/Box office 7839 8362/Brass Rubbing Centre 7930 9306/www. stmartin-in-the-fields.org). Leicester Square tube/Charing Cross tube/rail. **Open** *Church* 8am-6.30pm daily. *Brass Rubbing Centre* 10am-7pm Mon-Wed; 10am-10pm Thur, Sat; noon-7pm Sun. *Evening concerts* Thur-Sat & alternate Tue 7.30pm. **Tours** 11.30am Thur. **Admission** free. *Brass Rubbing* (LP) £2.90-£15 (special rates for groups & families). *Evening concerts* £6-£20. *Tours* free, phone box office to book tickets. **Credit** MC, V. **Map** p317 L7.

St Martin makes an inspired refuge from the touristy mass outside, especially during one of the free lunchtime or ticketed evening concerts (1pm and 7.30pm respectively; check the website for details). The interior of the church is an unusually bright and cheering sanctuary of sculptures, paintings and potted plants, all presided over by an intricately carved baroque ceiling. What makes St Martin such fun for children, though, is its fantastic 18th-century crypt, home not only to hearty self-service fodder at the excellent Café in the Crypt (*see p171*), but also to London's only Brass Rubbing Centre. Here kids can create their own lasting memento of medieval London, with knights and dragons among the images available. Rubbings – which take about an hour to complete – are supervised, and all materials provided (£2.90-£15 depending on the size of the brass). St Martin-in-the-Fields has been hosting London Musical Arts' popular family concerts since 2000. These fun-filled and informative afternoons bring a sense of enjoyment and discovery to music and give children the opportunity to learn about the orchestra, talk to the musicians and see their instruments up close at hand and hear about the stories behind the music. Family concerts take place on Saturday afternoons about four times a year; check the website for dates. Major renovations are finally under way to bring the beleaguered church and crypt up to date – under the patronage of Prince Charles, no less, who calls St Martin 'one of the vital parts of our national heritage'. Work should be completed by the end of 2007. *Buggy access. Café. Disabled access: ramp to church, toilet. Nearest picnic place: Leicester Square/Trafalgar Square. Shop.*

Tate Britain

Millbank, SW1P 4RG (7887 8008/www.tate.org.uk). Pimlico tube/88.77A, C10, bus. **Open** 10am-5.50pm daily. Late opening 6-10pm last Fri of mth. *Tours* 11am, noon, 2pm, 3pm Mon-Fri; noon, 3pm Sat, Sun. **Admission** (LP) free. *Temporary exhibitions* prices vary. *Tours* free. **Credit** MC, V. **Map** p317 L7.

'Old' Tate's collection of British fine art from 1500 to the present day includes a permanent collection that unites artists from Blake to Bacon in a grand riverside setting. This allows neighbouring galleries to focus on themes as diverse as 18th-century seascapes and visions of religious apocalypse, while still leaving several large halls free for staging regular temporary shows; until 28 August is Constable: The Great Landscapes, and there's Howard Hodgkin (14 June-10 Sept). Best of all is the Tate's ongoing effort to help younger audiences engage with and enjoy the art on display. The time-honoured Art Trolley is wheeled out every Saturday and Sunday and at weekends (11am-5pm), and it is packed with a wide range of make-and-do activities, while Tate Tales, on the first Sunday of each month, sees resident storytellers spinning yarns about individual works; on BP Saturdays, the entire gallery stages special events for children and their families, as well as practical workshops specially designed for teenagers (check website for dates). There's also a range of events for schools and a number of themed workshops during half-term and holiday breaks, as well as various activity bags, audio tours and a free Spot the Circle discovery trails waiting behind the information desk for little explorers. Tate Britain offers buggy storage, baby change facilities and healthy meals for children in its café and restaurant. You can nip swiftly to Tate Modern for another art fix via a trip on the Damien Hirst-decorated Tate-to-Tate boat. It runs every 40 minutes and it takes about 20 minutes to get from Millbank to Bankside, with a stop at the London Eye in between (£4.30, £2.15 under-16s family £10.80, discounts available for those with a valid Travelcard). *Buggy access. Café. Disabled access: lift, ramps, toilets. Nappy-changing facilities. Nearest picnic place: lawns (either side of gallery)/Riverside Gardens (by Vauxhall Bridge). Restaurant. Shop.*

Westminster Abbey

20 Dean's Yard, SW1P 3PA (7222 5152/tours 7654 4900/www.westminster-abbey.org). St James's Park or Westminster tube/11, 12, 24, 88, 159, 211 bus. **Open** *Nave & Royal Chapels* 9.30am-3.45pm Mon, Tue, Thur, Fri; 9.30am-7pm Wed; 9am-1.45pm Sat. *Abbey Museum & Chapter House* 10.30am-4pm Mon-Sat. *Cloisters* 8am-6pm Mon-Sat. *College Garden* Apr-Sept 10am-6pm Tue-Thur; Oct-Mar 10am-4pm Tue-Thur (last entry 1hr before closing). *Tours* phone for details. **Admission**

✖️ LUNCH BOX

For recommended restaurants and cafés in the area, see reviews pp162-84.

Café in the Crypt St Martin-in-the-Fields, WC2N 4JJ (7839 4342).

Cathedral Kitchen Westminster Cathedral, Victoria Street, SW1P 1QW (7931 6023).

Gallery Café National Gallery, Trafalgar Square, WC2N 5DN (7747 2885).

Inn The Park St James's Park, SW1A 2BJ (7451 9999).

Jenny Lo's Tea House 14 Eccleston Street, SW1W 9LT (7259 0399).

Laughing Halibut 38 Strutton Ground, SW1P 2HR (7799 2844).

McDonald's 155 Victoria Street, SW1E 5NA (7828 6911)

Pizza Express 85 Victoria Street, SW1H 0HW (7222 5270).

Ponti's Café 127 Victoria Street, SW1E 6RD (7828 7242).

The Portrait Restaurant National Portrait Gallery, St Martin's Place, WC2H 0HE (7312 2490).

Pret a Manger 62-65 Cockspur Street, WC2N 5DS (7932 5350).

Texas Embassy Cantina 1 Cockspur Street, SW1Y 5DL (7925 0077).

West Cornwall Pasty Company 35 Strutton Ground, SW1P 2HY (7233 3777).

£10; £6 11-15s, concessions; free under-11s with paying adult; £22 family (2+2). *Chapter House* free. *Abbey Museum* (EH/LP) free (audio guide £3). *Tours* £4. **Credit** AmEx, MC, V. **Map** p317 K9.

The location for every coronation since 1066, and a final resting place for many crowned heads (and bodies), Westminster Abbey has had a nave-ful of British royals. The abbey was consecrated in 1065, eight days before the death of Edward the Confessor. His body remains entombed in the abbey, although where, exactly, is unknown: it was removed from its elaborate shrine and reburied at an unmarked location during the Reformation. Elizabeth I is also interred here, as is Mary Queen of Scots. Poets' Corner is the final resting place of Geoffrey Chaucer, you can also see the graves of Charles Dickens, who is honoured to this day with a wreath to mark the anniversary of his death, as well as those of Dryden, Samuel Johnson, Browning and Tennyson. Several 20th-century martyrs (including Martin Luther King Jr) have been immortalised in 15th-century niches above the west door. Look out for the Coronation Chair, which bears the scars from the years it was left unprotected from the public and consequently is carved with many names – quite probably including Westminster School pupils – as well as the extraordinary nave (the highest roof in Britain at 31m (101ft) and a seemingly endless sea of stained glass. Escape the crowds in the serene College Garden which, at 900 years old, is one of the oldest cultivated gardens in Britain. The Abbey Museum (free to enter) is in the vaulted area under the former monks' dormitory in one of the oldest parts of the Abbey. There you'll find a collection of effigies and waxworks of British monarchs, such as Edward II and Henry VII wearing the robes they wore when alive. The Queen's Coronation robes are also on show. The Choir School holds an annual fête (11am-4.30pm, 15 July 2006), and there are also free concerts (12.30-2pm, Wed, 19 July-23 Aug 2006). Check the website in October 2006 for details of the magnificent Christmas services. Next door, St Margaret's Church (free to visit) is where the diarist Samuel Pepys and the former prime minister Churchill chose to be married (in 1655 and 1908 respectively). Sir Walter Raleigh is buried here.

Buggy access. Café. Disabled access: toilets. Nearest picnic place: college gardens (10am-6pm Tue-Thur)/ St James's Park. Shop.

Westminster Cathedral

Victoria Street, SW1P 1QW (7798 9055/tours 7798 9064/www.westminstercathedral.org.uk). St James's Park tube/Victoria tube/rail/11, 24, 211, 507 bus. **Open** 7am-7pm Mon-Fri, Sun; 8am-7pm Sat. *Campanile* Apr-Nov 9.30am-12.30pm, 1-5pm daily; Dec-Mar 9.30am-12.30pm, 1-5pm Thur-Sun. *Tours* by arrangement; phone for details. **Admission** free; donations appreciated. *Campanile* £3; £1.50 concessions; £7 family (2+2). *Tours* £2.50. **No credit cards. Map** p316 J10.

London's Catholic cathedral has relative newcomer status among Westminster's other religious edifices: the elaborate neo-Byzantine exterior (inspired by the Hagia Sophia in Istanbul) was completed at the beginning of the 20th century. Although the cavernous interior sparkles with coloured mosaics and marbled stone pillars – not to mention a cross the size of a semi-detached house hovering eerily above the altar – the high ceiling remains an ominous and unpainted black, casting a strange shadow over the many characters below who are crouched in prayer, crossing themselves with holy water or chatting

College Garden, **Westminster Abbey**.

quietly to the priest. Tourists are welcome (although they're respectfully asked not to break the reverie); the shop sells a neat little workbook that leads kids on an activity trail around the building, and the Cathedral Kitchen is on hand to provide half-time refreshments. If you have a head for heights, the 83m (273ft) Campanile Bell Tower is topped by a four-sided gallery with spectacular views across London; there's a lift all the way to the top. The tower is dedicated to St Edward the Confessor. It has one bell, named Edward, which was the gift of the Duchess of Norfolk, in 1910. Inscribed on the bell are the words: 'While the sound of this bell travels through the clouds, may the bands of angels pray for those assembled in thy church. St Edward, pray for England'.

Consult the cathedral's excellent website for details of choral and music recitals.

Buggy access. Café. Disabled access: ramp. Shop.

Kensington & Chelsea

Where the museums are big and very clever.

With three of London's most popular learned institutions, a royal palace and swathes of lovely parkland, the Royal Borough of Kensington and Chelsea has plenty to swagger about. Tops on the 'grand day out' itinerary is the world-renowned **Natural History Museum**, where there be dinosaurs (and lots of other things). The **Science Museum** shows how science touches all aspects of life, and there's great beauty in the **Victoria & Albert Museum**. But it's not all about learning in the Royal Borough. Hyde Park is a fine public space for picnics and sports. You can barely take a step in neighbouring **Kensington Gardens** without happening upon some tribute or other to the late Diana Spencer, as a leisurely stroll following the Diana, Princess of Wales Memorial Walk will reveal. The **Diana, Princess of Wales Memorial Playground** is a terrific for kids, and the **Diana, Princess of Wales Memorial Fountain** is an aptly controversial paddling pool that still attracts hordes of visitors on warm summer days). Stroll on for the oldest boating lake in the capital, the Serpentine, and **Kensington Palace**, birthplace of Queen Victoria in 1819 and home to the late princesses Diana and Margaret. 'South Ken' is also the home of the French Institute, which offers French lessons, a programme of French and English film screenings for young people called 'Ciné-teens and Kids' in November and a bilingual book fest in November. Details of forthcoming programmes are posted on the website www.institut-francais.org.uk.

Early 15th-century **Chelsea** was a fishing village, then from the late 18th until the early 20th century the area became popular with artists and writers – Dante Gabriel Rossetti and T S Eliot were among the creatives who lived here. Nowadays the area is synonymous with wealth, style and culture. Sloane Square, home to the acclaimed Royal Court Theatre, is the place to start a tour of Chelsea. The **Duke of York Square** nearby hosts a wintertime ice rink, fountains in summer and several upmarket cafés , including Gelateria Valerie for truly scrumptious

ice-creams. The **National Army Museum** and the Chelsea Royal Hospital, where the Chelsea Flower Show is held, are a short walk away. Also in the neighbourhood is the **Chelsea Physic Garden**. It can be reached via Flood Street, one of the many attractive side roads branching off King's Road. The prettiest is Glebe Place, which has a very picturesque little nursery school, tucked sweetly in the corner. The western end of King's Road is known as World's End. If you've walked all the way from the Royal Court you deserve to rest your tired legs in **Cremorne Gardens**, which has fine views over the river.

Baden-Powell House

65-67 Queen's Gate, SW7 5JS (7584 7031/www.scout base.org.uk). Gloucester Road or South Kensington tube. **Open** 7am-10pm daily. Closed 22 Dec-3 Jan. **Admission** free. **Credit** MC, V. **Map** p313 D10.
Robert Baden-Powell's memorial hostel was opened in 1961 and it provides accommodation for about 300,000 people from 30 different countries each year, with family rooms for visitors with children. There's an exhibition on the ground floor about the Chief Scout's life. During 2006, B-P House will be staging special events to celebrate the centenary of Scouting (Aug 2007). Be prepared: check the website for more information.
Buggy access. Café. Disabled access: toilet. Nappy-changing facilities. Nearest picnic place: Natural History Museum gardens. Shop.

Chelsea Physic Garden

66 Royal Hospital Road (entrance on Swan Walk), SW3 4HS (7352 5646/www.chelseaphysicgarden.co.uk). Sloane Square tube/11, 19, 239 bus. **Open** Apr-Oct noon-5pm Wed; 2-6pm Sun. *Tours* times vary, phone to check. **Admission** £6.50; £4 5-16s, concessions (not incl OAPs); free under-5s. *Tours* free. **Credit** *Shop* AmEx, MC, V. **Map** p313 F12.
The garden was set up in 1673, but the key phase of development was under Sir Hans Sloane in the 18th century. Its beds contain healing herbs and rare trees, dye plants and medicinal vegetables; plants are also sold. Public opening hours are restricted – because this is primarily a centre for research and education. That said, the education department organises activity days with interesting botanical themes over Easter and summer holidays. Activity days should be pre-booked, and are suitable for seven- to 11-year-olds (although there are some for four- to six-year-olds and nine- to 13-year-olds) and cost £5 per child per day. Phone or email education@chelseaphysicgarden.co.uk for

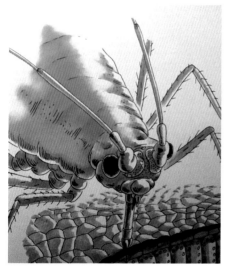

Around Town

Explore the world of creepy crawlies at the **Natural History Museum**. *See p87*.

a list of 2006 dates. Educational visits and teacher-training days can be arranged.

Buggy access. Café. Disabled access: ramp, toilet. Nappy-changing facilities. Shop.

Diana, Princess of Wales Memorial Playground

Near Black Lion Gate, Broad Walk, Kensington Gardens, W8 2UH (7298 2117/recorded info 7298 2141/www.royalparks.gov.uk). Bayswater tube/12, 148, 390 bus. **Open** *Summer* 10am-7.45pm daily. *Winter* 10am-6.45pm (or 1hr before dusk, if earlier) daily. **Admission** free. All adults & children over 12 must be accompanied by a child. **Map** p310 C7.

This commemorative play area is a wonderland for little ones. The focal point is a pirate ship aground in fine, white sand. Children enjoy scaling the rigging to the crow's nest and adore the ship's wheel, cabins, pulleys and ropes. During the summer months the mermaids' fountain and rocky outcrops are fab for water play. Beyond these shipshape glories lies the tepee camp: a trio of wigwams, each large enough to hold a sizeable tribe. The tree-house encampment has walkways, ladders, slides and 'tree phones'. The area's connection with Peter Pan's creator JM Barrie is remembered in images from the story etched into the glass in the Home Under the Ground. Many of the playground's attractions appeal to the senses: scented shrubs, whispering willows and bamboo are planted throughout, and footfall chimes and touchy-feely sculptures engage young visitors. Much of the equipment has been designed for use by children with special needs, including those in wheelchairs. There's plenty of seating for parents, and the newly refurbished café has a children's menu. During the school summer holidays there's

a programme of free entertainment, such as visits by clowns or storytelling sessions (11am, 1pm, 3pm Mon-Fri). Unaccompanied adults aren't allowed in, but they can view the gardens between 9.30am and 10am daily.
Buggy access. Café. Disabled access: toilet. Kiosk. Nappy-changing facilities. Nearest picnic place: Kensington Gardens.

Hyde Park

W2 2UH (7298 2100/www.royalparks.gov.uk). Hyde Park Corner, Knightsbridge, Lancaster Gate or Marble Arch tube/2, 8, 10, 12, 23, 38, 73, 94 bus. **Open** 5am-midnight daily. **Map** p311 E7.
Hyde Park is the largest of London's Royal Parks and was the first to be opened to the public. Year-round, the park's perimeter is popular with both in-line and roller-skaters,

as well as with bike- and horse-riders (there are riding schools near Rotten Row, part of the wide riding track around Hyde Park). If you're cycling, stick to the designated tracks; only children under ten are allowed to cycle on the footpaths. At the west side of the park is the Serpentine, London's oldest boating lake, which has its complement of ducks, coots, swans and tufty-headed grebes. You can rent rowing boats and pedalos from March to October. The Serpentine also has its own swimming club, whose members are so keen that they've been known to break the winter ice to indulge in their daily dip.

The park's innovative water feature, the Diana, Princess of Wales Memorial Fountain, is on a gentle slope near the Serpentine bridge and was opened by the Queen in July 2004. The circular structure, which was designed by American architect Kathryn Gustafson, is a Cornish granite channel filled with running water. The fountain's inaugural

Lovely **Glebe Place**. Chelsea *See p84*.

summer was troublesome: slippery stones, leaf-clogged pumps, algae and muddy banks resulted in its closure, but all such problems have been sorted out.

At the park's eastern end, near Marble Arch, is Speakers' Corner, the world's oldest platform for public speaking. The right to free speech is exercised here every Sunday. Every morning at 10.30am (9.30am Sun), the Household Cavalry emerge smartly from their barracks on South Carriage Drive and ride across the park to Horse Guards Parade, prior to the Changing of the Guard.
Buggy access. Cafés. Disabled access: toilets.

Kensington Gardens

W8 2UH (7298 2117/www.royalparks.gov.uk). Bayswater, High Street Kensington, Lancaster Gate or Queensway tube/9, 12, 28, 49, 148 bus. **Open** 6am-midnight daily. **Map** p310 C7.
These gardens cover 260 acres and meet Hyde Park at the Serpentine. The best element, as far as children are concerned, is the Diana, Princess of Wales Memorial Playground, but the Serpentine Gallery (*see p92*) should not be overlooked. No one could ignore the overblown Albert Memorial, complete with huge statue of Prince Albert, picked out in gold and seated under a 55m (180ft) spire and canopy (for guided tours ring 7495 0916). By Long Water there's a bronze statue of Peter Pan, built by Sir George Frampton in 1912 to honour his creator, JM Barrie. There's usually a Peter Pan-themed fun day to mark his birthday (in 2006 it's planned for 15 July; check the website for more details). Kensington Gardens is also home to what surely must be the poshest park café in the capital: the Orangery, a grand, glass-fronted building designed by Sir John Vanburgh in 1704. It's open daily throughout the year for morning coffee, light lunches and afternoon tea, and has a children's menu and high chairs. You can explore this parkland in around two hours at a leisurely pace and, as all the paths are asphalt, it's fine for pushing a buggy. For a walk that will take a couple of hours, begin at the Black Lion Gate, where you can start in the Diana, Princess of Wales Memorial Playground. Then follow the Broad Walk towards Kensington Palace, then on to the Diana, Princess of Wales Memorial Walk – it's marked by brass domes, one foot (30cm) in diameter, set into the path. The Memorial Walk actually follows a circular route that starts and finishes at Hyde Park Corner and measures a little over 11km (seven miles) in length. The formal Italian Gardens incorporate pretty fountains, although eagle-eyed infants will be far more interested in the small playground just up the slope. There are children's toilets near here.
Buggy access. Cafés. Disabled access: toilet. Nappy-changing facilities.

Kensington Palace

W8 4PX (7937 9561/booking line 0870 751 5170/ www.hrp.org.uk). Bayswater or High Street Kensington tube/9, 10, 49, 52, 70 bus. **Open** *Mar-Oct* 10am-6pm daily. *Nov-Feb* 10am-5pm daily. Last entry 1hr before closing. **Admission** (LP) incl audio guide £11.50; £9 concessions; £7.50 5-15s; free under-5s; £34 family (2+3). **Credit** MC, V. **Map** p310 B8.
William III and his wife Mary came to live in this Jacobean mansion in 1689, when Kensington was still a country village. The couple moved from Whitehall Palace to escape the smoggy air, which played havoc with William's asthma, having commissioned Sir Christopher Wren to alter the existing house into a palace. Since then, many royals have called it home. Queen Victoria, born and baptised

here, enjoyed living in Kensington so much that she awarded the borough its 'Royal' status. The Duke and Duchess of Kent have apartments in the palace. The palace is open for tours of the State Apartments (which you enter via Wren's lofty King's Staircase), the King's Gallery and the Queen's Apartments, where William and Mary lived quite simply. The most popular part is the Royal Ceremonial Dress Collection, which includes outfits worn by Princess Diana. An exhibition of photographs of Diana, Princess of Wales by Mario Testino will be on display until July 2007.
Buggy access. Disabled access: toilet. Nappy-changing facilities. Restaurant. Shop.

National Army Museum

Royal Hospital Road, SW3 4HT (7730 0717/ www.national-army-museum.ac.uk). Sloane Square tube/11, 137, 239 bus. **Open** 10am-5.30pm daily. Closed bank hols. **Admission** free. **Credit** *Shop* AmEx, MC, V. **Map** p313 F12.
Some eccentric exhibits and displays, together with an exciting programme of family events, make this museum dedicated to the British Army's 500-year history far more entertaining than the modern exterior might suggest. Sure, there are dry displays of regimental items – old uniforms, kit bags and the like – but highlights are many: The Road to Waterloo, a version of the famous battle starring 75,000 toy soldiers; the skeleton of Napoleon's beloved mount, Marengo; and Florence Nightingale's lamp. Children love the bizarre exhibits, such as the gruesome frostbitten fingers of Major 'Bronco' Lane, conqueror of Mount Everest. The Redcoats Gallery starts at Agincourt in 1415 and ends with the redcoats in the American War of Independence; The Nation in Arms covers both World Wars, with reconstructions of a trench in the World at War 1914-1946 exhibition, and a D-Day landing craft. There's more military hardware, including a hands-on Challenger tank simulator, up in The Modern Army exhibition. The museum's temporary exhibition, The Somme (1 July 2006 to early 2007), marks the 90th anniversary of one of history's bloodiest battles and is best suited to over-sevens studying World War I. Themed weekend events, which usually involve costumed interpreters and craft activities, have gone a long way to broadening the museum's appeal. Forthcoming topics in 2006 include the Somme (8-9 July), at which visitors can meet World War I soldiers (played by actors) and see letters, diaries, photos and newspapers from the time. The weekend is particularly suited to students aged 13 to 16 as it chimes in with the National Curriculum. There's also The Horse in War (16-17 Sept), which will include an outdoor event and equine-themed craft workshops; and Christmas Revolution (9-10 Dec), which will focus on the rebellion against British tax masters in New York 230 years ago.

The new Children's Zone, which opened in April 2006, has a baby play zone; building and music activities for toddlers; and a reading and art activity space for older ones. It can be booked by the hour for birthday parties.
Buggy access. Café. Disabled access: lift, ramps, toilet. Nappy-changing facilities. Nearest picnic place: benches outside museum/Chelsea Hospital grounds. Shop.

Natural History Museum

Cromwell Road, SW7 5BD (information 7942 5725/ switchboard 7942 5000/www.nhm.ac.uk). South Kensington tube. **Open** 10am-5.50pm Mon-Sat; 11am-5.50pm Sun. **Admission** free; charges apply for special exhibitions. **Credit** AmEx, MC, V. **Map** p313 D10.

Around Town

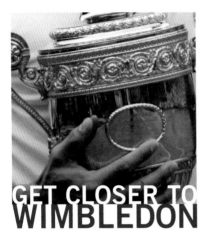

You couldn't see all 70 million plants, animals, fossils, rocks and minerals held in this giant museum in a month of Sundays. Young folk zoom in on the dinosaurs, but there's much more to wonder at (*see below* **Going for gold**). From the front entrance on the Cromwell Road, visitors enter the main hall of the Life Galleries, with its huge cast of a Diplodocus skeleton. If you turn left, you'll find yourself first in the Dinosaur Gallery, and then in the Human Biology section (gallery 22), with its interactive exhibits. From here, make your way to the blue whale (three buses long) via the stuffed mammals. Creepy Crawlies (gallery 33) has a colony of leafcutter ants and some robotic arthropods. To mug up on the Earth's different environments and biological diversity, Ecology (gallery 32) is the place. Spare some time for the Bird gallery (gallery 40); there's a stuffed dodo there, and an egg from the elephant bird.

The Earth Galleries can be accessed from Exhibition Road via an escalator that passes through a giant suspended globe. The earthquake simulation is always a winner. You'll find it and the volcanoes upstairs; the downstairs exhibits trace the history of our planet from the Big Bang to the present.

The Darwin Centre houses around 22 million specimens, with 450,000 stored in jars of alcohol – there's a mummified finger and whole monkeys in tanks. There are 14 free tours daily, each lasting half an hour, which allow punters (children must be at least ten years old) to encounter the scientists who work here; book your place on arrival at the museum. The Darwin Centre's second, final phase of development will store the insect and plant collections and is due for completion in 2008.

A special exhibition called Dino Jaws reveals what these gigantic creatures ate (30 June 2006 to May 2007). Until late August 2006, a free exhibition, The Ship: The Art of Climate Change, will present global warming from the point of view of a number of artists, writers and architects. Linked to the climate-change exhibition are a series of Family Climate Change Ice Workshops (Wed from mid July-Aug). The annual Wildlife Photographer of the Year competition, which includes a category for young photographers, runs from October to April every year. Outside, the Wildlife Garden (open Apr-Oct) provides a variety of British habitats for mammals, amphibians, insects and birds. New for 2006 are the Pond Life workshops; check the website for dates and times. Also due to return in 2006 is the Christmastime ice rink and fair, both run between November and January.

Buggy access. Cafés. Disabled access (Exhibition Road entrance): lift, toilet. Nappy-changing facilities. Nearest picnic place: indoor eating area/museum grounds. Restaurant. Shops.

Going for gold

Since it first opened its doors to the public in 1881, the Natural History Museum has been successfully entertaining and educating visitors of all ages, but when it comes to catering for families, it's second to none. No surprise, then, that this heavyweight in the world of museums won gold in the Family Friendly category at the 2005 Visit London Awards.

It's no mean feat helping visitors to navigate the 70 million items in its collection, let alone making it interesting and relevant to kids, but the museum manages the job admirably, thanks in no small part to an army of helpful staff well versed in the ways of small children let loose in large museums.

As with its two famous neighbours, don't attempt to visit every corner of the NHM in one trip – it simply won't be possible. Best to make a plan and take your time exploring a couple of topics. Another word of advice: arrive early at the weekend and in school holidays – on our visit in February half-term the queue snaked down from the main Cromwell Road entrance past the gates.

The museum's excellent website contains a wealth of information; most helpful is the 'parents survival guide', which helps parents prepare for a family visit. Here are downloadable floor plans, up-to-date 'what's on' listings, practical advice on topics from eating (picnics are encouraged, particularly for parents with allergic children, although there are several cafés and restaurants for healthy snacks and meals) to what to wear (tutu and stilettos… only joking; it's sensible shoes, of course). Also recommended on the website is the 'kids only' area, where science is enlivened by games to download and play, a list of 'cool' things to see in the museum, and a gallery of pictures.

You don't have to plan ahead, though. You'll find several free or low-cost activities at the information desk. The ever-popular Explorer Backpacks (ID deposit required) for under-sevens cover different topics – this summer's new addition has wildlife as its theme and is specially designed for use in the museum garden. Or pick up a themed Discovery Guide (40p-80p) – volcanoes or dinosaurs are good choices – linked to the National Curriculum and available in different versions for four- to 16-year-olds. The hands-on activities in the Investigate Gallery are usually mobbed by seven- to 14-year-olds. You can handle geological specimens in the Earth Lab. There are daily talks for schoolchildren – if you can drag them away from the motion-sensor animatronic T-Rex in the Dinosaur Gallery or the giant squid in the Darwin Centre (you'll need to book a behind-the-scenes tour to get to see this 8.5-metre (28-foot) spectacle.

You'll never get away without joining the scrum in the museum shop, but it's a good one, with science-related items and an abundance of dinosaur merchandise, and pocket-money priced stationery and souvenirs. The shop is near the main Cromwell Road entrance. One thing is guaranteed; you'll be footsore by the time you leave, so be warned that the Tube is often congested at museum chuck-out time on a Saturday (shoppers add to the crush). Stop for a bite to eat in one of the many eating places around South Ken (*see p171-2*) and go home later.

Around Town

Oratory Catholic Church

Thurloe Place, Brompton Road, SW7 2RP (7808 0900/ www.bromptonoratory.com). South Kensington tube/ 14, 74 bus. **Open** 6.30am-8pm daily. *Services* 7am, 10am, 12.30pm, 6pm Mon-Sat; 7am, 8am, 9am, 10am, 11am, 12.30pm, 4.30pm, 7pm Sun. **Admission** free; donations appreciated. **Map** p313 E10.

The second-largest Catholic church in the city (Westminster Cathedral occupies the top slot) is full of marble and mosaics. Many of the internal decorations are much older than the building itself: Mazzuoli's late 17th-century statues of the apostles, for example, once stood in Siena Cathedral. The church was used by Russian spies as a dead letter box during the Cold War. The Oratory's Junior Choir sings Mass at 10am on Sunday, and Schola, the boys' choir of the London Oratory School in Fulham (a reason many parents of secondary-transfer children in London discover popish associations), performs Mass on term-time Saturday evenings.

Buggy access. Disabled access: ramp. Shop.

Science Museum

Exhibition Road, SW7 2DD (7942 4454/booking & information line 0870 870 4868/www.sciencemuseum. org.uk). South Kensington tube. **Open** 10am-6pm daily. **Admission** free; charges apply for special exhibitions. **Credit** AmEx, MC, V. **Map** p313 D9.

It's no wonder visitors lose track of time when they come here; there are some 15,000 objects on display. The vast collection includes landmark inventions such as Stephenson's Rocket, Arkwright's spinning machine, Whittle's turbojet engine and the Apollo 10 command module. Children find the Science Museum a thrilling day out, spending hours learning through play at one of the museum's six play zones, each of which has been created with an age range or development stage in mind. Under-sixes dig the Garden area in the basement, where they can discover the principles of science in the three different zones: Water, Construction, and Sound and Light. On the ground floor, in the Wellcome Wing, the Pattern Pod introduces under-eights to patterns and repetition in the natural world. The Launch Pad is the museum's largest interactive gallery, with plenty to push, pull, look at and listen to. Several times a day, a 20-minute exploration of the concept of structure – in the form of a bubble show – takes place in the science show area. You might also encounter historical characters in the galleries – Albert Einstein, Amy Johnson or perhaps Thomas Crapper. These are played by actors, who help visitors get to grip with inventions and theories (ring 0870 870 4868 for a schedule of their appearances).

The Wellcome Wing embodies the notion of learning while having fun. There's also a five-storey IMAX cinema (£7.50-£9; £6-£7.50 3-16s; free under-3s). The interactive Energy Gallery explores how we power modern life in the 21st century – and beyond. In the Medical History Galleries on the often-neglected top floor, a new permanent gallery, Living Medical Traditions, challenges the notion that western medicine is superior. It takes on a 'guess the object' theme, encouraging families to think about four other global medicine traditions: Ayurveda (Indian), traditional Chinese, Unani Tibb (Islamic) and African. The museum is undergoing a ten-year-long revamp. The first gallery to be redeveloped was the Energy Hall on the ground floor; the Space galleries are currently being upgraded (work is due for completion by Feb 2007). The Photography and Cinematography Gallery has closed to make way for a bigger Launch Pad, to open in 2007.

Science Night sleepovers are held once a month (eight- to 11-year-olds, in groups of five or more), with an evening

Cremorne Gardens. *See p84.*

Paddling Pool
12 years and
under only

Big savings

with the
'extended' Family Railcard

60% off kids' fares

Adults save 1/3

Family size savings are waiting for you with a Family Railcard. Kids get 60% off and adults save 1/3 on most rail fares throughout Britain. It costs just £20 for a whole year and up to 4 adults and 4 children can travel on one card – they don't even have to be related.

Pick up a leaflet at any staffed train station or
call 08457 48 49 50 for the telesales number of your local Train Company.

of activities that might include creating slime or making balloon-powered buggies to take home. You have to book as much as two months ahead (24hr information line 7942 4747). The museum puts on free educational events and workshops every half-term and during school holidays – they can't be booked in advance, so turn up early on the day. To get advance details, sign up for the email newsletter on the museum's website or call the information line. *Buggy access. Cafés. Disabled access: lift, toilet. Nappy-changing facilities. Nearest picnic place: Hyde Park (outdoor); museum basement & 1st floor (indoor). Restaurant. Shop.*

Serpentine Gallery

Kensington Gardens (nr Albert Memorial), W2 3XA (7402 6075/www.serpentinegallery.org). Lancaster Gate or South Kensington tube. **Open** 10am-6pm daily. **Admission** free; donations appreciated. **Credit** AmEx, MC, V. **Map** p311 D8.

It may be housed in a 1930s tearoom, but this lovely, light gallery is a cutting-edge space for contemporary art. Its programme includes family days, artist-led workshops and trails relating to the current exhibitions; check the website for dates or to sign up for the email newsletter. Upcoming highlights at the gallery include photographs by Thomas Demand (until 20 Aug 2006) and contemporary works collected by artist Damien Hirst (Nov-Dec 2006). The 2006 summer pavilion will be designed by Dutch architect Rem Koolhaas along with Cecil Balmond, deputy chairman of structural engineering company Arup. The gallery is also involved in Fête de la Musique, a celebration of music and culture, which took place along Exhibition Road for the first time in June 2005. It is due to be repeated in summer 2006; check www.exhibitionroadmusicday.org for details. *Buggy access. Disabled access: toilets. Nappy-changing facilities. Nearest picnic place: Hyde Park/Kensington Gardens. Shop.*

Victoria & Albert Museum

Cromwell Road, SW7 2RL (7942 2000/www.vam.ac.uk). South Kensington tube. **Open** 10am-5.45pm Mon, Tue, Thur-Sun; 10am-10pm Wed & last Fri of mth. *Tours* daily; phone for details. **Admission** free; charges apply for special exhibitions. **Credit** *Shop* AmEx, MC, V. **Map** p313 E10.

There are thousands of beautiful objects in this stunning museum's collections of costumes, jewellery, textiles, metalwork, glass, furniture, photographs, drawings, paintings, sculpture and architecture from cultures across the world. One of the most fun ways to approach them is to simply wander through its halls, discovering treasures.

Home-grown delights – including the Great Bed of Ware – are housed in the British Galleries, where you'll find a range of interactive exhibits for children. There are plenty of ideas for filling rainy Sunday mornings and half-term holidays. Facilities for children include activity backpacks (available from the main entrance 10.30am-4.30pm Sat), which contain stories, games and objects linked to the collections. On Sundays (10.30am-5pm) children aged three to 12 flock to the Activity Cart, filled with art materials and worthy distractions. Family trails that keep children occupied for around 45 minutes are available daily. A wide range of well-organised activities is laid on in school holidays and at weekends; for details, see the website or call 7942 2211. In the Victorian Discovery Area, for example, there are corsets and crinolines to try on; you can also try your hand at building a model Crystal Palace or a chair. The 18th-Century Discovery Area has children making domestic objects, and there is tapestry to weave and armour to be tried out in the Tudor and Stuart Discovery Area. The Architecture Gallery and Study Centre is a little cramped, particularly if you're pushing a buggy. You can view videos, models, plans and descriptions of various architectural styles. The V&A's Photography Gallery presents work from the museum's famous collection.

The museum is undergoing an extensive ten-year refurbishment, so a number of galleries will temporarily close or relocate; call the booking office on 7942 2211 to check if a particular gallery is open. The stylish Kim Wilkie-designed Garden opened in July 2005; and the Morris, Gamble and Poynter rooms have been converted into a restaurant; the Jewellery galleries will be closed until 2008. Upcoming shows include Leonardo da Vinci: Experience, Experiment and Design (14 Sept 2006 to 7 Jan 2007) and Renaissance at Home (5 Oct 2006 to 7 Jan 2007). *Buggy access. Café. Disabled access: lift, ramps, toilets. Nappy-changing facilities. Nearest picnic place: Pirelli Gardens, museum garden & basement picnic room. Restaurant. Shop.*

 LUNCH BOX

For recommended restaurants and cafés in the area, *see reviews pp171-2*.

ASK 222 Kensington High Street, W8 7RG (7937 5540).

Benihana 77 King's Road, SW3 4NX (7376 7799).

Café Crêperie 2 Exhibition Road, SW7 2HF (7589 8947).

Carluccio's Caffè 1 Old Brompton Road, SW7 3HZ (7581 8101).

Ed's Easy Diner 362 King's Road, SW3 5UZ (7352 1956).

Gelateria Valerie 9 Duke of York Square, SW3 4LY (7730 7978).

Giraffe 7 Kensington High Street, W8 5NP (7938 1221).

Great Escape Café National Army Museum, Royal Hospital Road, SW3 4HT (7730 0717).

Green Fields Café 13 Exhibition Road, SW7 2HE (7584 1396).

Manicomio 85 Duke of York Square, SW3 4LY (7730 3366).

The Orangery Kensington Palace, Kensington Gardens, W8 2UH (7376 0239).

Oratory 234 Brompton Road, SW3 2BB (7584 3493).

Pâtisserie Valerie 215 Brompton Road, SW3 2EJ (7823 9971); 27 Kensington Church Street, W8 4LL (7937 9574).

Pâtisserie Valerie Left Wing Café, 81 Duke of York Square, SW3 4LY (7730 7094).

Paul Boulangerie 41 Thurloe Street, SW7 2LQ (7581 6034).

Pizza Express The Pheasantry, 152-154 King's Road, SW3 4UT (7351 5031).

Pizza Organic 20 Old Brompton Road, SW7 3DL (7589 9613).

Wagamama 26 Kensington High Street, W8 4PF (7376 1717).

North London

Even the scuzzy bits are gentrified now, but you can still run wild up north.

An urban idyll: **Primrose Hill**. *See p94.*

Around Town

Camden Town & around

In spite of its long-standing reputation as the spiritual home of drug-dealers, the homeless and Gothic teenagers – Camden is another of London's more fashionable middle-class addresses. The seedy side still exists, mostly in odd spots near the market or around the tube station, but shouldn't detract from the potential for a happy visit.

Open land and fields up until the 1790s, Camden then became home to scattered farms and a couple of cheap coaching inns. Even this far back, its reputation was of a dangerous landscape frequented by highwaymen – with a bit of imagination, kids can picture the gibbet that stood by the Mother Red Cap inn (now the World's End by the tube station), where highwaymen and other criminals of the day would be displayed, post hanging, for public viewing.

The major attraction, especially for teenagers, is bound to be the market at Camden Lock. Aside from people – over 100,000 on weekends – the

market is packed with stalls selling everything from junky jewellery, weird furniture and quirky art to customised fashion, tarot readings and oriental tableware. Head to the old Horse Hospital for a quieter mooch around stalls with antiques, original 1950s advertising and retro toys. Food has improved of late: a recent visit saw Moroccan, Cypriot and Japanese alongside good-quality bangers and mash, French crêpes, cookies and chocolate-drenched giant strawberries.

For a super-quick escape from the endless weekend crowds, head for the canal. Watch the lock in action as boats pass through, or catch a ride on one of the narrowboats that offer a passenger service up to Little Venice – a trip you could combine with a visit to the delightful Puppet Theatre Barge (*see p221*). Boats going west pass through London Zoo (*see p67*) and some allow you to hop off there for a visit. The 45-minute one-way trip passes elegant terraces with gardens backing on to the canal, willow-fringed towpaths and converted warehouses.

TOP 10 Nature Walks

North London is the bee's knees for flowers and trees, up hill and down dale. For more nature activities, taking place all over town, join the London Wildlife Trust (www.wildlondon.org.uk).

Abney Park Cemetery
A lovely old boneyard. *See p102.*

Barnsbury Wood
Islington's little woodland idyll. *See p100.*

Camley Street Natural Park
Pond-dipping, frog-watching heaven. *See p93.*

Dollis Valley Green Walk
A lovely part of the London Loop. *See p104.*

Gillespie Park
Islington's largest nature reserve. *See p100.*

Hampstead Heath
The ultimate urban nature destination. *See p96.*

Highgate Wood
This is Corporation country. *See p99.*

Parkland Walk
From Highgate to Finsbury Park. *See p99.*

Waterlow Park
Philanthropist's gift to North London. *See p99.*

Welsh Harp Reservoir.
Where nature and sports collide. *See p105.*

The borough of Camden stretches south to Holborn (*see p54*, where the library (32-38 Theobald's Road, WC1X 8PA, 7974 6342) houses Camden's Local Studies and Archives Centre, which is a lot more fun than the internet.

East of Camden Town, there are two other brilliant destinations. The **Camley Street Natural Park** is tucked away in the industrial hinterland of King's Cross and, just across York Way, you'll find the **London Canal Museum**, which has all the history of the local waterways. King's Cross Station has become an unlikely tourist attraction in the wake of Harry Potter fever. Camera-wielding families come for the newly installed sign: 'Platform 9¾'.

To the west of Camden Town, Primrose Hill has a reputation enhanced by the numerous famous folk who have opted to live – and bring up their kids – here. Separated from its brasher neighbour

only by a railway footbridge, the high street (Regent's Park Road) is café heaven. Trojka (No.101, NW1 8UR, 7483 3765) is an inexpensive and entertaining East European contribution – try the Hungarian chocolate torte.

Primrose Hill itself is a smallish park, with a nice play area that is secure for small children, and a big sandpit. There's a good local firework display on the weekend closest to Bonfire Night, but can get horribly crowded. If you're planning to eat out afterwards, book well in advance, as nearby restaurants get packed out.

Back over the railway footbridge in **Chalk Farm** is the revamped Roundhouse (7424 9991, www.roundhouse.org.uk, *see p219*). This place, with a strong focus on the arts and young people, is sure to become an amazing north London asset.

Camley Street Natural Park
12 Camley Street, NW1 0PW (7833 2311/www.wild london.org.uk). King's Cross tube/rail. **Open** *May-Sept* 9am-5pm Mon-Thur; 11am-5pm Sat, Sun. *Oct-Apr* 9am-5pm (or dusk) Mon-Thur; 10am-4pm Sat, Sun. Closed 20 Dec-1 Jan. **Admission** free. **Map** p315 L2.
The London Wildlife Trust's flagship reserve is tiny by national standards, yet manages to combine woods, ponds, marshes and flower meadows. The visitors' centre is a rustic cabin stuffed with bird, bat and spider studies, arty insect sculptures and a wealth of information on urban flora and fauna. Outside, hazel, rowan and silver birch trees offer shelter to many species of bird; the canal flowing by has waterfowl – coots, mallards and moorhens among them – and children are delighted with the dragonflies, grasshoppers and butterflies in the summer. *See also p97* **The Greening of King's Cross**.
Buggy access. Disabled access: toilets. Nappy-changing facilities.

Jewish Museum, Camden
Raymond Burton House, 129-131 Albert Street, NW1 7NB (7284 1997/www.jewishmuseum.org.uk). Camden Town tube. **Open** 10am-4pm Mon-Thur; 10am-5pm Sun. Closed public hols, incl Christmas Day, Jewish festivals. **Admission** (LP) £3.50; £2.50 OAPs; £1.50 5-16s, concessions; free under-5s; £8 family (2+2). **Credit** MC, V.
The history of the Jewish population of Britain, from medieval times up to the present day, is brought to life in this museum. Although it's undoubtedly of interest to students of history and world religions, it's neither too dry nor too academic for the young. The museum offers some fantastic monthly activities for children (pre-booking essential) – watch a puppet show, attend a lively storytelling session or make your very own Elijah's Cup with beading and metallic leaf. Permanent exhibits that draw crowds of youngsters include a sparkling, jewelled breastplate depicting the 12 tribes, a silver scroll case in the shape of a fish and a coconut-shell kiddush cup. The museum's up-to-date and extensive website is the best place to look for details of upcoming events – they also post art from children's sessions up online so you never know, the family art could make the leap from kitchen wall to world wide web.
Buggy access. Disabled access: lift, toilets. Nearest picnic place: Regent's Park. Shop.

London Canal Museum

12-13 New Wharf Road, N1 9RT (7713 0836/ www.canalmuseum.org.uk). King's Cross tube/rail. **Open** 10am-4.30pm Tue-Sun, bank hol Mon (last entry 3.45pm). **Admission** (LP) £3; £2 concessions; £1.50 8-15s; free under-8s. **Credit** MC, V. **Map** p315 M2.

This small shrine to life on Britain's canals is perfect for youngsters of all ages. Apart from panels of text relating the historic importance of the waterways, there is a real narrowboat to explore, complete with recorded domestic dialogue; a children's corner with canal-themed books and lots of pictures of Rosie and Jim to colour in; a life-size 'horse' in its stable; and videos showing life afloat in all its grimy grimness. A touch-screen display introduces visitors to the life and times of one Carlo Gatti. Gatti, sometime owner of the warehouse at 12 New Wharf Road, was an Italian-Swiss immigrant who rose from humble chestnut seller to wealthy ice-cream manufacturer simply by importing ice blocks from the frozen lakes of Norway. The ice was stored in two deep, circular ice wells below the warehouse – throw in a few pennies to appreciate the drop. The displays relating to the commercial history of ice-cream are also fascinating. The shop has some lovely, inexpensive artefacts with curious child appeal, from enamelware painted with 'castles and roses' to lace-and-ribbon plates. Regular craft sessions in the school holidays often involve recreating such items. Check out the 'what's on' section of the museum's website for information on temporary exhibitions and activities.

Buggy access. Disabled access: lift, toilets. Nappy-changing facilities. Nearest picnic place: museum terrace/canal towpath. Shop.

Hampstead & around

'An artistic and thoughtful little suburb of London' was how Forster described Hampstead in *A Passage to India.* That sums up this area pretty well, although most modern commentators can't resist mentioning champagne socialists and gargantuan house prices in the same breath. Hampstead was a place rich people went to live to escape the stench and disease of London in former times. It still has a villagey atmosphere, mainly due to its narrow streets and graceful period architecture. You step out from the tube station on to a very busy high street, but a short walk along East Heath Road takes you to north London's pride, Hampstead Heath. Willow Road joins the heath at Hampstead Ponds. You can take a play break in the playground opposite **2 Willow Road** (7435 6166). This sleek modernist house was built by Ernö Goldfinger in 1939 and is now open on a tour-only basis, so there's no chance of dragging bored under-11s round it. You get a good view of many rooms while pushing a swing, and it's amusing to think that James Bond's creator, Ian Fleming, hated the architect so much he named a villain after him. Up in the village itself are legions of cafés (though none, perhaps, so atmospheric as Louis Pâtisserie at 32 Heath Street, 7435 9908) and the pedestrian-only lanes make for peaceful shopping.

Hampstead has long been a favourite roosting place for artists and authors – witness the atmospheric **Keats House** and the **Freud Museum** (20 Maresfield Gardens, NW3 5SX, 7435 2002, www.freud.org.uk). It also boasts some of the finest dwellings in town. Modern artists get a kick out of the superbly refurbished **Camden Arts Centre** *(see p215)*, not far from the Freud Museum), where, even more importantly , there's a terrific café. **Burgh House** (New End Square, NW3 1LT, 7431 0144, www.burghhouse.org.uk), a Queen Anne house containing a small museum about the area's history, also has a pleasant café and garden away from the weekend crowds. **Fenton House** *(see below)* is picture perfect. Climb further up Hampstead Grove to reach the Hampstead Scientific Society Observatory (8346 1056). This is a charity that opens its doors to the celestially inclined – especially if they're well behaved – between September and April on clear Friday and Saturday evenings (8-10pm) and Sunday mornings (11am-1pm). Only think about coming if there are no clouds. A lot goes on during Science Week in March, call for details.

Camley Street Natural Park. *See p94.*

The daylight pleasures of **Hampstead Heath** – running wild, cycling, gathering conkers and climbing trees – are, obviously, the major attraction of the area. A good combination might be a walk through the Vale of Health (spot the blue plaque for DH Lawrence) to the top of Hampstead, then down the hill to the village for refreshments (there are several well-known chain restaurants here). Several of the pubs between heath and village have been made over into over-sophisticated eating places, but walking south on the heath to **South End Green** and the car park will bring you to Polly's (55 South End Road, NW3 2QB, 7794 8144), a nice place for tea. They also do a smashing wholesome breakfast that is decently priced for Hampstead. Alternatively, move on to the 'heath extension', or **Golders Hill**, where the park café (*see p178*), smooth, winding paths, playground, fallow deer and an aviary full of exotic birds await.

Fenton House

3 Hampstead Grove, NW3 6RT (7435 3471/information 01494 755 563/box office 01494 755 572/www.nationaltrust.org.uk). Hampstead tube/Hampstead Heath rail. **Open** *Mar* 2-5pm Sat, Sun. *Apr-Oct* 2-5pm Wed-Fri; 11am-5pm Sat, Sun, bank hols (last entry 4.30pm). *Tours* phone for times. **Admission** (NT) £4.90; £2.45 5-15s; free under-5s; £12 family. **No credit cards.**

A late 17th-century house enjoyed by adults for its William and Mary architecture, its award-winning garden and its quirky Benton Fletcher collection of early keyboard instruments: harpsichords, clavichords, virginals and spinets. Children enjoy it in a different way: a summer stroll through the orchard, vegetable garden and lawns is always agreeable, and the harpsichords, clavichords, virginals and spinets will probably be like no instrument they have ever seen before. There is also a porcelain collection that includes a 'curious grotesque teapot' and several poodles. Apple Day in October is celebrated in the orchard, and children may well be fascinated by the fortnightly summer concerts utilising instruments in the collection.
Baby slings for hire. Buggy access. Disabled access: ramp. Nappy-changing facilities.

Hampstead Heath

NW5 1QR (8348 9908/www.cityoflondon.gov.uk/ openspaces). Hampstead tube, Kentish Town tube/rail or Gospel Oak or Hampstead Heath rail/214, C2, C11 bus. **Open** dawn-dusk daily.
Hampstead Heath Ponds *Millfield Lane, N6 (7485 3873/www.cityoflondon.gov.uk/openspaces). Archway tube/Gospel Oak rail.* **Open** dawn-dusk daily. **Admission** £2; £1 concessions. *Season ticket* £100/yr; £60/yr concessions. Over-8s only.
Hampstead Lido *Gordon House Road, NW5 1QR (7485 3873/www.cityoflondon.gov.uk/openspaces). Tufnell Park tube/Gospel Oak rail.* **Open** *Oct-Apr* 7am-noon. *May-Sept* 7am-6pm daily. **Admission** 7-9am £2; £1 concessions. 10am-6pm £4.10; £2.50 concessions. *Season ticket* £100/yr; £60/yr concessions. All ages welcome.

The city's countryside, these rolling acres and wooded areas conspire to make Hampstead Heath feel larger and more rural than it really is. This undulating swathe of grassland, woodland and lakes is extensive enough, however (3.2 sq km), so it's possible to imagine yourself in several different places all on the same day. It's an inspiration for Londoners, who come from miles around to take the air. They toil up Parliament Hill to fly their kites or simply rest awhile, gazing down over the city for miles and miles. At the bottom of the hill families play tennis, bowls, *boules*; feed the ducks on the first lake or admire the model boats (occasionally noisy) on the second.

The heath is maintained by the Corporation of London. Lovely in winter, it really comes into its own during the warmer months. In recent years, the various ponds, which are fed by an underground stream thought to be the old River Fleet, have been cleaned up. Bathing is segregated, and since the Ladies Bathing Pond is located in a secluded enclosure, entry is barred to all males and to girls under eight. Consequently, family bathing is probably best undertaken in the far less rustic lido close to Gospel Oak station. The playground here has free access to a shallow paddling pool during the summer months (note that costumes must be worn even by the tiniest children). The adventure playground behind the athletics track has timber-framed play equipment, where ropes, tyres and ladders prove a challenge for athletic children.

Clowns, bouncy castles, magicians, storytellers and puppeteers perform free of charge in different locations each week (pick up a leaflet from the Parliament Hill information office). There are also tennis courses, learn-to-fish days, evening bat walks and imaginatively themed nature trails. Part of Hampstead Heath has been designated a Site of Special Scientific Interest by English Nature; this includes the area to the right of the tennis courts on Parliament Hill Fields, which is known locally as 'the secret garden', where children can sometimes engage in a spot of pond-dipping and beetle hunting. Call at the information centre to gain entry.
Buggy access. Cafés. Disabled access: toilets. Nappy-changing facilities.

Keats House

Keats Grove, NW3 2RR (7435 2062/www.cityoflondon. gov.uk/keats). Belsize Park or Hampstead tube/ Hampstead Heath rail/24, 46, 168 bus. **Open** 1-5pm Tue-Sun, bank hol Mon. **Tours** 3pm Sat, Sun. **Admission** £3.50; £1.75 concessions; free under-16s. Weekend tours incl in admission price. **Credit** MC, V.

You want to be a fan of Keats's poetry and the Romantics in general to appreciate the resonances in this house, so it's quite unlikely to be near the top of most children's visiting list. It is, however, on one of Hampstead's most beautiful streets, and kindly attendants from the Corporation of London make children welcome, providing line drawings of the house for children to colour in while their parents tour the august rooms that belonged to Keats's friend, Charles Brown. A chaise longue is set up in the position where Keats spent his days gazing out of the window after becoming ill in the 1820s, and the house is full of handsome pieces of antique furniture, portraits of the poet and his friends, and photocopied sheets of the poems. There's also a (new) tree in the garden near the spot where Keats is said to have sat writing 'Ode to a Nightingale'. During July and August 2006 there will be teddy bears' picnics at the house for children; call for details of other events.
Buggy access (ground floor only). Nearest picnic place: house gardens. Shop.

The greening of King's Cross

A generation ago most parents would have taken the long way round to avoid King's Cross. What wasn't given over to industrial developments and railway stations was seedy as Soho and rougher than Brixton Station after midnight. Then along came the Channel Tunnel Rail Link and suddenly things started to look much brighter. First came the Costas and Starbucks, bringing their own brand of mass-produced respectability to Euston Road. Then came culture, courtesy of the revamped British Library. More surprising was the arrival of green, open spaces, created by local residents on vacant lots, car parks and rooftops across King's Cross.

Today, a green revolution is sweeping across the area, providing new spaces for children and families to connect with the natural environment. The pioneer of the movement was the Camley Street Natural Park (*see p94*), which opened in 1985 on a small patch of wasteland squeezed between the Chunnel building site and Regent's Canal. From modest beginnings, the park has grown into one of London's most entertaining natural spaces for children. School groups cram into the living classroom every weekday during term time, and the park and nature rooms are open to the public daily except Friday, with loads of opportunities for little hands to get dirty.

Don't expect flower beds and topiary; the focus at Camley Street is on wild nature. Kids can fish for pond creatures in reed-filled marshes and spy on wild birds from scrub-wood nature hides. Probably the most enjoyable activity is turning over rotting logs in the woodpile to search for beetles, newts and other creepy crawlies. Nature-spotting guide sheets are provided for tiny naturalists and conservation days and environment-based activities take place throughout the year.

Hot on the heels of Camley Street came the Calthorpe Project (7837 8019/www.calthorpeproject.org.uk) on Gray's Inn Road. Camden Council planned to turn this patch of greenery into office space, but local residents campaigned for the creation of a community garden, and the authorities bowed to popular pressure. As well as horticultural training for adults, there are creative drop-in sessions for under-5s from Monday to Thursday and a popular crèche for shopping mums on Saturday morning – see the website for timings.

More recently, attention has shifted to the top floor, thanks to the efforts of Global Generation (7284 1054, www.globalgeneration.org.uk), a charity that provides nature experiences for inner city children. In 2005, the flat roof of 175 Gray's Inn Road was transformed into an airy outdoor classroom for pupils from local schools, many of whom rarely see a garden, let alone one laid out way above the city streets. Today, the roof forms part of an ongoing science project, exploring new techniques for recycling, water conservation, carbon balancing, natural insulation and encouraging natural diversity.

Living roofs are now planned for buildings across King's Cross, including parts of the Channel Tunnel Rail Link development. Probably the grandest living roof of all sits on top of the 35-storey Barclays Building at Canary Wharf. Despite being surrounded by some of the most expensive real estate in London, this lofty wild space is closed to everyone except the birds and bees. Of course, that's nothing compared to Beijing, which plans to cover 40 million square metres of rooftops with greenery in time for the Olympics in 2008.

For more on green roofs in London, visit www.livingroofs.org.

Around Town

London Canal Museum. *See p95.*

Kentish Town City Farm

*1 Cressfield Close, off Grafton Road, NW5 4BN
(7916 5421/www.ktcityfarm.org.uk). Chalk Farm tube
or Kentish Town tube/rail.* **Open** 9am-5.30pm daily.
Closed 25 Dec. **Admission** free; donations appreciated.
An absolute delight in almost any season, this city farm
stretches way beyond the farmyard into precious pasture-
land and well-tended vegetable gardens. Livestock-wise,
there are Aylesbury ducks, goats, pigs, horses, cows,
chickens, cats and rabbits, all of which seem to be busy
reproducing. In the gardens locals grow coriander, mooli
and curry plants, as well as more traditional allotment fare.
Orchards and enclosures for sheep line the railway line.

A pond with a dipping platform is full of frogs, and a riding school is the scene of weekend pony rides (1.30pm Sat,
Sun, weather permitting, £1). The railway arch forms an
impromptu proscenium for children's drama, while a classroom is used for a plethora of craft and play sessions. An
energetic education officer, welcomes school visits from
all boroughs and anyone can come to the Easter egg hunt,
May Day celebrations, Apple Day (October) and so on.
*Buggy access. Disabled access: ramp, toilet.
Nappy-changing facilities. Nearest picnic place: on the
farm.*

Kenwood House/Iveagh Bequest

*Hampstead Lane, NW3 7JR (8348 1286/www.english-
heritage.org.uk). Hampstead tube/Golders Green tube,
then 210 bus.* **Open** *Apr-Oct* 11am-5pm daily. *Nov-Mar*
11am-4pm daily. **Tours** by appointment only.
Admission free; donations appreciated. *Tours* £3; £2
concessions; £1.50 under-16s. **Credit** MC, V.
Strike out across Hampstead Heath from almost any
direction and a path will lead you to Kenwood House. Hot
chocolate and cream teas in winter or classy lemonade and
ice-creams in summer persuade small feet that the trek is
worthwhile, as the Brew House café (*see p178*), set in the
old kitchens, is the best, if a little pricey, catering venue for
miles around. The house is a white stucco mansion, built
in the classical style by Robert Adam in 1767-9 and
bequeathed to the nation in 1927. It houses the Iveagh
Bequest, a collection of paintings by Reynolds, Turner, Van
Dyck, Hogarth, Guardi and Boucher. There's also a vast
library. Of special interest to children are the annual Easter
egg hunt, St George's Day 'dragon trails', kite-making
workshops and spooky Hallowe'en storytelling days.

Volunteer group Heath Hands also has its office
here – it plans family events throughout the year; call for
details or pick up a leaflet at the visitors' centre in the
Kenwood House Estate Office. Left to their own devices,
most youngsters find ample amusement in the vicinity:
running through the Ivy Arch, hiding in the vast rhodo-
dendron bushes or rolling down the grassy slopes.
*Buggy access. Café. Disabled access: ramps, toilets.
Nappy-changing facilities. Shop.*

Highgate & Archway

A pretty, hilly village studded with estate agents
offices (testament to its desirability), Highgate is
forever associated with Dick Whittington. Legend
has it that the young man was walking away
from the city at the foot of Highgate Hill when
he heard the Bow bells peal out 'Turn again
Whittington, thrice mayor of London'. This
life-changing event is commemorated on the
Whittington Stone, near the hospital, and there's
a little statue of his famous cat here too.

Highgate Wood is a little piece of paradise, as
is Waterlow Park, donated to Londoners by the
low-cost housing pioneer Sir Sydney Waterlow in
1889, and containing **Lauderdale House**.

Next door, beautiful **Highgate Cemetery** (Swains Lane, N6 6PJ, 8340 1834, www.highgate-cemetery.org) is on the visiting list of many a tourist, much to the annoyance of the Friends of Highgate Cemetery, who prefer to play down the visitor pull of their historic patch. Children are discouraged from visiting unless they're coming to see the grave of a relative, but if you long to pay your respects to Karl Marx, Mary Ann Evans (aka George Eliot), Max Wall or any of the other admired figures who now repose in the Eastern Cemetery, you can bring children to this delightful boneyard, as long as they're well behaved. The Western Cemetery is out of bounds to casual visitors (adults and kids aged eight and over can pay £3 for a guided tour, which brings the departed to life and affords a chance to see the eerie catacombs).

A little further down the hill from the tube station is Shepherd's Close, from where you can access the pleasant, bramble-fringed Parkland Walk (which runs to Finsbury Park). Hornsey Lane, on the other side of Highgate Hill, leads you to the **Archway**, a grim Victorian viaduct spanning what is now the A1 and offering views of the City and the East End. Jackson's Lane arts centre (269A Archway Road, N6 5AA, box office 8341 4421, www.jacksonslane.org.uk) puts on shows for children most Saturdays, and a popular, large-scale pantomime at Christmas.

Highgate Wood/Queen's Wood

Muswell Hill Road, N10 3JN (8444 6129/www.cityof london.gov.uk/openspaces). Highgate tube/ 43, 134, 263 bus. **Open** 7.30am-dusk daily.
This large area of woodland has been tended by the Corporation of London and its trusty team of woodsmen (and women) since 1886, when the Lord Mayor declared the wood 'an open space for ever'. Carpeted with bluebells and wild flowers in spring and dappled with sunlight filtered by the trees, this corner of London really doesn't feel like London at all.

The wood is carefully managed: trees are coppiced in the traditional way, areas are fenced off to encourage new growth, boxes are provided for owls, bats and hedgehogs to live in, and everything that moves is chronicled. Most encouragingly, the bird population has increased dramatically in recent years, both in types and numbers. You can pick up leaflets about the wildlife in the visitors' information hut beside the café, or join one of the bird-identification walks or nature trails. The award-winning children's playground in this beautiful setting has been carefully planned to allow wheelchair-users and their more mobile friends to play together. The bridge and tower structure is accessible to buggies and wheelchairs, the sturdy swings are designed to be used by children who need more support, and there are Braille noticeboards. For sporty types, there's a football and cricket field (in front of the café), and exercise equipment has recently been installed among the trees.
Buggy access. Café. Disabled access: toilet. Nappy-changing facilities.

Lauderdale House

Highgate Hill, Waterlow Park, N6 5HG (8348 8716/ restaurant 8341 4807/www.lauderdale.org.uk). Archway tube/143, 210, 271, W5 bus. **Open** 11am-4pm Tue-Fri; 1.30-5pm Sat; noon-5pm Sun; phone to check weekend openings. *Restaurant* 9am-6pm Tue-Sun. Closed 24 Dec-mid Jan. **Admission** free. **No credit cards**.
The pretty, 16th-century Lauderdale House, once home of Nell Gwynne, is the centrepiece of Highgate's secluded park. A favoured venue for wedding receptions and other bashes, it's sometimes closed to the public. Saturdays, however, are sacrosanct, because that's when children come for their morning shows, usually aimed at the threes to eights. Ring for details of craft fairs, musical events, exhibitions by local artists and other events held in the arts centre. In the summer, weather permitting, the parkland surrounding the house hosts open-air shows. Whatever's on, it's lovely to sit on the terrace of the café and admire the view over a coffee and ice-cream or an Italian meal; book ahead if you fancy having Sunday lunch here. Fans of the house and park may join a free mailing list to be advised of upcoming events.

Beautiful Waterlow Park, in which the house is set, has several lakes, a toddlers' playground and picnic-friendly grassy slopes. Home to much wildlife the park also has an injured animal recovery centre. This is the largest park in Camden Council's care; and it's permanently staffed.

The Grade II-listed park has been restored in recent years, so now the 17th-century terrace garden is looking good and the depot building has become workshops, an activities room and toilets.
Buggy access (ground floor only). Café. Disabled access: toilets (ground floor). Nearest picnic place: Waterlow Park. Restaurant.

The gardens at **Fenton House**. *See p96.*

Around Town

Islington

An idyllic village in Tudor times, Islington was a handy venue for Henry VIII's hunting activities. Looking at this smart and fashionable area it's hard to believe that for more than a century and a half it went into a decline, when the opening of the busy Regent's Canal brought with it industrial slums in the 1820s. Creeping gentrification started in the late 1970s, has over the decades resulted in a very trendy Islington, whose smart Georgian squares and Victorian terraces shelter many of London's wealthier residents. The district is characterised by its mix of trendy bars, shops, and flourishing arts centres, many of which have plenty to offer children.

Islington has 11 theatres and is home to the Anna Scher Theatre School, where many *EastEnders* cast members learned their trade – the school has a five-year waiting list. The **Little Angel Theatre** (14 Dagmar Passage, N1 2DN, 7226 1787, www.littleangeltheatre.com) is a celebrated, purpose-built puppet theatre. Every June the area hosts a two-week festival of music, theatre and art, and there are regular exhibitions at the Business Design Centre on Upper Street. Wednesdays and Saturdays see antiques markets in pedestrianised **Camden Passage**.

Playground-loving kids rate **Highbury Fields**, wilder types prefer **Gillespie Park**, a nature reserve near the old art deco Arsenal stadium. Footie fans of the Gunner variety are still mourning the imminent removal of the club to the swish new 60,000-capacity Emirates Stadium down the road. The switch is planned for the start of the 2006/7 season. Occasional 90-minute guided tours, which end at the museum, take place at the £390m new ground (call 7704 4504 to book).

The other big park in the area is **Finsbury Park**, for which the borough of Islington shares responsibility with the boroughs of Haringey and Hackney. It's a great sprawling green space currently in the hands of the Finsbury Park Partnership, whose regeneration of the area is supposed to be complete by the time the project ends in 2006. There's no shortage of sporting facilities, notably the **Michael Sobell Leisure Centre** (Hornsey Road, N7 7NY, 7609 2166), with its climbing walls, trampolining, table tennis, squash and badminton, and mini ice rink. A star attraction for the under-threes is the Sobell Safari, an indoor playground on four floors, with tunnels, slides and ball ponds. Nearby, on Green Lanes, the **Castle Climbing Centre** (07776 176 007, www.geckos.co.uk) is one of London's top climbing venues, but always oversubscribed. You'll find it in a Grade II-listed Victorian folly

(previously a water tower) modelled on Stirling Castle. Within the grounds, in a separate building, is another ball pond.

Those who crave the scent of the countryside can commune with pigs at **Freightliners City Farm**, learn about green activities at the **Islington Ecology Centre** or take a short walk in Barnsbury Wood (Crescent St, N1). Rural flavours – in a form that trendy urban types can stomach (think ruby chard) – can be sampled every Sunday from 10am to 2pm at the Islington Farmers' Market (William Tyndale School Playground, Richmond Grove, behind Islington Town Hall, Upper Street N1, 7833 0338). Look out for happily picnicking families sampling their farmers' market goodies on the green. They're sensible: most eating places on Upper Street are expensive. The Turkish restaurants are great , however, with the three branches of the popular Gallipoli (No.102, N1 1QN, 7359 0630; Gallipoli Again, No.120, N1 1QP, 7359 1578; Gallipoli Bazaar, No.107, N1 1QP, 7226 5333) also serving hearty English breakfasts. The S&M Café (*see p175*) is also affordable, as is Giraffe (29-31 Essex Road, N1 2SA, 7359 5999; *see also p162*).

Chapel Market (on the street of the same name) is a gloriously downmarket bargain bin of fruit and vegetables, linen, partyware, toys and (not always durables), presided over by rowdy costers. It's still thriving, despite competition from the **N1 Shopping Centre** that links Liverpool Road with Upper Street. The centre has reliable childrenswear chains, restaurants like Wagamama and Yo Sushi!, and an eight-screen cinema.

Freightliners City Farm

Paradise Park, Sheringham Road, off Liverpool Road, N7 8PF (7609 0467/www.freightlinersfarm.org.uk). Caledonian Road or Holloway Road tube/Highbury & Islington tube/rail. **Open** *Summer* 10am-4.45pm Tue-Sun. *Winter* 10am-4pm Tue-Sun. Closed 25 Dec-1 Jan. **Admission** free; donations appreciated.
A stone's throw from Pentonville Prison, this city farm (next to the playground in Paradise Park) positively teems with life: there are rabbits, cows, goats, cats, pigs, as well as all kinds of poultry. The animals, many of them rare breeds, are impressive. Giant Flemish rabbits are the biggest you will see anywhere in London; guineafowl run amok in other animals' pens; exotic cockerels with extravagantly feathered feet squawk alarmingly in your path; bees fly lazily around their hives (if you're lucky you can buy restorative local honey). You can also buy hen and duck eggs of all hues, plus own-grown vegetables and plants when in season, and there's an organic market on Saturdays. Playschemes run during the summer holidays and are justifiably popular, ring for details. And, at any time of year, there is an overwhelming scent of straw and manure – bliss.
Buggy access. Café. Disabled access: toilets. Nappy-changing facilities. Nearest picnic place: farm picnic area. Shop .

A tribute to a mayoral cat near the **Whittington** Hospital. *See p98*.

Highbury Fields

Highbury Crescent, N5 1RR (7527 4971). Highbury & Islington tube/rail/19, 30, 43, 271 bus. **Open** *Park* 24hrs. *Playground* dawn-dusk daily.
Islington's largest outdoor space repays careful exploration. Hidden behind Highbury Pool and a series of high bushes is an unusual playground that combines old-fashioned thrills (such as a circular train demanding passenger propulsion, Flintstone-style, and a long, alarmingly steep slide) with more recent additions, like the flying fox and giant, web-like climbing frames. The outdoor tennis courts have been refurbished and are used by the excellent Islington Tennis Centre. A stroll across Highbury Fields can take you from busy Upper Street past imposing period terraces to Highbury Barn, a trendy enclave boasting several excellent food shops, restaurants and cafés.
Buggy access. Café.

Islington Ecology Centre

191 Drayton Park, N5 1PH (7354 5162/www. islington.gov.uk). Arsenal tube. **Open** *Park* 8am-dusk Mon-Fri; 9am-dusk Sat; 10am-dusk Sun. Closed Arsenal FC home matches. *Centre drop-in sessions* 2-4pm Tue, Thur; for other times phone to check. **Admission** free; donations appreciated.
This imaginative redevelopment of former railway land led to the founding of Islington's largest nature reserve: Gillespie Park. It has woodland, meadows, wetland and ponds, and the Ecology Centre is its educational heart. Staff are endlessly enthusiastic and helpful on the subject of all natural things in the borough. An events diary is published biannually with events suitable for families, from moth evenings to junk modelling. Nature-themed workshops run in the holidays.
Buggy access.

The Islington Museum

Islington Town Hall, Upper Street, N1 2UD (7527 2837). Highbury & Islington tube/rail. **Open** 11am-5pm Wed-Sat; 2-4pm Sun. **Admission** free.
The Islington Museum is housed in the former Assembly Hall, next to Islington Town Hall. It has two galleries: one houses a permanent collection illustrating, in an undeniably pedestrian way, the history of Islington from prehistoric times to World War II. The other has temporary exhibitions of work by local artists and community groups and on local history themes – the latter tend to be more fun.
Buggy access. Disabled access. Shop.

Stoke Newington

The popularity of Stoke Newington, in particular with families, grows year on year. Rumour has it that there are more buggies per square mile in 'Stokey' than anywhere else in London. Still pleasantly bohemian, the heart of the area nestled between Islington and Hackney is Stoke Newington Church Street, host to north London's best street festival every June. Visit on a regular weekend and you'll find a heap of great little independent shops, organic farmer's market, antique yard, a few good second-hand bookshops, and one of the best toy shops around – all on the one street. There's no shortage of places to grab a bite, all very child-friendly, or if the weather's good pick up a picnic (Fresh&Wild being one local option) and wander up the road to one of Stokey's great green spaces, **Clissold Park**. In inclement weather, parents denied proper park action might opt for the indoor over excitement encouraged by Stoke Newington's large and jolly adventure play centre, Zoomaround.

Around the corner from Church Street is the contrast of the High Street with its array of Turkish cafés and grocers displaying brightly coloured and often unusual fruit and veg. Azizia Mosque (117-119 Stoke Newington Road, London N16 0207 254 0046) is a real head-turner, a beautiful tiled blue Turkish mosque with a

Around Town

Top tiling at **Azizia Mosque**. *See p101.*

restaurant within. Heading south down the high street to dive into Stokey's rough-and-ready neighbour, Dalston, which has the biggest street market for miles around, full of Afro-Caribbean, Greek and Turkish wares .

Abney Park Cemetery & Nature Reserve

Stoke Newington High Street, N16 0LN (7275 7557/ www.abney-park.org.uk). Stoke Newington rail/73, 106, 149, 243, 276, 349 bus. **Open** dawn-dusk daily. *Visitors' centre* 9.30am-5pm Mon-Fri. **Admission** free.
A romantically decayed Victorian cemetery, Abney Park is a hub of conservation activity. An environmental classroom at the Stoke Newington High Street entrance is the scene of many free workshops for children and adults. Go on a mini beast hunt or take a tree tour and learn about the different varieties on site. The visitors' centre doubles as

a shop for guides to green London and other such environmentally aware literature. While still plainly a burial ground, the cemetery's decaying monuments – draped urns, angels, Celtic crosses, saints and shepherds – add Romantic interest to a local nature reserve where trees and plants are now in the ascendency.
Buggy access. Disabled access: toilet (visitors' centre). Shop.

Clissold Park

Stoke Newington Church Street, N16 5HJ (7923 3660). Stoke Newington rail/73, 149, 329, 476 bus. **Open** 7.30am-dusk daily. **Admission** free.
There is no tube station in Stoke Newington, but it is possible for energetic families to cycle to Clissold Park from Finsbury Park, utilising the parkland trails and the mercifully wide pavements along Green Lanes. The whole trip should take no more than 30 minutes – perhaps terminating at Clissold Park's café. The latter is set in a handsome,

listed Georgian building. There is lots to discover on a pleasant amble around Clissold Park: stroll over the river bridge and peek through the fences at some surprisingly friendly deer, rabbits, birds and goats. There are also several ponds supporting various waterfowl, an outdoor stage for children to cavort on whenever it is not in use by bands, and tennis courts that carers could use while kids are in the adjoining well-kitted-out playground. The courts are home to the Hackney wing of the City Tennis Centre (7254 4235); ring for details of its programme – family tennis evenings, junior clubs and tournaments, and coaching are all available. The bowling green here appears somewhat rundown, but the playground is lovely, with modern equipment and lots of shady picnic tables.

Buggy access (in park, steps at café). Café. Disabled access: toilets (in front of café). Nappy-changing facilities (on request).

Zoomaround

46 Milton Grove, N16 8QY (7254 2220/www. zoomaround.co.uk) Highbury & Islington tube, then 393 bus/73, 141, 341, 236, 476 bus. **Open** 9.15am–6.15pm Mon-Sat; 10am-6.15pm Sunday. **Admission** £2 under 1s, £3.50 1-3 years; £4.50 4 and over; free babes in arms and siblings under 1.

Approach Zoomaround from Albion Road and the squeals of delight coming from behind the glass bricks on one side of the building will tell you you've found the place. The source of this audible delight is a huge multi-level play frame filled with ball ponds, slides, rope swings, climbing nets and tunnels, all made of brightly coloured, padded plastic to bounce, crawl and climb up, down, across, inside and out. Toddlers have their own separate area, and carers can either squeeze through the child-size nooks and crannies in hot pursuit of little ones or sit and look on with some cake and a cappuccino from the café. Good home-cooked food is served, and there's a pleasant garden too.

Buggy access. Café. Pay & Display parking, free on weekends. Nearest picnic place: Butterfield Green.

Crouch End & Muswell Hill

These areas have become the settlement of choice for north Londoners looking for more space to breathe. Architecturally, they are blessed with a wealth of unspoilt Victorian and Edwardian housing (check out the scenery, pre-1890s building boom, at the Bruce Castle Museum *see p105*), which these days is becoming prohibitively expensive. This, together with decent primary schools, has made these areas popular with young families. Muswell Hill has a particularly villagey atmosphere and would be even more popular with commuters if it had got the transport links planned for it back in the 1940s, when there were moves to turn the now defunct railway into a tube line. Digging was abandoned, however, when construction workers came upon a deep pit filled with the remains of plague victims, and they refused to proceed any further.

The area's best-known attraction has to be the lofty **Alexandra Park & Palace**, but there are plenty of other green spaces. Priory Park in Middle Lane is great for cycling, rollerskating and football, and it has a paddling pool, formal gardens, tennis courts and the light, bright Rainbow Café, right next to the paddling pool, where real cake, organic drinks, proper coffee and plates of simple pasta are the order of the day. The park is the venue of the annual May fun run organised by the YMCA, a huge event for runners and families because of the children's races and free doughnuts.

Stationers Park, between Denton Road and Mayfield Road, has a good adventure playground, a pre-school children's play area and (free) tennis courts. Park Road Pools has both indoor and outdoor swimming pools, though the latter gets packed out on summer weekends. Hidden tracts of greenery off Park Road allow ample space for the North Middlesex Sports Club, plus various other tennis and cricket clubs; these are the scenes of various sport-related holiday playschemes and of after-school coaching.

There are so many family-oriented restaurants in the area that you'd stumble into one if you were blindfolded and spun round three times. Banners (*see p172*) is probably the most popular family-lunch place for families in Crouch End. Muswell Hill boasts branches of Giraffe (*see p162*) and the Fine Burger Company (*see p173*) and has a very special fish and chip shop called Toffs (*see p175*).

Alexandra Park & Palace

Alexandra Palace Way, N22 7AY (park 8444 7696/ information 8365 2121/boating 8889 9089/ www.alexandrapalace.com). Wood Green tube/ Alexandra Palace rail/144, W3 bus. **Open** *Park* 24hrs daily. *Palace times vary depending on exhibitions.* **Admission** free.

The Ally Pally (as it is affectionately known) has had some bad luck. It burned down twice – once in 1863, just weeks after opening, and once in 1980 – only to rise like a phoenix on each occasion as a grandiloquent place of public entertainment. The only trouble is that, on closer inspection, the buildings are still in need of repair. Such is the projected cost that progress towards a refurbishment programme is exceedingly slow. Outside, however, things are looking up. The children's playground has recently reopened after a thorough facelift as part of the park's £3.6m refurbishment project. All in all, the palace on the hill and its environs have much to offer, crumbliness notwithstanding. Chief interest for children is the ice-skating rink, along with (in summer) the boating lake and pitch-and-putt course. Walking around the park affords breathtaking views of London. There's plenty of space for picnics. In bad weather, try the café in the garden centre. Firework Night in November is excellent fun, with lots of room for spectators and pyrotechnics that can be seen for miles around.

Buggy access. Disabled access: lift, ramps, toilets. Nappy-changing facilities (ice rink). Nearest picnic place: picnic area by boating lake.

Around Town

Finchley

A popular, sprawling London suburb, Finchley has a settled Jewish and Japanese community and a general air of peace and prosperity. The three tube stations make it popular with London businessfolk and their families, and a preponderance of family-friendly facilities – parks, playgrounds, leisure centres and retail parks – mean that Finchley youth are well served until the lure of London's meaner streets has them taking the Northern Line south, usually to Camden Town.

A short way south of Finchley Central tube station – the heart of what was once a village and is now a rather dowdy cluster of small shops and cheap Turkish and Chinese restaurants – is **Avenue House** and its beautifully landscaped gardens, which were given to the nation in 1918. A five-minute walk north from the station gets you to Victoria Park, just off Ballards Lane between Finchley Central and North Finchley; here you'll find a bowling green, playground and tennis courts; in July the park also provides a venue for the Finchley Carnival.

For indoor entertainment, the **Great North Leisure Park** (Leisure Way, High Road, N12) – better known among the locals as Warner Village – is a US-style entertainment complex. The cinema, Finchley Vue cinema (0871 224 0240), has a Saturday morning kids' club. There's also an extremely popular swimming pool – a good spot for children's parties – kitted out with a vigorous wave machine and swirling currents for (as all the signs say) 'rough-and-tumble fun'. The Hollywood Bowl bowling alley (Leisure Way, High Road, N12 0QZ, 8446 6667, www.hollywoodbowl.co.uk) has a bar and a burger restaurant.

East Finchley's Phoenix Cinema (52 High Road, N2 9PJ, 8883 2233, www.phoenixcinema.co.uk) has children's films on Saturdays. The Old Manor House, on East End Road, is a cultural centre, which includes ritual baths, a school and the absorbing **Jewish Museum, Finchley**.

Should you decide to get away from it all *en famille*, try the **Dollis Valley Green Walk**, which forms part of the London Loop that encircles the city and links green spaces from Moat Mount, near Mill Hill in the north, to Hampstead Garden Suburb in the south. Setting off with a map is advisable, as the way isn't very well signposted; for more details, visit www.londonwalking.com.

Avenue House

17-19 East End Road, N3 3QE (8346 7812/ www.avenuehouse.org.uk). Finchley Central tube/ 82, 125 bus. **Open** *Ink Museum* 2-4pm Tue-Thur. **Admission** free; donations appreciated.

The land on which this handsome villa stands used to be known as Temple Croft Fields, after the Knights Templars who were granted it in 1243. The house was built in 1859 by Reverend Edward Coope. It was bought in 1874 by Henry Charles (Inky) Stephens, whose father invented blue-black ink. A Member of Parliament, Inky inherited a keen interest in writing fluids from his father, installing a laboratory in the house when he refurbished it. Stephens died in 1918, bequeathing Avenue House to the people of Finchley. Avenue House was formally opened to the public in 1928. Since then, it has been an important local facility for community meetings and events. The one-room Ink Museum commemorates Stephens father and son (Stephens' ink factory was once on the site of the Islington Ecology Centre, *see p101*) The rest of Avenue House is open to view only on certain days of the year – phone for details – but some of the rooms can be hired out, and it's undoubtedly a grand venue for children's parties. Otherwise, the grounds are open free of charge from 7am until dusk, and offer a pleasantly situated playground and buggy-accessible tree trail.

Buggy access. Café (Mar-Sept). Disabled access: toilet. Nappy-changing facilities. Nearest picnic place: Avenue House grounds. Shop.

Jewish Museum, Finchley

Sternberg Centre, 80 East End Road, N3 2SY (8349 1143/www.jewishmuseum.org.uk). Finchley Central tube/143 bus. **Open** 10.30am-5pm Mon-Thur; 10.30am-4.30pm Sun. Closed bank hols, Jewish hols, Sun in Aug. **Admission** (LP) £2; £1 concessions, 12-16s; free under-12s. **No credit cards**.

This more northerly branch of the informative Jewish Museum (*see p94*) focuses on Jewish social history. There's a reconstructed sewing workshop on the ground floor, which gives an idea of sweatshop life in the 19th century, and a display on the evolution of an East End family bagel business. Upstairs, an exhibition traces the life of Leon Greenman, a British Jew who survived Auschwitz. The Holocaust Exhibition may be considered too upsetting for young children, but staff leave it to the discretion of parents; the images are more likely to be understood by kids of at least secondary-school age. A new edition to the museum this year is Kindertransport, the moving story of the rescue of 10,000 children from Nazi Europe.

Buggy access. Café (lunchtimes Mon-Thur). Nearest picnic place: museum garden/Avenue House gardens. Shop.

Further north

The neighbourhoods of Tottenham and Haringey have sizeable Greek-Cypriot, Turkish Cypriot and Kurdish communities. Their respective cultures co-exist reasonably peacably on Green Lanes, where their food-related business success is evident in the kebab shops, olive- and honey filled-supermarkets and bakeries.

Spurs fans willingly make the pilgrimage to the frozen north and White Hart Lane, the home of **Tottenham Hotspur Football Club**, but for ordinary folk a good reason for striking out so northerly is **Bruce Castle**, an island of stateliness in run-down surroundings.

Further west, the North Circular (an escape route or a vehicle trap, depending on traffic) leads to **Brent Cross Shopping Centre** with its large range of chains and a handy crèche, thence to IKEA, purveyor of affordable flatpacks. It's not just the home furnishings that attract people here: take the Edgware Road if you have a yen for Japanese goods. **Oriental City** (399 Edgware Road, NW9 0JJ, 8200 0009) is a mall with several good places to eat, including a big self-service buffet. The shops are fascinating, with wind-dried ducks, odd-looking veg and oriental toiletries, though it's the amusement arcade that children love – and it's a lot less seedy than its counterparts in central London.

There's peace and quiet at the **Welsh Harp Reservoir** (Cool Oak Lane, NW9 3BG, www.brent.gov.uk). This huge body of water was created when a dam was built across the River Brent in the area between Old Kingsbury Church and the Edgware Road between 1833 and 1835. Not just a pretty spot, the Welsh Harp has been recognised as a Site of Special Scientific Interest. The informative environmental centre is a good starting point for nature trips. The leafy waterside areas provide space for games pitches, tennis courts, playgrounds and picnics.

Further north, in Hendon, the extensively revamped **Royal Air Force Museum Hendon** is a lavish tribute to the history of flying machines and the magnificent men who piloted them.

Bruce Castle Museum

Lordship Lane, N17 8NU (8808 8772/ www.haringey.gov.uk). Wood Green tube/Seven Sisters tube/rail, then 123 or 243 bus/Bruce Grove rail. **Open** 1-5pm Wed-Sun. **Admission** free.
This local museum, set in a beautiful 16th-century manor house and holding the entire collections of the borough of Haringey, is much appreciated for its weekend and holiday children's activities. Sunday afternoons (2-4pm) always see some craft session or other in progress; this means adults can peruse the photographs of local streets in Victorian times undisturbed (Muswell Hill as a muddy cart track; quaint shopfronts on north London high streets; rolling green pastures now built over with housing). The building itself was owned by successive generations of the Coleraine family and is said to be haunted by one of them still. More concrete is the lasting influence of Rowland Hill, a progressive schoolmaster on this site and subsequently a postal reformer: his ideas led to the formation of the Penny Post. He is featured in a room devoted to local inventors, which have plenty of buttons to push. Other displays, geared towards the war years, are popular with grandparents. The museum's archives may be visited by appointment; if you live in Haringey, there's a chance your street will be in a historic photo that may be copied to take home. The grounds make for good picnicking; there's a playground and a collection of antique postboxes.
Buggy access. Car park (in Church Lane, free). Disabled access: lift, toilet. Nappy-changing facilities. Shop.

Clown Town

222 Green Lanes, N13 5UD (8886 7520/www.clowntown.co.uk). Southgate tube/W6, 121, 329 bus; The Coppetts Centre, Coppetts Close, N12 0AQ (8361 6600/www.clowntown.co.uk). Arnos Grove tube/ 232 bus. **Open** 10am-7pm daily. **Admission** £3.50 per child; adults free. **No credit cards**.
A three-level multi-activity frame for adventures indoors, Clown Town has aerial runways, rope climbs and a spook room to attract those older children nearer the 1.45m (4.9ft) height limit. Toddlers and babies prefer the ball pond, toy cars and soft-shape toys.
Buggy access.

Royal Air Force Museum Hendon

Grahame Park Way, NW9 5LL (8205 2266/ www.rafmuseum.org). Colindale tube/Mill Hill Broadway rail/303 bus. **Open** 10am-6pm daily. Closed 1 Jan, 24-26 Dec,. *Tours* daily; times vary, phone for details. **Admission** free. *Tours* free. **Credit** MC, V.
The newly renovated RAF Museum makes a brilliant day out. The big exhibits – Camel, Tempest, Gypsy Moth, Mosquito, Harrier and so on – are parked at ground level or hung in dogfight poses from the rafters of the ultra-modern Milestones of Flight Gallery. As you take a break in the café, helicopter blades jut out above your head, while a little further on miniature parachutists go up and down in a tube or drop off a wire into the hands of kids eager to learn about the laws of gravity. More interactive games are available in the Aeronauts Gallery. Who could resist guiding a beach ball through hoops on a stream of hot air, or trying out the controls in a Jet Provost cockpit? Only the flight simulator (over-eights only) carries an extra charge; everything else is free. More low-key than the Milestones of Flight gallery are the atmospheric and dimly lit Battle of Britain Building, and the restored Grahame-White Aircraft Factory, with its pleasing architecture and beautiful biplanes, all string-and-canvas wings and polished wooden propellers.

Activities for children and adults take place all year: workshops include hot-air balloon-making, rocket science, and search and rescue role-playing. The workshops are always very popular, so book ahead. Quizzes, Pulsar Battlezone interactive laser games, face-painting, aircraft displays and giant garden games are also on the cards. The fun-packed Summer Festival Weekend at the end of August is a must.
Buggy access. Café. Disabled access: ramps, toilets. Lift. Nappy-changing facilities. Nearest picnic place: on-site picnic area. Restaurant. Shop.

Tottenham Hotspur Football Club

Bill Nicholson Way, 748 High Road, N17 0AP (8365 5000/ticket office 0870 420 5000/www.spurs.co.uk). White Hart Lane rail. **Open** *Tours* 11am Mon-Sat. **Admission** *Tours* £8; £5 under-16s, OAPs. **Credit** MC, V.
Tours of the pitchside, the tunnel, changing rooms, boardrooms and press rooms take place regularly, but the Saturday ones tend to be booked up well in advance. Tours cannot take place on a match day, nor the day before; indeed their regularity depends on a minimum number of customers, so don't turn up on spec. Tours last about an hour to an hour and a half, depending on how chatty the punters are. Finish in the megastore, where you can blow £50 on a shirt or 50p on a souvenir pencil.
Buggy access. Disabled access: toilet. Shop.

Around Town

East London

It's had some hard knocks, but this rough diamond can really sparkle.

Around Town

Spitalfields & around

The streets surrounding Spitalfields Market – once home to hard-working Huguenot families, whose skills in the silk-weaving trade supported their flight from religious persecution in France – are an architectural delight. Among them is Folgate Street, where you'll find **Dennis Severs' House**. Architectural merit won't mean much to the children, of course – the trick is to lure them to the area with promises of lunch in a Brick Lane curry house, or a burger at Bubba's famous pit barbecue inside the market square (Arkansas Café, *see p176*). The market itself, long a subject of strife between locals and developers, is now partially transformed. For better or worse, it is much smarter, and on Sundays you can browse hundreds of craft and fashion stalls there.

Sunday is without doubt the busiest day of the week in this neighbourhood. Thankfully, the sprawl of market stalls that extended at one point to Shoreditch High Street, petering out into pitiful bundles of cast-offs laid on the pavement, has been pruned back. Now the place to start is the northern end of **Brick Lane** and surrounding streets. Here, in front of some very trendy boutiques selling lifestyle products, chic baby clothes and vintage paraphernalia, you'll find remarkably cheap children's footwear, sports gear, leather jackets, DVDs and so on. (It is said that all the second-hand bicycles are stolen, so examine your conscience before you buy.)

In terms of culture, there is the **Whitechapel Art Gallery** (check for closure dates in 2006 as it is undergoing renovations), occasional exhibitions at Truman's Brewery on Brick Lane and, perhaps, a visit to Nicholas Hawksmoor's beautiful, Grade I-listed Christ Church (7247 7202; 11am-4pm Tue, 1-4pm Sun), which has a serene atmosphere and bags of space to shelter in. On Old Castle Street, the excellent Women's Library (7320 2222, www.thewomenslibrary.ac.uk), a former wash house, holds free exhibitions (9.30am-5.30pm Mon-Wed, Fri; 9.30am-8pm Thur; 10am-4pm Sat), as well as workshops and family activities in the summer holidays. The library holds the best collection relating to women's history in the country. The bright, contemporary Wash House Café on the first floor is a useful pit-stop, even for those with only a cursory interest in gender issues. The striking, rectangular Idea Store, (319-331 Whitechapel Road, E1 1BU, www.ideastore.co.uk) is one of several Idea Stores, a flagship project of Tower Hamlets council. Its ultra modern interior offers a state-of-the-art library, and learning and information services – among them a children's library, café and classrooms.

Off elegant Fournier Street (which runs alongside Christ Church towards Brick Lane), you'll find the minor jewel that is **19 Princelet Street**; unfortunately is open only occasionally. On Whitechapel Road, the **Whitechapel Bell Foundry** runs tours for over-14s. Pop into the foyer to see the huge frame of Big Ben surrounding the door. The **Royal London Hospital Archives & Museum** has more macabre attractions. And in the unprepossessing backstreets behind the hospital, scientists are busy growing tuberculosis and the like (not just for fun – they're researching new cures) in brand-new laboratories. In early 2007, the Centre of the Cell (64 Turner Street, E1 2AB, www.centreof thecell.org.uk) is due to open there too. This futuristic pod, suspended in air right above the boffinry, will contain high-tech exhibits and activities aimed squarely at getting small groups kids of all backgrounds excited about and intimate with cutting-edge medical research.

A tidy step north from Spitalfields you'll find yourself in Shoreditch and Hoxton, now one of London's most vibrant and dynamic social centres. The artists, such as Tracey Emin and Damian Hirst, who made it so, first flocked here in the 1990s because studio rents were cheap. They didn't bring a whole heap of family entertainment with them, however. The **Geffrye Museum**, is a gem, and provides a cultural impetus to visit Kingsland Road, whose other main asset is its plethora of inexpensive Vietnamese restaurants.

Hoxton Square, formerly Hoxton Fields, was where playwright Ben Jonson killed Gabriel Spencer in a duel in 1598. Fearless children will surely be interested in the possibility of a Sunday morning course in tightrope walking, trapeze work and so on at The Circus Space, set in a renovated generating station nearby (Coronet Street, N1, 7613 4141, www.thecircusspace.co.uk).

Whitechapels's **Ideas Store**. *See p106.*

Dennis Severs' House

*18 Folgate Street, E1 6BX (7247 4013/www.dennis
severshouse.co.uk). Liverpool Street tube/rail.* **Open**
2-5pm 1st & 3rd Sun of mth; noon-2pm Mon (following
1st & 3rd Sun of mth); Mon evenings (times vary;
booking required). **Admission** £8 Sun; £5 noon-2pm
Mon; £12 Mon evenings. No under-10s. **Credit** MC, V.
Map p319 R5.

Dennis Severs (1948-1999) is not the man you come to see
in this fully restored Huguenot house close to Spitalfields,
but his mark is on everything. Severs was an American
who came to the UK to study law but who fell in love with
the 18th century and lived in his house, *sans* bathroom,
modern cooking facilities or even electricity. During his
lifetime he narrated tours in which each room – from the
cellar, kitchen, dining room, smoking room and upstairs to
the bedrooms – was the scene of a different drama, covering eras from 1724 to 1914. A slightly laboured conceit
('You either see it or you don't' we are reminded on each
floor) makes a game of any tour here, which doesn't mean
they are suitable for children under ten – they're not.

Making your way around the house in silence, you seem
to chance upon the everyday activities and belongings of
a fictitious family of Huguenot silk-weavers. You may hear
their voices; you certainly feel the warmth of their log fires,
the scent of their pomanders, the gorgeous sheen of their
heavy silk drapes. It's as if the inhabitants only deserted
these rooms a moment before. A half-eaten meal is lovely
to behold – pineapples studded with glacéed fruits, pretty
glasses half-full of madeira, crystal sugar hanging on
strings like a frozen waterfall. Most striking of all is the
quality of light. Even several candles in one room will leave
you groping your way in the dark. Watch out, for this will
be the very moment when you notice the amber eyes of a
black cat staring impassively and rather spookily at you
from behind the bedpost. Equally impressive is the
contrast made between poverty and wealth as depicted,
say, in the chilly attic 'let out to a poor family of weavers',
with its sad items of damp washing strung across the room,
and the rather more comfortable merchants' quarters
below, where a fine tea table is set and the logs in the hearth
crackle. The house is still lived in, and no museum could
provide an experience quite like it.

*Nearest picnic place: Broadgate Circus (Liverpool Street
station) or Elder Street Gardens. Shop.*

Geffrye Museum

*136 Kingsland Road, E2 8EA (7739 9893/www.
geffrye-museum.org.uk). Liverpool Street tube/rail,
then 149, 242 bus/Old Street tube/rail, then 243 bus.*
Open 10am-5pm Tue-Sat; noon-5pm Sun, bank hol Mon.
Closed, 1 Jan, Good Fri, 24-26 Dec. **Admission** free;
donations appreciated. *Almshouse* £2; £1 concessions;
free under-16s. Under-8s must be accompanied by an
adult. **Credit** (restaurant, shop) MC, V.

This attractive, U-shaped building was constructed around
a deep, lawned courtyard as almshouses in 1715. In 1914
the place was converted into a furniture and interior design
museum. Now rooms represent different periods in
history, from the Elizabethan era to the present day, and
visitors walk past in a roped-off corridor, admiring the
changing tastes and styles of succeeding generations. This
is naturally a bit theoretical for young children, who tend
to perceive the displays as barely differentiated living
rooms, but fascinating for any adult interested in the history of design. What keeps the children occupied is a
thoughtful programme of activities. For example, on weekend afternoons there's an art trolley and a quiz desk.

The 17th- and 18th-century rooms were undergoing complete refurbishment as this guide went to press; they will
reopen in autumn 2006. While they are closed, a greater
emphasis is being placed on outdoor fun in the award-winning Herb Garden. The garden is open from April to
October each year, but the airy restaurant that overlooks
it is a pleasure year-round (and serves children's portions).
Summer Sundays take place once a month in June, July and
August, typically involving the making of lavender potions
and so on, with live music and plant sales.

The second, newer, half of the museum has space for
changing exhibitions downstairs; these are usually as
lively as the almshouses are static. From April to
September 2006 there's an audiovisual illusion of a home
by artists called the Light Surgeons. In winter, the
Christmas Past exhibition is always a hit, with each room
decorated for the festive season according to its period. The
museum also stages a Twelfth Night ritual (6 January),
when a Christmas tree is burned to the accompaniment of
cheers and mulled wine.

*Buggy access. Disabled access: lift, toilet. Nappy-
changing facilities. Nearest picnic place: museum
grounds. Restaurant. Shop.*

Around Town

TOP 10 | Eastern treasures

Docklands Light Railway
Not as high as a roller coaster, but just as rickety-feeling and the closest thing to being your own train driver. *See p115.*

Walthamstow Market
The longest in the UK, with 450 stalls selling everything, including endless sparkly bits of tat that kids love. *See p119.*

Thames Barrier Park
Great café, interesting landscape suited to hide-and-seek, now accessible via the DLR. *See p118.*

Mudchute City Farm
London's biggest urban farm's 'rural' setting contrasts with a skyscraper backdrop. See *p116.*

Idea Stores
Fab new-look libraries in Hackney and Tower Hamlets make the traditional public library seem positively Dickensian. *See p106.*

Museum of Childhood
We can't wait until it reopens in late 2006 after a sparkling refurb with great new facilities and displays. *See p111.*

Sutton House
Lively National Trust property with loads of hands-on activities for families. *See p111.*

Lee Valley reservoirs
Vast area of canals, reservoirs and conservation areas accessible by bike and foot. Watch out for the 'elevated Greenway' that promises to connect Olympic sites – may be built by 2007. *See p120.*

Museum in Docklands
The story of London's river, port and people, excitingly told. *See p116.*

Epping Forest
Wilder than Hampstead Heath, bigger than any park in the south or west. *See p121.*

19 Princelet Street
19 Princelet Street, Spitalfields, E1 6QH (7247 5352/ www.19princeletstreet.org.uk). Aldgate East tube/ Liverpool Street tube/rail. **Open** check website or phone for occasional open days. Group tours by appointment. **Admission** free; donations appreciated. **Map** p319 S5. This Grade II-listed building makes an unusual museum. First, it's the only one in Europe dedicated to immigration and cultural diversity. Second, the opening hours are infrequent, to say the least (just 17 days in 2006, including every day in Refugee Week, 18-25 June), in order that the fabric of the fragile building be preserved until trustees raise the £3 million required to open on a more permanent basis. Still, it's worth making an effort to join in on one of its rare open days, as they give you a rare opportunity to see inside this enchantingly crumbly silk merchant's home and hidden Victorian synagogue. No.19 was home to Huguenot silk weavers – you can still see a big bobbin hanging above the door – then to Irish dockers. In 1869 Eastern European Jews converted the house into a synagogue and, in the 20th century, it hosted English lessons for Bangladeshi women.

When families arrive these days, the adults are given a description of the house's history to peruse while they queue, and children get a quiz sheet to guide them round. On the ground floor and in the basement, the main exhibition, Suitcases and Sanctuary, was made by artists in collaboration with local schoolchildren. The kids wrote diary entries from the perspective of Huguenots fleeing persecution, acted out the plight of Irish families escaping the potato famine, and designed posters that might attract West Indian migrants; explainers are on hand to tell you about the house or their own experiences of the working synagogue. Upstairs, temporary exhibitions make the most of the atmospheric coloured skylights. Check the website or phone for details of opening dates and special events. *Buggy access. Nearest picnic place: Christ Church grounds.*

Royal London Hospital Archives & Museum
St Philip's Church, Newark Street, E1 2AA (7480 4823/www.brlcf.org.uk). Whitechapel tube. **Open** 10am-4.30pm Mon-Fri. Closed 24 Dec-2 Jan, bank hols & adjacent Tue. **Admission** free.
Along a backstreet and down some barely noticeable steps is the entrance to this fascinating museum, located in the former crypt of a late 19th century, early English style church, designed by Arthur Cawston, which has been extensively restored. The museum chronicles the history of the big hospital on parallel Mile End Road. The Royal London was founded in 1740 by a 22-year-old surgeon called John Harrison and was once the biggest general hospital in the UK. The 1934 X-ray control unit could have been created by a mad inventor from a sci-fi B-movie, but the museum is mostly a serious-minded affair. The development of nursing and childcare is traced through displays of starchy uniforms such as those worn by Florence Nightingale and war heroine Edith Cavell; there's a replica of the hat former patient Joseph Merrick (the 'Elephant Man') wore to conceal his swollen head and a forensics case with a copy of Jack the Ripper's notorious 'From Hell' letter. Most entertaining, however (and providing a welcome moment of rest if you have been dragging children about on foot all day), are the documentaries shown on a video screen, which date from the 1930s to the 1960s. Presenters speak in plummy, pre-war accents. We see children kitted out in pilot's goggles gratefully receive doses of ultra-violet light after the London smog prevented the natural synthesis of vitamin E, leading to rickets. In the footage keen young nurses talk passionately of their vocations as they cast down their eyes before the great male doctors in white coats. Priceless. *Buggy access. Café (in hospital). Disabled access: lift, ramp, toilet. Nappy-changing facilities (in hospital). Shop.*

Spitalfields City Farm

Weaver Street, off Pedley Street, E1 5HJ (7247 8762/ www.spitalfieldscityfarm.org). Shoreditch or Whitechapel tube. **Open** *Summer* 10am-4.30pm Tue-Sun. *Winter* 10am-4pm Tue-Sun. Closed 25 Dec-1 Jan. **Admission** free; donations appreciated.

Despite the usual funding problems, this is a particularly well-run community farm, established in 1978 after local allotments were lost to property developers. Gradually reorganising some of its land to make way for the East London Line extension, the farm currently has geese honking about, a daily goat-milking demo, mice and rabbits for stroking, and a full complement of cows, pigs and sheep. Poultry, gardeners and all the livestock produce free-range eggs, seasonal vegetables and manure (in that order). Keen eight- to 13-year-olds can join the Young Farmers Club, which runs a playscheme on Saturdays; there's also a jolly parent and toddler group for under-fives (Tue, Sun). Visitors can often enjoy donkey rides (£1) if the donkeys are up for it, and special annual events include a sheep-shearing day, an Eco Fair in July, the Spitalfields Show in September and Apple Day in October.

Buggy access. Disabled access: toilets. Nappy-changing facilities. Nearest picnic place: Allen Gardens. Shop.

Whitechapel Art Gallery

80-82 Whitechapel High Street, E1 7QX (7522 7888/ www.whitechapel.org). Aldgate East tube/15, 25, 254 bus. **Open** 11am-6pm Tue, Wed, Fri-Sun; 11am-9pm Thur. Closed 1 Jan 24-26 Dec. **Tours** 2.30pm Sun; phone to check dates. **Admission** free (variable entrance fee for one exhibition per year). **Map** p319 S6.

A £3.26 million grant from the Heritage Lottery Fund has enabled this cutting-edge art gallery to expand into the building next door, which used to be the public library. The work begins in November 2006 and is expected to last 18 months, during which time the gallery will be closed. The good news, however, is that when it reopens in autumn 2007, the extension will allow for major increases in the space available to the galleries and for school/community events, as well as adding a restaurant to the swish gallery café. The Whitechapel has a strong educational and community programme for children: when the gallery was founded in 1901, Reverend Canon Barnett insisted on it. So, while continuing its proud history of bringing excellent modern art to the East End (the gallery helped revive the fortunes of such then-neglected figures as George Stubbs and, amazingly, JMW Turner, as well as being the first place to exhibit Hockney and Gilbert & George), the Whitechapel has ensured that local schools benefit from a progressive programme of artist residencies, sometimes resulting in collaborative exhibitions. There are also exhibition-specific workshops, and each show is attended by family events and activity packs.

Buggy access. Café. Disabled access: lift, toilet. Nappy-changing facilities. Nearest picnic place: Altab Ali Park. Shop.

Whitechapel Bell Foundry

32-34 Whitechapel Road, E1 1DY (7247 2599/ www.whitechapelbellfoundry.co.uk). **Open** 9.30am-4.30pm Mon-Fri. *Tours* strictly by appointment 10am, 2pm Sat. No under-14s. **Admission** free. *Tours* £8. **Credit** MC, V.

Even if you have no interest in church bells, you'll be impressed by the foundry – Britain's oldest manufacturing company. It has been in continuous production since 1570; its most famous product was the 13.7 tonne Big Ben, cast in the 19th century. Anyone can pop in during office hours to see the little exhibition that illustrates the bell-founding process with miniature figures. A shop can set you up with handsome doorbells, and a handbell room introduces children to the gratifyingly easy techniques of producing music in a group with hand chimes. Tours of the foundry are open only to those aged 14 and over, but friendly staff are always willing to explain their techniques and terminology. 'Clappering', 'change ringing', 'five-tone peals' and so on are soon understood; just as the meaning of popular expressions like 'ringing the changes' is suddenly enhanced.

Disabled access: ramp (ground floor only). Shop.

Bethnal Green to Hackney

'Wiv a ladder, and some glasses
You could see, to 'ackney Marshes
If it wasn't for the 'ouses
In between.'

East of the Spitalfields cluster, the old-style East End begins to reassert itself. You'll find plenty of it on Bethnal Green Road, which is a market street, even on weekdays. Amid the many fast-food eateries, the lovely little caff E Pellicci (No.332, 7739 4873) is worth a visit. A sign in the window may say 'no buggies', but they are often accommodated in its general atmosphere of Italian

Columbia Road Market. *See p110.*

bonhomie. If you can get everyone up and out early enough, Columbia Road Flower Market (between Gosset Road and the Royal Oak pub, 8am-2pm Sun) makes a lovely morning excursion; if the garish colours of tightly packed plants fail to impress, there is the banter of the traders and the live music from pavement buskers adding to the pleasures of smoked-salmon bagels and Bath buns available on every corner. The mighty **Museum of Childhood at Bethnal Green** (www.museumofchildhood.org.uk) is closed for refurbishment until mid November 2006; but just next door, York Hall (Old Ford Road, E2 9PJ, 8980 2243, www.gll.org) has a decent swimming pool.

Hackney has been the subject of plans for improved transport links for well over a decade, and now that London's Olympic bid has been successful, there should be little to prevent the East London Line finally arriving here. In any case, with under-16s getting free bus travel, there's never been a better time to lose the train habit and hop on a north-bound bus.

The centre of Hackney is Town Hall Square on Mare Street, where you'll find the well-preserved old Hackney Empire (www.hackneyempire. co.uk), the cornerstone of Hackney's plan to create a 'cultural quarter'. Also central to this scheme is

Tiny Tudors at **Sutton House**. See p111.

Hackney Museum, housed in the Central Library opposite, and a large-scale local music venue, Ocean, just across the road. The latter went into receivership in 2004 but was due to reopen as this guide went to press.

For somewhere with such a definitively urban reputation, Hackney has a surprising number of green spaces – surprising, that is, until you learn that as late as the 19th century it was almost entirely rural. Adjoining the brilliant **Hackney City Farm**, Haggerston Park (Audrey Street, off Goldsmith Row, E2 8QH, 7739 6288) has pretty gardens beside a large pond, as well as places for ball games and BMX riding, and a spanking new, wood-built playground. Head north up Goldsmith's Row, cross Regent's Canal and you're on Broadway Market. The chi-chi establishments along this strip include chic but friendly gastropub the Cat & Mutton (No.76, 7254 5599, www.catandmutton.co.uk) and Holistic Health (64 Broadway Market, E8 4QJ, 7275 8434, www.holistic-health-hackney.co.uk), specialists in holistic therapies for tots. The area's sleek incomers buy their organic fruit and vegetables at the bustling Saturday farmers' market (www.broadwaymarket.co.uk), which has a dedicated Brat Park Corner. There's a play area with hopscotch, chess and draughts marked out on the ground, and storytelling and face-painting for under-sevens (12.30pm); the Broadway Knitters Club meets here monthly, supplying special giant needles so that children can have a bash. London Fields (Westside, E8) is right at the top of the market.

Further east, across the River Lee, lie 300 acres (120 hectares) of Hackney Marshes, a great place to take the air. It's fine kite-flying country and provides a muddy home for English Sunday League, American and Gaelic football, rugby and cricket. North up the river you'll find the very pretty Springfield Park, which looks east past the narrow boats of Springfield Marina and out over breezy Walthamstow Marshes. Refreshments are available at the child-oriented Springfield Park Café (8806 0444, www.sparkcafe.co.uk), in the White Lodge at the top of the park's steep hill.

Clowns International Gallery & Museum

All Saints Centre, Haggerston Road, E8 4HT (office hours only 0870 128 4336/www.clowns-international.co.uk). Dalston Kingsland or London Fields rail, then 38, 149, 236, 243 bus. **Open** noon-5pm 1st Fri of mth; other times by appointment. **Admission** free; donations appreciated.

Next to a church – where the annual Joseph Grimaldi memorial service is held in February, attended by 60 or more clowns in full motley and slap – is this colourful, one-room gallery devoted to the history of clowns. Manned by enthusiastic members of Clowns International, the gallery holds displays of pottery eggs painted with famous clowns' faces; sequinned and harlequinade costumes; original artworks, vintage posters and endlessly tumbling automata. The plethora of clown images is thought-provoking as well as jolly. 'Clown doctoring' proves to be the art of modern laughter therapy in hospitals; an old wooden 'slap-stick' shows you just how clowns were able to make comic slapping noises without inflicting pain. For details of the summer Clown Social or other events, check the website; the 'find a clown' section also allows you to find local member clowns and junior clowns. To arrange a workshop or school event, phone Mattie Faint on the listed number. *Buggy access. Disabled access: toilet. Nearest picnic place: Stonebridge Common (opposite). Shop.*

Hackney City Farm

1A Goldsmiths Row, E2 8QA (7729 6381/ www.hackneycityfarm.co.uk). Cambridge Heath Road rail, then 26, 48, 55 bus. **Open** 10am-4.30pm Tue-Sun & bank hol Mon. Closed 23 Dec-3 Jan. **Admission** free; donations appreciated.

The cobbled yard of a former brewery is a lovely setting for this inner-city haven. The scent of manure, plus a muted cacophony of clucking, quacking, honking and squeaking, is bound to make nature lovers smile, while occasional flower shows, weekly Indian head massage, children's pottery classes and other wholesome entertainments ensure the venue is lively in summer and winter. The animals are nicely varied: turkeys, geese, ducks, donkeys, rare breed pigs, calves, rabbits and guinea pigs are housed around the courtyard or swish their tails in the fields. The local propensity for bicycle theft (warnings are posted on every wall) is somewhat depressing but there are bike racks inside the farm, and the award-winning organic café, Frizzante (*see p176*), is a homely meeting place for middle-class mummies and babies every lunchtime. Outside, the well-established farm garden is lovely to sit in during summer. A new garden and plant nursery opened in spring 2006. Many keep-fit and craft activities take place at the farm in the evenings and are aimed at parents; children's workshops run throughout the holidays. Keen over-12s can also join the Young Farmers' Club, with activities every second and fourth Saturday of the month. The meeting room is available for children's parties. *Buggy access. Café. Disabled access: ramp, toilet. Nappy-changing facilities. Nearest picnic place: gardens. Shop.*

Hackney Museum

Technology & Learning Centre, 1 Reading Lane, off Mare Street, E8 1GQ (8356 3500/www.hackney. gov.uk). Hackney Central rail. **Open** 9.30am-5.30pm Tue, Wed, Fri; 9.30am-8pm Thur; 10am-5pm Sat. Closed bank hols. **Admission** free.

The Technology and Learning Centre is Hackney's version of an ultra-modern, light and glassy library, also known as an 'Ideas Store'; the museum occupies a sizeable area on the ground floor and is wonderfully accessible to children, who often wander in after school. Hackney's history certainly extends back 1,000 years, but instead of dreary pieces of flint, there's an Anglo Saxon log boat sunk into the floor and, beside it, a replica to load up with plastic fruits and pretend you're paddling off to market. Much is made of the borough's ethnic diversity (by no means a modern phenomenon), with one area devoted to shows put on by different community groups. A Jewish print shop, a traditional eel and pie shop, an air-raid shelter and a tabletop game in which participants move emergency vehicles to bomb sites as quickly as possible using magnetic wands are all part of the permanent displays. In summer 2006, an exhibition on Hackney's parks will involve interactive park-style games, and at all times, touch-screen computers let you trace family history or take a virtual tour of a Victorian house. During the closure of the Museum of Childhood, Hackney Museum will show rotating displays of the former venue's toy collections. There are also free Explorer Pads, full of activities, available at the entrance. Phone or check the website for details of exhibitions and the changing programme of drop-in events (family workshops are usually on the first Saturday of the month). *Buggy access. Café (Fab Food, next door). Disabled access: toilets. Nappy-changing facilities. Nearest picnic place: benches in square/London Fields. Shop.*

Kidzmania

28 Powell Road, Clapton, E5 8DJ (8533 5556). Clapton rail/38, 55, 56, 106, 253 bus. **Open** 10am-6pm daily. **Admission** £4 4-12yrs; £3.50 under-3s. **No credit cards.**

This indoor adventure centre is perfect for use as a children's party venue and activity centre. Kidzmania offers a safe and fun soft playcentre for children and has full on-site catering (special party menus can be prepared). There are ball rooms, slides and bouncy castles. *Buggy access. Café. Nearest picnic place: Hackney Downs*

Museum of Childhood at Bethnal Green

Cambridge Heath Road, E2 9PA (8983 5200/recorded info 8980 2415/www.museumofchildhood.org.uk). Bethnal Green tube/rail. **Open** 10am-5.50pm Mon-Thur, Sat, Sun. **Closed** daily until November 2006; 1 Jan 24-26 Dec. **Admission** free. Under-12s must be accompanied by an adult.

Note that the Museum of Childhood is closed until mid-November 2006. Established in 1872, as part of the V&A the Museum is now the UK's biggest collection of toys and childhood paraphernalia. You can enjoy neat cabinets that display board games, early electronic toys, puppets from all over the world and children's clothes from various periods. The huge doll's houses on the first floor draw a lingering crowd. The 'Good Times' play area, with its dressing-up box, sandbox and pier-end wonky mirrors sitting happily alongside interactive computer stations, was part of the last round of refurbishments completed in 2003.

The next stage, financed by a £3.5m grant from the Heritage Lottery Fund, will see a brand-new entrance hall, more space for community projects, and refurbished displays in the mezzanine galleries. *Buggy access. Café. Disabled: lift, ramps, toilet. Nappy-changing facilities. Nearest picnic place: museum grounds. Shop.*

Sutton House

2 & 4 Homerton High Street, E9 6JQ (8986 2264/ www.nationaltrust.org.uk). Bethnal Green tube, then 106 bus/Hackney Central rail. **Open** 12.30-4.30pm Thur-Sun (last entry 4pm). *Café & Gallery* noon-4.30pm Thur-Sun. Closed 23 Dec 2006-31 Jan 2007. **Admission** (NT) £2.50; 50p 5-16s; free under-5s; £5.50 family (2+2). *Tours* free, phone for details. **Credit** MC, V.

Around Town

This surprisingly child-friendly and handsome National Trust property offers a lot more than oak panelling and august portraits, though these are also splendid. Built of brick at a time when most houses were wattle and daub (1535), it was originally know as 'The Bryk Place'. Down some rickety steps in the cellar is a fascinating little exhibition explaining how bricks were made locally from 'brickearth', the sediment whipped up by winds at the end of the last Ice Age. At the very top of the house is an archive room where youngsters can access pictures of Hackney on computer, play with period toys and games and read panels about the Tudors, Georgians and so on in accordance with the school curriculum. In between are nicely differentiated rooms with harpsichords, tea sets, scratched drawings behind secret panels, spot-the-difference carvings, half- obliterated paintings of mythical beasts, and kitchen drawers that invite you to feel their contents through hand holes before opening them to see if your guess was correct. To help families enjoy these rooms, a free activity pack, designed for children aged three to 11, can be booked out from the Sutton House shop. The café is Hackney's best-kept secret and looks out through conservatory windows on to a school playground, so the entertainment at lunch is all skipping and hopping. A lively events programme features music, arts and crafts most weeks, with free family activity days on the last Sunday of each month.
Café. Disabled access: toilet. Nappy-changing facilities. Nearest picnic place: St John's churchyard. Shop.

Mile End to West Ham

The nondescript council estates that gather around the arterial Mile End Road would encourage few people to come here, but Mile End has two impressive parks: **Victoria Park** and **Mile End Park**, with the additional attraction of the **Ragged School Museum** nearby. The organic pub the Crown (223 Grove Road, E3, 8981 9998) overlooks Victoria Park, and Mile End Park has a plethora of affordable eateries below its 'green bridg. Towards town, you'll also find **Stepping Stones Farm**, with Stepney Green's bijou playground practically next door.

Further east is Bow, named in the 12th century after a bow-shaped bridge, built because Queen Mathilde (Henry I's wife) almost drowned trying to cross the River Lee. Here you'll find industrial heritage that predates the Victoriana – grain was being unloaded from boats for grinding at Three Mills as early as the 11th century – and then the new-look Stratford, the focal point for ambitious regeneration plans that will take in all of east London. Gerry Raffles Square provides both a cinema and the Theatre Royal Stratford East (8534 0310, www.stratfordeast.com), famous for its pantomimes. On the other side of the bus station lies Stratford's only die-cast kids' attraction: **Discover**. West Ham Park provides breathing space; there's a museum at **West Ham United Football Club**; and the stalls at Queen's Market (Tue, Thur-Sat) give Green Street a bit of zing.

Discover

1 Bridge Terrace, E15 4BG (8536 5563/www.discover. org.uk). Stratford tube/rail/DLR. **Open** *Termtime* 10am-5pm Tue-Sun. *School hols* 10am-5pm daily. **Admission** *Garden* free. *Story Trail* £3.50; £2.50 concessions; free under-2s. **Credit** MC, V.
In an area strikingly devoid of greenery or playspaces, this community-driven children's centre is an unexpected delight. Developed from a piece of wasteland in collaboration with local children, artists, musicians and others, Discover is an interactive 'story trail' that encourages the under-eights to give their imagination free rein. Outside, the Story Garden is a handsomely designed playground with monster's tongue-slide, raised stream, wooden playship and futuristic space vehicle. Inside, the principal character is a baby space monster called Hootah; children are told she visiting from the faraway planet, Squiggly Diggly, on a mission to collect new stories and take them home. To this end, kids are invited to stand in various Hootah 'cones', a sort of hairdryer affair that plays example stories and records any that the user cares to invent. In an atmosphere that is impressively calm as well as fun, children go on a trail involving a Lollipopter, an indoor river full of twinkling lights and a wooden footbridge that shouts 'Trip', 'Trap', baas like a sheep and gobbles like a troll. Inside the many low, softly lit 'caves' are machines that allow you to hear your own echo, manipulate string puppets or appear instantaneously onscreen in a film shot in the garden. Craft activities include making puppets with wooden spoons. In short, nothing is beyond this space for a child with a fertile imagination. Regular weekend drop-in activities include Stories in a Bag, during which children and a Story Builder create a tale using a random selection of objects, while bookable events for half-terms and holidays may include mask-making and home-made puppet shows. Discover also does parties for a gratifyingly low price of £6.50 per head.
Buggy access. Disabled access: ramp, toilet. Nappy-changing facilities. Nearest picnic place: ground-floor area. Shop.

Mile End Park

Locksley Street, E14 7EJ (7364 4147/children's park 7093 2253). Mile End tube. **Open** 24hrs daily.
Admission free.
Mile End Park is for many the quintessential modern urban park. The south end of the park has a great playground (funded by HSBC to the tune of £2m), with rope slide, scrambling wall, complicated climbing frame, swings and see-saw, as well as a dedicated area for under-fives. The Play Park is now enhanced by a refreshments kiosk and toilet, and the Play Pavilion hosts 'stay and play' sessions (phone for details). A little to the north, the go-kart track provides thrills and spills for older children, and the Adventure Park opened two years ago. There's a fully staffed drop-in centre for 11- to 17-year-olds, along with a dark-green youth shelter for teenagerly hanging out – the solar-powered lighting is indicative of the park's commitment to meeting environmental concerns. Placid strolls can be taken past the pretty fountain in the terraced gardens and over the 'green bridge' spanning Mile End Road, complete with trees growing above the passing traffic. Regent's Canal runs up the western side of the park, with bird life, cyclists and local fishermen in more-or-less happy coexistence. North of Mile End Road, thrill-seekers will find Mile End Climbing Wall (Haverfield Road, E3 5BE, 8980 0289) and nature lovers are able to potter around tranquil ponds

at the centre of the Arts Park and Ecological Park (pumped using power from a 9m- (30ft) tall wind turbine). The park also has a number of praiseworthy educational and community development aims, bringing sculptures into the park and holding temporary exhibitions (there's a children's art expo planned for the summer). The Mile End Town & Country Show (mid June 2006) offers a plethora of attractions, ranging from donkey cart rides and square dancing to weaving demonstrations, falconry displays and the opportunity to make your own boat… and, worryingly, to test it on the eco-ponds.
Buggy access. Café. Disabled access: toilets. Nearest picnic place: ground-floor area.

Ragged School Museum

46-50 Copperfield Road, E3 4RR (8980 6405/ www.raggedschoolmuseum.org.uk). Mile End tube. **Open** 10am-5pm Wed, Thur; 2-5pm 1st Sun of mth. Closed 24 Dec-1 Jan. *Tours* by arrangement; phone for details. **Admission** free; donations appreciated.

Any child who complains of boredom in the modern classroom deserves a trip to this museum, where s/he will be dressed in Edwardian cap and pinny, sat at an old wooden desk in strict rows with his/her classmates and instructed by a severe, costumed mistress to chant the lesson: as in 'H-A-T, hat! S-H-O-P, shop!' and so on. In fact, school groups seem to enjoy this regime – at least for a short time. The serious message is that life was tough for poor or orphaned children in the late 19th century. Dr Barnardo was the philanthropist who converted these particular canalside warehouses in 1877 into what became the largest of London's ragged schools. A typically sparse Victorian classroom has been recreated on the first floor, while the second floor has a replica Edwardian kitchen, with a fine array of outmoded domestic appliances (hand-turned meat mincers and toasting forks, for example). It's gratifying to hear the gasps of young visitors instructed in the art of boiling water in a large, heavy kettle on an open range for use in a tin bath requiring 12 or 15 kettle-fuls of water – and that's before getting started on the laundry. The local-history exhibition on the ground floor, Tower Hamlets: A Journey through Time, will be of more interest to adults than children, but if they live locally they may feel wistful about the lido that once enlivened Victoria Park in summer, and there is a humbling photograph of children queuing patiently for 'farthing bundles' of toys before the war. Another exhibition, Home, recalls family life in the 1950s with particular reference to the Ocean Estate, Stepney. In the basement you'll find the Towpath Café. Family workshops on the first Sunday of each month give members of the public access to the re-enactments, while school holidays offer structured, themed events for children: under-sixes can enjoy arts and crafts activities, storytelling and sometimes cookery and music sessions; trails and workshops entertain the six to 12s. The shop specialises in East End history and has an impressive selection of books on the subject.
Buggy access (ground floor only). Disabled access: toilet. Nappy-changing facilities. Nearest picnic place: Mile End Park. Shop.

Stepping Stones Farm

Stepney Way (junction with Stepney High Street), E1 3DG (7790 8204). Stepney Green tube. **Open** *Apr-mid Oct* 10.30am-4pm Tue-Sun, bank hols. *Mid Oct-Mar* 10.30am-dusk Tue-Sun, bank hols. **Admission** free; donations appreciated.

Punctuated by ruined walls and a hillock on which sheep graze, this sprawling farm is part allotments, part animal enclosures – and there are lots of animals. The larger ones come in twos, ark-style. A couple of donkeys grace the entrance opposite a toddlers' play area full of plastic tractors; two cows stand in a big field on the other side. Smaller animals are to be found in a pleasing muddle: long-eared rabbits sitting among bantams, ferrets and stoats standing up to look at you from inside their hutches, chickens and pigs amiably eating together. It's not the tidiest of farms, but old railway carriages full of straw bales look poetic and, just opposite, St Dunstan's Church makes a lovely antique backdrop. There's also a wildlife pond and picnic area, and the activities room is stocked with arts and crafts materials. Annual events include an Easter egg hunt, Christmas on the Farm and ever-popular summer weekend activities; phone for details.
Buggy access. Café. Disabled access: toilet. Nappy-changing facilities. Shop.

Three Mills Island

Lea Rivers Trust, Three Mill Lane, E3 3DU (River Lee Tidal Mill Trust 8980 4626/schools programmes 8981 0040/www.leariverstrust.co.uk). Bromley-by-Bow tube. **Open** *House Mill* May-Nov 2-5pm Sun. Phone to check other times. *Funday Sundays* Mar-Dec 11am-5pm 1st Sun of mth. **Admission** *Mill* £2; free under-16s (incl tour). **No credit cards.**

The House Mill, built in 1776, is the oldest and largest tidal mill left standing in Britain. It was used to grind the grain for gin distilling. Taken over in 1989 as part of a big restoration project by the Tidal Mills Trust, it now has a visitors' centre that provides a history of the area, maps for walkers, a little souvenir shop and a café. Outside, Riverside Green and Three Mills Green are pleasant for picnicking and strolling. The first Sunday of the month is Funday Sunday (usually Mar-Dec, phone to confirm), during which children are able to take part in a variety of workshops, often with some sort of an environmental theme. The Christmas Fayre (early December) usually attracts huge numbers of people.
Buggy access. Café. Disabled access: lift, toilet (in Tesco if House Mill is closed). Nearest picnic place: Riverside Green/Three Mills Green.

Victoria Park

Old Ford Road, E3 5DS (8985 1957/www.tower hamlets.gov.uk). Mile End tube/Cambridge Heath or Hackney Wick rail/8, 26, 30, 55, 253, 277, S2 bus. **Open** 6am-dusk daily. Closed 25 Dec.

Victoria Park was opened in 1845 after demands for more public space were met with an extraordinarily generous £100,000 in donations. With wide carriageways, lampposts and wrought-iron gates, the park was conceived as the Regent's Park of the East End, and is the largest area of formal parkland this side of town. Poverty-stricken locals made good use of the park's two lakes as baths, but somehow there are still fish in the Western Lake (you can help deplete the stock by getting a free fishing licence); Britain's oldest Model Boat Club convenes around the other lake, near Crown Gate East, every second Sunday. There's a fallow deer enclosure on the east side, and tennis courts, a bowling green, and football, hockey and cricket pitches. Stop off for refreshments at the Lakeside Pavilion Café and watch the geese, swans and ducks play under the fountain.
Buggy access. Café. Disabled access: toilets. Nappy-changing facilities.

Around Town

Newham City Farm. *See p118.*

West Ham Park

Upton Lane, E7 9PU (8472 3584/www.cityoflondon. gov.uk). Stratford tube/rail/104, 238 bus. **Open** 7.30am-30mins before dusk daily.

West Ham Park was opened with much aplomb in 1874. It was designated 'open public grounds and garden for adults, children and youth' and decreed that the City of London should maintain the Park forever at its own expense. Today West Ham Park is as neat and civilised as ever, with pretty ornamental gardens and lovely trees. It's one of the few London parks to have its own plant nursery. The playground, which has a full-time attendant in summer, has some impressive climbing apparatus, a wooden prairie locomotive to clamber on and a Wendy house corner. There are 12 tennis courts (the annual tennis clinic is held in June), three cricket nets (Essex CCC run free training for under-16s in July), two match-quality cricket tables, two football pitches (one all-weather), a running track and a rounders area. The pre-war paddling pool (late May-Aug) is another attraction. From late July to August there are children's events on Monday and Friday afternoons; a bouncy castle arrives each Wednesday; and there are occasional Sunday concerts. An ice-cream van lingers tantalisingly close to the playground (from noon daily, Easter to Oct).

Buggy access. Disabled access: toilet. Nappy-changing facilities.

West Ham United Football Club

Boleyn Ground, Green Street, E13 9AZ (8548 2748/ www.whufc.com). Upton Park tube. **Open** *Museum/ shop* 9.30am-5pm Mon-Sat; phone to confirm. Closed 25 Dec. **Admission** *Museum* £6; £4 concessions, 5-16s; free under-5s; £15 family (2+2). *Tours* £10; £5 concessions, 5-16s; free under-5s. **Credit** MC, V.
West Ham United is celebrating its return to the Premiership with a refurbishment of the museum. So far, it has cost a cool £4 million and tells the story of the club from its origins in 1895 as the Thames Iron Works FC through glory days under Ron Greenwood to the ups and downs of the present. Those who aren't fans of the claret and blue go for the Champions Collection: it includes the World Cup winners' medals of Sir Geoff Hurst, Bobby Moore and Martin Peters. Book in advance if you're visiting on a match day. With the refurbishment in progress, opening times may be erratic, and admission prices are also under review. Visitors are advised to phone first. *Bars. Buggy access. Disabled access: toilet. Shop.*

Docklands

In the decade since the 1990s recession, Docklands has become a rather chipper destination. More than just the modern alternative to a City address for financiers, this part of London has plenty of entertainment options, even for visitors whose suits are still in the wardrobe – though the thicket of tower blocks now crowding iconic Canary Wharf Tower proves the bankers are still here in numbers. The best way to get around Docklands is on the Docklands Light Railway (DLR; 7363 9700, www.tfl.gov.uk/dlr). With various extensions over the years, the DLR now reaches from Bank in the City to Beckton in the east, and from Lewisham south of the Thames to Stratford to the north. The real beauty of the network is that much of it runs on raised tracks, making the journey a sightseeing pleasure. Pick quiet times (weekdays after 10am and before 5pm) and the kids can sit in the front windows of the train and pretend to drive.

To take things a step more touristy, and make the most of this riverside destination, snap up a Rail & River Rover ticket (£10.50 adult, £5.25 children, free under-5s, £65 family), which combines travel on the DLR with trips on City Cruises sightseeing boats (*see p30*). Disembark at Tower Pier to check out the marina of St Katharine Docks, with its flashy yachts and Thames barges. Then stroll the ten minutes past Tower Bridge and the Tower of London (for both, *see p52*) to the DLR station at Tower Gateway. Alternatively, stay on board and enjoy the views until you reach Greenwich Pier (for Greenwich's numerous attractions, *see p125*), then take the DLR back under the river for more sightseeing on the Isle of Dogs. If you want to dock at Canary Wharf itself, there's a fast commuter service.

The westernmost point to fall under the Docklands banner is Wapping (the name derives from Wapol, old English for marsh). It's now very des res, but until well into the 19th century, convicted pirates were brought at low tide to Execution Dock (at Wapping New Stairs), hanged and left in chains until three tides had washed over them. A rather new-looking noose dangles from the 16th-century Prospect of Whitby pub (57 Wapping Wall, E1, 7481 1095), which has a splendid riverside courtyard. A couple of pirate ships (sadly, you can't board either) reside in dry docks by the ornamental canal at the usually deserted Tobacco Docks mall. Food options here all point in one direction: the newly opened and much appreciated Lilly's (75 Wapping High Street, E1, 7702 2040), which blends seamlessly into the vista of chic warehouse conversions, serving brunch on weekends and excellent comfort food, from lamb shanks to fish and chips, the rest of the time. Big leather booths make for comfy family dining too. Between Wapping and the Isle of Dogs is Limehouse, so called because medieval lime kilns once stood here. A century ago this was a bustling commercial port; now it's a marina with posh yachts and jolly narrowboats, surrounded by luxury flats. The impressively lofty white church north-east of the basin, St Anne's Limehouse, was designed by Hawksmoor between 1712 and 1724; the kids will probably manage to raise a little interest for the man-sized pyramid in the north-west corner of the churchyard. More importantly, the basin is a good starting point for canal walks: head north up Regent's Canal for Mile End Park (*see p112*), or take a longer walk north-east on Limehouse Cut to Three Mills Island (*see p113*).

The Isle of Dogs is the pre-eminent destination for visitors – not something many people would have said during the docks' long years of post-war decline, nor during the divisive redevelopments of the 1980s. You can explore all the area's history, as well as such arcane areas of debate as to whether the Isle of Dogs is an island and what dogs have to do with it (answers: not really, not much), at the excellent **Museum in Docklands**. It stands in a row of converted warehouses, most of them cafés of one sort or another, on a cobbled quayside overlooking the water – lovely in bright weather, if a little windy. The museum is across the bouncing bridge (it's supported on floats) from Cabot Square, which looks up at Canary Wharf.

The impact of Cesar Pelli's 244-metre-high (800-foot) monster edifice, actually called One Canada Square, may have been diminished by the duller buildings that now surround it, but it's still a stunner. Tables outside Carluccio's Caffè (Nash Court, E14 5AJ, 7719 1749) provide a good vantage

Around Town

point if you're peckish. The kids might enjoy finding artworks along Canary Wharf's public sculpture trail (click the 'Lifestyle' link at www.canarywharf.com or phone 7418 2000 for a map). They include bits of floor or wall or more impressive pieces like Pierre Vivant's Traffic Light Tree, and oddities like Constance de Jong's Speaking of the River – riverside benches with concealed loudspeakers in the arms, triggered when people sit down. The fountain in Cabot Square is lovely, and there are benches, but the Japanese Garden beside the Jubilee Line tube station is the best place to picnic. There are chain shops in the mall (Gap Kids, HMV), as well as a Waitrose and a Marks & Spencer for the sandwich ingredients. Indeed, when you see how peaceful the pristine Docklands shopping malls are at weekends, you may well wonder why you don't patronise them instead of your local shopping centre; the contrast is wonderfully relaxing.

A south-bound DLR ride from Canary Wharf takes you to Mudchute, once just a dump of silt dug out of Millwall Dock. In the 1970s locals fought off property developers to ensure the place was preserved as an unlikely park and natural habitat, with lovely **Mudchute City Farm** the principal result. There's also an uninspiring playground by the station and lots of flat green grass for running about on. You can walk to Island Gardens (cross the main road from the eponymous station) with its unbeatable view of Greenwich over the Thames. There's also the spookily drippy and echoing Victorian foot tunnel under the river; the attendant-operated lifts (7am-7pm Mon-Sat, 10am-5.30pm Sun) are large enough for a fleet of buggies, but it's quite a long walk through to the Cutty Sark (see p126). You're not allowed to cycle through the tunnel.

Mudchute City Farm

Pier Street, Isle of Dogs, E14 3HP (7515 5901/ www.mudchute.org). Crossharbour, Mudchute or Island Gardens DLR. **Open** 9am-4pm daily. Closed 25 Dec-1 Jan. **Admission** free; donations appreciated.
Mudchute offers what is surely East London's most surreal experience: standing in a vast meadow full of cows that may or may not be bulls, while taking in, beyond the fence that could be your nearest escape route, the New York-style skyscrapers of Canary Wharf. By far the largest of the city farms, Mudchute is perhaps best approached from Mudchute station, where you are obliged to walk on a raised path past parkland and allotments, spying the llamas only sporadically through the trees as you trudge. It seems to be, as your small companions might point out, 'the country here.' The closer you get, the more audible the sounds of farm animals such as ducks, chickens and pigs. But a level of sponsorship from wealthy local businesses has also equipped this farm with a serious equestrian centre, and everything is spick and span. Local kids can join the pony club or Young Farmers' Club, and everyone,

wherever they live, can enjoy summer arts and crafts workshops and play schemes. There's a small aviary and petting corner for cuddling guinea pigs and bunnies, a volunteer-run café (usually open mid morning to early afternoon) and, during school hols, a shop for cannily selected model farm toys and riding accessories. The farm is also a charming site for a 64-place nursery (10am-5pm Wed-Sun), along with a garden centre specialising in plants for urban gardens.
Buggy access. Café. Disabled access: toilet. Nappy-changing facilities. Shop.

Museum in Docklands

No.1 Warehouse, West India Quay, Hertsmere Road, E14 4AL (0870 444 3857/recorded info 0870 444 3856/www.museumindocklands.org.uk). Canary Wharf tube/West India Quay DLR. **Open** 10am-6pm daily. Closed 1 Jan, 24-26 Dec. **Admission** (annual ticket, allows for multiple visits) £5; £3 concessions; free under-16s. **Credit** MC, V.
This £15m museum, which shares its collection with the Museum of London (see p51), is housed in a beautiful, Grade I-listed Georgian warehouse overlooking the cobbled quayside. Spread over three floors, the museum tells the story of 'London's river, port and people' from Roman times to the Docklands redevelopment. First, Tony Robinson enthusiastically narrates the city's Roman history on a series of touch screens. Then you pass models of London Bridge, narwhal tusks, a dangling gibbet cage and a reconstructed quay. The business of importing goods by boat over the centuries is illustrated everywhere with reconstructed coffee and tea offices, vast weighing machines, coils of rope, model ships and computer diagrams of the lock systems used in the docking process. Most impressive for children is Sailortown, a gloomy and foul-smelling alleyway depicting the Victorian sailors' murky milieu, complete with pub and poky front room. The Docklands at War gallery is as moving as it is vivid – much helped by period black and white footage. Sections covering more recent history include a discussion of the effects of containerisation and an environmental gallery detailing the wildlife that lives along the river, as well as a fun, push-button display on the river and recycling. The reward for taking in so much information is surely the Mudlarks Gallery, which is so popular that (free) entry is by timed ticket. There, under-12s can build Canary Wharf Tower out of soft-play bricks, try to balance cargo in the hull of a clipper, try on a deep-sea diver's helmet or dig around in the wonderfully messy Foreshore Discovery Box, with its archaeological treasures buried in gravel and flowing water. Under-fives have their own soft-play area. A plethora of events run by the museum includes dramatic narratives from costumed actors playing, for example, the pub landlady in Sailortown or an Asian sailor, and holiday and half-term craft and handling events; check the website for details or to join the mailing list.
Buggy access. Café. Disabled access: lift, toilet. Nappy-changing facilities. Nearest picnic place: quayside benches, refectory. Restaurant. Shop.

SS Robin Gallery

SS Robin Trust, West India Quay, Hertsmere Road, E14 4AE (7538 0652/www.ssrobin.org). West India Quay DLR. **Open** Feb-Nov noon-6pm Wed-Fri; noon-4pm Sat. **Admission** free. **Credit** AmEx, MC.
The *SS Robin* Trust is a registered arts, educational and heritage charity housed on board the newly restored cargo

Memories of China: Limehouse tales

The Gerrard Street Chinatown, bustling with restaurants and shops, has a short history – it developed in the post-war period largely as a result of the new fashion for Chinese food. But the Chinese presence in London goes back much further than that. London's original Chinatown grew up in east London, around Limehouse, in the latter half of the 19th century, to provide a home for a transient population of Chinese sailors.

It was an insular community, and overt racism and the language barrier helped keep it that way. Most English people had no real notion of Chinese culture – instead, they built up a picture based on the lively novels of the period. Key to their plots were contemporary images of the Chinese as opium traffickers, white slavers and sexual predators preying on innocent white girls. To the average Englishman or woman, Limehouse was a sinister quarter, and its denizens, the mysterious 'Chinks', the epitome of the dangerous Other.

Sax Rohmer boosted the notoriety of Limehouse by making it the headquarters of his evil genius, Fu Manchu, criminal mastermind: 'Imagine a person, tall, lean and feline, high-shouldered, with a brow like Shakespeare and a face like Satan, a close-shaven skull, and long, magnetic eyes of the true cat-green. Invest him with all the cruel cunning of an entire Eastern race, accumulated in one giant intellect... the yellow peril incarnate in one man,' he wrote in *The Insidious Fu Manchu*. Thomas Burke was a little kinder. His bestselling collection of Chinatown love stories, *Limehouse Nights*, published in 1916, summed up the thrilling, exotic, oriental otherness of Limehouse, captured in earlier works of fiction such as Oscar Wilde's *The Picture of Dorian Gray* (1891) and Conan Doyle's *The Man With the Twisted Lip* (1887): 'There was the blue moon of the Orient. There, for the bold, were the sharp knives, and there, for those who would patiently seek, was the lamp of the young Aladdin.'

East London had two main concentrations of the Chinese population: Limehouse Causeway and neighbouring Pennyfields, where – more sober accounts often related – Chinese men set up shops, laundries and cafés, worked hard and played a little mah jong, interspersed with smoking pipes of opium. Hostility erupted into violence on occasion in these neighbourhoods. Resentment over the Chinese workers 'signing on' with ships in the port as their money ran out, plus hostility towards the inevitable mixed marriages that arose in a community devoid of Chinese women, led to riots in the early years of the 20th century. In 1908 and 1912 English sailors attacked Chinese workers as they attempted to sign on outside the East India Dock trade offices.

But the wider demonisation of the Chinese was as much related to the criminalisation of drug-taking as to intermarriage and competition for jobs. In the early 19th century, opium and its derivatives had been sold legally and widely tolerated. The advent of the temperance movement changed all that. And since the Chinese were often the source of opium, the feeling that they controlled such a wicked trade seemed to strike at the very heart of British society and Empire.

These days little or nothing remains of architectural interest in Limehouse to inspire visitors seeking the old Chinatown. The best way to explore the history of the Chinese in this part of London, then, is to revel in the literature and photographs of the late Victorian and Edwardian eras. Images of crime, opium dens and gambling joints blur the reality of a small workaday immigrant community that only reached 600 people at its peak before World War I. Both impossibly romantic and hellish, the Limehouse slums of the lurid Victorian imagination – and the so-called 'yellow peril' who lived in them – held a perverse appeal.

hold of the *SS Robin* – the world's oldest complete steamship. World-class temporary documentary photography exhibitions take place here from February to November. One of the latest projects, in conjunction with *The Times* Education Supplement, uses the theme of identity and relates to the government's plans to introduce identity cards in the UK. Children are asked to imagine that they could take their own picture, and asked what would it look like? Would it be a self-portrait or a picture of a favourite friend, food or clothing? A digital camera is provided to enable the kids to take pictures and explore the ways we define ourselves. A competition will be run, and winning entries and 'best of the rest' will feature as a gallery on the TES website and as an exhibition at the *SS Robin* Gallery. The forecastle of the ship, previously the ship's crew accommodation, is currently being restored by volunteer conservation team and is due to become a dedicated classroom in 2006.
Bookshop. Café. Nearest picnic place: Cabot Square.

East of Docklands

The DLR splits after Westferry station: one branch goes south via Island Gardens station to Lewisham in south-east London (*see p129*), the other east via Poplar to Beckton. At the end of 2005 a new spur of the network opened, which runs directly from Canning Town via London City Airport and the marvellous **Thames Barrier Park**. Even if you are not flying out of the country, the view of the airport, with its landing strip poised between the two docks still full of water, is impressive.

Meanwhile over Connaught Bridge, on the north side of Royal Albert Docks, is the London Regatta Centre (Dockside Road, E16 2QD, 7511 2211). Sit

Around Town

and watch rowers puff and pant, or planes taking off and landing at the airport, from the Regatta Centre's restaurant and bar. A footbridge over Royal Albert Way takes you into Beckton District Park (Stansfeld Road, E6 5LT, 8430 2000 ext 23639), which has a wild-flower meadow and woodland walk, plus a good-sized lake at its northern end. The Millennium Tree Trail takes you past 50 trees from five different continents. There are play areas, cricket and football facilities, a trim trail and a summer snack kiosk.

To the south, **North Woolwich Old Station Museum** is next to the North Woolwich Silverlink station, near the tidy Royal Victoria Gardens. A foot tunnel to the south bank that takes you to **Firepower** (*see p130*), but the free Woolwich ferry (8921 5968, www.greenwich.gov.uk), which takes pedestrians and cars across the river every 10 minutes daily, is always fun.

Eastbound, Beckton is the last DLR stop. Lovers of the outdoors are well served by Docklands Equestrian Centre (2 Claps Gate Lane, E6 7JF, 7511 3917), the little **East Ham Nature Reserve** and **Newham City Farm**. Otherwise, Beckton is mainly new builds and retail parks.

East Ham Nature Reserve

Norman Road, E6 4HN (8470 4525). East Ham tube/ Beckton DLR. **Open** *Nov-Feb* 10am-5pm Tue-Fri; 1-4pm Sat, Sun. *Mar-Oct* 10am-5pm Mon-Fri; 2-5pm Sat, Sun. Closed bank hols. **Admission** free.
The East Ham Nature Reserve combines a little museum with the largest churchyard in London, with beguilingly shaggy nature trails. The museum comprises two rooms: one contains an 1893 schoolroom to terrify the kids, a wartime kitchen to terrify the mums and a real incendiary bomb that will help nobody relax; the other has a case of stuffed birds and mammals, all looking a bit weary, plus a case each of beetles and butterflies.
Buggy access. Disabled access: toilet. Nearest picnic place: grounds.

Newham City Farm

Stansfeld Road, E16 3RD (7474 4960/recorded info 7476 1170). Royal Albert DLR/262, 300, 376 bus. **Open** *Summer* 10am-5pm Tue-Sun, bank hols. *Winter* 10am-4pm Tue-Sun. Closed 1 Jan, 25 Dec. **Admission** free; donations appreciated.
Having taken on extra staff in the last year, Newham City Farm is now open six days a week. The farmyard animals (a shire horse, cows, Kune Kune pigs, sheep, goats, poultry) take centre stage, but there are also littler chaps (rabbits, guinea pigs, a ferret) and a house of finches, a kookaburra and a buzzard. The farm's school programme is well established, and there are plans to improve the facilities for casual visitors. There are picnic areas and, depending on volunteer availability, refreshments. Fun days offer the likes of sheep-shearing demonstrations, rides on a shire-horse-drawn cart and felt-making. The Young Volunteer scheme gets kids involved.
Buggy access. Café. Disabled access: toilets. Nearest picnic place: grounds.

North Woolwich Old Station Museum

Pier Road, E16 2JJ (7474 7244/www.newham.gov.uk). North Woolwich rail/101, 473, 474 bus. **Open** *Jan-Nov* 1-5pm Sat, Sun. *Newham school holidays* 1-5pm daily. **Admission** free. **No credit cards**.
The Old Station Museum is a low-key affair, but at certain times in the school holidays can prove a highly entertaining day out. The museum contains carefully preserved old engines, timetables, signs and other relics from the age of steam travel. There's an old ticket office and plenty of models and information, but the children will probably tire of that and clamour to rush round to the back and poke around Coffee Pot (a Victorian commuter train from the 1890s) and Pickett (from the 1940s). They can climb all over Dudley the Diesel, which will sometimes even be able to take them for a spin (nothing too adventurous, just along the platform and back). There's outside play equipment and, indoors, a Brio layout, a computer running a Thomas the Tank Engine programme, and the Hornby Virtual Railway. The museum's small shop sells souvenirs and snacks. During school holidays, drop-in Wednesday afternoon arts and crafts sessions keep fledgling railway buffs amused. Staff permitting, there are weekend soft-play sessions (1.30-2.30pm). Do ring before you set out, however.
Buggy access. Disabled access: ramps, toilets. Nappy-changing facilities. Shop.

Thames Barrier Park

Barrier Point Road, off North Woolwich Road, E16 2HP (7511 4111/www.thamesbarrierpark.org.uk). Canning Town tube/DLR, then 474 bus. **Open** dawn-dusk daily. **Admission** free.
With its utterly modern landscaping, French-style avenues of trees and view over the silver shoe-shapes of the Thames Barrier itself, this park is an unexpected delight. The Barrier's visitor centre is actually on the south side (*see p131*), but that hardly matters as long as you know how it works and can enjoy the river breezes, since there is no access to the barrier even if you approach via the visitor centre. On one side of the park is a concrete and granite channel the width of a small motorway. Called the Green Dock, it is filled with fragrant honeysuckle and wavy yew hedges, giving it excellent hide-and-seekability – with the two pedestrian bridges overhead adding a whole extra dimension to the game. At the riverfront is the Pavilion of Remembrance, which commemorates those who lost their lives in the Blitz. It is made of undulating beechwood, with similarly shaped granite benches below that make excellent skateboard ramps. The flat lawns are beautifully manicured, perfect for picnics and games. There's a playground packed with apparatus; a basketball hoop and five-a-side court for sporty folk; and plenty of ducks, geese, swans and oyster catchers picking around the gleaming mudflats. The park is fantastic for waterfowl watching, in fact. Grey herons also feed along the shore at low tide and large numbers of teal and shelduck join the mallards at both low and high tide. Mournful cormorants can be seen drying themselves or feeding in the river.

The tea pavilion has the distinction of serving the best coffee in Docklands, and for a fraction of the cost of many of the chains. It's a great refuge from the wind on chilly days; you can even hide inside and watch your kids play through the massive plate-glass windows.
Buggy access. Café. Disabled access: toilet. Free parking. Nappy-changing facilities.

Walthamstow & Wanstead

Walthamstow has a split personality. Five minutes' walk east of Walthamstow Central (the last stop north on the Victoria line) you'll find yourself in curiously rural Walthamstow Village. Around St Mary's Church the atmosphere may be villagey, but the history is grisly: Vinegar Alley was once a trench full of the stuff, intended to prevent pestilence spreading from the mass graves of Black Death victims in the churchyard. The half-timbered Ancient House opposite pre-dates the Plague, although the current incarnation is a painstaking 1934 restoration designed to look authentically saggy. Pamphlets recounting such history are available at the **Vestry House Museum**. Orford Road boasts the Village Kitchen (No.41, 8509 2144) and the Village pub (No.31, 8521 9982), which has a patio.The rest of Walthamstow is as busy as the Village is quiet, especially the street market, which runs the length of Walthamstow High Street and lays reasonable claim to being Europe's longest street market, (it's open Tuesday to Saturday). It is a terrific venue for bargain hunters, which naturally includes all children. Picture books, remaindered socks, batteries for toys and Asian stores selling sparkly jewellery and bindis for £1 will send most under-11s to consumer heaven. Lloyd Park, on Forest Road, lies to the north, with the **William Morris Gallery** at the southern entrance, near a scented garden for the visually impaired, an aviary of budgies and cockatiels, and a lake with strangely black water. At the far end of the park is a play area and skate park. Across the North Circular Road the art deco façade of **Walthamstow Stadium** is worth a look; this greyhound track runs family race days, and its restaurant, the Stowaway Grill, does dogs' dinners in a good way. The Walthamstow Marshes are at the end of Coppermill Lane (you might prefer to cycle or drive there: it's a good 15-minute walk from St James Street rail station). Ideal for picnics and walks by the River Lee, the marshes are where doughty Sir Edwin Alliot Verdon Roe made the first all-British powered flight on 23 July 1909 in his triplane *Yellow Terror*, flying roughly 300 metres (900 feet). The marshes employ a low-tech method of horticultural maintenance: a herd of cows is let loose in July to munch the grass until it's all gone, usually by January the following year. East of Walthamstow, Wanstead is another urban village – as local homeowners are proud to point out. There's another St Mary's church, Grade I listed and dating to 1790, but the attraction for visitors, especially those with kids, is Wanstead's greenery: Wanstead Flats and, especially, **Wanstead Park**.

Vestry House Museum

Vestry Road, E17 6HZ (8509 1917/www.lbwf.gov.uk). Walthamstow Central tube/rail. **Open** 10am-1pm, 2-5.30pm Mon-Fri; 10am-1pm, 2-5pm Sat. Closed 1 Jan, 25, 26 Dec, bank hols. *Tours* groups only, by prior arrangement. **Admission** free.

At different times a home, a police station and a workhouse, this lovely little museum has displays that are thoroughly engaging, even for children. One room is devoted entirely to vintage toys and games; another is got up as a Victorian parlour; on the ground floor you can see a reconstructed police cell, complete with waxen figures dressed as village bobby and arrested drunk. Other displays are pleasingly domestic: carpet beaters, meat mincers and knife sharpeners survive as quaint relics of the housewife's former lot. The relandscaping of the pretty walled garden, including building an airy space to house one of the first cars built in Britain, has resulted in more room for children's activities, which should be in full flow by summer 2006 since the appointment of a new curator.

Buggy access (ground floor only). Disabled access: toilets (ground floor only). Nappy-changing facilities. Nearest picnic place: museum garden (closed 1-2pm). Shop.

Walthamstow Stadium

Chingford Road, E4 8SJ (8531 4255/www.ws greyhound.co.uk). **Admission** free Mon, Fri; £3-£6 Tue, Thur, Sat. Free under-15s. **Racing** from 2.15pm Mon; from 11am Fri; from 7.30pm Tue, Thur; Sat. **Credit** *Restaurant* MC, V.

Any institution that plays 'Run, Rabbit, Run' on its telephone system must hold some interest for children, and indeed 'going to the dogs' on Saturday night remains a popular family outing hereabouts. It's fun – and even educational if you consider that gambling is a part of everyday life, for its costs may be learned here for low stakes. But first, the know-how. If you pass through the Popular entrance you only pay £3, whereas the Main Enclosure costs £6 (for adults; children go free). The difference is crucial: in the latter, you are close to the start and finish, while in the former you only glimpse a sort of canine streak as six dogs hurtle after an orange fluorescent 'rabbit'. For this reason the atmosphere in the main enclosure tends to be jollier; the somewhat dilapidated playground located in the middle is only sporadically inhabited by older kids disenchanted with the racing. Under-11s are often riveted. Bets may be placed for as little as 10p at the Microtote, so ekeing out pocket money over an evening should pose no problem (although only the over-18s in the party are allowed to place bets.) All this, plus the anthropological interest of excited punters, po-faced tic-tac men and many bags of chips – what more could you ask? *Buggy access. Disabled access: ramps, toilets. Nappy-changing facilities. Restaurant.*

Wanstead Park

Warren Road, E11 (8508 0028). Wanstead tube. **Open** dawn-dusk daily. **Admission** free.

Nowadays, Wanstead Park is managed by the City of London as part of Epping Forest. Heavily wooded, it also has several beautiful water features (the Ornamental Water and the three ponds – Perch, Heronry and Shoulder of Mutton). At the fenced-off end of the Ornamental Water is a ruined grotto, built in the early 1760s with a boathouse below and a domed, shell-encrusted chamber above; it's now all tumble-down romantic. The other important ruin in the park is the Temple, once a fancy summerhouse,

Around Town

which has the park toilets to one side. Both (the grotto and Temple, not the toilets) are Grade II listed, but the children will probably get far more excited by the ball-throwing and kite-flying possibilities on the extensive grassy area between the Temple and the tea stall. The park's WrenConservation and Wildlife Group (www.wren-group.fsnet.co.uk) is a good point of contact for sociable nature lovers. There is an annual programme of assorted activities in the park, including family walks (book on the listed number), a bluebell walk and all manner of drop-in arts and craft sessions.
Buggy access. Café. Disabled access. Free parking.

William Morris Gallery

Lloyd Park, Forest Road, E17 4PP (8527 3782/ www.lbwf.gov.uk/wmg). Blackhorse Road tube, then 123 bus. **Open** 10am-1pm, 2-5pm Tue-Sat; 1st Sun of mth. Closed 25, 26 Dec, 1 Jan, bank hols. *Tours* phone for details. **Admission** free; donations appreciated.

It is tempting to think of Walthamstow's most famous son, the designer and socialist William Morris, as a genial 19th-century forebear of IKEA. After all, he wished beautiful things to be produced for the masses, and his social conscience yearned to improve the lives of the working people; it's just too bad that craftsmanship and low prices do not sit happily together. At any rate, this handsome, moated building on Forest Road was his childhood home. The area was still rural when Morris lived here, and the love of nature evident in many of his textile and furniture designs is said to spring from his many boyhood forays into nearby Epping Forest. The rooms are now kept as galleries, showing as many artefacts by Morris's friends and collaborators as by the man himself. Paintings by Edward Burne-Jones contain wildly romantic depictions of angels and damsels; those of Frank Brangwyn are full of incident and colour. Kids will doubtless find the furniture dull as ditchwater, but there's consolation in freely available ceramic tiles, which encourage them to examine ceramic tiles narrating such stories as Beauty and the Beast. To the rear of the house, invisible from the road, is Lloyd Park, with its aviary full of birds, hillock and moat.
Buggy access. Disabled access: ramp (ground floor). Nearest picnic place: Lloyd Park. Shop.

Lee Valley Regional Park

Starting east of Hackney (*see p109*) and heading north-east all the way into Hertfordshire, Lee Valley Regional Park is a network of lakes, waterways, parks and countryside areas that covers a vast area on either side of the River Lee. There's plenty to do, though a gentle guided walk is a good way to start. The park's ideal for picnics, walking or fishing; it's well signposted and open year-round. It's also a nature lover's paradise. There are said to be 32 species of mammals making their home in the park, not to mention 21 species of dragonfly. Waymarked walks, some providing easy buggy access, take you to see orchids, grasshoppers and water lilies. The birdwatching is excellent: winter brings 10,000 migrant waterbirds from chillier climes, and summer is the time to enjoy the kingfishers. Other attractions include the Lee Valley Riding Centre

Product testing at the **Royal Gunpowder Mills**.

(Lea Bridge Road, E10 7QL, 8556 2629) and the much-loved Lee Valley Cycle Circuit (Quarter Mile Lane, E10 5PD, 8534 6085), next to the M11 extension. The Lee Valley Boat Centre (Old Nazeing Road, Broxbourne, Herts EN10 6LX, 01992 462 085, www.leevalleyboats.co.uk) is the place to hire a boat by the hour or book a narrowboat holiday. The small and fascinating town of Waltham Abbey is a good point of access. It has plenty of cafés and shops and an Augustinian abbey: founded in 1060 by King Harold, it is also reputed to be where he was buried. Once one of the largest in the country, the abbey had its own farm, fishponds and brewery; only the gateway, a few walls and a stone bridge remain, but the gardens contain a variety of public artworks, and there's a Sensory Trail highlighting the natural history of the area. The exciting **Royal Gunpowder Mills** and **Epping Forest** are but a ten-minute drive from the town.

Lee Valley Park Farms

Stubbins Hall Lane, Crooked Mile, Waltham Abbey, Essex EN9 2EG (01992 702 200/www.leevalley park.org.uk). Broxbourne or Waltham Cross rail. **Open** *Mar-Oct* 10am-4.30pm daily. Closed Nov-Feb. **Admission** £4.20; £3.70 concessions; £3.20 3-16s; £17 family (2+3); free under-3s. **Credit** MC, V.
Hayes Hill Farm is a rare-breeds centre, with a 'Tudor Barn' for sheltered picnics, a restored gypsy caravan and an adventure play area. Visitors can watch the milking of cows (from 2.30pm daily) at the nearby commercial farm, Holyfield, and talk to the farmer via an intercom. Livestock includes sheep, goats, cows, llamas and even water buffalo. There's also the Pet Centre, where you'll meet all sorts of little furry and scaly things. There are guided tours for school parties and tractor-trailer rides (1.45pm weekends, school holidays, Apr-Oct, weather permitting), as well as special events, no doubt involving pumpkins and pine trees, for Hallowe'en and Christmas.
Buggy access. Café. Disabled access: ramps, toilets. Nappy-changing facilities. Shop.

Royal Gunpowder Mills

Beaulieu Drive, Waltham Abbey, Essex EN9 1JY (01992 707 370/www.royalgunpowdermills.com). Waltham Cross rail, then 213, 250, 251 bus. **Open** *29 Apr-1 Oct 2006* 11am-5pm Sat, Sun (last entry 3pm), bank hols; 10.30am-2.30pm daily for school groups. **Admission** £6; £5 concessions; £3.25 5-16s; free under-5s; £18.50 family (2+3). **Credit** MC, V.
The Royal Gunpowder Mills were involved in the making of explosives for more than 300 years. Gunpowder production began here in the 1660s; later, the manufacture of guncotton, nitroglycerine, cordite paste and the highly explosive tetryl was undertaken; and after World War II the mills were a research centre for non-nuclear explosives and propellants. Few of the more than 20 historic buildings on the 175-acre site have been renovated, in a deliberate attempt to convey their long and complex past. The Visitors Centre runs an introductory film, as well as having an informative, hands-on exhibition that concentrates on the human story behind gunpowder. You can explore the extremely dangerous process of nitroglycerine manufacture, try on workers' boots and use their tools, or put cannon balls into a chute. A 'guided land train' (actually a tractor and trailer) takes visitors on a woodland tour (£1.50; £1 children). The educational programme offers Victorian Life, Home Front and (seasonal) Victorian Christmas sessions, as well as Explorer programmes that cover everything from investigations of the natural surroundings to the making of air-powered paper rockets. Costumed re-enactments (such as the Guy Fawkes Experience, 23-24 Sept 2006) are popular and usually involve some kind of live firing. New acquisitions include two locomotives, the Woolwich and the Carnegie, which are being cleaned up and having steps installed – let the scrambling commence!
Buggy access. Café. Disabled access: lift, ramps, toilets. Nappy-changing facilities. Nearest picnic place: on site. Shop.

Epping Forest

The biggest public space in London, Epping Forest (www.cityoflondon.gov.uk/openspaces) is a gift for walkers, riders and cyclists, not to mention wildlife fans. It is 19 kilometres long and 35 kilometres across (12 miles by 22 miles) and was saved from development by the Corporation of London in 1878. Commoners still have grazing rights and, each summer, English Longhorn cattle can be seen chewing the cud. The forest contains Iron Age earthworks and two listed buildings – the Temple in Wanstead Park (*see p110*) and the fully restored, 16th-century Queen Elizabeth's Hunting Lodge (Rangers Road, E4 7QH, 8529 6681; under-16s must be accompanied by adults). The latter has a quiz trail, as well as opportunities for dressing up as a Tudor; in the kitchen area, you can smell food made from 400-year-old recipes. If you're coming to Epping Forest by public transport, be prepared for some exercise Chingford railway station gives access to the Hunting Lodge and some lovely strolls. Loughton and Theydon Bois (Central Line) are the forest's nearest Tube stops, though it's a two-mile (three-kilometre) uphill walk from both – a struggle for some adults, let alone small and easily bored children. The best advice is to get a map and plan your route in advance – or use the car. At High Beech car park there's a small tea hut, as well as the Epping Forest Information Centre (High Beech, Loughton, Essex IG10 4AF, 8508 0028, www.eppingforest.co.uk, May-Sept 10am-5pm Mon-Sat, 11am-5pm Sun; Oct-Apr 11am-3pm Mon-Fri, 10am-4pm Sat, 11am-4pm Sun), with a children's area, disabled toilet and shop. For a real back-to-nature feeling, between May and September you can pitch your tent at the Debden House campsite (Debden Green, Loughton, Essex IG10 2NZ, 8508 3008; £6/night, £3/night children) and listen to the owls hoot.

Around Town

South-east London

Follow the Thames for naval-gazing fun.

Rotherhithe

A shipbuilding village for centuries, Rotherhithe had a less edifying role during the 18th century, when it was the centre of London's whaling trade. The area relinquished its links with whaling in 1864, and showed a rather more benign face to marine mammals when half of south London turned out to weep for the ill-fated bottlenose whale that ventured up the Thames in January 2006.

The old wharves, warehouses and seafarers' pubs still have an air of the salty seadog about them. One pub, the Angel, on Bermondsey Wall East, has a smugglers' trapdoor. Another, the Mayflower, on Rotherhithe Street, recalls the Pilgrim Fathers who sailed from here in 1620.

Most visitors to this history-steeped area call in at **St Mary's Rotherhithe** (St Marychurch Street, SE16 4JE, www.stmaryrotherhithe.org), a church built by local sailors in 1715. Many are disappointed to find they have to glimpse its treasures, including a communion table made from timber from the Battle of Trafalgar gunship *Temeraire*, through a vandal-proof glass partition. Come for a Sunday service to get closer. Nearby, the **Brunel Museum** celebrates the world's first underwater tunnel.

TOP 5	River views

Docklands
From Wolfe Monument, Greenwich Park (*see p127*).

Thames Barrier
From the Woolwich Ferry (*see p130*).

Laban
From the Docklands Light Railway (*see p125*).

The O₂
From the Cutty Sark Tavern (Ballast Quay, off Lassell Street, Greenwich, SE10 9PD, 8858 3146).

Wapping
From the Thames River Walk outside the Brunel Museum (*see p122*).

The Norwegian Church and Seaman's Mission lies at the mouth of the Rotherhithe car tunnel. There are several Scandinavian churches around here, harking back to Nordic sailors and their Viking ancestors who settled in the area. Across Jamaica Road lies **Southwark Park**. South of here, and across the London Bridge-bound railway tracks is South Bermondsey – Millwall FC territory. The streets around the stadium are in line for a £100-million facelift in time for the 2012 Olympics.

Leaving Southwark Park in an easterly direction brings you to Rotherhithe's retail quarter, the Surrey Quays Shopping Centre, and attendant leisure activities, including a massive cinema, a branch of Hollywood Bowl (7237 3773) and the Surrey Docks Watersports Centre (*see p267*).

Wild green spaces nestle uneasily amid all the urban newbuild. Lavender Pond and Nature Park (Lavender Road, SE16 5DZ) was created from a dock inlet in 1981. The Pumphouse Educational Museum (7231 2976, www.thepumphouse.org.uk) is used for school groups. Other ecology parks, promoted by the Trust for Urban Ecology and its volunteers, include Russia Dock Woodland and Stave Hill Ecological Park.

The Brunel Museum

Brunel Engine House, Railway Avenue, SE16 4LF (7231 3840/www.brunel-museum.org.uk). Rotherhithe tube. **Open** 1-5pm daily. **Admission** £2; £1 concessions, 13-16s; free under-12s; £5 family (2+2). **No credit cards.** The Brunels, father and son (Sir Marc and Isambard Kingdom), worked together to create the world's first underwater tunnel. Work began in 1825 and was finally completed in 1843, with Isambard nearly drowning in the process. The story of what the Victorians hailed as 'the Eighth Wonder of the World' is told in this museum, housed in the original engine house. The tunnel itself is now used by the East London tube line.

Isambard Kingdom Brunel was born in 1806, and there's plenty going on in and around the museum in his bicentenary year. A timely refurbishment has made the museum a sight more family-friendly. There are activity packs for children and a popular summer playscheme in the new sculpture garden. The museum also owns a giant Brunel figure with a steaming stovepipe hat, which is wheeled out for high days and holidays, including the Bermondsey Carnival (8 July 2006) and Rotherhithe Festival (16 July 2006). There is also free entry during Open House weekend (16-17 Sept).

Buggy access/storage. Nearest picnic place: museum gardens & riverbank. Shop.

Around Town

Greenwich. *See p125.*

Discovery Planet

*Surrey Quays Shopping Centre, Redriff Road, SE16
7LL (7237 2388/www.discovery-planet.co.uk). Canada
Water tube.* **Open** 10am-6pm Mon-Sat; 11am-5pm Sun.
Admission *2-10s* £3.99 Mon-Fri; £4.99 Sat, Sun.
Under-2s £3.49 Mon-Fri; £4.49 Sat, Sun. **Credit** (over
£10) MC, V.
This huge indoor area filled with brightly coloured tubes,
tunnels, ball ponds and slides gives a children two hours
of climbing, sliding, bashing and throwing themselves
about. Check the website for party information.

Southwark Park

*Gomm Road, SE16 2UA (park rangers 7740 1665/art
gallery 7237 1230/www.cafegalleryproject.org). Canada
Water tube.* **Open** *Park* 8am-1hr before dusk daily.
Gallery (during exhibitions) Summer noon-6pm Wed-
Sun. Winter 11am-4pm Wed-Sun. Phone ahead to check.
Admission free.
The Metropolitan Board of Works first opened Southwark
Park to the public in 1869, making it London's oldest
municipal park. In 1998 the park was given a new bandstand, bowling pavilion and children's play area. Local
artists, old and young, are well supported by the Café
Gallery Project, with various exhibitions held throughout
the year. Don't miss the special Children's Exhibition with
associated workshops (19-27 Aug 2006; booking essential)
and the big annual Open Exhibition (19 Nov-10 Dec 2006),
which always features children's work.
*Buggy access. Café. Disabled access: toilet. Nappy-
changing facilities (in gallery).*

Surrey Docks Farm

*Rotherhithe Street, SE16 5EY (7231 1010/www.surrey
docksfarm.org). Canada Water tube, then 225, 381 bus.*
Open 10am-5pm Tue-Sun. Closed 18 Dec 2006-3 Jan
2007. **Admission** free (except for school parties &
playschemes); donations appreciated.
A riverside location, a yard patrolled by overfriendly goats
and sheep (buy a bag of grain in the café then try fending
them off), and paddocks and loose boxes filled with donkeys, cattle and various poultry breeds (plus a resident
blacksmith who runs metalwork courses) make this city
farm a favourite of ours. Since the café has reinvented itself
as Nabo, a haven of healthy eating (think herbal teas and
Fair Trade flapjacks), we've started coming at lunchtime.
Raised beds by the riverside yield organically grown vegetables and herbs, some of which are for sale, supplemented by bought-in organic veg. Honey, fresh eggs and
compost are also sold when available. Outside the café, the
river walk beckons. Children enjoy sitting on the bronze
donkey that stands among the animal sculptures just outside the farm. Can you spot the mouse?
*Buggy access. Café. Disabled access: ramps, toilets.
Nearest picnic place: riverside. Shop.*

Deptford & Greenwich

The 2012 Olympics promises much for both
these riverside enclaves, but five years before
that, the sporting folk of Deptford and Greenwich
will be out in force for the Grand Départ of the
Tour de France 2007. The cyclists will stream
through from Bermondsey, across Deptford Creek,
through Greenwich town, past the Millennium

Dome and on to Woolwich and Erith en route to
Kent; their journey will end in Canterbury.
 Stellar sporting events aside, the regeneration
of Deptford continues. Even the station is being
given a facelift. Deptford's famously diverse high
street, with its market, independent shops and
cafés, runs parallel to the more trafficky Church
Street. The area's arty types gather along
Creekside, to the east. Deptford's creek is the
tidal reach of the River Ravensbourne, a tributary
of the Thames. The shoreline here – known as
Greenwich Reach – is earmarked for a massive
regeneration project. Take time on your way to
the river to admire **St Nicholas's Church** on
Deptford Green; known as the sailors' church,
it dates from 1697 and has timber-shivering
skulls and crossbones carved on the gate piers.
If you walk along Creekside to where it joins the
Thames, you'll see the striking **Laban** dance
centre (*see p229*) to your right. Non-dancing
visitors are allowed into the reception area,
café and grounds. Just beyond the railway
bridge lies the **Creekside Centre** and to the
left is the original railway viaduct. The Ha'penny
Hatch footbridge, which crosses the creek, opened
in 2002. To the right, the sewage pumping station
is part of Bazalgette's system of the 1860s.
 East of Deptford lies historic maritime
Greenwich, a UNESCO World Heritage Site.
Henry VIII built a palace here, the Palace of
Placentia. For nearly 200 years, from around
1450 to 1650, it was one of the main royal palaces
of England, before being torn down and replaced
by Sir Christopher Wren's **Old Royal Naval
College**. In January 2006, while part of the site
was being dug up for a new car park, remains
of the old palace's chapel were discovered. After
conservation, they'll be displayed either here or
at the Museum of London.
 River trips from central London to Greenwich
(Thames Cruises, 7930 3373, www.thames
cruises.com; Catamaran Cruises, 7987 1185 or
City Cruises, 7930 9033, www.citycruises.com)
take you to Greenwich Pier, just by the weathered
old tea clipper, the **Cutty Sark**. The Docklands
Light Railway (DLR) offers the Rail & River Rover
(7363 9700, www.dlr.co.uk), a family pass that
is also valid on City Cruises. Not far fom the pier
is the 250-year-old **Greenwich Market**, open
Thursdays to Saturdays – but for how much
longer? Like many street markets today, its future
looks uncertain as the landlord, the Greenwich
Hospital Charity, considers maximising its assets.
 From the riverside it's a ten-minute walk (or you
can take the park's shuttle bus) up the steep slopes
of Greenwich Park to the Royal Observatory. This
building looks all the more stunning at night,

Around Town

Deptford Creekside – ripe for regeneration. *See p125.*

partly due to the spectacular bright green Meridian Line Laser, illuminating the path of the Prime Meridian Line across the London sky.

From Greenwich, the Thames Path can take you to the Greenwich Peninsula, dominated by the structure formerly known as the Millennium Dome, now rechristened the O_2. The area has seen an increase in activity following Meridian Delta's £5 billion regeneration project. Work has begun on the construction of Millennium Square, all part of the plan to make this once-derelict part of the riverscape a brand-new town and offshoot of Olympics 2012 action. Before the big event, however, the O_2 will be in use as a venue for the Tutankhamun and the Golden Age of the Pharaohs exhibition in November 2007. The structure will also host the 2009 World Gymnastics Championships.The peninsula is also home to the **Greenwich Peninsula Ecology Park**, a pleasant riverside walk away from the O_2.

Creekside Centre

14 Creekside, SE8 4SA (8692 9922/ www.creeksidecentre.org.uk). Greenwich DLR/rail.
Open phone for scheduled events. **Admission** £1.50. **No credit cards**.
Take a walk on Deptford's Creekside to enjoy a selection of regular weekend activities for families. Check the website for details and to sign up for the Creekside Centre's mailing list. You might even see a kingfisher flash by. *Buggy access. Disabled: toilets. Nappy-changing facilities.*

Cutty Sark

King William Walk, SE10 9HT (8858 3445/www.cutty sark.org.uk). Cutty Sark DLR/Greenwich DLR/rail.
Open 10am-5pm daily (last entry 4.30pm). *Tours* Mon-Fri; depending on availability. **Admission** £5; £3.90 concessions; £3.70 5-16s; free under-5s; £12.50 family (2+3). *Tours* free. **Credit** MC, V.
Launched in 1869 from Dumbarton on the Clyde, the *Cutty Sark* took tea to China and wool to Australia. It is now a museum, and the world's only Grade I-listed ship. The lower hold contains a large collection of figureheads from merchant ships, and activities for families take place most weekends. Restoration works on the *Cutty Sark* are due to start in her dry dock in October 2006, so visitors are urged to take the opportunity of coming aboard before the autumn closure (the ship will be closed from 1 October until the end of January 2007). From February 2007 the ship will remain open to the public during the conservation programme for visitors to join on-site 'hard-hat tours'. *Buggy storage. Nearest picnic place: Cutty Sark Gardens. Shop.*

Fan Museum

12 Crooms Hill, SE10 8ER (8305 1441/www.fan-museum.org). Cutty Sark DLR/Greenwich DLR/ rail. **Open** 11am-5pm Tue-Sat; noon-5pm Sun. Closed 1 Jan, Easter, 25 Dec. **Admission** £4; £3 concessions; free under-7s; free OAPs, disabled 2-5pm Tue. **Credit** *Shop* MC, V.

Elegant and idiosyncratic, this museum is restful to tired adult sensibilities but probably a bit wasted on young children. Over-tens with artistic leanings, however, admire the exhibitions of hand-held fans. There are more than 3,000 in the collection (only a proportion is displayed at any one time). Look out for one of the more recent acquisitions: a fan painted around 1889 by Walter Richard Sickert (1860-1942). Painted in gouache on vellum, it depicts the artiste Little Dot Hetherington performing on stage at the Old Bedford Theatre, Camden. A new temporary exhibition is mounted every four months or so. The summer 2006 display, Come to the Ball, presents Victorian fans and posyholders. If you visit on a Tuesday or Sunday afternoon you'll be able to take tea in the Orangery. Check the website for exhibition dates and details of fan-making workshops.
Buggy access. Disabled access: lift, toilet. Nearest picnic place: Greenwich Park. Shop.

Greenwich Park

Blackheath Gate, Charlton Way, SE10 8QY (visitors centre 8858 2608/www.royalparks.org.uk). Cutty Sark DLR/Greenwich DLR/rail/Maze Hill rail/1, 53, 177, 180, 188, 286 bus/riverboat to Greenwich Pier. **Open** 6am-dusk daily.
Officially one of the best parks in England since winning a Green Flag award, Greenwich has it all – fab views, teeming wildlife, roly-poly hills, an observatory at the top and a museum at the bottom, an excellent café, playgrounds, boating and entertainments. It's the oldest and, we think, loveliest Royal Park, whose proud connections go back to Tudor times. Henry VIII hunted here, and there's an ancient husk of an old oak tree, which the monarch is said to have danced round with his then paramour, Anne Boleyn. The dead tree has a more vigorous neighbour – a new oak was planted on the site by Prince Philip to mark his wife's golden jubilee. A grassland enclosure serves as a sanctuary for deer, foxes and birds. It's home to the Greenwich Park Secret Garden Wildlife Centre where, from a specially built deer hide, children can enjoy close-up views of the resident wild red and fallow deer (open last Wed of the month; booking required).
Just outside the top gates, across Charlton Way, a group of saddled and resigned donkeys give rides to children on sunny weekends – fitting for a park that is going to host the equestrian events at 2012's Olympics. Free fun for under-tens is provided by the Royal Parks' summer entertainments programme and includes alfresco theatricals, plus circus skills and craft workshops (31 July-1 Sept 2006; phone 7298 2078 or check the website for details).
Buggy access. Cafés. Disabled access: toilets. Nappy-changing facilities.

Greenwich Peninsula Ecology Park

Thames Path, John Harrison Way, SE10 0QZ (8293 1904/www.urbanecology.org.uk). North Greenwich tube/108, 161, 422, 472, 486 bus. **Open** 10am-5pm Wed-Sun. **Admission** free.
A pond-dipping, bird-watching haven run by the Trust for Urban Ecology for English Partnerships. The park is reserved for schools on Mondays and Tuesdays. The rest of the week, it's all yours. A wetland area with woodland, marsh, meadow, lakes and streams, it supports frogs, toads, dragonflies and many bird species, and hosts a wide variety of children's entertainment. Children are plied with various quizzes and trails to follow as they explore, as well

as regular activities involving pondlife, mud and gumboots. The centre's dragonfly-themed Open Day takes place on 18 June this year, and the Frog Day is usually the first weekend in March. The summer play event runs from the end of July to early September.
Buggy access. Disabled access: toilet. Nappy-changing facilities. Nearest picnic place: Southern Park.

National Maritime Museum

Romney Road, SE10 9NF (8858 4422/information 8312 6565/tours 8312 6608/www.nmm.ac.uk). Cutty Sark DLR/Greenwich DLR/rail. **Open** *July, Aug* 10am-6pm daily. *Sept-June* 10am-5pm daily. *Tours* phone for details. **Admission** free; donations appreciated. **Credit** *Shop* MC, V.
This light, bright, modern museum charting our life at sea is a splendid place to be – especially on a rainy Sunday, when amiable staff welcome children to the Upper Deck for various maritime-themed artistic endeavours. School hols and weekends see all kinds of involving activities and storytelling sessions for children, although just wandering round the place is a lark. The more you explore the more you find to do. Even if you don't visit during school holidays, there are interactive computer terminals dotted around and games of quoits to play in the excellent Life at Sea Exhibition on Level 3. The very hands-on All Hands Gallery is also located here; children can play with a variety of exhibits, including Morse code machines, ships' wheels and a cargo-handling model. Family events for summer 2006 include August's all-pervading Treasure Island theme, so dig out your eye patches and wooden legs.
Other permanent galleries include Planet Ocean, all about the mysteries of the sea, where visitors can have a go at making whirlpools on special machines; Explorers is devoted to pioneers of sea travel (the exhibition includes evocative and spooky artefacts from the *Titanic* – cutlery, plates, a ceramic piggy bank); Passengers is a paean to glamorous old ocean liners; and Maritime London tells the capital's nautical history through old prints and model ships. On the ground floor, you'll find the Neptune Planetarium, a temporary attraction in use while the Royal Observatory's Time and Space project is being developed. Purchase tickets for shows at the main entrance. Upstairs, Seapower covers naval battles from Gallipoli to the Falklands, and the Art of the Sea is the world's largest maritime art collection. June 2006 sees the opening of Nelson's Navy, a new gallery displaying around 250 objects from the Museum's collections, highlighting the Royal Navy in the late Georgian period, the role played by Vice-Admiral Horatio Nelson and the impact of his death at the Battle of Trafalgar upon cohesion and morale.
Costumed actors and storytellers entertain the kids with crafts and stories during weekends and school holidays, and no young pirate can leave without plundering the gift shop; it runs the vaguely nautical gamut from dolphin water pistols for 50p to models of HMS *Victory* for £85.
Buggy access. Café. Disabled access: lifts, ramps, toilets. Nappy-changing facilities. Nearest picnic place: Greenwich Park. Restaurant. Shop.

Old Royal Naval College

King William Walk, SE10 9NN (8269 4747/tours 8269 4791/www.greenwichfoundation.org.uk). Cutty Sark DLR/Greenwich DLR/rail. **Open** 10am-5pm daily (last entry 4.15pm). *Tours* by arrangement. **Admission** free. **Credit** *Shop* MC, V.

Around Town

Built by Sir Christopher Wren in 1696, the buildings that comprise the Old Royal Naval College were originally a hospital, then a naval college; they are now part of the University of Greenwich. The public can admire the rococo chapel and Painted Hall, a tribute to William and Mary that took artist Sir James Thornhill 19 years to complete. In 1806 the body of Lord Nelson was laid in state here for thousands to pay their respects. Free organ recitals take place in the chapel on the first Sunday of each month. The Greenwich Gateway Visitor Centre (a council-run tourist information office, 8269 4747) is in the Pepys Building, where there's also an exhibition on 2,000 years of Greenwich history, the story of the Royal Hospital for Seamen and information on other Greenwich attractions.

At weekends and during school holidays, the College runs events and historical re-enactments. Visitor participation is encouraged during performances of character actors playing, for example, pirate Grace O'Malley, diarist Mr Pepys or pensioned sailor Joe Brown, who tell their stories in the Painted Hall. Pirate workshops (16 July 2006), special events such as the Nelson's Navy activity weekend (7, 8 Oct 2006) with its cannon and musket demonstrations, or the Big Draw sketching Hall of Fame art event (14 Oct 2006) make this one of our favourite places in London for free family fun. Make a date to skate too: the courtyard will be iced over as usual to form a seasonal rink from 2 December 2006. And don't miss the Christmas craft workshop (20, 21 Dec 2006), either. Check the website and book ahead for events.

Buggy access. Café. Disabled access: toilet. Nappy-changing facilities. Nearest picnic place: Naval College grounds. Restaurant. Shop.

Queen's House

Romney Road, SE10 9NF (8312 6565/www.nmm.ac.uk). Cutty Sark DLR/Greenwich DLR/rail. **Open** *Jan-June, Sept-Dec* 10am-5pm daily. *Jul, Aug* 10am-6pm daily. Last entry 30mins before closing. *Tours* noon, 2.30pm daily; phone to check. **Admission** free; occasional charge for temporary exhibitions. *Tours* free. **Credit** (over £5) MC, V.

Designed in 1616 by Inigo Jones for James I's wife, Anne of Denmark, Queen's House was handed, in an unfinished state, to Charles I's queen, Henrietta Maria. The House of Delights, as it was dubbed, was finally finished in 1640, 24 years after the original commission. The house is now home to the National Maritime Museum's impressive art collection, which includes portraits of famous maritime figures and works by Hogarth, Gainsborough and Lely. A fascinating exhibition on the ground floor charts the house's former life as a boarding school for the sons of sailors. The Queen's House is also home to a ghost, famously captured on film by a couple of Canadian visitors in 1966 but spotted as recently as 2002 by a gallery assistant. A colonnade connects the building to the National Maritime Museum (*see p127*). In November 2006 the Art for the Nation exhibition will bring together 200 of the museum's most significant works for an in-depth display of maritime-themed paintings, combining important works by Hogarth, Reynolds and Turner and including recent acquisitions and paintings that have not yet been seen by the public. Family Sundays (last Sunday of every month) see party games, performances, dancing, and art and craft activities; phone to check what's on before setting out.

Buggy access. Disabled access: lift, ramps, toilets. Nappy-changing facilities. Nearest picnic place: Greenwich Park.

Ranger's House

Chesterfield Walk, SE10 8QX (8853 0035/www.english-heritage.org.uk). Blackheath rail/Greenwich DLR/rail/53 bus. **Open** *Mar-late Sept* 10am-5pm Wed-Sun & bank hols. *Oct-Dec* group bookings only. Closed Jan-Feb 2007. **Admission** £5.50; £4.10 concessions; £2.80 5-16s; free under-5s. **Credit** MC, V.

This red-brick villa – formerly the official residence of the Greenwich Park Ranger – was built in 1720. It now contains the collection of treasures amassed by German-born millionaire Julius Wernher, who made his fortune in the South African diamond trade. Wernher died in 1912. His priceless collection of 19th-century art, still family-owned, includes jewellery, bronzes, tapestries, furniture, porcelain and paintings, and is one of the most unusual in the world. Displayed in 12 elegant rooms, it shows what Britain's richest man liked to spend his dosh on – enamelled skulls, miniature coffins and jewel-encrusted reptiles are just some of the unusual items that caught Wernher's eye.

Buggy storage. Disabled access: lifts, toilets. Nearest picnic place: Greenwich Park. Shop.

Royal Observatory

Greenwich Park, SE10 9NF (8312 6565/www.rog.nmm.ac.uk). Cutty Sark DLR/Greenwich DLR/rail. **Open** 10am-5pm daily (last entry 4.30pm). *Tours* phone for details. **Admission** free. *Tours* free. **Credit** MC, V.

Four new galleries devoted to the history of timekeeping opened in the home of Greenwich Mean Time early in 2006. The galleries, which contain chronometers dating back to the 13th century, are part of the £15m refurbishment of the old Observatory. Built for Charles II by Wren in 1675, this observatory now examines the life of John Flamsteed, the Royal Astronomer, who was assigned the task of mapping the heavens. A series of set-piece rooms evokes the Flamsteed household. Elsewhere, there are cases and cases of clocks and watches, from hourglasses to a mind-bogglingly accurate atomic clock. The dome houses the largest refracting telescope in the country – and eighth-largest in the world. In the courtyard is the Prime Meridian Line – star of a billion snaps of happy tourists with a foot in each zone. You can pay £1 to receive a certificate marking your visit.

The onion dome at the Royal Observatory holds occasional observing evenings using the 28-inch refractor. Book ahead on 8312 8565 for events on 2 and 3 November, and 1 and 30 December 2006, and a winter stars special on 26 January 2007. Check the website for times and prices.

The planetarium in the South Building closed in 2005. A state-of-the-art planetarium is being built as part of the Time and Space Project – a redevelopment of the 330-year-old observatory that should, by spring 2007, open up one-third of the site previously closed to visitors.

Buggy access (courtyard only). Nappy-changing facilities. Nearest picnic place: Greenwich Park. Shop.

Blackheath & Lewisham

Windswept **Blackheath** is kite-flying central and home to many sports clubs: the Royal Blackheath Golf Club (established 1745), the Blackheath Hockey Club (1861) and the Blackheath Football Club (1862), which plays rugby union. Nearby Blackheath Village has great shops and cafés, but the traffic can be depressing. Blackheath Conservatoire (*see p234*) is the area's arts focus. On Sundays there's a farmers' market in Blackheath station car park.

South-west of Blackheath lies rough old **Lewisham**, more than ready for its promised regeneration programme. It is planned that the Lewisham Borough section of the Thames Gateway project will provide 120,000 new homes in a development that will stretch to the Isle of Sheppey.

If you keep walking down the fancifully named Lewisham Promenade, you'll end up in Catford, with its landmark black-and-white cat over an ugly shopping centre, the beautiful old art deco **Broadway Theatre** and trees lit up by blue light bulbs. Lewisham borough has many parks, the best of which are the stunning Sydenham Wells Park (Wells Park Road, SE26) and **Manor House & Gardens**. **Mountsfield Park** (Stainton Road, SE6) hosts People's Day (8 July 2006), an annual festival. Near Mountsfield's bowling green on Hither Green Lane, a local winter sanity-saver for parents comes in the form of **Kids Korner**, an indoor adventure playground (0870 011 9293).

Age Exchange Reminiscence Centre

11 Blackheath Village, SE3 9LA (8318 9105/www.age-exchange.org.uk). Blackheath rail. **Open** 10am-5pm Mon-Sat. **Admission** free. Groups must book in advance, for a small charge. **Credit** MC, V.

A registered charity that aims to improve the quality of life for older people by emphasising the value of memories, Age Exchange has created a nostalgic museum experience. Mock-ups of everyday life in the 1930s include a grocer's and old-fashioned sweet shop stocked with contemporary comestibles like rosy apples, and a sitting room with nostalgic toys, a stove, old-style furnishings and crockery. There's also a little café and theatre space at the back. The centre's programme of exhibitions is based around older people's memories – check the website for dates of future attractions.

Buggy access. Café. Disabled access: lift; toilets. Nearest picnic place: centre gardens. Shop.

Manor House & Gardens

Old Road, SE13 5SY (park 8318 1358/library 8852 0357/www.lewisham.gov.uk). Hither Green rail. **Open** *Café & park* 8am-dusk daily. *House & library* 9.30am-5pm Mon, Sat; 9.30am-7pm Tue, Thur. **Admission** free.

Currently awaiting its facelift, this 1772 manor house, once the home of illustrious banker George Baring, is now one of London's grandest local libraries. Visit on a Tuesday morning with your pre-schoolers for the parent-and-toddler session. In the garden is an ancient ice house, which

War stories: the **Imperial War Museum**. *See p131.*

opens to the public occasionally. The park outside, with its central lake, raised platform for wildfowl feeding and unchallenging play area, is all the better for the child-friendly park café and its menu of simple, own-made hot meals, ice-cream, drinks and snacks.
Buggy access. Café. Disabled access: toilets.

Charlton & Woolwich

The once well-to-do area of **Charlton** still retains its villagey charm around the church and remnants of the green. **Charlton House** is the main attraction. Its terrace looks out over grim-looking Charlton Park. **Maryon Wilson Park**, across the road, is more pleasant. It has a small farm (organised tours only, call 8319 4253 for details). The northernmost part leads to Woolwich Church Street and the river, spanned by London's lifeline, the **Thames Barrier**.

The future's bright for Woolwich. This section of riverside London has not only had a starring role in the 2006 film *Children of Men*, but is also in line for a huge cash injection. Work has begun on the much-anticipated Woolwich Arsenal DLR extension, which will run under the Thames from King George V station at North Woolwich to Woolwich Arsenal. The line should be finished in 2009. Add to that the Thames Gateway Bridge plan to connect Thamesmead and Beckton north of the river, and it looks as if this area's days are a depressing backwater are numbered. Looking at the high street today, though, it's hard to imagine that this part of London will ever be upmarket. The street's rather limp claim to fame is as the venue for the first-ever UK McDonald's (opened in 1974, trivia fans).

Come to Woolwich for **Firepower**, the artillery museum, located in the old buildings of the Woolwich Arsenal. Established in Tudor times as the country's main source of munitions, by World War I the Arsenal stretched 51 kilometres (32 miles) along the river, had its own internal railway system and employed 72,000 people. Much of the land was sold off during the 1960s, but the main section, with its lovely Georgian buildings, has been preserved. South of here, the Royal Artillery Barracks has the longest Georgian façade in the country. For more on the Arsenal, visit the **Greenwich Heritage Centre**. Another highlight is the free **Woolwich Ferry** (8921 5968, www.woolwich.gov.uk), whose diesel-driven boats replaced a paddle steamer that was in use until 1889. The ferry takes pedestrians and cars across the river every ten minutes. The trip to the north shore lands you by North Woolwich Old Station Museum (*see p118*) and Royal Victoria Gardens. Just by the ferry terminal on the south bank is the Waterfront Leisure Centre (Woolwich High Street, SE18 6DL, 8317 5000).

Charlton House

Charlton Road, SE7 8RE (8856 3951/www.greenwich. gov.uk). Charlton rail/53, 54, 380, 422 bus. **Open** *Library* 2-7pm Mon, Thur; 10am-12.30pm, 1.30-5.30pm Tue, Fri; 10am-12.30pm, 1.30-5pm Sat. *Toy library* 10.30am-12.30pm, 1.30-3.30pm Mon, Tue, Fri. **Admission** free.
Built in 1612, Charlton House was home to the tutor of Henry, eldest son of James I. These days it's a community centre and library, but glimpses of its glorious past can be seen in the creaky oak staircase, marble fireplaces and ornate plaster ceilings. The library has a good children's section (activities take place 10.30am Mon); this is also home to the Charlton Toy Library (8319 0055). Outside, the venerable mulberry tree, dating back to 1608, bears fruit every summer, and if the locals don't ransack it first, the creative cooks in the delightful tea rooms here put mulberry chutneys, crumbles and cakes on the menu. Visit at 1pm on a Friday, and you'll be treated to a free concert by musicians from the Trinity College of Music.
Buggy access. Café. Disabled access: lifts, ramps, toilets. Nappy-changing facilities. Nearest picnic area: Charlton House grounds.

Firepower

Royal Arsenal, SE18 6ST (8855 7755/www.firepower. org.uk). Woolwich Arsenal rail. **Open** *Nov-Mar* 10.30am-5pm Fri-Sun (last entry 4pm). *Apr-Oct* 10.30am-5pm Wed-Sun (last entry 4pm). **Admission** (LP) £5; £4.50 concessions; £2.50 5-16s; free under-5s; £12 family (2+2 or 1+3). **Credit** MC, V.
The Gunners might be more commonly associated with a not very British north London premiership team, but down here the rather more heroic gunners – soldiers of the Royal Artillery – are celebrated loudly. Occupying some converted Woolwich Arsenal buildings close to the river, Firepower is a popular destination for children and their families during the school holidays (although it's quite fun playing 'spot the sister' among their ranks as this museum is definitely one for the boys). Firepower occupies two sites. On entry, march through to the Gunnery Hall, bristling with preserved artillery pieces, some centuries old. A Real Weapons Gallery allows the firing of (mini) cannons and other hands-on gunner activities. Don't miss the introductory cinema presentation in the Breech Cinema, followed by a multimedia, floor-shaking run through to the various wars the Royal Artillery have been party to. A new exhibition, Dragons: The Artillery of the East, starring some of the most interesting cannon from China, Burma, Borneo and Japan, runs until September 2006. The Gun Pit café – recently refurbished to include squashy sofas, hot dishes of the day and decent coffee, as well as a good value child's picnic box (*see p173*) – is also on this site.

Across the courtyard (where, during the hols, whey-faced children can join a drill class run by a barking sergeant in combats) is another building containing a huge collection of trophy guns and the Cold War Gallery, which focuses on the 'monster bits' (ginormous tanks and guns). Of most interest to children, however, is the first-floor Command Post, where £1.50 buys you a go on the brilliant Rolling Rock climbing wall, or a paintball target session. Both activities are supervised by staff/soldiers in fatigues. Special events take place throughout the year. 'Camouflage' party packages for little birthday soldiers are available (details on 8312 7111).
Buggy access. Café. Disabled access: ramps, toilets. Lift. Nappy-changing facilities. Nearest picnic place: riverside. Shop.

Greenwich Heritage Centre

Artillery Square, Royal Arsenal, SE18 4DX (8854 2452/www.greenwich.gov.uk). Woolwich Arsenal rail. **Open** 9am-5pm Tue-Sat. **Admission** free. **No credit cards**.

The history of the borough of Greenwich, with particular emphasis on the rise and fall of the Royal Arsenal in Woolwich, is the subject matter here. Visitors with family in the area can use the archives to find out about their fore-bears. The centre has a large collection of historical sources – books, maps, drawings and manuscripts, an archaeo-logical archive and natural history specimens. Phone for details of events and activities, including a free Saturday Club for children (10.30am-noon), which may include art and craft activities for five- to 12-year-olds.

Disabled access: lifts, ramps, toilets. Nappy-changing facilities. Nearest picnic area: Riverside Park. Shop.

Thames Barrier Information & Learning Centre

1 Unity Way, SE18 5NJ (8305 4188/www. environment-agency.gov.uk). North Greenwich tube/Charlton rail/riverboats to & from Greenwich Pier (8305 0300) & Westminster Pier (7930 3373)/177, 180 bus. **Open** *Apr-late Sept* 10.30am-4.30pm daily. *Late Sept-Mar* 11am-3.30pm daily. Closed 24 Dec-2 Jan. **Admission** *Exhibition* £1.50; £1 concessions; 75p 5-16s; free under-5s. **Credit** MC, V.

The Barrier, spanning the 520m (1,700ft) Woolwich Reach, is the world's largest adjustable dam. It was built in 1982 at a cost of £535m; since then it has saved London from flooding at least 67 times. The small Learning Centre explains how it functions and has a map that shows which parts of London would be submerged if it stopped work-ing. Time your visit to see the barrier in action: every September there's a full-scale testing, with a partial test closure once a month (phone for dates). Campion Cruises (8305 0300) runs trips from Greenwich (Mar-Oct only). *Café. Shop.*

Kennington & the Elephant

The situation for children in this area has improved dramatically since Charlie Chaplin endured a ghastly Kennington childhood. Any child who likes cricket is on to a surefire winner: they'll be awed by the refurbished Oval Cricket Ground, where the 2005 giant-slaying took place. Kennington Park has come up a bit too, since it used to be renowned for public executions. Not far away, the old Bedlam lunatic asylum now houses the **Imperial War Museum**, beside which is Geraldine Mary Harmsworth Park, providing welcome refuge from traffic-choked Lambeth Road.

Elephant and Castle, once the 'Piccadilly Circus of south London', is now arguably the city's greatest eyesore: two nights of sustained bombing during the Blitz in 1941 made it the worst-hit area in the capital, and cynics would argue that it has hardly improved since. The tarnished red façade of its moribund shopping centre, which straddles one of the most congested roundabouts in London, still inspires loathing among locals, but redemption could be imminent in the form of a long-overdue £1.5 billion redevelopment, slated to begin turning the area into a pedestrianised town centre with modern housing, shops, leisure facilities and a new tram system. Sadly, the shopping centre isn't due for demolition until 2010.

Brit Oval

Kennington Oval, SE11 5SS (ticket office 7582 7764/ 6660/tours 7820 5750/www.surreycricket.com). Oval tube. **Open** *Ticket office* 9.30am-4pm Mon-Fri. *Tours* by arrangement; phone for details. **Admission** varies; depending on match. **Credit** MC, V.

Interest in occasional tours of London's most famous skewed circle has enjoyed a certain resurgence since September 2005, but the Brit Oval has long been a land-mark venue in the history of national and international cricket. The £24m LCS stand, unveiled in 2005, has added new terraces, a community education centre and a swanky aerofoil roof. Membership of the new under-18s Hollioake Club – named after the late Ben Hollioake, Surrey captain between 1997 and 2003 – costs £15 for the season, includ-ing free entry to all games (the last domestic match of 2006 is 12 Sept). The Oval offers Outreach coaching for 250 London schools, as well as school tours, educational work-shops and tournaments (including a girls-only series). The club has also developed a second community cricket ground – used for training by Kennington United – at Kennington Park.

Buggy access. Café. Disabled access: ramps, toilets. Nappy-changing facilities. Shops.

Imperial War Museum

Lambeth Road, SE1 6HZ (7416 5000/www.iwm.org.uk). Lambeth North tube/Elephant & Castle tube/rail. **Open** 10am-6pm daily. **Admission** free; donations appreciated. *Exhibition* prices vary. *Audio guides* £3.50-£3. **Credit** MC, V.

The extensive collections of 'important' military weapons are no doubt a specialist interest. Much more interesting – if no less disturbing – are the WWI and II galleries, dis-playing poetry by Wilfred Owen, Siegfried Sassoon and their contemporaries, as well as a reconstructed Somme trench and a look at life on the home front. Between the two galleries there's a countdown clock-face, whose minute hand ticks off the number of people killed in war, while the new Children's War exhibition, open until 2008, explores the conflict of 1939-45 through the eyes of chil-dren and features a revamped 1940s house with interac-tive exhibits, boxes full of wartime treasures and dressing-up clothes. The Secret War exhibition takes you on a whirlwind tour of British espionage. There's also a 200-seat cinema that shows drama and documentary footage of conflicts through history. The Holocaust Exhibition, on the third floor, traces the history of anti-Semitism and the rise of Hitler. Unsuitable for children under 14, it's the vast collection of salvaged shoes, clothes, spectacles and other mementoes, as well as tes-timonials from survivors that break the heart. On the fourth floor, Crimes Against Humanity, covering geno-cide and ethnic violence in our time, leaves you in no doubt about the pointlessness of war (over-16s only). Temporary exhibitions include Great Escapes (until

3 Sept 2006), and The Animals' War (14 July 2006-22 Apr 2007), illustrating the range of jobs bestowed upon animals – from cats and dogs to camels, dolphins and elephants – in modern warfare. The educational programme offers audio guides, workshops and talks by costumed actors, especially during school holidays.
Buggy access. Café. Disabled access: lifts, ramps, toilets. Nappy-changing facilities. Nearest picnic place: Geraldine Mary Harmsworth Park. Shops.

Camberwell & Peckham

It inspired Mendelssohn's famous 'Spring Song' – which was only a success after he changed its name from 'Camberwell Green' – and was once rural enough to give rise to a new species of butterfly (the Camberwell Beauty, identified in 1748), but today Camberwell is a place better known for one of south London's busiest, smog-veiled crossroads. These days you're as likely to find old drunks on the benches of Mendelssohn's famous green as children using its playground. For a breath of fresh air, most locals tend to retreat to nearby Burgess Park or the more bosky Ruskin Park. Not that Camberwell is without

charm; the steady influx of swanky boozers suggests that local gentrification is taking root, and there are amenities to be found – the Blue Elephant Theatre stages occasional family plays, for example, and annual open days at Camberwell College of Arts have hands-on workshops for minors.

The college also has a hand in the regeneration of neighbouring Peckham: in 2006 architect Will Alsop is returning to his 2000 RIBA award-winning Peckham Library where, in the courtyard, he'll be constructing an open-air exhibition centre for Camberwell students, with a café, a bookshop and 'the most amazing lavatory in London'. It's all part of an ongoing change in fortunes for this neglected area. That said, there's still a long way to go: the Peckham Pulse health club (7525 4999, www.fusion-lifestyle.com) saw red faces all round when its 'state-of-the-art' swimming pool had to close (it won't re-open until late 2006). Community forums like New Peckham Varieties (*see p230*) keep spirits up, however. The high street, diverse though it is, is characterised by a grubby mix of bargain warehouses and open-fronted butchers.

Horniman Museum. *See p134.*

A safer bet is to head up the road to Peckham Rye Common, where William Blake claimed to have been visited by his first angel, and where – more recently – a Heritage Lottery Fund-financed makeover gave it gravelled paths, reshaped gardens and a small concrete skateboard park. Less sculpted, but infinitely more sublime, is nearby **Nunhead Cemetery**.

North-east from Nunhead is New Cross, the only part of south-east London with a tube station. Various sites of Goldsmith's College, part of the University of London, occupy the buildings along here. The Ben Pimlott Building, a dramatic glass and steel construction with a metal sculpture that sits astride the fifth-floor terrace, is diverting. The main source of fun is away from the traffic, on the airy slopes of the redeveloped Telegraph Hill Park.

Burgess Park
Albany Road, SE5 0RJ (park rangers 7525 1066/ www.southwark.gov.uk). Elephant & Castle tube/rail then 12, 42, 63, 68, 171, 343 bus. **Open** 24hrs daily. **Admission** free.
At first glance, Burgess Park looks dull, flat, featureless and unlikely to win any prizes for beauty but, community-wise and parenthood-wise, it's a godsend. Planned in 1943, the construction involved demolishing terraced housing and relocating many residents to the now-notorious Aylesbury Estate. In an area in dire need of community initiatives, Burgess Park has attractions for all ages. For young tearaways, there's a busy little kart track (7525 1101), an adventure playground, an indoor games room and an award-winning BMX track. Then there's Chumleigh Gardens, home to Southwark Rangers, which has a café and features various garden styles: English country, fragrant Mediterranean, meditative Islamic, and flamboyant Caribbean. The Heart Garden is a fruit and vegetable patch planted, tended and harvested by those with long-term illnesses. On Wednesdays and Thursdays throughout the year, the Peckham Sure Start programme organises creative outdoor games and activities for families with young children (phone for details). Festivals include Vibrations (5 Aug 2006) and the South American Carnaval del Pueblo (6 Aug 2006).
Buggy access. Café. Disabled access: toilets.

Livesey Museum for Children
682 Old Kent Road, SE15 1JF (7635 5829/www.livesey museum.org.uk). Elephant & Castle tube/rail, then 53 bus. **Open** 10am-5pm Tue-Sat (last entry 4.30pm). Closed bank hols. **Admission** free.
The first library in Camberwell (opened in 1890), the Livesey was converted into a museum and reopened in 1974 by the poet laureate, Sir John Betjeman. Since then, it has developed into an interactive children's museum, showing temporary hands-on exhibitions for under-12s, their families, carers and teachers. There's an agreeable little courtyard area for play, and regular holiday workshops centre on current museum exhibitions: a recent display of the Throne of Weapons – a chair made from guns decommissioned following the civil war in Mozambique – saw children urged to bring in old toy guns and create a similar exhibit of their own. The Myths and Legends

exhibition runs until 26 August 2006 and has interactive games, puppet shows and storytelling for smaller tots. The museum closes over the summer holidays; phone for details of new exhibitions and events.
Buggy access. Nappy-changing facilities. Nearest picnic place: museum courtyard.

Nunhead Cemetery
Limesford Road or Linden Grove (entrances), SE15 3LP (information 7732 9535/www.southwark.gov.uk). Nunhead rail. **Open** *Summer* 8am-7pm daily. *Winter* 8am-4pm daily. **Tours** 2pm last Sun of mth. **Admission** free; donations to Friends of Nunhead Cemetery appreciated. *Tours* free.
An atmospheric Victorian cemetery with a restored chapel at its heart. Volunteers work on the land around the broken statues and stone monuments that have been upturned over time by tree roots and ivy, although the plot clearance is carried out with a view to ensuring that Nunhead keeps its overgrown charm. The tree-filled cemetery is a nature reserve and offers some fine views of the city from its highest points. There are guided tours on the last Sunday of each month, meeting at the Linden Grove gates at 2pm.
Buggy access.

Peckham Library
122 Peckham Hill Street, SE15 5JR (7525 2000/ www.southwark.gov.uk). Peckham Rye or Queen's Road rail/12, 36, 63, 171 bus. **Open** 9am-8pm Mon, Tue, Thur, Fri; 10am-8pm Wed; 10am-5pm Sat; noon-4pm Sun. **Admission** free.
Family activities that take place inside Will Alsop's funny-looking library include creative baby and toddler sessions every Tuesday morning (10.30am) and the Sure Start reading group for under-fives the same afternoon (1.30pm). At both, kids are encouraged to make use of the wide selection of children's books on the fourth floor. There's a Homework Club on Mondays and Fridays (4-7pm), craft sessions on Tuesdays, and meetings of the Teenage Reading Group (TRG) on the second Tuesday and Family Reading Group (FRG) on the last Thursday of each month. There is also an extended programme of holiday workshops. The square outside hosts a farmers' market on Sunday mornings.
Buggy access. Disabled access: lift, toilets. *Nappy-changing facilities.*

South London Gallery
65 Peckham Road, SE5 8UH (7703 6120/www.south londongallery.org). Peckham Rye rail/12, 36, 171, 345 bus. **Open** noon-6pm Tue-Sun. Closed 1 Jan, bank hol Mon, 25, 26 Dec. **Admission** free.
This gallery gives some way towards supporting extravagant claims about Peckham becoming the next Hoxton. Work on display tends towards the cutting edge: artists including Tracey Emin and Bill Viola have exhibited here in the past, and the gallery has a forward-thinking approach and futuristic atmosphere. Family workshops are fine-tuned to tie in with current exhibitions: a recent show by the German artist Daniel Roth exploring the watery history of Peckham – named after ancient River Peck – saw kids out in the open air erecting temporary structures inspired by the local landscape.
Buggy access. Disabled access: lift, ramp, toilets. Nappy-changing facilities. Nearest picnic place: gallery garden (during summer).

Around Town

Dulwich & Herne Hill

The popularity of Dulwich with young families isn't hard to fathom: its leafy streets, upmarket amenities and abundance of wide open spaces make it one of London's most pleasant places to raise children. Dulwich Village is a gem, and the 'village' tag entirely justified. Many settle here with one eye on their offspring and the other on Dulwich College, with its stately brick campus, bulletproof reputation for rugger and formidable roster of literary alumni (Michael Ondaatje, Raymond Chandler, PG Wodehouse). The affiliated Edward Alleyn Theatre – named after the Elizabethan actor and founder of the College – has a programme of dramatic entertainment (*see p222*). Dulwich Picture Gallery offers an artistic education at a less eye-watering cost than the public school. Every May the annual Dulwich Festival brings the village to life for young ones. There's also a small open-air skateboard park opposite West Dulwich station. Sydenham Hill Wood, on the other side of the A205, is a rambler's paradise, comprising one of the last remaining tracts of the old Great North Wood that once stretched from Deptford to Selhurst.

Neighbouring East Dulwich isn't quite so sylvan as West Dulwich, but it remains a popular destination for young parents – thanks to the number of child-friendly pubs, restaurants and cafés on Lordship Lane, gentrified almost beyond recognition in the last few years. The northernmost end has a children's playground on Goose Green and the East Dulwich Community Centre (8693 4411) has just been kitted out with a new playground. Further west, Herne Hill has a range of family-friendly pubs and restaurants on Half Moon Lane, as well as Brockwell Park, a slightly grittier, hillier alternative to Dulwich Park.

Dulwich Park

College Road, SE21 7BQ (park rangers 8693 5737/ www.southwark.gov.uk). North Dulwich or West Dulwich rail. **Open** 8am-dusk daily.
The park was formally landscaped in 1890, but had served as a scenic retreat long before that. Queen Mary was a regular visitor (one of the park's four gates is named after her). Visitors today are treated to the Pavilion Café (*see p179*), a super playground, boat hire on the lake, novelty bike hire from London Recumbents (8299 6636, www.london recumbents.co.uk) and a number of gardens (including the original American Garden, home to one of London's largest collections of rhododendrons and azaleas, as well as herons, cormorants and the occasional kingfisher). Plans to open a glamorous new boathouse had to be put on hold for financial reasons, but a temporary boathouse will be running pleasure boats in the interim, and, from late 2006, a new community officer will be running a programme of

children's activities from the Francis Peek Centre, housed in the cricket pavilion (schools only; phone for details). *Buggy access. Café. Disabled access: ramps, toilets. Nappy-changing facilities.*

Dulwich Picture Gallery

Gallery Road, SE21 7AD (8693 5254/www.dulwich picturegallery.org.uk). North Dulwich or West Dulwich rail/P4 bus. **Open** 10am-5pm Tue-Fri; 11am-5pm Sat, Sun, bank hol Mon. Closed 1 Jan, Good Friday, 24-26 Dec. **Tours** 3pm Sat, Sun. **Admission** £4; £3 concessions; free under-16s. *Exhibitions* £3; free under-16s. *Tours* free. **Credit** MC, V.
Widely held to be the first purpose-built art gallery in the country, this neo-classical building – designed by Sir John Soane in 1811 – also remains one of the best. Despite being of modest size, the gallery houses an outstanding collection of work by European Old Masters and offers a fine introduction to the baroque era through pieces by Rembrandt, Rubens, Poussin and – batting for the home team – the great Thomas Gainsborough. The programme of children's activities is comprehensive enough to be almost confusing, but rest assured there's something for all ages. It costs between £50-£60 per five-week term, and there are school-holiday courses (Art in the Garden runs on Wednesdays during the summer hols and costs just £2 per child) and workshops. Best of all are the free Art Play afternoons (2-3.30pm, first Sun of every month), which offer parents and their children (aged over four) the chance to engage in artist-led activities across a range of subjects and creative media. Check the website for details and fees of all courses and classes.

Exhibitions for 2006 include a retrospective of the work of Rembrandt and his contemporaries (until 3 Sept) and little-known German painter Adam Elsheimer (20 Sept-3 Dec), while Venetian artist Canaletto will be the subject of an exhibition in 2007 (24 Jan-15 Apr).
Buggy access. Café. Disabled access: ramps, toilets. Nappy-changing facilities. Nearest picnic place: gallery gardens. Shop.

Horniman Museum

100 London Road, SE23 3PQ (8699 1872/ www.horniman.ac.uk). Forest Hill rail/122, 176, 185, 312, P4 bus. **Open** 10.30am-5.30pm daily. **Admission** free; donations appreciated. **Credit** *Shop* MC, V.
Travelling tea trader Frederick J Horniman assembled a great number of curiosities, first in his home at Forest Hill and later in this jolly art nouveau museum, which was left to the people of London in 1901. The recently smartened-up Natural History Gallery has spooky skeletons, pickled animals, stuffed birds and insect models in old-fashioned glass cases, all presided over by a large, rather threadbare, overstuffed walrus on a centre plinth. Meanwhile, the atmospheric World Cultures exhibition offers an astonishing 80,000 objects sourced from across the earth: kids tend to gravitate straight towards the shrunken heads. The Music Room comprises the third permanent exhibition: here you'll find the walls hung with hundreds of instruments of every type, with touch screens on tables for you to hear their sound and a Hands On room for visitors to bash away at world instruments such as Thai croaking toads and an Irish bodhrán. There's also an under-fives book zone, cases of exotic reptiles and an observation beehive in the Environment Room. The aquarium reopens this year after a £1.5m overhaul (*see p135* **Tanks for the Horniman**). Under-fives' and family storytelling takes

Tanks for the Horniman

These days it's an overgrown patch of rubble and partially collapsed walls, but in 1871, when the world's largest marine aquarium opened in Crystal Palace Park, its many displays brought the oceans to generations of land-locked Londoners. Ironic, then, that while plans for the restoration of Crystal Palace Park flounder unconvincingly, it's up to the modest **Horniman Museum**, a short drive down the hill, to bring those same wild waters back to life.

Summer 2006 sees a £1.5 million overhaul for the Horniman's basement aquarium. More than 200 aquatic and animal species will be housed in 14,000 litres of water across seven separate zones, the better to explain the challenges now faced by the world's delicate ecosystems.

'It's going to be a greatly enhanced space,' says Kerwin Porter, the aquarium manager. 'Frederick Horniman, the museum's founder, wanted to show the Victorian public the living natural world close up, and we've tried to stay true to his vision.'

This new aquarium is as entertaining as it is educational. The British Pond Life Zone wows kids with its viewing den located inside a hollow willow tree; it also boasts an interactive learning area to magnify wee beasties ordinarily beyond the scope of the human eye. Similarly, the Drifters Zone has a hypnotic display of jellyfish suspended in a

dramatically lit cylindrical tank closely simulating the currents of the open ocean; there are also 3D images illustrating how sea plankton constitutes the building blocks of the marine food chain and helps regulate the Earth's climate.

Elsewhere, the Seashores Zone brings Britain's threatened coastlines to life, with a fully functioning North Devon rock pool complete with crabs, shellfish and realistic wave surges. There's plenty of tropical colour too: more exotic habitats reconstructed at the new aquarium include a Fijian coral reef, a Caribbean mangrove swamp and a stunning South American rainforest teeming with bizarre creatures like the monkey frog and the starlight catfish.

All told, the refitted aquarium boasts enough gadgetry and simulated exotic environments to enchant everyone, but it's not all state-of-the-art wizardry: the Victorian-style parlour aquarium of the Drawn to Water Zone features a painting of sea anemones by the eminent British naturalist Philip Henry Gosse, a colleague of Charles Darwin, who is credited with coining the word 'aquarium' in the mid 1800s. Gosse was also a friend of Alfred Cort Haddon, who helped Horniman set up the first aquarium here, in 1903. It seems a fitting gesture, more than a century later, as the museum prepares to illuminate the oceans for yet more generations of Londoners to come.

place on Fridays and Saturdays. School holidays and Saturdays see art and craft workshops, and there are Hands On activity workshops throughout the year (pick up a What's On leaflet for details).

Forthcoming attractions include a display of decorative artefacts from Amazonian rainforest tribes, and an exhibition documenting the life of Crow Indians in 21st-century America (both until 31 Oct 2006). A showcase of Cambodian Khmer silk costumes runs until February 2007. Outside, the delightful gardens boast a pets corner, an elegant conservatory and a picnic spot with superb views. The café is a welcome pit stop in colder weather.
Buggy access/storage. Café. Disabled access: lift, ramps, toilets. Nappy-changing facilities. Nearest picnic place: Horniman Gardens. Shop.

London Wildlife Trust Centre for Wildlife Gardening

28 Marsden Road, SE15 4EE (7252 9186/www.wild london.org.uk). East Dulwich rail. **Open** 10.30am-4.30pm Tue-Thur, Sun. **Admission** free.
The London Wildlife Trust has been reclaiming derelict land for nature reserves for over two decades, and this centre – created on a disused bus depot – is one of its best. Its attractions include areas of wildlife-friendly woodland and marshland, a herb garden, pond area and a nursery for plants and trees. Local families can fill their own gardens with greenery raised here, for a donation to the LWT. The visitors' centre has tanks of fish and stick insects, and a sandpit play area goes down well with toddlers. Every March, families descend on the centre for

Frog Day, a celebration of spring with children's games, frog-spotting and craft-based activities. For £15 a year, eight- to ten-year-olds can join the Wildlife Watch Club. As members, they can take part in outdoor activities like pond-dipping and bat-walking.
Buggy access. Disabled access: toilets. Nappy-changing facilities. Nearest picnic place: wildlife garden.

Crystal Palace

When Joseph Paxton moved his enormous glass centrepiece from the Great Exhibition in Hyde Park to a hilltop estate in Sydenham's Great North Wood in 1852, he turned a relatively unknown suburb of London into the cultural and entertainment capital of the capital. The building was a showcase for creative and industrial achievements from around the world and could be seen from the farthest corners of the city. Its surroundings blossomed as a result; new houses, amenities and transport links were built to accommodate the influx, and Crystal Palace looked all set to redefine London's cultural heritage – until 1936, that is, when the building was destroyed in the country's largest peacetime fire of the 20th century. These days, the crumbling remains of the park – statuary, graffitied stone stairs to nowhere, a motley collection of bizarre

Leafy **Dulwich**. *See p134.*

dinosaurs – lend the otherworldly air of a lost civilization. The local sports centre does its best to drag the place into the 21st century (hosting various national athletics championships, and the occasional rock concert), but its grim mid-60s architecture isn't exactly easy on the eyes. The enigmatic Crystal Palace Museum offers an insight into this epic chapter of London's history. There's little to see or do locally other than marvel at the size of the 222-metre (728 feet) Crystal Palace television transmission tower, although there are a handful of child-friendly places to grab a bite of lunch on the high street.

Crystal Palace Museum

Anerley Hill, SE19 2BA (8676 0700). Crystal Palace rail. **Open** 11am-5pm Sun, bank hol Mon. **Admission** free.

To find out more about the majestic exhibition that gave this area its name, pop into this friendly museum, housed in the old engineering school where John Logie Baird invented the television. The museum is entirely volunteer-run, so opening hours are limited, but school groups are welcome on weekdays provided teachers book a few weeks ahead. The 'exhibition of an exhibition' includes some enchanting Victorian artefacts from the original Hyde Park production, as well as video and audio presentations about the great glass building. A small Logie Baird display marks the birth of home entertainment; from June 1934 the

Baird Television Company had four studios at Crystal Palace. The Crystal Palace Foundation, which runs the museum, hosts an annual Victorian weekend at the Penge entrance to the park (1, 2 July 2006).
Nearest picnic place: Crystal Palace Park. Shop.

Crystal Palace Park

Thicket Road, SE20 8DT (8778 9496/www.bromley. gov.uk). Crystal Palace rail/2, 3, 63, 122, 157, 227 bus. **Open** 7.30am-dusk daily. **Admission** free.
The London Development Agency is now in charge of negotiating the hurdles that have dogged the redevelopment of Crystal Palace Park for years: not the least of them are financial, although the question of how large a landmark Londoners really want is a matter for ongoing consultation. Until the work is finished, the decaying terraces of Joseph Paxton's enterprise remain a highly atmospheric place to potter; all the more haunting when you think how many generations of Londoners were once wowed in what is now effectively a wasteland. So far, the 'monsters' (the remains of a Victorian prehistoric theme park created by Benjamin Waterhouse-Hawkins), restored in 2003, stand around the freshly landscaped tidal lake, the hornbeam maze has been replanted, and we're all waiting for the animals to return to the little farm. The National Sports Centre, although in need of cosmetic attention, has a busy programme of events for all ages and abilities and one of the few Olympic-sized (50m/160ft) pools in London.
Buggy access. Café. Disabled access: toilets. Nappy-changing facilities.

Further south-east

Watling Street, the pilgrims' way out of London en route to Canterbury, is now the A207, and the villages it passed through are London suburbs, such as Bexleyheath, where the National Trust's Red House (13 Red House Lane, 8304 9878), once the home of William Morris, attracts a mixed crowd of artists and historians.

Between Bexleyheath and Welling, huge Danson Park contains an 18th-century Palladian villa, but lively children may be more interested in the park (ranger service 8304 9130), with its woods, lakes and terrific watersports centre (8303 2828), which organises a wacky annual all-nations polo tournament in August. Danson Park's annual show takes place 1-2 July 2006. More delightful parkland and a stunning Tudor mansion can be enjoyed at **Hall Place**, just up the road in Bexley.

The area around Eltham and Bexley is dotted with meadows and woodlands. **Oxleas Wood,** across the Shooters Hill Road, is an 8,000-year-old piece of woodland, dating back to the Ice Age. The wood was to be uprooted in the mid 1990s – until a campaign stopped the bulldozers. Its paths link up with the Green Chain Walk (8921 5028, www.greenchain.com), a 64-kilometre (40-mile) network starting near the Thames Barrier (*see p131*) and ending at Crystal Palace. The Oxleas Wood path starts at Erith and takes in the remains

of 12th-century **Lesnes Abbey**, a fine picnic place with tower-block views to the north.

Organic **Woodlands Farm** can be found just off Shooters Hill (the name of this area of Kent as well as the road that leads to it from near Blackheath). Across the A20, the village of **Chislehurst** has its very own Druids' caves.

Further west, beyond Bromley, Croydon is one of London's busier southern suburbs, with a tram system, the Whitgift Centre and the **Croydon Clocktower**. The Warehouse Theatre Company (62 Dingwall Road, 8681 1257, www.warehousetheatre.co.uk) offers drama workshops during the holidays and children's productions on Saturdays.

If you're prepared to venture out through the London Borough of Bromley as far as Orpington, pay a visit to Down House (Luxted Road, Downe, 01689 859 119/www.english-heritage.org.uk), former home of Charles Darwin, which in 2005 became a World Heritage Site. Down was the scientist's home for 40 years and includes his experimental garden and 'thinking path'. It's open Wednesday to Sunday only (phone English Heritage for details).

Chislehurst Caves

Old Hill, Chislehurst, Kent BR7 5NB (8467 3264/ www.chislehurstcaves.co.uk). Chislehurst rail. **Open** 9am-5pm Wed-Sun. *Tours* hourly; phone for details. **Admission** (LP) £5; £3 5-15s, OAPs; free under-5s **Credit** MC, V.
The spooky caves and passageways at Chislehurst were carved out of the hillside by Druids digging for chalk and flint (they also came here to make grisly human sacrifices). In due course, the Romans were to extract chalk from here and, more recently, the caves were used as a World War I ammunition dump and, in the 1930s, a mushroom farm. But the caves became famous during World War II, when they were Britain's largest bomb shelter.
The 45-minute lamp-lit tour covers less than a mile, taking in the Druid altar and cave church. It's not strenuous, but it isn't for the claustrophobic. If you fancied it, you could even have a birthday party in the café here.
Café. Shop.

Croydon Clocktower

Katharine Street, Croydon, Surrey CR9 1ET (box office 8253 1030/tourist information 8253 1009/ www.croydon.gov.uk/clocktower). East Croydon or West Croydon rail/George Street tram. **Open** *Clocktower & library* 9am-7pm Mon; 9am-6pm Tue, Wed, Fri; 9.30am-6pm Thur; 9am-5pm Sat. *Clocktower Café* 9.30am-5.30pm Mon-Sat. Closed bank hols. *Tourist Information Centre* 9am-6pm Mon-Wed, Fri; 9am-5pm Sat. *Museum & galleries* Closed until Sept 2006. **Admission** free.
Croydon Clocktower, built in 1896, is a splendid Victorian building – a stark contrast to all the surrounding office blocks. Its museum is closed for refurbishment until September 2006. The David Lean Cinema has a kids' club (11am Sat) and special screenings for parents and carers

Around Town

Alfresco eating at **Eltham Palace**.

accompanied by babies. Braithwaite Hall, the centre's theatre, hosts weekend and holiday theatre productions for children every month. To find out what's on, pick up a brochure or check the website. The library hosts story, music and art sessions and runs a homework help club.
Buggy access. Café. Disabled access: lifts, ramps, toilets. Nappy-changing facilities. Nearest picnic place: Queen's Gardens.

Eltham Palace

Court Yard, off Court Road, SE9 5QE (8294 2548/ www.elthampalace.org.uk). Eltham rail. **Open** *Apr-Oct* 10am-5pm Mon-Wed, Sun. *Nov-Mar* 10am-4pm Mon-Wed, Sun. Closed 22 Dec-31 Jan. **Admission** *House & grounds* (incl audio tour) £7.60; £5.70 concessions; £3.80 5-16s; free under-5s; £19 family. *Grounds only* £4.80; £3.60 concessions; £2.40 5-16s; free under-5s. **Credit** MC, V.
A royal residence from the 13th century through to Henry VIII's heyday, Eltham Palace fell out of favour in the latter part of Henry's reign, after which it fell into ruin. Its Great Hall, the most substantial surviving medieval hall outside the Palace of Westminster, was used as a barn for many years. It was not until 1931 that the wealthy Stephen

Courtauld, a patron of the arts, commissioned a thoroughly modern house to stand among the relics of the old palace. The Great Hall, with its stained glass and hammer beam roof, was pressed into service for glamorous society parties, concerts and banquets. The interior is all polished veneer and chunky marble, with mod cons such as concealed lighting, underfloor heating and a room-to-room vacuuming system. Even the Courtauld's beloved pet ring-tailed lemur, Mah-Jongg, lived the life of Riley in his special lodgings. The grounds are beautifully restored, and the tearoom and shop have a distinctly 1930s flavour.
As well as free quiz sheets and trails for children, various family-friendly events are laid on for visitors throughout the year. The gardens are used for open-air performances of Shakespeare during the summer, and there's a 1930s dance experience (14 Sept 2006) and a Birds of Prey display (24, 25 Oct 2006) for families to look forward to. Check the website for details.
Buggy storage. Café. Disabled access: lift, toilets. Nappy-changing facilities. Nearest picnic place: palace grounds. Shop.

Hall Place & Gardens

Bourne Road, Bexley, Kent DA5 1PQ (01322 526574/ www.hallplaceandgardens.com). Bexley rail/132, 229, 492, B15 bus. **Open** *Apr-Oct* 10am-5pm Mon-Sat; 11am-5pm Sun, bank hols. *Nov-Mar* 10am-4pm Tue-Sat. **Admission** free. **Credit** *Shop* MC, V.
This enchanting Tudor mansion, on the banks of the River Cray, was built nearly 500 years ago for the Lord Mayor of London, Sir John Champneys. Its fine panelled Great Hall, with minstrels' gallery, is a favourite venue for music societies and chamber groups, and the extensive gardens, with their topiary, herb garden, model allotments and sub-tropical plant houses, have won several Green Flag awards. A new environmental-education garden in the walled nursery has a pond-dipping area (to catch 'mini beasts'), a small meadow and a Tudor knot garden. In the Austen Gallery there's a hands-on Science Project exhibition about lasers and lights (5 Aug-2 Sept 2006), and regular art and photography exhibitions take place in the Chapel and Dashwood galleries. Half-term art and craft activities cater for children aged from three years; phone for details. Easter and summer holidays see egg trails, garden festivals and open-air theatre productions, while Christmas is celebrated with merry workshops, dressing-up, craft fairs and carols.
Buggy access. Café. Disabled access: lifts, ramps, toilets. Garden centre. Nappy-changing facilities. Shop.

Woodlands Farm

331 Shooters Hill, Welling, Kent DA16 3RP (8319 8900/www.thewoodlandsfarmtrust.org). Falconwood rail/89, 486 bus. **Open** 9.30am-4.30pm daily. **Admission** free; donations appreciated.
This large community farm, covering 89 acres, straddles the boroughs of Greenwich and Bexley and is a thriving organic enterprise, with a lovely cottage and wildlife garden, orchards and meadows. There are some noisy geese and hens, a flock of sheep, a cow and a pair of Shetland ponies called Ted and Bob. A core staff keeps the place ticking over, but volunteers are welcome to don their gumboots and help out. The farm hosts educational group visits, giving lessons on farm-animal care, conservation, composting and the history of farming. Keep an eye on the website for events and activities (such as orienteering, pond-dipping and Lambing Day).
Buggy access. Nearest picnic place: farm grounds. Shop.

South-west London

Urban grit gives way to happy valley in London's nappy belt.

Battersea Park Children's Zoo.
See p141.

Vauxhall & Stockwell

On the cusp of Zone 2 and central London, Vauxhall is impressively well connected: alongside the tube and rail station is a futuristic bus station with solar panels. Vauxhall's other eye-catching structure is the riverside 'Spy Central', the MI6 headquarters flanking Vauxhall Bridge, featured in *The World Is Not Enough*.

Vauxhall is plagued by round-the-clock heavy traffic, exacerbated by the fruit and flower wholesalers of New Covent Garden Market. Happily, though, there's a fine selection of green spaces for families to enjoy – admittedly, these are less exotic than the 18th-century local hotspot Vauxhall Pleasure Gardens (the plain Spring Gardens is all that remains).

At Vauxhall Park (junction of South Lambeth Road and Fentiman Road, SW8), there many

facilities, including a One O'Clock Club and a model village. The taste (and smell) of country life comes from **Vauxhall City Farm**. Neighbouring Stockwell has Slade Gardens Adventure Playground (Lorn Road, SW9, 7737 3829) and Larkhall Park (Courland Grove, SW8). Stockwell Bowl Skatepark, nearer Brixton (*see p140*) has been popular with local kids since the 1970s.

The local Portuguese community is reflected in the cafés and shops along South Lambeth Road. Overall, community spirit is a mark of this part of town – take the housing co-operatives of Bonnington Square, where residents created a 'secret garden' from a former bombsite. Oasis Children's Venture (7720 4276) is run by local residents and has a nature garden, a kart track and a cycle centre; its projects have included after-school environmental workshops, where kids have produced their own 'Recycling For Kids' leaflets.

Vauxhall City Farm

165 Tyers Street, SE11 5HS (7582 4204). Vauxhall tube/rail/2, 36, 44, 77 bus. **Open** 10.30am-4pm Wed-Sun. Closed 1wk in late summer, phone to check. **Admission** free; donations appreciated.
Founded on derelict land in 1977, and run by an enthusiastic team of staff and volunteers, Vauxhall City Farm attracts around 12,000 visitors a year. The sociable livestock reared in its grassy paddocks – against a backdrop of big city buildings – include cows, pigs, sheep, poultry, donkeys and horses; many breeds have won awards in farm shows. Various education, refugee and gardening groups meet at the farm; it also runs Sunday art classes, offers subsidised riding lessons for local children, and has a popular after-school club and summer playscheme. *Buggy access. Disabled access: toilet. Nappy-changing facilities.*

Brixton

Culturally rich Brixton has transformed itself radically from it 19th-century roots as a prototype suburb into South London's buzziest residential area. With a rough-around-the-edges charm, it's most famous for its nightlife and live venues such as Brixton Academy (accompanied under-18s are admitted to some gigs). Still, there's plenty to do before dark – such as exploring the diverse wares of cheap 'n' cheerful Brixton Market; dating back to 1870, its stalls now offer everything from Afro-Caribbean food to children's clothes. The street running alongside is Electric Avenue, so-called because it was one of London's first streets to be lit by electricity; it is namechecked by Eddy Grant's single (a hit in 1983 and 2001). The restored Ritzy Cinema (*see p218*) used to be one of nine local picture houses; it's well worth catching the Kids' Club matinées every Saturday. For a hot summer day, few attractions could beat Brockwell Lido – as most of South London seems to agree.

Brockwell Park

Dulwich Road, SE24 0PA (7926 0105). Herne Hill rail. **Open** 7am-dusk daily.
It has a south-eastern postcode,but this park is Lambeth's responsibility, and it's most valued by the people of bustling Brixton. Brockwell Hall is the looming landmark in the park, which originally opened to the public in 1892 and has retained much of its 19th-century character. The place has shown signs of wear and tear in recent years, but a successful Heritage Lottery Fund bid promises to spruce things up nicely. Park plus points include play facilities for a broad age range (playgrounds, a BMX trail and multi-sports pitch), duck ponds and an increased live entertainment schedule, including music festivals and a free fireworks display around 5 November. The annual Lambeth Country Show (15-16 July 2006) is a massive hit with families, with quirky entertainment such as farmyard displays, live music, a miniature railway, food stalls and a 'vegetable animal' craft competition.
Of course, the art deco Brockwell Lido is a reason to visit in its own right; the unheated outdoor pool comes into its own during a hot summer (see www.thelido.co.uk for 2006

opening times); there's also a paddling pool for water babies. A proactive users' group (www.brockwell lido.com) ensures that there is plenty going on despite funding difficulties, with an excellent seasonal programme of kids' activities including 'Whippersnappers' music workshops for the under-fives.
Buggy access. Café. Disabled access: toilets. Nappy-changing facilities.

Streatham

Ever since Roman Londinium, this part of town has been a major thoroughfare; today, traffic-choked Streatham High Road is reviled for its famously ill looks. Streatham may have long ago given way to urban sprawl, but it is a well-used hive of weekend activities for active youngsters. Its buses and three railway stations make access easy, too. The Streatham Ice Arena (*see p265*) has long been an essential destination, and there's also fun to be had at the Streatham Megabowl (*see p270*) and Playscape Pro Racing (*see p261*). Streathamites call the combined attractions of rink, track and bowling lane the Streatham Hub and they campaigned for improvements to the facilities here. Their saviour has come in the form of Tesco, which has agreed to fund a new top-flight rink with swimming pool in exchange for putting a supermarket in the area. Mayor Ken and Wandsworth Council have approved the plans, which should be completed by 2009.
As far as the great outdoors is concerned, Streatham's welcome designation as a conservation area has drawn more attention to local green sites. Streatham Common includes woodlands, a wild flower area and a charming 'secret' garden known as the Rookery, and hosts such lively annual events as 'Kite Day' (www.streathamkiteday.org.uk) and Streatham Festival's arty entertainment programme (1-14 July 2006, www.streathamfestival.info).

Battersea

Clapham Junction station, which has long held the title of Britain's busiest railway station, is the main gateway to Battersea. Numerous steps and no lift mean it's tricky to negotiate with a pushchair, though. Once in the area, however, family-friendly pursuits are within easy reach. You could walk to the cafés and chic shops of Northcote Road (leading to Wandsworth's 'Nappy Valley', *see p142*) or trot up Lavender Hill to Battersea Arts Centre (Lavender Hill, SW11 5TN, 7223 2223, www.bac.org.uk), whose innovative programming has made it a *Time Out* Live Awards nominee. This convivial venue hosts regular projects such as BAC YPT, an open-access theatre group for 12-to 25-year-olds. Kids of all ages enjoy the Latchmere Leisure Centre (*see p268*), which also has a popular line in birthday pool parties.

Battersea Park is a year-round delight to explore, from the live events surrounding its pretty lake, to kids' hotspots, including an adventure playground and zoo.

The iconic Battersea Power Station still looms large on the skyline – but for how long? A major commercial/cultural project is planned here, but as this guide went to press, the site still looked dormant. Proposals to demolish the famous chimneys have provoked a fierce debate.

Battersea Park Children's Zoo

Queenstown Road, Battersea Park, SW11 4NJ (7924 5826/www.batterseazoo.co.uk). Sloane Square tube, then 19, 137 bus/Battersea Park or Queenstown Road rail/156, 345 bus. **Open** 10am-5pm daily. **Admission** £5.95; £4.50 3-15s; free under-2s; £18.50 family (2+2). **Credit** MC, V. **Map** p313 F13.

A zoo of small, sweet things, whose new owners (who also run an otter sanctuary in the New Forest) have pitched it just right for small children. Adults think it's perfect too. Everything looks spick and span, the notices are clear and informative, and the animal enclosures are clean, roomy and well kept. Staff are as delightful as the animals. The most entertaining residents have to be the playful otters, whose antics – playing with pebbles and chasing each other in and out of the stream – drew large crowds on a freezing January day. Children have lots of fun with the meerkats; little ones can actually pop their heads up in their enclosure, which they access via a tunnel – their heads are protected by see-through plastic viewing bubbles. We also loved the mouse house, especially all those little mice living it up in their own doll's house, just like Tom Thumb and Hunka Munka in Beatrix Potter's *Tale of Two Bad Mice*. Other friendly creatures include talking mynah birds and parrots, cuddlesome sheep and goats, rather bossy turkeys, wide-eyed monkeys, Shetland ponies and loads more. The shops's strong on pocket-money-priced toys, and there's plenty of space for a picnic if you don't fancy spending money in the Lemon Tree café. Another reason why so many families think South-west is best.
Buggy access. Café. Disabled access: ramps, toilets. Nappy-changing facilities. Shop.

Battersea Dogs & Cats Home

4 Battersea Park Road, SW8 4AA (7622 3626/ www.dogshome.org). Vauxhall tube/rail, then 44 bus/ Battersea Park or Queenstown Road rail/344 bus. **Open** *Viewings* 1-4pm Mon-Fri; 10.30am-4pm Sat, Sun. Closed 1 Jan, Good Friday, 25, 26 Dec. **Admission** £1; 50p 5-16s, concessions; free under-5s. **Credit** *Shop* MC, V.

While it's obviously not a conventional tourist attraction, this world-famous sanctuary for canines and felines (founded in 1871) is open to casual visitors as well as those who are set on adopting a furry friend. Responsible ownership is key – and the diligent staff here will vet all candidates to ensure they're right for the pet they're paying to rescue; this process could take several visits, and many of Battersea's rescued dogs are best suited to child-free homes. Still, this is still a fascinating destination for animal-loving kids, including a souvenir and accessory shop, a café and a collection of tributes to dogs and their owners. They offer sessions on how to choose and train your puppy or kitten, and kennels can also be 'sponsored' via their bright website.
Buggy access. Café. Disabled access: lift, ramp, toilet. Nearest picnic place: Battersea Park. Shop.

TOP 10 Pleasure gardens

Bonnington Square
A unique 'secret garden' filled with lavender and love and perfect for picnics. *See p139.*

Cherry Garden & Orangery, Ham House
Fruitful plots in landscaped grounds. *See p149.*

Climbers & Creepers, Kew Gardens
This indoor garden is better for a high-energy scrambles than serene rambles. *See p148.*

The Rookery, Streatham Common
Hidden amid woodlands and wild flowers, Streatham's saving grace. *See p140.*

The Isabella Plantation, Richmond Park
A woodland garden that's ablaze with colour in spring and early summer. *See p147.*

The Japanese Garden, Kew Gardens
One of many beautiful places to wander and meditate in Kew Gardens. *See p148.*

The Rose Garden, Morden Hall
Swoon at the scent of 2,000 gorgeous blooms in the summer months. *See p145.*

Hampton Court Palace
Stunning formal gardens fit for a cardinal and a king. Lose the kids during a wander in the famous maze. *See p150.*

Marble Hill House
You'll hardly believe you're in London on a ramble in the tree-filled riverside parkland and gardens. *See p150.*

Walled Garden, Brockwell Park
A bee- and butterfly-filled haven of peace, the garden is a lovely place to toddle, even while it's awaiting a much-needed makeover. *See p140.*

Welcome to Nappy Valley

Not for nothing did the leafy enclave between Wandsworth Common and Clapham become known as Nappy Valley. The claim that it has the highest birth rate in Europe may be hard to verify, but a quick stroll around the pleasant streets provides all the empirical evidence you'll need: au pairs push buggies; mummies lunch with offspring in tow; swathes of spruced-up schoolchildren fill the streets. In short, children are everywhere.

So what is the draw? Nappy Valley is so popular that people are prepared to pay £600,000 for a family home here, and houses have been known to make £2million– and there isn't even a Tube station. In fact, some property prices have tripled in the last 15 years, with particularly sought-after areas including the Magdalen Park Estate and the Nightingale Triangle.

Desirable school catchment areas, enviable open spaces and family-oriented local amenities are among the attractions cited by residents. Nico Sissons is a mother of two who moved here 13 years ago. 'We originally came here for more green space; in those days, it was less crowded than places like Fulham,' she explains. 'There is a good community here, with local One O'Clock clubs and sports facilities, and the atmosphere's quite buzzing; you still get the sense that you're in London, thanks to the train and bus links.' Well-off young couples, it seems, fix on Nappy Valley even before they've conceived their first: 'People do seem to come here to have children,' reports Nico. 'A young couple will move in, and nine months later, they've had their first baby.'

Of course, there is the odd downside to this capital idyll. In addition to property-price pressures, parents here share the common London concern that the quality of education doesn't continue from primary to secondary level. 'Local schools are better for younger children than older kids,' Nico says.

The Nappy Valley effect has brought artisan bakers, frou-frou boutiques (for parents and children) and upmarket child-friendly cafés to the area hubs of Northcote Road and Bellevue Road. But amid the immaculate smugness, you'll still find the odd surprise. Take the Lucky Parrot (2 Bellevue Parade, SW17 7EQ, 8672 7168), purveyor of 'glorious frivolata' for 30 years. The parrot in question, Apollo the African Grey, perches by the till, and the shop window serves as a community noticeboard. On our last visit one notice read 'Shut Guantanamo'.

Battersea Park

SW11 4NJ (8871 7530/boating lake 7262 1330/ www.wandsworth.gov.uk). Sloane Square tube, then 19, 137 bus/Battersea Park or Queenstown Road rail. **Open** 8am-dusk daily. **Map** p313 F13.

The marshy fields that this park was built on were originally used for market gardens, and more excitingly, for duelling. The Duke of Wellington fought an (abortive) duel at Battersea Fields in 1829. The riverside park laid out here in 1858 and recently has undergone an extensive restoration project. It genuinely offers a retreat for people of all ages, with facilities ranging from water features (a boating lake, fountains and riverside promenade) to its state-of-the-art sporting facilities and play areas, including a toddlers' playground and colourful adventure playground for children aged eight to 15 (8871 7539). Tennis coaching is available to anyone over eight on the floodlit courts, a range of cycles can be hired from London Recumbents (7498 6543; Sat, Sun, bank holidays, school holidays), and open fishing is available from mid June to mid March (for permit information, contact 8871 7530). Battersea Park is also home to a rich array of wildlife, including migratory birds and rare butterflies; the London Wildlife Trust runs nature reserves within its grounds. When you're feeding the ducks there are a whole load of other waterfowl to look out for, including herons, cormorants, grebes, and black swans.

The Gondola al Parco café (7978 1655) has tables overlooking the boating lake and live music during summer evenings – but the loveliest landmark remains the lofty Peace Pagoda, donated in 1985 by Japanese monks and nuns to commemorate Hiroshima Day. It stands serenely opposite the Children's Zoo, in the centre of the park's northern edge.

Buggy access. Café. Disabled access: toilets. Nappy-changing facilities.

Clapham & Wandsworth

Gentrification is key to this part of the capital – but the history of Wandsworth borough goes considerably further back; its name is thought to have derived from a Saxon tribal leader known as Wendel. Both Wandsworth Common and Clapham Common have great recreational features (the latter regularly hosts summer events, from live music to skateboard tournaments), upholding the area's tradition for breezy green spaces. The London Wildcare Centre (previously Wandsworth Environment Centre) on Wandsworth Common has unfortunately ceased its public opening hours due to lack of funds; however, special events are planned for summer 2006 – check the website for details (Wandsworth Common, Dorlcote Road, SW18 3RT 8871 3863, www.londonwildcare.org). The district between the Commons has earned the nickname 'Nappy Valley' (*see above* **Welcome to Nappy Valley**) thanks to its high proportion of young families; soaring house prices and chi-chi shops and cafés (particularly along Northcote Road, with its bustling market) lend the place an aspirational air. Clapham Old Town, north-east of the common, also has an upmarket high street, with plenty of places to eat out and the excellent Clapham Picture House (*see p216*).

Even Wandsworth's formerly grim Arndale Centre has scrubbed up in recent years – it's now the Southside mall (Wandsworth High Street, www.southsidewandsworth.com), and includes a multiplex Vue cinema. Alongside, King George's Park has seen better days, but it remains popular for its playgrounds and sports facilities, including the **Kimber BMX/Adventure Playground** and the football pitches and indoor play area at Wandle Recreation Centre (Mapleton Road, SW18 4DN, 8871 1149, www.kinetika.org), on the banks of the River Wandle. These are slightly off the beaten track, but worth travelling to if you're in charge of any two-wheel tearaways or a team of dedicated footie players.

The River Wandle, which flows out of ponds at Carshalton and Beddington in Surrey, bisects the meadowland around **Morden Hall Park** (*see p142*) and flows towards Wandsworth. The 15-kilometre (nine-mile) Wandle Trail (www.wandletrail.org) runs alongside the river between Wandsworth and Carshalton, passing through grim industrial landscape and newly regenerated wildlife havens. Towards Earlsfield, down Magdalen Road, lurks **It's a Kid's Thing**.

It's a Kids Thing

279 Magdalen Road, SW18 3NZ (8739 0909/ www.itsakidsthing.co.uk). Earlsfield rail. **Open** 9am-6pm daily. **Admission** £4 over-2s; £3 under-2s; £1 siblings under 18mths. *Activities* prices vary; check website for details.

On our last visit to this award-winning family-run indoor adventure play centre, both our three-year-old 'tester' and her baby sister had a whale of a time – the former tearing through its two-tier playzone, the latter in a special, more cuddly soft play area. Parents can keep a watchful eye from the café, which offers nursery food for all ages, or bury themselves blissfully in the daily papers, which are provided for grown-up fun. There's also an imaginative programme of activities (such as capoeira for five- to seven-year-olds) and a separate party room. It's a very popular local spot, so consider booking ahead, to avoid disappointment and tantrums.

Buggy access. Café. Disabled: toilets. Nappy-changing facilities. Nearest picnic place: Wandsworth Common.

Kimber BMX/Adventure Playground

King George's Park, Kimber Road, SW18 4NN (8870 2168). Earlsfield rail, then 44 or 270 bus. **Open** *Termtime* 3.30-7pm Tue-Fri; 11am-6pm Sat. *Holidays* 11am-6pm Mon-Sat. **Admission** free.

Bright multilingual 'welcome' signs mark the entrance to the playground. Aimed at under-16s, Kimber has all the usual variously challenging platforms, ropes, tyres and ladders, big swings, little swings and monkey bars, plus the added attractions of a basketball court and a compact BMX track. If kids don't have their own bike to skid around on, they can usually hire one at the playground (though do phone ahead to check availability). For showery days there's also an indoor games room with table tennis, as well as kitchens and arts and crafts rooms. The five ramps of the skateboard park are open to anyone who brings their own protective clothing.

Buggy access. Disabled access: ramp, toilet. Shop.

Lady Allen Adventure Playground

Chivalry Road, SW11 1HT (7228 0278/www.kids-online.org.uk). Clapham Junction rail. **Open** *Term-time* 10am-5pm Tue (under-8s only); 3-5pm Wed-Fri; 10am-noon Sat. *School holidays* 10am-3pm Tue (under-8s only); 10am-noon Mon, Wed-Fri. **Admission** free; £1 suggested donation per non-disabled child appreciated.

On the north-west corner of Wandsworth Common, this well-designed playground lets children with special needs and disabilities swing, slide, climb ropes, dangle off monkey bars and generally muck about with their mates in a very safe, well-supervised environment. This is a free, council-run service for children with disabilities who are Wandsworth residents; self-referral is by telephone. Families must phone ahead of visiting. Non-disabled children are also admitted (open access times listed above). *Buggy access. Disabled access: ramps, toilets. Nappy-changing facilities. Nearest picnic place: indoor & outdoor seating.*

Wandsworth Museum

The Courthouse, 11 Garratt Lane, SW18 4AQ (8871 7074/www.wandsworth.gov.uk). Clapham Junction rail, then 39, 77A, 156, 170, 337 bus/Wandsworth Town rail/28, 37, 44, 220, 270 bus. **Open** 10am-5pm Tue-Fri; 2-5pm Sat, Sun. Closed bank hols. **Admission** free. **Credit** *Shop* MC, V.

This tiny space crams in a history of Wandsworth from prehistoric times to the present day. Displays include an Ice Age fossilised skull of a woolly rhino (found during the construction of Battersea Power Station), a model of Wandle Mills, a World War II air-raid shelter and a Southfields chemist's shop. The downstairs museum area exhibits such treasures as an Iron Age sword and scabbard unearthed on the Thames foreshore at Wandsworth, cooking and farming tools from Wandsworth's Roman period, and swords, scabbards and

Around Town

Babies who lunch on **Northcote Road**.

Wimbledon Lawn Tennis Museum.

sundry weaponry from the medieval villages of Batricesage (Battersea), Baelgeham (Balham), Puttenhythe (Putney) and Totinge (Tooting). Interactive exhibits let children make a brass rubbing of a Putney knight or get their hands on an ancient flint hand-axe or a Roman helmet. A favourite term-time trip for local schools and school-holiday venue for families, the museum offers activities geared towards both the under-sixes and children aged six and above; advance booking is recommended for these. Some are connected with the exhibitions, others link in with nationwide events, such as Black History Month and The Big Draw (both in Oct).
Buggy access. Disabled access: toilet. Nappy-changing facilities. Nearest picnic place: King George's Park/ Old Burial Ground. Shop.

Tooting

Tooting's roots stretch back to Roman times, when its high street connected London with Chichester. Its history has been both bucolic and industrial, and nowadays it's a popular commuter base with elements of both. Tooting Common is a woody open space with a great playground and sports facilities – notably Tooting Bec Lido (8871 7198, www.slsc.org.uk), which opened in 1906 and is Europe's biggest open-air pool.

The area is home to a well-established Asian community, so has a wealth of Indian grocery markets. During festivals such as Eid or Diwali, illuminations are strung along Tooting High Street and Upper Tooting Road. There are some excellent South Asian restaurants here too – these might not offer kids' menus, but the atmosphere is reliably family-orientated.

Wimbledon

Wimbledon comes to world attention in June, when its world-famous annual Lawn Tennis Championships take place; they started here in 1877, and their history is documented in the **Wimbledon Lawn Tennis Museum**, which reopened after refurbishment in spring 2006. At any time of year, though, Wimbledon's town centre is accessible and family-friendly. Many amenities are based in the Centre Court shopping centre adjoining the station; an Odeon multiplex cinema is just across the road, and, further along the Broadway, there's further entertainment to be had at Wimbledon Theatre and the superb Polka Theatre for Children, which is always worth a visit (*see p225*). Southbound, towards Colliers Wood, there's the vast **Tiger's Eye** indoor adventure playground for boisterous under-nines.

Outdoor pursuits are always well served, thanks to Wimbledon Common's lovely nature trails, horse rides, cycle paths, sports facilities – and resident Wombles, according to Elisabeth Beresford's classic books. A wealth of green spaces includes Wimbledon Park, which has a boating lake, and the stately Morden Hall Park, which has meadows, wetlands and waterways. At the south of the common, Fishpond Wood & Beverley Meads nature trail (entrance near Beverley Meads car park at the end of Barham Road, SW20) is open at all times. The trail leads you through oak avenues and coppiced hazel woodland that has a profusion of bluebells in springtime. Seasonal ponds have plenty of amphibians and dragonflies.

Venture further south from Wimbledon, or alternatively follow the Northern Line to the bitter end, and you will be rewarded with **Morden Hall Park**, a former deer park on the River Wandle.

Deen City Farm & Community Garden

39 Windsor Avenue, SW19 2RR (8543 5300/ www.deencityfarm.co.uk). Colliers Wood tube, then 200 bus. **Open** 10am-4.30pm Tue-Sun, bank hol Mon. **Admission** free; donations welcome.
Founded in 1978, this community farm has pigs, goats, rabbits and poultry alongside rare breeds, which include Jacob sheep, fluffy alpacas Kimby and Milo, and Derek the white peacock. Deen City works as an educational resource for all ages, with volunteer schemes for those who fancy getting their hands dirty; it now boasts a successful parent and toddler group. Children's activities include Young Farmer days for eight to 13 year-olds, who can learn to feed, groom and clean out the animals during the school holidays. The riding school has facilities for the disabled and runs Own a Pony days (bookings on 8543 5858; it is advisable to book well ahead, as the days are popular). *Buggy access. Café. Disabled access: toilet. Nappy-changing facilities. Shop.*

Morden Hall Park
Morden Hall Road, Morden SM4 5JD (8545 6850/
www.nationaltrust.org.uk). Morden tube. **Open** 8am-
6pm daily. Closed 1 Jan 25-27 Dec. **Admission** free.
Credit *Shop* AmEx, MC, V.
This is National Trust-owned parkland of uncommon
beauty. The Morden Hall of the name is run as a private
restaurant, so public access centres meadows, woodland
and a network of waterways (the River Wandle flows
through the park). Between May and September the rose
garden bursts into around 2,000 blooms, but the park gives
South Londoners a reviving dose of countryside all year
round. The Snuff Mill Environmental Centre, housed in one
of several historic buildings in the park, has been
refurbished with improved accessibility, and its activities
include a nature club for parents and children (phone 8545
6852 for details). Craftspeople, furniture restorers and
artists occupy many of the old estate buildings, and the
Riverside Café is a beautiful place from which to admire
the surrounds while having tea.
Buggy access. Café. Disabled access: toilets. Nappy-
changing facilities. Shop.

Tiger's Eye
42 Station Road, Wimbledon, SW19 2LP (8543
1655/www.tigerseye.co.uk). Colliers Wood or South
Wimbledon tube. **Open** *Termtime* 10am-6pm Tue-Sun.
Holidays 10am-6pm daily. **Admission** £5.50 6yrs &
over; £4.99 2-5s; £2.50 under-2s. Height limit 4ft 9
inches. **Credit** MC,V.
Tiger's Eye is a vast barn of an indoor playcentre for
children up to the age of ten, with ball ponds, scramble
nets, soft play areas and slides. The jungle themed centre
also hosts parties for children.
Buggy access. Cafe. Disabled access: ramps, toilets.
Nappy changing facilities.

Wimbledon Lawn Tennis Museum
Centre Court, All England Lawn Tennis Club, Church
Road, SW19 5AE (8946 6131/www.wimbledon.org/
museum). Southfields tube/39, 93, 200, 493 bus.
Open 10.30am-5pm daily. *During championships*
spectators only. *Tours* Phone or check website for
details. **Admission** *Museum* £7.50; £6.25 concessions;
£4.75 5-16s; free under-5s. *Museum & tour* £14.50; £13
concessions; £11 5-16s. **Credit** AmEx, MC, V.
This museum was reopened in 'new and improved' form
at Easter 2006, with further interactive elements – for
instance, a chance to compare wooden and contemporary
racket grips, a virtual reality tour and a section on players' fashion. As ever, its celebration of the glorious game
includes memorabilia from famous players, views of the
Centre Court and an education programme. The eclectic
collection of artefacts has grown to include memorabilia
such as Victorian flannels, racket presses and tea sets, trophies from former champions, even 'I love Wimbledon'
souvenirs. There's also a library (admission by
appointment only, closed during the Championships) and
art gallery. Multilingual audio guides are available, and
you can take a tour of the whole jolly complex, including
Court No.1, the players' boards and the hallowed Centre
Court, where the finals are played.
   School groups have always been well catered for, with
the museum's Education Unit running classroom activities and workshops for children up to the age of 11, as well
as presiding over a developing programme for secondary
school or college-based visitors. Family activities happen

throughout the year, including historical workshops, which
acquaint visitors with famous faces from Wimbledon's
past, among them Maud Watson, the petticoat-clad first
Ladies Champion back in 1884, William Renshaw, seven
times Wimbledon Champion in the 1880s, and William
Coleman, head groundsman in the 1920s, who tells his visitors all about the Centre Court grass, the pony roller and
horse boots. Visit the website for dates and times for 2006.
Buggy access. Café. Disabled access: lift, toilet. Nappy-
changing facilities. Shop.

Wimbledon Windmill Museum
Windmill Road, Wimbledon Common, SW19 5NR
(8947 2825/www.wimbledonwindmillmuseum.org.uk).
Wimbledon tube/rail. **Open** *Apr-Oct* 2-5pm Sat; 11am-
5pm Sun & bank hols; school groups by appointment
only. **Admission** £1; 50p children, concessions.
No credit cards.
John Betjeman wrote a verse tribute – 'Old Surrey Working
Woman' – to this Wimbledon landmark as part of the
Wimbledon Windmill Restoration Appeal. The old dear,
built in 1817, is still working, but only on high days and
holidays. It's believed to be the only remaining example of
a hollow-post flour mill in this country, and its restored
two-storey interior is full of display cases containing
working models of many other types of windmill, each with
a button to push to watch the sails go round. Other
hands-on exhibits feature various pieces of grain-grinding
equipment, including pestles and mortars and hand querns
(grinding stones). Such items are put to good use during
occasional children's workshops. Dioramas, tool and
machinery displays, videos, sieving and weighing exhibitions and a small Robert Baden-Powell exhibition (the
founder of the Scout movement wrote *Scouting For Boys*
here in 1908) make up the rest of the museum. Run and
maintained by the Wimbledon Windmill Museum Trust,
the museum relies on volunteers and the painstaking work
of Wimbedon-based architect Norman Plastow, who
crafted all the detailed models inside.
Buggy access (ground floor). Café. Car park. Shop.

Bucolic Morden Hall Park.

Around Town

That's edutainment at **Eddie Catz**.

Putney & Barnes

Putney's riverside suburb draws thousands of spectators in person (and millions more on TV) to watch the annual Varsity Boat Race, starting out from the University Stone, near Putney Bridge, and ending just over four miles away in Mortlake. The trees and parkland along the river lend a sense of Putney's rural history – although it's in sharp contrast to the modern luxury flats and busy high street nearby. Local amenities include a three-screen Odeon cinema, and the invariably busy Putney Exchange Shopping Centre; **Eddie Catz** also opened its first children's 'edutainment' centre here in 2005 – with different playzones for various ages, from bouncing babies to energetic tweenies. This play centre, with its interactive video game and pleasant café, hosts school-holiday activities throughout the year.

Putney Heath is a lengthy stretch of rugged beauty that eventually adjoins Wimbledon Common. Once the haunt of highwaymen, it isn't particularly geared towards kids' play today. The best option for playgrounds is the riverside King George's Park, which also has tennis courts; this is a charming and lively little park, and it usually hosts a Bonfire Night display.

Neighbouring Barnes exudes even more of an upmarket, village-like atmosphere – although it also draws glam rock devotees to the shrine of musician Marc Bolan, who was killed in a car crash near Barnes Common on 16 September 1977. A very different – and very widely recommended – visitors' attraction here is the **WWT Wetland Centre**; you can ride the dedicated 'Duck Bus' to this lovely nature reserve.

Eddie Catz

68-70 High Street, Putney, SW15 1SF (0845 201 1268/www.eddiecatz.com). Putney Bridge tube. **Open** 9.30am-6.30pm Mon-Sat; 10am-5pm Sun. **Admission** £5 over 3s; £4.50 under-3s; £3.50 under-2s. **Credit** MC, V.
This first-floor play centre and café is a big, bright, clean space, bordered by windows and mirrors, where £5 buys excited children access to interactive video games, table ice-hockey and a themed adventure play frame. There's an innovative programme of workshops such as 'Mad Science', which gave kids a chance to build rockets and robots; themes vary, so check the website for upcoming bookings. None of these edutainments is allowed to dominate the central café area, where adults can wallow unmolested, with the newspapers.
Buggy access. Café. Disabled access: lift, toilets. Nappy-changing facilities. Shop.

WWT Wetland Centre

Queen Elizabeth's Walk, SW13 9WT (8409 4400/ www.wwt.org.uk). Hammersmith tube, then 33, 72, 209 (alight at Red Lion pub) or 283 (Duck Bus direct to Centre) bus. **Open** *Summer* 9.30am-6pm daily. *Winter* 9.30am-5pm daily (last entry 1hr before closing). *Tours* 11am, 2pm daily. *Feeding tours* 3.30pm daily. **Admission** £7.25; £6 concessions; £4.50 4-16s; free under-4s; £18.50 family (2+2). *Tours* free. *Feeding tours* free. **Credit** MC, V.
Opened in May 2000, this reserve has quickly built a reputation as the best urban base in Europe for watching nature. One of nine Wetland Visitor Centres, the London site, a mere 6.5km (four miles) from the West End, supports a range of rare or threatened wildlife. There are at least 150 species of bird, such as the Hawaiian goose, white-headed duck, red-breasted goose and blue duck. The site has 27,000 trees and 300,000 aquatic plants, and in summer, 300 varieties of butterfly flutter by. The centre is divided into a permanent section, where the exotic and endangered waterfowl are given appropriate (notwithstanding the English weather) habitats to play in, and open water lakes, reedbeds and mudflats that attract scores of insects, with

flocks of migratory birds not far behind them. If the weather's atrocious, it's possible to view parts of the reserve from indoors through CCTV cameras, but it's best to get outside with the binoculars (which can be rented here) and head for one of the three strategically placed hides. Young children might find it hard to keep quiet within the hides, so they're probably best off sticking to the permanent habitats, or joining one of the centre's impressively informed guides for a tour. The visitors' centre has various bird identification displays, and the Water's Edge café combines pretty good grub with an outdoor terrace. There's an excellent programme of seasonal activities for children (check the website or phone for details), with late opening, bat walks and and barbecues during the summer. A brand-new children's play area with landscaped wet/dry zones, called eXplore, is due to open in July 2006; it's certain to draw even more flocks of young visitors.

Buggy access. Café. Car park. Disabled access: lifts, toilet. Nappy-changing facilities. Shop.

Richmond & Kew

Elegant Richmond-upon-Thames has traditionally attracted wealthy residents, from royalty – including Henry VII, who built Richmond Palace in 1501 (its remains can be found on picturesque Richmond Green), and Elizabeth I, who sought recreation here before her death in 1603 – to rock stars and celebrities, such as Pete Townshend and Jerry Hall. This remains a strikingly scenic borough overall, very well suited to families thanks to its expansive open spaces (although it's still well-connected to London, via rail and tube); indoor entertainment can be found at Richmond Theatre, a beautiful, ornate Victorian venue that regularly offers children's shows and musicals (The Green, Richmond, TW9, 0870 060 6651, www.richmondtheatre.net).

One westbound stop along on the District Line, Kew is world-famous for its majestic **Royal Botanic Gardens**, while the town itself is a pleasant, sedate place for a family stroll.

East Sheen Common Nature Trail

East Sheen Common, Fife Road, SW14 7EW (Ranger 8876 2382/Borough Ecology Officer 8831 6125). Hammersmith tube, then 33 bus/Mortlake rail, then 15min walk. **Open** dawn-dusk daily. **Admission** free.
East Sheen Common, an attractive green expanse, is owned by the National Trust and run by the London Borough of Richmond. It is home to a small nature trail that runs through 13 areas of woodlands, ponds and streams marked with orange posts. A wildlife-watching leaflet, available from the resident ranger, tells you about the animals and insects that live around here. You'll be lucky if you see the badgers (unless you wander round here in the stilly watches; they have an active nightlife), but visit in spring and you should hear a frogs croaking and woodpeckers tapping. Summer brings butterflies to the meadow flowers and woodland floor; autumn provides berries for the birds. Contact the ranger for details of children's activities and guided walks.

Museum of Richmond

Old Town Hall, Whittaker Avenue, Richmond, Surrey TW9 1TP (8332 1141/www.museumofrichmond.com). Richmond tube/rail. **Open** 11am-5pm Tue-Sat. Closed public hols. **Admission** free.
Given its right royal connections, it's only fitting that Richmond should have a museum that parades its regal history, detailing the lives of silver-spooned former residents, from the 12th-century Henry I to Elizabeth I four centuries later. There are permanent and temporary displays including local art, and the broad programme of children's activities includes workshops for pre-schoolers. Harry the Herald's Saturday Club, for six- to 11-year-olds, takes place on the third Saturday of every month (10-11.15am, £2 per child). An under-fives club, Mini-Heralds, takes place on the third Wednesday of every month (2-2.40pm, £1 per child). Free trails and drop-in activities change with the museum's various exhibitions, so consult the website for details.

Buggy access. Disabled access: lift, toilets. Nearest picnic place: Richmond Green/riverside. Shop.

National Archives

Kew, Richmond, Surrey TW9 4DU (8876 3444/ www.pro.gov.uk/education). Kew Gardens tube, then 10min walk/65, 391 bus, then 5min walk. **Open** 9am-5pm Mon, Wed, Fri; 10am-7pm Tue; 9am-7pm Thur; 9.30am-5pm Sat. *Tours* 11am, 2pm Sat (booking necessary). **Admission** free. *Tours* free.
The erstwhile Public Record Office is now known as the National Archives. Devoted to keeping the records of 1,000 years of central government and the law courts, the Archives brings these documents to life with imaginative family-friendly activities at its Education and Visitor Centre. The museum spans British history from the Domesday Book to the Festival of Britain, and the millions of historical documents, some relating to the lives of every-day people, go back as far as the Norman Conquest. School-holiday family events often involve dressing up, storytelling and craft sessions based around exhibition themes. Check the website's excellent online resources for details or call the interpretation department on 8392 5202. The Learning Curve a free online teaching and learning resource, following the History National Curriculum from Key Stages 2 to 5, is well worth a look.
Buggy access. Café. Disabled access: lifts, toilet. Nappy-changing facilities. Nearest picnic place: National Archives grounds. Shop.

Richmond Park

Holly Lodge, Richmond, Surrey TW10 5HS (8948 3209/www.royalparks.gov.uk). **Open** *Summer* 7am-30mins before dusk. *Winter* 7.30am-30mins before dusk. **Admission** free
Extensive Richmond Park, 13km (eight miles) across its widest point, is the biggest city park in Europe and rivalled only by Epping Forest as the nearest London gets to wild countryside. Picturesque herds of red and fallow deer roam freely, a source of much fascination to children, but do bear in mind that these seemingly shy and gentle wild animals can be fierce in autumn during the rutting season. The whole family needs to pay heed to the signs that warn you not to get too close. Besides the deer, the park is home to numerous varieties of bird, fish and, apparently, 1,000 species of beetle. Tucked away in the middle of the park is the Isabella Plantation, a secluded and tranquil woodland garden. It's primarily home to acid-loving plants such as

Around Town

The new Alpine House at **Kew Gardens**.

camellias, azaleas and rhododendrons, and is best seen in all its glory in early summer or late September. Criss-crossed with streams and ponds, stepping stones and wooden bridges, it makes fun walking for children. There are also plenty of benches and grassy glades where you can picnic. The park's Petersham Gate has a playground, not far from here is King Henry VIII's Mound. Follow the twisting path up this leafy hillock and, from the top, you'll have a spectacular view right across London. On a clear day, the London Eye and St Paul's Cathedral can easily be made out. Alternatively, you could stroll along Terrace Walk, a famous Victorian promenade that stretches all the way from the philosopher Bertrand Russell's childhood home, Pembroke Lodge (now a licensed café, and a good lunch spot for the picnic-less), and beyond the park to Richmond Hill, continuing the wonderful views.

A great way to see the park is by bike: a well-kept cycle path rings the perimeter. If it's too much hassle to bring your own bicycles, it's possible to hire them from Roehampton Gate (07050 209 249/7581 1188). Adult bikes with tag-alongs (for the over-fives) and child-seats are available, as are children's bikes for those who have already learned how to ride without stabilisers.

Between June and March, fishing is available at Pen Ponds by paid permit from Holly Lodge (child concessions available); for details, call 8948 3209. Like all the Royal Parks, Richmond hosts a summer events programme for families, see the notice at the gate lodge or on the website. *Café.*

Royal Botanic Gardens (Kew Gardens)

Richmond, Surrey TW9 3AB (8332 5655/information 8940 1171/www.kew.org.uk). Kew Gardens tube/rail/ Kew Bridge rail/riverboat to Kew Pier. **Open** *Apr-early Sep* 9.30am-6.30pm Mon-Fri; 9.30am-7.30pm Sat, Sun. *Early Sep-late Oct* 9.30am-6pm daily. *Late Oct-early Feb* 9.30am-4.15pm daily. *Early Feb-late Mar* 9.30am-5.30pm daily (last entry 30mins before closing). **Tours** 11am, 2pm daily. **Admission** (LP) £11.75; £8.75 concessions, late entry (4.45pm); free under-17s. **Credit** AmEx, DC, MC.

The 300 acres of gardens, split into 47 areas, are a massive amount of ground to cover – but small visitors will always make a beeline for the brilliantly designed Climbers & Creepers adventure playground, which opened in June 2004. Kids aged three to nine have great fun climbing into a giant flower to 'pollinate' it, clambering through an illuminated blackberry tangle, and digging for 'fossilised plants', while real live insects buzz through see-through habitats; all the while, they're actually learning about the importance of plant and animal relationships. Climbers & Creepers is the base for new Midnight Ramble sleepovers, which give eight- to 11-year-olds and accompanying guardians the chance to track local wildlife like badgers and bats, and earn prizes; scheduled dates for 2006 are 12 May, 17 June, 8 July and 28 October (£40 per head, booking subject to availability).

If you're exploring the gardens on foot, pick up a free map at the ticket office. Little legs might prefer to ride the Kew Explorer people-mover, which plies a circular route around the gardens (£3.50; £1 concessions, under-17s). Gordon the Garden Gnome (of CBBC animation fame) points out an interactive trail specially aimed at kids.

Overall, Kew's monuments, gardens, buildings and landscapes are divided into eight zones. Most visitors start at the Entrance Zone, which has the Broad Walk, Nash conservatory and the Orangery restaurant. This leads to the Pagoda Vista Zone, with the glorious Japanese Gateway taking you to the serene gardens of Peace, Activity and Harmony. Perhaps most popular of all is the Palm House Zone. The glass-constructed building (designed by Decimus Burton and Richard Taylor in 1848) has exotic plants from Africa, Asia and America, and a series of spiral staircases that allows you to view them all from a gallery. The Palm House has its resident record-breakers in the form of the oldest pot plant in the world and the tallest palm under glass. Kew's latest glasshouse, the £800,000 Alpine House, designed by Wilkinson Eyre Architects, opened in spring 2006. The Syon Vista Zone, with – obviously enough – views of Syon House across the Thames, is dominated by an artificial lake. The Western Zone, which was once part of Richmond Gardens, has a bamboo garden and the Japanese Minka House (used for workshops, displays and events). The Riverside Zone runs alongside the Thames. It contains the newly opened Kew Palace and the 17th-century-style Queen's Garden.

There are cafés and restaurants dotted throughout Kew Gardens, but on a fine day you can't beat a picnic. Art exhibitions and live music during the summer, and a winter ice rink in front of the Temperate House (check website for dates) ensure that this place is a year-round treat.

Buggy access. Cafés. Disabled access: ramps, toilets. Nappy-changing facilities. Nearest picnic place: grounds. Restaurants. Shop.

Further south-west

Stunningly scenic greenery and historic splendour are all within easy reach of the capital; hop aboard a south-bound train from Clapham Junction station, or just follow the undulating Thames into Surrey. Nearby Kingston-upon-Thames has pretty riverside paths alongside its busy pedestrianised shopping hub, while Richmond and sporty Twickenham offer an increasingly tranquil, genteel ambience.

The pretty southern reaches of the river towards well-to-do Twickenham are lovely spots to ride a bike around, and there's the Thames Path for walkers. Way out on the westerly reaches of Twickenham, pretty Crane Park Island (entrance on Ellerman Avenue, TW1, 8755 2339, www.wildlondon.org.uk) is one of the London Wildlife Trust's staffed reserves. It used to be the old Hounslow Gunpowder Mills, but is now a peaceful haven surrounded by the River Crane, where woodland, scrub and reedbeds provide a home for the increasingly scarce water vole. Work is now in progress to turn the tower, an imposing relic of the old mills, into a nature study centre.

The area has a number of gracious historic buildings. Overlooking the river from Marble Hill Park, **Marble Hill House** is a perfect example of a Palladian villa. Neighbouring **Orleans House** (Riverside, Twickenham TW1 3DJ, 8831 6000, www.richmond.gov.uk) was built in 1710 for James Johnston, William III's secretary of state for Scotland, but later it became home to the exiled Duke of Orléans – hence the name. **Ham House** is another favourite: a handsome, red-brick, riverside mansion with a beautiful, well-kept garden. Carrying on along the river past Twickenham, you'll eventually come to the **Museum of Rugby** inside Twickenham Stadium.

From Twickers, the river passes by the busy shopping centre of Kingston-upon-Thames, then curves around to **Hampton Court Palace**. Once the country seat of Cardinal Wolsey, the palace was taken over by Henry VIII, who liked it so much he spent three honeymoons here.

For a real day-trip retreat, try Box Hill (www.nationaltrust.org), where the lovely woodland and chalk downs are traditionally popular with cyclists and ramblers, and even helped to inspire Jane Austen's 1815 novel *Emma*. The views from its summit make for a memorably great outdoors experience.

Ham House

Ham Street, Ham, Richmond, Surrey TW10 7RS (8940 1950/www.nationaltrust.org.uk). Richmond tube/rail, then 371 bus. **Open** *House* mid Mar-Nov 1-5pm Mon-Wed, Sat, Sun. *Gardens* 11am-6pm or dusk Mon-Wed, Sat, Sun. Closed 1 Jan, 25, 26 Dec. *Tours* Wed (pre-booking essential). Phone for membership details & prices. **Admission** (NT) *House & gardens* £8; £4 5-15s; free under-5s; £19 family (2+2). *Gardens only* £4; £2 5-15s; free under-5s; £9 family (2+2). **Credit** AmEx, MC, V.
Built in 1610, this lavishly restored riverside mansion was originally home to the Duke and Duchess of Lauderdale, and it was occupied by the same family until 1948. Today the interiors boast exemplary original furniture, paintings and textiles. The landscaped grounds include the Cherry Garden, with a central statue of Bacchus, the South Garden and the maze-like Wilderness, besides an Orangery with a terrace café. Ham House is reputedly one of Britain's most haunted houses, and its regular family events include entertaining Ghost Tours (suitable for over-fives; a torch-lit adult version is also available). In 2006, there's also a Restoration-themed exhibition, plus alfresco theatre in the garden in the summer, egg trails for Easter, art and craft open days for the August bank-holiday weekend, more spooky tours for Hallowe'en and all manner of of carols, feasts and art and craft events for Christmas (check the website for details).
Café (high chairs). Disabled access: lift, toilets. Nappy-changing facilities. Parking (free). Shop.

Around Town

Grand old **Ham House**. *See p150.*

Hampton Court Palace

East Molesey, Surrey KT8 9AU (0870 751 5175/ recorded info 0870 752 7777/www.hrp.org.uk). Hampton Court rail/riverboat from Westminster or Richmond to Hampton Court Pier (Apr-Oct). **Open** *Palace* Mar-Oct 10am-6pm daily. Nov-Feb 10am-4.30pm daily (last entry 1hr before closing). *Park* dawn-dusk daily. **Admission** *Palace, courtyard, cloister & maze* £12.30; £10 concessions; £8 5-15s; free under-5s; £36.40 family (2+3). *Gardens only* £4; £3 concessions; £2.50 5-15s; free under-5s; £12 family. *Maze only* £3.50; £2.50 5-15s. **Credit** AmEx, MC, V.
Breathtakingly beautiful, 'Magnificence-upon-Thames', is a very apt name for this most lavish of palaces. This sumptuous monument stands testimony to the rule of Henry VIII – although it was originally commissioned by Cardinal Wolsey in 1514. For the following two centuries, Hampton Court was a focal point in English history: Elizabeth I was imprisoned in its tower by her elder sister Mary I; Shakespeare performed here; and after the Civil War, Oliver Cromwell went against the puritanical grain and moved in. Little wonder, then, that there's so much to explore here. Hampton Court's beautifully imposing buildings span over six acres, with costumed guides adding a lively dimension to its state apartments, court-yards and cloisters. On selected bank holidays and week-ends, Tudor cookery demonstrations take place in the impressively vast kitchens, where children love the bubbling cauldrons and various game bird carcasses awaiting preparation for the pot). The gardens (over 60 acres of them) are a draw in their own right; Hampton

No pond-dipping at **Hampton Court Palace**.

Court's famous maze, a longtime family favourite, has been nicely spruced up in recent years, and now includes a sound installation. The oldest maze (open to the public) in the land, it was planted between 1689 and 1694, and is pretty easy to get lost in. Special events run throughout the year – blockbusters to look out for include the Hampton Court Palace Music Festival (June-July) and the Hampton Court Flower Show (3-9 July 2006), which attracts hoards of horticulturalists from the shires. Themed activities during the school holidays include Sports for the King and Fool in August 2006, when the palace recreates a series of fun outdoor activities that once delighted Henry VIII, including jousting, archery, hunting, shooting and laughing at jesters. For about six weeks from the beginning of December to mid January (call or check the website for 2006-7 dates) the west front of the palace is iced over for a scenic skate rink and Frost Fayre.
Buggy access. Café. Car park. Disabled access: lift, toilets. Nappy-changing facilities. Nearest picnic place: palace gardens/picnic area. Restaurant. Shops.

Marble Hill House

Richmond Road, Middx TW1 2NL (8892 5115/ www.english-heritage.org.uk). Richmond tube/rail/ 33, 90, 290, H22, R70 bus. **Open** *late Mar-Nov* 10am-2pm Sat; 10am-5pm Sun. *Tours* noon, 3pm Tue, Wed. **Admission** (EH, LP) £4; £3 concessions; £2 5-15s; free under-5s; £10 family (2+2). Price includes tour. **Credit** MC, V.
This stunning Thameside villa, once home to Henrietta Howard, mistress of King George II, was built in the 1720s with an £11,500 cash present from the king. The property is filled with Georgian objects and paintings, and it is also known for its stunning Honduran mahogany staircase. Marble Hill House hosts events throughout the year, including Easter trails, open-air concerts, such as the annual Jazz Café Picnic, and craft workshops. Guided tours can be taken of the house and its surrounding acres of parkland, and the house is connected by ferry to Ham House just across the river.
Nappy-changing facilities. Nearest picnic place: Marble Hill Park. Shop.

Museum of Rugby/ Twickenham Stadium

Twickenham Stadium, Rugby Road, Twickenham, Middx TW1 1DZ (0870 405 2001/www.rfu.com/ microsites/museum). Hounslow East tube, then 281 bus/Twickenham rail. **Open** *Museum* 10am-5pm Tue-Sat; 11am-5pm Sun (last entry 30mins before closing). *Tours* 10.30am, noon, 1.30pm, 3pm Tue-Sat; 1pm, 3pm Sun. Closed 1 Jan, Easter Sun, 24-26 Dec, Sun after match days. **Admission** Combined ticket £9; £6 concessions; £30 family (2+3). Advance booking advisable. **Credit** AmEx, MC, V.
This sports museum experienced increased interest following England's 2003 World Cup Rugby triumph, although enthusiasm might have waned somewhat given the team's poor showing in 2006. Non-match days see tours of the stadium, during which visitors can walk down the players' tunnel, look at the England dressing room and drop in on the Members' Lounge, the President's Suite and the Royal Box. The World Rugby Room tackles the game on an international level, while regular exhibitions reveal the history of such legendary teams as the All Blacks. Fans can admire sporting memorabilia dating back to 1871.
Buggy access. Disabled access: toilet. Restaurant. Shop.

West London

The best western postcodes command high prices, and families love them.

Bayswater & Paddington

Paddington Station, forever connected with the hard-staring bear (*see p154* **Please look after this bear**) is, less amusingly, where Victoria and Albert terminated their first train journey. Their train rushed along at a then heart-stopping 44 miles per hour (70km/h), which reputedly delivered the prince pale and shaken to this station, designed by Isambard Kingdom Brunel in 1851. The station also turned the area into a place of arrivals and departures, leading to a patchwork of downmarket squares fronted by grubby hotels for a transient population.

Today, the Paddington Basin development project is restoring land on either side of the Grand Union Canal with futuristic offices (including a swanky new M&S headquarters), arty bridges, waterside housing and a range of amenities and entertainments. Free walking tours (7313 1011, www.paddingtonwaterside.co.uk) get this fascinating area into perspective for visitors. One of them, starting at the Paddington Bear's statue and heading over to Peter Pan's in Hyde Park, is aimed at children, while other walks cover Brunel and the area's other famous pioneer, Alexander Fleming. Fleming discovered penicillin in St Mary's Hospital, thereby revolutionising modern medicine and earning a Nobel Prize.

Further south, the Bayswater Road skirts the north side of Hyde Park. Overpowering traffic makes it a less pleasant walk than it might be, but it's worth a stroll on Sundays, when the metal gates in front of the park display roughly a mile of paintings by aspiring artists; the quality varies dramatically, but the open-air setting makes a change from stuffy galleries. Queensway, towards the road's western end, was named after Queen Victoria, who used to ride her horse here en route to Kensington Palace. The main target for kids is Queens, the bowling alley and ice rink (*see p265*).

Whiteleys shopping centre (7229 8844, www.whiteleys.com) is a three-floor retail nirvana that retains its Edwardian charm (marble floors, sculpted water features, a glass domed ceiling) despite holding the unfortunate honour of being Hitler's favourite London building (he intended to make it his headquarters following victory in Europe). The third floor has an eight-screen UCI cinema and various chain restaurants and there is a Gymboree Play and Music Centre on the first floor. Bayswater is characterised by its large Chinese, Arabic and Persian communities, which accounts for the abundance of Oriental and Middle Eastern cafés and restaurants.

Alexander Fleming Laboratory Museum

St Mary's Hospital, Praed Street, W2 1NY (7886 6528/ www.st-marys.nhs.uk). Paddington tube/rail/7, 15, 27, 36 bus. **Open** 10am-1pm Mon-Thur; other times by appointment. Closed bank hols. **Admission** (LP) £2; £1 concessions, 5-16s; free under-5s. **No credit cards.** **Map** p313 D5.

Alexander Fleming made his momentous chance discovery of penicillin in this very room on 3 September 1928, when a Petri dish of bacteria became contaminated with some kind of mysterious mould. The museum is Fleming's laboratory recreated, with displays and a video that celebrate both his life and the role of penicillin in fighting disease. The staff run tours for family and school groups, and other visitors get a guided tour as part of the entrance fee. *Disabled access: toilets (in hospital). Nearest picnic place: Hyde Park. Shop.*

Paddington Basin has scrubbed up well.

Around Town

TOP 10 Urban Idylls

West London veers eccentrically between pretty, affluent neighbourhoods and pug-ugly, traffic-blighted inner city streets. Here's our pick of the former category.

Bedford Park, Ealing
London's first garden suburb and still an exclusive residential area. See p157.

Bishops Park
A hugely popular riverside ornamental park containing Fulham Palace, adjoining the loveliest allotments in London. See p155.

Chiswick Mall
Spectacular Georgian homes here have mini gardens across the road next to the Thames, facing Chiswick Eyot (a long narrow island on the Thames). See p157.

Holland Park
White stucco houses border a pretty, wooded park with added peacocks and open-air theatre. See p155.

Little Venice
Serene canalside walks past painted houseboats with geraniums, one of which even contains a puppet theatre. There are few prettier scenes in London. See right.

Parson's Green
A family-friendly, popular urban village (with a village green), close to Fulham Broadway. See p155.

Portobello Road
With a market forever associated with Julia and Hugh, this winding road is a perfect place to browse, shop and enjoy coffee and cakes at a Portuguese patisserie. See p153.

River Brent
The waterway that gave Brent Lodge Park its name has some stunning riverside walks. See p159.

Strand on the Green
The Thames Path here is perfect for a Sunday toddle. See p157.

Turnham Green
Delightful shops and the air of a posh Gloucestershire village make it lovable. See p157.

Maida Vale, Kilburn & Queen's Park

FM-savvy kids may recognise the name from the regular sessions recorded in the BBC 1 Maida Vale studio, but the reality of Maida Vale is more Mozart than Metallica; a picturesque community of Regency mansions, many of them white stucco numbers that crowd the canalside of **Little Venice**. Every May Day weekend, narrowboats from across the country travel here for the lovely Canalway Cavalcade (*see p28*). The Cavalcade also heralds a special performance from the unique and very sweet 50-seat Puppet Theatre Barge (www.puppetbarge.com), one of London's real treasures, which spends the winter moored in Little Venice putting on regular performances for adults and children, before embarking on its summer tour of the Thames (June-Oct). From Little Venice, it's possible to follow the canal all the way to Camden Lock, stopping for refreshments along the way at Café Laville (Little Venice Parade, W2 1TH, 7706 2620), and taking in sights such as the infamous 'Blow Up Bridge' (originally destroyed when a barge, loaded with gunpowder, detonated beneath it; evidence of the blast can still be seen on a neighbouring tree) or, further up, London Zoo (*see p67*). Little legs not up to the slog can board a London Waterbus (www.londonwaterbus.com) – traditional narrowboats that wind their way between Little Venice and Camden Lock or London Zoo (via a private water gate), and through the creepy Maida Vale Tunnel.

Rembrandt Gardens, next to Little Venice, is a quiet spot for repose and a picnic in fair weather. At Meanwhile Gardens, on the other side of the canal, there's a concrete skateboard bowl for aspiring Z-Boys – just make sure they take a helmet. The area's largest official outdoor space, however, is Paddington Recreation Ground, best known for its association with Roger Bannister, who trained here before breaking the four-minute mile in 1954. These days the park is home to a cricket ground, bowling green, gym and various tarmac courts for tennis, basketball and football.

Further north, **Queen's Park** is a real beauty: well maintained and with regular bandstand entertainers to keep kids amused in summer. Nearby Kilburn is characterised by a crowded, largely uninspired high street littered with chain stores and cafés, but it's a place rescued from obscurity by the delightful Tricycle Theatre & Cinema (*see p214*), which runs a year-round programme of Saturday children's plays and movies, as well as workshops and several oversubscribed youth theatre groups, two of them specifically for Jewish and Muslim children.

Queen's Park

Kingswood Avenue, NW6 6SG (park manager 8969 5661/info@queenspark.gov.uk). Queen's Park tube/rail. **Open** 7.30am-dusk daily. **Admission** free.

This Corporation of London park has wardens to maintain fair play, so parents with wandering children feel safer than in larger, less visibly staffed parks. There's a playground with a giant sandpit and adjacent paddling pool (open in summer), and a small enclosure of goats, ducks and chickens, as well as rotund guinea pigs and rabbits that keep small children busy for ages. At the northern end of the park is a wild, overgrown area with a nature trail signposted with pictures of the mini beasts you are likely to find there. A very pleasant, refurbished café is great for own-made cakes and locally made Disotto's ice-cream. Active bodies can enjoy the pitch-and-putt area, *pétanque* enclosure and six tennis courts. There's a programme of lively kids' entertainment taking place at the bandstand during the summer holiday (3-4pm Mon, Wed, Fri), although the main focus of family activities in the park falls on the annual Queen's Park Day, which in 2006 takes place on 10 September and features an abundance of fancy dress competitions, face-painting and plenty of 'He's behind you' puppeteering.

Buggy access. Café. Disabled access: toilet. Nappy-changing facilities.

Notting Hill

Cynics may claim that little has changed since the time when Notting Hill was known as the Piggeries for its 3:1 ratio of pigs to people, . Notting Hill has been put on the tourist map following Hugh and Julia's on-location larks in the 1999 comedy of the same name, but it also became synonymous with swanky celebrity life. Consequently, long-term residents rail against over gentrification, but the spiralling house prices and proliferation of smart amenities do something to ease the pain. Among the latter are some of the most media-centric kids' fixtures in the capital, including weekly script-writing classes for 14- to 18-year-olds at the Gate Theatre (7229 5387, www.gatetheatre.co.uk) and the Youth Culture TV centre (8964 4646, www.yctv.org), which gives 11- to 20-year-olds a head start in the television industry with free classes in writing, acting and programme production.

Not that things have always been so fancy. In the 1950s, Notting Hill was a reluctant hub for racial tensions between working-class whites and the unwelcome influx of Afro-Caribbean immigrants, many of whom were crammed into squalid tenement blocks by the millionaire landlord and shameless racketeer Peter Rachman. August 1958 saw four days of race riots – Britain's first – centred on Pembridge Road, where West Indian homes were attacked by white gangs, many of them bussed in especially. The following August saw the first Notting Hill Carnival take place as an assertion of cultural identity and solidarity. The carnival remains the area's defining event, second in the world only to Rio in terms of sheer scale, and annually turning the entire neighbourhood into a festival of colours and flavours, with masquerades, steel bands, decorative floats and more sound systems than you could shake a paper plate of curried goat at. Its reputation for bringing short, sharp spikes to the annual crime charts continues to court controversy, but increasing commercialism and a strong police presence has made the carnival safer than ever, and never more so than on the Bank Holiday Sunday, a designated children's day (www.lnhc.org.uk).

Year-round children's entertainment comes courtesy of the Electric and Gate cinemas (*see p216* for both). Portobello Road – the 'street where the riches of ages are stowed' immortalised in *Bedknobs and Broomsticks* – continues to provide one of the quirkiest outdoor markets on earth, filled with unexpected treasures (and plenty of tat), although prices seem to be rising as rapidly as the surrounding residences'. These days you'll find as much garden-variety fruit and veg as you will organic focaccia breads with feta and fennel, but it's still a glorious retro experience, especially on a Saturday. Speaking of retro experiences, the new **Museum of Brands, Packaging and Advertising** may reduce nostalgic parents to jelly with its images of yesteryear. Children will just have to humour them.

There's an excellent range of recreational and sporting facilities beneath the A40, which bisects Ladbroke Grove. The Westway Sports Centre (1 Crowthorne Road, W10 6RP, 8969 0092, www. westway.org/sports) has London's finest indoor (and outdoor) climbing wall, often overlooked in favour of its self-important competitor, the Castle in Manor House. The Westway Stables (20 Stable Way, Latimer Road, W10 6QX, 8964 2140, www.westwaystables.co.uk) organises riding lessons and pony-based birthday parties. Then there's the awesome Bay Sixty6 Skate Park (*see p264*). Kensington Leisure Centre, just across the way (Walmer Road, W11 4PQ, 7727 9747), has sporting facilities and something for the tinies in the form of Bumper's Back Yard, a littler version of **Bramley's Big Adventure**.

Local green lungs include Avondale Park, which has a playground, although parents are swayed by the proximity of Kensington Gardens. An eerie ramble can be enjoyed at Kensal Green Cemetery, north of the Grand Union Canal. A Victorian graveyard with a Greek Revivalist chapel and catacombs (over-12s only), it's the final resting place for many, including Isambard Kingdom Brunel and the author William Thackeray.

Please look after this bear

King's Cross Station may have platform 9¾, but Paddington has a bear. Paddington Bear, from Darkest Peru. However, unlike in the story, Michael Bond first met Paddington in Selfridges. It was Christmas Eve, 1957, and he was looking for a present for his wife, Brenda, when he chanced upon 'a small bear, looking, I thought, very sorry for himself as he was the only one who hadn't been sold'. Bond took the bear home and, some months later, sitting in front of his typewriter, he wrote: 'Mr and Mrs Brown first met Paddington on a railway platform. In fact, that was how he came to have such an unusual name for a bear, for Paddington was the name of the station.'

Bond had served in the army during World War II. He still had vivid memories of columns of refugees trudging along dusty roads, leaving behind everything they had once known, and evacuated children with labels tied around their necks and all their possessions in tiny suitcases. The small bear, sitting outside the Lost Property Office at Paddington Station, was just like that (apart from the fact that he was a bear, that is).

Around Town

Although Paddington was in many ways a furry wartime refugee, the world in which Bond placed him was more reminiscent of England between the wars. When Paddington moved into Mr and Mrs Brown's home at No.32 Windsor Gardens (Lansdowne Crescent in Bond's mind), he found the sort of middle-class household that no longer seems to exist. The children, Judy and Jonathan, both boarded at public schools, while Mrs Bird, the housekeeper, was based on a familiar pre-war figure: a widow of the Great War, reduced to making ends meet by housekeeping.

In fact, the terrible conflicts of the 20th century cast long shadows on the books. Wanting a character who could understand something of what it was like for Paddington to find himself a stranger in a strange land, Bond introduced the bear to Mr Gruber, the Hungarian keeper of an antiques shop on the Portobello Road. Michael Bond had met many Hungarians during his time working for the BBC Monitoring Service, and had been impressed with their kindness and philosophical approach to life's hardships. Paddington and Mr Gruber, like so many exiles, would sit and talk for hours of their lost homes, although they tended to prefer cocoa and buns to the more usual cigarettes and coffee.

But despite the loss that's hinted at in the books, Paddington remains a kind and thoughtful bear throughout, a reminder of a now-distant England, where people raised their hats before saying 'Good afternoon', and always said 'After you'. But lest politeness be mistaken for weakness, beware Paddington's hard stare, calculated to produce an uncomfortable blush in even the most supercilious of officials.

Bramley's Big Adventure

136 Bramley Road, W10 6TJ (8960 1515/ www.bramleysbig.co.uk) Latimer Road tube. **Open** *Term-time* 10am-6pm Mon-Fri; 10am-6.30pm Sat, Sun. *Holidays* 10am-6.30pm daily. **Membership** £15/yr. **Admission** *Members* £2/£2.50 under-2s; £3.50/£4 2-5s; £4/£4.50 over 5s. *Non-members* £3/£3.50 under-2s; £4.50/£5 2-5s; £5/£5.50 over-5s (Mon-Fri/Sat, Sun). Under-1s free. **Credit** AmEx, MC, V.

An indoor playground under the Westway flyover, Bramley's contains a giant three level playframe with slides, ball pools, swings, climbs, spooky den, giant balls, sound effects and separate under fives and baby areas. The whole shebang provokes such a deafening reaction in hordes of crazed kids that it makes neighbouring Latimer Road tube station sound like a nunnery by comparison. *Café. Disabled access: toilets. Nappy-changing facilities. Shop.*

Museum of Brands, Packaging and Advertising

2 Colville Mews, Lonsdale Road, W11 2AR (7908 0880/www.museumofbrands.com) Ladbroke Grove or Notting Hill Gate tube/23 bus. **Open** 10am-6pm Tue-Sat; 11am-4pm Sun (last entry 1hr before closing). **Admission** £5.80; £2 7-16s; £3.50 concessions; free under-7s. **Credit** MC, V.

Opened in December 2005, this is an eccentric time capsule that shouldn't be missed by anyone who goes weak at the knees when confronted by original boxes of Bassett's Liquorice Allsorts or Rowntree's Black Magic. Comprising the collection of renowned consumer historian Robert Opie (who began his obsession aged 16, when he decided to file rather than bin a Munchies wrapper), the museum charts the evolution of consumer society over the last 200 years, covering tastes and trends influenced by Victorian leisure pursuits, the advent of the radio, the chipper thrift of the wartime 1940s and the liberal revolution of the swinging '60s. The displays are clearly geared towards nostalgic adults, but historically minded children may be amused by the antiquated toys, magazines and comics on show – not to mention old versions of their favourite chocolate wrappers. Maltesers looked quite different, you know. *Buggy access. Café. Disabled access: toilet. Nappy-changing facility. Shop.*

Holland Park

West London doesn't get much better bred than Holland Park. Its name is derived from Holland House, built in 1607 and the scene of endless society parties courtesy of its 19th-century hostess, Lady Holland, who regularly had the likes of Byron, Wordsworth and Dickens round for tea. The building was bombed in the World War II (only the east wing was saved, comprising now the most refined youth hostel in the capital), but its remains are still to be found in the park, also famed for wooded walks, landscaped gardens, a café, play areas and various sporting facilities.

Another local building worth an ogle is Leighton House (12 Holland Park Road, W14 8LZ, 7602 3316), formerly the live-in studio of the Victorian artist and president of the Royal Academy Frederic Leighton, built at a time when Leighton and his peers were struggling to found an 'artists' colony'. Tracking down other buildings from this period (William Burges's medieval folly, the Tower House, on 29 Melbury Road, or the Peacock House on Addison Road, which hosts a craft fair every December)makes for a highly amusing architectural history trail. For Victorian grandeur, however, you can't beat a tour of the **Linley Sambourne House**, erstwhile home to the prolific *Punch* cartoonist of the same name.

Holland Park
Ilchester Place, W8 6LU (7471 9813/www.rbkc.gov.uk/ Ecology Centre 7471 9809). Holland Park tube/9, 27, 28, 49 bus. **Open** 8am-dusk daily. **Map** p314 A9.
This beautiful park has a series of paths through wild forested areas, which take you past imperious peacocks and plenty of squirrels and rabbits. The Ecology Centre provides site maps, nets for pond-dipping and information on local wildlife. It also hosts half-term and holiday activities (insect hunts, magpie walks, animal-footprint investigations) and meetings of the local Wildlife Watch group, the junior branch of the Wildlife Trust (www. wildlondon.org.uk). Elsewhere, there's a smart Italian café, with modern glass walls. The remains of Holland House (it suffered irreparable damage from German bombers during a World War II raid) are at the centre of the park, its murals and fountains making it a lovely spot to sit. The house's restored east wing contains a youth hostel, though one without family rooms, sadly. It also provides a backdrop for the open-air theatre, whose summer programme of opera and Shakespeare is popular for family outings. The peaceful Japanese Garden has a pond

full of Koi carp, which fascinate children, and the adventure playground keeps the over-fives entertained. Of most interest to youngsters is Whippersnappers (7738 6633, www.whippersnappers.org), for weekly musical and puppet workshops. Also in the park are tennis courts and two art spaces, the Ice House and the Orangery. The lovely North Lawn is busy with families and picnickers throughout the summer.
Buggy access. Café. Disabled access: toilets. Nappy-changing facilities. Restaurant.

Linley Sambourne House
18 Stafford Terrace, W8 7BH (7602 3316 ext 300 Mon-Fri only/7938 1295 Sat, Sun/www.rbkc.gov. uk/linleysambournehouse). High Street Kensington tube. **Tours** 10am, 11.15am, 1pm, 2.15pm, 3.30pm Sat, Sun; other times by appointment only. Maximum of 12 on each tour. Pre-booking essential. **Admission** £6; £4 concessions; £1 under-18s. **Credit** MC, V.
Map p314 A9.
Edward Linley Sambourne was a Victorian cartoonist, famous for his work in *Punch*. His house, which contains almost all its original fittings and furniture, can be visited only in the context of the terrific and slightly eccentric tours. They are each guided by a costumed actor (especially popular with children is gossipy housekeeper Mrs Reffle, who provides a cheeky insight into Victorian family life and tells a few jokes along the way), and there's a visitors' centre where children can participate in craftwork sessions relating to objects in the house. On Sundays holders of a Kensington & Chelsea library card are admitted free if they make an advance booking. *Shop.*

Earl's Court & Fulham

The huge exhibition centre synonymous with Earl's Court was erected in 1937; before that, the site was used as a funfair and showground, with Buffalo Bill's Wild West show of 1891 proving to be its biggest draw, pulling in roughly 15,000 visitors daily. These days, the 18,000-capacity venue hosts regular industry trade shows, awards ceremonies and conferences and the occasional rock concert, despite echoey acoustics.

Much of Earl's Court's once-grand Victorian housing has been sliced up into the rather pokier flats and bedsits favoured by Australians and New Zealanders on their obligatory world tours. There's a paucity of open spaces, but the rambling, overgrown Brompton Cemetery provides a last resort in more ways than one.

Most parents retreat to Hammersmith or Fulham for their fresh-air fixes. An abundance of greenery along the riverside, most notably the picturesque Bishop's Park, with its boating lake, teahouse and a popular One O'Clock Club, makes it splendid for a walk. The slightly dilapidated playgrounds and paddling pool were due for a refurbish in spring 2006, as was neighbouring Fulham Palace, on the receiving end of a £3 million lottery refit. No less hallowed grounds can be found at Craven Cottage,

Around Town

the riverside home stadium of Fulham FC, and the infinitely more plush Stamford Bridge, manor for Mourinho's boys at Chelsea FC. Guided tours of each are available throughout the year (75 minutes; from £8.50 adults, £5.50 children), and the latter also has a megastore. Well-off families can make use of the stunning grounds and sports facilities at the exclusive Hurlingham Club; less minted parents can still wheel their tots around Hurlingham Park (Hurlingham Road, SW6), where rugby and football pitches, tennis courts and a running track take pride of place.

The Fulham Broadway end of the Fulham Road, which starts at South Kensington, caters for the entertainment needs of the many families living in the Parson's Green urban village. There's a Pottery Café (735 Fulham Road, SW6 5UL, 7736 2157) and a nine-screen Vue cinema in the Fulham Broadway shopping centre.

Museum of Fulham Palace

Bishop's Avenue, off Fulham Palace Road, SW6 6EA (7736 3233). Hammersmith or Putney Bridge tube/ 220, 414, 430 bus. **Open** *hours vary; phone for details.* **Tours** *times vary, phone to check.* **Admission** *Museum free; under-16s must be accompanied by an adult. Tours £3; free under-16s.* **No credit cards.**
The official residence of the Bishops of London from 704 until 1973, Fulham Palace has some buildings dating back to 1480, although the main house is 16th century. The moat has gone, but some of its trench is still visible. The museum traces the buildings' histories and has some funny exhibits, not least a mummified rat – and thanks to a successful lottery bid, it is also undergoing a major restoration. Extensive building work will continue until the end of 2006, until when the museum will open only on Wednesdays, Saturdays and Sundays (2-4pm). Children's workshops (suitable for six- to 14-year-olds) run during the school holidays, most of them relating to Roman, Tudor and Victorian eras, and there's a rolling programme of exhibitions (the most recent – the Romans' Green Invasion – studying the plants and foods brought to the British Isles by the Romans). Ring to check what's coming up. Leave plenty of time to admire the lovely grounds, planted with rare trees, which provide sanctuary from the busy Fulham Palace Road. The walled kitchen garden is full of fragrant and pretty herbs and rare plants.
Buggy access. Disabled access: toilet (in palace). Shop.

Shepherd's Bush & Hammersmith

Shepherd's Bush is very much a suburb in transition. It wasn't until the railway arrived here in the early 1900s that urbanisation really began to take hold, but already the area is light years from its rural heyday, when stockmen on their way to Smithfield Market would graze their flocks on what became known as Shepherd's Bush Common. These days, the Common is little more than a glorified roundabout, but the ongoing

White City development to the north should change all that. There are plans for the single largest shopping centre in Greater London (150,000 square metres) and some seriously improved local transport links.

Until then, however, central Shepherd's Bush remains a rather grungy place – an image bolstered by the number of rock legends bred here (members of The Who, the Sex Pistols, the eponymous Bush and – more recently – Pete Doherty), not to mention the regular gigs held at the Empire, one of London's greatest rock venues. Future rockers should enrol at the Music House for Children at nearby Bush Hall (*see p235*).

Nor are the Bush's entertainment ties merely musical: the Beeb also broadcast many shows (*Wogan, Crackerjack* and *This Is Your Life*, among others) from the Empire until 1991. The telly-obsessed can still take backstage tours of the BBC studios at nearby Wood Lane (tickets need to be booked in advance and the minimum age is nine years; call 0870 603 0304 to book a ticket). Those seeking an induction into the dramatic arts are better off in Hammersmith, where the Dramatic Dreams Theatre Company (8741 1809, www.dramaticdreams.com) runs children's workshops at the Riverside Studios. Albert & Friends Instant Circus (Hammersmith, Ealing, & West London College, Glidden Road, W14 9BL, 8237 1170) offers children's classes in stilt-walking, unicycling and generally clowning around. The biggest local draw for pint-sized Pinters, however, is the Lyric Theatre (*see p224*).

Children who support Queens Park Rangers FC (*see p274*) are on to a very good thing. Their Loftus Road headquarters is a hub of community football for young people, and their soccer schools and party packages are great value. For more information, phone 8740 2509.

Ravenscourt Park

Ravenscourt Road, W6 0UL (www.lbhf.gov.uk). Ravenscourt Park tube. **Open** *7.30am-dusk daily.* **Admission** *free.*
In summer the packed paddling pool is the most popular part of this family-friendly park, but it also has three play areas, including a pre-school (two- to five-year-old 8748 3180) offering a Fathers' Club (2-4pm Sat) for much-needed bonding between babes and their overworked old men (a Grandparents' Club is expected to be up and running by the summer). A One O'Clock Club operates during half terms and holidays. There's a big pond, a nature trail and a scented garden for the visually impaired. Kids with spare energy can use the skateboarding ramp or enjoy a game of tennis. The café is open all year round and is conveniently positioned for the playground. There's a flower show and children's fair in July, and an annual Fun Day, with bouncy castles and face-painting (1 Aug 2006).
Buggy access. Café. Disabled access. Nappy-changing facilities.

Chiswick

A most desirable suburb, with great transport links, amenities and pretty riverside walks, Chiswick is devastatingly attractive to families. Its popularity isn't a recent phenomenon: prehistoric tools found in the grounds of **Syon House** suggest this was one of London's first human settlements, and while the proximity of Heathrow and the M4 may not have been the draw then that they are today, we can't fault their taste.

Chiswick's villagey feel is embodied by its many parks and traditional high streets. Turnham Green, for example, is surrounded by shops, traditional housing and the town hall, with a small church at its centre. Acton Green Common – the site of a hostile confrontation between the cavaliers of King Charles I and the forces of the Earl of Essex in 1642 – makes for an idyllic spot to stretch out and watch the cricket in summer. Picnic materials are available from the many delis on adjoining Turnham Green Terrace: cheese-making may have been Chiswick's forte in the 18th century, but these days you'll also find smart butchers and traditional fishmongers. North of Turnham Green station lies the gracious acreage of London's first suburb, Bedford Park, laid out in a rural setting in 1875 by Jonathan Carr.

The lion's share of Chiswick's charm can be found beside the river: a leisurely stroll along its banks reveals all manner of wholesome outdoorsy activities for all the family, not to mention varied local wildlife and delightful views. Chiswick Pier is home to the popular Chiswick Canoe Club (www.chiswickcanoeclub.co.uk), which runs canoe polo sessions (indoor and outdoor) for over-eights, as well as kayaking for those who simply fancy pottering about on the Thames. Lesser salty seadogs will be reassured to know that the pier also houses one of London's four lifeboat stations (the brightly coloured boats can usually be seen bobbing on the water). The Chiswick Pier Trust (www.chiswickpier.org.uk) organises all kinds of waterborne family events throughout the year, including a Party on the Pier day in June, with food and drink stalls, music and boat trips – some of them organised by the Chiswick Sea Cadets (8399 8201, www.chiswickw4.com/seacadets), a maritime club for local kids aged ten to 18 years.

Keep walking on to Duke's Meadows, a green expanse occupied by the Duke's Meadow Golf Club (8995 0537, www.golflessons.co.uk) – which offers junior group coaching on Saturday afternoons – and cricket pitches, tennis courts and boathouses. Carry on beyond Chiswick Bridge to enjoy Strand-on-the-Green, a picturesque former fishing community; these days it is more congested with buggies than boats, as hordes of weekend walkers descend on the numerous family-friendly pubs that line the water, and muddy their boots frolicking on the bay at low tide. Annie's Café (162 Thames Road, 8994 9080) has a children's menu as well as toys and books.

The area has enough entertainments and educational diversions to engage kids all year round. The Kew Bridge Steam Museum, for example, is a blessing for Thomas fans of all ages. The fantastic Musical Museum (8560 8108, www.musicalmuseum.co.uk) should reopen in spring 2006 after moving from its old site in St George's Church to a new premises 150 metres up the high street, where it will once again unveil its world class collection of (often self-playing) acoustic oddities, including player pianos, orchestrions, wurlitzers and a theremin, producer of eerie sci-fi soundtracks since the year dot. The riverside arts venue Watermans (40 High Street, Middx TW8 0DS, 8232 1010) has an eclectic programme of children's entertainment covering drama, puppetry and musical workshops.

For sporting endeavours, there's the Brentford Fountain Leisure Centre (*see p268*). Further north, the private Park Club (East Acton Lane, W3 7HB, 8743 4321) runs a rolling programme of sporting activities and workshops for children, and is home to both the Ark in the Park crèche and childcare centre as well as Urban Parx, a place for children and young people aged eleven years and over, who don't give a stuff about the correct spelling of the word 'parks' to meet and chill out.

More historical adventures await at Syon Park, where, luckily for kids less than enamoured of old mansions, the surrounding grounds have all manner of child-friendly amusements. Regular animal encounter sessions take place at the Tropical Forest, there's a motorised bike track and an indoor adventure playground. The London Butterfly House, which has wowed generations with its tropical hothouse of fluttery friends, creepy crawlies and exotic birds, may close its doors for the last time on 31 October 2006, after a bid to relocate to nearby Gunnersbury Park was scuppered by red tape – catch it while you still can. Gunnersbury Park has a boating lake, some mock Gothic ruins, a miniature golf course and the Gunnersbury Park Local History Museum (8992 1612; open Apr-Oct 11am-5pm daily; Nov-Mar 11am-4pm daily), which runs local-interest exhibitions and regular tours, talks and workshops. Nearby, the Kids Cookery School (*see p233*) was turning children on to good home cooking with unusual or unfamiliar ingredients way before the heroic Mr Oliver put them off their turkey twizzlers for good.

Around Town

Kew Bridge Steam Museum, an awesome Victorian powerhouse.

Chiswick House

Burlington Lane, W4 2RP (8995 0508/www.english-heritage.org.uk). Turnham Green tube, then E3 bus to Edensor Road/Hammersmith tube/rail, then 190 bus/Chiswick rail. **Open** *Apr-Oct* 10am-5pm Wed-Fri, Sun; 10am-2pm Sat. Last entry 30mins before closing. Closed Nov-Mar. *Tours* by arrangement; phone for details. **Admission** (EH/LP) incl audio guide £4; £3 concessions; £2 5-16s; free under-5s. **Credit** MC, V.
Walking through the gardens of Chiswick House you'll come across obelisks hidden among the trees, a classical temple, a lake and a cascading waterfall. Families come here on summer days for a picnic. You can also take a jaunt along the river, which is only a stone's throw away. Burlington's Café, in the grounds of Chiswick House, is lovely. A multi-million pound restoration of the grounds looked likely to go ahead at time of going to press after first stage approval from the Heritage Lottery Foundation. English Heritage also stages activity days and occasional re-enactments here: check its website for details.
Buggy access. Café. Disabled access: stairlift, toilet. Nearest picnic place: Chiswick Park. Shop.

Gunnersbury Triangle Nature Reserve

Bollo Lane, W4 5LW (8747 3881/www.wildlondon. org.uk). Chiswick Park tube. **Open** *Reserve* 24hrs daily. *Information* Jun-Sep 10am-4.30pm Tue-Sat. Oct-May 10am-4.30pm Tue, Sun. **Admission** free.
This area of land enclosed by railway tracks is run by the London Wildlife Trust, which organises regular outdoor activities for kids, including practical conservation workshops (old clothes and stout footwear required). In all, this expanse of woodland, pond, marsh and meadow is home to a range of wildlife, and during the summer there's a full-time warden and free, drop-in activities for youngsters, such as craft workshops, mask-making sessions and mini beast safaris. There's also an annual summer open day each June. When the small information cabin is open (throughout the summer, but only on Tuesdays and Sundays in winter) you can pick up trail leaflets, find out about guided tours or hire a net for a spot of pond-dipping. *Buggy access.*

Kew Bridge Steam Museum

Green Dragon Lane, Brentford, Middx TW8 0EN (8568 4757/www.kbsm.org). Gunnersbury tube, then 237 or 267 bus/Kew Bridge rail/65, 391 bus. **Open** 11am-5pm Tue-Sun, bank hol Mon. Closed 1 Jan 23-26 Dec, Good Friday. *Tours* times vary; phone or check website, book in advance. **Admission** (LP) *Mon-Fri* £4.25; £3.25 concessions; free under-16s. *Sat, Sun* £6.50; £5.50 concessions; free under-16s. Under-16s must be accompanied by an adult. **Credit** MC, V.
This Victorian riverside pumping station has had to cut back on the firing of its historic Cornish beam engines after a 65% rise in its gas bill (we know the feeling), but it's still 'all systems go' on certain weekends throughout the year (phone for information on the next one). Other steam engines, however, will be running every weekend, and kids can still ride the working narrow gauge steam locomotive, Cloister (Sun, Mar-Nov). During the school and bank holidays, there's a lot of action, because the Education Department and volunteers run family activities. The popular Tower Open Days are now combined with special Behind the Scenes tours of the museum but places are limited, so you'll have to book well in advance. Children, unfortunately, are not allowed to climb the 261 steps to the top of the tower because the handrails are too high – but adults will enjoy the impressive view.
Buggy access. Café (Sat, Sun). Disabled access: lift, ramps, toilet. Nappy-changing facilities. Nearest picnic place: Kew Green. Shop.

Syon House

Syon Park, Brentford, Middx TW8 8JF (8560 0881/ London Butterfly House 8560 0378/Tropical Forest 8847 4730/Snakes & Ladders 8847 0946/www.syon park.co.uk). Gunnersbury tube/rail, then 237, 267 bus. **Open** *House* mid Mar-late Oct 11am-5pm Wed, Thur, Sun, bank hol Mon (last entry 4.15pm). *Gardens* Mar-Oct 10.30am-5pm daily. Nov-Feb 10.30am-4pm daily. (last entry 45min before closing). *Tours* by arrangement; phone for details. **Admission** *House & gardens* £7.50; £6.50 concessions, 5-16s; free under-5s; £17 family (2+2). *Gardens only* £3.75; £2.50 concessions, 5-16s; free under-5s; £9 family (2+2).

Tropical Forest £5; £3.75 3-15s; free under-3s; £15 family (2+3). *Butterfly House* £5.25; £4.25 concessions; £3.95 3-16s; free under-3s; £16 family (2+2). *Snakes & Ladders* £3.50 under-2s; £4.50 under-5s; £5.50 over-5s; adults free. Reduced rate after 4pm. **Credit**
Shop MC, V.

This is a gracious, turreted Tudor mansion, developed from a building dedicated to the Bridgettine Order. Following the Dissolution of the Monasteries, it was dedicated to providing Henry VIII with another country seat. Each room seems more impressive than the last, from the grand Roman hallway to the Red Drawing Room, with its crimson silk walls and Roman statues. On Sundays a wooden mini steam railway travels through the trees and around the flowerbeds. Regular family-friendly workshops include demonstrations and re-enactments of Stuart life in the mid-17th century (29 Oct 2006), and there'll be a summer exhibition (until 16 July) charting the ongoing excavation of the original Syon Abbey, discovered three years ago by Channel 4's *Time Team*.

Most children – let's be realistic – find more thrills in the other attractions set out in the grounds. The London Butterfly House won't be here after October 2006, but there's always the Tropical Forest (formerly known as the Aquatic Experience) with regular 'animal encounters' sessions. Children yearn for Snakes & Ladders, an indoor adventure playground designed like a castle, with three tiers of play areas, including slides, hanging ropes and enormous ball pools. There's also an indoor motorised bike track (£1/ride) and a café. Bring a picnic in summer, as the nicest eating locations are outside, although the cafeteria has a selection of hot meals and a junior menu.
Café. Nappy-changing facilities. Nearest picnic place: Syon House Gardens/Syon Park. Shop.

Further west

As you'd expect, there's a roughly proportional relationship between distance from the city centre and the number of parks available for rambling in. Ealing, at the western end of the District Line, is no exception, with an abundance of open spaces including Ealing Common (close to the congested Uxbridge Road) and Horsenden Hill, the latter an erstwhile Stone Age settlement that now constitutes the highest point in the borough to enjoy stunning views across London and great kite-flying opportunities.

During the Covent Garden London Transport Museum's period of closure (*see p74*), its Acton Depot (7379 6344, www.ltmuseum.co.uk), which already boasts 370,000 items, will be pressed into service as a repository for the museum's displays. Petrolheads can also marvel at the collection of hogs and choppers at the London Motorcycle Museum (8575 6644, www.motorcycle-uk.com) in Greenford's Ravenor Park, which also has a playground and an annual carnival.

The banks of the River Brent are a cheerful picnic spot in clement weather. There are pleasant riverside walks in either direction – don't miss the Hanwell Flight of Locks, seven locks in close

succession just north of Osterley Park. These days, this park is ungraciously bisected by the M4, but stately **Osterley House** remains a great place to visit, its 18th century interiors are magnificent and family events are numerous. By far the magnetic north of seasonal family entertainment, however, is Walpole Park, which hosts much of the Ealing Summer Festival (July, Aug; 8579 2424, www.ealing.gov.uk) and is also home to Sir John Soane's **Pitshanger Manor**. Nearby, Questors Theatre (12 Mattock Lane, W5 5BQ, 8567 0011, www.questors.org.uk) runs a highly respected term-time youth theatre for children aged six to 16.

There are also numerous sporting facilities in Ealing; the most interesting is the Gurnell Leisure Centre (Ruislip Road East, W13 0AL, 8998 3241, www.leisureconnection.co.uk), which boasts an Olympic-sized pool. Riders tack up at Ealing Riding School (*see p263*), and Brent Valley Golf Course (Church Road, W7 3BE, 8567 1287) is good for beginner golfers.

Southall, west of Ealing, has London's largest Asian community. Wednesdays usher in the capital's last surviving agricultural market in Southall Park, where kids can marvel at horses being auctioned. Unsurprisingly, fine curries are served in the restaurants round here. The Sri Guru Singh Sabha Gurdwara (Alice Way, Hanworth Road, Hounslow TW3 3UA, www.sgss.org) opened in 2003: with a capacity of 3,000 people, it is the largest Sikh temple outside India, second in size only to the Golden Temple in Amritsar. The **Shri Swaminarayan Mandir Temple**, to the north of Southall, is a monument to Hinduism.

The Heathrow Airport Visitor Centre (Newall Road, Middx UB3 5AP (8745 6655, www.heathrow-airport-guide.co.uk) has, since 1995, introduced its visitors to flying by means of flight simulators, interactive metal detectors and plenty of hands-on activities. The centre is closing in spring 2006 for a three-to-four month refurbishment; phone for updated information. Nearby **Hounslow Urban Farm** brings kids back to earth with a bump, a baa and a cock-a-doodle-doo. Still further out of town, Hounslow Heath (450 Staines Road, Hounslow TW4 5AB, 8577 3664) is one of London's largest nature reserves. There's an information centre near the Staines Road entrance, where a warden will provide you with information on local wildlife and nature trails.

Brent Lodge Park

Church Road, W7 3BL (8825 7529). Hanwell rail/E1, E2 bus. **Open** *7.30am-dusk daily. Maze & animals* May-Aug 10.30am-6pm daily. Apr, Sept, Oct 10.30am-5pm daily. Nov-Mar 10.30am-4pm daily.

Around Town

Admission £1; 50p concessions, 3-16s; free under-3s. **No credit cards.**
Walk up the hill from the Millennium Maze, planted in 1999, for the hub of activities in this sweet and well-maintained local park, There's a café and a playground with an animal centre, housing a handful of primates (some white-lipped tamarins being the most recent addition to the monkey house) as well as reptiles, amphibians, birds and plenty of domestic pets, such as bunnies and guinea pigs. The centre organises children's activity days in the summer months: phone for more information.
Buggy access (no access to animal area). Café. Disabled access: toilet.

Hounslow Urban Farm

A312 at Faggs Road, Feltham, Middx TW14 0LZ (8751 0850/www.hounslow.info/urbanfarm). Hatton Cross tube, then 20min walk or 90, 285, 490 bus. **Open** 10am-4pm daily. **Admission** £3.50; £2.75 concessions; £2 2-16s; under-2s; £10 (2+2) family. **No credit cards.**
This is London's largest community farm, so thre's plenty to see. There are pigs, goats, numerous varieties of duck, Exmoor ponies and more, with feeding time at 3.30pm daily. The farm has a conservation programme – endangered and historic breeds of domestic livestock are reared here. Most fascinating is a visit during the breeding season: turn up at the right time and you could be lucky enough to see brand new lambs, goats or even a litter of piglets. Orphan lambs need to be bottle-fed and children are sometimes allowed to help. There's a playground (with, we're delighted to report, pedal tractors), a picnic area and a kiosk for food and refreshments.
Buggy access. Café. Disabled access: toilet. Nappy-changing facilities.

Eating out in **Osterley House** grounds.

Osterley House

Osterley Park, off Jersey Road, Isleworth, Middx TW7 4RB (8232 5050/recorded information 01494 755 566/www.nationaltrust.org.uk/osterley). Osterley tube. **Open** *House* late Mar-Oct 1-4.30pm Wed-Sun, bank hol Mon. *Park* 9am-7.30pm daily. *Tours* by arrangement; minimum 15 people. **Admission** (NT) *House* £5.10; £2.50 5-15s; free under-5s; £12.80 family (2+3). *Park* free. **Credit** *Tearoom/shop only* MC, V.
Osterley House was built for Sir Thomas Gresham (founder of the Royal Exchange) in 1576, but transformed by Robert Adam in 1761. Adam's revamp is dominated by the imposing colonnade of white pillars before the courtyard of the house's red-brick body. The splendour of the state rooms alone makes the house worth the visit, but the still-used Tudor stables, the vast parkland walks and the ghost said to be lurking in the basement add to Osterley's allure. The 18th century pleasure grounds have been restored and look very fine. Visitors can also take advantage of their foray out of town to buy home-grown produce in the farm shop. Children can pick up a house trail from the office to help them explore; regular kiddie events include kite-making workshops, interactive historical tours of the house, bluebell walks, outdoor performances and the annual free Osterley Day in July, always full of arts and fun. Family Fun Days take place on Mondays in August: phone or check the website for more information.
Baby slings for hire. Buggy access (not when busy). Café. Car park (£3.50/day, NT members free). Disabled access: lift, toilet. Nappy-changing facilities. Nearest picnic place: front lawn/picnic benches in grounds. Shop.

Pitshanger Manor & Gallery

Walpole Park, Mattock Lane, W5 5EQ (8567 1227/ www.ealing.gov.uk/pmgallery&house). Ealing Broadway tube/rail/65 bus. **Open** *May-Sept* 1-5pm Tue-Fri, Sun; 11am-5pm Sat. *Oct-Apr* 1-5pm Tue-Fri; 11am-5pm Sat. Closed bank hols. **Tours** by arrangement; phone for details. **Admission** free. *Audio guide* £1.
Most of Pitshanger, a beautiful Regency villa, was rebuilt 1801-3 by Sir John Soane. His individual ideas in design and decoration make this a very special place. Among the exhibits is the Hull Grundy Martinware pottery collection, and there is an art gallery where contemporary exhibitions are held, plus a lecture and workshop programme for all ages. The manor is also home to the Waitrose Children's and Young People's Gallery, for exhibitions of artwork by local children and young people.
Buggy access. Disabled access: lift, ramp, toilet. Nearest picnic place: Walpole Park.

Shri Swaminarayan Mandir Temple

105-119 Brentfield Road, NW10 8LD (8965 2651/ www.swaminarayan.org). Wembley Park tube, then BR2 bus/Neasden tube, then 15min walk. **Open** 9.30am-6pm daily. **Admission** (LP) free. *Exhibition* £2; £1.50 6-15s; free under-6s. **Credit** AmEx, MC, V.
Built in 1995, this beautiful Hindu temple is an extraordinary structure, intricately carved by master sculptors. Much of the stone was sent to India to be carved and then brought back to Neasden – at a cost of more than £10m. An inspirational place to visit, the temple also has a permanent exhibition, with a video, called Understanding Hinduism; so it's particularly useful for those in Years 6 and 7 studying world religion.
Buggy access. Café. Disabled access: lift, toilet. Nappy-changing facilities. Shop.

Around Town

Consumer

Eating

Food glorious food, warm welcomes and high chairs.

Consumer

In this child-centred age, any restaurant that banned children would be roundly criticised, so most proprietors will say (some through clenched teeth) they admit infants. It's up to parents to work out whether their children are going to be stiffly tolerated or positively welcomed. Our selection of restaurants includes those that are legends in their own lunchtimes as far as children are concerned (**TGI Fridays**, the **Rainforest Café**), whose child-friendliness is worn like a badge of honour (literally, in TGI Friday's case). We've also chosen friendly neighbourhood burger bars and cafés that are well placed for park outings and sightseeing, but may not have special menus and seating arrangements for small children. Staff in these places, however, do know how to look after a family group and sashay round straying toddlers without having a sense-of-humour failure. Wherever appropriate, we have included contact details for other branches of restaurants listed in this chapter, but not all branches have the same facilities. It's always wise to book a table where possible, because some of the places listed below become pretty busy, especially at weekends and during school holidays. For handy places to eat while sightseeing in a particular area of central London, look for the **Lunch box** round-ups in the **Around Town** section (see pp30-160).

South Bank & Bankside

Bankside

32 Southwark Bridge Road, SE1 9EU (7633 0011/ www.banksiderestaurants.co.uk). Mansion House or Southwark tube/Blackfriars or London Bridge tube/rail. **Lunch served** noon-3pm Mon-Sat. **Dinner served** 6-10pm Mon-Sat. **Meals served** noon-7pm Sun. **Main courses** £9.90-£20. **Set meals** £13.50 2 courses, £18 3 courses. **Service** 12.5%. **Credit** AmEx, DC, MC, V. **Map** p318 P8.

A friendly restaurant near Shakespeare's Globe, Bankside comes into its own on a Sunday, when you can enjoy fantastic roasts with meat sourced from Borough Market. Also on the menu are brasserie favourites, such as fish and chips and sausage and mash or big steaks with fat or thin chips. The cheese course comes from Neals Yard (who have an outlet near the market). The children's menu offers sausage, chicken goujons or fish from £5.95. On Sunday lunchtimes a clown or magician causes a diversion. *Entertainment: clown, magician (12.30-4pm Sun). High chairs. No-smoking tables.*

Cantina del Ponte

Butlers Wharf Building, 36C Shad Thames, SE1 2YE (7403 5403/www.conran.com). Tower Hill tube/London Bridge tube/rail. **Lunch served** noon-3pm daily. **Dinner served** 6-11pm Mon-Sat; 6-10pm Sun. **Main courses** £9.50-£15.50. **Credit** AmEx, DC, MC, V. **Map** p319 R8.

We like this Conran venue because it's lowkey and by the river; when the terrace isn't too busy it's a gift for children. So too is the fulsome Italian welcome given to the *bambini.* The Cantina has done away with its children's menu but now has a much better system of offering 'a little pasta, a little pizza' in junior portions, or letting the kids choose a small portion of whatever they like the look of on the menu. We like the slow-roasted meat dishes, and the pizza primavera. Be warned: it is quite smart and as such is favoured by business folk at lunch during the week. *Buggy access. Tables outdoors (20, terrace).*

fish!

Cathedral Street, Borough Market, SE1 9DE (7407 3803/www.fishdiner.co.uk). London Bridge tube/rail. **Meals served** 11.30am-11pm Mon-Thur; noon-11pm Fri; noon-10.30pm Sun. **Main courses** £9.95-£16.95. **Credit** AmEx, MC, V. **Map** p317 M8.

This is an impressive-looking restaurant for families, handy for the children of the choir in the cathedral next door (parents treat them to a slap-up feed here if they do a good solo). Kids can have fish and chips, tuna bolognese or chicken goujons and chips, as well as ice-cream and a soft drink, for £6.95 while their parents debate whether to push the boat out and have halibut. We recommend the classic battered cod and chips for an eye-watering £11.95 (sadly the children's version uses a slightly flabbier batter, but our small companion didn't mind). A large notice-board tells of the superior pedigree of the fish (Icelandic cod, organically reared salmon, posh veg from Borough Market next door) to make you feel better about the bill. *Buggy access. Children's menu (£6.95). Crayons. High chairs. No-smoking tables. Tables outdoors (24, pavement).*

Giraffe

Units 1&2, Riverside Level 1, Royal Festival Hall, SE1 8XX (7928 2004/www.giraffe.net). Waterloo tube/rail. **Open** 8am-11pm Mon-Fri; 9am-11pm Sat; 9am-10.30pm Sun. **Main courses** £7.95-£10.95. **Set meals** (5-7pm) £6.95 2 courses; (7-11pm) £8.95 2 courses. **Credit** AmEx, MC, V. **Map** p317 M8.

The latest Giraffe to descend on London is this, most central, branch. Like its ten siblings, the spacious premises in the Royal Festival Hall exude warmth, colour and good cheer. This welcome is extended to children, which is why this mini chain is consistently at the top of the Most Child-Friendly Restaurant charts. Generous opening hours mean you can drop in for coffee, brunch or cocktails as well as meals. Children can choose from their

Gracelands. *See p174.*

own menu (fried or scrambled eggs, beans, sausage – veggie or pork – and fries or mash, chicken, with good ice-cream and juice thrown in for £5.25) or opt for a squarer meal from the main menu. We love the vegetarian meze starter (it can be made carnivorous with the addition of a rosemary lamb skewer) and the spicy chicken wings. The vegetarian burger, stuffed with grilled pepper, houmous, beetroot, rocket and halloumi is a delight, as are the noodle and salad dishes. The biggest treat has to be the white chocolate and crushed Toblerone cheesecake.
Balloons. Buggy access. Children's menu (£5.25 noon-3pm Mon-Fri). Crayons. Disabled: ramp, toilets. High chairs. Nappy-changing facilities. No smoking. Tables outdoors (20, terrace). Takeaway service.
Branches: throughout town. Phone or check website.

Konditor & Cook

10 Stoney Street, SE1 9AD (7407 5100/www.konditor andcook.com). London Bridge tube/rail. **Meals served** 7.30am-6pm Mon-Fri; 8.30am-5pm Sat. **Main courses** £2-£5. **Credit** AmEx, MC, V. **Map** p319 P8.
It's famous for its cakes, and let's face it, once the children have clocked the deservedly legendary brownies, banoffi slices, lemon meringue pies, treacle tarts and Curly Whirly (chocolate and vanilla) cake, that's all they'll want. But you should try the savouries too. We loved our pizza squares with their crispy bases and toppling toppings, and the salmon pasta. The interior is minimalist, with bare floorboards and bench seating. Even the drinks are well thought out, including cheering juices from the Innocent range and organic fizzy juices.
Buggy access. No smoking. Tables outdoors (1, pavement). Takeaway service.
Branches: 22 Cornwall Road, SE1 8TW (7261 0456); 46 Gray's Inn Road, WC1X 8LR (7404 6300).

Loco Mensa

3B Belvedere Road, SE1 7GP (7401 6734). Waterloo tube/rail. **Open** noon-10.30pm Mon-Thur; noon-11pm Fri; 10.30am-11pm Sat; 10am-10.30pm Sun. **Main courses** £6.95-£14.95. **Credit** MC, V. **Map** p317 M8.
Conveniently placed for the London Eye and the Aquarium, this super-friendly Italian café tends to get overlooked by the hordes searching for sustenance along the main riverside drag. That's a shame, as this place is great for children. The menu, which gives them pizza or spaghetti with a soft drink and ice-cream for £5.95, is good for this area and the other Italian specialities, such as cannelloni, fettuccine, mozzarella salad and delicious panna cotta were generous in proportion and well prepared.
Buggy access. Children's menu (£5.95). Disabled access: toilet. High chairs. Nappy-changing facilities. No-smoking tables. Tables outdoors (10, terrace). Takeaway service.

The City

Shish

313-319 Old Street, EC1V 9LE (7749 0990/www. shish.com). Old Street tube/rail. **Meals served** 11.30am-11.30pm Mon-Fri; 10.30am-11.30pm Sat; 10.30am-10.30pm Sun. **Main courses** £4-£10. **Credit** AmEx, MC, V. **Map** p309.
The menu is eclectic and ever changing at this colourful canteen-like restaurant, which ambitiously sets out to cover cuisine from Turkey to Indonesia – the Silk Road route. It's

a lot of ground to cover, and we have complained before that a little less diversity and a little more consistency might be an idea. Families don't complain, though, as there's plenty to nourish and entrance children, from the first-rate juice bar in the main restaurant (try the striped mixed fruit juice), to the well-stocked bread basket that sustains you while you decipher the menu (although there's an extra charge for this). The £4.25 kids' menu offers fish cakes, Mediterranean chicken or a falafel and houmous wrap (all served with rice, chips or salad), followed by an ice-cream or sorbet. Tasty, healthy and great value.
Buggy access. Children's menu (£4.25). Disabled access: toilet. High chairs. Nappy-changing facilities. No smoking. Takeaway service.
Branches: 71-75 Bishops Bridge Road, Bayswater, W2 6BG (7229 7300); 2-6 Station Parade, Willesden Green, NW2 4NH (8208 9290).

Smiths of Smithfield

67-77 Charterhouse Street, EC1M 6HJ (7251 7950/ www.smithsofsmithfield.co.uk). Farringdon tube/rail. **Meals served** *Ground-floor bar/café* 7am-4.30pm Mon; 7am-5pm Tue-Fri; 10am-5pm Sat; 9.30am-5pm Sun. **Main courses** £3.50-£8.50. **Credit** AmEx, MC, V. **Map** p318 O5.
Smiths is four floors of eating and drinking, but the main event for families is in the ground-floor café/bar, an industrial-scale space with bare brick-walls. Here, the options for breakfast, brunch and snack times are just right for children. A big dreamy milkshake is a must, particularly the nutty, banana-y Cheeky Monkey, then there are bacon sandwiches, eggs and bacon, substantial porridge, chip butties and yummy waffles. A great place for a Saturday lunchtime blowout.
Buggy access. Disabled access: lift, toilets. High chairs. Nappy-changing facilities. Tables outdoors (6, pavement). Takeaway service.

Holborn & Clerkenwell

Bank Aldwych

1 Kingsway, WC2B 6XF (7379 9797/www.bank restaurants.com). Holborn tube. **Breakfast served** 7-10.30am Mon-Fri. **Brunch served** 11.30am-3pm Sat; 11.30am-4.30pm Sun. **Lunch served** noon-3pm Mon-Fri. **Dinner served** 5.30-11pm Mon-Sat. **Main courses** £12.50-£32. **Set meal** (lunch, 5.30-7pm, 10-11pm) £13.50 2 courses; £16 3 courses. **Credit** AmEx, DC, MC, V. **Map** p315 M6.
One of the most successful 1990s high-style makeovers, Bank was once a bank and still has a high-finance feel to it. Don't be alarmed, though; for all its glassy sleekness , with long metal chefs' stations and mirrored walls, Bank's friendly, and the staff are splendid with children. A children's menu is available at lunch or brunch. You can have dishes like chipolatas and mash or linguine with tomato sauce followed by sticky toffee pud and ice-cream. Grown-ups have a rather more sophisticated à la carte menu (delicate seared tuna with miso dressing or organic salmon with broccoli and mousseline sauce, or classic eggs benedict and scrambled eggs and smoked salmon for brunch). At weekends, there's a brunch-time activities table with crayons, puzzles and toys.
Booking advisable. Buggy access. Children's menu (£7.25). Crayons (weekends only). Disabled access: toilet. High chairs. Nappy-changing facilities. Toys.

wagamama

great for little
grown ups too!

wagamama.com

Bloomsbury & Fitzrovia

Abeno

47 Museum Street, WC1A 1LY (7405 3211). Holborn or Tottenham Court Road tube. **Meals served** noon-10pm daily. **Main courses** £6.95-£42. **Set lunches** £7.50-£19.80 incl miso soup, rice. **Credit** AmEx, DC, JCB, MC, V. **Map** p317 L5.

An appealing Japanese bolt-hole, Abeno's culinary style, *okonomiyaki* (literally, 'cooking what you like'), makes a humble meal of vegetables and/or meat mixed with batter much more exciting by setting the action at your table. OK, the waitress does all the actual cooking – from mixing your ingredients and depositing them on the table-top hot plate, to flipping your 'pancake' – but you decorate the result with a choice of mayonnaise, fruit and vegetable sauce, dried seaweed, shaved fish and chilli sauce. It's fun to watch and the results are delicious and finger-friendly.
Buggy access. High chairs. Takeaway service.
Branches: Abeno Too, 15-18 Great Newport Street, WC2H 7JE (7379 1160).

Carluccio's Caffè

8 Market Place, W1W 8AG (7636 2228/www.carluccios.com). **Meals served** 7.30am-11pm Mon-Fri; 10am-11pm Sat; 10am-10pm Sun. **Main courses** £4.85-£10.95. **Credit** AmEx, MC, V. **Map** p314 J6.

The original West End branch of what has become a widespread chain, this is our favourite Carluccio's because it has plenty of outside tables for watching the world go by. The staff are always pleased to see children, and we're always delighted to pig out on the fabulous classic and regional Italian dishes. Main courses, such as risotto, or fried swordfish, are generous, then there are the wonderful breads, olives, breadsticks and pastries that children enjoy lunching off. Finish with own-made *gelati* and sorbets, or warm frothy milk or hot chocolate, and all seems right with the world, unless you have to head home past Oxford Circus.
Buggy access. Children's menu (£4.95 incl drink). Crayons. Disabled access: toilets. High chairs. Nappy-changing facilities. No smoking. Tables outdoors (15, pavement). Takeaway service.
Branches: throughout town. Phone or check website.

North Sea Fish Restaurant

7-8 Leigh Street, WC1H 9EW (7387 5892). Russell Square tube/King's Cross tube/rail/68, 168 bus. **Lunch served** noon-2.30pm, **dinner served** 5.30-10.30pm Mon-Sat. **Main courses** £7.95-£17.95. **Credit** AmEx, MC, V. **Map** p315 L3/4.

Handy for the British Museum, this retro-looking fish and chip establishment requires big appetites. It's just brilliant on a cold foggy day to come here and fill up on jumbo-sized battered cod and haddock, with golden, floury chips in a basket, own-made tartare sauce and mushy peas. Portions are so large you'd do well to just ask for the legendary spare plate for anyone under seven. Try to leave a space for apple crumble and custard or sherry trifle; only the greedy can manage this. Leave at a waddle.

Buggy access. High chair. No-smoking tables. Takeaway service.

Tas

22 Bloomsbury Street, WC1B 3QJ (7637 4555/ www.tasrestaurant.com). Russell Square or Tottenham Court Road tube. **Meals served** noon-11.30pm Mon-Sat; noon-10.30pm Sun. **Main courses** £5.65-£14.45. **Credit** AmEx, MC, V. **Map** p315 L5.

This branch of the Anatolian mini chain is well placed for sustenance following a hike around the British Museum. It may not have any of the obvious trappings of child-friendliness – play areas and colour-in menus aren't an option – but families love it. The food is made for sharing, and baskets of bread and pots of olives and houmous arrive as you sit down. Choosing from the four mixed meze menus gives you falafel, fetta cheese salad, lamb or chicken shish, borek (pastries) and more of that delicious own-made bread, and the children can select a little sample of each to fill their thoughtfully provided empty plates. The staff engage with kids, explaining each dish, suggesting chips on the side if the cous cous or speciality rice pilaf seems too exotic. They're also generous with the puddings, such as the sticky sweet baklava or the mousse-filledchocolate cake, especially if they're to be shared. The fussiest feeder can find something to get their teeth into at Tas.

Buggy access. Disabled access: toilets. High chairs. Nappy-changing facilities. No-smoking tables. Takeaway service.
Branches: throughout town. Phone or check website.

Marylebone

Fairuz

3 Blandford Street, W1H 3AA (7486 8108/8182). Baker Street or Bond Street tube. **Meals served** noon-11.30pm Mon-Sat; noon-10.30pm Sun. **Main courses** £9.95-£13.95. **Set meals** £18.95 meze; £26.95 4 courses. **Cover** £1.50. **Credit** AmEx, MC, V. **Map** p314 G5.

A fold-back frontage with pavement seating and a Mediterranean-flavoured interior entice passing trade to this accomplished Lebanese restaurant, where the staff are usually welcoming to children. The menu has an expansive offering of around 50 hot and cold meze – all great for little fingers to dip into. Fluffy falafel comes with a miniature pot of tahini; chicken livers are made child-friendly with a marinade of lemon and pomegranate juice, and there's plenty of bread to dip into various yoghurty dishes. Of the mains, farouj mousakhan is a stand-out – a duvet of flatbread filled with chicken pieces smothered in fried onions and parsley and baked in the oven.

Booking advisable. High chairs. No-smoking tables. Tables outdoors (4, pavement). Takeaway service.

Fishworks

89 Marylebone High Street, W1U4QW (7935 9796/ www.fishworks.co.uk). Baker Street, Bond Street or Regent's Park tube. **Lunch served** noon-2.30pm, **dinner served** 6-10.30pm Tue-Fri. **Meals served** noon-10.30pm Sat, Sun. **Main courses** £10.90-£22. **Credit** AmEx, MC, V. **Map** 314 G5.

Many children are fascinated by fish stalls, so the display in the windows of Fishworks is a conversation point. The fishy dishes, all created from carefully sourced, ultra-fresh seafood, are spectacular. We adore the roasted skate and the hearty fish soup. Children can eat well for nothing: own-made fish cakes or fingers, or mussels, or anything else on the kids' menu, is free with an adult purchasing a main course. Otherwise, the junior menu is £4.95.

Children's menu (£4.95). High chairs. No smoking.
Branches: throughout town. Phone or check website.

Hard Rock Café

150 Old Park Lane, W1K 1QR (7629 0382/www. hardrock.com). Hyde Park Corner tube. **Meals served** 11.30am-12.30am Mon-Thur, Sun; 11.30am-1am Fri, Sat. **Main courses** £8.45-£15.95. *Minimum* (when busy) main course per person. **Credit** AmEx, DC, MC, V. **Map** p316 H8.

Time was when everyone visiting London queued in gormless fashion to bag a table at this rock 'n' roll-themed restaurant. Everyone's a bit more sensible thes days, and the restaurant's bigger anyway, but the Hard Rock still holds a lasting attraction for children, who are treated very nicely here. It has everything a child could want: face-painting at certain times, a Lil' Rocker children's menu with all kinds of ketchup-covered pizza, pasta and, of course, burger creations (plus a free colouring book and crayons), as well as themed activities from time to time (Hallowe'en parties and the like). Waitresses wear mini-skirts and charm little boys. The hamburgers here are OK, the salads huge and quite main-course-orientated, the noise is loud and the cheesy nachos moreish.

Buggy access. Children's menu (£6.50). Crayons. Disabled access; toilet. Entertainment: face-painting Sat, Sun. High chairs. Nappy-changing facilities. No-smoking. Tables outdoors (10, pavement).

Hong Kong

6-7 Lisle Street, WC2H 7BG (7287 0352). Leicester Square or Piccadilly Circus tube. **Dim sum served** noon-5pm daily. **Meals served** noon-11.30pm Mon-Thur; noon-midnight Fri, Sat; 11am-11pm Sun. **Main courses** £5.50-£10.50. **Set lunch** £10 3 courses. **Credit** AmEx, JCB, MC,V. **Map** p317 K7.

This is another Chinatown favourite of ours, mostly because the dim sum is so very good. Seafood lovers adore the king prawn dumplings and the crispy seafood rolls, and the pan-fried chive dumplings are the ultimate comfort food. Even the day-glo sweet-and-sour dishes earn applause for excellent flavour. The scope and quality of the lunchtime menu (which includes pictures of all the dumplings – a handy detail for explaining dishes to the young 'uns) continues to improve alongside the service – congenial every time we visit.

Buggy access. High chairs. Takeaway service.

Masala Zone

9 Marshall Street, W1F 7ER (7287 9966/ www.realindianfood.com). Oxford Circus tube. **Lunch served** noon-3pm Mon-Fri; 12.30-3.30pm Sun. **Dinner served** 5.30-11pm Mon-Fri; 6-10.30pm Sun. **Meals served** 12.30-11pm Sat. **Main courses** £6-£12. **Credit** MC, V. **Map** p314 J6.

This is a top zone for curry-loving families. It has everything you could want: a share-worthy menu, low prices, exemplary service, fascinating decor and lots of room for family groups to let their hair down. A great-value

Consumer

menu encompasses crisp and savoury Bombay beach snacks, meal-in-one plates, rare regional dishes (undhiyu and lentil khichdi – a mushy rice mix – for instance), properly prepared curries and satisfying thalis. The children's menu delivers accessible dishes in portions small enough (and with a familiar little pile of crisps on the side) to encourage even the most reluctant palates. *Buggy access. Children's menu (£3.75 incl ice-cream). High chairs. No smoking. Takeaway service.* **Branches**: 80 Upper Street, N1 0NU (7359 3399); 147 Earl's Court Road, SW5 9RQ (7373 0220).

Planet Hollywood

13 Coventry Street, W1D 7DH (7287 1000/ www.planethollywoodlondon.com). Piccadilly Circus tube. **Meals served** 11.30am-1am Mon-Sat; 11.30am-12.30am Sun. **Main courses** £8.50-£19.95. **Credit** AmEx, DC, MC, V. **Map** p317 K7.
It's noisy, it's brash, there are screens everywhere, and the menu is all about steaks, shakes, burgers and fries, with choc-chip brownies for afters. What's there for a tween not to like? Beleaguered parents who would like a chance to enjoy their juicy burger and very good chips in peace are less enamoured. Service is amused and indulgent. *Balloons. Booking advisable (weekends; limited reservations Sat). Buggy access. Children's menu (£7.95 incl drink & ice-cream). Crayons. High chairs. Nappy-changing facilities. No-smoking tables.*

Rainforest Café

20 Shaftesbury Avenue, W1D 7EU (7434 3111/ www.therainforestcafe.co.uk). Piccadilly Circus tube. **Meals served** noon-10pm Mon-Thur; noon-8pm Fri; 11am-8pm Sat; 11.30am-10pm Sun. **Main courses** £9.75-£16. **Credit** AmEx, MC, V. **Map** p317 K7.
Drag them from the ground-floor shop bit, where a talking tree preaches sustainability while you try to sustain equilibrium, to the basement restaurant. Here, animatronic apes, elephants and parrots continue to pump up the excitability levels. Children find the Rainforest Café delightful; indeed they fare better with the menu than the adults do. But grown-ups can take comfort from the number of organic items on the Rainforest Rascals kids menu. At £10.25 including dessert it's a bit pricey, and they could at least give hyperventilating children free mineral water to help wash it down. As it is, you have to pay £1.80 for a small bottle of Robinson's Fruit Shoot – a massive mark-up for a sickly squash packaged in a highly unsustainable way. Dishes such as meatballs, salmon pasta and pork and beef 'jungle spears' use organic ingredients, but others – chicken goujons, bangers and burgers – do not. Puds are a medley of jelly, whipped cream, caramel, chocolate, ice-cream and Smarties. Few young children get through two courses, so save money by ordering a small adult dish and help polish off the children's food. *Bookings not accepted Sat. Buggy access. Children's menu (£10.25 incl dessert). Crayons. High chairs. Nappy-changing facilities. No smoking.*

Royal Dragon

30 Gerrard Street, W1D 6JS (7734 1388). Leicester Square or Piccadilly Circus tube. **Dim sum served** noon-5pm daily. **Meals served** noon-3am daily. **Main courses** £6.50-£10. **Credit** AmEx, MC, V. **Map** p317 K7.
We've been coming here for years; ever since a small child in our party chose the restaurant because of its fiery name.

It's another one with a good dim-sum menu and smart, friendly staff who obligingly translate the menu for you. Children are keen on the seaweed rolls and deep-fried dumplings and the tasty chicken and prawn fried rice. For those in a more adventurous mood, dishes on the main menu such as mui-choi kau-yuk (a generous portion of excellent earthenware-cooked pork with preserved vegetables) are also worth a punt. *High chair. Takeaway service.*

Covent Garden

Belgo Centraal

50 Earlham Street, WC2H 9LJ (7813 2233/www.belgo-restaurants.com). Covent Garden tube. **Meals served** noon-11pm Mon-Thur; noon-11.30pm Fri, Sat; noon-10.30pm Sun. **Main courses** £8.95-£16.95. **Set lunch** (noon-5pm) £5.95 1 course. **Credit** AmEx, DC, MC, V. **Map** p315 L6.
Grown-up *Time Out* reviewers are a bit sniffy about this subterranean mussel merchant, but we say it's a great-value way to feed the family: two kids eat free when accompanied by an adult ordering from the à la carte menu. The chain's trademark bivalves are the best thing on the children's menu, which is otherwise sausages, chicken and so on. The wide selection of Belgian beers is another plus, as far as parents and older siblings are concerned. *Buggy access. Children's menu (£4.95 or free with adult purchasing main course). Crayons. Disabled access: lift, toilets. High chairs. No-smoking tables.* **Branches**: Belgo Bierodrome, 44-48 Clapham High Street, SW4 7UR (7720 1118); Belgo Bierodrome, 67 Kingsway, WC2B 6TD (7242 7469); Belgo Bierodrome, 173-174 Upper Street, N1 1XS (7226 5835); Belgo Noord, 72 Chalk Farm Road, NW1 8AN (7267 0718).

Ottolenghi. *See p174.*

Consumer

Bodean's

10 Poland Street, W1F 8PZ (7287 7575/www. bodeansbbq.com). Oxford Circus or Picccadilly Circus tube. **Lunch served** noon-3pm, **dinner served** 6-11pm Mon-Fri. **Meals served** noon-11pm Sat; noon-10.30pm Sun. **Main courses** £8-£14. **Service** 12.5%. **Credit** AmEx, MC, V.

This is what they call 'good eatin'' down South (US, that is, not Portsmouth), but it's not a place for vegetarians, smokey barbecued meat being the main point of it. A rack of baby back ribs is chewy meaty perfection here (the children's menu lists a mini version, alongside chicken or sliced turkey or ham, with ice-cream to follow). Order some gorgeous tomatoey baked beans and crisp fries to go with the barbecue and you'll think you're in heaven. The atmosphere is laid-back class, with leather banquettes, wood-panelled walls and baseball perpetually on the flat-screen television.

Children's area. Children's menu (£5 incl ice-cream). High chairs. Nappy-changing facilities. No-smoking tables. Takeaway service.

Branches: 4 Broadway Chambers, Fulham Broadway, SW6 1EP (7610 0440); 169 Clapham High Street, SW4 7SS (7622 4248).

Hamburger Union

4 Garrick Street, WC2E 9BH (7379 0412/www. hamburgerunion.com). Leicester Square tube. **Meals served** 11.30am-9.30pm Mon, Sun; 11.30am-10.30pm Tue-Sat. **Main courses** £3.95-£6.95. **Credit** MC, V. **Map** p317 L7.

Mighty good burgers, oozing juice and served in a robust bun packed with salad, cost only a tiny bit more than a superchain equivalent and taste about a hundred times better. Sides of fries, salad and coleslaw are served in

chunky bowls. It's a clean, pleasant place to have lunch (although it's apt to get busy in peak hours) and even red-meat avoiders are happy – there are chicken and vegetarian options.

Buggy access. High chairs. No smoking. Takeaway service.

Branches: 25 Dean Street, W1D 3RY (7437 6004); 341 Upper Street, N1 0PB (7359 4436).

PJ's Grill

30 Wellington Street, WC2E 7BD (7240 7529). Covent Garden tube. **Brunch served** noon-4pm daily. **Meals served** noon-midnight Mon-Sat. **Main courses** £7.95-£13.95. **Credit** AmEx, DC, MC, V. **Map** p317 L6.

There's a theatrical ambience to this long, narrow West End restaurant. The walls are plastered with old film posters and the tables are surrounded by little brass plaques with the names of regulars, many of whom have acted or crewed at the numerous nearby theatres. There's a big pre- and post-theatre rush. The menu is an appetising blend of old-fashioned dishes and more creative cuisine, with some great classics like crispy duck for starters and linguini or chicken noodle salad. The children's menu lists fish and chips, chicken and chips and pasta with tomato sauce, all good quality.

Buggy access. Children's menu (£4.95). High chairs. Nappy-changing facilities. No-smoking tables.

Rock & Sole Plaice

47 Endell Street, WC2H 9AJ (7836 3785). Covent Garden or Leicester Square tube. **Meals served** 11.30am-10.30pm Mon-Sat; noon-9.30pm Sun. **Main courses** £8-£14. **Credit** MC, V. **Map** p315 L6.

There has been a chippy on this site since 1871. In clement weather the outside seats get packed – and the young

Rainforest Cafe

A WILD PLACE TO SHOP AND EAT®

Rainforest Cafe is a unique venue bringing to life the sights and sounds of the rainforest.

Come and try our fantastic menu!
With a re-launched healthy kids menu, including gluten free, dairy free and organic options.

15% DISCOUNT
off your final food bill*

Offer valid seven days a week.
Maximum party size of 6.

020 7434 3111

20 Shaftesbury Avenue, Piccadilly Circus, London W1D 7EU

www.therainforestcafe.co.uk

*Please show this advert to your safari guide when seated.
Cannot be used in conjunction with any other offer.

waiting staff shoo away takeaway customers hoping to rest their legs. Taramasalata, Efes Turkish beer and pitta point to the current proprietor's Turkish roots, but the name of the game is good old-fashioned British fish and chips. On good fish days, large portions of thick, creamy cod and haddock come encased in just-right golden batter, accompanied by crisp, rough-cut chips. You can go all sophisticated and choose sardines or dover sole if you're that way inclined, but we reckon the poor beleaguered cod is the business. The impressive fish and whale mural in the basement is worth a detour to the loo.
Buggy access. Tables outdoors (10, pavement). Takeaway service.

Smollensky's on the Strand

105 Strand, WC2R 0AA (7497 2101/www.smollenskys. co.uk). Embankment tube/Charing Cross tube/rail. **Meals served** noon-11pm Mon-Wed; noon-11.30pm Thur-Sat; noon-5.30pm, 6.30-10.30pm Sun. **Main courses** £8.95-£21.95. **Credit** AmEx, DC, MC, V. **Map** p317 L7.

To our mind, the main reason for lunching here at the weekend is the children's entertainments (clowns, face-painters and so on). so we're always surprised by the number of loving couples sharing the experience. Perhaps they're considering starting a family and feel that if they can endure this, they're ready. Whatever. Children love this place, and we're fond of it, because the service is friendly and the food is, on the whole, pretty well presented, if unimaginative, international fare. We've enjoyed the crispy wun tuns in the past, and, more recently, delighted in starters of mushroom tart and spicy chicken skewers. Steak is the main attraction, with such options as sirloin with béarnaise sauce and ribeye with peppercorn sauce. Each was large, tender and cooked precisely as requested. And on the children's menu, mini burgers, chicken goujons and penne pasta to keep little hands occupied; older children might prefer the rather more serious options of jambalaya or steak with fruit salad to follow (although they may not be able to resist the little ones' gingerbread man and ice-cream; we can't). Fun packs keep everyone busy.
Booking advisable. Buggy access. Children's menu (£3.95-£7.95). Crayons. Entertainment: clown, magician, Nintendo games, face-painting (Sat, Sun lunch). High chairs. No smoking. Play area (under-7s).

TGI Friday's

6 Bedford Street, WC2E 9HZ (7379 0585/www. tgifridays.co.uk). Covent Garden or Embankment tube/Charing Cross tube/rail. **Meals served** noon-11.30pm Mon-Sat; noon-11pm Sun. **Main courses** £7.45-£17.95. **Credit** AmEx, MC, V. **Map** p317 L7.

You can rely on TGI staff to be chirpy and pleased to see you, however many buggies and babycarriers you're touting. This is especially true at the weekends, when there's sometimes a face-painter in situ. The children's menu now promises less salt in the food, a mineral water, crudités and fruit options to counteract the lure of Pepsi floats, chips and Malteser sundaes. Hmmm, wonder which the kids would choose? It's pretty good value, though. Tasty burgers, fish fillets, spaghetti bolognese or penne pomodoro options cost from £3.45, and big thrills like dirt and worm pie (ice-cream with chocolate shavings and jelly worms), milkshakes and fruit smoothies are just a couple of quid. Then there's all that good cheer, and plenty of room

to make a right mess in your booth without the staff turning a hair. Adults' dishes are pretty good; we've enjoyed a grand salmon steak, meaty ribs, lovely onion rings and delicious, creamy, pudding-like cocktails in the past. Children don't care whether a place is cool or not. Uncool it may be, but fun it undoubtedly is.
Balloons. Buggy access. Children's menu (from £3.45). Crayons. Disabled access: lift, toilets. Entertainment: occasional face-painting (noon-5pm Sat, Sun). High chairs. Nappy-changing facilities. No smoking.
Branches: throughout town. Call or check the website.

Westminster

Café in the Crypt

Crypt of St Martin-in-the-Fields, Duncannon Street, WC2N 4JJ (7839 4342/www.stmartin-in-the-fields.org). Embankment tube/Charing Cross tube/rail. **Lunch served** 11.30am-3pm Mon-Sat; noon-3pm Sun. **Dinner served** 5-7.30pm Mon-Wed, Sun; 5-10pm Thur-Sat. **Main courses** £5.95-£7.50. **Set meal** £5.25 soup & dessert. **Credit** (over £5) MC, V. **Map** p317 L7.

This echo-chamber self-service café is hidden in the centuries-old crypt below St Martin-in-the-Fields church, so it's worth visiting for atmosphere alone. A daily rotating menu offers a selection of canteen food, such as salads, meat and two veg, or the occasional salmon fillet with new potatoes, doled out to tray-carrying diners by uniformed staff. A children's sandwich box costs £3.95 and is available during school holidays and art weekends.
High chairs. No-smoking tables. Takeaway service.

Texas Embassy Cantina

1 Cockspur Street, SW1Y 5DL (7925 0077/www. texasembassy.com). Embankment tube/Charing Cross tube/rail. **Meals served** noon-11pm Mon-Wed; noon-midnight Thur-Sat; noon-10.30pm Sun. **Main courses** £7.50-£22. **Credit** AmEx, DC, MC, V. **Map** p317 K7.

Touristy and friendly, this restaurant can get really packed (even at lunchtime), so don't come expecting a haven of tranquillity. Do come here, though, because, even though the sound system twangs with country music, the food's good. The tortilla chips are fresh, light and free and the chicken enchiladas are cheesy and well spiced. Nachos are great, too. For children the Tex Mex options are augmented by less scary hamburgers and hot dogs, but we think they would prefer the Texas flavours.
Balloons. Buggy access. Children's menu (main meals £4.75). Crayons. High chairs. Nappy-changing facilities. No smoking. Tables outdoors (8, pavement).

Kensington & Chelsea

Big Easy

332-334 King's Road, SW3 5UR (7352 4071/ www.bigeasy.uk.com). Sloane Square tube, then 11, 19, 22 bus. **Meals served** noon-11.30pm Mon-Thur; noon-12.30am Fri; 11am-12.30am Sat; 11am-11.30pm Sun. **Main courses** £8.85-£27.50. **Set lunch** (noon-5pm Mon-Fri) £7.95 2 courses. **Credit** AmEx, MC, V. **Map** p313 E12.

'Put a li'l South in yo' mouth' is the motto here, which does sound a little worrying, but there's no need to stand on ceremony here. The Big Easy is raucous, buzzing and

Consumer

very friendly. Evenings are a bit boozy, so we'd recommend lunchtime only for young families. The food is excessive (vast steaks, hunks of lobster, buckets of shellfish), all perfectly cooked and served with cheerful efficiency. Children who feel they wouldn't be able to do justice to such largesse would be better off with the menu destined for them, although it's less than adventurous: typically, hot dogs, fish fingers, ribs, burgers or chicken dippers to sustain them as they indulge in a bit of crayon work or play with their balloon. Big Easy is popular with homesick Yanks.

Balloons. Buggy access. Children's menu (£6.95, dessert £2.95-£4.75). Crayons. High chairs. Nappy-changing facilities. No-smoking tables. Tables outdoors (5, pavement). Takeaway service.

Blue Kangaroo

555 King's Road, SW6 2EB (7371 7622/www.theblue kangaroo.co.uk). Fulham Broadway tube/Sloane Square tube, then 11, 19, 22 bus. **Meals served** 9.30am-7.30pm daily. **Main courses** £6.95-£13.80. **Credit** AmEx, MC, V. **Map** p312 C13.

Children eat well and at this oft-praised family diner, and the adults don't do half badly either, as the food has been terrific every time we've visited. Traditionalists might baulk at the nets, slides, ball ponds and tunnels in the basement, as they're not exactly conducive to sitting quietly at the table, but it's great for the grown-ups to be able to linger over their meal or coffee while their young companions (aged four to seven) play. The brasserie menu is all modern classics; we always love the pumpkin risotto and the excellent salmon fishcakes or the very finbe fish in beer batter with chips, and can heartily recommend the goat's cheese salad or massive chicken sandwich with melted cheese and rocket, or the full English at breakfast time. The children's menu has superior, own-made versions of kiddy standards: chicken or fish goujons, spaghetti, penne, cottage pie made with organic meat, and lovely puddings, such as ice-cream puzzle pieces or banana boats. Service is affable and unflappable.

Buggy access. Children's menu (£5.45 incl drink). Disabled access: toilet. High chairs. Nappy-changing facilities. Play area. No smoking.

Boxwood Café

The Berkeley, Wilton Place, SW1X 7RL (7235 1010/ www.gordonramsay.com). Hyde Park Corner or Knightsbridge tube. **Lunch served** noon-3pm Mon-Fri; noon-4pm Sat, Sun. **Dinner served** 6-11pm daily. **Main courses** £12.50-£25. **Service** 12.5%. **Credit** AmEx, MC, V.

We can't believe that Gordon Ramsay would have any truck with the balloon and wax-crayon end of kiddie catering, but here, in this handsome, relaxed restaurant in the posher-than-posh Berkeley Hotel, a children's menu is available. Mr Ramsay, as a father of four, is committed to feeding them right, but has said in the past he doesn't want them to get a taste for poncey restaurants. The dishes on the menu aren't poncey, then, but they're a little more expensive than you'd expect to pay for junior portions, at £7.50 per main. They're great, though, and parents can rest assured that all the dishes are made with the highest quality ingredients. Children can have fish and chips with pea purée, or a wonderfully savoury macaroni cheese or spaghetti with proper meatballs. There are doughnuts (beautiful own-made, sugar-dusted things), elderflower jelly or yummy black forest gâteau.

Booking advisable. Children's menu (£7.50 mains). Crayons. Disabled: ramp, toilet (in hotel). High chairs. No smoking.

Top Floor at Peter Jones

Peter Jones, Sloane Square, SW1W 8EL (7901 8003/ www.johnlewis.com). Sloane Square tube. **Meals served** 9.30am-6.30pm Mon-Sat; 11am-4.30pm Sun. **Main courses** £7.50-£9.50. **Credit** MC, V.

Trust John Lewis to run a popular self-service canteen that isn't designed to clog your arteries and try your patience. Occupying the summit of the sleekly renovated Peter Jones at Sloane Square, the Top Floor offers magnificent views of London towards Kensington Gardens, along with a hot and cold buffet. The sandwiches are good, especially the vegetable and goat's cheese tortilla wrap, there are children's packed lunch boxes and some fine scones, tiramisu and cheesecakes. We've also sampled a very toothsome Sunday roast here. Never knowingly undersold, silver service is also available on the second floor, in a bijou cocktail bar of a restaurant just the other side of women's lingerie, although that's perhaps one to try without the kids.

Buggy access. Children's menu (£2.50, free baby food with adult purchase). Disabled access: lift, toilets. High chairs. Nappy-changing facilities. No smoking.

North London

Banners

21 Park Road, Crouch End, N8 8TE (8292 0001/ booking line 8348 2930/www.bannersrestaurant.co.uk). Finsbury Park tube/rail, then W7 bus. **Meals served** 9am-11.30pm Mon-Thur; 9am-midnight Fri; 10am-4pm, 5pm-midnight Sat; 10am-4pm, 5-11pm Sun. **Main courses** £8.95-£14.75. **Set lunch** £6.25-£6.95 soup or salad & side dish. **Credit** MC, V.

The daytime crèche-like atmosphere of this Crouch End institution gives way to a hipper, mellower atmosphere after 7pm, when the sprogs have been put to bed. Until that witching hour, however, the place is a home from home for young families, who get through huge quantities of coffee, crayons and colouring books. The food is consistently enjoyable, if unsubtle. We adore the garlic chips and big stuffed sandwiches, the lasagne and the jerk chicken. Children can choose from a menu that lists sausage and mash with gravy, chicken breast and chips, burgers, beans on toast and pasta. There's also a special £1.50 baby meal of cheesy mash and baked beans.

Buggy access. Children's menu (£2.55-£5). High chairs. No smoking (9am-7pm Mon-Fri).

Benihana

100 Avenue Road, NW3 3HF (7586 9508/www. benihana.co.uk). Swiss Cottage tube. **Lunch served** noon-3pm daily. **Dinner served** 5.30-10.30pm Mon-Sat; 5-10pm Sun. **Set meals** *Lunch* £8.75-£25 4 courses. *Dinner* £17-£50 6 courses. **Credit** AmEx, DC, MC, V.

Teppanyaki means 'grilled on a ploughshare', and Benihana, an international chain of Japanese restaurants owned by an ex-Olympic wrestler, has built its success in creating a performance out of such grilling techniques (but without using the actual agricultural implement). Diners sit at large, half-moon-shaped teppanyaki tables and make their selection of meat and/or fish (teriyaki

Need a packed lunch?

You're out for a day's sightseeing but couldn't be bothered to make a packed lunch. The big museums and attractions have got your number. Most museum cafés now provide a jolly box of sandwiches and snacks for their youngest visitors. Prices and quality vary wildly, as is evident from the ten we've tried, listed below.

British Museum
The Gallery Café's brightly decorated boxes (£3.95) contain a ham or cheese sandwich, a carton of drink, a piece of fruit and a chocolate bar, which was a substantial but not-so-healthy Mars Bar when we visited. *See p61.*

Firepower
Ration Packs in the Gun Pit café cost just £1.95 and usually include a jam or chocolate spread sandwich, a Penguin biscuit, crisps, juice and sweets or a lolly. *See p130.*

Imperial War Museum
The Millburns-run café has a £2.99 lunch pack consisting of a ham or cheese sandwich, juice, piece of fruit and packet of crisps. *See p131.*

London Zoo
The Oasis Café's pick-and-mix lunch box costs £4.95, but all the food items a child can choose (sandwich, fruit, muffin, cake) are organic. There's fruit juice or milk to drink. *See p67.*

Museum of London
The Digby Trout café does a children's lunch box for £3.50. Inside is a brown roll, cream cheese, a piece of fruit, a bottle of Robinson's Fruit Shoot, a chocolate biscuit and a jelly. One children's lunch box is free with an adult meal (£5.50-£5.85) during school holidays. *See p51.*

National Maritime Museum
The children's lunch box available at the Upper Deck Coffee Bar costs £3.99. This buys a sandwich and a choice of four other items from the food on display for the purpose: cheese snips, grapes, crudités, crispy cakes and fruit yoghurts. *See p127.*

Natural History Museum
The Gallery Restaurant can furnish children with a lunch box for £3.95. It's full of organic goodies, namely a cheese sandwich, juice, crisps and a biscuit bar. *See p87.*

RAF Museum
Many of the items in the café's kids' lunch box are made on site. There are own-baked baguettes (filled with tuna, ham or cheese), mini brownies, organic apple or orange juice, a bag of mixed dried fruit, grapes and a choice of another piece of fruit – fantastic value at £3.50. *See p105.*

Science Museum
The Revolution Café does a children's packed lunch for £3.95. The box contains a brown roll with a choice of fillings, crisps, a piece of fruit, a chocolate biscuit and a drink. The award-winning Deep Blue Café near the Dana centre will provide a hot meal for children for £4.25. *See p91.*

Tower of London
The Digby Trout restaurant's lunch box for children (£3.95) features a castle design for boys, or crown for girls. Children can pick five items from a range that includes a finger roll filled with jam, Marmite or Dairylea, carton of fruit juice, jelly, Penguin bar, Mini Cheddars, bag of raisins or cherry tomatoes and bite-sized brownies, shortbread or flapjacks. *See p53.*

steak, tuna or chicken, prawns, filet mignon, lobster tails), after which the chefs claim centre stage. Knives are released from holsters, and vegetables and fish are sacrificed for the chefs to show off their (admittedly awesome) cutting skills. The grilled items, spiced up with mustard and ginger dips, are all fresh and healthy-tasting, but it's the preparation that everyone comes for. Pepperpots fly through the air, to squeals of delight from the youngsters.
Buggy access. Children's menu (£9.50-£13.50 6 dishes incl ice-cream, noon-3pm Sun). Disabled access: toilets. High chairs. No-smoking tables. Takeaway service.
Branches: 37 Sackville Street, W1S 3DQ (7494 2525); 77 King's Road, SW3 4NX (7376 7799).

Camden Arts Centre
Corner of Arkwright Road & Finchley Road, Swiss Cottage, NW3 6DG (7472 5516/www.camdenarts centre.org). Finchley Road tube/Finchley Road &

Frognal rail. **Meals served** 10am-5.30pm Tue, Thur-Sun; 10am-8.30pm Wed. **Main courses** £2.95-£6.50. **Credit** MC, V.
The café at this chic arts centre fills a corner of the ground floor and spills out into a garden. For the menu, think imaginative sandwiches and meze platters, or a daily special such as plump, juicy salmon and dill fish cakes, children's portions of which are offered. The focus is on locally sourced food – plus toast and Marmite and Kit-Kats.
Buggy access. Disabled access: ramps, toilets. High chairs. No smoking. Reduced portions for children. Tables outdoors (10, garden). Takeaway service.

Fine Burger Co
256 Muswell Hill Broadway, Muswell Hill, N10 3SH (8815 9292/www.fineburger.co.uk). Highgate tube, then 43, 134 bus. **Meals served** noon-11pm Mon-Sat; noon-10pm Sun. **Main courses** £5.25-£8.95. **Credit** AmEx, MC, V.

We have found that it's possible to become addicted to the thick, malty shakes here, and the hand-cut chips are amazing. The burgers are fine, like most other gourmet burger places, but a little more expensive for a slightly less impressive meat patty, showily encased in ciabatta with a pile of salad. We prefer this branch to the more self-regarding Islington one. Bantering staff convey a variety of burgers from an open kitchen into a modern dining space that seems as suited to beer-supping trendies as it does to milkshake-slurping families. The kids' menu gives them a smaller fine burger and chips.
Balloons. Buggy access. Children's menu (£4.95-£5.50). Crayons. High chairs. Nappy-changing facilities. No smoking. Takeaway service.
Branches: throughout town. Call or check the website

Gracelands

118 College Road, NW10 5HD (8964 9161). Kensal Green tube. **Open** 8am-5pm Mon-Fri; 9am-3pm Sat; 10am-2pm Sun. **Main courses** £2.50-£5. **Unlicensed. Corkage** no charge. **Credit** MC, V.
This is one of those thrown-together, friendly local cafés that every neighbourhood deserves, but few get. It's so child-friendly, and the food is so delicious, that it scooped the *Time Out* Best Family Restaurant gong for 2005, even if it is slightly off the beaten track. Eating goes on at scrubbed wooden tables; playing is confined to a well-equipped play area at the front, which has a book c orner, a home corner and a big squashy sofa. Food is all made on the day, and there's usually a nourishing hot dish of the day, such as chicken provencale. There are quiches, a wide selection of salads and sandwiches and artisan breads and filling cakes, or organic ice-cream or yoghurt and honey. The own-made banoffi pie is particularly delicious and goes well with the strong, fragrant coffee. Children can have a frothy 'babycino'.
Buggy access. Children's menu). High chairs. No smoking. Tables outdors (4, pavement; 3, garden). Takeaway service. Toys.

Haché

24 Inverness Street, Camden Town, NW1 7HJ (7485 9100/www.hacheburgers.com). Camden Town tube. **Meals served** noon-10.30pm Mon-Sat; noon-10pm Sun. **Main courses** £4.95-£10.95. **Service** 12.5%. **Credit** AmEx, DC, MC, V.
Voted best burger bar in the *Time Out* Eating Awards 2005. Haché's burgers are made with the French steak *haché* (meaning, chopped) in mind. The meat, premium Aberdeen Angus, served in a plump and juicy style, is the star of the show. Burgers are beautifully presented, with salad, and the chips are as crisp and golden as they should be. It's a stylish place, but very friendly and welcoming to children (you get Smarties with the bill). Parents are impressed by the extensive wine list, but the zesty smoothies should not be missed.
Buggy access. High chairs. No smoking. Takeaway service.

Mangal II

4 Stoke Newington High Street, Dalston, N16 8BH (7254 7888). Dalston Kingsland rail/76, 149, 243 bus. **Meals served** noon-1am daily. **Main courses** £7-£12. **No credit cards.**
Families, both Turkish and English, fill up Mangal II on a Sunday. Children love the grilled chicken and pide and saç bread; their parents go for the substantial fried lamb's liver and grilled aubergine as well as lamb kebabs – tender

medallions of fillet lamb held together with a cocktail stick – and spicy beef or lamb sausages known as Sucuk. This restaurant, with its neutral green walls and vaulted blue ceiling, is a step upmarket from the original Mangal café, and from the Mangal Turkish pizza shop across the way at No.27, but prices remain keen. Service is always friendly and relaxed, but not particularly fast.
Buggy access. High chairs. Takeaway service.

Marine Ices

8 Haverstock Hill, Chalk Farm, NW3 2BL (7482 9003). Chalk Farm tube/31 bus. **Meals served** noon-3pm, 6-11pm Mon-Fri; noon-11pm Sat; noon-10pm Sun. **Main courses** £5.20-£9.60. **Credit** MC, V.
More than 70 years old, run by descendants of the original owner, this popular ice-cream parlour and restaurant has a *famiglia* atmosphere. There always seem to be exited children in here, usually with their sights fixed on the traditional gelateria at the back, whose fantastic ice-cream menu is famed far and wide. The more modern restaurant at the front serves pizza, pasta and a few meatier Italian meals. The savoury dishes are reliable and enjoyable; we had a big bowl of steaming, impressively large mussels, bresaola and spaghetti alle vongole and an interesting, scampi based pasta dish and it was all excellent. Then it's time for pudding: whether lavished with sauces and toppings in a novelty glass or served as a simple scoop astride a wafer, the ice-cream is something special.
Buggy access. High chairs. No smoking. Takeaway service.

Ottolenghi

287 Upper Street, Islington, N1 2TZ (7288 1454/ www.ottolenghi.co.uk). Angel tube/Highbury & Islington tube/rail. **Meals served** 8am-11pm Mon-Sat; 9am-7pm Sun. **Main courses** (lunch) £7.50-£11.50; (dinner) £15-£25. **Credit** MC, V.
Ottolenghi is the second branch of the busy Notting Hill deli/café of the same name. The all-white modernist interior, with its long communal dining tables and space-age chairs, has a typically Islington look, but the food displays, in a riot of Mediterranean colours, are head-turning. Choose from breakfast dishes (granola or pastries), cakes, sandwiches and other savouries, all made on the premises. The breads, created by renowned master baker Dan Lepard, are baked on site to his recipes and include focaccia, rye, huge grissini and an excellent sourdough. Among the marvellous French-style creations are rich and intensely flavoured lemon and mascarpone tarts with polenta crusts, or fruit tarts made on packed crumble bases with almond cream. Main dishes (which change daily) could be loosely described as southern Mediterranean, using influences from Iran to Morocco. Stunningly displayed, they're a riot of colour and form.
Buggy access. Disabled access: toilet. High chairs. No smoking. Reduced portions for children (£3.50). Tables outdoors (2, pavement). Takeaway service.
Branches: 63 Ledbury Road, W11 2AD (7727 1121); 1 Holland Street, W8 4NA (7937 0003).

La Porchetta

147 Stroud Green Road, Finsbury Park, N4 3PZ (7281 2892/www.laporchetta.co.uk). Finsbury Park tube/rail. **Open** 3pm-midnight Mon-Fri; noon-midnight Sat, Sun. **Main courses** £5.10-£9.60. **Credit** MC, V.
The Stroud Green branch of this expanding Italian chain with a persistent pig theme still comes in for most praise for child-friendliness; the one in town is a little too cramped

and busy (see the website for the address). It's extremely cheap and the pizzas, of which there are 26 varieties, are pretty good. Prices run from £5.10 for the margherita to £7.50 for the Pizza Speck. Pasta lovers can indulge in one of the 35 dishes based round this staple. Children are offered smaller portions on pasta dishes.
High chairs. No-smoking tables. Reduced portions for children (pasta). Takeaway service.
Branches: throughout town. Call or check the website.

S&M Café

4-6 Essex Road, Islington, N1 8LN (7359 5361).
Angel tube/19, 38 bus. **Meals served** 7.30am-11.30pm Mon-Thur; 7.30am-midnight Fri; 8.30am-midnight Sat; 8.30am-10.30pm Sun. **Main courses** £2.50-£7.95. **Credit** MC, V.
You choose your sausages from a big list that includes butcher's classics and veggie variants, then you select the type of mash and gravy you want from a smaller list. The result is served Beano-style, with sausages poking out of a generous mash mountain. The menu changes seasonally, so for spring and summer there are lighter sausage delights, such as a pleasant Italian-style sausage with tomato, or a lean spring lamb with mint. Children can choose the same, only smaller, on their menu, which also offers chicken nuggets or fish fingers and plus a drink. A portion of ice-cream costs £1 extra. The Islington branch of this growing mini chain is lovely-looking, with a vintage 1920s blue-and-chrome interior. S&M does comforting breakfasts; boiled egg and soldiers is £1.50.
Buggy access. Children's menu (£3.50).
Branches: 268 Portobello Road, W10 5TY (8968 8898); 48 Brushfield Street, E1 6AG (7247 2252).

Tiger Lil's

270 Upper Street, Islington, N1 2UQ (7226 1118/ www.tigerlils.com). Highbury & Islington tube/rail.
Meals served 6-11pm Mon-Thur; noon-3pm, 6-11pm Fri; noon-midnight Sat; noon-11pm Sun. **Main courses** £7.90-£12.65. **Credit** AmEx, MC, V.
Here's an entertaining way to turn your children on to cooking (and saving an ungodly mess in the kitchen). Tiger Lil's is a DIY restaurant where you assemble your own raw ingredients – including a wide range of vegetables – from a huge selection, choose a cooking oil and sauce, then watch chefs stir-fry them in a central cooking area. The fizz and clatter of flaming wok adds to the drama, and young families are actively encouraged through the portals with the promise that under fives eat free with a paying adult. The quality of the food is pretty good, and a tasteful modern interior is another plus point.
Booking advisable weekends. Buggy access. Children's menu (£5.65). Crayons. Disabled access: toilets. High chairs. Nappy-changing facilities.

Toff's

38 Muswell Hill Broadway, Muswell Hill, N10 3RT (8883 8656). Highgate tube, then 43, 134 bus.
Meals served 11.30am-10pm Mon-Sat. **Main courses** £7.95-£17.50. **Set meals** (11.30am-5.30pm Mon-Sat) £7.95 1 course incl tea/coffee. **Credit** AmEx, DC, MC, V.
Toff's dark-panelled dining room, which you get to through a pair of saloon-style swing doors (children love them) is beyond the takeaway zone, decorated with photographs of Victorian fish markets, signed celebrity snaps and the odd gold disc. The nationality of the ownership

Crown & Greyhound. *See p177.*

can be guessed from the presence of calamares, Greek salad and taramasalata on the menu. If you can, try the fish soup: thick and delicious, but not always available. Batter or matzo, grilled or fried – the fish options are numerous. Haddock is expertly cooked, white and flaky in a crisp, golden batter, while chips come big and yellow. Fruit flan, apple pie and similar puddings are apparently offered, but we've never had enough room left to find out. Another big bonus: the affordable children's menu is well executed.
Buggy access. Children's menu (£2.95-£3.50). Crayons. Disabled access: toilets. High chairs. No-smoking tables. Takeaway service.

Wagamama

11 Jamestown Road, Camden, NW1 7BW (7428 0800/www.wagamama.com). Camden tube. **Meals served** noon-11pm Mon-Sat; noon-10pm Sun. **Main courses** £5.60-£9.25. **Credit** AmEx, DC, MC, V.
Everyone's a bit blasé about noodle bars – a high-street staple nowadays – but it pays to remember that Wagamama is one of the originals, and one of the best. And one of the most successful too, with 20 branches in London alone and outlets as far afield as Australia and Dubai. This north London outpost is bright and spacious. A gleaming, smoke-free environment, perky staff and a wholesome menu are appealing – though not everyone likes the communal tables and resultant noise. For children, there's chicken katsu (chicken breast fried in breadcrumbs) with dipping sauce, rice and shredded cucumber, or vegetarian or chicken noodle dishes for just £3.50. To drink, choose from raw juices, beer, wine, saké – or drown your unhealthy self in gallons of free green tea.

Buggy access. Children's menu (£2.95-£4.25). Disabled access: toilets. High chairs. Nappy-changing facilities. No smoking. Takeaway service.
Branches: throughout town. Phone or check website.

East London

Arkansas Café
Unit 12, Old Spitalfields Market, Whitechapel, E1 6AA (7377 6999). Liverpool Street tube/rail. **Lunch served** noon-2.30pm Mon-Fri; noon-4pm Sun. **Dinner served** party bookings only, by arrangement. **Main courses** £5-£14. **Credit** MC, V. **Map** p319 R5.
Carnivorous children beyond high-chair age, with healthy appetites, will get the most out of this most authentic barbecue restaurant, presided over by the gregarious Bubba. Hovering on the edge of Spitalfields Market, it's a justifiably popular lunching spot. Bubba cooks huge piles of tender beef brisket, pork ribs, duck and juicy chicken. It's a show that the kids will love, and the smell of all that sizzling meat will set mouths watering. Customers sit on a mishmash of church pews and garden chairs. Service is efficient and polite, although you may have to wait if you arrive at peak times on a Sunday. Puddings are unsubtle and gorgeous – pecan pie, chocolate cake and cheesecake are a struggle to get down after the first course, but children might like to share a portion.
Buggy access. Disabled access: toilet (in market). No-smoking tables. Tables outdoors (16, terrace inside market, Sun only). Takeaway service.

Faulkner's
424-426 Kingsland Road, Dalston, E8 4AA (7254 6152). Dalston Kingsland rail/67, 76, 149, 242, 243 bus. **Lunch served** noon-2.30pm Mon-Fri. **Dinner served** 5-10pm Mon-Thur; 4.15-10pm Fri. **Meals served** 11.30am-10pm Sat; noon-9pm Sun. **Main courses** £8.90-£17.90. *Minimum* £4. **Credit** MC, V.
Yet another tradtional fish and chip shop that's been given a bit of a makeover by its new Turkish owners. Like many before them, they've added taramasalata and houmous to the starter list, but left the main event as good as it ever was. Fresh, fresh fish comes grilled, battered or crusted in matzo meal; it's served with strapping chunky chips, robust mushy peas and own-made tartare sauce. Comfort staples such as cherry pie, sherry trifle and spotted dick are among the puds. Service is kind, especially to children.
Buggy access. Children's menu (£4.90). Disabled access: toilet. High chairs. No-smoking tables. Takeaway service.

Frizzante at City Farm
1A Goldsmith's Row, Hackney, E2 8QA (7739 2266/ www.frizzanteltd.co.uk). Bus 26, 48, 55. **Meals served** 10am-5.30pm Tue-Sun. **Main courses** £4.50-£7.50. **Credit** AmEx, DC, MC, V.
Hackney City Farm's delightful Italian café chalks up a different, tempting menu every day, as well as providing some excellent breakfast fry-ups. Location is all, of course, especially when you've brought a young family for lunch, and this place has pigs, poultry, cattle and space to play, making it one of the most popular spots for Sunday lunch in London, when, of course, you can't book, and you may have to queue for a table. Interesting meal choices on our last visit included a delightful list of well-dressed salads, to go with a pumpkin and spinach pie, salade niçoise, spaghetti with mussels, lean, roasted poussin and a very

creamy moussaka. If the children don't fancy the specials, there are excellent thin pizzas and various pasta options.
The new branch of Frizzante, at the Unicorn Theatre (*see p225*), is rather more sophisticated-looking than its bucolic big sister, except when it's full of children. The menu is much more geared to quick working lunches and coffee breaks, so there are excellent stuffed sandwiches and a few hot dishes. We had arancini with mushrooms, a breadcrumbed ball of mozzarella-cheesy risotto, with a peppery rocket salad.
Buggy access. Children's menu (£2.50-£3.50). Disabled access: toilets. High chairs. No smoking. Tables outdoors (7, garden). Takeaway service. Toys.
Branch: Unicorn Theatre, 147 Tooley Street, SE1 2HZ (7645 0500).

Jones Dairy Café
23 Ezra Street, Bethnal Green, E2 7RH (7739 5372/ www.jonesdairy.co.uk). Bus 26, 48, 55. **Open** 9am-3pm Fri, Sat; 8am-2pm Sun. **Main courses** £4-£7. **No credit cards.**
Ezra Street, with its cobbled stones and old lamps, is occasionally called upon to cover for Victorian London, so you may recognise it from a variety of films. The centuries-old façade of the old dairy, where this café now resides, is also a historic London landmark. On Sunday mornings, when the Columbia Road Flower Market is in full bloom, Jones is overrun by families and green-fingered types well aware that it has the best bread in the area and the finest bagels this side of Brick Lane. On Fridays and Saturdays, though, it's a far more sedate operation, dishing up daisy-fresh brunches to locals sat around a large farmhouse table or, in summer, on the peaceful street outside. The menu is tiny (poached or scrambled eggs, kippers, salads, cheesecake), but you can't really go wrong with any of it. A shop around the corner offers a wider range of breads, a worthwhile selection of cheeses and a small assortment of other picnic-friendly temptations.
Buggy access. High chair. No smoking. Tables outdoors (3, patio). Takeaway service.

Royal China
30 Westferry Circus, Docklands, E14 8RR (7719 0888/ www.royalchinagroup.co.uk). Canary Wharf tube/DLR/ Westferry DLR. **Meals served** noon-11pm Mon-Thur; noon-11.30pm Fri, Sat; 11am-10pm Sun. **Dim sum served** noon-4.45pm daily. **Main courses** £7-£50. **Dim sum** £2.20-£4.50. **Set meal** £30 per person (minimum 2). **Credit** AmEx, DC, MC, V.
We cannot rave enough about this restaurant, with its inspiring views over the Thames and adventurous menu. Most guests eating here seem to be ethnic Chinese – a good sign if ever there was one. This is a venue for serious Chinese dining and its location means you don't find the long queues and hasty atmosphere of other Royal China branches (*listed below*). On a warm spring evening, park the buggy outside, decant the kids on to the terrace and divide your time between pondering the menu and admiring the view. There's plenty to interest young and old in both. Whole king prawns deep-fried and encrusted with a paste of salted duck's egg yolk is a favourite, and we'll always remember the crisp sesame prawn rolls, and sliced duck in a special sauce. On the dim sum menu the little dumplings generously stuffed with scallops can be singled out for further praise. Staff are all smiles and very friendly towards the children whenever we visit.

Disabled access: toilet. High chairs. Nappy-changing facilities. Tables outdoors (23, terrace). Takeaway service.
Branches: 40 Baker Street, W1M 1BA (7487 4688); 13 Queensway, W2 4QJ (7221 2535); 68 Queen's Grove, NW8 6ER (7586 4280).

Sông Quê

134 Kingsland Road, Shoreditch, E2 8DY (7613 3222). Bus 26, 48, 55, 67, 149, 242, 243. **Meals served** noon-3pm, 5.30-11pm Mon-Sat; noon-11pm Sun. **Main courses** £4-£9.20. **Credit** MC, V.
We're into the name means 'rustic river', which sums up this rough-around-the-edges local Vietnamese diner, with its fake ivy decor, rather well. The menu is long and authentic, the food delicious. Like a culinary excursion through Vietnam, the assortment of dishes covers specialities from all regions – the aromatic pho (soup with noodles) from Hanoi, minced shrimp on sugar cane from Hue and the southern Vietnamese pancakes filled with pork, prawns and beansprouts; these are very popular with junior diners. Try the cold goi cuon (literally 'rolled salad'), which consist of cool, soft, rice paper rolls usually containing prawns, pork, herbs and rice vermicelli and served with a peanutty sauce. Vegetarian versions are also available. Puddings are a strange, acquired taste: see how you get on with the 'three-colour pudding' of gelatinous red bean, mung bean, tapioca and coconut-milk paste.
Buggy access. High chairs. No-smoking tables. Takeaway service.

Story Deli

3 Dray Walk, The Old Truman Brewery, 91 Brick Lane, E1 6QL (7247 3137). Liverpool Street tube/rail. **Meals served** Winter 8am-5pm daily. Summer 9am-10pm daily. **Main courses** £4-£9. **Credit** AmEx, MC, V. **Map** p319 S5.
A stylish deli-cum-pizzeria that's constantly besieged by hungry trendy types and their offspring, which must be a trial for the staff, who have to negotiate steep steps lined with flour sacks to get to the food in this former Truman Brewery. Diners sit communally around one of the enormous tables, perched on cardboard-box stools, waiting patiently for their food (staff, bless them, may be overwhelmed by their duties when there's a rush on). Another table displays bowls of salad and quiches. Otherwise the menu consists of breakfasts, the odd special (a whopping, strongly flavoured kedgeree topped with a feather-light herb omelette), pizzas and alluring cakes and tarts. Pizzas are superb, with bubbly thin bases, tomato and mozzarella toppings, and top-notch extras.
No smoking. Reduced portions for children. Tables outdoors (6, pavement). Takeaway service.

South-east London

Au Ciel

1A Calton Avenue, Dulwich Village, SE21 7DE (8488 1111). North Dulwich rail/P4, 37 bus. **Snacks served** 8.30am-5.30pm Mon-Sat; 10am-5.30pm Sun. **Snacks** £1.95-£2.95. **Credit** MC, V.
This fragrant French café is a perfect place for Saturday morning hot chocolate and croissants after an early romp in Dulwich Park. The bread and pastries are from the Sally Clarke range so they're not cheap, but the quality is tip-top. We also recommend the house hot chocolates,

partnered with a slice of excellent cake. There are French chocolates from Valrhona, and fresh pâtisserie from Didier (French bakers) and De Baere (Belgian). It's all comforting, luxurious and guilt-inducing, unless you're a breastfeeding mother who needs those calories. Better rush round the park a few times more if you're not.
Tables outdoors (2, pavement). Takeaway service.

Crown & Greyhound

73 Dulwich Village, SE21 7BJ (8299 4976). North Dulwich rail. **Open** 11am-11pm Mon-Wed; 11am-midnight Thur-Sat; noon-10.30pm Sun. **Meals served** noon-10pm Mon-Sat; noon-9pm Sun. **Main courses** £6.50-£13.90. **Credit** AmEx, MC, V.
'The Dog' is legendary among parents (even those whose offspring are quite grown up now) for being a fine place for Sunday lunch with the family. It's a large pub, with jolly staff and a number of highchairs for groups dominated by minor diners. Those free of childish companions tend to stay in the front section, but at the back there are squashy sofas and a less pubby vibe. On weekdays dedicated children's meals are limited to sausage and mash (vegetarian or meaty bangers) or pasta, although children are welcome to have small portions of chips or sandwiches and bar snacks. The Carvery (Sundays only) is visited by hungry families after a traditional roast. On summer Fridays, when the weather's warm and evenings are rosy, a barbecue gets fired up in the big garden.
Disabled access; toilets. High chairs. Nappy-changing facilities. No-smoking tables. Reduced portions for children (£3.50-£5). Tables outdoors (20, garden).

Domali Café

38 Westow Street, Crystal Palace, SE19 3AH (8768 0096/www.domali.co.uk). Gypsy Hill rail. **Meals served** 9.30am-11pm daily. **Main courses** (lunch) £3.90-£9.90. **Credit** MC, V.
A friendly brasserie/café with cocktails for the evening crowd and substantial snacks and sandwiches for families who want to lunch out in the garden on a sunny day. The long breakfast menu plus the huge range of toasties and sandwiches are the strengths; you can have a simple peanut butter and banana combo for £2.30 or go for the full vegetarian fry-up (non-meat sausages). Ribollita – a classic Tuscan bean and cabbage stew packed with vegetables and topped with cheese – is great, nutritious comfort food. Children's portions are available, and the chunky chips are fabulous.
Buggy access. High chairs. No-smoking tables. Reduced portions for children (£1.45-£3.50). Tables outdoors (10, garden).

The Green

58-60 East Dulwich Road, SE22 9AX (7732 7575/ www.greenbar.co.uk). East Dulwich rail/37, 185 bus. **Open** 10am-11pm daily. **Breakfast served** 10am-noon, **lunch served** noon-5pm, **dinner served** 6-11pm daily. **Main courses** £9.95-£12.95. **Set lunch** £8.50 2 courses; £11.50 3 courses; (Sun) £15.95 3 courses. **Service** 10%. **Credit** AmEx, MC, V.
This youngish, trendyish restaurant/bar/arts space makes room for high chairs, so family groups touting toddlers blend in graciously with child-free parties. A children's menu is available (pasta or cod goujons, say, served with a drink and pudding). The main menu is the business. Starters of, for example, own-made tomato and basil soup, salmon fish cakes or well-dressed gnocchi pave the way

Consumer

Go out to eat

Park cafés aren't always great. Some are still in the dark ages, thrusting instant coffee, Slush Puppies and Kit Kats at innocent strollers. Others are terrific. We list the second category below.

Brew House

Kenwood, Hampstead Lane, Hampstead Heath, NW3 7JR (8341 5384). Bus 210, 214. **Open** *Oct-Mar* 9am-dusk daily. *Apr-Sept* 9am-6pm daily (7.30pm on concert nights). **Credit** (over £10) MC, V.
Occupies part of the basement and terrace of neo-classical Kenwood House, whose large outdoor tables set amid glorious flower beds and massed hanging baskets are always at a premium in warm weather. Inside are high ceilings, lightly frescoed walls and quaint village-style signposts that point out the cake stand (as if you could miss the huge chunks of carrot cake, pineapple pavlova, scones, and gooseberry cheesecake) and guide you around the jam-packed service area. Homely grub matches the setting perfectly. *Buggy access. Children's menu (£2.50-£3.95). High chairs. Nappy-changing facilities. No smoking (inside). Tables outside (400, garden). Takeaway service.*

Chumleigh Gardens Café

Chumleigh Gardens, Burgess Park, SE5 0RJ (7525 1070). Elephant & Castle tube/rail, then 12, 42, 63, 68, 171, 343, P3 bus. **Open** 9am-5pm Mon-Fri; 10am-5pm Sat, Sun. **Main courses** £3-£5. **Licensed. Credit** MC, V.
This café, in one of the few attractive bits of Burgess Park, occupies two large rooms in a mellow enclave of almshouses set around nicely tended lawns. The chaotic-looking kitchen turns out big, wholesome meals on old china plates; delicious, light quiches, full breakfasts, generous sandwiches and a rib-sticking lasagne and chips combo. There's sometimes jazz on a Sunday. Outdoor seating is in the Islamic section of Chumleigh Parks's globally themed gardens. There's no specific children's menu but there are chips, fry-ups, and sandwiches, crisps, confectionery and fizzy pop to keep them happy. *High chairs. Toys.*

Common Ground

Wandsworth Common, off Dorlcote Road, SW18 3RT (8874 9386). Wandsworth Common rail. **Open** 9am-5.15pm Tue-Fri; 10am-5.15pm Sat, Sun. **Main courses** £3.50-£9. **Unlicensed. Credit** MC, V.
Common Ground is a happy place to idle away an hour or two. Warm, friendly staff skilfully avoid treading on contented toddlers (there are many well-cuddled toys), and effortlessly maintain a relaxed atmosphere. The cosy back room – with room enough to play – is a heavenly retreat on a winter's day. The food is own-made; a goat's cheese, baby spinachand pine nut tart was the lunch of choice on our visit. There are also cakes and sandwiches and a selection of mini meals – pasta, chicken strips, Marmite sandwiches, cookies, cakes and babycinos – for children. *Children's menu. High chairs. Toys.*

Garden Café

Inner Circle, Regents Park, NW1 4NU (7935 5729/www.thegardencafe.co.uk). Baker Street or Regents Park tube. **Open** 10am-dusk daily. **Main courses** £4.25-£12.95. **Licensed. Credit** MC, V.
The spacious interior of the 40-year-old Garden Café in Regents Park had a makeover in 2005 and now looks rather chic. There's plenty of space inside for little tots to run around with wobbly ice-creams. If it's sunny, the outdoor area surrounded by rose beds is heavenly. The menu has classics like prawn cocktail, ploughman's lunches, super puds and sandwiches and cakes. *Tables outdoors.*

Golders Hill Park Refreshment House

North End Road, Golders Green, NW3 7HD (8455 8010). Golders Green or Hampstead tube. **Meals served** *Summer* 9am-dusk daily. *Winter* 10am-dusk daily. **Main courses** £3-£7. **No credit cards.**
Always a choice spot for freshly made ice-cream, this Italian-run park café has a lovely, bright, clean glasshouse interior and a good selection of cakes and drinks. The savoury menu includes a long list of salads and pasta dishes, plus an extended children's menu. We love the summer bowls of strawberries and cream and big wedges of refreshing watermelon. *Children's menu (£3-£5). High chairs. Nappy-changing facilities. No smoking. Tables outdoors (25, terrace). Takeaway service.*

Inn The Park

St James's Park, SW1A 2BJ (7451 9999/www.innthepark.com). St James's Park tube. **Open** 8am-11pm Mon-Fri; 9am-11pm Sat; 9am-10pm Sun. **Main courses** £11.50-£14.50. **Credit** AmEx, MC, V. **Map** p317 K8.
This is an attractive lakeside wood-and-glass pavilion with glazed walls that slide back in clement weather. Part British restaurant (don't have a stroke when you see the prices), part all-day café, it's a lovely place for a family meal. There are great ice-creams, afternoon teas and cakes and breakfasts. Children get their own menu of chicken and chips or sausage and mash. *Buggy access. Children's menu (£7.50). Disabled access: toilets. High chairs. No smoking (inside).Tables outdoors (40). Takeaway service.*

Pavilion Café

Dulwich Park, off College Road, Dulwich, SE21 7BQ (8299 1383). North Dulwich or West Dulwich rail. **Open** *Summer* 9am-6pm (with some late evenings) daily. *Winter* 9am-dusk daily. **Main courses** £3.50-£6.50. **No credit cards.**
This welcoming space is just what you'd hope to find down Dulwich way. The glass-fronted pavilion, decorated with striking contemporary art (for sale) and large bunches of fresh flowers, can be opened up on hot days, with plenty of tables inside, though it's a bit of a squeeze outside. The café has a relaxing vibe even when busy. Sweets, lollies, ice-creams, English breakfasts and the usual sandwiches and cakes are available, but the Pavilion goes a step further, with the likes of orange-blossom and ginger cake, and tender pork marinated with rosemary, served in flatbread with salad and apple and cinnamon sauce. Produce is free-range and locally sourced. Children's parties are a speciality.
Buggy access. Children's menu (£1.50-£3.50). Disabled access: toilets . High chairs. Nappy-changing facilities. Tables outdoors (11, terrace). Takeaway service. Toys.

Pavilion Café

Highgate Woods, Muswell Hill Road, N10 3JN (8444 4777). Highgate tube. **Open** *Summer* 8am-8pm daily. *Winter* 9am-dusk daily. **Main courses** £6-£8.95. **Licensed**. **Credit** AmEx, MC, V.
This little treasure is popular, and rightly so, thanks to its tasty, beautifully presented food and location in Highgate Woods. We enjoyed a mixed platter of dips and smoked mackerel and a lovely steak with onion. For children there's pasta, fish, chicken goujons and chips and mini eaters are welcome into the evening. The setting is perfect for jazz on Thursday or Friday evenings.
Children's menu (£3). Tables outdoors.

Pavilion Tea House

Greenwich Park, Blackheath Gate, SE10 8QY (8858 9695). Blackheath rail/Greenwich rail/DLR. **Open** 9am-5pm Mon-Fri; 9am-6pm Sat, Sun. **Main courses** £4.95-£8.50. **Licensed**. **Credit** MC, V.
This is a lovely spot, where the soup, salads and sandwiches are of the gourmet variety. Puddings and cakes go down well with a nice pot of tea. Children have a small selection of hot options, or can just stick to cake and ice-cream. The garden is safely hedged off from the central thoroughfare.
Children's menu. High chairs. Tables outdoors.

Ravenscourt Park Café

Paddenswick Road, W6 0UL (8748 1945). Ravenscourt Park tube. **Open** *Summer* 9am-5.30pm daily. *Winter* 9am-4pm daily. **Main courses** £5.50-£7.50. **Unlicensed**. **No credit cards.**
A pleasant park stop that caters for lunchtime blowouts and mid-afternoon snacks. Light meals include own-made soups and sandwiches or Cumberland sausages with lentils, and pasta dishes. If the lemon curd bread and butter pudding's on, go for it. Children's meals include free-range nuggets and fish fingers.
Children's menu. Tables outdoors.

Springfield Park Café

White Mansion Lodge, Springfield Park, E5 9EF (8806 0444/wwwsparkcafe.co.uk). Stamford Hill or Stoke Newington rail. **Open** *Apr-Oct* 10am-6pm daily. *Nov-Mar* 10am-4pm daily. **Main courses** £3.90-£5.90. **Unlicensed**. **No credit cards.**
Order at the counter, beside a big sculpture of a dog, from a pretty fabulous menu: Springfield Special sandwiches (roasted veg and halloumi, perhaps), own-made soups, tasty cakes, shakes and organic juices. The lawn out front rolls down towards the River Lea and the Springfield Marina. Children are very much welcomed, and they'll find plenty of treats on the menu.
Tables outdoors.

for top quality mains. All that we sampled was attractively presented and carefully seasoned. Calf's liver on a pad of crushed, buttery Jersey Royals in a fruity gravy is pink and succulent, and the salmon steak sports a delicious, crispy skin. The pudding list lists a seasonal fruit crumble and a hot chocolate pud served with pistachio ice-cream. *Buggy access. Children's menu (£6.95-£7.95). Disabled: toilets. High chairs. No-smoking tables.*

Joanna's
56 Westow Hill, Gipsy Hill, SE19 1RX (8670 4052/ www.joannas.uk.com). Crystal Palace or Gipsy Hill rail. **Brunch served** noon-6pm Mon-Sat. **Meals served** 10am-11.15pm Mon-Thur; 10am-11.30pm Fri, Sat; 10am-10.30pm Sun. **Main courses** £9-£16. **Credit** AmEx, MC, V.
This bright, welcoming and spacious brasserie has an upbeat soundtrack, attentive staff and a menu with a classic British feel. Reasonably priced lunchtime favourites include Somerset oak-smoked ham, eggs and fries and traditional roast beef with a giant yorkshire pudding and fresh vegetables. The pricier à la carte menu, on the other hand, lists steaks, lamb cutlets, battereed fish or moules (served either marinière or with a Thai curry twist). The brunch/lunch menu seems great value and is served alongside a children's version that includes a scoop of creamy Guernsey ice-cream in a range of flavours (toffee and nut for us). You can reserve the old train carriage if you're with a family group and want a space to yourselves. *Buggy access. Children's menu (£4.95-£5.95 incl ice-cream). High chairs. Tables outdoors (5, pavement).*

Olley's
65-69 Norwood Road, Herne Hill, SE24 9AA (8671 8259/www.olleys.info). Herne Hill rail/3, 68 bus. **Meals served** 5-10.30pm Mon; noon-10.30pm Tue-Sun. **Main courses** £8.45-£18.45. **Credit** AmEx, MC, V.
A serial award-winner, Olley's, underneath the railway arches, is a fantastic fish and chip restaurant, some say the best in town. Its popularity has forced the owners to expand the premises to fit in more tables, but the decor still has that 'rancho de luxe' look. Once inside, you'd never guess you were in a couple of knocked together railway arches. Children get their own diminutive menu, while adults can tuck into starters such as Neptune's Punchbowl (creamy fish soup), prawn cocktail and specials. Chips are pre-blanched then fried in groundnut oil for a two-tone crunchy shell and soft inside; we're told the batter for the fish is kept cold to ensure a crisp, even coating. We were pleased to see that *Time Out*'s own 'Guy Diamond Experience' (lemon sole fillet and chips) was still on the menu last time we visited. Staff are ridiculously friendly and helpful, tempting you with puddings (apple pie, gourmet ice-creams) you won't ever be able to finish. *Children's menu (£4). High chairs. Tables outdoors (12, pavement). Takeaway service.*

El Pirata
15-16 Royal Parade, Blackheath, SE3 0TL (8297 1880). Blackheath rail. **Meals served** noon-midnight daily. **Main courses** £8-£13. **Tapas** £3.20-£4.90. **Credit** AmEx, DC, MC, V.
Friendly, spacious and well positioned for pre-prandial Blackheath footie and kite-flying, the pirate ticks all the family-friendly boxes. The tapas list (38 hot items, seven cold), though hardly authentic and adventurous, is extensive enough for the whole family to find something

Crumpet

they like. The emphasis is mainly on bestsellers, such as patatas bravas, tortilla, pinche de pollo and various seafood and salad-based items. Puddings are limited to popular staples, such as ice-creams, bombes, fried bananas and crêpes, but the service is always sweet, espcially towards children, for whom the chef will rustle up a cheeseburger and chips if the Spanish specials don't suit. *Buggy access. High chairs. Tables outdoors (5, pavement).*

South-west London

Blue Elephant
4-6 Fulham Broadway, Fulham, SW6 1AA (7385 6595/www.blueelephant.com). Fulham Broadway tube. **Lunch served** noon-2.30pm Mon-Fri; noon-4pm Sun. **Dinner served** 7pm-midnight Mon-Thur; 6.30pm-midnight Fri, Sat; 7-10.30pm Sun. **Main courses** £9.50-£28. **Set buffet** (Sun lunch) £22 adults, £11 children (4-11 years). **Credit** AmEx, DC, MC, V.
Imagine a Vegas floorshow in Fulham and you'll have some idea of what to expect from this successful Thai restaurant, part of an international chain. Its jungle of foliage, with trickling fountains, wooden bridges and cascades of flowers is sometimes called kitsch by adults but loved by kids, who enjoy being fussed over by formally

Buggy access. Children's menu (£2.25-£4). High chairs. Tables outdoors (3, pavement; 8, garden). Takeaway service.

Crumpet

66 Northcote Road, Battersea, SW11 6QL (7924 1117). Clapham Junction rail. **Open** 9am-6pm Mon-Sat; 10am-6pm Sun. **Main courses** £3.95-£6.95. **Credit** AmEx, MC, V.

There's plenty of room for a fleet of buggies in this relaxed and friendly café, and there's a jolly sort of raised play area at the back. The staff are saints in the face of awkward requests from spoilt customers (the pregnant ones are the worst) and cake-lobbing toddlers. Crumpet is all about wholesome lunches (quiche, soups, sandwiches) proper teas (there are 22 different varieties of the cup that cheers), and the best sandwiches ever, made with real butter and fresh ingredients – our roasted salmon and salad sandwich, in a doorstep of granary, served with vegetable chips on the side, was perfection, and so was a club sandwich loaded with ham and chicken. A child's lunch of cheese toasted fingers was golden and oozy (they do great pasta for kids, too); an expertly assembled quiche of the day is served with salad in generous proportions. Cakes made by local mummies are typically yummy; we were particularly tempted by the multi-coloured fairy cakes but opted instead for the always reliable chocolate fudge cake. You could stay here all afternoon; many mothers seem to. *Buggy access. Children's menu (£1.45-£3.95). Disabled access: toilets. High chairs. Nappy-changing facilities. Play area (under-5s). Tables outdoors (2, pavement). Takeaway service.*

The Depot

Tideway Yard, 125 Mortlake High Street, SW14 8SN (8878 9462/www.depotbrasserie.co.uk). Barnes Bridge or Mortlake rail/209 bus. **Lunch served** noon-3pm Mon-Fri; noon-4pm Sat, Sun. **Dinner served** 6-11pm Mon-Sat; 6-10.30pm Sun. **Main courses** £9.95-£15. **Set meal** (Mon-Thur) £12.50 2 courses; £15.50 3 courses. **Credit** AmEx, DC, MC, V.

Cool, calm and collected, this 20-year-old riverside establishment effortlessly conjures that laid-back brasserie vibe. With gleaming woodwork and well-spaced tables, it's best visited in the day or at sunset for impressive views over the Barnes bend of the Thames. The main winning ingredient, however, is the menu, with its long list of simple, well-executed dishes, such as a meze dish of serrano ham and asparagus in season to start, salade niçoise, risotto and roasted pollock with squash and braised fennel. If that sounds a mite too sophisticated for the junior palate, there's a less challenging children's menu, listing the likes of grilled chicken, sausages, pasta and fish cakes. The weekday set menu is an affordable way to sample the Depot's winning ways, and there are roasts on Sundays. *Buggy access. Children's menu (£5.50 incl ice-cream). Crayons. High chairs. Nappy-changing facilities. No-smoking tables. Tables outdoors (8, courtyard).*

Dexter's Grill

20 Bellevue Road, Wandsworth, SW17 7EB (8767 1858/www.tootsiesrestaurants.co.uk). Wandsworth Common rail. **Meals served** noon-11pm Mon-Fri; 11am-11pm Sat; 11am-10.30pm Sun. **Main courses** £6.25-£14.40. **Credit** AmEx, MC, V.

Owned by the same company as Tootsies (*see p184*) – Dexter's has that familiar, amiable ring to it. This Dexter's

dressed waiting staff. The food is delicious and powerfully flavoured. A platter of starters brings chicken legs; plump spring rolls; crisp sweetcorn cakes; and baby corn wrapped in pastry – each with a different dipping sauce. Also good is the khantoke platter, which includes a distinctive mussaman curry, aubergine and okra in chilli paste, and stir-fried beef. During the Sunday buffet, an entertainer wanders about with face-paints. *Buggy access. Crayons. Delivery service. Disabled access: toilets. High chairs. Nappy-changing facilities. Takeaway service.*

Boiled Egg & Soldiers

63 Northcote Road, Battersea, SW11 1ND (7223 4894). Clapham Junction rail. **Open** 9am-6pm Mon-Sat; 9am-4pm Sun. **Main courses** £4-£10. **No credit cards.**

A jolly institution on the most family-friendly street in London, this café is great for breakfasts and nursery teas, although a huge menu lists a whole lot more than egg and toast. We've been let down by our choice of lunch here in the past, but always enjoy the steak or bacon sandwiches, the ice-cream and the cakes. It's also really good to be able to park your family in a café and sit down to simple fare, such as beans or Marmite on toast, thus escaping the usual kiddie burger/chips/pizza choices.

is our favourite, being spacious and handy for Wandsworth Common. During the day, it's full of young affluent families, and the well-trained staff pander to their every need, however irritating they're inclined to be. So child-friendly is it, there's a kind of kiddie heaven at the back, with sweeties and ice-creams galore. This is all part of Dexter's excellent meal deals for children. The menu for junior diners is in two parts: for £4.95 they can choose from classic American (burgers, hot dogs, babyback ribs and fries, breakfasty fry-up or fish and chips; £6.25, however, gives them a choice from a wholly organic list that includes chicken bolognese, sweet vegetable noodles, spaghetti and meatballs or cheesy pasta bake. Both options throw in a soft drink and the chance to build your own sundae for your pud. Brilliant, and the rather more grown-up options, such as main-course salads, steaks and big, excellent burgers, go down very well indeed.

Buggy access. Children's menu (£4.95-£6.25 2 courses incl drink and dessert). Crayons. Disabled access: toilets. Entertainment: face-painting noon-3pm Sun. High chairs. Nappy-changing facilities. No-smoking tables. Tables outdoors (8, balcony terrace). Takeaway service. **Branches**: throughout town. Phone or check the website.

Don Fernando's

27F The Quadrant, Richmond, Surrey TW9 1DN (8948 6447/www.donfernando.co.uk). Richmond tube/rail. **Meals served** noon-3pm, 6-11pm Mon, Tue; noon-11pm Wed-Sat; noon-10pm Sun. **Main courses** £7.95-£12.95. **Tapas** £3-£7. **Credit** AmEx, MC, V.
This little corner of Spain right next to Richmond station is a splendid place for a family meal. It's run by a Spanish family, who always seem pleased to see children and are happy to recommend items from the extensive tapas list to newcomers to the cuisine. Firm favourites include pinche de pollo and patatas fritas (chicken and chips by any other name), but there are many other little dishes to sample, such as grilled squid, lentil stew, chickpeas, tortillas and garlicky prawns. Add plenty of bread and perhaps some spare chips on the side, and the table is covered. Main meals, such as paella, lamb with rosemary or swordfish add to a highly traditional, but tasty collection.
Buggy access. Children's menu (£7.25 incl soft drink & ice-cream). High chairs. No-smoking tables. Tables outdoors (6, pavement).

Gourmet Burger Kitchen

44 Northcote Road, Battersea, SW11 1NZ (7228 3309/ www.gbkinfo.co.uk). Clapham Junction rail. **Meals served** noon-11pm Mon-Fri; 11am-11pm Sat; 11am-10pm Sun. **Main courses** £5.45-£7.40. **Credit** MC, V.
What does it take for a burger bar to brand itself 'gourmet'? Would it be the presence of knives and forks, the real cheese in the cheesburgers or the lack of Mc prefixes? Gourmet Burger Kitchen scores on these points, but has a more genuine claim to the tag in the shape of the 100% Aberdeen Angus Scotch beef this mini chain always uses. The thick patties are cooked to your liking (medium-rare to well done), and served in a sourdough roll topped with sesame. The burgers here have dominated the high-quality fast-food market, gathering foodie awards galore. The range of imaginative burger varieties (a Kiwiburger comes with beetroot, egg and pineapple) means the adventurous need never tire of the menu. Other toppings include smoky barbecue sauce, fresh garlic mayo, pesto and many other tempting ingredients. These are the highest burgers in town – some measure six

inches so kids will need two hands to eat them, unless, of course, they order the mini version from the children's menu. Don't forget the chips, which are golden on the outside and fluffy in the middle: near perfect.
Buggy access. Children's menu (£3.95). High chairs. No smoking. Tables outdoors (4, pavement). **Branches**: throughout town. Phone or check the website.

Light House

75-77 Ridgeway, Wimbledon, SW19 4ST (8944 6338). Wimbledon tube/rail, then 200 bus. **Brunch served** 10am-noon Sun. **Lunch served** noon-2.30pm Mon-Sat; 12.30-3.30pm Sun. **Dinner served** 6.30-10.30pm Mon-Sat. **Main courses** £11.50-£16.50. **Set lunch** (Mon-Sat) £14 2 courses, £16.50 3 courses; (Sun) £18 2 courses, £23 3 courses. **Service** 12.5%. **Credit** AmEx, MC, V.
South-western parents rave about this place, which they say gets the balance right between welcoming families and being grown up about its creative, Italian-inspired menu, which includes piquant starters of *bocconcini*, asparagus and beetroot with pumpkin seeds or a delicious avocado and almond salad, followed by a lovely fettucini and asparagus dish. For children, the offerings are less adventurous but equally well made: linguini with own-made tomato sauce, pizza, grilled chicken or salmon. Prices for children are charged according to their size and appetite, so pasta for a two-year-old may only set you back a couple of quid, whereas a hungry ten-year-old might be charged £7.50 for their large chicken portion.
Crayons. Disabled access: toilets. High chairs. No-smoking tables. Reduced portions for children. Tables outdoors (5, terrace).

Newtons

33-35 Abbeville Road, Clapham, SW4 9LA (8673 0977/www.newtonsrestaurants.co.uk). Clapham South tube. **Open** noon-4pm, 6-11pm Mon-Sat; noon-10.30pm Sun. **Main courses** £9.50-£15. **Set lunch** (noon-4pm Mon-Sat) £8 2 courses; £10.50 3 courses. **Credit** AmEx, MC, V.
A bit of an elder statesman in these parts, Newtons was around before the area became so trendy, and was thoughtfully providing for family groups before it became *de rigueur*. The menu is kept simple, with about nine starters and nine mains, with a very popular weekend set menu (the Sunday roast is much appreciated). All the dishes are attractively presented and a lot of care goes into quality of ingredients. Some of the seasonal vegetable dishes seem a cut above your average brasserie dish – we were impressed with our watermelon and green bean salad, a light precursor to our roast pork and sea bass mains. Children can either choose a mini portion of what the grown-ups are having or else opt for more conventional kiddie grub (nuggets, chips, chicken and so on). A few coveted pavement tables are great for summer grazing.
Buggy access. Children's menu (£6 incl dessert). High chairs. No-smoking tables. Reduced portions for children. Tables outdoors (7, terrace).

Petersham Nurseries

Petersham Nurseries, Petersham Road, Petersham, near Richmond, Surrey TW10 7AG (8940 5230). Richmond tube/rail, then 65 bus or half-hour walk. **Open** *Summer* 10.30am-4.30pm Tue-Sat; 11.30am-4.30pm Sun, Mon. *Winter* noon-2.30pm Wed-Sun. **Main courses** £15-£22. **Credit** MC, V.

This idyllic spot was awarded the Best Alfresco Dining prize at the *Time Out* Eating Awards 2005. It's a garden centre and café, surrounded by paddocks, meadows and woodland, between Richmond Hill and the Thames. A lazy lunch or tea-time at Petersham Nurseries is well-earned culmination of a morning out in the (sort of) country. The kitchen, sited in an old shed, has a cottage-like charm, but the food is delivered with panache, using quality produce, often grown on site. The menu changes daily –a blackboard outside the door lists the day's specials – we've sampled summer gazpacho, seared salmon fillets and adorable little chocolate pots with strawberries on top. The good life doesn't come cheap in Petersham, but all the meats and dairy produce are organic and the fish are line-caught. There's no children's menu, but smaller appetites are allowed for with reduced-priced portions, or the kids can feast happily off own-made lemonade, cream teas and heavenly cakes. This is a perfect venue for sunny days, but bear in mind the limited opening hours before you set out. *Buggy access. Disabled access: toilets. High chairs. No smoking (indoors). Tables outdoors (12, garden).*

Slurp

104-106 Streatham High Road, SW16 1BW (8677 7786). Streatham Hill rail. **Open** noon-3pm, 5-11pm Mon-Fri; noon-11pm Sat; noon-10pm Sun. **Main courses** £5.50-£9.50. **Set lunch** (Mon-Fri) £5 main course & drink. **Credit** MC, V.

What child can resist an outfit called Slurp, especially if it sells noodles? Not ours, although most could not resist the plates of egg-fried rice either. It's a simple sort of noodle bar, with huge plates of noodles with prawns, pork, chicken and colourful vegetables, and variations on Far Eastern themes in the form of classic dishes from Thailand, Japan and China. Good food in simple surroundings – great for those after-school treat days. *High chairs. No-smoking tables. Takeaway service.* **Branch**: 138 Merton Road, SW19 1EH (8543 4141).

Victoria

West Temple Sheen, East Sheen, SW14 7RT (8876 4238/www.thevictoria.net). Mortlake rail/ 33, 337 bus. **Breakfast served** 7-9.30am Mon-Fri; 8-10am Sat, Sun. **Lunch served** noon-2.30pm Mon-Fri; noon-3pm Sat; noon-4pm Sun. **Dinner served** 7-10pm daily. **Main courses** £10.95-£19.95. **Credit** AmEx, MC, V.

An atmosphere more redolent of a country hotel than a trendy gastropub means that the Victoria is well set up to satisfy families without winding up the sprogless. There's plenty of room for the two groups to escape one another, especially in the summer, when the pretty garden and play area is in use. The cooking is definitely a notch above (in quality and pricing) what you'll find in many gastropubs. Everyone enjoys a plate of own-made bread, dips and a bowl of olives to start, and the risottos and seasonal

Nursery tea at **Boiled Egg & Soldiers**.

asparagus starters are lso lovely. Simple mains, such as Charolais rump steak or frilled salmon with Jersey royal potatoes, are beautifully cooked and presented. Children can enjoy pasta, chicken, or sausage with mash and broccoli from their own menu. We all love the puddings, especially if the profiteroles or chocolate mousse is on. *Buggy access. Children's menu (£4.50-£5.50). High chairs. Nappy-changing facilities. No smoking (dining area). Play area. Tables outdoors (9, garden & play area).*

West London

Babes 'n' Burgers

275 Portobello Road, Notting Hill, W11 1LR (7727 4163/www.babesnburgers.com). Ladbroke Grove tube. **Meals served** 11am-11pm daily. **Main courses** £3.50-£9.95. **Credit** MC, V.
This extremely child-friendly burger bar has books and toys to distract the tots, organic fare on the menu and enough healthy options to satisfy the most neurotic skeletal mother (of which there are many round here). The management put more chairs and tables in what was a rather isolated playroom and everything is sensibly wipe clean. The menu lists organic burgers, chicken breast, tofu vegetarian alternatives, substantial breakfasts and a long list of smoothies and wheatgrass-based health drinks, as well as hot drinks and fizzy pop. The chips and organic ketchup is a favourite post-nursery sustainer, even if your mummy is picking at sprouted mung beans and cogitating about whether a wedge of banana cake will spend a lifetime on the hips.
Buggy access. Children's menu (£4.95 incl drink). Disabled access: toilets. High chairs. No smoking. Toys.

Bush Garden Café

59 Goldhawk Road, Shepherd's Bush, W12 8EG (8743 6372). Goldhawk Road tube. **Meals served** 8am-7pm Mon-Fri; 9am-5pm Sat. **Main courses** £3.50-£4.60. **Credit** (over £10) AmEx, MC, V.
The health-conscious of Shepherd's Bush have taken to this higgledy-piggledy café and deli next to the tube station. It's particularly useful for parents, because there's a garden and play area for children. The menu is chalked up on a big board over the counter, where cheerful young staff whisk up smoothies, warm pastries and advise on the contents of the colourful salad display. We love the salads; there's usually a nice beetrooty one, a more substantial bean or buckwheat, plenty of mixed leaves and a fine tomato and mozzarella. The soups are a good bet on a chilly day, and we've also enjoyed scrambled eggs and salmon bagels for breakfast. Own-made cakes are a treat and the ice-creams and smoothies make a good, sweet ending too.
Buggy access. High chairs. Nappy-changing facilities. No smoking. Tables outdoors (5, garden).

Moroccan Tagine

95 Golborne Road, Ladbroke Grove, W10 5NL (8968 8055/www.moroccantagine.net). Ladbroke Grove or Westbourne Park tube/23 bus. **Meals served** noon-11pm daily. **Main courses** £5.50-£7.90. **Credit** MC, V.
The quality of the food here belies the humble setting. Moroccan Tagine, run by Hassan, a Berber from the Atlas mountains, has an excellent menu. There are no fewer than six types of lamb tagine (this slow simmered stew takes its name from the shallow earthenware dish it's cooked in). There are lamb tagines with okra, with prunes and almonds or green peas and artichokes. The meat is beautifully tender from its long simmer: the ultimate comfort food. If you're a fish, not flesh, eater, there's also a good showing of seafood – children always love the grilled calamares and the fish platter with salad. Couscous is fluffy and moreish, and the version with stewed chicken with olives or onions and sultanas makes a lovely meal. Complimentary olives are another plus point. Finish with refreshing mint tea, so no alcohol is served. An exotic treat for children with adventurous palates.
Buggy access. High chairs. No-smoking tables. Tables outdoors (8, pavement). Takeaway service.
Branches: throughout town. Phone or check website.

Rotisserie Jules

133A Notting Hill Gate, Notting Hill, W11 3LB (7221 3331/www.rotisseriejules.com). Notting Hill Gate tube. **Meals served** noon-11pm daily. **Main courses** £5.75-£10.75. **Credit** AmEx, MC, V.
Anyone who has a craving for chicken and chips (which, let's face it, encompasses pretty much all children and most adults) will find what they're looking for here. The children's dish of drumsticks and french fries costs £4.95, a quarter of a chicken with a side dish (salad or fries) is £5.75. A serving of ratatouille or gratin dauphinoise makes a more nutritious alternative to chips and is good value at £2.50. For afters, there's apple tart, Häagen Dazs or own-made chocolate mousse. Very nice.
Buggy access. Children's menu (£4.95). Delivery service. Disabled access: toilets. High chairs. No-smoking tables. Table outdoors (1, pavement). Takeaway service.
Branch: 6-8 Bute Street, SW3 3EX (7584 0600).

Tootsies Grill

120 Holland Park Avenue, Holland Park, W11 4UA (7229 8567/www.tootsiesrestaurants.co.uk). Holland Park tube. **Meals served** 9am-11pm Mon-Thur, Sun; 9am-11.30pm Fri, Sat. **Main courses** £5.95-£12.50. **Credit** AmEx, MC, V.
At this branch of one of our favourite family restaurants, big windows look out over leafy Holland Park Avenue and old posters portray both British and American themes. Like many Tootsies branches, the place is heaving on Saturday and Sunday lunchtimes, but the pleasant staff seem to be hand-picked for unflappability. For starters, seafood lovers enjoy both the prawns and calamares with a chilli dipping sauce, and vegetarians like the meze dips. We don't like to pass on the excellent burgers, served with salad, mayo and fries, which cost from £6.95 for the unadorned beef version. Among t he fancier numbers, the jalapeño is a favourite, or there's an organic beef one, or a chicken and goat's cheese version; but we can't say we would really fancy the burger called the Works, in which grilled pineapple is just one of a multitude of toppings. Children, plied with wax crayons and colouring-in while they wait, have a choice of burgers, hot dogs, ribs or organic pasta meals, with drinks and a build-your-own sundae option for pudding. Junior heaven. As are the butterscotch milkshakes, a legend in our lunchtime.
Balloons. Buggy access. Children's menu (£4.95-£6.25 incl drink & dessert). Crayons. High chairs. No smoking. Tables outdoors (3, pavement). Takeaway service.
Branches: throughout town. Phone or check website.

Shopping

Crack open those piggy banks.

This city's inelegant sprawl makes it impossible to do justice to all the fashion, toy and equipment retailers we've discovered over the years. The following is a selection of our faves, from the big-name department stores to more obscure locals you may have to get on your bike to find. There isn't room to list every one of London's historic street markets, either, but don't let the children miss out on the bustle of the East End's **Brick Lane**, **Spitalfields**, **Columbia Road** and **Walthamstow** markets (*see p106-121*); also worth checking out are Battersea's **Northcote Road** (*see p142*), west London's **Portobello Market** (*see p153*), foodie heaven **Borough Market** (Bankside, *see p37*) and teen's dream **Camden Market** (*see p93*).

All-rounders

Daisy & Tom

181-183 King's Road, Chelsea, SW3 5EB (7352 5000/ www.daisyandtom.com). Sloane Square tube, then 11, 19, 22, 49 bus. **Open** 9.30am-6pm Mon, Tue, Thur, Fri; 10am-7pm Wed, Sat; noon-6pm Sun. **Credit** AmEx, MC, V. **Map** p313 E12.

Get shod at **Selfridges**. *See p186.*

This attractive shop splits its diverse wares over two levels. On the first floor are nursery equipment and furniture, a toy department and a 'girls' room'. On the second are clothes and shoes. The biggest thrill is the mini carousel (rides are at 11am, 1pm, 3pm, 5pm Mon-Sat; 11am, 3pm Sun). Another attraction is the half-hourly puppet re-enactment of *Peter and the Wolf*. As well as the vast selection on sale (everything from sulky Bratz dolls and jolly Lego kits to £2,000-plus handmade rocking horses), there are toys around for children to try out. In the book department, a central area has big beanbags and cushions. Shaggy children can be shorn by the resident hairdresser (£8 for fringe trim, £16 for a first cut with certificate). Among the 12 different brands of pushchair are Boz by Baby Comfort, Silver Cross and Bugaboo. The clothing department carries Daisy & Tom in abundance, Timberland, Elle, Catimini and more.
Buggy access. Disabled access: ramp, toilet. Hairdresser. Mail order. Nappy-changing facilities. Play area.

Harrods

87-135 Brompton Road, Knightsbridge, SW1X 7XL (7730 1234/www.harrods.com). Knightsbridge tube. **Open** 10am-8pm Mon-Sat; noon-6pm Sun. **Credit** AmEx, DC, MC, V. **Map** p313 F9.

Harrods is the mother of all upscale department stores and a very exciting place for children to be let loose in. Staff are friendly and, in the big toy department at least, tot-tolerant, even playful. Each enormous, colourful room on the fourth-floor children's universe has its own theme or collection and pumping music. Clothes begin with baby-cool pieces from modish labels like No Added Sugar and go through ultra-smart tweedy garb to streetwear along the lines of O'Neill and Quiksilver. Couture 'casualwear' with styles for newborns onwards includes mini togs by Burberry, Christian Dior, Moschino and Armani. The excellent Bunny London (*see p193*) also has a collection here. The shoe collection includes Start-rite, Naturino and Instep. The toy rooms have big-name construction sets, games, tons of stuffed cuddly animals, cars, dolls, costumes and more. There is face-painting, haircutting and lots of interactive fun during the holidays and on selected weekends. The nursery department carries all the famous names prams and buggies, cots, beds and high chairs.
Buggy access. Café. Car park. Delivery service. Disabled access: lift, toilet. Hairdressing. Mail order. Nappy-changing facilities.

John Lewis

278-306 Oxford Street, Oxford Circus, W1A 1EX (7629 7711/www.johnlewis.co.uk). Bond Street or Oxford Circus tube. **Open** 9.30am-7pm Mon-Wed, Fri, Sat; 9.30am-8pm Thur; noon-6pm Sun. **Credit** MC, V. **Map** p314 H6.

At nearly 150 years old, John Lewis's upstanding consumer values – courtesy and quality coming as standard – combined with its comforting 'never knowingly undersold'

motto, make it every canny parent's friend. The fourth-floor children's department can be relied on for excellent nursery equipment, the widest-ranging school uniform selection and some very attractive fashions for the younger generation. The service in the shoe department is exemplary (the fairly standard fitting procedure is done thoroughly and sensitively; stock consists of sturdy Clark's and Start-rites, along with trendier Kangaroos, Tods, Nike and Puma brands). The spacious toy department contains a pleasant balance of toys of the moment and educational playthings, and there are plenty of toys left out for children to test. Pregnant women enjoy the in-store nursery advice service, where experts can help them decide on the baby paraphernalia they will need. There's also a car-seat fitting advisory service.
Buggy access. Cafés. Delivery service. Disabled access: lifts, toilets. Mail order. Nappy-changing facilities.

Mothercare

461 Oxford Street, W1C 2EB (7629 6621/ www.mothercare.com). Marble Arch tube. **Open** 9am-8pm Mon-Sat; noon-6pm Sun. **Credit** AmEx, MC, V. **Map** p314 G6.
For all things infant-related, Mothercare should be your first stop. This three-floored branch has everything on your list for that first mad dash before baby arrives – breast-pads, wipes, muslins and nappies, high chairs and cots – plus most things you'll need for later – not least, a decent range of easy-fold, bus-friendly buggies (from £30) and more elaborate travel systems with carrycots and car seats involved. Prices are reasonable for all the basics. In the baby clothing department, for example, newborns' scratch mits and hats sell from £1.50, a pack of three sleepsuits costs £12 and cute little T-shirts for boys and girls cost from £6. Although still a bit pink and blue in the respective girl/boy collections, the styles are far less staid than you would imagine, and the Moda maternity wear is worth a gander for the nine-month weight-gain period.
Buggy access. Delivery service. Disabled access. Mail order. Nappy-changing facilities.
Branches: throughout town. Check website for details.

Selfridges

400 Oxford Street, Oxford Circus, W1A 1AB (0870 837 7377/www.selfridges.com). Bond Street tube. **Open** 10am-8pm Mon-Wed, Fri; 9.30am-9pm Thur; 9.30am-8pm Sat; noon-6pm Sun. **Credit** AmEx, DC, MC, V. **Map** p314 G6.
Comprehensive merchandising tactics combine with a slick of razzle dazzle to make Selfridges an awesome monument to consumerism. Children gambolling around the third floor Kids' Universe aren't overawed, however. They'd rather be in the ground-floor sweetie section (*see p196* **Sugar rush**) or in a store with a bigger, brasher toy department. If you're not after designer stuff, Kids' Universe can disappoint, as it's not great for basics. The atmosphere is quite teenybopperish, Girls Aloud blares on the sound system and white, shiny pods contain the gear (Burberry, Moschino, Caramel, Emilie et Rose). There are toys, sticker stations, sweetie displays, partywear and fairy frocks. There's also a Buckle My Shoe store. Sale items help keep the expense down. Beach-bum labels (O'Neill, Quiksilver) are down on the first floor, which is dominated by sportswear, bikes and skateboards.
Buggy access. Cafés. Car park. Delivery service. Disabled access: lifts, toilet. Mail order. Nappy-changing facilities.

Educational

Books

Several of the toyshops listed on pp206-212 also stock a useful selection of children's picture books.

Bookseller Crow on the Hill

50 Westow Street, Crystal Palace, SE19 3AF (8771 8831/ www.booksellercrow.com). Gypsy Hill rail. **Open** 9am-7.30pm Mon-Fri; 9.30am-6.30pm Sat; 11am-5pm Sun. **Credit** AmEx, MC, V.
The Crow family's book-filled nest is a Crystal Palace landmark, and Justine Crow's thoughts on literature and domestic dramas are a must-read in *Families South East*. There's a wealth of baby, toddler, child, teen, parent and grandparent literature alongside modern classics for youth – Rosen, Horowitz, Wilson and Rowling. It's a good general bookshop, so grown-ups need not feel excluded.
Buggy access. Mail order. Play area.

Bookworm

1177 Finchley Road, Temple Fortune, NW11 0AA (8201 9811/www.thebookworm.uk.com). Golders Green tube. **Open** 9.30am-5.30pm Mon-Sat; 10am-1.30pm Sun. **Credit** MC, V.
This much-loved specialist children's bookshop has cosy spaces for reading, and the stock is exemplary: shelf after shelf of everything from reference books for projects such as the Victorians or the Romans to the latest fiction. Twice-weekly storytelling sessions for under-fives take place on Tuesdays and Thursdays (2pm), when badges and stickers are handed out and not-so-literary friendships forged. Local authors, occasionally drop by for signings.
Buggy access. Disabled access. Mail order.

Children's Book Centre

237 Kensington High Street, Kensington, W8 6SA (7937 7497/www.childrensbookcentre.co.uk). High Street Kensington tube. **Open** 9.30am-6.30pm Mon, Wed, Fri, Sat; 9.30am-6pm Tue; 9.30am-7pm Thur; noon-6pm Sun. **Credit** AmEx, MC, V. **Map** p312 A9.
This two-storey treasure trove has toys, board games, stationery, T-shirts and dressing-up clothes downstairs. There is a PC set up at the back for staff to demonstrate new computer games and for children to have a go at playing them. Of course, they should be spending their time browsing through the large book selection. The range on the ground floor covers all ages and tastes, from larger picture books and the Dr Seuss titles for new readers to a range for sophisticated consumers of teen literature.
Buggy access. Mail order.

Children's Bookshop

29 Fortis Green Road, Fortis Green, N10 3HP (8444 5500). Highgate tube, then 43, 134 bus. **Open** 9.15am-5.45pm Mon-Sat; 11am-4pm Sun. **Credit** AmEx, MC, V.
Quiet, well-stocked and roomy, this shop provides a famously good atmosphere in which to take in the row upon row of neatly ordered shelves, full of colour and interest, with small themed displays and a children's corner with picture books at floor level. Book-related events are publicised in the quarterly newsletter, which also carries helpful, personal reviews of new titles.
Buggy access. Mail order. Regular author visits.

Story time at **Tales on Moon Lane**. *See p189.*

caramelbaby&child

what
gorgeous clothes and accessories for babies and children of 3 months to 12 years
what else
hair salon every Wednesday and Saturday
in also**caramel** for the most stylish of cuts
call 020 7730 2564 for an appointment
where
caramelbaby&child
291 Brompton Road
London SW3 2DY
Tel: (0)20 7589 7001
also**caramel**
259 Pavilion Road
London SW1X 0BP
Tel/Fax: (0)20 7730 2564
Selfridges concession
3rd Floor Oxford Street
London W1
when
Monday to Saturday 10am-6pm
Sunday noon-5pm
web
www.caramel-shop.co.uk

Daunt Books

*51 South End Road, NW3 2QB (7794 8206/
www.dauntbooks.co.uk). Belsize Park or Hampstead
tube.* **Open** 9am-6pm Mon-Sat; 11am-6pm Sun.
Credit MC, V.
This branch of Daunt has a wonderfully cosy, low-
ceilinged play area, with stacks of picture books and
comics, and mini-beanbags to lounge on while reading
them. There isn't a single children's classic missing, and
for grown-ups, what better way to take a tranquil stroll
down memory lane than by leafing through *The Little
Prince*, Enid Blyton and Dr Seuss?
Buggy access. Mail order. Play area.
Branches: 193 Haverstock Hill, NW3 4QG (7794 4006);
83 Marylebone High Street, W1U 4QW (7224 2295); 112-
114 Holland Park Avenue, W11 4UZ (7727 7022).

Golden Treasury

*29 Replingham Road, Southfields, SW18 5LT (8333
0167/www.thegoldentreasury.co.uk). Southfields tube.*
Open 9.30am-6pm Mon-Fri; 9.30am-5.30pm Sat;
10.30am-4.30pm Sun. **Credit** MC, V.
It's a pleasure to spend time with the kids in this excellent children's bookshop, where everything here is laid
out for maximum impact, and a buggy-friendly ramp
allows ease of progress through the store. All phases and
crazes are covered. There's a fairy and princess section,
a large section is devoted to Horrible Histories and attendant strands, then there's the less interesting official educational section with various 'browbeat your child
through SATs' type guides for insecure parents. There's
a Dr Seuss tower, a pretty cabinet devoted to Beatrix
Potter, mini picture books from Red Fox (just £1.50), a
large collection of favourite baby and toddler books, and
reads for ages eight to 12, and teens.
Buggy access. Delivery service. Play area.

Lion & Unicorn

*19 King Street, Richmond, Surrey TW9 1ND (8940
0483/www.lionunicornbooks.co.uk). Richmond tube/rail.*
Open 9.30am-5.30pm Mon-Fri; 9.30am-6pm Sat; noon-
5pm Sun. **Credit** MC, V.
We don't believe that many more books can be jammed
into this long established, award-winning bookshop,
which counts the late, great Roald Dahl among its first
visiting authors. There's a wall of signed photos and
mementos from all the children's writers who've visited
over the years, and still they come (check the website for
details of such visits, and for regular Saturday storytelling sessions). Every children's book worth reading is
sold here; displays are broken up into Current Favourites,
children's picture books, reads for eight to 12s, and teen
books. One wall of shelves is devoted to reference books
and dictionaries.
Buggy access. Mail order.

Owl Bookshop

*209 Kentish Town Road, Kentish Town, NW5 2JU
(7485 7793). Kentish Town tube.* **Open** 9.30am-6pm
Mon-Sat; noon-4.30pm Sun. **Credit** AmEx, MC, V.
Children's titles in this general bookshop are sorted by age
and interest. There are usually deals to be had: three for
two on picture books is a long-standing favourite, and various other rotating discounts. The shop hosts readings by
local children's authors and, in term-time, schoolchildren
come to listen (join the mailing list for times).
Buggy access. Mail order.

Tales on Moon Lane

*25 Half Moon Lane, Herne Hill, SE24 9JU (7274 5759/
www.talesonmoonlane.co.uk). Herne Hill rail/3, 37, 68
bus.* **Open** 9.15am-5.30pm Mon-Sat; 11am-4pm Sun.
Credit MC, V.
This bookshop has a warm community feel. Every
Tuesday and Thursday a storyteller and playleader runs
Once Upon a Story, for pre-school children (£4 per session).
Tales also hosts regular events centred round local authors
and illustrators. It has a sofa where children can curl up
with a good book (with a view to getting parents to buy it).
As well as all that, there is a very wide range of picture
books and tapes, and novels and reference books for all
young readers from toddlers to teenagers.
Buggy access. Mail order.

Victoria Park Books

*174 Victoria Park Road, E9 7HD (8986 1124/
www.victoriaparkbooks.co.uk). Bethnal Green tube.*
Open 10am-5.30pm Tue-Sun. **Credit** MC, V.
A bright little space – its centre occupied by a children's
table and chairs, plus toys – Victoria Park Books has
divided its stock into user-friendly sections: history (plenty
of Horrible Histories and more), art, stories from around
the world, dinosaurs, reference, masses of baby and toddler books, a Ladybird corner and more. There are also sections for fiction by age; teenagers are particularly well
catered for, and there is some adult fiction too (plus parenting books). There is a reading group for under-fives, on
Friday morning at 10am.
Buggy access. Delivery service. Play area.

Musical instruments

Chappell of Bond Street

*50 New Bond Street, Oxford Circus, W1S 1RD (7491
2777/www.chappellofbondstreet.co.uk). Bond Street
or Oxford Circus tube.* **Open** 9.30am-6pm Mon-Fri;
9.30am-5pm Sat. **Credit** AmEx, MC, V. **Map** p316 H6.
Established in 1811, Chappell offers the largest range of
printed music in Europe. A Yamaha specialist, the store is
also renowned for keyboards – many musicians drop in to
tickle the ivories. Certain instruments (typically flutes,
saxes, clarinets, trumpets) may be hired on a rent-to-buy
scheme, but quarter- and half-size instruments must be
purchased; the child is measured beforehand. Recorders
are the most popular instruments for youngsters to begin
on; Yamaha does colourful ones for about £6.
Delivery service. Mail order.

Dot's

*132 St Pancras Way, Camden Town, NW1 9NB
(7482 5424/www.dotsonline.co.uk). Camden Town
tube/Camden Road rail.* **Open** 9am-5.30pm Mon-Sat.
Credit MC, V.
Run by an experienced music teacher, Dot's has new instruments – mostly stringed and wind – costing from, say, £5
for a recorder, £40 for a guitar and £59 for a violin. There's
also a rent-to-buy scheme, with hire costs eventually off-
setting the purchase price should a child show consistent
interest. The great joy here is receiving unpressured advice
in a friendly setting. A noticeboard has advertisements for
tuition and second-hand instruments, along with information about Dot's own recorder club. There's also an instrument repair service.
Mail order.

Consumer

Born. *See p192.*

Dulwich Music Shop

*2 Croxted Road, Dulwich, SE21 8SW (8766 0202).
West Dulwich rail/3 bus.* **Open** 9.30am-5.30pm Mon,
Tue, Thur-Sat; 9.30am-7.30pm Wed. **Credit** AmEx,
MC, V.
Staff can help out if you're looking to invest in used or new
instruments and sheet music, and there's a range of price
lists for wind, brass and string instruments, including hire
and buy-back prices. Reeds, strings and cleaning cloths are
also sold, alongside knick-knacks, gifts, CDs and stationery. There's also a repair service. Recorders, for those
early days of parent-torture, cost from £4.99.
Buggy access. Mail order.

Northcote Music

*155C Northcote Road, Battersea, SW11 6QB (7228
0074). Clapham Junction rail.* **Open** 10.30am-6pm Mon-
Sat. **Credit** MC, V.
This is a tiny little place, so if too many Battersea mummies descend at the same time for their darling's first
recorder (£4.99), it's a bit of a crush. Northcote squeezes
string, percussion and wind instruments into the space, as
well as brass and digital equipment, and there's an on-site
workshop for any instrumental mishaps. Classical sheet
music is sold, as well as other musical styles, from show
tune books to Christina Aguilera.
Buggy access. Delivery service. Mail order.

Robert Morley & Co

*34 Engate Street, SE13 7HA (8318 5838/www.morley
pianos.com). Lewisham DLR.* **Open** 9.30am-5pm Mon-
Sat. **Credit** MC, V.
This family firm is reassuring in its dealings with nervous
parental investors. To see if a child is really serious about
owning a piano, they'll hire one out to the family, asking
for an initial fee of £250 to include delivery, then monthly
rental starting from £30. If, after a year, the family are still

keen on the piano, they can buy it, and get half their rental
payments off the price, plus half the delivery charge.
Buggy access. Delivery service.

Equipment & accessories

Babyworld

*239 Munster Road, Fulham, SW6 6BT (7386 1904/
www.babyworldlondon.co.uk). Fulham Broadway tube
then 211, 295 bus.* **Open** 10am-6pm Mon-Wed, Fri;
10am-5.30pm Sat. Closed Thur. **Credit** AmEx, MC, V.
Friendly staff here can tell you the best transport systems
for precious cargoes. Most popular with parents of newborns these days is the latest Bugaboo pram and accessories, whose chassis can hold either a carrycot or a buggy
seat for older babies and toddlers. Other pram and buggy
ranges are by Chicco, Maxicosy and Stokke. There are also
toys from Lamaze and a load of nursery accessories.
Buggy access. Delivery service. Mail order.

Chic Shack

*77 Lower Richmond Road, Putney, SW15 1ET
(8785 7777/www.chicshack.net). Putney Bridge
tube, then 14, 22 bus.* **Open** 9.30am-6pm Mon-Sat.
Credit MC, V.
These compact premises on two floors are filled with beautiful things for the home, but the stuff for babies and children's rooms is especially lovely – from knitted teddies and
snowy bedlinens and shawls to superbly finished nursery
furniture. Items are inspired by French and Swedish 18th-
century design, and can also be designed to order. It's not
cheap, but prices reflect quality. Sturdy little white cot beds
cost from £499; toy storage chests are £285. Chic Shack
also offers a range of fabrics for curtains and upholstery,
as well as nursery and christening gifts.
Buggy access. Delivery service. Mail order.

Dragons of Walton Street

23 Walton Street, Knightsbridge, SW3 2HX (7589 3795/www.dragonsofwaltonstreet.com). Knightsbridge or South Kensington tube. **Open** *9.30am-5.30pm Mon-Fri; 10am-5pm Sat.* **Credit** *AmEx, MC, V.* **Map** *p313 E10.*

Veteran hand-painter of nursery furniture Rosie Fisher opened her first Dragons shop in 1979. After 25 years in the business, the name is synonymous with top quality, exclusive baby rooms. Everything you could ever want in a nursery, including curtains, cots, sofas, chaises longues and tiny chairs, is made to order. You come in, choose your item and paint or fabric scheme. Favourite themes include fairies, soldiers, animals and flowers, but customers are encouraged to come up with their own ideas. Such finery doesn't come cheap: expect to pay £2,000 for a special artwork bed, and between £3,500 and £10,000 for a rocking horse. There are toys as well as furniture: money boxes (£10); dolls' houses (£250-£550), and wooden toys and teddy bears.
Buggy access. Delivery service. Disabled access. Mail order.

Lilliput

255-259 Queenstown Road, Battersea, SW8 3NP (7720 5554/0800 783 0886/www.lilliput.com). Queenstown Road rail. **Open** *9.30am-5.30pm Mon, Tue, Thur, Fri; 9.30am-7pm Wed; 9am-6pm Sat; 11am-4pm Sun.* **Credit** *MC, V.*

Product literature and baby services (aromatherapy for children?) just inside the door includes Lilliput's own leaflet entitled Equipment You Need When Having a Baby. A number of young staff are on hand to demonstrate the huge number of prams and buggies (from £30 folding buggies to an £850 Silver Cross carriage pram), cots, cot beds, cabinets and changing tables, bedding, bath equipment, towels and toys. There's clothing for babies and toddlers too.
Buggy access. Delivery service. Mail order. Nappy-changing facilities. Play area.

Mini Kin

22 Broadway Parade, Crouch End, N8 9DE (8341 6898). Finsbury Park tube/rail, then W7 or 41 bus. **Open** *9.30-5.30pm Mon-Sat; 10.30am-4.30pm Sun.* **Credit** *MC, V.*

Mini Kin has a children's hairdressing salon with animal-themed seats and the possibility of mini makeovers. Baby haircuts start at £10; the special first haircut, with lots of fuss, certificate and samples, costs £14.95. Little girlies love the full princess treatment (£29.95), which involves glitter, hypoallergenic products, peel-off nail varnish and goodies, plus photos to take home. Otherwise, this sizeable venue stocks natural bath and hygiene products (including the SOS range for eczema), Bugaboo buggies, Baby Björn, carriers, potties and stools, adorable bootees and Nurtured by Nature merino wool sleepsuits. Everyone adores Angulus shoes (Itsy Bitsies for the little squirts from £21, leather shoes for older toddlers are more expensive). *Buggy access. Disabled access. Nappy-changing facilities. Play area.*

Nursery Window

83 Walton Street, South Kensington, SW3 2HP (7581 3358/www.nurserywindow.co.uk). Knightsbridge or South Kensington tube. **Open** *10am-6pm Mon-Sat.* **Credit** *AmEx, MC, V.* **Map** *p313 E10.*

If you want your newborn to snuggle into the finest cashmere, linen and lambswool, look no further than Nursery Window. Quality bedlinen in 100% cotton with pink or blue bunnies, stripes or spots costs from £14 for pillowcases; then there are softer-than-soft blankets, towels, cot bumpers and quilts. That all-important snowy cobweb shawl costs from £24.95 in wool or cotton, or, if you choose cashmere, £115. As well as the soft stuff, there's a wide range of nursery furniture that comes in two ranges; affordable white-painted pine (cot £380) or covetable solid oak (cot £550), plus accessories and gift sets.
Buggy access. Delivery service. Mail order.

Rub a Dub Dub

15 Park Road, Crouch End, N8 8TE (8342 9898). Finsbury Park tube/rail, then 41 or W7 bus. **Open** *10am-5.30pm Mon-Fri; 9.30am-5.30pm Sat; 11am-4pm Sun.* **Credit** *MC, V.*

Ways of getting babies and children to and fro and seated comfortably are the forte here. The knowledgeable owner chooses stock with care – you'll find the excellent Bugaboo three-in-one pushchair-cum-pram, carrycot- and car-seat-adaptable travel system; the posture-reforming Tripp Trapp high chair (£137); and Nomad travel cots that fold to backpack size and double as a UV tent (£125). Also available is Stokke's Xplory baby buggy, which elevates your little darling above nasty car fumes (£499). There are softer, fun things too, like wheely bugs in bird and bumblebee shapes for whizzing around the house (£50 for a small model, £55 for a larger size). Every conceivable brand of eco-friendly nappy and bottom cream is stocked, and look out for the German Moltex nappies: 30% gel, 70% biodegradable and entirely free of bleach.
Buggy access. Delivery service. Disabled access. Mail order. Nappy-changing facilities. Play area.

Environmentally friendly

If you're thinking of a washable nappy system, the staff at Green Baby can offer advice. Shaped nappies with easy-fit waterproof coverings are a

Consumer

viable alternative to disposables. **Bambino Mio** (0160 488 3777, www.bambinomio.co.uk), the **Ellie Nappie Company** (www.elliepants.co.uk) and **Little Green Earthlets** (0143 581 1555, www.earthlets.co.uk) also sell real nappies and environmentally friendly cleaning products. Try **Snazzypants** (0845 370 8440, www.snazzypants. co.uk) for washable nappies in soft organic cotton. Organic cotton babywear, with gift sets (printed cotton bodysuit and terry cardi, for example), as well as fab, fairly-traded cotton casuals for children aged up to ten can be ordered from **People Tree** (7739 0660, www.peopletree.co.uk).

Born
168 Stoke Newington Church Street, N16 0JL (7249 5069/www.borndirect.com). Finsbury Park tube/rail, then 106 bus/73, 393, 476 bus. **Open** 9.30am-5.30pm Tue-Sat; noon-5pm Sun. **Credit** MC, V.
Born specialises in natural, organic, Fair Trade and practical products, and staff are programmed to dispense sensible advice to customers. Thus, you'll get the lowdown on how your expensive Bugaboo or Stokke pushchairs and prams, or Tripp Trapp high chairs and cots work; you can also try on a wide range of babyslings (Wilkinets and Hippy Chick are just two of the choices). There are natural lambskins, cotton sleeping bags, wool baby blankets and organic baby bath products and unguents. Breastfeeding mum with sore nipples can buy Lansinoh, the purest lanolin ointment for protection. Cotton nappies are a big part of the Born philosophy; demonstrations are available and trial packs are on sale. Toys are by Heimess and other companies that use only renewable materials.
Buggy access. Delivery service. Disabled access: ramp. Mail order. Nappy-changing facilities. Play area.

Green Baby
345 Upper Street, Islington, N1 0PD (7359 7037/mail order 0870 240 6894/www.greenbaby.co.uk). Angel tube. **Open** 9.30am-5.30pm Mon-Fri; 9.30am-6pm Sat; 11am-4pm Sun. **Credit** MC, V.
If you're about to pop or you've just dropped, make this your first port of call. It has clothing basics for the newborn and sheets made from 100% organic cotton, nappy balms and baby lotions based on pure lanolin, sweet almond oil and cocoa butter, and nursery furniture made of beech from sustainable forests. Green Baby clothing is made in South India, as part of a community project that supports the education and employment of young girls.
Buggy access. Delivery service. Mail order.
Branch: 5 Elgin Crescent, W11 2JA (7792 8140); 4 Duke Street, TW9 1HP (8940 8255); 52 Greenwich Church Street, SE10 9BL (8858 6690).

The Natural Mat Company
99 Talbot Road, Notting Hill, W11 2AT (7985 0474/www.naturalmat.com). Ladbroke Grove tube. **Open** 9am-6pm Mon-Fri; 10am-4pm Sat. **Credit** MC, V.
Infants may safely snooze cuddled up in the organic cotton and wool sheets, blankets, sleeping bags and fleeces sold here. Handmade cot mattresses – tufted in wool or mohair on coconut fibre, natural latex or even Chinese horsetail hair cores and wrapped in unbleached cotton herringbone ticking – are unique to the company and cost

from £65 for a standard mattress. The giant American fleeces make fabulous playmats for the nursery and are machine washable (£68). Cots and nursery furniture in painted and natural wood finishes are also sold. Baby clothes, T-shirts and pyjamas in cotton cost from £14.50, but for luxury textile overload you can blow £45.50 on a cashmere sleepsuit and hope the nappy cover does its job.
Buggy access. Delivery service. Mail order.

Fashion

Budget

Adams
Unit 11, Surrey Quays Centre, Redriff Road, Rotherhithe, SE16 7LL (7252 3208/www.adams. co.uk). Surrey Quays tube. **Open** 9.30am-6pm Mon-Wed, Fri, Sat; 9.30am-8pm Thur; 11am-5pm Sun. **Credit** AmEx, MC, V.
Affordable playwear, babywear and school uniform essentials mean Adams is a reliable, if slightly uninspiring option. It's always worth having a butcher's at the end-of-season sale rails. On our last visit we picked up some light-up Hallowe'en slippers for a couple of quid, a pair of bright baby tights for £1.50 and some extremely cheap purple jellies for the beach.
Buggy access. Disabled access.
Branches: throughout town. Check website for details.

H&M
103-111 Kensington High Street, Kensington, W8 5SF (7368 3920/www.hm.com). High Street Kensington tube. **Open** 10am-7pm Mon-Wed, Fri, Sat; 10am-8pm Thur; noon-6pm Sun. **Credit** AmEx, MC, V. **Map** p312 A9.
Once you've located the nearest sizing chart (bear in mind the sizes come up big, our seven-year-old is swamped in her age four to five denim shorts), you can have fun selected a basketload of fashionable gear for boys and girls in this spacious basement store. There are also racks of extremely sweet baby clothes, with little T-shirts and three-button vests from £3.99. Teeny-tiny hats and socks cost from £1.25 – perfect for parcelling up and sending to new arrivals. Accessories are brilliant: jewellery, bags, hair clips and bands, wallets with chains, keyrings and sweatbands. Children who get bored with selecting their look can watch cartoons on the telly. This is our favourite place for childrenswear.
Buggy access. Disabled access: lift. Nappy-changing facilities. Play area.
Branches: throughout town.

Designer

Amaia
14 Cale Street, Chelsea, SW3 3QU (7590 0999). Sloane Square or South Kensington tube. **Open** 10am-6pm Mon-Sat. **Credit** MC, V.
Amaia is a welcome addition to smart little Chelsea Green, already home to a fishmonger, a baker (well, Jane Asher cakes) and a picturesque toyshop (Traditional Toys, *see p212*). It's run by friendly Amaia and her partner Sergolene, whose aim is to dress children their age, rather than in mini versions of adult street fashions. Prices are reasonable for beautifully made 100% wool coats with velvet collars (£125),

jackets and pinafores (from £45), three-quarter- length trousers, kilts, cardigans and polo necks (£25), cords and button-through shirts. Colours are unusual for us Brits: there are chocolate brown sweaters, moss green skirts and trousers, camel tweed skirts and powder blue cord coats.
Buggy access. Delivery service. Disabled access. Mail order.

Bunny London
7627 2318/www.bunnylondon.com.
The beautiful hand-sewn dresses that make-up artist Debbie Bunn used to make for her god-daughter were noticed by no less a celebrity mum than Madonna. Pictures of little Lourdes in Bunny London created a global interest in the label, whose distinctive colours, patterns and textures of fabric make the limited-edition garments must-haves among both celebrity and ordinary mortal parents of daughters. The collection includes delicately embroidered pieces, coats in vintage fabrics and pretty little blousons. It's available in baby sizes (two-18 months) and child sizes (two to 12 years). The dresses sell from about £60. As we went to press, Debbie Bunn had moved out of her South Bank workshop and boutiques and was looking

Dress with a difference at **Bunny London**.

for new premises. Her designs for girls can be seen at Harvey Nichols (109-125 Knightsbridge, SW1X 7RJ, 7235 5000) and Paul Smith (Westbourne House, 122 Kensington Park Road, W11 2EP, 7727 3553).

Caramel Baby & Child
291 Brompton Road, South Kensington, SW3 2DY (7589 7001/www.caramel-shop.co.uk). South Kensington tube. **Open** 10am-6pm Mon-Sat; noon-5pm Sun. **Credit** AmEx, MC, V. **Map** p313 E10.
Ring the bell to enter this chicer-than-chic designer outlet for tots whose label-led parents are prepared to pay through the nose to trendify their offspring. The deliciously cuddly stripy cashmere pullover by Baby Caramel for babies of six months costs £95, for instance; and a dusky pink goatskin gilet for a baby girl of 12 months is £133. There are little Prada trainers (£90), and summer collections comprise floaty, hip dresses and shirts to be worn with teeny Birkenstocks. Favourites are fresh and floral dresses by Caramel (£65), Marni (£132) and Quincy (£49), and the Prada ballerina pumps (£80). Rompers, skirts and trousers for children up to ten, plus miniature wellies, lamb's wool-lined papooses (£220) and a finger puppet set (£40) widen the store's appeal. The branch stocks books and toys and has a hairdressing service on Saturdays and Wednesdays (book in advance).
Buggy access (single only). Mail order.
Branch Also Caramel, 259 Pavilion Road, SW1X 0BP (7730 2564).

Catimini
52 South Molton Street, Mayfair, W1Y 1HF (7629 8099/www.catimini.com). Bond Street tube. **Open** 10am-6.30pm Mon-Wed, Fri, Sat; 10am-7pm Thur; 11.30am-5.30pm Sun. **Credit** AmEx, MC, V. **Map** p314 H6.
This sophisticated, classic, sometimes kooky French label is a cheerful provider of outfits to get babies and children up to age ten noticed. The everyday range is strong on stripes, animal and floral patterns, but the Catimini Atelier line favours easy formality: dresses and skirts for girls in white, yellow, pink and orange, and suave linen suits for boys. No attention to detail is spared: girls can have matching socks, tights, shoes and dresses, along with light rain-coats and headscarves, adorable cotton knit cardigans, or, for *l'hiver*, chunkier toggle cardigans in vibrant and earthy colours, tweedy skirts and dresses. Boys get puffa jackets, button sweaters and warm cords. The shop assistants are friendly and helpful. Prices are on the high side (expect to pay from £60 for the distinctive knitwear).
Buggy access. Disabled access. Mail order. Play area.

Frocks Away
79-85 Fortis Green Road, Fortis Green, N10 3HP (8444 9309). Highgate tube, then 43 or 134 bus. **Open** 9.30am-5.30pm Mon-Sat. **Credit** AmEx, MC, V.
Polished floorboards and old-fashioned shopfittings set the shabby-chic tone in this north London store. For children up to age 12 there are flowery tights in wooden hosiery drawers; church pews are used to seat fidgets while their feet are measured; and little wooden stands display adorable headgear. There's a good range of clothes for women and children, including Petit Bateau, Ali Bali, Contrevents et Marres and Balu, plus shoes from Start-rite, Geox, Primigi and Diesel.
Buggy access. Disabled access. Play area.

Consumer

Jake's

*79 Berwick Street, Soho, W1F 8TL (7734 0812/
www.jakesofsoho.co.uk). Oxford Circus tube.* **Open**
11am-7pm Mon-Sat. **Credit** AmEx, MC, V.
Map p314 J6.
Buy your child a hand-printed T-shirt by Soho's Jake and
help make a little lad's prospects brighter. Jake is a little
boy with cerebral palsy and a percentage of the profits
made on the clothing range for adults and children up to
age eight go towards his future. T-shirts with 'Elvis Loves
You', 'Weapon of Mass Destruction' and 'Lucky Seven'
logos are popular in the celebrity world (Jamie Cullum,
McFly and Mr Beckham) and cost £15. Other items in the
childrenswear range include Aran jumpers, sweatshirts
and pants, combat trousers and baseball caps.
Buggy access. Disabled access. Mail order.

Jakss

*463 & 469 Roman Road, Bethnal Green, E3 5LX
(8981 9454/www.jakss.co.uk). Bethnal Green tube,
then 8 bus.* **Open** 10am-5.30pm Tue-Sat. **Credit**
AmEx, DC, MC, V.
Eat your heart out Knightsbridge: the Roman Road has all
the labels a toddler never knew he wanted. At number
No.463, the collections are for babies up to children aged
six. Infants as young as three months can be right little
fashion victims in pinky purple Burberry checks (£48 for
a skirt or £55 for a classic buff check pinafore). Otherwise,
there's Oilily, Fornarina, Timberland, DKNY and D&G. It
all continues for the two to 14 age group at No.469, where
there's a full range of Burberry outerwear. The Miss Sixty
line for girls is bold and eyecatching; which eight-year-old
wouldn't prefer cuddling up in the swirly green fringed
long cardigan (£75) instead of a sensible gabardine? End-
of-season sales encourage buying big for growing into.
Buggy access. Mail order.

Membery's

*1 Church Road, Barnes, SW13 9HE (8876 2910/
www.specialdresscompany.co.uk). Barnes Bridge rail.*
Open 10am-5pm Mon-Sat. **Credit** AmEx, MC, V.
Membery's offers the kind of special-occasion wear that
warms granny's cockles. You can bribe small boys into
rather gorgeous blue or white linen shorts suits with dou-
ble-breasted shirt with blue piping (from £39, all fully
washable). Wee girls look demure in crisp, yellow birds'
eye piqué dresses in 100% cotton (from £34, also machine
washable). Heirloom-type christening robes are also sold.
Made-to-measure bridesmaids' dresses are available for all
ages. Christening gifts, such as personalised framed pictures, are another speciality. Membery's lovely own label
shares space with more relaxed but pricier casualwear
from Catimini, Marèse, IKKS and Petit Bateau.
Buggy access. Delivery service. Play area.

Notsobig

*31A Highgate High Street, Highgate, N6 5JT (8340
4455). Archway or Highgate tube.* **Open** 10am-6pm
Mon-Sat; 11am-5pm Sun. **Credit** MC, V.
Tiny outfits by Quincy, Cacharel, Braez, Essential Girls,
Maharishi, No Angel and Agatha Ruiz de la Prada hang
on the walls; there is silver and gold jewellery for babies,
many items with precious stones; and Little Chums T-
shirts sit in organza bags alongside sweet handmade soft
toys. Halfway down the windy stairs are French-looking
tea sets and assorted knick-knacks, and at the bottom, hap-

hazardly arranged fancy-dress costumes by Bandicoot
Lapin (there aren't always loads in the shop, but you can
order the one you want before the big event; from £60).
Buggy access. Delivery service. Mail order. Play area.

Oilily

*9 Sloane Street, Knightsbridge, SW1X 9LE (7823
2505/www.oilily-world.com). Knightsbridge tube.*
Open 10am-6pm Mon, Tue, Thur-Sat; 10am-7pm
Wed. **Credit** AmEx, MC, V. **Map** p313 F9.
There are Oilily collections in many children's boutiques,
but this is the only London store dedicated to the Dutch
label. The clothes are exuberant gatherings of orange,
green, pink and blue with stripes and flowers and little
details on flounced dresses and skirts. There are also
embroidered jeans, and prettily detailed bags, sandals, hats
and accessories. Stuff for boys doesn't shy away from the
prints but hardens up the colours a bit. Expect to pay about
£70 for a girl's dress. Babywear is similarly bold.
Buggy access. Mail order. Play area.

Patrizia Wigan

*19 Walton Street, Knightsbridge, SW3 2HX (7823
7080/www.patriziawigan.com). Knightsbridge or South
Kensington tube.* **Open** 10.30am-6.30pm Mon-Fri;
10.30am-6pm Sat. **Credit** AmEx, MC, V. **Map** p313 E10.
Quintessentially English, the PW brand name has long
been favoured by royals and celebrities. The beautifully
made, classic styles for children aged up to eight are
designed to last beyond fashion fads and pass down
through generations, which makes the £89 hand-smocked
dresses for tiny girls seem reasonably good value; likewise
the stunning christening gowns from £195. There are
pressed linen shorts for boys, kilts and velvet dresses for
winter parties, and pageboy and bridesmaid outfits made
to order. Gifts, baby accessories and furniture are also sold.
*Buggy access. Delivery service. Nappy-changing facilities.
Play area.*

Rachel Riley

*82 Marylebone High Street, Marylebone, W1U 4QW
(7935 7007). Baker Street or Bond Street tube.*
Open 10am-6pm Mon-Sat. **Credit** AmEx, MC, V.
Map p314 5G.
Riley's unmistakable 1950s retro look is reminiscent of a
Loire Valley attic, and all the clothes for babies, boys and
girls have a rare beauty. Try a smocked floral dress (£79),
or the bishop neck dress with matching bloomers (£59).
Toddler boys can do a Little Lord Fauntleroy in a sailor
set of pale blue shirt and dark blue long shorts (£75), but
there's less showy stuff too. It's all built to last, with moth-
er-of-pearl buttons and hand-embroidery.
Buggy access. Delivery service. Mail order. Play area.
Branch: 14 Pont Street, SW1X 9EN (7259 5969).

Ralph Lauren

*143 New Bond Street, W1S 4ES (7535 4600/
www.polo.com). Bond Street tube.* **Open** 10-6pm
Mon-Wed, Fri, Sat; 10am-7pm Thur; noon-5pm Sun.
Credit AmEx, DC, MC, V. **Map** p314 6H.
It may look a little too patrician for some parents' tastes,
but the trademark preppy look translates quite distinc-
tively into miniature form. Some items, such as £185 hacking jackets for two-year-olds and £8 bibs for people with
more money than sense induce snorts of derision, but we
admired the pretty, bright plaid kilts and miniskirts for

Sugar rush

Today's generation of Haribo-fuelled children don't know what they've missed. It's not easy, these days, to show them the exquisite pleasure of old-fashioned classics, such as cola cubes, chewing nuts, pineapple chunks and sour apples. Sold in 50 gram (two-ounce) portions by a sweet shop proprietor, they are hard, but not impossible to find. To show kids what a heavenly prospect a real sweet shop can be, skip down south to **Hope & Greenwood**. Here you'll find jars and jars of nectar from the gods: sherbert pips, lemon bon bons, bullseyes, floral gums, Tom Thumb drops and the rest. Local children bundle in here after school for their sugar fix.

A Gold, Traditional Foods of Britain is a delightful shop that would be at home in a 1950s village. Regional products from all over the British Isles are a speciality, but confectionery is an irresistible draw. Come here for your bonbons, liquorice torpedoes, floral gums and nostalgic drinks such as dandelion and burdock.

Another handsome outlet for traditional sweet treats is the venerable department store **Fortnum & Mason** (181 Piccadilly, W1A 1ER, 7734 8040). The food hall here may be famous for its caviar, tea and whiskey marmalade, but children will be inexorably drawn to the chocolates and sweets (oh, happy day if there are free samples on the counter!). Beautifully packaged gifts of sugared almonds, rhubarb and custard, toffee bonbons and humbugs cost £5 for a 250g tin, or £1.75 for a portion of 100g. Not quite so posh, but rather more hands-on is the bright and beautiful sweet department at **Selfridges** (*see p186*). Here the children can go mad at the Jelly Belly counter, where there's the biggest range of flavours we've ever seen. Then there are the lollipops, the marshmallows, the jellies, the chocs, and the tummy ache if you don't exercise some restraint.

Naturally sweet, if less colourful, the **Hive Honey Shop** is owned by a beekeeper (look out for the wall of bees near the counter) and sells, as well as jars of honey and beeswax, honey fudge, sucky sweets with a liquid honey centre and honey chocolates. You can even kid yourself they're doing you some good.

A Gold, Traditional Foods of Britain
42 Brushfield Street E1 6AG (7247 2487/ www.agold.co.uk). Liverpool Street tube/rail. **Open** 11am-8pm Mon-Fri; 10am-6pm Sat; 11am-6pm Sun. **Credit** AmEx, MC. V.

Hive Honey Shop
93 Northcote Road, SW11 6PL (7924 6233/ www.thehivehoneyshop.co.uk). Clapham Junction rail. **Open** 10am-5pm Mon-Sat. **Credit** MC, V.

Hope & Greenwood
20 North Cross Road, East Dulwich, SE22 9EU (8613 1777). East Dulwich rail/12, 40, 176, 185 bus. **Open** 10am-6pm Mon-Sat; 10am-5pm Sun. **Credit** AmEx, MC, V.

little girls (£48); the warm rugby shirts in a rainbow of colours; bold, lambswool jumpers, pullovers and brightly striped cardigans. Items such as five-pocket, unadorned (save the little Polo logo) jeans, tennis shoes, windcheaters and cable knits are so well finished and only priced a little above similar items in high-street chains.
Delivery service. Mail order. Nappy-changing facilities.

Sasti
8 Portobello Green Arcade, 281 Portobello Road, Ladbroke Grove, W10 5TZ (8960 1125/ www.sasti.co.uk). Ladbroke Grove tube. **Open** 10am-6pm Mon-Sat; 11am-4pm Sun. **Credit** AmEx, MC, V.
Sasti is the affordable end of individual, British-made, designer clothes for children. Little girls love the frill and flounce skirts in unusual fabrics and prints. Babies from six months look so sweet in the bright red fleece dinosaur suit (£28), and the Pow! or Zap! tops (£20) are loved by the whole family. Whatever the season, the stock is colourful, some is flamboyant and all is pretty unusual.
Buggy access. Delivery service. Mail order. Nappy-changing facilities. Play area.

Semmalina-Starbags
225 Ebury Street, Pimlico, SW1W 8UT (7730 9333/ www.starbags.info). Sloane Square tube. **Open** 9.30am-5.30pm Mon-Sat. **Credit** AmEx, MC, V. **Map** p316 G11.

A large fibreglass tree with fairy lights in its branches greets you, a little bridge takes you from the front section (all party-bag toys and trinkets) to the clothes and dressing-up costumes at the back. There's no denying the clothes for children are sweet; we adored the little knits with crystal buttons (from £40), the silky sequinned kaftans for little girls and the little logoed T-shirts in presentation boxes. There are clothes by the Danish company Miniature and a variety of other designers. Among the toys are vintage items from the 1950s. Starbags is a party-bag service for parents too busy to concoct their own. In the basement, there's Papillon, a shoe shop with Hunter wellies, and ballet pumps in unusual shades.
Buggy access. Delivery service. Nappy-changing facilities.

Tartine et Chocolat
66 South Molton Street, Mayfair, W1K 5SX (7629 7233). Bond Street tube. **Open** 10am-6pm Mon-Sat. **Credit** AmEx, MC, V. **Map** p314 H6.
Blissfully French and posh, T&C has a whole range of products for babies and under-11s, including clothes, children's scents (from £30), soft toys and gifts. The pink and blue detailing is tempered by snowy-white sleepsuits, little dresses or baby shoes. Prices might make you choke on your tartine: sleepsuits with a soft and velvety finish (delightfully presented) cost from about £40; classic casuals (linen shorts, dresses, wool coats) for children cost much more.
Buggy access. Delivery service. Mail order.

Selfridges. *See p186*.

Consumer

Their Nibs

214 Kensington Park Road, Notting Hill, W11 1NR (7221 4263/www.theirnibs.com). Ladbroke Grove or Notting Hill Gate tube. **Open** 9.30am-6pm Mon-Fri; 10am-6pm Sat; noon-5pm Sun. **Credit** AmEx, MC, V.

A generously proportioned play area at the back makes visiting this shop with under-fives a treat. While the subjects play, their minders can riffle through the racks, selecting floaty dresses, fairy dresses, party dresses and baby dresses (£20-£35), cashmere baby cardigans (from £40) and embroidered combats and long-sleeved T-shirts (from about £30). A sale rail may yield some terrific bargains. The selection of vintage clothes, including some nasty 1970s stuff – starts at about £10. There are wooden baby toys with bells on by Heimess, Nurtured by Nature babyclothes and distinctive hair accessories. Haircuts cost from about £7; phone to find out when the hairdresser is next in).
Buggy access. Delivery service. Disabled access: ramps. Mail order. Play area.

Tiddleywinks

414 Roman Road, Bethnal Green, E3 5LU (8981 7000). Bethnal Green tube, then 8 bus. **Open** 10am-5.30pm Mon-Sat. **Credit** AmEx, MC, V.

Heavyweight designers in miniature mode are represented in this packed little shop. Tiny tots can be dressed up in Baby Dior, Marèse, Coco and Confetti; there are little

trimmed cardigans, all-in-one sleepsuits, pretty dresses and dinky dungas for little scraps in pushchairs. The fun starts, of course, when they're toddling in their fancy little shoes and boots by Eli and selecting their own outfits by DKNY, Kenzo, Moschino Sulk and Miss Grant. For boys there are suits, jeans by Diesel and quilted jackets.
Buggy access. Delivery service. Mail order.

Tots

39 Turnham Green Terrace, Chiswick, W4 1RG (8995 0520/www.totschiswick.com). Turnham Green tube. **Open** 10am-6pm Mon-Sat; noon-5pm Sun. **Credit** AmEx, MC, V.

This select little boutique for babies and children up to about 12 tricks out modish mites in Miniman, Absorba, Berlingot and Catimini baby clothes, with little leather and fake fur booties by Robeez. Sweatshirts, hoodies, shorts and anoraks by Quiksilver, Timberland and O'Neill are all lined up for older children looking to adopt an outdoorsy look. Girlie girls can have a ball with sticky-out net skirts from Kenzo and zingy designs from Oilily.
Buggy access. Disabled access. Play area.

Trendys

72 Chapel Market, Islington, N1 9ER (7837 9070). Angel tube. **Open** 10am-6pm Mon-Sat; 10am-4pm Sun. **Credit** AmEx, MC, V.

Chapel Market may be a throwback, but Trendys is very firmly established in the 21st-century world of aspirational fashionwear for tinies. So there's Pringle and Burberry babywear among the more traditional Absorba, Cacharel and Jean de la Lune, Diesel jeans for wee girls and Kickers and D&G footwear. The clothes go up to age 14 or so, and regular sales means that you will pick up some bargains if you visit often.
Buggy access. Disabled access.

Mid-range & high street

Biff

41-43 Dulwich Village, Dulwich, SE21 7BN (8299 0911). North Dulwich rail/P4 bus. **Open** 9.30am-5.30pm Mon-Fri; 10am-6pm Sat. **Credit** MC, V.
Dulwich Village's own little children's empire takes up two shop fronts, joined at the back by a Start-rite shoe area, which also has PE pumps and ballet shoes. In the baby side of the shop there are little striped togs by Weekend à la Mer, teddy-like fleeces by Seesaw and Petit Bateau, sleepsuits, rompers, vests and cardies from IKKS, Jean Bourget, Berlingot and Catimini, as well as Grobags. For older children up to 16 there's a big Quiksilver and O'Neill presence, as well as shirts by Ben Sherman and separates and coats by French Connection. Shoes aren't limited to Start-rite; there are Skechers and Hush Puppies too. The little ones' side has a small play area, and service in both is friendly.
Buggy access. Disabled access. Mail order. Play area.

Gap Kids

122 King's Road, Chelsea, SW3 4TR (7823 7272/ www.gap.com). Sloane Square tube. **Open** 10am-7pm Mon-Sat; noon-6pm Sun. **Credit** AmEx, MC, V. **Map** p313 11F.
Clothes for babies to teens in this ubiquitous chain always score a hit. Just as for the adults upstairs, there are jeans to suit all tastes, from slim-cut bootlegs for the girlies to spacious carpenter-style denims for lads who like to have their boxers on display above their trousers. Tiny jumpers and summer Ts look good on toddlers, and the accessories are distinctive, with funky floral rucksacks and school accessories for the girls and camouflage-style essentials for the lads. Gap's sale rails are a boon for thrifty parents.
Buggy access. Delivery service. Disabled access. Nappy-changing facilities.
Branches: throughout town. Check website for details.

Iana

186 King's Road, Chelsea, SW3 5XP (7352 0060/ www.iana.it). Sloane Square tube. **Open** 9am-6pm Mon, Tue, Thur, Fri; 9am-7pm Wed; 10am-6.30pm Sat; 11am-6pm Sun. **Credit** AmEx, DC, MC, V. **Map** p313 F11.
Practical and chic Italian outfits for children up to age 14 include some bargains, such as pretty white baby vests with crotch poppers (£6 for two) and light, bright long-sleeved T-shirts from £11.50. This is a useful find if you don't want to see your child in the high-street fashions everyone's wearing, but haven't quite got the budget for the designer brands.
Buggy access. Delivery service. Disabled access. Mail order. Play area.
Branch: Putney Exchange Shopping Centre, Putney High Street, SW15 1TW (8789 2022).

Igloo

300 Upper Street, Islington, N1 2TU (7354 7300/ www.iglookids.co.uk). Angel or Highbury & Islington tube. **Open** 10am-6.30pm Mon-Wed; 9.30am-7pm Thur-Sat; 11am-5.30pm Sun. **Credit** AmEx, DC, MC, V
This fashion and toy stop for babies and children aged up to eight is owned by two women with five young children between them. This, their sixth 'baby', holds some unexpected treasures. To wear, there are classics by Petit Bateau, Triple Star and cheeky shirts by Bob & Blossom. Other fashions suitable for the child around town are separates by Miniature (skirts from £29) and those rainwear bestsellers – macs, sou'westers and gumboots in pastel pink and powder blue florals by Blue Fish. At the back a Start-rite shoe shop is ready with the fitting gear. In the front are all the toys, as well as comic cuddlies from Zooflies. Pocket-money-priced toys are good for party bags too. Children can also get their hair cut (fringe trim £5).
Buggy access. Delivery service. Disabled access. Mail order. Nappy-changing facilities. Play area.

Jigsaw Junior

190-192 Westbourne Grove, Notting Hill, W11 2RH (7727 0322/www.jigsaw-online.com). Notting Hill Gate tube. **Open** 10.30am-6.30pm Mon; 10-6.30pm Tue, Wed, Sat; 10am-7pm Thur, Fri; noon-6pm Sun. **Credit** AmEx, MC, V. **Map** p310 A6.
Children can take a silver slide instead of the stairs down into the basement level where all the Jigsaw Junior stuff is. The look is richly textured but relaxed, which is echoed in the antique shop fittings: glass-fronted cabinets, framed mirrors and chairs with silk-covered cushions. It's girls only – pretty long-sleeved T-shirts or broderie anglaise sun tops, velvet-trimmed cardigans and sumptuous floppy dresses. Tops cost from £18, skirts about £30.
Buggy access. Disabled access. Mail order. Play area.
Branches: throughout town. Check website for details.

JoJo Maman Bébé

68 Northcote Road, Battersea, SW11 6QL (7228 0322/www.jojomamanbebe.co.uk). Clapham Junction rail. **Open** 9.30am-5.30pm Mon-Sat; 11am-5pm Sun. **Credit** MC, V.
This reasonably big branch of the increasingly popular Jojo brand, but it always seems to be chock-a-block with double buggies and flutey-voiced Clapham mammas. We know why they come. The clothes for babies, toddlers and infants are a happy combination of classics (80% wool duffle coats, £40), essentials (two-pack animal print sleepsuits, £16), and very pretty (cord flared skirts with velvet trim, £14). There are lots of brightly striped fleeces and sweatshirts, and easy-wash cottons for comfort, and children look positively delicious in everything. Maternity wear can be found at the back, and nursery essentials are available too, either in-store or via the catalogue.
Buggy access. Delivery service. Disabled access. Mail order. Nappy-changing facilities.
Branches: 3 Ashbourne Parade, 1259 Finchley Road, Golders green, NW11 0AD (8731 8961); 80 Turnham Green Terrace, Chiswick, W4 1QN (8994 0379).

Monsoon

Unit 25, The Market, Covent Garden, WC2 8AH (7497 9325/www.monsoon.co.uk). Covent Garden tube. **Open** 10am-8pm Mon-Sat; 11am-6pm Sun. **Credit** AmEx, MC, V. **Map** p317 L7.

Boys and girls are provided for in this busy branch dedicated to children. Many adult Monsoons, both in the West End and on high streets countrywide, also have children's clothes alongside their adult collections. The baby range (two months and upwards) includes delicate little dresses (about £26) and cardies in beautiful shades. The clothes are extremely pretty for older girls, who look sweet in tiered skirts with ribbon detail from £30 and 'baby kitty' ribbon bow cardigans (£24). The T-shirts have attractive detailing (from £12) and the lined dresses (from £34) are superb. For little boys there are smashing striped lambswool jumpers or the hooded, blue striped London Transport one (our favourite, £30). Cords and jeans for older lads are well priced at £24.

Buggy access. Mail order.
Branches: throughout town. Check website for details.

O'Neill

5-7 Carnaby Street, Soho, W1F 9PB (7734 3778/ www.oneilleurope.com). Oxford Circus tube. **Open** 10am-7pm Mon-Wed, Fri, Sat; 10am-8pm Thur; noon-6pm Sun. **Credit** AmEx, MC, V. **Map** p316 J6.
This season's – every season's – skater jeans, sweats, tees, caps and beanies are perfect for school hols filled with skateboarding, surfing and – for the lucky ones – snowboarding. Other attractions include button-through and collared shirts, 20 styles of sweatshirt (and hoodies) for boys, pleated skatey miniskirts, tighter Ts, winter fleeces and cardies, and summer vests and cropped trousers for girls. Prices start at £15 for a T-shirt; O'Neill's classic chunky hoodies from £40.
Buggy access (ground floor only). Mail order.
Branch: Bluewater Shopping Centre, Kent DA9 9SJ (01322 623 300); 9-15 Neal Street, WC2H 9PU (7836 7686).

Petit Bateau

106-108 King's Road, Chelsea, SW3 4TZ (7838 0818/www.petit-bateau.com). Sloane Square tube. **Open** 10am-6.30pm Mon-Tue, Fri, Sat; 10am-7pm Wed-Thur; noon-8pm Sun. **Credit** AmEx, MC, V. **Map** p313 F11.
The nautical look (not so much sailor suits as *milleraies* stripes in softest 100% cotton, three-button necklines and jerseys with whales on them) is as popular as ever in this classic French chain. Few babyclothes have enjoyed such long-lasting appeal. This is the largest London branch, with a drawing table for tots and a full range of baby, children's and womenswear. We adore the striped vests (£12), but then stripes are everywhere, from the gorgeous pastel-striped velour sleepsuits (£22-£45) to the cotton sundresses (£30), swimsuits (£20-£25) and T-shirts (£15-£20) for boys and girls. Girls get dark purples, bright pinks and bottle greens and some lovely floral pattern

Trotters. *See p203.*

dresses to wear with mohair jumpers. Boys look good in soft denims, logo T-shirts and padded jackets. *Buggy access. Delivery service. Mail order. Nappy-changing facilities. Play area.* **Branches**: throughout town, check website for details.

Popcorn

121 Stoke Newington Church Street, N16 0UH (7241 1333). Finsbury Park tube/rail, then 106 bus/73, 393, 476 bus. **Open** 10am-6pm Mon-Sat; 11am-5pm Sun. **Credit** MC, V

This crowded little addition to a fashionable street that gets more family-friendly by the month has clothes for children aged up to six, with the emphasis on babies and tod-

dlers. There are quirky tie tops and pants by Duckie Beau, sloganising T-shirts by Toby Tiger and other distinctive fashions from French Connection for Kids, Eat Your Greens, Ollie, Uttan and Brightbots. The shoe department has a fitting service, and there's a whole load of baby accessories, such as Kari Me slings, first shoes in a gift box, Hippy Chick hip seats and a range of baby toys. *Buggy access. Play area.*

Quackers

155D Northcote Road, Clapham, SW11 6QB (7978 4235). Clapham Junction rail, then 319 bus. **Open** 9.30am-5.30pm Mon-Fri; 10am-5.30pm Sat. **Credit** MC, V.

Push the button

New cot, trad toys or a top day out for your teenager. It's all available online...

Aspen & Brown

www.aspenandbrown.com/0870 011 0511. The website for well-known, quality welcome baby or christening gifts. Personalised baby cushions (£45) go down a storm, and we love the dancing-ducks music box (£16.95). Nursery gift sets include sterling silver christening mementoes, lambskin blankets and personalised bath towels.

Bright Minds

www.brightminds.co.uk/0870 442 2144. Sparky ideas that make learning fun. Footie fans will love the fabric and velcro football chart wall hanging (£29.99), and they'll be sharpening their maths skills when they tot up the top teams' scores and rank them. Software such as Become a British Isles Explorer (£9.99) makes geography effortless, and fun projects include a six-metre-long (3ft 3in) wordsearch puzzle (£7.99).

Bump to 3

www.bumpto3.com/0870 606 0276. Useful products, such as Grobag sleeping bags to stop children kicking off the bed covers (prices start at £21.95) and UV sunsuits and hats to keep the rays at bay (from £24.95).

Days to Amaze

www.daystoamaze.co.uk/0870 240 0635. If a birthday tea at home doesn't cut it, maybe the kids would prefer hurtling down a hill inside a giant inflatable ball? Sphering, as it's known, is one of the thrills on offer here (£49 for two), though there are gentler alternatives, including shadowing a zoo keeper for day (£149 for two). Age and height restrictions apply on some of the activities.

Decorative Country Living

www.decorativecountryliving.com/01400 273 632. Genuine whimsy for the nursery is on offer from former fashion editor Amanda Knox's small but

gorgeous collection. Stock changes as each piece is a one-off, but you'll find 1950s children's watering cans, a tiny china tea set (£18), cushions made from vintage French nursery rhyme fabric (£25) and fabulously shabby-chic 1940s single floral quilts (around £55).

Hawkin's Bazaar

www.hawkin.com/0870 429 4000. We'll keep on hoping a Hawkin's will open nearer London, but until that fine day we'll have to lose ourselves in the brilliant catalogue. Pocket-money prices apply for such must-haves as hair-growing cat soap (£3.99), magnetic marbles (£1.99), flexifaces (99p) or fortune-telling fish (99p for 12). Then there are all the bath treats, practical jokes, make and do kits and party-bag fillers.

Into the Blue

www.intotheblue.co.uk/01959 578 100. Great for junior adventure-seekers, this site offers adrenalin-charged experiences such as a go-karting session (for three or more, £35 per person, suitable for over-eights), a quad-bike safari or junior off-roading at venues all around the country. For youngsters (and parents) with nerves of steel, junior flying lessons or microlighting are also on offer (age and height restrictions operate).

Kidzcraft

www.kidzcraft.co.uk/01793 327 022. Everything you need for making stuff, from basic acrylic paint sets (£3) and glue spreaders to activity kits. The scrapbooking sets are good value at £5, including patterned shapes, frames, stickers and trimmings to immortalise those memories (separate kits for boys and girls). There are mask-making, fabric-painting, pottery-decorating and jewellery-making kits too.

Labour and Wait

www.labourandwait.co.uk/7729 6253. At this über-trendy hardware store you'll find a carpentry set, with small-sized but functional

Consumer

The well-preserved maters of Battersea regularly shove their Bugaboos into this shop, where they are greeted in a friendly fashion by the proprietor Veronica McNaught, who presides over the wide range of clothes for children aged up to ten. Labels for smart babies include the German brand Kanz, as well as always-delightful Petit Bateau. There's a good deal of affordable, individual pieces by Whoopi, with vintage-looking floral pinafores for girls (£24.99), as well as a selection of cosy coats and cardies for winterwear. Alongside the No Added Sugar T-shirts, there are statement makers by Toby Tiger, and must-haves for toddlers include excellent, pretty rainwear by Blue Fish and Kidorable gumboots that masquerade as ladybirds or frogs (£13.95). Juniors whose feet are just size four can have their Kidorables presented in a box and labelled 'my first wellies'. How adorable. *Buggy access.*

Quiksilver

Units 1 & 23, Thomas Neal Centre, Earlham Street, Covent Garden, WC2H 9LD (7836 5371/ www.quiksilver.com). Covent Garden tube. **Open** 10am-7pm Mon-Sat; noon-6pm Sun. **Credit** AmEx, MC, V. **Map** p315 L6.

This iconic label, started in the 1960s in Torquay (that's Torquay, Australia) by surfers Alan Green and John Law and a pair of revolutionary board shorts, is a label of choice even for those who never ride the waves. Snow- and

---

tools; a frame knitting kit (£18), a make-your-own crystal radio (£20) and a mini cleaning kit (£15), complete with wooden pegs, chamois and enamel bucket and pan. Junior gardeners love the scaled-down trowel, hoe, gloves and spade combo (£12).

Letterbox

www.letterbox.co.uk/0870 600 7878.
Huge range of personalised items, from duffle bags in an array of colours (£19.99) and director's chairs (£29.99) to smaller stuff including pencils, torches and lunchboxes. Good crop of traditional toys such as wooden boats (from £10.99), and dressing-up sets for both sexes.

The Little Experience

www.the-little-experience.com/01903 889 500.
You'll find great inspiration for kids' parties, from a sack-race kit (four sacks, four rosettes and a pennant finishing line) to a knit-your-own-mouse pack (both at £14.99). There are cooking materials for a bake-it prince or princess party (£6.99), including shortbread mix, cookie cutters and dragées. When you buy from the website, 50p is donated to Great Ormond Street hospital.

Mini Boden

www.boden.co.uk/0845 677 5000.
Practical enough to please parents, funky enough to mollify children, this casual collection offers clothes for children from nought to 14. The range includes nightwear and shoes too.

Mitty James

www.mittyjames.com/0845 612 0240.
If your nippers turn blue on breezy British beaches, this range of long towelling robes with hoods should warm their cockles. Nautical stripes in a range of bright colours are on offer (£28.95 for size six to 12 months, £29.95 for age six to seven). There's also a selection of sweet, retro swimwear for little girls.

Pedlars

www.pedlars.co.uk/01330 850 400.
This family business offers an eclectic mixture of toys, family games, music, books and more. A build-your-own rocket kit costs £16.50, a flying gyroscope that travels over 200 metres (660 feet) is £8.50. Pricier items include a covetable go-kart with BMX wheels (£179.50). There's also a nice selection of one-off antique Enid Blyton hardbacks.

Talking Book Shop

www.talkingbooks.co.uk/7491 4117.
An excellent selection of contemporary and classic children's books, from Arthur Ransome's *Swallows and Amazons* (£15.19) to Jacqueline Wilson's *Love Lessons* (£15.99) are available on tape, CD and MP3.

Urchin

www.urchin.co.uk/0870 112 6006.
Great kids' accessories include retro coat hooks (£7.99), original but affordable lighting (a colour-change light panel bedside lamp, £31.99) and simple but fun ideas such as plastic jelly moulds in zingy colours (£6.99 a set). It's all available alongside more mundane aspects of childcare, including a range of products to zap headlice.

Win Green

www.wingreen.co.uk/01622 746 516.
Brilliant children's handwoven cotton play tents that can be used inside or out. A small country cottage with a light aluminium frame is £180, a large knight's castle is £215. The cute candy gingham hanging tent (£145) is a bestseller; it's neat enough to fit into a bedroom.

The Woolshed

www.woolshed.co.uk/8444 8529.
London-based Woolshed has delightful hand-knitted children's clothes all made in the UK, from natural fibres. Groovy colourful striped jumpers for toddlers cost around £34.

Consumer

skateboarders choose from hard-wearing loose-cut jeans, T-shirts, shorts, shoes and thick, warm hoodies for those evenings on the beach. Expect to pay from £15 for T-shirts, £39 for boys' jeans and around £40 for girls'.
Buggy access.
Branches: 11-12 Carnaby Street, W1F 9PH (7439 0436); Unit 7, 12 North Piazza, Covent Garden, WC2E 8HD (7240 5886).

Tomboy Kids

176 Northcote Road, Clapham, SW11 6RE (7223 8030/www.tomboykids.com). Clapham Junction rail. **Open** 10am-5.30pm Mon-Fri; 10am-6pm Sat. **Credit** MC, V.
This spacious shop has fashionable gear for children and young people. Nothing is too twee, although the Fair Isle Choo Choo knits for babies are cuddly. For older children there's outerwear by French Connection and Quiksilver, and labels like IKKS cater for all ages. We love the vibrantly striped vests and underwear by Molo. During the summer there's a wide range of cool swimwear and flip flops by Reef, and in winter there are plenty of hoodies and warm jackets from Timberland.
Buggy access.

Trotters

34 King's Road, Chelsea, SW3 4UD (7259 9620/ www.trotters.co.uk). Sloane Square tube. **Open** 9am-7pm Mon-Sat; 10.30am-6.30pm Sun. **Credit** AmEx, MC, V. **Map** p313 F11.
A clothes and toyshop that caters for various peripheral needs as well, this is the sort of place you can't get children to leave. They can have their hair cut (£12.50 age three and under; £14 older children) while watching the colourful fish in the massive aquarium. Those needing new shoes can bounce around in the spacious Start-rite shoe zone, where there's a large silver car to play on. We like the clothes by Chelsea Clothing Company for babies and children, soft little trousers for babes from £14.99, nice pyjamas and cosy dressing gowns. Other labels include RiverWoods and Bob & Blossom. There are toys from Jellicat and Lollipop accessories, and there's a small section of books with lots of Dr Seuss.
Buggy access. Delivery service. Hairdressing. Mail order. Nappy-changing facilities.
Branches: 127 Kensington High Street, W8 5SF (7937 9373).

Zara

333 Oxford Street, W1C 2HY (7518 1550/www. zara.com). Oxford Circus tube. **Open** 10am-8pm Mon-Sat; noon-6pm Sun **Credit** AmEx, MC, V.
The Spanish giant's bid for global domination means that children's fashions have to fall in with the 'cheaper than it looks' formula that has made Zara such a huge success. Certainly the clothes in the nought to teens department are well priced, and some of them very likeable: knitwear from just £8 includes extremely useful cosy jumpers, scarves and hats for winter. There are some great cord, cotton and tweed shifts and skirts for the girls, and distinctive little rompers and jackets for small babies. Some styles may seem too fussy for children used to the street style of Gap or the more winsome (and cheaper) quirkiness of H&M. There's plenty to appeal here, though, and the underwear and baby basics are worth going back for.
Buggy access. Nappy-changing facilities.
Branches: throughout town. Phone or check website.

Second-hand

Boomerang

69 Blythe Road, Olympia, W14 0HP (7610 5232). Kensington (Olympia) tube/rail. **Open** 10am-6pm Tue-Sat. **Credit** AmEx, DC, MC, V.
Crammed with babies' and children's clothes and toys, Boomerang is the sort of place you keep coming back to. There's a good selection of sleepsuits, kids' separates and shoes, and loads of generally useful baby paraphernalia. Stock changes every season, and you can offload your children's hand-me-downs for a share of the asking price. To save time trawling through the rails, let the owner know what sort of thing you're after.
Buggy access. Nappy-changing facilities.

Little Trading Company

7 Bedford Corner, The Avenue, Chiswick, W4 1LD (8742 3152). Turnham Green tube. **Open** 9am-5pm Mon-Fri; 9am-4.30pm Sat. **No credit cards.**
A mark of this area's smartness is the fact that, on our last visit, alongside the buggies and high chairs lined up outside the shop was a well-preserved navy-blue carriage pram of the type that sells for £850 new. LTC was offering it for £350. Items are sold on a profit-share or sale-or-return basis, and among the stock you can find sports kit, baby accessories and equipment, including car seats, clothes for all ages and books, toys, DVDs and videos. These may be watched by children who come in for a haircut (Wed, Fri, Sat; ring for an appointment). New stuff is also sold, including soft leather first shoes by Starchild.
Buggy access. Play area.

Merry-Go-Round

12 Clarence Road, Hackney, E5 8HB (8985 6308). Hackney Central rail. **Open** 10am-5.30pm Mon-Sat; 11am-5pm Sun. **Credit** AmEx, MC, V.
This is every green parent's dream. The recycling possibilities provided by the mountains of baby stuff we're encouraged to buy are fully exploited by this excellent and unusually large agency. As well as what look like new and barely used car seats hanging from the ceiling, there are pushchairs and high chairs, babywalkers and nursery equipment. In the basement are clothes and other items for children aged from two to teenage. Previously owned clothes are more likely to be Gap than Gucci, but we saw a well-preserved Polo Ralph Lauren shirt for just £3.50.
Buggy access. Nappy-changing facilities. Play area.

Pixies

14 Fauconberg Road, Chiswick, W4 3JY (8995 1568/ www.pixiesonline.co.uk). Chiswick Park or Turnham Green tube. **Open** *Term time* 10am-4.30pm Mon-Fri; 10am-3pm Sat. *School hols* 10am-4.30pm Wed-Fri; 10am-3pm Sat. **Credit** AmEx, MC, V.
A clothing and equipment agency full of new and nearly new clothes, accessories and baby equipment, Pixies can furnish you with quality items such as Stokke high chairs, car seats and pushchairs, buggy boards (these are sold new too), and, for summer, UV bodysuits and swim shoes. The quality clothing is sensibly arranged into school uniforms, babywear and items for older children clearly labelled with age and price. The company also offers the Babytalk consultation service, (£40 per hour), offering advice on equipment and clothing for your new baby.
Buggy access. Delivery service. Disabled access. Mail order.

Consumer

Bought the T-Shirt?

Why give in to mainstream cute? You might no longer feel comfortable wearing band shirts (though you still sleep in your old Clash one), but your kids can. At **Planet Boo** (www.planet boo.co.uk) you'll find iconic album covers from the Ramones, Smiths, Clash, Sex Pistols, Blondie and more. And they're just £8 – the cheapest we've found anywhere. New designs are introduced as demand dictates, so if you really, really need a Metallica tee for a mini-me, let them know.

Cult movie posters beloved of students are still selling strong at **Vinmag** (39-43 Brewer Street, W1R 3SD, 7439 8525, www.vinmag.com) and are available as T-shirts too. The kids range includes *The A-Team* and *Planet of the Apes*, but any design can be scaled down to kids' sizes and printed to order (£10.99-£12.99). The possibilities are endless: *Barbarella*, *Godzilla*... even Sid James. Film stars (Monroe, Hepburn, Connery, Bruce Lee) can be found on tees and hoodies at **www.stardustkids. co.uk** (also from 294 Milkwood Road, SE24 0EZ, 7737 0199). The company also does rompers emblazoned with 'ASBO', 'Drama Queen' and 'The Incredible Sulk'; baby booties with 'LOVE' and 'HATE' on each foot (£10), and Routemaster vests (£12, age one to three years, perfect for parents pining after London's much-loved bus) make kooky gifts.

Nappyhead (www.nappyhead.co.uk) sells father-and-child sets ('Who's the Daddy?' and 'Who's the Babby?', £30), and 'Good Cop'/'Bad Cop' tees for twins (£24). **Nippaz With Attitude** (www.nippaz.com) is popular with urban-cool celebrity parents; Madonna's a fan. Did Lourdes and Rocco wear 'Muthasucka' bodyvests (£16.99)?

A browse through the babies and kids section at **www.moretvicar.com** reveals a dozen stylish and contemporary designers. Lonely hearts ads (... You had a red balloon, I was on the swings...) from Eat Yer Greens, and Takkoda's humorous

dressed-up animals are fun. Celebrities' favourite Jakes and London fashion label Uniform are among the other contemporary designers available.

Lisa Quinn started **Snuglo** at Spitalfields market in 1999 and has collected a fan base including Michael Stipe and Toni Collette. Her funky range is typified with hip, grown-up colours and bold lettering: 'I Want Chips, Chocolate and Cake'; 'I Love Sweeties, Shopping and Shoes' – and are available from www.snuglo.com (tees £15.95-£17.95, sleepsuits £18.95) and Fenwick. Snuglo's signature spaceman design is also very, very cute.

No Added Sugar (www.noadded sugar.co.uk) produces edgy kids' clothes – the 'Lock Up Your Daughters!' tee is a fave; 'Enjoy Milk'; and 'Enjoy Chocolate', in traditional Coca Cola-style graphics are also bestsellers (£15.50-£18.30).

At **www.dribble factory.com** you'll find designs in flock, puff and glitter prints: 'Evil Dictator'; 'Be Nice – Don't Forget Who Chooses Your Nursing Home'; 'I (heart) Boobies' (£13). More slogan kidswear can be found at **www.tots planet.co.uk**.

Groovy parents can kit their rainbow children out for Glastonbury in ethically sourced, tie-dye and patchwork clothing from **www.susumama.co.uk**; and for Goths, there are pentacle t-shirts (in black, of course).

Alternative parents should also check out US sites **www.theretrobaby.com**, **www.80stees.com** and **www.babywit.com** for slogans like: 'My Mama Drinks Because I Cry'; as well as Sonic Youth and Hendrix rock shirts. And possibly working its way over here from across the pond, there's **Happy Bunny**, a hugely popular and gleefully cruel kids' line of T-shirts and stationery. Middle America retirees have been publicly vocal about their offence at shirts proclaiming: 'Seriously – Old People Have To Go!'; and, 'Run Along and Die Now'. Honestly, what happened to Pingu and Hello Kitty?

Shoes

Brian's Shoes

*2 Halleswelle Parade, Finchley Road, Temple Fortune,
NW11 0DL (8455 7001/www.briansshoes.com).
Finchley Central or Golders Green tube.* **Open** 9.15am-
5.30pm Mon-Sat; 10.30am-1.30pm Sun. **Credit** MC, V.
This 35-year-old children's shoe shop has helpful staff and
is conveniently close to Bookworm (*see p186*). It offers
Timberland, Start-rite, Ricosta, Babybotte, Nike and
Kickers, as well as a range of Italian designer shoes.
Buggy access. Disabled access.

Instep

*45 St John's Wood High Street, St John's Wood, NW8
7NJ (7722 7634/www.instepshoes.co.uk). St John's
Wood tube.* **Open** 9am-6pm Mon-Sat; 11am-5pm Sun.
Credit AmEx, MC, V.
A one-stop store for children's footwear, conveniently close
to Regent's Park. It offers a massive range of shoes, sandals, boots and trainers, as well as all the 'extras', such as
football boots, ballet shoes, plimsolls and gumboots. The
mature, helpful staff are all trained shoe fitters. Labels
stocked include DKNY, D&G, Babybotte, Mod 8,
Birkenstock and Ricosta. Expet to pay around £30 for
expertly fitted baby shoes, ansd from £50 for fantasy
delights from Italy.
Buggy access. Disabled access.
Branches: throughout town. Check website for details.

One Small Step One Giant Leap

*3 Blenheim Crescent, Notting Hill, W11 2EE (7243
0535/www.onesmallsteponegiantleap.com). Ladbroke
Grove or Notting Hill Gate tube.* **Open** 9am-6pm
Mon-Sat; 11am-5pm Sun. **Credit** MC, V.
This growing chain of award-winning specialist children's
shoe shops continues to make giant leaps into parents'
good books, and it's quite obvious why. Everything is
beautifully set out, and the range of brands, both fashionable and reliable, is quite astonishing. Babies can have
chubby feet encased in Starchild soft-leather protectors in
a wide range of designs; then there are Start-rites, Asters
from France, swanky Roberto Cavalli and Pinco Pollino
from Italy, trendy Skechers, Puma, Diesel and
Birkenstocks, sturdy Geox and Kickers and many, many
more. Prices go from £15 for baby shoes, to £34 for sensible Start-rites and a bit more for the posh continentals.
Buggy access. Mail order.
Branches: 409 Upper Richmond Road West, SW14
7NX (8487 1288); 49 Northcote Road, SW11 1NJ (7223
9314); Putney Exchange, 1st floor, High Street, SW15
1TW (8789 2046).

Shoe Station

*3 Station Approach, Kew, Surrey TW9 3QB (8940
9905/www.theshoestation.co.uk). Kew Gardens tube.*
Open 10am-6pm Mon-Sat. **Credit** MC, V.
Run by two women with seven children between them, this
little shop near the station has children's shoes for every
occasion in sizes from 18 to 40. Brands available include
Start-rite, Ricosta, Aster, Naturino, Babybotte, TTY,
Giesswein, Mod8, Pom d'Api, GEOX, Kenzo, Nike, Puma,
Birkenstock, Primigi, Freed and Daisy Roots. Football
boots, ballet shoes, slippers and gumboots are also cov-
ered. Staff are trained Start-rite fitters.
Buggy access. Play area.

Stepping Out

*106 Pitshanger Lane, Ealing, W5 1QX (8810 6141).
Ealing Broadway tube.* **Open** 10am-5.30pm Mon-Fri;
9.30am-5.30pm Sat. **Credit** MC, V.
A Start-rite agent first and foremost, Stepping Out stocks
plenty of Ricosta, Mod8 and Kenzo as well. Experienced
assistants specialise in advising on shoes for children with
mobility problems, with local GPs often referring kids here;
lots of styles provide extra support, but manage to be fashionable too (Le Loup Blanc, for example, is perfect for kids
with weak ankles).
Buggy access. Play area. Nappy-changing facilities.

Sportswear

Most parents' idea of hell would be to slog down
Oxford Street's sports emporia looking for child-
sized trainers and sports kit. We'd advise against
it and would instead direct you to the pleasant
places listed below.

Ace Sports & Leisure

*341 Kentish Town Road, Kentish Town, NW5 2TJ
(7485 5367). Kentish Town tube.* **Open** 9.30am-6pm
Mon-Wed, Fri, Sat; 9.30am-7pm Thur. **Credit** AmEx,
MC, V.
There are walls of footwear for all sports, as well as junior
rackets, footballs, bats and swimming equipment. Brands
include Puma, Adidas, Reebok and Nike. There are small
baseball mitts (£20), children's cricket balls and bats, junior tennis
rackets, ping-pong balls in bright colours, tracksuits, swim
nappies, goggles, earplugs and nose clips – everything, in
fact, to get kids active.
Buggy access. Disabled access.

Decathlon

*Canada Water Retail Park, Surrey Quays Road, SE16
2XU (7394 2000/www.decathlon.co.uk). Canada Water
tube.* **Open** 10am-7.30pm Mon-Thur; 10am-8pm Fri;
9am-7pm Sat; 11am-5pm Sun. **Credit** MC, V.
An enormous sports emporium that fills up two hangars,
Decathlon endears itself to us because the young staff spend
a good deal of time sprinting about and being helpful. On
our last visit, one was kicking a football about with a small
boy while his parents cogitated over skiing equipment.
There are loads of bargains, particularly on the clothing sale
rails. Aisles are devoted to footie, athletics, equestrian sports,
golf, fishing, cricket, watersports… you name 60 sports,
they've got the stuff for them. The bike section is very large.
Buggy access. Delivery service. Disabled access.

Lillywhites

*24-36 Regent Street, SW1Y 4QF (0870 333 9600/
www.sports-world.com). Piccadilly Circus tube.* **Open**
10am-9pm Mon-Sat; noon-6pm Sun. **Credit** AmEx, MC,
V. **Map** p317 K7.
Good for mainstream sports gear, Lillywhites has unfortunately given up on equipment for pricier pursuits (riding, diving and so on) for more urban activities. This
presumably is because it's now part of the Sports Soccer
group. Children's mini football kits, as well as those essential goalie gloves and team socks, are in good supply. It's
not always easy to find a member of staff.
Buggy access. Disabled access.

Consumer

Ocean Leisure

*11-14 Northumberland Avenue, Charing Cross,
WC2N 5AQ (7930 5050/www.oceanleisure.co.uk).
Embankment tube.* **Open** 9.30am-7pm Mon-Fri;
9.30am-5.30pm Sat. **Credit** MC, V. **Map** p399 L8.
This watersports emporium takes up two shops underneath the arches. One's all sailing and scuba, the other is
mostly surfing. Some of the gear comes in very small sizes.
Short-sleeved wetsuits (£44) are on hand for those freezing forays into the North Cornish surf, while full-length
steamer suits (£74.99) are for less intrepid winter users.
There's a good range of Reef sandals and neoprene
Aquashoes (£6) in small sizes, as well as baby life jackets,
fins, masks and snorkels, and even scuba equipment (from
age eight). The Chiswick branch is a diving specialist and
has a swimming pool for lessons.
Buggy access. Disabled access. Mail order.

Slam City Skates

*16 Neal's Yard, Covent Garden, WC2H 9DP (7240
0928/www.slamcity.com). Covent Garden tube.* **Open**
10am-6.30pm Mon-Sat; noon-5pm Sun. **Credit** AmEx,
MC, V. **Map** p315 L6.
This is teen heaven, with a range of possibilities for the
very small. Skateboard decks, T-shirts, the skate shoes of
the moment (the littlest is UK size three), rucksacks and
accessories are all sold here. Although there's no stock dedicated to children, most are happy to buy the small Slam
City T-shirt and grow into it. Shoes include chunky Nikes,
Vans, Etnies and Emerica.
Mail order (0870 420 4146).

Soccerscene

*56-57 Carnaby Street, Soho, W1F 9QF (7439 0778/
www.soccerscene.co.uk). Oxford Circus tube.* **Open**
9.30am-7pm Mon-Wed, Fri ; 9,30am-7.30pm Thur,
Sat; 11.30am-5.30pm Sun. **Credit** AmEx, MC, V.
Map p314 J6.
Scaled-down replica kits are available for most of the popular teams, especially the sainted Arsenal and ever-popular Man U and Chelsea. Rugby kits are upstairs. There are
also balls, boots, shin pads, trainers, socks, boxes, scarves
and hats. Service is helpful.
Delivery service. Mail order.
Branch: 156 Oxford Street, W1D 1ND (7436 6499).

Speedo

*41-43 Neal Street, Covent Garden, WC2H 9PJ (7497
0950). Covent Garden tube.* **Open** 10am-7pm Mon-
Wed, Fri, Sat; 10am-8pm Thur; noon-6pm Sun. **Credit**
AmEx, MC, V. **Map** p315 L6.
The no-nonsense Speedo brand has traditionally catered
for lane swimmers who want comfort and coverage, but it
also sells beachwear, towelling capes, sun-tops and knee-
length sunsuits (£23) with up to 98% UV protection. The
junior range is cool for swimming lessons. There are children's accessories too: come for swim nappies, armbands,
snorkels, goggles and caps that match your swimsuit.
*Buggy access. Delivery service. Disabled access.
Mail order.*

Urban Chaos

*Unit 26, Thomas Neal Centre, Earlham Street, Covent
Garden, WC2H 9LD (7836 9060/urban-chaos.co.uk).
Covent Garden tube.* **Open** 11am-7pm Mon-Sat; noon-
6pm Sun. **Credit** MC, V. **Map** p315 L6.

The friendly Antipodien lads here can usually find smallish T-shirts with the right logos or 26in waist baggy pants
and small-size skate shoes by, perhaps, DC. Adolescents
salivate over the huge board display.
Buggy access. Disabled access: lift. Mail order.
Branches: Throughout town.

Wigmore Sports

*79-83 Wigmore Street, Marylebone, W1U 1QQ (7486
7761/www.wigmoresports.co.uk).* **Open** 10am-6pm
Mon-Wed, Fri, Sat; 10am-7pm Thur. **Credit** AmEx,
MC, V. **Map** p314 G6.
London's only racket sport specialist is great fun to visit.
Disciplines covered include tennis, squash, badminton and
more, and there's a 'try before you buy' practice wall. If
you have a child inspired by Andy Murray, check out the
junior stock. Excellent tennis shoes by K-Swiss, Adidas,
Nike and others (£30-£40) are stocked in half sizes from
12 up; shorter rackets (from 50cm/19in; £15-£100) and
softer balls are a speciality.
*Buggy access. Delivery service. Disabled access.
Mail order.*
Branches: Harrods, 87-135 Brompton Road, SW1X
7XL (7730 1234); Selfridges, 400 Oxford Street, W1A
1AB (0870 8377 377).

Toyshops

Bikes

Chamberlaine & Son

*75-77 Kentish Town Road, Camden, NW1 8NY
(7485 4488). Camden Town tube.* **Open** 8.30am-6pm
Mon-Sat. **Credit** AmEx, MC, V.
Hundreds of bikes are suspended from the ceiling and
walls in this shop. In addition, there are reclinable Hamax
baby seats (£62.99), Phillips trailer buggies (from £120)
and tagalongs (£120-£160) – a safe way to travel greenly
with the kids. A new child's bike costs about £100; first
service is free.
*Buggy access. Delivery service. Disabled access.
Mail order.*

Edwardes

*221-225 Camberwell Road, Camberwell, SE5 0HG
(7703 3676/5720). Elephant & Castle tube/rail, then
12, 68, 176, P3 bus.* **Open** 8.30am-6pm Mon-Sat.
Credit AmEx, MC, V.
Bikes for children aged two to 12, including Pro Bike,
Bronx and Giant ranges, are supplemented by useful accessories such as bike seats, jolly helmets, trailers and tag-
alongs to fix to adult bikes (from £89). Repairs for slipped
chains, punctured tyres and damaged wheels are all dex-
terously carried out. Service is cheery.
Buggy access. Delivery service. Disabled access. Mail order.

Two Wheels Good

*143 Crouch Hill, Crouch End, N8 9QH (8340 4284/
www.twowheelsgood.co.uk). Finsbury Park tube, then
W7 bus.* **Open** 8.30am-6pm Mon-Sat. **Credit** AmEx,
MC, V.
This bike shop combines the cool side of adult biking with
a good range of kids' equipment – the children's versions
of Trek, which cost from about £130, are the smartest.
There are helmets (by Met, £20) and Trek trailers (£250,

Herbie takes centre stage at the **Disney Store**.

converts to a stroller) and tagalongs (from £100, geared and ungeared), plus Bobike child seats (£70).
Buggy access. Disabled access.
Branch: 165 Stoke Newington Church Street, N16 0UL (7249 2200).

Fun & games

Cheeky Monkeys
202 Kensington Park Road, Notting Hill, W11 1NR (7792 9022/www.cheekymonkeys.com). Notting Hill Gate tube, then 52 bus. **Open** 9.30am-5.30pm Mon-Fri; 10am-5.30pm Sat; noon-5pm Sun. **Credit** MC, V.
Map p310 A6.
The Notting Hill Monkey is strong on presentation and good at stocking unusual, attractive and fun products. Pride of place on our last visit went to a most impressive ten-in-one games table for £250. An enduring bestseller is the beautiful, shaggy rocking sheep for babies and toddlers to ride (£49.99). Smart wooden toys from the Toy Workshop include a fantastic pirate ship, then there are arty-crafty items, such as Hama Beads and knitting sets. Role play toys are handsome – the adorable wooden kitchen units standing at around two feet high (from about £70) are highly covetable. Pocket-money toys cost from about £1.99. Fancy-dress outfits are sold, and there's a bookshop in the basement of this branch.
Buggy access. Disabled access. Mail order (website only).
Branches: Throughout town.

Disney Store
360-366 Oxford Street, W1N 9HA (7491 9136/www. disneystore.co.uk). Bond Street tube. **Open** 10am-8pm Mon-Sat; noon-6pm Sun. **Credit** AmEx, MC, V.
Map p314 J6.
This most central branch of the highly coloured Disney Store has a high turnover. Selling fast on our last visit were Mr Incredible dressing-up costumes, Mr I talking dolls (£10) and Mrs I stretch dolls (£8). Other dressing-up costumes include Peter Pan, Snow White, Tinkerbell and Buzz (costumes from £20). There's children's underwear, night-

wear and casuals emblazoned with favourite characters, then there's the tableware, stationery, lunch bags and boxes and cuddly toys. Enduring favourites are the character dolls and, of course, the classic DVDs.
Buggy access. Disabled access. Mail order.
Branches: 9 The Piazza, Covent Garden, WC2E 8HD (7836 5037); 22A & 26 The Broadway Shopping Centre, W6 9YD (8748 8886).

Early Learning Centre
36 King's Road, Chelsea, SW3 4UD (7581 5764/www. elc.co.uk). Sloane Square tube. **Open** 9.30am-7pm Mon-Fri; 9.30am-6pm Sat; 11am-6pm Sun. **Credit** AmEx, MC, V. **Map** p313 F11.
Dedicated to imaginative play for babies and young children, ELC is such a good friend to parents that you miss it when the children grow out of the stuff, from about the age of nine. Everything is sturdy, brightly coloured and reasonably priced. There are some things ELC does extremely well – for example, simple, soft-bodied baby dolls. Another bestseller is the affordable wooden train sets that link together just like Brio but are cheaper. Then there are the wonderful art materials, play animals and farms, playhouses and pop-up tents, swings, sandpits, paddling pools, picture books and story and song tapes, science sets and arty-crafty kits. This branch holds play sessions for toddlers on Tuesdays (9.30-11am), but not from mid September to early January, when every inch of space is taken up with Christmas stock.
Buggy access. Delivery service. Mail order.
Branches: throughout town. Check website for details.

Fun Learning
Bentall's Centre, Clarence Street, Kingston-upon-Thames, Surrey KT1 1TP (8974 8900). Kingston rail. **Open** 9am-6pm Mon-Wed, Fri, Sat; 9am-8pm Thur; 11am-5pm Sun. **Credit** MC, V.
We make no apology for sending you out of town to Fun Learning, because it's one of the best toyshops we know. Yes, everything's more or less educational (although we're not sure how some of the nuttier outdoor toys, such as

Consumer

Stomp Rockets and screeching slingshot-type missiles might fit into that category). There are large sections devoted to puzzles and number games, art and craft activities, and science experiments. Affordable pocket-money-priced items include balloon-making gunk, bouncy balls, puzzles, magnifying glasses and other curiosities. Less affordable are the stunt kites and the extremely tempting Observer 60 Altaz Refractor Astronomical Telescope (£99), which will show you lunar craters, Saturn's rings, Jupiter's moons, star clusters and nebula.
Buggy access. Disabled access.
Branch: Brent Cross Shopping Centre, NW4 3FP (8203 1473).

Hamleys

188-196 Regent Street, W1B 5BT (0870 333 2455/ www.hamleys.com). Oxford Circus tube. **Open** 10am-8pm Mon-Fri; 9am-8pm Sat; noon-6pm Sun. **Credit** AmEx, DC, MC, V. **Map** p314 J6.
This most famous toyshop is an over-exciting experience that can produce tears before bedtime for children who don't understand credit limits. Parents tend to throw tantrums over prices, crowds and queuing at the tills. Most must-have toys are here, though prices seem to build in a margin for the convenience of getting everything under one roof. The ground floor accommodates most mayhem and a mountain of soft toys. The basement is the Cyberzone, full of games consoles and high-tech gadgetry. The first floor has items of a scientific bent, plus a lurid sweet factory and a branch of the Bear Factory, where children can have a bear custom-made (from £9.99). On the second is everything for pre-schoolers. Third is girlie heaven – Barbie World, Sylvanian Families and departments for dressing up, make-up and

so on. Fourth has remote-controlled vehicles, plus die-cast models. Fifth is Lego World. Kids can have their birthday party here – typically on a Sunday morning – and Hamleys can also arrange Christmas parties and other events.
Buggy access. Café. Delivery service. Disabled access: lift, toilet. Mail order. Nappy-changing facilities. Play areas.

LEGO ®

Unit 7, The Bentall Centre, Wood Street, Kingston-upon-Thames, Surrey KT1 1TR (8546 1280/ www.lego.com). Kingston rail. **Open** 9.30am-6pm Mon-Wed, Fri; 9.30am-8pm Thur; 9am-6pm Sat; 11am-5pm Sun. **Credit** MC, V.
Like this one, most Lego branches reside in suburban or out-of-town shopping centres, where there's space enough to create a huge 'pick a brick' wall, which consists of a multitude of Perspex containers full of various Lego brick permutations for customers to pick and mix to their choice. Otherwise you can buy special pieces (such as Duplo figures for tots) singly (from 35p) or big presentation boxes of Lego knights and castles, Harry Potter Lego and various other themed sets.
Buggy access. Nappy-changing facilities. Play area.

Little Rascals

140 Merton Road, Wimbledon, SW19 1EH (8542 9979). South Wimbledon. **Open** 9am-5.30pm Mon-Sat. **Credit** AmEx, MC, V.
A splendid little local shop full of unusual wooden toys, clothes and gifts for babies, Little Rascals is run by a helpful, friendly woman who can advise on top presents for toddlers and infants. Last visit we were very taken by a Christopher Robin-style wooden trolley with swivelly front wheels for just £20 – perfect for taking all your soft

'I bought it on eBay'

Since eBay, the online auction site, launched in the UK in 1999, more than ten million people have used it. And with toys traded on eBay worldwide accounting for a staggering $2.1 billion a year, it's clear that parents are part of this bidding frenzy. Even Cherie Blair is at it – she bought a Winnie the Pooh clock on the site.

People can find themselves drawn to toy shopping on eBay for all sorts of reasons. One parent first logged on in search of rare Yu-Gi-Oh! cards for his son's collection – now, there's parental devotion for you. Kids themselves aren't allowed to buy on eBay, but there's nothing to stop them cruising around it like any other shop and then telling their parents what they want.

As well as individuals trading second-hand goods, lots of busy stores maintain a presence on the site. Desperate parents, finding the Christmas must-have toy is sold out are buying from shops or wholesalers overseas and getting the goods shipped over in time for the big day. Last Christmas it was the PlayStation PSP, which was available on eBay from stores in Hong Kong.

Of course, the possibility of saving money is one of the site's big draws. One PSP model was on sale in London shops for £260 but available for £181 on eBay. And the system is pretty

convenient: after the initial hassle of setting up your eBay and PayPal accounts, purchases only take a matter of minutes. Don't kid yourself that it's completely hassle-free, though, particularly in the run-up to Christmas, when there are a lot more bidders sniffing around the more popular toys. 'If there are 36 seconds left on a bid, I'll usually wait 30 seconds, then put mine in,' explains one seasoned toy bidder. 'But there are a lot of other bidders at Christmas, so you have to second guess what they are going to offer.' If this sounds far too stressful and competitive buyers can often go for a 'buy now' price, which is usually a bit higher than the auction price would be.

A teddy bear sells on eBay every two minutes, a toy car every 26 seconds – what toy shop can emulate those sales figures? One would imagine · that toy retailers would be shaking in their shoes. But Derek Markie of the British Association of Toy Retailers insists his members aren't worried. 'I don't think at the moment the trend is high enough to be a significant factor in the high street,' he said, and though buying on the internet may be convenient, no one has yet managed to replicate online the excitement, ambience, instant gratification and – well – magic, of buying from a toyshop. Hamleys needn't panic just yet.

toys out for a picnic in the Hundred Acre Wood. Other gifts could include paint-your-own bird feeders, brightly coloured macs, souwesters and gumboots and simple games and puzzles.
Buggy access.

Mystical Fairies

12 Flask Walk, Hampstead, NW3 1HE (7431 1888/ www.mysticalfairies.co.uk). Hampstead tube. **Open** 10am-6pm Mon-Sat; 11am-6pm Sun. **Credit** MC, V.
Around 2,000 fairy products find a patch in this amazing shop. Fairy creatures hang from the ceiling on beaded swings, endure being shaken inside glitter-storm bubbles and lend their wings to little girls' rucksacks. Much energy is going into fairy bedwear: canopies, bed covers, slippers, dressing gowns, pyjamas and duvet covers are available for around £20. Fairy dresses come from So Fairy Beautiful and Frilly Lilly in addition to favourite Lucy Lockett, and there are also Disney princess costumes. The Enchanted Garden in the basement is a splendid space for parties; it's also home to Fairy Club and Fairy School.
Buggy access. Mail order. Nappy-changing facilities.
Branches: Bluewater Shopping Centre, Kent, DA9 9SR (01322 624 997).

Toys R Us

760 Old Kent Road, Peckham, SE15 1NJ (7732 7322/ www.toysrus.co.uk). Elephant & Castle tube/rail, then 21, 56, 172 bus. **Open** 9am-8pm Mon-Fri; 9am-7pm Sat; 11am-5pm Sun. **Credit** AmEx, MC, V.
The Peckham branch of the chain of spacious toy warehouses, usually found in suburban retail parks, is the most central Toys R Us we know. All branches stock industrial quantities of the toy of the moment. Inexpensive bikes (from £39.99), trikes, ride-on tractors and go-karts (£89.99), car seats and buggies are other attractions. The party paraphernalia is pretty good too: themed paperware, silly hats, balloons and party bags with their various plasticky fillings. This is the cheapest place to buy big-name board games and is a consistently good bet for the unshakeable Action Man, Barbie and My Little Pony brands.
Buggy access. Car park. Delivery service. Disabled access: toilet. Nappy-changing facilities.
Branches: throughout town. Check website for details.

Local toyshops

Art Stationers/ Green's Village Toy Shop

31 Dulwich Village, Dulwich, SE21 7BN (8693 5938). North Dulwich rail. **Open** 9am-5.30pm Mon-Sat. **Credit** MC, V.
If it's art supplies – paint boxes, pastels, crayons, easels, paper, stationery – you want, stay in the front section, where party paperware, cards and craft kits are also sold. Most children canter to the back section, however, where Brio, Sylvanian Families, Playmobil, Crayola, Lego and other giants of the toy kingdom sit temptingly on the crowded shelves. Dolls' house furniture and dressing-up clothes are also sold. The staff remain cheerful even during the after-school rush for pocket-money-priced must-haves (stickers, stretchy aliens, yo-yos, rings, bubbles – this is an excellent place to fill party bags inexpensively). They are happy to advise on toys for all occasions.
Buggy access.

Fagin's Toys

84 Fortis Green Road, Muswell Hill, N10 3HN (8444 0282). East Finchley tube, then 102 bus. **Open** 9am-5.30pm Mon-Sat; 10am-3pm Sun. **Credit** MC, V.
This is the sister shop of Word Play in Crouch End (*see p211*), and it has a similar feel: it's a lovely big space and the stock is sensibly chosen. There is almost nothing faddy here; the owner sticks with her favourites (Galt, Orchard, Brio, Lego, Playmobil, Sylvanian Families). Row upon row of games yields to an art corner with paint, art, sewing and henna kits by John Adams and, of course, Galt, and the Jellycat stuffed animals are hugely popular. A large table at the front is chock-a-block with novelties, sweeties, pens and pretty much everything else a child might want to blow their pocket money on.
Buggy access. Disabled access. Play area.

Happy Returns

36 Rosslyn Hill, Hampstead, NW3 1NH (7435 2431). Hampstead tube. **Open** 10am-5.30pm Mon-Fri; 10am-6pm Sat; noon-5.30pm Sun. **Credit** MC, V.
A good range of Galt crafts, from Octons and paints to hair art, is complemented by Crayola art equipment. There are cheap and cheerful items like police helmets, swords and feather boas, but otherwise it's all proper boxed toys – Sylvanian Families (from £10.99 per doe-eyed family), bubble machines (£9.99), sailing yachts, Wolfhammer games and action figures. There are some useful party-ware products such as printed helium balloons (£2.99 each), cheap party-bag treats and higher-quality mixed packs of presents (good value at £2.50 for four gifts) to be perused.
Buggy access.

Patrick's Toys & Models

107-111 Lillie Road, Fulham, SW6 7SX (7385 9864/ www.patrickstoys.co.uk). Fulham Broadway tube. **Open** 9.30am-5.30pm Mon-Sat. **Credit** MC, V.
For once, boys get the lion's share of the goods. This is the main service agent for Hornby and Scalextric, so expect lots of tracks and model trains. Outdoor sports get a look in with kites, bikes and garden games, while war buffs will find enough to engage in full-scale combat. There's a choice of dolls' houses with all the furniture miniature Victorians could wish for, or Barbies, Bratz and Sindies for those in search of a more modern version of womanhood. There is also a large selection of cheap party gifts.
Buggy access. Delivery service (local). Disabled access.

Play

89 Lauriston Road, Victoria Park, E9 7HJ (8510 9960/www.playtoyshops.com). Bethnal Green or Mile End tube/277, 388 bus. **Open** 10am-5.30pm Mon-Sat; 11am-4pm Sun. **Credit** MC, V.
This exciting toyshop on two floors always has customers. We certainly blew the Child Benefit when we visited. There's lots for everyone to covet: little girls love the pretty, flower fairy melamine tableware and sparkly glasses, the Lily Dolls downstairs and the range of Pintoy dolls' houses, furniture and people. Everyone wants to cuddle the Gund soft toys and play with the Geomag, Lego, Galt and Playmobil. Downstairs there are books and musical instruments by New Classic Toys. There's a whole range of dressing-up stuff and messy play products (glitter, glue, dough, beads and paints) alongside trinkets by Jellycat and Lucy Lockett and party paperware.
Buggy access. Play area.

Consumer

QT Toys

*90 Northcote Road, Clapham, SW11 6QN (7223 8637).
Clapham Junction rail.* **Open** 9.30am-5.30pm Mon-Sat.
Credit MC, V.
It's a bit of a tight squeeze in here if you're in with a couple of parents with pushchairs. It's not that the shop is small, but the breadth of stock is vast. You can find most stuff at QT, from tacky plastic waterpistols and pocket-money toys, to big brand-name items – Barbie, Bratz, Brio and Lego. Then there's a whole wall crowded with craft kits, modelling toys and stationery, various educational toys, such as a fine times-tables board with little wooden tablets bearing the answers. Gorgeously detailed Schleich animals include farm and safari park livestock, wildlife and cantering horses for knights and soldiers. Small children can find their dollies, buggies, push-along trucks and pull-along dogs; there's stuff for the garden too, such as paddling pools, sandpits, swings and scooters.
Buggy access. Disabled access. Mail order. Nappy-changing facilities. Play area.

Route 73 Kids

*92 Stoke Newington Church Street, Stoke Newington,
N16 0AP (7923 7873/www.route73kids.co.uk).
Finsbury Park tube/rail, then 106 bus/73, 393, 476 bus.*
Open 10am-5.30pm Tue-Sun. **Credit** MC, V.
Take the No.73 bendy to this brightly coloured, personable shop for traditional toys, pocket-money toys, educational toys and various children's favourites that aren't toys. Brio trains and track, Plan wooden toys and Galt marble runs and art equipment are in the first category; items such as

rubber fish, mini pencils, bubbles and mini cars are in the second; books, puzzles, jigsaws and word games make up the third. As for the non-toys, there are Daisy Roots soft leather shoes, Lollipop hair accessories and dear little printed pyjamas in boxes by Bedlam (£20). Route 73 is strong on crafts (face-paints, friendship bracelets, beads, glitter, glue and clay) and, in summer, it stocks outdoor toys, including play sand and sandpit toys.
*Buggy access. Delivery service (local). Disabled access.
Mail order.*

Snap Dragon

*56 Turnham Green Terrace, Chiswick, W4 1QP (8995
6618). Turnham Green tube.* **Open** 9.30am-6pm Mon-Sat; 11am-5pm Sun. **Credit** MC, V.
Playtime looks exceedingly promising at this bright red shop, where dolls like the always pinkly attired Baby Annabell and dolly pushchairs line up against pouty-mouthed Bratz and Smoby sit-and-rides. For imaginative play there are dolls' houses, accessories and figures by Pintoy, as well as sets and scenes from Playmobil. A wide range of family games includes Twister, Buckaroo and the more cerebral Scrabble. Then there are the kits, balls, rockets and remote-control cars for outdoor play.
Buggy access. Delivery service (local). Mail order.

Toy Station

*6 Eton Street, Richmond, Surrey TW9 1EE (8940
4896). Richmond tube/rail.* **Open** 10am-6pm Mon-Fri; 9.30am-6pm Sat; noon-5pm Sun. **Credit** (over £8) MC, V.

Play. *See p209.*

There are so many toys jostling for attention in the window of this old-fashioned, two-storey toyshop that children are saucer-eyed before they even get in. Inside, there's a great display of Schleich and Papo farm animals, wild animals, sea creatures, knights and soldiers. Forts and castles are also stocked – they're bestsellers. Elsewhere, there are Nikko remote-control vehicles (Mini Cooper £24.99); dolls' houses and traditional wooden toys by Pintoy and Plan; dolls, including Baby Annabell; there's a whole load of Playmobil in the basement, along with the fancy dress costumes and accessories, and party equipment.
Buggy access. Disabled access.

Toystop
80-82 St John's Road, Clapham, SW11 1PX (7228 9079). Clapham Junction rail. **Open** *9.30am-6pm Mon-Sat; 11am-5pm Sun.* **Credit** MC, V.
A spacious toyshop that devotes a section to Warhammer sets and accessories, a large wall to Sylvanian Family sets (from £10.99) and plenty of space to Playmobil and Lego. Then there are the dolls, including Bratz and Barbie. Angelina Ballerina also finds favour here. Near the till, a large table is taken up with party-bag-type toys (stretchy smiley men, notebooks, fortune-telling fish, magnetic stones, wobbly ladybirds). There's also a huge sticker tower, outdoor toys, including kites, diablos and stomp rockets, new and classic board games, puzzles, a small selection of books, make-up cases, novelty stationery, mini racing cars, beads, bangles and baubles.
Buggy access.

Word Play
1 Broadway Parade, Crouch End, N8 9TN (8347 6700). Finsbury Park tube/rail, then W7, 41 bus. **Open** *9am-5.30pm Mon-Sat; 11am-5pm Sun.* **Credit** MC, V.
A good half of the display space in this well-loved Crouch End fixture is devoted to children's books. Then there are lots of craft supplies, plus popular building toys such as Bionicles or Geomag at sensible prices. New in are those adorably detailed Schleich toys: little figures such as farm animals, knights and soldiers (£1.99-£6.99) and, for £69.99, a great castle. Little pocket-money dolls (£1.25) are at the high end of the pocket-money spectrum here: a low '£2 and under' table-top is full of penny dreadfuls, devil bangers and fortune-telling fish for 10p.
Buggy access. Disabled access.

Traditional toys

Benjamin Pollock's Toyshop
44 The Market, Covent Garden, WC2E 8RF (7379 7866/www.pollocks-coventgarden.co.uk). Covent Garden tube. **Open** *10.30am-6pm Mon-Sat; 11am-4pm Sun.* **Credit** AmEx, MC, V. **Map** p317 L7.
Cross behind the disused shopfront reading 'Pollock's Theatre', dodge the waffle stand, hike up some steep stairs, and discover a kooky haven. Best known for its toy theatres, Pollock's is a wonderland for young thesps but is hugely enjoyed by all. The most popular paper theatre to assemble is Jackson's (£7.95), with set and characters for the ballet *Cinderella*. The Victorian Gothic version features a nativity play, and there's an Elizabethan one (£8.95) that puts on *A Midsummer Night's Dream*. Other items on sale include marionettes, glove and finger puppets, and music

boxes (£37.50). Quirky pocket-money toys include cardboard masks (£1.40) and pocket compasses (£1.99).
Mail order.

Bob & Blossom
140 Columbia Road, E2 7RG (7739 4737/www.boband blossom.com) Old Street tube/rail/55 bus. **Open** *9am-3pm Sun.* **Credit** MC, V.
Not quite a toy shop, Bob & Blossom is probably best described as a 'children's lifestyle shop' (stop sniggering), with beautiful Danish wooden Noah's Ark sets, those trademark trendy, tiny T-shirts emblazoned with cheeky mottos, Mexican jumping beans and spinning tops – and prices ranging from £1 to £50. For the parents, there are books with titles like *How to Have a Babe and Be a Babe*. Classic toy cars and wooden musical instruments will have us all exclaiming, 'I used to have one of those!' Because the shop is on Columbia Road, owner Kirsten Harris decided to coincide trading hours with the hugely popular Sunday flower market. The shop is doing a roaring trade despite being open just six hours a week.
Buggy access. Mail order.

Compendia Traditional Games
10 The Market, Greenwich, SE10 9HZ (8293 6616/ www.compendia.co.uk). Cutty Sark DLR/Greenwich rail. **Open** *11am-5.30pm daily.* **Credit** MC, V.
The ultimate shop for a rainy day, Compendia has the traditionals – chess, backgammon, dominoes – as well as an appealing range of more obscure games from around the world to suit all ages. If you've had enough Cluedo, check out Champagne Murders (a murder-mystery game for ages eight to adult). Little ones have fun with Coppit – a wobbly hat game – but the drug-smuggling board game Grass is, of course, adults only.
Buggy access. Delivery service. Disabled access. Mail order.

Farmyard
63 Barnes High Street, Barnes, SW13 9LF (8878 7338/www.thefarmyard.co.uk). Barnes or Barnes Bridge rail. **Open** *10am-5.30pm Mon-Fri; 9.30am-5.30pm Sat.* **Credit** MC, V.
Traditional toys and games for newborns to eight-year-olds are corralled into the Farmyard, which has its own personalised range of wooden toys, models and kits. Small children (and this adult) can't resist Pintoy's smartly painted Rolling Slope, which has a range of wooden cars that descend in clicketty-clack fashion – it's mesmerising and costs £59.99 (a smaller, natural wood version is £32.99). There are also quirky imports, such as Uncle Milton's Ant Farm (a £5.99 plastic 'farm' area into which you release your ants and watch them at work), several shelves of fairy/princess stuff, and a wide range of tiny collectibles, such as weeny clay animals (Clay-mates). Dressing up for that all-important party could also prompt a trip here – there's a concise collection of dressing-up clothes.
Buggy access. Delivery service. Play area.
Branch: 54 Friar's Stile Road, Richmond, Surrey TW10 6NQ (8332 0038).

Kristin Baybars
7 Mansfield Road, Gospel Oak, NW3 2JD (7267 0934). Kentish Town tube/Gospel Oak rail/C2, C11 bus. **Open** *11am-6pm Tue-Sat.* **No credit cards.**
This miniaturist's paradise is also a fairytale come true for any child capable of looking without touching. You have

Consumer

to knock to gain entry, but what you'll see inside is the biggest, most jaw-dropping array of tiny scenes and houses outside a craft fair. Show enough interest and decorum, and you'll be ushered into the inner sanctum – room after room of amazing little worlds, including a house full of dogs, a macabre execution scenario and an old-fashioned store for mourning jewellery. The dolls' house kits aren't prohibitively expensive (£70 buys you massive Regency affair), and it's well worth investing a few pounds in tiny accessories; there's plenty at pocket-money prices, though collectors are liable to invest a good deal more.
Buggy access.

Never Never Land

3 Midhurst Parade, Fortis Green, N10 3EJ (8883 3997). East Finchley tube. **Open** 10am-5pm Tue, Wed, Fri, Sat. **Credit** MC, V.
A shop crammed with old-world delight. Best known for its dolls' houses – high-quality structures (from £85) – and individually sold bits and pieces that really do fit together, Never Never Land also sells affordable alternatives, such as conservatories (£20) and shops (£57.50). The owner is adept at sourcing unusual wooden toys (such as dancing musical frogs, £8.99) and also stocks baby-safe toys. There is lots of pocket-money potential here too, in addition to the dolls' house content: bright Russian dolls (£6.99), gorgeous tiny Chinese cloth purses (99p) and colourfully hewn German knights.
Buggy access. Mail order.

Puppet Planet

787 Wandsworth Road (corner of the Chase), Clapham, SW8 3JQ (7627 0111/07785 541 358/www.puppetplanet.co.uk). Clapham Common tube. **Open** 9am-4pm Tue-Sat; regular storytelling on Sun, phone to check. Also open by appointment. **Credit** AmEx, DC, MC, V.
A specialist shop and hospital for tangled marionettes, Puppet Planet is run by Lesley Butler, whose passion for stringed characters extends to her children's party service. Puppets sold include classic Pelham characters, traditional Indian and African marionettes, Balinese shadow puppets, and vintage carved and felt hand-puppets from Germany. Prices go from a couple of quid for a finger puppet to quite a bit more for the more expressive models.
Buggy access. Delivery service. Disabled access. Mail order. Play area.

Rainbow

253 Archway Road, Archway, N6 5BS (8340 9700/ www.rainbow-toys.co.uk). Highgate tube. **Open** 10.30am-5.30pm Mon-Sat. **Credit** MC, V.
The dressing-up costumes here are among the best in town: Spiderman and *Star Wars*, with light sabre, are very popular, as are ballerina outfits and Lucy Lockett fairy dresses. There are lots of quality wooden Pin and Plan Toys, including sit-and-rides and tricycles (£30-£50). There are reasonably priced dolls' houses (£45-£75) and accessories. Orchard Toys – games and puzzles manufactured in the UK and linked to Key Stages in the National Curriculum and Early Learning objectives – are another speciality. Mobiles and paper lampshades got up as hot air balloons (£5.75) hang from the ceiling, and puppets are much in evidence, as are Gund bears. Display counters offer assorted marbles, kids' jewellery and such dolls' house furnishings as tiny plates of food, coat-hangers or books (from 15p).

There's a useful website and a nifty little mail-order business to supplement the treasure-stuffed shop itself.
Buggy access. Delivery service. Mail order. Nappy-changing facilities. Play area.

Soup Dragon

27 Topsfield Parade, Tottenham Lane, Crouch End, N8 8PT (8348 0224/www.soup-dragon.co.uk). Finsbury Park tube/rail, then 41, W7 bus. **Open** 9.30am-6pm Mon-Sat; 11am-5pm Sun. **Credit** MC, V.
Soup Dragon started out as a market stall selling unusual kids' clothing, toys and nursery items. These days there are more nursery products, high chairs, slings, a wide selection of Grobag sleeping bags and some wonderfully colourful baby clothes. The toys are the mainstay, however, with soft toys for babies from La Maze, fancy dress in classic forms like ballerina for girls and king/Native American for boys. Then there are the Groovy Girl dolls (£8.90); pretty dolls' houses (£79 for an impressive Victorian version, £65 for a contemporary house with flat-screened television and glass walls); and a mini-kitchen play area. The community noticeboard is excellent, and bargain hunters may leave an email address to be advised of the bi-monthly warehouse sales. The website has a near-complete list of stock.
Buggy access. Disabled access. Mail order. Play area.
Branch: 106 Lordship Lane, SE22 8HF (8693 5575).

Traditional Toys

53 Godfrey Street, Chelsea, SW3 3SX (7352 1718/ www.traditionaltoy.com). Sloane Square tube, then 11, 19, 22 bus/49 bus. **Open** 10am-5.30pm Mon-Fri; 10am-6pm Sat. **Credit** AmEx, MC, V. **Map** p313 E11.
This terrific little toyshop near Chelsea Green fills every nook and cranny with games, books and toys. There's a wide range of toys at pocket-money prices – such as farm animals, bouncy balls, stickers and toy soldiers, plus painted ride-on toys for the nursery and a bright-red wooden fire engine (£63). Shelves hold Breyer model ponies, Brio train sets, boats, dolls, teddies by Steiff, Gund and the North American Bear Company, sturdy wooden Noah's Arks and much more. Don't miss the fantastic fancy-dress section – sheriffs, knights, elves and fairie –, plus accessories for imaginative games, such as shields, swords, helmets and breastplates, a miniature bow-and-arrows set and hobbyhorses (£45). There's also a catalogue of costumes that may be ordered from the store.
Buggy access.

Tridias

Sheen Road, Richmond (0870 420 8632/www. tridias.co.uk). Richmond tub/raile. **Open** 9.30am-5.30pm Mon-Sat; 11am-4pm Sun. **Credit** MC, V.
Staff could never hope to get the full Tridias range in here, but anything customers need from the extensive catalogue can be ordered. There are shelves stocking intriguing chemistry and science experiment sets (for about £30), but there's also plenty of party equipment. Outdoor toys include croquet, cricket and swingball sets. Otherwise, expect to find a range of dressing-up clothes, Brio, tool kits, marble runs, garages and cars, farms and animals, dolls' houses and accessories, plenty of educational books and board games. Popular items include a stage for puppet shows (£34.99), wizard puppets (£6.99 each) and an ace wooden rocking horse (£759, including delivery). Party stuff includes some lovely decorated tableware and party bag gifts to suit all budgets.
Buggy access. Mail order (0870 443 1300).

Activities

Arts & Entertainment

Get out more! There's inspiration around every corner in this city.

Imagination is key to enjoying the best arts and entertainment in the capital. It's easy to spend a fortune on a trip to your local multiplex, but there's a more sociable – and bargain – option in the form of children's film-club screenings for just a couple of quid at cinemas such as the **Clapham Picturehouse** or the **Ritzy Cinema**. There's even high culture for little ones; the **English National Opera** continues its popular interactive family workshops based around famous operas, for a reasonable £3. Over at the friendly **Jackson's Lane** community centre, innovative classes have included 'Mini Mozart' singalongs for parents and toddlers (£4.50). A number of free options exist too, such as activity packs at art galleries (try the weekend and holiday Art Trolley at **Tate Britain**) or the creative adventures of the **Learning Centre** at Somerset House.

London's handful of venues dedicated to young audiences was augmented in 2005 with the opening of the **Unicorn Theatre For Children**.

Arts Centres

Transformation work continues on the South Bank Centre. The refurbished Royal Festival Hall is due to reopen in June 2007, with a revamped ballroom and foyer, and improved acoustics, seating and technical design in the main auditorium. In the meantime, events are taking place in the **Queen Elizabeth Hall** and **Purcell Room** venues (*see below*). For updates, check www.rfh.org.uk. Over in Camden, the historic Roundhouse and its youth-focused Creative Centre is relaunching in spring 2006.

Barbican Centre

Silk Street, The City, EC2Y 8DS (box office 7638 8891/cinema hotline 7382 7000/arts education programme 7382 2333/www.barbican.org.uk). Barbican tube/Moorgate tube/rail. **Open** *Box office (in person)* 9am-8pm Mon-Sat; noon-8pm Sun, bank hols. *Gallery* 11am-8pm Mon, Wed, Fri, Sat, Sun; 11am-6pm Tue, Thur.* **Admission** Library free. *Exhibitions, films, shows, workshops* phone for details. **Membership** (BarbicanCard) £20/yr. Film Club £7.50/yr/family. **Credit** AmEx, MC, V. **Map** p318 P5.

A well-organised programme of family-oriented events and activities includes the weekly Family Film Club. A diverse mix of international movies is screened for kids aged five to 11 and their parents, with Saturday Special workshops on the last Saturday of every month – booking ahead is generally recommended. Less regularly, the Barbican hosts mini-seasons and events for families, including the annual Animate The World! cartoon-fest in the summer, and the London Children's Film Festival in November. The children's classic concerts enchantingly combine music and storytelling.

Buggy access. Café. Disabled access: lift, toilet. Nappy-changing facilities. Restaurants. Shop.

Queen Elizabeth Hall & Purcell Room

South Bank, SE1 (box office 0870 380 4300/www. rfh.org.uk). Waterloo tube/rail. **Open** *Box office (in person)* 11am-8pm daily. *Foyer* 10am-10.30pm daily. **Admission** prices vary; phone for details. **Credit** AmEx, MC, V. **Map** p317 M8.

Two separate auditoriums in the same riverside building, these South Bank stalwarts have absorbed many of the events that would normally take place in their bigger sibling, the Royal Festival Hall, which is being refurbished. Although these venues have quite a 'serious' feel (the Purcell Room in particular is more of a chamber music venue), their accessible layout and variety of family events mean that young visitors don't miss out – recent programming has included the Chinese State Circus and the Imagine Children's Literature Festival. On occasional weekends, you'll get some great free matinée workshops.

Buggy access. Café. Disabled access: infrared hearing facility, lift, toilet, . Nappy-changing facilities.

Tricycle Theatre & Cinema

269 Kilburn High Road, Kilburn, NW6 7JR (box office 7328 1000/www.tricycle.co.uk). Kilburn tube/ Brondesbury rail. **Open** *Box office* 10am-9pm Mon-Sat; 2-9pm Sun. *Children's shows* 11.30am, 2pm Sat. *Children's films* 1pm Sat. **Tickets** *Theatre* (Sat) £5; £4 advance bookings. *Films* (Sat) £4; £3 under-16s, concessions. **Credit** MC, V.

This is a venue with a real community feel, and the Tricycle's range of children's activities incorporates various after-school classes, covering drama, dance and performance. Half-term and holiday workshops allow kids to get creative with everything from learning street dance to growing a mini-garden. Details can be found on the website, which also lists the regular Saturday film screenings and stage shows.

Buggy access. Disabled access: lift, ramps, toilet. Nappy-changing facilities. Restaurant. Shop.

Art galleries

Many of London's major galleries include free arty activity packs to enhance the experience for young visitors – it's always worth asking about these. Besides the listings below, check Around Town (*pp29-160*) for information on activities in the South Bank's **Tate Modern** (*see p40*) and **Hayward Gallery** (*see p33*), Westminster's **National Gallery** (*see p81*) and **Tate Britain** (*see p82*), the grand **Royal Academy of Arts** in Piccadilly (*see p73*), the **Wallace Collection** in Marylebone (*see p69*), the bijou **Dulwich Picture Gallery** in south-east London (*see p134*), and east London's **Whitechapel Art Gallery** (*see p109*).

Camden Arts Centre

Corner of Arkwright Road and Finchley Road, Camden, NW3 6DG (7472 5500/www.camdenartscentre.org). Finchley Road tube/Finchley Road & Frognal rail. **Open** 10am-6pm Tue, Thur-Sun; 10am-9pm Wed. Closed bank hols. **Admission** free. **Credit** *Shop* MC, V.
Camden Arts Centre's makeover by Tony Fretton Architects has created more light and space in this attractive building while keeping its lovely entrance arches, terrazzo flooring and tall, stone dressed windows. The three new galleries host exhibitions, a state-of-the-art ceramics studio and a busy programme of courses for adults and children. Typically, half-terms feature two-day courses in, say, clay and mixed media for £40 (£24 concessions). Four different term-time courses cater for young people of different age groups. More casually, drop into the excellent café and gardens (*see p173*) for great coffee, sandwiches and snacks.
Buggy access. Café. Disabled access: lifts, toilets. Nappy-changing facilities. Shop.

Learning Centre

Somerset House, Strand, WC2R 0RN (7420 9406/ recorded information 7848 2526/www.courtauld.ac.uk). Covent Garden, Holborn or Temple (closed Sun) tube. **Open** *Gallery* 10am-6pm daily (last entry 5.15pm); noon-6pm 1 Jan; 10am-4pm 31 Dec. *Tours* pre-booked groups only; phone for details. **Admission** *Gallery* £5; £4 concessions; free under-18s, UK students. Free to all 10am-2pm Mon (not bank hols). **Credit** MC, V. **Map** p317 M7.
Somerset House, with its striking courtyard, summer fountain jets and picturesque winter ice rink, comprises three galleries – the Courtauld's fine art collection, the imperial-style Hermitage Rooms and the gem-studded Gilbert Collection. Its Learning Centre has an innovative programme of workshops and events. Free Saturday afternoon workshops run throughout the year, with child-friendly adventures including detective trails and storytelling. One recent session involved creating artwork inspired by the Gilbert Collection's gold treasures – a glittering hit with our eight-year-old artist. On the first Thursday of each month, Art Start classes cater for families with children under five (free). Holiday activities include the likes of printmaking or clay sculpture; a small fee may be charged for materials; booking is essential. Art packs and paper trails are available all year round.
Buggy access. Café. Disabled access: lift, toilet. Nappy-changing facilities. Shop.

Unicorn Theatre for Children. *See p225.*

London International Gallery of Children's Art

O2 Centre, 255 Finchley Road, Finchley, NW3 6LU (7435 0903/www.ligca.org). Finchley Road tube. **Open** 4-6pm Tue-Thur; noon-6pm Fri-Sun. **Admission** free; donations requested. **No credit cards.**
LIGCA celebrates the creativity of children from around the world. Far-reaching exhibitions have ranged from the young talent showcase of Tokyo's Artscape competition, to photographs taken by children from London's ethnic minority communities. Saturday morning art and storytelling workshops cater for five- to 12-year-olds, and cost £5; plans are afoot to resume activities for very young kids. Arty birthday parties can be booked here, including a one-hour session with an art teacher (themes include mobile making and tie-dye). As it is run by volunteers, ringing to confirm opening hours is advised.
Buggy access. Disabled access: lift, toilet. Nappy-changing facilities (O2 Centre).

Orleans House Gallery

Riverside, Twickenham, Middx TW1 3DJ (8831 6000/ www.richmond.gov.uk). St Margaret's or Twickenham rail/33, 490, H22, R68, R70 bus. **Open** *Apr-Sept* 1-5.30pm Tue-Sat; 2-5.30pm Sun, bank hols. *Oct-Mar* 1-4.30pm Tue-Sat; 2-4.30pm Sun, bank hols. **Admission** free; donations appreciated. **Credit** MC, V.
The 18th-century Orleans House is down a secluded riverside path surrounded by acres of woodland, and it resembles a decaying country seat more than a centre for living arts. The collections are less stuffy than you might

imagine, though, and the gallery's Coach House education centre hosts workshops tying in with events such as Black History Month (Oct). There's a similarly upbeat series of year-round activity workshops for kids, with after-school sessions (3.45-5pm Wed, Thur) for five- to nine-year-olds available alongside the Star Club (4-5.15pm Mon), the latter offering those aged seven to ten a place to try their hands (and feet) at dance and drama. Both are £6 per session, and worth booking in advance. For more information, phone to be put on the mailing list.
Buggy access. Disabled access: ramp, toilet. Nappy-changing facilities. Nearest picnic place: Orleans House Gallery grounds, Marble Hill Park or riverside benches. Shop.

Cinemas

The bright lights of Leicester Square are bound to beckon if you're after a blockbuster multiplex blowout – it's home to the West End flagships of **Vue** (0871 224 0240, www.myvue.com) and the **Odeon** (0871 224 4007, www.odeon.co.uk), and to the **Empire** (0870 010 2030). However, it's a pricey experience. If your kids are film fans, the following picture palaces are definitely worth a visit – many offer workshops and special events (*see also p214* **Arts Centres**).

BFI London IMAX

1 Charlie Chaplin Walk, South Bank, SE1 8XR (0870 787 2525/www.bfi.org.uk/imax). Waterloo tube/rail. **Open** 12.30-9.30pm Mon-Fri; 10.30am-9.45pm Sat, Sun. **Admission** £7.90; £4.95 4-15s; £6.50 concessions; ; free under-4s; add-on film £5.50 extra per adult, £3.95 extra per child. **Credit** AmEx, MC, V.
This London landmark houses the biggest cinema screen in the UK – over 20m (65ft) high and 26m (85ft) wide. Kids enjoy wearing 3D glasses to watch special IMAX films such as *Deep Sea* or *Haunted Castle* – here, storylines are secondary to the fantastic effects that seem to leap from the screen, this could be a bit intense for very young viewers. During the summer, mainstream films are shown here (though rarely in 3D); *Superman Returns* gets the IMAX treatment in 2006, and, from August, *The Ant Bully*. Christmas brings festive entertainment, such as 3D screenings of *The Polar Express* – ticket prices for these special events are usually higher.
Buggy access. Café. Disabled access: lift, toilets. Nappy-changing facilities.

Clapham Picturehouse

76 Venn Street, Clapham, SW4 0AT (0870 755 0061/ www.picturehouses.co.uk). Clapham Common tube/35, 37 bus. **Open** *Box office* (phone bookings) 9.30am-8.30pm daily. *Film club* activities 11.15am, screening 11.45am Sat. **Tickets** £3; members £2. **Membership** £4/yr. **Credit** MC, V.
Kids' film clubs and parent-and-baby screenings were pioneered at this stylish cinema. Parents with infants under one year can bring the babies to the long-running Big Scream! club at 10.30am every Thursday. Park prams in the bar, and watch a movie from an updated roster of blockbuster and art-house films without having to worry about disturbing the audience. Meanwhile, the Kids' Club offers

Saturday matinées for three- to ten-year-olds. Staff organise craft and activity workshops before the show and prize competitions afterwards. Young members also have the opportunity to go into the projection room and start the film on their birthday.
Buggy access. Café. Disabled access: toilet (Screens 3 & 4 only). Nappy-changing facilities.

Electric Cinema

191 Portobello Road, Notting Hill, W11 2ED (7908 9696/www.electrichouse.com). Ladbroke Grove or Notting Hill Gate tube/52 bus. **Open** *Box office* 9am-8.30pm Mon-Sat; 10am-8.30pm Sun. *Children's screenings* 11am, 1pm Sat (depending on film length; call to check). **Tickets** £4.50 (all ages). *Workshops* £2.50. **Credit** AmEx, MC, V. **Map** p310 A7.
With its film-star looks (red leather armchairs, wall friezes and a sumptuous bar), this is one of London's most exclusive cinemas. For membership, you must apply in writing, be accepted by a committee made up of local residents and businessmen, and then pay up to £250 per year. One perk is that members receive two free tickets for every Kids' Club screening. These show classic films and preview new releases, with occasional arts activities. Parents and their babies (up to one year) can enjoy special Electric Scream! screenings on Mondays and Tuesdays at 3pm (except bank holidays).
Buggy access. Disabled access: lift, toilet. Kiosk.

Gate Cinema

87 Notting Hill Gate, W11 3JZ (0870 755 0063/ www.picturehouses.co.uk) Notting Hill Gate tube. **Open** *Box Office* 11am-8.30pm daily *Children's screenings* 11.30am Sat. **Tickets** £4; £3 members. **Membership** £4/yr. **Credit** AmEx, MC, V.
The Gate runs a Saturday Kids' Club with pre-screening activities. Games like pin the tail on the donkey begin at 11am; screenings start at 11.30am.
Buggy access. Kiosk.

Greenwich Picturehouse

180 Greenwich High Road, SE10 8NN (8853 0484/ www.picturehouses.org.uk). Cutty Sark DLR. **Open** *Box Office* 11am-10pm daily. *Kids' Club screenings* 11.30am Sat. *Membership* £4.50/yr. **Tickets** £3 members; £4.50 non-members, adults. **Credit** MC, V.
The Greenwich Picturehouse, a four screener with tapas bar attached, opened in September 2005. Part of the reliably right-on Picturehouse group, the Greenwich branch has a children's club (doors open at 11am on Saturday for an 11.30am start) and a Big Scream! for parents and babies on Fridays at 11.30am.
Buggy access. Café. Disabled: lift, toilet. Kiosk. Nappy-changing facilities.

Movie Magic at the NFT

National Film Theatre, South Bank, SE1 8XT (box office 7928 3232/www.bfi.org.uk/moviemagic). Waterloo tube/rail. **Open** *Box office* phone bookings 11.30am-8.30pm daily. Personal callers 5-8.30pm Mon-Thur; 11.30am-8.30pm Fri-Sun. *Film club* times vary; usually Sat, Sun, school hols. **Tickets** *Children* £1 film, £5.50 workshop & film. Prices vary, phone to confirm. *Adults* £7.20 members, £8.20 non-members. **Membership** £29.95/yr. **Credit** AmEx, MC, V. **Map** p317 M8.

families
Have great days out at Tate

A visit to Tate is child's play...

There's loads to do for **FREE** at Tate Britain – from terrific trails and imaginative activities on the *Art Trolley*, sponsored by Tate & Lyle, to creative workshops and special holiday events. The BP British Art Displays are also free and there are reduced price family tickets to all major exhibitions.

Sign up for free families email bulletins to find out more: www.tate.org.uk/bulletins

Tate Britain
Millbank
London SW1P 4RG
⊖ Pimlico or Vauxhall
⇌ Vauxhall
🚢 Millbank Pier

Open daily 10.00–17.50
Open first Friday of every month until 22.00
Closed 24–26 December

Call 020 7887 8888
www.tate.org.uk/families

BP British Art Displays 1500–2006

bp
Supported by BP

Photo: Richard Eaton

Drama for development

'Don't put your daughter on the stage, Mrs Worthington,' sang Noel Coward. 'The profession is overcrowded/The struggle's pretty tough.' Sounds like sage advice – but these days, there is an alternative to stage-school stereotypes of pushy parents and their precocious progeny. London has an established clutch of drama courses where the spotlight is on creative play – and the aim is expressly to encourage confidence and self-esteem in young students.

One of the first such schools to launch in Britain was **Allsorts** (*see p228*) set up by actresses Melissa Healy and Sasha Leslie in 1992. Allsorts classes bring role-playing and improvisation, rather than song and dance routines, to the fore; props are also kept to a minimum, to encourage young imaginations to run free.

'We don't tend to get show-off children; many kids are very shy but still love performing,' explains Melissa. 'When we put on a performance, it's about what the children have created with our guidance – this week, the little ones are doing colours; for instance, they'll do a yellow adventure, maybe ride on a cloud and go to the sun.

'It's not a snazzy show, and we rarely use something that's already been written. Work with the older kids might broach subjects like bullying, although we're not claiming to be psychologists; it's more of an outlet for expression. Parents are welcome to come in, but it's usually a work in progress.'

While group sizes are kept small, Allsorts has around 300 students overall, taking part in activities from school workshops to private classes on Fridays and Saturdays, with a fairly broad age range, from four to 16. 'We've got one girl who started at five and stayed with us; she's 16 now. We've even got some 17–year-olds who are still hanging in there!' Clearly they're having too much fun to leave.

For even younger children, **Perform** (*see p231*) was founded in 2000 and concentrates on encouraging the natural potential of four- to eight-year-olds, with workshops encompassing 'Move and Feel', 'Listen, Speak and Sing' and 'Create and Imagine' sections. For even tinier talents, there's the recently launched 'Mini Ps' classes, which cater for 'Crawlers, Walkers and Talkers' from six months upwards.

The aforementioned schools run classes across the capital, but **Helen O'Grady's Academy** (*see p228*), created by a Perth-based drama teacher, seems globally prolific. It opened its first UK school in Croydon in 1994; there are now several in the capital, 47 UK branches overall, not to mention franchises from Malta to Dubai. There's no written work for its students (ranging from five to 17) and no star system – just an emphasis on high-energy activities and kids together onstage.

'We run a self-development programme for children, and it's geared to be great fun, too,' explains Nigel Le Page, the Academy's UK director. 'It's inevitable that many of our children will be approached by stage and TV companies, but it's not something that we actively encourage. All of the skills they've learned – looking people in the eye, feeling good about themselves – are useful, whatever they decide to do in life.'

These classes certainly aren't a budget option – signing up for consecutive sessions could stretch to hundreds of pounds, although Allsorts and Perform do offer free trial classes – but enthusiasts see them as a neatly structured investment. Your children may not get to see their names in lights, but they'll feel like little stars all the same.

For a list of Performance Workshops, *see p228*.

Movie Magic is the NFT's programme of films for children under 16. Sometimes the movies are classics of yesteryear, so nostalgic parents might want to tag along. At other times, there are previews of the new film of the moment. Accompanying workshops cover innovative themes, such as Claymation techniques, and are usually aimed at seven- to 12-year-olds. Booking in advance is recommended. From autumn 2006, the NFT building will undergo renovation; the main cinema spaces will remain intact, with promised additions including archive viewing stations, a Filmstore and gallery space. *Buggy access. Café. Disabled access: ramp, toilet. Nappy-changing facilities.*

Rio Cinema

103-107 Kingsland High Street, Dalston, E8 2PB (7241 9410/www.riocinema.co.uk). Dalston Kingsland rail/Liverpool Street tube/rail, then 67, 77, 149 bus. **Open** *Box office 2-9pm daily. Film club 4.15pm Tue (term-time only); 11am Sat.* **Tickets** *£2; £1 under-15s.* **Credit** *AmEx, MC, V.*

The Rio is a fun, friendly place where children can watch a mixture of mainstream and alternative entertainment. The Kids' Club intersperses the latest blockbusters with occasional classics. Membership is free, and comes with a card that's stamped on each visit; children get a free visit after ten stamps. Kids under five must be accompanied. A parent-and-baby club (under-ones only) operates on Tuesdays and Thursdays at lunchtime; it costs £5 (£4 concessions). *Café. Disabled access: toilet.*

Ritzy Cinema

Brixton Oval, Coldharbour Lane, Brixton, SW2 1JG (0870 755 0062/www.ritzycinema.co.uk). Brixton tube/rail. **Open** *Box office 10.15am-9.30pm daily. Film club 10.30am Sat.* **Tickets** *£3; £1 under-14s.* **Credit** *MC, V.* Opened in 1911 as one of the UK's first purpose-built cinemas, the Ritzy has survived various owners, near demolition and significant development in the 1990s to become one of London's finest. Tender age is no restriction to enjoying its delights: two Kids' Club films are shown

every Saturday – the first aimed at under-sevens, the second at over-sevens. During school holidays the club also operates on Tuesdays and Thursdays, with related activity sessions, competitions and special events often set up at short notice. The Ritzy also has a programme of Watch with Baby matinées, on Fridays at 11am, open to parents with under-ones only. Membership costs £1 (tickets £4); bottle-warming and pushchair-parking facilities are provided, and after the film, parents can mingle in the bar with complimentary tea or coffee.
Buggy access. Café. Disabled access: lift, toilet. Nappy-changing facilities.

Stratford Picturehouse
Theatre Square, Stratford, E15 1BX (8522 0043/ www.picturehouses.co.uk). Stratford tube/rail/DLR. **Open** *Box office* Phone bookings 9am-9pm daily. *Film club* 10.30am Sat. **Tickets** £2 members; £3 non-members. **Membership** £4/yr. **Credit** MC, V.
The eastern wing of the Picture House family, Stratford has plenty of attractions for families and children, including a film club with creative activities, fun and games that take place after a screening. The club is suitable for three-to ten-year-olds and costs £4 a year to join, with film tickets costing £2. Kids' Club membership entitles you to the 1st film free. Members receive a quarterly newsletter and the chance to enter competitions, win prizes, and start the film on their birthday. The sanity-saving Big Scream, for parents who can't escape their babies, takes place on Tuesdays at 10.30am (£4; no membership fee).
Buggy access. Café. Disabled access: ramps, lifts, toilets. Nappy-changing facilities.

Music venues

English National Opera
The Coliseum, St Martin's Lane, Covent Garden, WC2N 4ES (education 7632 8484/box office 7632 8300/www.eno.org). Leicester Square tube. **Open** *Box office* 10am-8pm Mon-Sat. **Tickets** £15-£82. **Credit** AmEx, DC, MC, V. **Map** p315 L7.
This bastion of high culture has earned a reputation for sparky accessibility – thanks in part to the enjoyable Family Days run by its ENO Baylis department, and its dedicated Clore Education Room. Workshops offer kids aged seven and above, their families and carers, a chance to explore the ENO's current production for just £3 each. Family opera packages are available separately for the matinée performance afterwards. A free crèche is provided for under-sevens, subject to availability. ENO Baylis also runs courses for different age groups, including Saturday Live! workshops for seven- to 18-year-olds at St Marylebone School in central London (7935 9501); check the ENO website for full details.
Disabled access: ramp, toilet.

Roundhouse
Chalk Farm Road, NW1 8EH (7424 9991/Box office 0870 389 1846/www.roundhouse.org.uk). Chalk Farm tube. **Open** *Box office* 11am-6pm Mon-Sat. **Tickets** £10-£25. **Credit** MC, V.
In the 1960s, this former engine shed became legendary for concerts by the likes of Led Zeppelin and Jimi Hendrix. It has been refurbished and reopens as north London's biggest performance venue in June 2006, with the Aargentinian avant-garde spectacle 'Fuerzabruta' in the

Main Space (not suitable for under-12s) and 'The Foolish Young Man' in Studio 42. While not all of the shows staged will be for families, creative opportunities for young people lie at the heart of the project. The Roundhouse Studios for 13 to 25-year-olds will give up to 10,000 young people a year access to the new facilities, including music, TV and media, with advice and mentoring from artist tutors and creative professionals. For information about programmes and events, visit the website.
Café. Disabled access: ramp, toilet. Nappy-changing facilities. Restaurant. Shop.

Royal Albert Hall
Kensington Gore, South Kensington, SW7 2AP (7589 8212/www.royalalberthall.com). South Kensington tube. **Open** *Box office* 9am-9pm daily. **Tickets** £5-£150. **Credit** AmEx, MC, V. **Map** p313 D9.
This splendid rotunda venue hosts the BBC Proms from July to September each year. Two annual Blue Peter Proms and the outdoor Proms In The Park extend this classical music extravaganza to younger audiences. There's a smart education department, with projects levelled at children and local students. Family-friendly entertainment here has included *The War Of The Worlds* musical. Forthcoming programming was due to be announced as we went to press; check the website for details.
Buggy access. Café. Disabled access: lift, ramp, toilet. Nappy-changing facilities. Restaurant (booking necessary). Shop.

Royal College of Music
Prince Consort Road, South Kensington, SW7 2BS (7589 3643/www.rcm.ac.uk). South Kensington tube/ 9, 10, 52 bus. **Map** p313 D9.
The RCM'S junior tuition is tailored to students 'of an exceptionally high standard'. If that doesn't deter you, applications (for children aged eight to 17) are by audition and are, of course, heavily oversubscribed. Lessons – which run in conjunction with the school term (8am-5pm Sat) – focus almost exclusively on classical instruments. Families are perhaps best off keeping an eye on the programme of (usually free) performances staged by pupils throughout the year.
Café. Disabled access: lift, toilet.

Wigmore Hall
36 Wigmore Street, Marylebone, W1U 2BP (7935 2141/education 7258 8240/www.wigmore-hall.org.uk). Bond Street or Oxford Circus tube. **Open** *Box office* 10am-7pm Mon-Sat; 10.30am-6.30pm Sun. **Tickets** £10-£25. **Credit** AmEx, DC, MC, V. **Map** p314 H5.
This art deco recital hall has endured a great deal over the years, not least two world wars. Thankfully, the interior remains virtually unaltered, with marble, warm wood panelling and plush red seating. Performances are classical, but regular young fiddlers' days introduce violinists from Grade 2 upwards to playing folk fiddle (ages 12-18, £10). There's also a programme of family events, starting with the sadly oversubscribed Chamber Tots music and movement classes for two- to five-year-olds (£6 children, adults free; maximum of three sessions per child). For children five and over, there are two family concerts each term (£3 children, £6 adults). Themed family days such as 'Mozart Magic', with storytelling and the chance to compose personalised minuets, are highly praised.
Buggy access. Disabled access: toilet. Nappy-changing facilities. Restaurant.

Drama classes and Holiday Courses
for ages 4-16

Held in Fulham, Kensington,
Hampstead & Queens Park

For a free trial class or
information pack

t: 020 8969 3249 / 020 8871 4987

e: info@allsortsdrama.com
w: www.allsortsdrama.com

Eddie Catz

CHILDREN'S EDUTAINMENT CENTRE

For kids 0-10

Playframe • Interative video games • Air hockey
Dance, music and fun classes for all ages
Baby massage • Kiddie Rides • Kids' parties
Holiday camps • Café restaurant
TV lounge • Internet access & WiFi • Fully air-conditioned

Open 7 days a week

1st Floor, 68-70 Putney High Street, SW15 1SF
Tel 0845 201 1268 www.eddiecatz.com

THE INTERNATIONAL SMASH HIT!

STOMP

'IDEAL FOR KIDS'

SUNDAY TELEGRAPH

VAUDEVILLE THEATRE
0870 890 0511

The Strand, London WC2

MATINEES THUR, SAT AND SUN AT 3PM

Theatre

Puppets

Little Angel Theatre

14 Dagmar Passage, off Cross Street, Islington, N1 2DN (7226 1787/www.littleangeltheatre.com). Angel tube/Highbury & Islington tube/rail, then 4, 19, 30, 43 bus. **Open** *Box office* 10am-6pm Mon-Fri; 9.30am-4.30pm Sat, Sun. **Tickets** £7.50-£8.50; £5-£6 under-16s. **Credit** MC, V.

Established in 1961, the Little Angel remains London's only permanent puppet theatre. Performances offer a spin on classics, such as *Sleeping Beauty In The Wood*, as well as multicultural folk tales, involving just about every kind of puppet under the sun. Most productions are aimed at audiences aged five and over, with occasional adaptations for very young audiences. A Saturday Puppet Club runs over ten weeks, in conjunction with most major productions (£70, £50 concessions); these are for kids only, so parents must wait for one of the family fun days (during school holidays) for their chance to play with the puppets. *Buggy access. Disabled access: ramps, toilet. Kiosk. Nappy-changing facilities. Shop.*

Puppet Theatre Barge

Opposite 35 Blomfield Road, Little Venice, W9 2PF (7249 6876/www.puppetbarge.com). Warwick Avenue tube. **Open** *Box office* 10am-8pm daily. *Children's shows* term-time Sat, Sun; school hols daily. Phone for times. **Tickets** £7.50; £7 under-16s, concessions. **Credit** MC, V.

One of the capital's most enchanting assets, the Puppet Theatre Barge's combination of puppet shows – courtesy of Movingstage Productions – and unusual location is unique. Small and cosy (there are just 50 seats), the barge is moored on the scenic towpath in Little Venice between November and June, with a variety of performances held on Saturday and Sunday afternoons (3pm), and more frequent daytime and evening slots during school holidays. Between July and October, the barge floats off on a summer tour of the Thames, stopping off to perform at picturesque riverside towns (Henley, Clifton, Marlow and Richmond). During this period, children's shows take place at 2.30pm and 4.30pm.

Touring companies

These London-based theatre companies are specialists in children's performances and tour all over the country. Their work is innovative, exciting and enchanting. Check their websites for more tour details.

Kazzum

7539 3500/www.kazzum.org.

Since its inception in 1989, Peter Glanville's Kazzum collective has toured schools, theatres, libraries, parks and festivals with diverse projects; including works aimed at under-sixes, reworkings of international classics, and interactive installations for under-11s. As well as educational programmes and residencies, it runs Pathways, a programme of work relating to the experiences of refugee children. Upcoming productions include an update of the South Asian epic *The Ramayana* (from Sept 2006), and a UV/Black Light Theatre puppetry show (May 2007).

Oily Cart

8672 6329/www.oilycart.org.uk.

Oily Cart's forte is brilliantly innovative, multi-sensory productions conceived to fire the imaginations of two theatrically excluded groups – very young children and children with special needs. The company's work has developed into a truly interactive art form, utilising large multi-sensory spaces or 'wonderlands', where groups of children can not only watch, but also become part of the performance. *Hippety Hop* was the first-ever hip hop musical for the under-fives. Other shows have included acrobats, a soft play maze and a world made of paper.

Pop-Up Theatre

7609 3339/www.pop-up.net.

Founded in 1982, the pioneering Pop-Up has made a name for itself creating multi-media theatre for audiences aged under 11. Development projects include Dramatic Links workshops (held at the Robert Blair School in north London), where writers collaborate with schoolchildren to produce relevant scripts. Pop-Up's Equal Voice interactive theatre sessions tour schools, opening up the art form for kids from all backgrounds. The company's portable Offstreet stage allows certain shows to take place on any flat six-square-metre space.

Quicksilver Theatre

7241 2942/www.quicksilvertheatre.org.

Producing and performing new plays across Britain, Quicksilver aims to give children a positive introduction to theatre. Over 25 years, this collective has developed a rapport with young crowds. Its long-running touring production *Teddy in the Rucksack* (ages three to five) gets a child from the audience to star in the final act.

Theatre Centre

7729 3066/www.theatre-centre.co.uk.

Founded in 1953 by the late Brian Way, a pioneering director, educator and writer, Theatre Centre works internationally, in schools, colleges, theatres, arts centres and community spaces. The company has not only secured a reputation for on-stage excellence and technical invention, but also champions more challenging writing; books of plays can be purchased online. In 2006, Theatre Centre's production for over sevens in collaboration with the Unicorn Theatre – *Journey to the River Sea* – earned rave reviews from *The Guardian* and *Time Out*. Future tours were being developed as we went to press; check the website for further details.

theatre-rites

c/o Battersea Arts Centre, Lavender Hill, SW11 5TN (7228 0504/www.theatre-rites.co.uk).

Theatre-rites, with puppet supremo Sue Buckmaster as artistic director and visionary installation artist Sophia Clist as associate artist, is a unique, creative and exciting company; its shows feed young children's imagination and stick in their memory. A reputation for site-specific work was cemented by 1996's astounding *Houseworks*, which took place in a Brixton home. Since then there have been *Millworks*, *Cellarworks*, *Shopworks* and *Hospitalworks*, various installations and some delightful smaller-scale touring shows, such as the bumptiously musical *In One Ear* tour, still on the performance circuit through the first half of 2006. In 2007 there will be a tour of *The Thought That Counts* show for four-to-seven-year olds.

Activities

Venues

London's few dedicated children's theatres are a treat for young audiences. However, most of the places below are mainstream adult venues that regularly schedule family-friendly shows (usually with additional performances during the school holidays). *See also p219* **The Roundhouse**.

The Albany

Douglas Way, Deptford, SE8 4AG (8692 4446/ www.thealbany.org.uk). Deptford rail/bus 21, 36, 47, 136, 171, 177, 188, 225. **Open** *Box office* 9am-9pm Mon-Fri; 10am-5pm Sat. **Tickets** *Family Sunday* £5; £3 under-16s, concessions. **Credit** MC, V.
Serving the community of Deptford since the late 19th century, this now multi media arts centre retains a lively neighbourhood focus, and its regular Family Sunday brunch performances (from noon) entertain children with specially written musical plays, while the oldsters can relax with the Sunday papers and 'sweet sounds'.
Buggy access. Café. Disabled access: lift, ramp, toilet. Nappy-changing facilities.

artsdepot

5 Nether Street, North Finchley, N12 0GA (8369 5454/ www.artsdepot.co.uk). Finchley Central or Woodside Park tube. **Open** *Box office* 10am-5.30pm Mon-Sat; noon-5.30pm Sun (later during shows). **Tickets** free-£15. **Credit** MC, V.
The stylish artsdepot houses the 400-seat Pentland Theatre. However, most children's performances take place in the smaller 150-seat studio – shows run on Sundays at 3pm – while the foyer and public spaces are used for seasonal specials. A comprehensive learning programme involves all ages from one-year-olds to adults, and has courses ranging from drama to visual arts. Customising For Kids is a fashionable new option for eight- to ten-year-olds; the Depot Youth Theatre also puts on regular performances.
Buggy access. Café. Disabled access: lift, ramp, toilet. Nappy-changing facilities.

BAC (Battersea Arts Centre)

Lavender Hill, Battersea, SW11 5TN (7223 2223/ Puppet Centre 7228 5335/www.bac.org.uk). Clapham Common tube, then 345 bus/Clapham Junction rail/77, 77A, 156 bus. **Open** *Box office* 10.30am-6pm Mon-Fri; 4-6pm Sat, Sun. *Puppet Centre* 2-6pm Mon, Wed, Sat. **Tickets** £3.50-£6.50. **Membership** suggested discretionary donation of £30 or £150. **Credit** AmEx, MC, V.
Interactive innovation and a distinctly enthusiastic spirit have set the respected BAC apart, belying the fact that this institution (nominated for a *Time Out* Live Award in 2005-6) has long been strapped for cash. BAC's popular Scratch workshops allow writers to test projects in progress and develop them with audience participation; the infamous *Jerry Springer The Opera* was developed here, so you could be helping with a future West End smash. Young drama queens (and kings) can take part in the (oversubscribed) Young People's Theatre groups, which take kids from the age of 12 and work towards an end-of-term performance (Wed evenings; £45 per term, £30 concessions).
Buggy access. Café. Disabled access: lift, toilet. Nappy-changing facilities.

Broadway Theatre

Catford Broadway, Catford, SE6 4RU (8690 3428/ www.lewishamyouththeatre.com). Catford or Catford Bridge rail/75, 181, 185, 202, 660 bus. **Open** *Box office* 10am-6pm Mon-Sat. **Tickets** £3.50-£22. **Credit** AmEx, MC, V.
Home to the Lewisham Youth Theatre Group (see **Performance Workshops**, *p228*), this listed art deco building is scruffy Catford's pride and joy. Children's shows often take place on Saturday mornings in the intimate 100-seater studio, although the main auditorium (400 seats) has been used for family entertainment such as the spooktacular musical *Rentaghost* and pantos. There are also film screenings on 'dark' nights between shows – compensating just a little for the fact that Lewisham is devoid of cinemas, a shocking state of affairs in our book.
Buggy access. Café. Disabled access: lift, toilet. Nappy-changing facilities.

Chicken Shed Theatre

Chase Side, Southgate, N14 4PE (8292 9222/www. chickenshed.org.uk). Cockfosters or Oakwood tube. **Open** *Box office* 10am-6pm Mon-Fri; 10am-5pm Sat. **Tickets** *Workshops* £5/hr; £3.50/hr under-16s. **Shows** £4-£18.50. **Credit** MC, V.
Chicken Shed was founded in 1974, on the premise that performing arts belong to everyone who wants to join in. This inclusive policy has currently attracted around 700 members of every background. The resulting productions are among London's liveliest, with political dramas like *Globaleyes* programmed alongside Shakespeare. There are groups for the young, so there's nothing to deter little stars except the waiting lists. Performances take place in one of four creative spaces, including an outdoor amphitheatre during the summer. Chicken Shed's hallmark is the communication between age groups: toddlers act alongside adults, and everyone mucks in for the Christmas show.
Buggy access. Café. Disabled access: lift, toilets. Nappy-changing facilities. Restaurant. Shop.

Colour House Children's Theatre

Merton Abbey Mills, Watermill Way, Merton, SW19 2RD (box office 8640 5111/www.wheelhouse.org.uk). Colliers Wood tube. **Open** *Box office* 10am-5pm daily; 1hr before show. **Shows** 2pm, 4pm Sat, Sun. **Tickets** £7. **No credit cards**.
Tucked in the midst of Abbey Mills' weekend craft market, this bijou riverside venue regularly lends a zany twist to fairytale classics such as *Pinocchio*; our only problem has been the uncomfortable seating. After-show birthday parties with a mini disco can also be arranged.
Buggy access. Disabled access: toilet. Nappy-changing facilities (in Merton Abbey Mills). Shop.

The Edward Alleyn Theatre

Dulwich College, Dulwich Common, SE21 7LD (8299 9232/www.dulwich.org.uk/drama). West Dulwich rail/ Brixton tube/rail, then 3, P4, P13 bus. Box office around performance times only. **Tickets** £5-£6; £3.50-£4 under-16s, concessions. **No credit cards**.
This 250-seat theatre hosts child-friendly performances throughout the year. The Edward Alleyn also runs theatre schools over Easter, the summer holidays and October half-terms: two separate classes cater for seven- to 11-year-olds and 12- to 16-year-olds; ring for full details.
Buggy access. Disabled access: toilets.

Spit, spot! Or things will get nasty! **Mary Poppins**. *See p228.*

Hackney Empire

291 Mare Street, Hackney, E8 1EJ (8510 4500/box office 8985 2424/www.hackneyempire.co.uk). Hackney Central rail/38, 106, 253, 277, D6 bus. **Open** *Box office* 10am-6pm Mon-Sat; 1hr before show on Sun. **Tours** 1st Sat of mth; phone for times. **Tickets** prices vary, phone for details. *Tours* £5; £4 concessions. **Credit** MC, V.

This East End variety theatre dates back to 1901 – Charlie Chaplin performed here – and was saved from demolition in the 1980s and revamped in 2004. Shows take in comedy to orchestral works, while the education programme includes workshops run by professionals as well as the Artist Development Programme for 40 east Londoners aged 12 to 16. Saturday workshops for seven- to ten-year-olds and 11- to 16-year-olds cover acting to MC-ing.
Buggy access. Disabled access: toilet. Nappy-changing facilities.

Half Moon Young People's Theatre

43 White Horse Road, Stepney, E1 0ND (7709 8900/ www.halfmoon.org.uk). Limehouse DLR/rail. **Open** *Box office* 10am-6pm Mon-Fri; 9am-4pm Sat. **Tickets** £4. **Credit** MC, V.

The Half Moon is a bastion of creativity, encouraging participants regardless of race, gender, ability or financial situation – an estimated 32,000 individuals take part in its activities. The fully accessible theatre has an annual calendar of performances for kids from birth right up to 17 years. Children can join one of eight youth theatre groups, which meet weekly during term-time (£3 per session, £1.50 concessions), working towards a final show. The aim is to improve self-expression and confidence. Committed participants often filter into the larger productions.
Buggy access. Disabled access: ramps, lifts, toilets. Nappy-changing facilities.

Jackson's Lane

269A Archway Road, Highgate, N6 5AA (box office 8341 4421/administration 8340 5226/www.jacksons lane.org.uk). Highgate tube. **Open** *Box office* 10am-10pm daily. **Tickets** £4.75. **Credit** MC, V.

This arts centre housed in an old church crams in around 60 activities a week. These range from an after-school club for five- to 11-year-olds (3.30-6pm Mon-Fri; £7 per session) to off-the-cuff sessions with visiting groups like Kaos! Organisation, and include everything from ballet to street dance and martial arts to trapeze. Prices vary: an 11-week performance course, Crazee Kids, might cost £88, while a Mini Mozart singalong for babies and toddlers is just £4.50. All events are oversubscribed, so phone in advance. There's a family treat every weekend during termtime (occasional weekdays during school holidays).
Buggy access. Café. Disabled access: ramps, toilet. Nappy-changing facilities.

Activities

Activities

Lauderdale House

*Highgate Hill, Waterlow Park, Highgate, N6 5HG
(8348 8716/www.lauderdale.org.uk). Archway tube,
then 143, 210, 271, W5 bus.* **Open** *Box office* 30mins
before performance; advance bookings not accepted.
Tickets £4.50; £3 concessions. **No credit cards.**
This rustic manor-house-turned-arts-centre backs on to
picturesque Waterlow Park. Its programme includes dance
and drama courses; the junior versions cater for kids aged
three and upwards, as do most of the drawing, painting
and music workshops. Saturday matinées feature
puppetry, music and magic from professional touring
companies; school holidays inspire various family days,
including the annual spooky Hallowe'en Walk and the Jazz
in the Park festival for cool dudes.
Buggy access. Café. Disabled access: toilet.

Lyric Hammersmith Theatre

*Lyric Square, King Street, Hammersmith, W6 0QL
(0870 050 0511/www.lyric.co.uk). Hammersmith tube.*
Open *Box office* 9.30am-7pm Mon-Sat (until 8pm on
performance days). **Tickets** £12-£25 adults; £6 under-
16s concessions, students; £6 16-25s (restrictions
apply). **Credit** MC, V.
Within the Lyric's glassy modern façade, you'll find an
antique auditorium – a Victorian proscenium-arch
playhouse, no less. But despite this historical aesthetic, the
Lyric remains one of London's most future-focused
theatres in terms of children's programming, particularly
embracing cutting-edge companies like Oily Cart (*see
p221*). Lyric Studio, a one-hundred seater black box space
is home to the mix – a boundary busting collection of
companies and artists who are making their new pieces of
work with the Lyric. Some of that work goes public; some
of it doesn't, but there's a packed programme of readings,
works in progress and performances, and a chance to
experience the work of the next generation of theatre
makers and hear voices that are rarely heard in the theatrical mainstream. Most childrens' events also take place
in this purpose-built studio, and many are produced in
conjunction with schools. Café Brera provides an airy,
child-friendly pit stop, with seats outside. Check the
website for regular updates of the Lyric's workshops,
which range from pre-performance activities and holiday
courses to START training schemes, which pair teenagers
interested in performing arts with young adult mentors in
fields as varied as choreography and rapping.
*Buggy access. Café. Disabled access: lift, toilet. Nappy-
changing facilities.*

Nettlefold Theatre

*West Norwood Library, 1 Norwood High Street, West
Norwood, SE27 9JX (7926 8070/www.lambeth.gov.uk).
West Norwood rail/2, 68, 196, 468 bus.* **Open** *Box
office* 9am-9pm Mon-Fri; 9.30am-6pm Sat. **Tickets**
£3.50. **Credit** (advance only) MC, V.
A 200-seat theatre built into West Norwood Library that
runs one child-orientated show per month (usually on a
Saturday). More regularly, the energetic Bigfoot Theatre
Company (0870 011 4307, www.bigfoot-theatre.co.uk) runs
drama, singing, and dance and movement classes here for
eight-year-olds and over; they take place between 10am
and noon every Saturday during termtime, with half-term
and school-holiday activities organised on an ad hoc basis.
*Buggy access. Disabled access: lift, toilet. Nappy-
changing facilities.*

The classy Portobello-based **Electric Cinema**. *See p216.*

New Wimbledon Theatre

*The Broadway, Wimbledon, SW19 1QG (0870 060
6646/www.theambassadors.com/newwimbledon).
Wimbledon tube/rail.* **Open** *Box office* 10am-6pm Mon-
Sat (until 8pm performance days); 10am-5.30pm Sun.
Credit AmEx, MC, V.
A glimmer of the West End on a suburban high street, the
New Wimbledon Theatre presents a steady flow of tour-
ing hits. Highlights in 2006 so far have had a family-friend-
ly slant, from the Disney musical *Beauty and the Beast* to
Edward Scissorhands. A number of shows specifically for
kids are programmed throughout the year, and the end-of-
year panto is a jolly jape.
Disabled access: lift, toilet. Shop.

Open Air Theatre

*Inner Circle, Regent's Park, Marylebone, NW1 4NU
(box office 0870 060 1811/www.openairtheatre.org).
Baker Street tube.* **Tickets** £8-£32.50; £15 under-16s.
Credit AmEx, MC, V. **Map** p314 G3.
Shakespeare is the thing at this lovely open-air venue,
where whispering trees surround the stage and where, in
2006, children might enjoy the lighter musical confection
of *The Boyfriend* (18 July-9 September). The production of
Babe The Sheep-Pig, based on Dick King-Smith's classic
story, should be an ideal family-pleaser (1-26 August 2006);
it's recommended for ages six and above, though all are
welcome. If rainy weather stops play, tickets will be
exchanged for a later performance – subject to availability – but umbrellas and blankets are always advisable.
Café. Disabled access: toilet.

Polka Theatre

*240 The Broadway, Wimbledon, SW19 1SB (8543
4888/www.polkatheatre.com). South Wimbledon tube/
Wimbledon tube/rail, then 57, 93, 219, 493 bus.* **Open**
Phone bookings 9.30am-4.30pm Mon; 9am-6pm Tue-Fri;
10am-5pm Sat. *Personal callers* 9.30am-4.30pm Tue-Fri;
10am-5pm Sat. **Tickets** £5-£10. **Credit** AmEx, MC, V.
This beautifully designed young person's theatre has
earned its place in generations of young hearts since it
launched in 1979. Daily shows are staged by touring companies in the main auditorium (10.30am, 2pm), with weekly performances – often puppet-based – taking place in
the Adventure Theatre, dedicated to babies and toddlers.
There are also in-house productions, workshops and
storytelling sessions for families and schools. Book for
school-holidays workshops, as well as getting involved in
the Polka Youth Theatre, where the professional team
helps young people to put on shows. The venue is
baby-friendly, and the cheerful café is open from Tuesday
to Saturday. There's a complimentary ice-cream for every
child taking part in the free monthly World of Stories
drop-in event. Look out for literature events featuring
much-loved children's authors, such as Jacqueline Wilson.
*Buggy access. Café. Disabled access: lift, toilet. Nappy-
changing facilities.*

Royal National Theatre

*South Bank, SE1 9PX (box office 7452 3000/
information 7452 3400/www.nationaltheatre.org.uk).
Waterloo tube/rail.* **Open** *Box office* 10am-8pm Mon-
Sat. **Credit** AmEx, DC, MC, V. **Map** p317 M8.
Between its three theatres (the Olivier, the Lyttleton and
the Cottesloe), the NT's consistently top-notch programme
is traditionally adult-orientated, although occasional

productions might appeal to children – Philip Pullman's
His Dark Materials was staged here. Things change during the summer holidays, when the theatre puts on free
mini shows – anything from jazz to modern circus acts –
and activities in cordoned-off areas of the foyer or (weather permitting) at the riverside, where you can picnic on a
patch of AstroTurf. Don't miss the annual free outdoor
Watch This Space festival (7 July-2 September 2006), comprising over 100 world-class shows.
*Cafés. Disabled access: lift, toilet. Nappy-changing
facilities. Restaurant. Shop.*

Shakespeare's Globe

*21 New Globe Walk, Bankside, SE1 9DT (7401 9919/
tours 7902 1500/www.shakespeares-globe.org).
Mansion House tube/London Bridge tube/rail.* **Open**
Box office (theatre bookings, 5 May-8 Oct 2006) 10am-
6pm daily. **Tours** Oct-Apr 10am-5pm daily. **Tickets**
£5-£31. *Tours* £9; £7.50 concessions; £6.50 5-15s; free
under-5s; £25 family (2+3). **Credit** AmEx, MC, V.
Map p318 O7.
Young kids won't be inclined to sit – or stand – through
the performances at this reconstructed venue. Still, the
building itself should capture their imagination. The
Globe has a dedicated education department. A huge range
of talks, tours and activities – many of them conducted by
staff in full period costume – takes place with schools during term time, while holiday workshops and excellent
seasonal events open the floor to families.
*Café. Disabled access: lift, toilet. Nappy-changing
facilities. Restaurant. Shop.*

Unicorn Theatre for Children

*147 Tooley Street, Bankside, SE1 2HZ (0870 053
4534/www.unicorntheatre.com). London Bridge
tube/rail.* **Open** *Box office* 9.30am-6pm Mon-Fri; 10am-
6pm Sat; noon-5pm Sun. **Credit** MC, V. **Map** p319 R9.
Opened in December 2005, the new Unicorn Theatre is the
result of a three-year collaboration with local school
children, whose thoughts are incorporated into the
£13-million design. Its two performance spaces include the
300-seater Weston Theatre and more intimate Clore
Theatre; so far they have hosted a vibrant, critically
acclaimed programme for audiences aged four and above.
Family Days get everybody together for performances and
themed workshops, and cost around £24 per participant.
Buggy access. Café. Disabled access.

The Warehouse Theatre

*62 Dingwall Road, Croydon, Surrey CR0 2NF (8680
4060/www.warehousetheatre.co.uk). East Croydon rail.*
Open *Box office* 10am-6pm Mon-Sat; extended opening
hours on performance days. **Tickets** £6; £4.50 2-16s.
Credit AmEx, MC, V.
Its location in a converted Victorian warehouse tucked
behind East Croydon station makes this place easy to miss
on your first visit, but once found you won't forget it.
Theatre4Kidz matinées take place every Saturday at 11am
(£6 adults, £4.50 children), while a variety of touring shows
entertain those as young as two. Particularly notable is the
ongoing success of the Croydon Young People's Theatre
(CRYPT), which offers a creative base for 13- to 16-year-
olds. CRYPT meets between 2pm and 5pm every Saturday
during termtime, and puts on an annual show in July. The
fee per term is a bargain £10; application forms are available online.
Disabled access: lift, toilet (bar only).

Activities

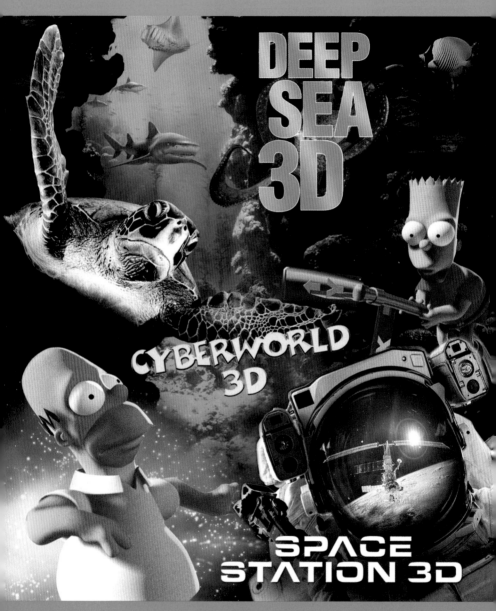

Young Vic

66 The Cut, Waterloo, SE1 8LZ (box office 7928 6363/ www.youngvic.org). Southwark tube/Waterloo tube/rail. **Open** *Box office* 10am-6pm Mon-Fri. **Tickets** prices vary; phone for details. **Credit** MC, V. **Map** p318 N8.
Built in 1970 as a temporary offshoot of the Old Vic theatre, the Young Vic's longevity demonstrates what a valuable theatrical asset this is, for all ages. The award-winning venue was closed for essential repairs at the time of writing; a rejuvenated auditorium is due to reopen in June 2006, with new foyers and plusher dressing rooms and a 130-seat studio theatre. While the improvements are going on, the theatre is being run from temporary offices in Kennington Park.
Buggy access. Café. Disabled access: lift, toilet. Nappy-changing facilities. Restaurant.

West End shows

With the exception of *Billy Elliot*, the shows below are suitable for children of all ages. Less-developed attention spans may find some more suitable than others (many clock in at over two hours), and very young children are advised to avoid the West End and go instead to one of the more intimate kid-specific venues in other parts of town (*see p221*), where plays are shorter, house lights brighter and the bangs less likely to scare.
For an alternative introduction to Theatreland, the **Society of London Theatres** (7557 6700, www.officiallondontheatre.co.uk) organises **Kids Week** (18 August-1 September 2006). Juniors get in free (with accompanying adults) to West End shows and, best of all, get to take part in the pre-performance workshops. For more on Kids Week and the best family-friendly theatre information in London, subscribe to the free family bulletin on the SOLT website. SOLT's Kids Club also runs a Saturday morning theatre club at the Theatre Museum in Covent Garden (*see p77*), but you have to book as places are limited.

Billy Elliot

Victoria Palace Theatre, Victoria Street, Victoria, SW1E 5EA (0870 895 5577/www.billyelliotthe musical.com). Victoria tube/rail. **Times** 7.30pm Mon-Sat. *Matinée* 2.30pm Thur, Sat. **Tickets** £17.50-£55. **Credit** AmEx, MC, V.
The musical version of the BAFTA-winning film, about the motherless miner's son who discovers a talent for ballet by accident, has 17 songs by Elton John. Its website has a warning reminding us that it contains strong language and scenes of confrontation, which gave the film its 15 rating. Not for the under-eights.

Blood Brothers

Phoenix Theatre, Charing Cross Road, St Giles's, WC2H 0JP (0870 060 6631/www.theambassadors. com). Tottenham Court Road tube. **Times** 7.45pm Mon-Sat. *Matinée* 3pm Thur; 4pm Sat. **Tickets** £17.50-£45. **Credit** AmEx, MC, V. **Map** p315 K6.
Willy Russell's multi-award-winning folk opera has ultimately tragic lead characters – and some great tunes. It

tells the story of separated twins reunited in later life and deals with issues of family ties and class divisions. The ending may upset very young children.

Daddy Cool

Shaftesbury Theatre, Shaftesbury Avenue, WC2H 8DP (0870 906 3798). Tottenham Court Road tube. **Times** 7.30pm Mon-Thur, Sat; 8.30pm Fri. *Matinée* 5pm Fri; 3pm Sat. **Tickets** £17.50-£45. **Credit** AmEx, MC, V. **Map** p315 K6.
Yet another musical based on pop hits (this time, Boney M's disco classics), *Daddy Cool* stars So Solid Crew's Harvey in a London-set tale of rival gangs and romance. As we went to press, it was scheduled to open in May 2006.

Fame: The Musical

Aldwych Theatre, Aldwych, WC2B 4DF (0870 400 0805/www.famethemusical.co.uk). Charing Cross tube/ rail. **Times** 7.30pm Mon-Thur, Sat; 8.30pm Fri. *Matinée* 5.30pm Fri; 3pm Sat. **Tickets** £15-£42.50. **Credit** AmEx, MC, V. **Map** p317 M6.
This energetic stage adaptation hit the West End in 1995, spawning a touring version before returning to the capital. The story – revolving around a bunch of leotard-clad, tantrum-throwing wannabes at New York's High School of the Performing Arts – will appeal to drama queens of all ages. Expect some risqué songs.

Guys And Dolls

Piccadilly Theatre, Denman Street, W1V 8DY (0870 060 0123/www.theambassadors.com). Piccadilly Circus tube. **Times** 7.30pm Mon-Sat. *Matinée* 2.30pm Wed, Sat. **Tickets** £20-£55. **Credit** AmEx, MC, V. **Map** p316 J7.
This Broadway musical romance, centring on New York gamblers, was brightly revived in 2005. Much of the excitement here is inspired by its leading men – Ewan McGregor made his musical debut in the role of suave Sky Masterson, followed by *EastEnders* heart-throb Nigel Harman.

Les Misérables

Queen's Theatre, Shaftesbury Avenue, Soho, W1D 8AS (0870 890 1110/www.lesmis.com). Leicester Square tube. **Times** 7.30pm Mon-Sat. *Matinée* 2.30pm Wed, Sat. **Tickets** £12-£47.50. **Credit** AmEx, DC, MC, V. **Map** p315 K6.
An enduring musical adaptation of Victor Hugo's tale of revolution in 19th-century France: 20 years since its London première, *Les Misérables* is still impressive. The Les Miz Kids' Club also runs here twice a month, and gives kids aged 8-15 a chance to tour backstage and re-enact a scene from the show for £15.

The Lion King

Lyceum Theatre, Wellington Street, Covent Garden, WC2E 7RQ (0870 243 9000/www.ticketmaster.co.uk). Covent Garden tube. **Times** 7.30pm Tue-Sat. *Matinée* 2pm Wed, Sat; 3pm Sun. **Tickets** £20-£52.50. **Credit** AmEx, MC, V. **Map** p317 L7.
Most children are familiar with the film version of this Disney classic. The beauty of this production lies in the elaborate staging. Expect awesome set designs, a combination of puppetry and live actors (there are 25 different animals represented in the show), and a fabulous cocktail of West End choruses and African rhythms.

Activities

Lord of the Rings

www.lotr.com.
A buzz of Middle Earth proportions surrounds this musical adaptation of the Tolkien epic; its London premiere was delayed because of difficulties in finding a large enough venue – as we went to press, it was slated to open at the Dominion Theatre (268 Tottenham Court Road, W1) in November 2006. LOTR made its world stage debut earlier in the year, in Toronto. With a budget of £11.5 million (making it London's most expensive musical to date), it promises to be precious indeed.

Mamma Mia!

Prince of Wales Theatre, Coventry Street, Soho,
W1V 8AS (0870 850 0393/www.ticketmaster.co.uk).
Piccadilly Circus tube. **Times** 7.30pm Mon-Thur, Sat; 8.30pm Fri. *Matinée* 5pm Fri; 3pm Sat. **Tickets** £25-£49. **Credit** AmEx, MC, V. **Map** p317 K7.
It may be thin on story, but what *Mamma Mia!* lacks in dramatic development it more than makes up for with feelgood musical numbers.

Mary Poppins

Prince Edward Theatre, Old Compton Street, Soho,
W1D 4TP (0870 850 9191/www.marypoppinsthe
musical.co.uk). Leicester Square tube. **Times** 7.30pm Mon-Sat. *Matinée* 2.30pm Thur, Sat. **Tickets** £15-£55. **Credit** AmEx, MC, V. **Map** p315 K6.
All together now: supercalifragilisticexpialidocious! Cameron Mackintosh's smash-hit stage version of PL Travers's magic nanny is closer to the darker original than the spoonful-of-sugar Disney film, but it still has the old singalong favourites and spectacular dance numbers, choreographed by Matthew Bourne. Children under three aren't allowed in, and the website advises against bringing anybody under seven.

Stomp

Vaudeville Theatre, Strand, Covent Garden, WC2R
0NH (0870 890 0511/www.stomp.co.uk). Charing
Cross tube/rail. **Times** 8pm Tue-Sat. *Matinée* 3pm Thur, Sat, Sun. **Tickets** £16-£38.50. **Credit** AmEx, MC, V. **Map** p317 L7.
Kids who like smashing pans together will adore this hyperactive show. The cast finds music in the most obscure objects – including the kitchen sink – and the whole noisy extravaganza feels as vital as it did when it originated in 1991. Just remember to hide the saucepans and bin lids before you leave home.

Performance workshops

Allsorts

Office: 34 Pember Road, NW10 5LS (8969 3249/
www.allsortsdrama.com). Classes and locations vary.
Fees from £85/one-hour class; sibling discount 20%.
Credit AmEx, MC, V.
Previous drama experience isn't necessary to join up at Allsorts, as the focus of these Saturday classes and holiday workshops (held at various school venues) is to boost kids' confidence and communication skills through lively role-playing activities in close-knit groups. Ages range from four years up to 16, and bespoke drama workshops at home can also be booked.

Centrestage

Office: 117 Canfield Gardens, West Hampstead,
NW6 3DY (7328 0788/www.centrestageschool.co.uk).
Classes 10am-1pm, 2-5pm Sat. **Fees** £260/12wk term.
Credit AmEx, MC, V.
Centrestage offers Saturday drama, singing and dance classes for three- to 17-year-olds at its two branches, in Holland Park and Hampstead. The approach is intensive – kids are encouraged to grasp fundamental skills, such as improvisation and diction, before trying out different performance styles. There are also week-long workshops, concluding in a collective show. Student intake is limited; there are usually between 10 and 16, students per class.

Dance Attic

368 North End Road, Fulham, SW6 1LY (7610 2055/
www.danceattic.com). Fulham Broadway tube. **Fees**
from £50/11wk term; phone for individual class prices.
Credit (shop) MC, V.
The overall range of performance classes here is staggering, setting Dance Attic apart from any pretenders. Students must pay for daily/monthly membership besides class fees; reduced rates are available for teens. Children under ten are encouraged to take part in Saturday morning workshops on tap (for over-fives) and ballet (for over-threes), the latter working towards RADA exams. Both cost £5 per hour-long session. There's also a shop, stocking children's dance wear.

Dramarama

Holiday courses: South Hampstead High School,
Maresfield Gardens, NW3 5SS. Term-time classes:
South Hampstead Junior School, Netherhall Gardens,
NW3 5RN (both 8446 0891/www.dramarama.co.uk).
Finchley Road & Frognal rail. **Fees** prices available on request. **No credit cards.**
Dramarama for boys and girls of all abilities, was founded by Jessica Grant. It runs a number of Saturday workshops for kids aged three and above. More intensive theatrical tuition leads 11- to 14-year-olds into their LAMDA (London Academy of Music and Dramatic Art) speech and drama exams. Half-term and holiday workshops, in which participants devise and perform a play of their own, last five days. Birthday parties for six- to 14-year-olds include imaginative games and the chance for kids to act in their own mini shows.

Helen O'Grady's Children's Drama Academy

Office: Northside Vale, Guernsey, GY3 5TX (01481
200 250/www.helenogrady.co.uk). **Classes** times vary; phone for details. **Fees** £66/12wk term.
No credit cards.
Drama teacher and actress Helen O'Grady started her after-school acting classes in Perth, Australia in 1979. Her aims were to provide a self-development through drama programme for children. Her empire now runs more than 37 academies across Britain. Children aged five to 17 attend a one-hour workshop each week, with courses spread across three terms. Skills are developed depending on age: the lower and upper primary groups (five to eight and nine to 11 respectively) nurture self-esteem through clear speech and fluent delivery; the Youth Theatre (13- to 17-year-olds) develops more progressive techniques, including improvisation and monologues. A production is devised and performed at the end of every third term.

Arts & Entertainment

Hoxton Hall

*130 Hoxton Street, Hoxton, N1 6SH (7684 0060/
www.hoxtonhall.co.uk). Old Street tube/rail.* **Classes**
times vary; phone for details. **Fees** £15/term.
No credit cards.
In this unique venue – a refurbished Victorian music hall
– eight- to 11-year-olds can experiment and compose at
leisure in the junior music class, working individually or
in groups. They can also perform in front of an audience
or record their work on CD. The parallel junior arts class
encourages fledgling talent by usingvaried resources and
materials. Both the Junior Drama and Youth Drama
groups, for eight to 11- year-olds and 11- to 18-year-olds,
respectively, give kids a free hand in writing and producing a performance piece for the main hall.

Laban

*Creekside, Deptford, SE8 3DZ (8691 8600/
www.laban.org). Deptford rail.* **Classes** times vary;
phone for details. **Fees** prices vary; phone for details.
Credit MC, V.
Thoroughly modern Laban offers a variety of performance
classes for all ages, as well as contemporary dance and
music shows. The award-winning building houses 13 separate studios, where dance courses cater for all; young children are particularly encouraged to explore inventive
movement, while the annual Children's Show (8 July 2006)
showcases student performance from toddlers to teenagers.
Touring performances in the theatre are combined with
lectures and educational workshops.

Lewisham Youth Theatre

*Broadway Theatre, Catford Broadway, Catford, SE6
4RU (8690 3428/www.lewishamyouththeatre.com).
Catford or Catford Bridge rail.* **Classes** *Junior Youth
Theatre* (8-11s, 11-13s) 90 mins Wed, Sat; *Senior Youth
Theatre* (8-13s, 14-21s) phone for specific times. *ROAR!
Children's Theatre* 11.30am Sat (3-8s & families). **Fees**
free, £5 refundable deposit. **Tickets** *All* £3.50. **No
credit cards**.
Driven by the admirable conviction that theatre should be
fully accessible (free, with no auditions), LYT's youth
programmes have a high standard, and a reputation for
solid, innovative variety. All classes work towards full
productions. ROAR! Children's Theatre performances are
presented to young children and their families on Saturday
mornings in this lovely art deco theatre. Junior Youth
Theatre is divided into two groups, catering for eight- to
11-year-olds and 11- to 13-year-olds, but there is some
crossover with the Senior Youth Theatre for young people
aged between 14 and 21. Most recruitment takes place
through schools, but some places are allocated on a
first-come-first-served basis. Workshops take place after
school as well as at weekends.

London Bubble Theatre Company

*5 Elephant Lane, Rotherhithe, SE16 4JD (7237 4434/
www.londonbubble.org.uk). Bermondsey or Rotherhithe
tube.* **Open** *Box office* 10am-6pm Mon-Fri. **Classes**
times vary; phone for details. **Fees** £37.50/11wk term.
Credit MC, V.

The Lewisham Arthouse. *See p233.*

Activities

In October 2005, the London Bubble Theatre Company launched its Everybody's Theatre project, enabling children and adults to boost their performance skills in a collective company. This has proved an immediate hit, and continues the company's ethos – to present theatre that is both unusual and accessible. Its wonderfully atmospheric promenade show shows have previously toured many unconventional venues, including London parks and woods. Summer 2006 sees a tour of Metamorphoses, which will include a major participatory project involving up to 75 people of all ages. In 'Myths, Rituals and Whitegoods' stories from Ovid will be interwoven with stories exploring mankind's relationship with consumer goods.

Bubble's Youth Theatre groups include five- to seven-year-olds (4.30-6pm Tue) and 13- to 17-year-olds (2-4pm Sat); fees can be paid per term (£37.50, £17.50 concessions) or per session (£4, £2 concessions), and the first class is a free 'taster'.

Millfield Theatre School

Silver Street, Edmonton, N18 1PJ (box office 8807 6680/www.millfieldtheatre.co.uk). Silver Street rail, then 34, 102, 144 bus/217, 231, W6 bus. **Classes** (4-5s) 10.30am-noon, (6-7s), 12.30-2pm, (8-16s), 11am-2pm, Sun; 14-19s), 6.30-9pm Fri. Fees (4-5s and 6-7s) £85/10wk term; (8-16s) £165/10wk term; 14-19s £120/10wk term. **Credit** MC, V.
Millfield Arts Centre presents a regular calendar of musicals, comedies and mainstream drama, besides some perky touring children's shows (including many TV adaptations like *Engie Benjy*), in its 362-seat venue. The in-house Silver Street Youth Company is divided into three age groups, honing the dramatic instinct of neighbourhood thesps from four to 19. The courses run throughout termtime, meeting on Fridays or Sundays, with performances throughout the year, including a seasonal panto. Talented young actors (14-25 years) could progress to Millfield Youth Theatre, via auditions.

National Youth Music Theatre

www.nymt.org.uk.
Happy news – this much-loved, historic and all-encompassing producer of challenging theatre for young people has finally overcome the danger of folding through 'deplorable' (Jude Law) lack of funding. NYMT relaunched with gusto in October 2005, when its Royal Gala starred such alumni as *Little Britain*'s Matt Lucas. Details of auditions and regional workshops are updated on its website – 2006 productions include Howard Goodball's Shakespeare-inspired musical *The Dreaming*. Stage-management opportunities appeal to young behind-the-scenes stars. Here's to the next fantastic 28 years!

New Peckham Varieties

Magic Eye Theatre, Havil Street, Camberwell, SE5 7SD (venue 7703 5838/office 7708 5401/www.npvarts.co.uk). Elephant & Castle tube/rail, then 12, 45A, 171 bus. **Classes** times vary; phone for details. **Fees** £2.50-£3. **Credit** MC, V.

Dance, then, whoever you may be

It's an eternal problem for dance organisations: how do you persuade talented boys to give classical and contemporary dance a try? Despite ballet being thrust to the forefront with the success of *Billy Elliot* (*see p227*), negative stereotypes persist. Dance in general is growing in popularity – and is seen as a viable career – thanks to the ubiquitousness of the pop video. However, boys are still reluctant to try classical dance even if it will deliver definite benefits to other dance forms they practise. Kate Prince, who teaches street dance at **Pineapple** and is principal of dance company Zoonation (www.zoonation.net), says: 'It's when you suggest a ballet class to improve their strength that you run into problems. Pride gets in the way.'

However, organisations are fighting back and finding innovative ways to encourage reluctant male talent. Staff at the groundbreaking **Laban** (www.laban.org), which teaches contemporary dance, knew from their community work that boys were interested in their popular youth classes, but weren't putting themselves forward. They concluded that those boys who might want to give contemporary dance a try were intimidated about entering a class full of girls and thus Pick up the Pace was born. The project aims to encourage boys and young men into contemporary dance and is now in its second year. There are weekly classes for 8-11s, 12-15s and 16-22s. The 8-11s group has been the most successful, consistently full and with with a long waiting list (but people do drop out along the way, so it's worth putting your child's name down). Boys learn creative dance – in a typical class they are given a range of movements from the contemporary canon, then encouraged to add their own. The centre discovered that after a while most of the students feel comfortable enough to join a mixed class.

The project finishes in July 2007, but a dedicated class for boys will carry on in some form. Laban has been in discussions with the **George Piper Dance Company** (www.gpdances.com) to broaden the project. George Piper is a resident ballet company at Sadler's Wells, with an extensive education programme. It has also found that boys weren't being encouraged to try contemporary dance or ballet and in 2005 started a project, Peace Process to redress the balance. Its workshops incorporate film and music, with the kids cutting a DVD at the end. At present the company only works with schools but it also hosts workshops at the annual **Connect Festival** at Sadler's Wells. Connect, and another Sadler's Wells event, **Breakin' Convention** (for both, see www.sadlerswells.com), are both good places for boys (and girls) to spark an interest in a wider range of dance, with workshops – for all standards from beginner to professional – and youth performances to inspire children to try styles they might otherwise dismiss out of hand.

Varieties by name and by nature – New Peckham Varieties' popular youth arts programme has worked at the heart of this multicultural neighbourhood for 21 years, offering 11- to 16- year-olds a grounding in dance, drama, musical theatre and circus skills. Workshops run throughout the week, with Saturday classes at the local Oliver Goldsmith School. Highlights include Bouncing Babies And Funky Tots, which gets under-fours grooving, while the Boys' Dance Class (ages eight and above) has convinced male teens to learn ballet alongside jazz and street dance. Twice a year, professional actors team up with NPV's Theatre School students to present new musical shows for families.

Nifty Feet!

7266 5035.
Lynn Page is best known for training young actor Jamie Bell for the blockbuster film *Billy Elliot* – and the young leads in the stage musical of the same name. Ever since, she has been swamped by likely lads hoping to effect a similarly spectacular transformation. Thus Nifty Feet! was born, bringing ballet to the capital's two- to 16-year-olds by way of vibrant, mixed classes that defy the medium's somewhat starchy stereotype. The key to Page's success is cunning: using popular tunes, she hooks the kids in with urban dance tuition that only slowly (and with her subjects hardly noticing it) turns into ballet lessons without the slippers. These classes are mainly run on Saturdays in Richmond, Kingston, Dulwich and Wimbledon. Phone or log on to the website for an information pack.

Perform

c/o Perform Media, 66 Churchway, Somers Town, NW1 1LT (0845 400 4000/www.perform.org.uk). Euston tube/rail. **Classes** times vary; phone for details. **Fees** £125/10wk term (weekday); £180/10wk term (weekends). **Credit** MC, V.
This ever-expanding company runs drama, dance and singing classes across London and the south-east. Workshops, with holiday courses available, are aimed at four- to eight-year-old children. They're geared towards building up those four all-important Cs: confidence, communication, concentration and coordination. Sessions include movement games, singing and improvisation. A free trial session means you can gauge your child's interest before making a financial commitment. 'Experience' holiday workshops last for a week, with youngsters developing and presenting a mini performance. In April 2006, Mini Ps was launched to extend the experience to tots between six months and four years and their parents. Check the website for your nearest venue. Phone for details of the children's party service.

Pineapple Performing Arts School

7 Langley Street, Covent Garden, WC2H 9JA (7583 5289/www.pineapplearts.com). Covent Garden tube. **Classes** 1-2pm (8-11s), 2-3pm (12-16s) Sat; 11am-noon (3-4s), 11am-2pm (5-12s), 2-5pm (13-18s) Sun. **Fees** £90/12wk term 3-4s; £295/12wk term over 4s. *Trial class* £25. *Registration fee* £30-£35. **Credit** MC, V. **Map** p315 L6.
One of Britain's premier performing-arts schools, Pineapple offers many in-demand courses. These are for students aged five to 18; infants can participate in Pineapple Chunks classes every Sunday. Classes fall into three categories: dance, drama and singing, each divided into workshops running over three terms.

The Place

16 Flaxman Terrace, Bloomsbury, WC1H 9AB (box office 7121 1080/classes 7388 8430/www.theplace.org.uk). Euston tube/rail. **Classes** times vary; phone for details. **Fees** from £80-£90/11wk term; £5 discount for 2nd or subsequent class taken by same student or a sibling. **Credit** MC, V.
The Place is home to both the London Contemporary Dance School and the touring Richard Alston Dance Company. A programme of shows runs throughout the year, but the Place ethos is that anyone can learn to dance: the centre is accessible to all ages, as well as to the disabled; there is, however, a daunting waiting list. The Saturday programme offers classes for five- to 18-year-olds, combining free-form expression with fundamental dance techniques. There are also occasional and striking 'Offspring' performances for young people in the adjoining Robin Howard Dance Theatre.

Royal Academy of Dance

36 Battersea Square, Battersea, SW11 3RA (7326 8000/www.rad.org.uk). **Classes** times vary; phone for details. **Fees** call for details.
The RAD dance school offers a diverse range of activities for children aged from as young as two and a half. Activities include ballet, jazz and contemporary dance, drama, singing, creative movement, musical theatre and classes in excerpts from ballets.

Stagecoach Theatre Arts

Head office: The Courthouse, Elm Grove, Walton-on-Thames, Surrey KT12 1LZ (01932 254 333/www.stagecoach.co.uk). **Fees** *Term-time classes* £285 (£142.50 for 4-7s). **Credit** MC, V.
Stagecoach has mushroomed into the world's most prolific part-time theatre school – currently it has more than 560 venues nationwide (over 60 of them in London) and many more abroad. Courses run parallel to school terms and break down into three hours of professional tuition per week (one in dance, one in drama and one in singing). Two performances are given annually, which keeps the enthusiasm going. Other incentives include medals for consistent achievement. Excitingly for ambitious children, there's an in-house agency to represent the most promising talents. All venues take kids aged seven to 16, and most run Early Stages introductions, with shorter sessions for ages four and above. Holiday workshops are also available.

Sylvia Young Theatre School

Rossmore Road, Marylebone, NW1 6NJ (7402 0673/www.sylviayoungtheatreschool.co.uk). Marylebone tube/rail. **Classes** times vary; phone for details. **Fees** *Classes* £75/13wk term. *Summer school* (10-18s) £250/wk. **No credit cards**.
Sylvia Young's alumni span stage, screen and pop charts (Billie Piper, Blue's Lee Ryan and numerous *EastEnders* soapstars, to name a few). The tuition, from rehearsal rooms to recording studio, develops an interest in all aspects of performance art. It's a famously oversubscribed full-time stage school (with around 150 pupils aged ten to 16), as well as a Saturday school (for students aged four to 18); it also runs Thursday evening classes. The holiday school runs a theatre-skills course for eight-to 18-year-olds in July and a six-day musical-theatre workshop for ten- to 18-year-olds in August.

Activities

Activities

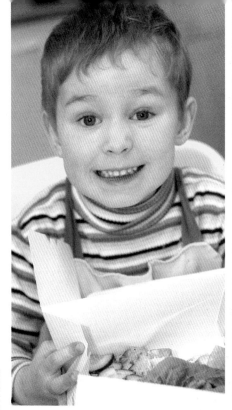

Yummers! **The Kids' Cookery School**.

Workshops & Activities

For performance workshops, *see p228*.

Busy Kids London

7823 5037/www.busykidslondon.co.uk. **Classes** times vary, phone for details. **Fees** from £25. **No credit cards.**
Busy Kids aims to introduce children to a host of exhilarating activities that will help build their confidence. Young gardeners can learn how to grow plants at the Chelsea Physic Garden, filmmakers can make a mini movie under expert supervision, and younger children can take part in Photogram, a day of making collages, prints and pictures, or Yogatots – where a story is told using yoga positions. Other packages include cooking, magic or storytelling.

Archaeology

Museum of London Archaelogy Service

Mortimer Wheeler House, 46 Eagle Wharf Road, Hoxton, N1 7ED (7410 2200/www.molas.org.uk).
The Museum of London's Archaeology Service (MoLAS) runs various digs and activities for families. Its Young Archaeologists Club, for children aged ten to 16, meets weekly at the Pumphouse Educational Museum in Rotherhithe. Check the website for details.

Art

Art 4 Fun

Various venues (head office 8449 6500/www.art4 fun.com). **Fees** *Workshops* & *courses* phone for details. **Credit** MC, V.
Booking is advisable, though not compulsory, at these creative café-shops, where children choose a ceramic item (from £3.50) and get busy decorating it with water-based paints. Pieces are then fired and glazed in the café, to be picked up later: a studio fee (£5.95 per person) covers the process. Workshops run throughout the year for kids and adults, covering sand-painting, tie-dyeing and stamp-making.

The Art Yard

318 Upper Richmond Road West, Mortlake, SW14 7JN (8878 1336/www.artyard.co.uk). Mortlake rail/33, 337, 493 bus. **Classes** *Termtime* 9am-6pm Mon-Fri. *School hols* 9.30am-3.30pm Mon-Fri. **Fees** phone for details. **No credit cards.**
Creative kids aged five and above love getting their hands dirty at this busy (and pleasingly messy), OFSTED-registered outlet. Many children come for two-day workshops (9.30am-3.30pm, bring a packed lunch and wear old clothes) during the school holidays, and have great sociable fun creating improvised art works (painting to collage and papier mâché) and listening to music. Themed special events have included a *Doctor Who* day.

Children's Workshops in Clay

Lewisham Arthouse, 140 Lewisham Way, Lewisham, SE14 6PD (8694 9011/www.shirley-stewart.co.uk).
Lewisham Arthouse is a co-operative based in a handsome Grade II listed building with an amazing marble staircase. Artists rent studio space here, and Shirley Stewart is one of them. Her throwing and studio pottery workshops for children aged from five are held during termtime only, but extra sessions can be arranged for the holidays. Pottery parties are also available.

Pottery Café

735 Fulham Road, Parsons Green, SW6 5UL (7736 2157/www.pottery-cafe.com). Parsons Green tube/ 14, 414 bus. **Open** 11am-6pm Mon; 10am-6pm Tue, Wed, Fri, Sat; 10am-10pm Thur; 11am-5pm Sun. **Credit** MC, V.
The Pottery Café, one of London's first decorating studios, is much favoured around holiday time for lovingly crafted presents. Visitors return to collect their works of art, after they've been glazed and fired.
Buggy access. Café. Disabled access. Nappy-changing facilities. Shop.
Branch: 332 Richmond Road, Twickenham, Surrey TW1 2DU (8744 3000).

Cooking

Art of Hospitality

St James Schools, Earsby Street, Olympia, W14 8SH (7348 1755/www.artofhospitality.co.uk). **Open** 10.30am-12.15pm Sat. **Classes** £25 per child. **No credit cards.**
The Art of Hospitality is a department of St James Schools that holds well-organised cookery courses and demonstrations. The kitchen is designed to allow 12 children to participate in practical classes. Courses are taught by professional cooks, invited guest chefs and specialists of different ethnic cuisines.

Junior Masterclasses

City Café, City Inn Westminster, 30 John Islip Street, Westminster, SW1P 4DD (7630 1000/www.citycafe. co.uk). **Classes** 2.30-5.30pm 12 Aug 2006; phone for details of other dates. **Fees** £35. **Credit** MC, V.
The City Café Westminster is a sleek and professional setting for these entertaining and informative cookery sessions, where eight- to 12-year-olds learn about fresh ingredients and help to prepare a delicious meal; the fee includes full recipes of the day's dishes and a cool-looking City Café apron. Junior Masterclass children's parties can be arranged on request. On our last visit we made some fabulously colourful fruit and yoghurt smoothies, learned all about different fish species and how to make foolproof and healthy vegetarian pasta dishes.

The Kids' Cookery School

107 Gunnersbury Lane, Acton, W3 8HQ (8992 8882/ www.thekidscookeryschool.co.uk). Acton Town tube. **Open** *Office* 9am-5.30pm Mon-Fri. **Fees** *Half-term & school hols only* £15/75mins; £30/2.5hrs; £50/5hr incl lunch. **No credit cards.**
A totally inclusive project aimed at promoting culinary skills, healthy eating and food awareness among children of all ages and backgrounds. Events and classes teach kids in a deliciously hands-on way about new ingredients and equipment, encouraging them to touch, smell, taste and feel different foods. Cookery workshops are designed to the young chefs' needs (dietary requirements can be catered for); there are a maximum of 12 students in each cookery session, so everyone gets a piece of the culinary action.

Activities

Modern languages

Club Petit Pierrot

7385 5565/www.clubpetitpierrot.uk.com.
This high-profile language club offers fun French lessons for children from eight months to nine years old across London. The lessons, given by experienced native speakers, are in French with an emphasis on the children learning through play and having fun communicating in French with confidence. Groups are kept small, and the club caters for all levels. Parent and toddler groups, morning, afternoon, after-school, Saturdays and holiday clubs (painting, cooking, sand and water play and so on) are all available. Fees vary (from £90 per term).

Easy Mandarin

7828 2998/www.easymandarinuk.com.
It's all very well being fluent in French and German, but these days kids want a language club that's really going to stretch them. Step forward Ms Wu, whose fun-filled Knightsbridge-based Saturday morning Chinese classes for ages nine to 13 are going down a storm.

French & Spanish à la Carte

7 Revelstoke Road, Wimbledon, SW18 5NL (8946 4777/www.frenchandspanishalacarte.co.uk).
This language school gives south London's ambitious two- to five-year-olds a head start with its weekly playgroups (Tuesday and Thursday, or Wednesday and Friday mornings), involving an hour of activity and an hour of free play while a teacher chats to them in French or Spanish. After-school and holiday courses are offered for older children, and adult tuition is also available.

Le Club Tricolore

10 Ballingdon Road, Wandsworth, SW11 6AJ (7924 4649/www.leclubtricolore.co.uk).
Everything is learned orally at Tricolore, by means of role-playing or singalongs. After-school classes, Saturday morning activities and holiday workshops dish cookery, crafts and treasure hunts, all in a French atmosphere. The club is aimed at children aged three to 11, and operates in venues across London – phone for details of your nearest. Fees vary (£135 for a ten-week course).

Music

Blueberry

8677 6871/www.blueberry.clara.co.uk.
Since 1991 Margo Random's classes have grown across south and west London. In the weekly parent-and-toddler groups (ages nine months to three years), parents have a good sing-song to an accompanying guitar and guide their offspring through the actions. Big Kids Blueberry (two- to four-year-olds) builds on the singing with more games, but without the aged ps; an 11-week term costs £60. Blueberry birthday parties (between £85-£95 for a 45-minute session) include such activities as dancing with bubbles, or – space permitting – a 'giant parachute'.

Centre for Young Musicians

Morley College, 61 Westminster Bridge Road, Waterloo, SE1 7HT (7928 3844/www.cymlondon.demon.co.uk).
Every Saturday during termtime CYM hosts a programme of choirs, ensembles, masterclasses and instrumental lessons for the musically talented. The Main Centre is open to youngsters who already play an instrument at any stage, subject to audition. It also acts as an umbrella organisation for London boroughs that provide instrumental lessons for beginners; there are 13 satellite centres – phone to find your nearest.

Fanfare

The Conservatoire, 19-21 Lee Road, Blackheath, SE3 9RQ (8852 0234/www.conservatoire.org.uk). Blackheath rail. **Fees** £129/term. **Credit** MC, V.
The Blackheath Conservatoire's Fanfare programme is aimed at children aged five to 11. An innovative new scheme for beginners, it combines the fun of learning with others with individual tuition over one year. Participants receive a free book and CD so they can practise at home, and in their lessons get to make a lot of noise and make friends. If your child does not own one, instruments can be hired from the store.

Guildhall

Silk Street, Barbican, EC2Y 8DT (7628 2571/ www.gsmd.ac.uk). Barbican tube/Moorgate tube/rail.
This world-class conservatoire runs the coveted Junior Guildhall instrumental training for gifted children on Saturday mornings. Entry is by audition, and standards are extremely high, but a String Training Programme has also been introduced for newcomers aged four to 11, including instrumental training and music appreciation. The Guildhall's Drama Course (13-18 year-olds) involves a more informal audition process.

London Suzuki Group

Various venues (01372 720088/www. londonsuzukigroup.co.uk).
Dr Shinichi Suzuki's teachings that talent is inherent in all newborn children inspired a ground-breaking school of music in Japan. This led to the foundation of the London Suzuki Group in 1972; its teachers (covering violin, cello and piano) apply Dr Suzuki'various venuess methods to enhance the natural ability of children aged three to mid teens. The key is learning through listening, and then playing for pleasure; no previous musical experience is necessary. Classes are held after school and at weekends, and are for members only.

Monkey Music

Various venues (01582 766 464/www. monkeymusic.co.uk).
'All rhythm and no blues', this pre-school music company has franchises all over the country, focusing on children aged from six months to four years. Weekly 30-minute classes encourage social and musical skills within a fun, and friendly environment, using a catchy combination of songs, percussion instruments and colourful visuals.

Musical Express

Various venues (8946 6043/www.musicalexpress.co.uk).
Flautist and music therapist Jenny Tabori believes that all children possess an inherent enjoyment of music and sound, and her successful Musical Express classes give youngsters the means to express themselves and develop social skills, with instruments and 'action songs'. Small classes for over- and under- twos take place all over south London and Surrey; parents and carers stay and share the experience throughout each session.

Working those elbows at the **Pineapple Performing Arts School**. *See p231.*

Music House for Children

Bush Hall, 310 Uxbridge Road, Shepherd's Bush, W12 7LJ (8932 2652/www.musichouseforchildren.co.uk). Shepherd's Bush tube. **Fees** phone for details. **Credit** MC, V.

The Music House offers a broad medley including instrumental tuition, art activities (for kids aged 14 and under) and a Saturday Club. Home tuition is tailored to the needs of the student; the Music House has over 200 tutors on its books. Holiday workshops encompass many age groups and interests and give pre-teens a chance to try their hand at costume and stage design. Future pop and rock stars (8-15 years) enjoy the in-house Creative recording studio, where they can get to grips with professional technology to capture their own sounds. Personally tailored themed parties can also be arranged.

Wildlife

Oasis Children's Nature Garden

Larkhall Lane & Studley Road, Stockwell, SW4 (7498 2329). Stockwell tube. **Open** *After-school Club* 3.30-5.30pm Tue-Fri. *Termtime* 10am-3.30pm Sat. *School hols* 10am-noon, 2-4pm Mon-Fri. **Admission** 25p.

Reclaimed from wasteland, the Nature Garden is one of three projects run by the Oasis Children's Venture (the others are cycling and karting centres). It provides a serene environment in an inner-city area, and its after-school club, which includes pond-dipping and gardening, as well as arts and crafts or woodwork activities, is very popular. Environmental workshops are run in school holidays.

Roots & Shoots

The Learner Centre, Walnut Tree Walk, Lambeth, SE11 6DN (7587 1131/www.roots-and-shoots.org). Lambeth North tube. **Open** *Jan-Apr, Aug-Dec* 9.30am-4pm Mon-Fri. *May-July* 9.30am-5pm Mon-Fri; 10am-2pm Sat. Phone before visiting. **Admission** free; donations welcome.

Roots & Shoots is a Lambeth-based charity organisation that has offered vocational training for young people for more than 20 years. Various outdoor activities take place around its tranquil one-acre grounds. R&S has introduced the pleasures of tending a simple urban garden to a large number of London's youngsters, many of them children with disadvantages and/or disabilities. The site is also a popular destination for school groups; David the outreach worker guides them through the garden's diverse insects, animals and wildflowers, and explains how the delicious London honey is collected from the resident bees (the centre is also home to the London Beekeepers Association). Special activities are organised in conjunction with events such as National Apple Day (Oct).

Parties

A perfect party? Call in the professionals.

Parties are no longer a matter of popping balloons, sulking over the pass the parcel and overdosing on jelly. Today it's all about themes: you can have drama parties, craft parties, science parties, GCSE coursework parties (OK, we made that one up), sports parties, even yoga parties – all manner of improving activities must now be completed before children can get their hands on the Twiglets. Our party directory lists a wide range of such activity organisers, as well as entertainers, cake-makers, partyware and dressing-up shops, and our favourite London party venues. Where possible, we've given a rough guide to prices for the party people and places we've listed below, but as most entertainers and organisers prefer to tailor their service, be aware that prices need to be negotiated on application.

Activities

Arts & crafts
For more pottery cafés, see p233.

Crawley Studios
39 Wood Vale, Forest Hill, SE23 3DS (8516 0002). Forest Hill rail. **Open** daily (by appointment only). **No credit cards.**
Marie Lou runs all-week pottery-painting parties for small groups of children in her studio. The cost usually depends on what's to be painted – selections range from popular animal ornaments (around £8) to cups and bowls (£5-£20 including firing charge). Items are ready for collection a week later. A conservatory area is available for refreshments (£3 a head).

Eazi Beadzi
01843 600 502/07713 102 498/www.eazibeadzi.co.uk. **No credit cards.**
Here's a pretty idea – jewellery-making parties for six- to 12-year-olds. The Beadzi people come along with beads, gems, wire and fixings (tailored to the children's age and ability) and help the partygoers make something to treasure. Prices start at £150 for 90 minutes, plus £6 per child.

Nellie's Arty Time Parties
01433 631 694/07710 479 852/www.dk.com/ nellieshepherd. **No credit cards.**
Fenella Shepherd can transform a venue into a mermaid's underwater palace, a robot world or a cyberdelic spaceship, all with arty activities thrown in. Artist-themed affairs (Dalí or Picasso, for instance) give an educational angle; children can try producing their own piece in the artist's

style. Prices for this bespoke service vary, but a starting price is £500 for two hours. If that's out of your range, fear not. Nellie's workshops in schools and community centres, and her books, such as *My Party Art Class* (Dorling Kindersley, £6.99), give the lowdown on doing it yourself.

Cookery

Cookie Crumbles
8876 9912/www.cookiecrumbles.net. **Credit** MC, V.
Chef Carola Weymouth offers an introduction to cooking with her food-themed parties, during which children prepare their own tea. Menus have been tailored to suit little chefs from as young as four. For older children, there are 'disco diva' and 'pirate bounty' themes. A two-hour party starts at £165 (plus VAT) for six kids; the price covers everything from shopping to mopping up.

Gill's Cookery Workshop
7 North Square, Golders Green, NW11 7AA (8458 2608). Golders Green tube. **No credit cards.**
Gill Roberts's parties cater for 12 children (£10 per extra child, up to a maximum of 20). Children can decide on their own themes or menus to make on the day. Gill's two-day holiday classes for six- to 13-year-olds cost £90; Saturday morning sessions for three- to eight-year-olds are £25.

Face-painting & make-up

Magical Makeovers
01932 244 347/07957 681 824/www.magical makeovers.com. **No credit cards.**
Slap enthusiasts aged six to 16 can enjoy a pampering party with any number of companions. All make-up is provided, along with hair accessories that the partygoers can keep afterwards. MM now hosts spa parties with facials and manicures for older girl groups. Prices start at £140 for eight participants (up to two hours).

Mini Makeovers
8398 0107/www.minimakeovers.com. **No credit cards.**
Beauty parties (hair, make-up and nails) for girls aged from five to 13 allow younger children to indulge fairy and princess fantasies, while older girls can learn dance routines or parade on a catwalk. All guests receive a pink party bag with hair accessories, bracelet or necklace. Optional extras include a limousine service. Prices start from £160 for eight.

Performance
For clubs and companies that run term-time music and drama courses as well as staging parties, see pp228-31.

Puppet Planet.

Club Dramatika!

8883 7110. **No credit cards.**
Vicky Levy offers fun-packed drama parties for birthday kids with thespian leanings. Parties cost £80 for one hour, £150 for two. Vicky also runs after-school sessions in north London for children aged three and over; call for details.

Little Actors Theatre Company

0800 389 6184/www.dramaparties.com.
No credit cards.
Little Actors can set up role-play or storytelling games with such ever-popular themes as princesses, pirates and superheroes for children aged three years and older. Prices start at £110 an hour; phone for details.

Puppet Planet

787 Wandsworth Road (corner of the Chase), SW8 3JQ (7627 0111/07785 541 358/www.puppetplanet.co.uk).
Credit MC, V.
Lesley Butler's brilliant puppet shop is a great place for a party. Puppets perform favourite tales, then the kids can roll up their sleeves to make their own puppets to take home. Get in touch to find out about other puppet-themed parties for all ages.

Tiddleywinks

8964 5490/www.tiddleywinks.co.uk. **No credit cards.**
Kate Gielgud turns up at your house, in character, to narrate and direct a play in which the kids act, dance and sing their way through one of many themes (*Bugsy Malone,*

Annie, Sleeping Beauty and *Chitty Chitty Bang Bang* are favourites). Thespians aged nine and over can work on a comedic murder mystery to be presented as a showpiece at the end. Prices start at £220 for two hours; all costumes and props are provided.

Science

Mad Science

0845 330 1881/www.madscience.org.uk. **Credit** MC, V.
Fancy experimenting with rocket launchers, hovercrafts and candy floss on that special day? If that sounds like your kids' idea of fun, you can hire a Mad Scientist to create a crazy escapade for groups between the ages of five and 11, and take comfort in the fact that the fun may go some way to improving the science GCSE scores. The scientists involve the children through a combination of interactive experiments, jolly group activities and demonstrations. The basic rate for parties (for up to 20 children) starts at £195 for one hour 15 minutes, rising to £235 for a two-hour full party package that includes eight to ten demonstrations and hands-on experiments.

Sport

Campaign Paintball

Old Lane, Cobham, Surrey KT11 1NH (01932 865 999/www.campaignpaintball.com). Effingham Junction rail. **Credit** MC, V.
The people at Campaign Paintball insist that warlike combat is just a cover for the centre's primary objective:

After all that **Time Out** how about some **Time In** with NICKELODEON

nick.co.uk

ART GALLERY

team-building. But children prefer to be lone heroes and infiltrate enemy camps. By planning a Sunday attack, they get the centre when it's free of office bodkins, and a party package (£24.95 per head) offers kids 300 paintballs to fire at will between 9.30am and 4pm, with a barbecue lunch and awards ceremony afterwards.

Delta Force

01483 211 194/www.paintballgames.co.uk.
Credit MC, V.
The biggest name in UK paintballing, Delta Force has branches all over the country; there are several near enough to the M25 to be convenient for Londoners (choose from Billericay, Hemel Hempstead, Bidbrough, Watford, Upminster, Effingham and Cobham). Children have to be over 11 to participate in the fun. For £12.50 per head, they get 150 paintballs to fire between 9.15am and 4pm, plus a barbecue lunch. If you're planning a large manoeuvre, every 15th person goes free. Players are carefully supervised throughout the day.

League One Sports Academy

8446 0891/www.leagueone.co.uk. **No credit cards**.
Coach Danny Grant organises sporty activities for children aged between five and 11, ranging from basketball, football and cricket to mini Olympics. Varying skill levels don't generally prove an issue, as the coaches will cater for everyone's needs. Parties (prices vary, call for details) cover all equipment, the coaches' fees and a winner's trophy for the birthday child. Venue hire can be arranged for an extra charge. League One also offers after-school and Saturday morning programmes, plus holiday courses in the Hampstead area.

Mallinson Sports Centre

Bishopswood Road, N6 4NY (8342 7272).
Highgate tube. **Credit** MC, V.
Attached to sporty Highgate school for boys, the Mallinson Sports Centre offers two weekend party packages. On Saturday mornings, under-sevens can enjoy an hour on a bouncy castle followed by packed lunches (bring your own) in the social room (from £200 for an hour and 45 minutes). Eight- to 15- year-olds take part in a more comprehensive sporting experience that may involve basketball, hockey or football (from £235). This package involves an hour of supervised team play, as well as half an hour in the pool and then 45 minutes in the social room, giving partygoers a chance to congratulate their fellow teammates on the day's top scores over lunch (provided by parents). Party packages are also available during school holidays.
Buggy access. Nappy-changing facilities.

Paintball Centre

Homeward, Horsley Road, Effingham, Surrey KT11 3JY (0800 917 0821/www.paintballgames.co.uk).
Effingham Junction rail, then 10min walk. **Open** *Phone enquiries* 9am-5.30pm Mon-Fri; 8.30am-4pm Sat, Sun. **Credit** MC, V.
Each soldier gets 150 paintballs to fire off during a morning and early afternoon, with a barbecue lunch laid on as the young guns debrief. The day runs from 9.15am to 4pm; helmets, equipment and overalls are provided. Prices start at £17.50 per head (11- to 17-year-olds, minimum of 20 kids on weekdays).
Canteen.

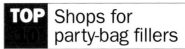

TOP Shops for party-bag fillers

Cheeky Monkeys
Unusual, attractive and fun toys. *See p207.*

Fagin's Toys
Plenty of choice, but nothing faddy. *See p209.*

Happy Returns
Ready-made packs of presents. *See p209.*

Hawkin's Bazaar
Catalogue packed with cheap treats. *See p200.*

Never Never Land
Crammed with old-world delight. *See p212.*

Rainbow
Display counters full of trinkets. *See p212.*

Route 73 Kids
Plenty at pocket-money prices. *See p210.*

Toystop
Beads, bangles and lucky fish. *See p211.*

Tridias
All sorts of toys and great tableware. *See p212.*

Word Play
Books and toys in Crouch End. *See p211.*

Pro-Active 4 Parties & Entertainment

0845 257 5005/www.proactive4parties.co.uk.
No credit cards.
Pro-Active's Premier Football theme is in a league of its own, putting junior teams through a series of tournaments and shoot-outs (£180-£260), while the Sports Combo parties and 'mini Olympics' cover sports from basketball to ultimate frisbee. 'Mayhem' parties for groups of four- to 11-year-olds encompass circus skills, magic, competitions and discos; themed parties for junior gladiators and aspiring wizards (both from £225) are also available. Pro-Active can also set up events in your garden (provided, of course, it's big enough to accommodate a horde of active kids) or a local sports hall.

Cakes

Amato Caffè/Pasticceria

14 Old Compton Street, Soho, W1D 4TH (7734 5733/www.amato.co.uk). Leicester Square or Tottenham Court Road tube. **Open** 8am-10pm Mon-Sat; 10am-8pm Sun. **Credit** AmEx, DC, MC, V.
Map p315 K6.
Many of Amato's bespoke cakes can be further personalised with pictures of the birthday child (from £33.50). For a young film fan, the chefs can create everything from free-standing cake versions of *Star Wars* character R2-D2 (from £150) to designs capturing the Starship Enterprise or an ancient Egyptian scene. The very extravagent can spend up to £3,500.
Buggy access. Delivery service.

Activities

Activities

Alexandra Palace Ice Rink
For £8.50 per head, kids get a brief lesson in skating techniques before a session on the rink, followed by drinks and sandwiches. *See p103.*

Art 4 Fun
Ceramic-painting parties can be set up in your home or can take place in the company's café-shops. Costs vary, phone for details. *See p233.*

The Art Yard
Kids get to choose what they'd like to make from an imaginative list (T-shirt painting to funky bags). Parties cost £16 per child. *See p233.*

Bramley's Big Adventure
Bramley's parties come in Bronze, Silver and Gold versions. Bronze is the cheapest option (75 minutes play, plus a meal and party bag from £8 per head). Gold parties cost from £13. *See p154.*

Chislehurst Caves
A private tour of the spooky tunnels, finishing off with a buffet in the Caves Café costs £50 (maximum 20 kids and four adults), plus £3.95 per child for party food. *See p137.*

Coram's Fields
At weekends, rooms – with kitchen facilities – may be rented, costing from £38 for an afternoon session. Parents provide food and entertainment. *See p63.*

Discover
A two-hour birthday-party booking gives children the first hour playing in Discover's magical Story Trail, then a trained 'story builder' leads hands-on activities like badge-making. All for a bargain £6.50 per child (minimum 15 children). *See p112.*

HMS Belfast
A party room (seating up to 23 children) in the World War II battlecruiser residing at Bankside costs £75/day to hire; catering can be arranged, or else bring your own. Captain Corky's private tour is £100 extra. *See p45*

London Dungeon
Little horrors can have a birthday party here. The price (from £17 per head) includes a tour, an hour in the café's games centre, a themed photograph and a well-filled party bag. *See p38.*

London International Gallery
Musical drawing and origami make variations on the traditional art party theme. Prices start at £125 (plus material expenses). *See p215.*

London Zoo
Parties cost from £15 per child (one adult free with every ten kids). This fee includes entry to the zoo, party animal invitations, goody bags and animal masks, party game leaflets, stickers and a hot or cold party meal. *See p67.*

Lyric Hammersmith Theatre
Parties are for a minimum of five and a maximum of 30 kids. Food is served after the 11am or 1pm performances; the Café Brera hosts party teas from £4.50-£5.50 per child. Parents usually bring the cake. *See p224.*

Michael Sobell Leisure Centre
A selection of party ideas include a gambol round the centre's indoor safari playground facilities (£70-£130), or mixed sports parties with netball, basketball, badminton (£70 for up to 20 kids). Trampolining parties (£87) begin with a lesson; ice-skating parties (£130) come with skates and a lesson. Parents provide the edibles. *See p100.*

Mile End Climbing Wall
Parties for over-eights get an experienced instructor to every eight climbers (costs £58; 90 minutes of climbing and abseiling). Parties end in the padded 'monkey room'. *See p113.*

Playscape Pro Racing
Racing parties for eight- to 16-year-olds, with an hour on the track, cost from £215 for ten drivers, £322.50 for 15 (90 minutes) and £430 for 20 (over two hours). Full training and safety gear are provided, and there's a medal presented to the birthday boy or girl at the end. *See p260.*

Pottery Café
This café offers one all-inclusive two-hour party package (£17.50 per child), which pays for the equipment needed, refreshments, invitations and some colourful decorations. *See p233.*

Puppet Theatre Barge
A brilliant place for a birthday party. Tickets for performances are £7 for kids and £7.50 for adults, and for £50 extra the boat can be rented out for an hour of fun and feasting (parents bring the food). Kids can have a private performance, with an hour on the barge afterwards for £350. *See p221.*

Science Museum
Young children can enjoy the Garden, then eat lunch at the Deep Blue restaurant for £4 a head – a personalised cake costs £24. IMAX cinema parties include a meal (£11 per head); add on £2 for a simulator ride. For £30 per person (minimum five children) you can book a sleepover. *See p91.*

Theatre Museum
Full-on theatricals in Covent Garden include drama birthday parties (£200 for a maximum of 15 children, supervising adults go free). *See p77.*

Westway Sports Centre
Available activities include tennis, football and indoor climbing. Invitations are provided, along with equipment and relevant training. Prices range from £125-£195 for 12 to 24 children, with catering available as an optional extra. *See p154.*

The Cake Store

111 Sydenham Road, Sydenham, SE26 5EZ (8778 4705/www.thecakestore.com). Sydenham rail. **Open** 8am-5.30pm Mon-Sat. **Credit** MC, V.
A cake-lover's paradise, this shop also displays its full catalogue of treasures on its website. It's a fine place to order a birthday cake; standard eight-inchers sell from £19.95, decorated with a Happy Birthday and the name of the birthday girl or boy. If you want to go more fancy, the Cake Store will knock up a cake with your child's photo on the icing, make little marzipan or icing decorations of choice, or rig up a fairy castle, robot and the like.

Cakes4Fun

100 Lower Richmond Road, Putney, SW15 1LN (878 9039/ www.cakes4fun.co.uk). Putney Bridge tube/Putney rail/14 bus. **Open** noon-5pm Mon; 10am-5pm Tue-Sat. **Credit** MC, V.
Cake queen Carolyn and her team make eye-poppingly perfect celebration cakes. For children's birthdays, the range goes from Nemo to Bob the Builder, and from Barbie to spacecraft, ships, castles and animals. Or you can ask them to design something just for you at the initial consultation. The most popular designs are baked in sponge with a variety of jam and buttercream fillings and finished in soft icing, but a rich fruit option can also be arranged. Decorations can include sugarcraft figures and flowers, models and edible photos, as well as 2D and 3D cake sculptures. Most people come here for really fancy 3D designs (Carolyn's reputation has spread far and wide), but prices start from £55 for an eight-inch round cake.

Choccywoccydoodah

47 Harrowby Street, Lisson Grove, W1H 5EA (7724 5465/www.choccywoccydoodah.com). Edgware Road or Marble Arch tube. **Open** 10am-2pm Tue-Fri; 11am-6pm Sat. **Credit** MC, V. **Map** p311 F5.
Choccy creations made here can even be coated with dyed chocolate to match your party's colour scheme. The £25 house cake yields eight to ten portions, 70 portions cost £100; hand-moulded figures and novelty chocs can be added as party table extras.
Buggy access. Delivery service.

Chorak

122 High Road, East Finchley, N2 9ED (8365 3330). East Finchley tube/263 bus. **Open** 8.30am-6.30pm daily. **No credit cards.**

Choccywoccydoodah.

Chorak's handmade party cakes embellished with icing versions of famous characters, such as Shrek, come in two sizes, with the price also depending on whether you opt for a flat cut-out design or a 3D shape. Small cakes contain around 20 portions and cost from £50; large creations begin at £65.
Buggy access. Disabled access.

Dunn's

6 The Broadway, Crouch End, N8 9SN (8340 1614/www.dunns-bakery.co.uk). Finsbury Park tube/rail, then W7 bus/Crouch Hill rail/41, 91 bus. **Open** 7am-6pm Mon-Sat; 10am-5pm Sun. **Credit** MC, V.
For five generations now, Dunn's has been turning out themed party cakes of all descriptions, ranging from photos of your child to Thomas the Tank Engine or Hello Kitty (from £39.60). Bespoke designs can be iced to order.
Buggy access. Delivery service.

Jane Asher Party Cakes

22-24 Cale Street, South Kensington, SW3 3QU (7584 6177/www.jane-asher.co.uk). South Kensington tube/11, 19, 211 bus. **Open** 9.30am-5.30pm Mon-Sat. **Credit** AmEx, MC, V. **Map** p313 E11.
Visit the shop or check out the website to see Ms Asher's range of cake ideas for children. You can order cakes in the form of 3D castles, ladybirds or gorillas and much much more; prices start at £35. Some cake mixes and Jane Asher sugarcraft materials are also available in the shop, should you prefer to bake your own.
Buggy access. Delivery service. Disabled access. Mail order.

Maison Blanc

102 Holland Park Avenue, Holland Park, W11 4UA (7221 2494/ www.maisonblanc.co.uk). Holland Park tube. **Open** 8am-7pm Mon-Thur, Sat; 8am-7.30pm Fri; 8.30am-6pm Sun. **Credit** MC, V.
Any of the MB gateaux can be decorated with a greeting. Other fab ideas for cakes can be whipped up to suit.
Branches: throughout town. Check website for details.

Margaret's Cakes of Distinction

224 Camberwell Road, Camberwell, SE5 0ED (7701 1940/www.purple-pages.com/margarets). Elephant & Castle tube/rail, then 12, 35, 45, 68, 171, 176 bus. **Open** 9am-5pm Mon-Sat. **No credit cards.**
This West Indian bakery turns out distinctive, fairly priced personalised cakes. A simple round sponge cake sandwiched with buttercream or jam can be embellished with

cute little marzipan figurines and costs from £43.95. Alternatively, a 12in (30cm) cake in the shape of a favourite character or animal can be ordered for £80.50. *Buggy access. Disabled access.*

Pierre Péchon

127 Queensway, Bayswater, W2 4XJ (7229 0746/ www.croquembouche.co.uk). Bayswater or Queensway tube. **Open** 7am-7pm Mon-Wed; 7am-8pm Thur-Sat; 8am-7pm Sun. **Credit** MC, V. **Map** p310 C6.
For inspiration, a catalogue of past work is available and PP can add iced messages, characters or a picture from a photographic print if you want. Prices for a 12in (30cm) cake start at £59.10 (33 portions). *Buggy access.*

Primrose Bakery

07802 275 205/www.primrosebakery.org.uk.
If you want pretty home-made party cakes for your little ones but don't have time to whip them up yourself, this chi-chi outfit could be your solution. It allows you to order online and have them delivered to your door instead (if you live in London). Beautifully iced cup cakes made with organic eggs, fresh milk and butter, with a choice of sprinkles, sugar flowers and letters, cost £1 for a mini version, £1.50 for full-sized, plus delivery. Or you can collect from their Primrose Hill HQ. Large cakes, ideal for birthday candles, start at £25.

Costumes

Mail order

Hopscotch

Summer Wood, Puttenham Heath Road, Compton, Guildford, Surrey GU3 1DU (01483 813 728/ www.hopscotchdressingup.co.uk). **Open** *Phone orders* 9.30am-5.30pm Mon-Fri. **Credit** MC, V.
There's a huge choice of costumes on the Hopscotch website, with everything from knights and princesses to soldiers and mermaids, as well as accessories (crowns, fezzes and wands) to sharpen up any outfit. We like the helpful way Hopscotch can supplement your home-made efforts with their well-finished headgear (dragon head in fun fur for £9.95) or supply the whole jolly outfit (adorable dragon suit, £29.95).

J&M Toys

46 Finsbury Drive, Wrose, Bradford, West Yorks BD2 1QA (01274 599 314/fax 01274 591 887/ www.jandmtoys.co.uk). **Open** *Phone enquiries* 9am-5.30pm Mon-Fri. **Credit** MC, V.
Firefighters, fairies, pirates, cowgirls, Vikings, dragons, nurses. Jim and Melanie's comprehensive range includes over 150 dressing-up costumes and accessories, available in age ranges three to five and five to eight. The company has been manufacturing and supplying outfits for almost 20 years. The owners are also medieval enthusiasts, so regal robes, Robin Hoods and a nice range of knights' armour, with wooden swords and shields, are also to be found. J&M is also a boon at that nativity time of year – angels and wise men are tricked out nicely. It's all surprisingly cheap: the majority of costumes cost no more than £15, with discounts on group purchases. Orders are taken online, by post or fax.

Shops

For more toyshops and children's boutiques with dressing-up gear, *see pp185-212.*

Angels

119 Shaftesbury Avenue, St Giles's, WC2H 8AE (7836 5678/www.fancydress.com). Leicester Square or Tottenham Court Road tube. **Open** 9am-5.30pm Mon-Fri. **Credit** AmEx, MC, V.
Angels has a large collection of costumes, props and make-up for children and adults covering many themes. For girls, the Dorothy (*Wizard of Oz*) outfit is rather appealing (£27), while boys can choose from a number of superheroes like Batman or the Hulk. The 'costume treasure chests' are a great gift idea, coming filled with dressing-up outfits and accessories (from £33.50 for three outfits). *Buggy access. Disabled access. Mail order.*

Escapade

150 Camden High Street, Camden Town, NW1 0NE (7485 7384/www.escapade.co.uk). Camden Town tube. **Open** 10am-7pm Mon-Fri; 10am-6pm Sat; noon-5pm Sun. **Credit** AmEx, MC, V.
Escapade make many of its costumes in-store, with all manner of characters catered for – you can opt for a cuddly bear or a kitten, a comedy vegetable item, a well-rendered Cinderella or perhaps a dandified Prince Charming. For instant action heroes, ready-made kits can be bought from around £10 for the most basic, going up to £30 for the full Batman or Thunderbird set. Three-day costume hire costs £30-£65, with a £50 deposit. *Buggy access. Delivery service. Disabled access. Mail order.*

Harlequin

254 Lee High Road, Lewisham, SE13 5PR (8852 0193). Hither Green rail/Lewisham rail/DLR/21, 261 bus. **Open** 10am-5.30pm Mon, Tue, Thur-Sat; 10am-1pm Wed. **Credit** MC, V.
Harlequin is the place to come for your Legolas, or if superheroes are more your bag, there's everyone from Batman (and Robin) to Spidey (£24.95). Cheaper alternatives are available in the form of Indians and ninjas or a set of sheriff accessories. The Elvis kid's jumpsuit (£16.95) is a blast. *Buggy access. Disabled access.*

Pantaloons

119 Lupus Street, Pimlico, SW1V 3EN (7630 8330/ www.pantaloons.co.uk). Pimlico tube. **Open** 11am-6pm Mon-Wed, Fri; 11am-8pm Thur; 10am-6pm Sat. **Credit** AmEx, MC, V.
A dressing-up and balloon specialist that caters for both adults and children, Pantaloons can make sure your party animal looks the part. Budget costumes cost from as little as £10, but you're more likely to hand over £30 for the full Disney regalia. Big production costumes, such as the 'step-in' horse, can also be hired, and elaborate disguises, including wigs and masks, are available too. *Buggy access. Delivery service. Disabled access. Mail order.*

Preposterous Presents

262 Upper Street, N1 2UQ (7226 4166). Highbury & Islington tube./rail. **Open** 10am-6pm Mon-Sat. **Credit** MC, V.

Activities

Preposterous Presents. *See p243*.

A quirky shop full of all kinds of party fripperies, along with jokes of the whoopee cushion, itching powder and fake blood school of humour. Fancy dress is the predominant feature here, with plenty of stage make-up, latex heads, stick-on wizards' beards for the Dumbledore effect and junior-sized costumes (expect to pay £22 for a dalmation or Scooby Doo outfit).

Deals on wheels

The Party Bus

01753 548 822/www.childrenspartybus.co.uk.
This colourful mobile party venue (a converted single-deck bus) holds up to 24 children, with on-board events tailored to the age group in question (from four- to nine-year-olds). Expect games and comedy magic for younger ones, and a mobile disco experience for older kids. For £300-£350 the bus stays at your house for two hours, and provides all the catering except the cake. The added bonus is that when the music stops, the mess just disappears into the sunset.

Wonder Years

8288 0814/0800 458 0852/www.limousine hireheathrow.com.
Wonder Years supplies a chauffeur-driven stretched limo with leather seats, fairy lights and mirrored ceilings. Soft drinks are provided, and each car can legally seat up to eight people; minimum charge is £125 for one hour; additional hours are charged at £50.

Entertainers

More information on the entertainers we've listed can be found on their websites, if they have them, and their prices coaxed out of them by phone.

Ali Do Lali

01494 774 300.
The magic tricks and illusions perfected by Ali over a 30-year career suit all age groups. The very young enjoy storytelling and more gentle trickery; fire-eating and the sawing in half of parents are saved for the older kids. Prices available on application.

Amigo's Magic

8480 8176/www.amigosmagic.co.uk.
Fancy a spot of plate-spinning at the party? Get out the best china for your friend, Simple Simon, Magic Circle member and friendly face of Amigo's. He can also bring his own brand of karaoke, balloon-modelling and magic. Prices start at £120 for an hour.

Billy the Disco DJ

8471 8616/www.billythediscodj.co.uk.
Billy's disco for party children aged five to 11 years includes limbo contests, disco lights, face-painting and temporary tattoos, pop quizzes and karaoke. He charges £150 for a 90-minute do.

Blueberry Playsongs Parties

8677 6871/www.blueberry.clara.co.uk.
A parent-and-toddler music group with nine branches in London (check the website for details), Blueberry sends entertainers to parties of children aged one to six for 45 minutes of guitar-led singing and dancing. Prices start at £75 for 20 children, and include balloons and a present for the birthday boy or girl.

Boo Boo

7727 3817/www.mr-booboo.co.uk.
Boo Boo is part clown, part magician, part comic. His two-hour shows for three- to eight-year-olds incorporate music, balloon-modelling, dancing and general buffoonery; older kids get a Boo Boo disco party.

Chris Howell

7376 1083/www.christopherhowell.net.
Chris Howell is a member of the Magic Circle and uses magic, music and storytelling to narrate an adventure in which the children are encouraged to play an active part. The story is followed by a game with balloon-animal prizes. Hour-long parties for four- to six-year-olds start at around £100.

Foxy the Funky Genie

7692 5664/www.foxythefunkygenie.com
Genie magic, ventriloquism, games, dancing, karaoke, marionettes and more from the multi-talented Owen Reid.

Jenty the Gentle Clown

8527 4855/07957 121 764.
Parties for children aged two to 11 include singing, banjo music, puppets, storytelling, balloon-modelling, face-painting and limbo dancing. Choose the activities to suit your child's tastes. Gentle Jenty charges £145 for one hour or £195 for two.

John Styles

8300 3579/www.johnstylesentertainer.co.uk.
The antique art of ventriloquism is practised by Mr Styles and his team; he also does a Punch & Judy show, balloon modelling and magic.

Juggling John

8938 3218/www.jugglersetc.com.
John Haynes is the man behind the Jugglers Etc agency, which supplies unicyclists, stilt-walkers, storytellers and fire-eaters (mind the curtains!). One- or two-hour shows, depending on age (one-year-olds upwards can be catered for), cost around £140-£275.

Lee Warren

8670 2729/07973 337 575/www.sorcery.org.uk.
Lee combines sorcery with audience participation. The hour-long shows – for four- to eight-year-olds – cost from £110 for a performance in your own home or £120 in a hired hall, and Lee says he's able to deal with nearly any size of audience (eight minimum).

Lisa the Disco Diva

8891 3046/07778 122 277/www.childrenspartieslondon.co.uk.
Lisa's large collection of mobile DJ and disco equipment includes bubble and smoke machines, mirrorballs and fancy lights. She can design a party according to a child's desires and choreograph a whole dance routine to a favourite tune; kids can then do their new grooves for

Activities

barbican

theatre · art · dance
film · education · music

0845 120 7531 Box off
Reduced booking fee online
www.barbican.org.u

London's most exciting film events and activities for children and families!

Every Saturday morning
Barbican Cinema 1

Family Film Club

- a great place to watch new and classic children's films from around the world
- free activities and workshops each week
- tickets from just £2.50!

www.barbican.org.uk/familyfilmclub

18 – 26 Nov 2006
Barbican and venues across London

The London Children's Film Festival 2006

- the very best of contemporary children's world cinema
- premieres and previews of new UK releases
- a chance to meet the stars of the films
- creative workshops with professional film and animation artists
- schools screenings and education activities

www.londonchildrenfilm.org.uk

The London Children's Film Festival is presented in partnership with

iCO independent cinema office

Supported by

FILM LONDON

UK FILM COUNCIL
LOTTERY FUNDED

CITY OF LONDON

Third largest funder of the arts in the UK

grown-ups, or just party the rest of the afternoon away on their own. Events cater for boys and girls aged four and upwards, with games, magic and competitions included in the high-energy, two-hour package. Prices start from £170.

Little Blisters

8392 9093/www.childrensentertainment-surrey.co.uk.
Parties for three- to seven-year-olds may star Flossie the Fairy, Sea Lily the Mermaid or Kitty the Magical Pussy Cat. Shows with stories, song and dancing last one or two hours (£100-£220), with games, prizes and face-painting.

Lydie's Children's Parties

7622 2540/www.lydieparties.com.
Musician, mime artist and dancer Lydie can transform your home into a themed party kingdom for a make-believe extravaganza for up to 26 children, and promises to clean up afterwards too. Parties cost from £365 for two hours.

Magic Mikey

0808 100 2140/www.magicmikey.co.uk.
High-profile Magic Mikey brings with him a disco, lots of games ideas, Rocky the Super Racoon, and – of course – his magic show, to entertain children up to 12 years old. Prices cost from £250 for a two hour party package.

Merlin Entertainments

8866 6327/www.merlinents.co.uk.
Choose from a long list of performers, with everything from caricaturists and comedy waiters to fortune-tellers and fire-eaters on Merlin's books. Prices start at £120 for a one-hour performance, or £150 for a more interactive two-hour show. Merlin also organises circus and clown workshops for parties with age groups of three upwards; they'll bring the necessary equipment to a suitable venue of your choice.

Mr Squash

8808 1415/www.mr-squash.co.uk.
Mr Squash travels all over London with his musical puppet show, balloon tricks, singalongs and funny stories. Well known on the playgroup circuit, he's experienced in engaging the very young (two- and three-year-olds), but his parties are suitable for children aged up to six. His puppet friends, performing in a band, invite audience participation, especially from the birthday boy or girl. Mr Squash charges £150-£175 for a one-hour set.

Pekko's Puppets

8575 2311/www.pekkospuppets.co.uk.
Stephen Novy's puppet plays are aimed at children aged three to 11, with shows for under-fives packing in two shorter tales with lots of singing and audience participation. The repertoire for older children includes Celtic folk tales, popular classics and chillers like *Dracula*, all enacted from one of Mr Novy's two mobile booths (from £140 for one hour).

Peter McKenna

7703 2254/07956 200 572.
Magic Circle member Peter McKenna appears in a variety of guises to suit various age groups – and performs tricks with a degree of competence rarely seen at children's parties. Illusions might include levitating, sawing parents in half and decapitating audience members (fear not,

noone's ever left a party minus their head), but there are always less alarming routines for little ones. Discos, party games and goody bags are all available by arrangement. Prices start at £90 for one hour, £145 for two.

Professor Fumble

01395 579 523/www.professorfumble.co.uk.
Professor Fumble's routine involves repeatedly bungling his tricks, juggling like a seasoned amateur and sitting in his own custard pies. Shows can last one or two hours (from £115 or £160 respectively); the former include balloon animals for the kids and – where space permits – a chance for party-goers to have a crack at spinning plates or walking on small stilts. Longer performances allow for Fumbling versions of old party games.

Silly Millie the Clown

7823 8329/www.sillymillietheclown.co.uk.
Silly parties for three to twelve year olds include magic, balloon animals, singalongs, puppets all wrapped up in general daftness. Prices cost from £85 an hour.

Equipment hire

Disco

Young's Disco Centre

2 Malden Road, Chalk Farm, NW5 3HR (7485 1115/ www.londondiscohire.co.uk for equipment hire/ www.steveyoungdisco.co.uk for DJs). Chalk Farm tube. **Open** by appointment only. **Credit** MC, V.
Young's is the place to hire disco equipment. A state-of-the-art sound system comes with a DJ for two hours (£200), and karaoke set-ups are available from £80. You can add a smoke machine or industrial bubble blower (both from £15), popcorn and candy-floss makers (from £50 each), or even fake snow machines (£20). A DIY children's party package with a sound system and disco lights can be hired over 24 hours for a bargain £60.
Buggy access. Delivery service. Disabled access.

Fairground

PK Entertainments

01344 626 789/07771 546 676/www.fairandfete.co.uk. **No credit cards**.
What do you get for the child who has everything? An indoor fairground might be a start. PK Entertainments can set up a basic package (from £250) in your living room, with mini bouncy castle, bucking bronco and stalls of the pop-gun variety; those with more capacious sitting rooms (along the lines of a ballroom, perhaps?) can even request a toboggan run. Outdoor events start at about £250 for 20 kids, though a full-blown fair can be built for roughly £500 (roundabouts, swingboats and all).

Marquees

Sunset Marquees

Welsback House, 3-9 Broomhill Road, Putney, SW18 4JQ (8741 2777/www.sunsetmarquees.com). East Putney tube. **Open** 8am-6pm daily. **No credit cards**.
If a giant, child-filled tent sounds like a fab idea, Sunset should be able to supply you with everything you need to

Activities

make it a reality. A basic package with 3m by 3m (10ft by 10ft) tent starts from £190 (plus VAT), with lighting, furniture, candy-floss machines, heating and carpeting supplied for an extra charge.

Organisers

Action Station

0870 770 2705/www.theactionstation.co.uk.
Specialising in interactive magical storytelling for younger children (four to six), with mermaids, witches, fairies and princesses, Action Station also offers themed parties for older children; drama, cheerleader and film make-up parties cost from £147 for an hour, £200 for two. The agency's books also brim with unicyclists, jugglers and the like.

Adam Ants

8959 1045/www.adamantsparties.com.
Adam Ants can conjure up a number of entertainers adept in the arts of music-making, magic and balloon-modelling. Party accessories, including ball ponds and bouncy castles, may be hired (from £55) along with kid-o-gram characters (from £85). Catering can also be organised.

Boo! Productions

7287 9090/07768 311 068/www.booproductions.com.
Boo! Productions (previously Crechendo Events) specialises in bespoke themed parties. If you only need an entertainer, prices start at around £235 for two hours, but you're looking at £893 plus for a full themed party service. But with Boo! Productions' promise of 'we will find it, build it or bake it', it would appear that staff will try to accommodate any crazed ideas you can dream up.

Laurie Temple & the Party Wizard Children's Company

8951 9469/07951 596 240/www.thepartywizard.co.uk.
Entertainer Laurie Temple and his team run a host of parties lasting for one or two hours that can feature magic, balloons, juggling, junior discos, puppetry, storytelling and face-painting, as well as themes such as popstar discos and crazy circus workshops. A wide range of party budgets are catered for, and prices can range from £130 to £180 (one hour), and from £175 to £250 (two hours).

Mystical Fairies

12 Flask Walk, Hampstead, NW3 1HE (7431 1888/ www.mysticalfairies.co.uk). Hampstead tube. **Open** 10am-6pm Mon-Sat; 11am-6pm Sun. **Credit** MC, V.
For parties shimmering with fairy dust, disco fun, gauzy outfits borrowed from the shop (*see p209*) and an 'enchanted garden', MF charges £350. This is for an on-site party package, including invitations, tableware, an entertainer and costumes. Home parties (lasting two hours) can work out cheaper (£200). If you'd like the good fairies to tailor a party to your child's needs, ask for a quotation. Prices quoted don't include VAT.
Buggy access. Mail order.

Puddleduck Parties

8893 8998/www.puddleduckparties.co.uk.
Puddleduck can put together flexible packages that encompass all those party necessities such as catering (inclusive

of tableware), decorations and entertainers. 'Teddy bears' picnics' can be arranged for the smaller ones, otherwise there's drama, sport or disco parties for all ages, starting from around £200 for two hours of fun.

Splodge

7350 1477/www.planetsplodge.com.
Splodge specialises in highly creative, themed corporate parties and family fun days; anything from a treasure hunt in Kensington Gardens to having Santa Claus arrive on your doorstep in puffs of coloured smoke can be arranged. Tailor-made packages might include party teas, invites, party bags, decorations, a video and a face-painter, all personalised according to the family's wishes. For 20 kids, such parties cost from around £500.

Taylor-Made Entertainment

07974 901 215/www.taylor-madeentertainment.com.
TME can provide the wherewithal for discos, with lights, scented smoke, bubbles and karaoke. It will also organise makeover artists, facepainters, musicians, and party MCs. Supplying entertainment for young and easily bored guests at weddings is another speciality.

Twizzle Parties

8789 3232/www.twizzle.co.uk.
Famed for organising various children's 'film premiere' parties (*Wallace & Gromit: Curse of the Were-Rabbit* and *Madagascar*, to name but two), Twizzle is capable of building themed events for all ages. While toddlers will enjoy a 'nursery rhymes and singalong fun' party, older children will thrill to themes including pirates, Action Man and ballerinas; Twizzle can also organise or street-dance parties for older siblings (from £150 for one hour or £250 for two). Wannabe pop stars can make their own CD in a recording studio (from £350 for two hours, up to 16 kids), taking a copy away to play at home. A choreographed video to accompany the musical masterpiece can also be arranged; prices on application.

Paraphernalia
Mail order

Baker Ross

Enquiries 8523 2733/phone orders 0870 458 5440/ www.bakerross.co.uk. **Credit** MC, V.
A great favourite with PTA fundraisers, Baker Ross stocks a vast range of little gifts that are suitable for prizes and bagfillers, as well as a huge range of craft supplies. Pocket-money toys – multi-coloured stretchy lizards (£2.64 for 12) or temporary Halloween tattoos (£7.92 for a box of 144) – are always popular with the younger generation. Phone or visit the website for a catalogue.

CYP

01279 444 707/www.cyp.co.uk. **Credit** AmEx, MC, V.
This company's selection of party tapes and CDs provides ideal backing music for traditional children's party games like pass the parcel, or musical chairs; they are equally suited to tot-friendly disco dancing. The ultimate pop party CD is £4.99 – which, with 70 minutes of hits (from big chunks of Abba to 'Mambo No.5'), is definitely the cheap alternative to hiring a DJ.

Pekko's Puppets. *See p247.*

Just Balloons

8560 5933/www.justballoons.com. **Credit** AmEx, MC, V.
Balloons can be personalised with messages or photographs (the latter costing £125 for 100). Foil balloons come in a range of styles from £2.95 each, while customised party banners start at £47. Delivery in central London is around £15.

Party Directory

01252 851 601/www.partydirectory4kids.co.uk.
Credit MC, V.
This mail-order catalogue covers everything required for a successful celebration. Fans of *The Incredibles* can enjoy themed tableware (cups to tablecloths ranging from 23p to £2.75), while wearing glitzy party headdresses (£1.50 for a set of five). There are loads of ideas for party-bag fillers too.

Party Pieces

01635 201 844/www.partypieces.co.uk. **Credit** MC, V.
A huge range of reasonably priced tableware (from around 25p an item) includes famous faces like Winnie the Pooh, Scooby Doo and Nemo, while themes for older kids include macho camouflage or girly popstar sets with matching party bags and invitations. There are loads of party bag-fillers, traditional games (a pin the eyepatch on the pirate version of the donkey's tail original is £2.45), and a whopping range of banners, balloons and assorted decorations.

Party Supplies Direct

01437 563 068/www.partysuppliesdirect.co.uk.
Credit MC, V.
An extremely useful online warehouse of discounted party essentials. You can order balloons, party-bag fillers, decorations, a vast range of themed tableware (including Harry

Potter) and all sorts of other stuff, and most of it's quite a bit cheaper than in the shops. It deals with requests too.

Your Party by Post

0845 408 4812/www.yourpartybypost.co.uk. **Credit** MC, V.
Themed children's partyware and gifts: everything from banners, balloons and games to thank-you notes.

Shops

Balloon & Kite Company

613 Garratt Lane, Earlsfield, SW18 4SU (8946 5962/ www.balloonandkite.com). Earlsfield rail. **Open** 9am-6pm Mon-Fri; 9am-5.30pm Sat. **Credit** MC, V.
Balloons are available in rubber or foil (from £1 or £2.99 a piece), bearing pictures of any number of favourite screen heroes; names can be added to Happy Birthday variants while you wait (from £3.99 each). There's themed paper tableware and banners, while kites (from £10) make good last-minute gifts. Goody-bag stuff starts at 99p a pack.
Buggy access. Delivery service. Disabled access: ramps. Mail order.

Balloonland

12 Hale Lane, Mill Hill, NW7 3NX (8906 3302/ www.balloonland.co.uk). Edgware tube/Mill Hill Broadway rail/221, 240 bus. **Open** 9.30am-5.30pm Mon-Fri; 10am-5.30pm Sat. **Credit** MC, V.
Balloonland's range of products can make children's parties look spectacular. Regular balloons start from 20p each and come in a wide variety of shapes and sizes. The choice is inflated further by designer creations (balloon clusters, jumbo balloon trees, balloons attached to soft toys

or chocolate boxes), as well as themed tableware and decorations. Loot-bag gifts are also available here.
Buggy access. Delivery service. Disabled access. Mail order.

Bouncing Kids

127 Northfield Avenue, Ealing, W13 9QR (8840 0110/www.bouncing-kids.com). Northfields tube/West Ealing rail. **Open** 9am-5.30pm Mon-Sat. **Credit** MC, V.
West London residents come here for their paperware, balloons, costumes and party-bags, but anyone who lives within a 25-mile radius of Ealing can hire one of the range of bouncy castles, tables and chairs, badge-making machines and parachute games. The proprietors are a mine of information about entertainers and organisers (and whether you can actually fit a bouncy castle into a pocket handkerchief – a peculiarly London problem). Check the website for details.
Delivery service. Mail order.

Circus Circus

176 Wandsworth Bridge Road, Fulham, SW6 2UQ (7731 4128/www.circuscircus.co.uk). Fulham Broadway tube. **Open** 10am-6pm Mon-Sat. **Credit** AmEx, MC, V.
If you have a particular kids' party theme in mind, Circus Circus will supply everything needed to put it together. That means that cakes can be baked (from £95), balloons blown up, bouncy castles organised and entertainers brought to your front door as part of the service. Children's costumes (from £10.99) and accessories – such as wigs, masks, wands and weapons, invitations, goody bags and boxes, ribbons, streamers and balloons – can all be purchased in the store, where tableware comes in more than 70 popular themes.
Buggy access. Delivery service. Disabled access: ramp. Mail order. Play area.

Mexicolore

28 Warriner Gardens, Battersea, SW11 4EB (7622 9577/www.pinata.co.uk). Battersea Park or Queenstown Road rail/44, 137 bus. **Open** by appointment daily. **No credit cards.**
Proper piñatas (not the cheapo cardboard ones you can buy at supermarkets) at Mexicolore are made from decorated papier mâché in a number of designs that can be filled by parents with fruit, sweets or small toys. Pick up a small bull or a star for around £19.95 or, if you prefer, maybe something a little larger, such as a donkey design that'll set you back £40 and last about five minutes in the hands of manic, stick-wielding children.
Buggy access. Mail order.

The Non-Stop Party Shop

214-216 Kensington High Street, Kensington, W8 7RG (7937 7200/www.nonstopparty.co.uk). High Street Kensington tube/10, 27, 391 bus. **Open** 9.30am-6pm Mon-Sat; 11am-5pm Sun. **Credit** MC, V. **Map** p312 A9.
The Non-Stop Party people have quite a selection of party headwear, from starchy would-be aristocrat top hats to some corking battered Australian bushwhacker affairs – and with the most basic plastic hats starting at a mere 99p, there are some affordable options too. Other than the titfers, expect to find plastic animal masks (£2.50) and – to complete the look – face-crayons, wigs and false noses, along with all sorts of theatrical make-up.
Delivery service (balloons only). Mail order.

Oscar's Den

127-129 Abbey Road, St John's Wood, NW6 4SL (7328 6683/www.oscarsden.com). Swiss Cottage tube/West Hampstead tube/rail/28, 31, 139, 189 bus. **Open** 9.30am-5.30pm Mon-Sat; 10am-2pm Sun. **Credit** AmEx, MC, V.
In addition to organising parties for the rich and famous (the prime minister has utilised them in the past for his kids), Oscar's Den coordinates celebrations for all budgets, and its range of services runs from face-paints to year-round firework displays. Ball ponds, bouncy castles (from £45) and big toys (seesaws, slides, pedal cars and more, from £10) are permanently for hire.
Buggy access. Delivery service.

Party Party

11 Southampton Road, Gospel Oak, NW5 4JS (7267 9084/www.partypartyuk.com). Chalk Farm tube/Gospel Oak rail/24 bus. **Open** 9.30am-5.30pm Mon-Sat. **Credit** MC, V.
Party Party has a bespoke piñata service, offering any character, animal or object you can think of. A piñata Spiderman or football, for example, can cost from £10, while more unusual, made-to-order designs are around £50 each. It also stocks a medley of party-bag fillers, along with decorations that encompass everything from themed tableware to mirrorballs.
Buggy access. Delivery service.

Party Superstore

268 Lavender Hill, Clapham, SW11 1LJ (7924 3210/ www.partysuperstore.co.uk). Clapham Junction rail/39, 77, 345 bus. **Open** 9am-6pm Mon-Wed, Fri, Sat; 9am-7pm Thur; 10.30am-4.30pm Sun. **Credit** AmEx, MC, V.
The first floor of the Superstore stocks children's party accessories, fancy-dress costumes (from £7.99), eye-masks and novelty hats (from £1.99) and wigs (from £2.99). There are also more than 50 themed tableware collections, many of which are suitable for children, as well as practical jokes, hundreds of balloons, mock jewellery, party-bag fillers, and a collection of cake decorations and candles.
Buggy access. Delivery service. Disabled access. Mail order.
Branch: 43 Times Square, High Street, Sutton, Surrey SM1 1LF (8661 7323).

Purple Planet

Greenhouse Garden Centre, Birchen Grove, Kingsbury, NW9 8SA (8205 2200/www.purpleplanet.co.uk). Wembley Park rail, then 182, 297 bus. **Open** 10am-5pm Mon-Sat; 10.30am-4.30pm Sun. **Credit** AmEx, MC, V.
Visit Purple Planet if you want to wow your party guests with your boundless creativity. This wonderful shop has a vast arts and crafts section, and staff run regular card-making workshops and free in-store demonstrations. Many party items are available: helium balloons from 90p, a selection of themed tableware and, most importantly, the fine and beautifully detailed selection of sugarcraft accessories and cookie cutters (90p-£19.99) for which the Planet is known. When it comes to the birthday centrepiece, there's everything you could think of for a truly magnificent cake, from opulent fountain candles (£2.50 each) to edible paint.
Buggy access. Car park. Delivery service. Disabled access: ramp, toilets. Mail order.

Activities

Sport & Leisure

It's ready, set, go! as London children prepare to raise their game.

There has never been a better time for kids to get sporty in London. The success of the London bid to host the 2012 Olympic and Paralympic Games has pushed sport and physical activity high up the political agenda, so money is at last being spent on improving the health of our children. If you don't already know the acronyms SSCo (School Sport Co-ordinator) and PESSCL (PE, School Sport and Club Links), you soon will: these are major initiatives designed to make a connection between what goes on inside the school gates and the clubs and activities available outside.

The government's aim is for all children to do at least two hours of high-quality PE and sport a week, with 75 per cent of schools required to meet that target by the end of 2006. PESSCL is intended to increase the percentage of five- to 16-year-olds who are members of an affiliated sports club from 14 per cent in 2002 to 20 per cent in 2006.

This ambitious strategy has also put the onus on sports clubs to implement child-protection policies and putting together development plans for which they can receive funding. Gone are the days when sports clubs were accountable to noone but their own brass-buttoned committees. Now, transparency is the keyword. For example, if you are looking for a club for your children to join, ask whether the club has a child-welfare officer. If not, demand to know why and proceed with caution.

Many sports have implemented a Sport England-backed quality assurance scheme to show that their clubs are 'safe, effective and child-friendly'. Any club that holds, or is working towards, a Clubmark or Charter Standard award should operate to high ethical standards. There will be a structured coaching and match play programme with qualified instructors and an ethos that places equal value on all children, not just the most talented. To find out more about how the Clubmark scheme works, visit www.sportengland.org.

Not all children enjoy competitive team games, and the aim of this section is to show the wide range of sport and fitness options available in the capital. Some activities are more aesthetic than athletic, while others can be enjoyed without the need for ten teammates, expensive equipment and a referee. There's one word to remember whatever your children choose, though: sport is about fun!

Sports to do

Athletics

With 18 different disciplines in 'track and field', not to mention the more winter-oriented cross-country, most children find at least one event they're good at. Many first encounter athletics through the popular Sportshall programmes used in schools, which employ soft javelins, relay races and specially designed jumping boards to create an exciting two-hour package. The same skills are developed in clubs, where keen athletes have the chance to join a training group under the guidance of a coach. Membership usually costs around £25-£40 per year, plus a fee for track use.

Maureen Jones (8224 7579) is a senior UK Athletics (www.ukathletics.net) coach who organises Run, Jump, Throw courses during the school holidays at several tracks in south London for children aged eight to 12.

The following clubs also have well-established sections for young athletes:

Belgrave Harriers (Battersea) *Kim Collier (07816 620 807/www.belgraveharriers.com).*
Blackheath & Bromley Harriers (Bromley) *John Baldwin (01825 768 193/www.bandbhac.org.uk).*
Havering Mayesbrook AC (Hornchurch/Dagenham) *Jean Tierney (01708 341 547/www.havering-mayesbrook.org).*
Newham & Essex Beagles AC (Plaistow) *Lesley Richardson (07958 459 123/www.neb 2005.co.uk).*
Shaftesbury Barnet Harriers (Barnet) *(8202 6478/www.sbharriers.co.uk).*
Thames Valley Harriers (Shepherd's Bush) *Kathy Davidson (01895 676 513/www.thamesvalley harriers.com).*
Victoria Park Harriers & Tower Hamlets AC (Mile End) *Alf Vickers (07832 251 478/ www.vphthac.org.uk).*
Windsor, Slough, Eton & Hounslow AC (Windsor/Eton) *Dennis Daly (01753 686 169/ www.wseh.info).*
Woodford Green AC with Essex Ladies (Woodford) *(8550 9788/Club HQ 8505 5575/www.wgel.org.uk).*

South of England Athletics Association
4th Floor, Marathon House, 115 Southwark Street, SE1 0JF (7021 0988/www.seaa.org.uk).

The SEAA has details of other clubs around London. There's also a directory at www.british-athletics.co.uk.

Badminton & squash

The success of Nathan Robertson and Gail Emms at the Athens Olympics in 2004 did wonders for badminton's image. Both badminton and squash have excellent junior development programmes and are not saddled with the social preconceptions that bedevil tennis. For more information, contact the **Badminton Association of England** (01908 268 400, www.badmintonengland.co.uk) or **England Squash** (0161 231 4499, www.englandsquash.co.uk). The respective websites for the sports have club searches.

These clubs have junior badminton and/or squash programmes; phone for prices and times:
Dulwich Sports Club *Burbage Road, SE24 9HP (7274 1242/www.dulwichsquash.com). Herne Hill rail.*
New Grampian Squash Club *Shepherd's Bush Road, W6 7LN (7603 4255/www.newgrampians.co.uk). Hammersmith tube.*
New Malden Tennis, Squash & Badminton Club *Somerset Close, New Malden, Surrey KT3 5RG (8942 0539/www.newmaldenclub.co.uk). Malden Manor rail.*
Southgate Squash Club *Walker Cricket Ground, Waterfall Road, N14 7JZ (8886 8381/www.southsquashclub.co.uk). Southgate tube.*
Wimbledon Racquets & Fitness Club *Cranbrook Road, SW19 4HD (8947 5806/www.wsbc.co.uk). Wimbledon tube/rail.*

Baseball & softball

Both these sports are attracting more participants because of their wide range of programmes for kids of both sexes, all ages and abilities. Schemes like Pitch, Hit & Run and Play Ball teach the basics in schools and clubs to children aged from six. Check www.playballwithfrubes.com. For more information, contact **BaseballSoftballUK** (7453 7055/www.baseballsoftballuk.com). The **London Baseball Association** (www.londonsports.com) also runs skills clinics.

The following clubs have junior programmes:
Essex Arrows (Waltham Abbey) *Phil Chesterton (07890 280 118, www.essexarrows.com).*
London Meteors Baseball & Softball Club (Finsbury Park) *Neil Warne (07770 381 308/ www.londonmeteors.co.uk).*
Windsor Baseball & Softball Club (Windsor) *John Boyd (07769 655 496/www.baseballsoftballuk.com).*

Basketball

There are basketball clubs all over the capital playing in local leagues, and the sport is extremely well organised at junior level, with competitions

Activities

right up to national standard. The famous Topcats programme in Brixton has produced numerous international players. To find out more, contact regional development manager Steve Alexander (8968 0051) or the **English Basketball Association** (0870 774 4225/www.basketball england.org.uk).

The following clubs have junior programmes:

Brixton Topcats Brixton Recreation Centre
Station Road, SW9 8QQ (contact Jimmy Rogers 7737 3354/brixtontopcats@hotmail.com). Brixton tube/rail.

Croydon Flyers (girls) *Lewis Sports Centre, Maberley Road, SE19 2JH (8657 1566/www.croydon flyers.com).*

Hackney Academy *SPACE Centre, Hackney Community College, Falkirk Street, N1 6HF (7613 9525). Old Street tube/243 bus.*

Boxing

The success of Amir Khan, first at the Athens Olympics and more recently as a professional, has shown that boxing can be an exciting, disciplined and intelligent activity. The sport at amateur level has an impressive safety record, and youngsters are simply not powerful enough to inflict the sort of damage that has disfigured some parts of the professional game.

To find a local club, contact the London regional secretary on 7252 7008 or use the search facility on the Amateur Boxing Association of England's website (www.abae.co.uk).

Circus skills

It's not usually kids who are petrified at the thought of walking tightropes or dangling from trapezes – it's their parents. Circus skills are thrilling to learn and develop excellent all-round physical fitness. They are often popular with children turned off by ball games on muddy fields. Rest assured that the circus schools listed below give safety the highest priority.

Albert & Friends' Instant Circus

8237 1170/www.albertandfriendsinstantcircus.co.uk.
Albert the Clown (aka Ian Owen) runs Instant Circus workshops to teach children skills such as juggling, diabolo, and stilt-, ball- and wire-walking. Many of his students go on to join the Albert & Friends' performing troupe – the UK's largest children's circus theatre, which also tours abroad.

The Circus Space

Coronet Street, N1 6HD (7613 4141/www.thecircus space.co.uk). Old Street tube/rail.
There's a Sunday morning 'Little Top' course for eight- to 11-year-olds; older children can choose static and flying trapeze, juggling, trampoline and acrobatics.

Jackson's Lane Community Circus

269A Archway Road, N6 5AA (8340 5226/ www.jacksonslane.org.uk). Highgate tube.
Classes are offered in unicycling, juggling and acrobatics.

Climbing

This is a seriously addictive sport, and its problem-solving requirements (you climb with your head as well as your body) have been shown to have a knock-on effect in the classroom.

London's indoor centres all cater for children (aged from around eight), with safe sessions run by qualified instructors. For general information on climbing, contact the **British Mountaineering Council** (0870 010 4878/www.thebmc.co.uk).

Castle Climbing Centre

Green Lanes, N4 2HA (07776 176 007/www.geckos. co.uk). Manor House tube.
Overwhelming popularity means that the only way for children to climb here is by private tuition (£35hr plus £10 admission and kit hire) or at a weekend birthday party (£125 for six children, £225 for up to 12). For both, you'll need to book in advance.

Mile End Climbing Wall

Haverfield Road, E3 5BE (8980 0289/www.mileend wall.org.uk). Mile End tube.
This centre runs children's beginner sessions (£6) every Friday evening, with skills sessions on Saturday and Sunday mornings. Birthday parties can be held here and there is a summer holiday programme.

Westway Climbing Complex

Westway Sports Centre, 1 Crowthorne Road, W10 6RP (8969 0992/www.westway.org/sports/wsc/climbing). Latimer Road tube.
This impressive centre challenges all levels of climbing skill, and its big, chunky holds are perfect for kids. There are after-school classes on Mondays Wednesdays, from 4.30pm to 6pm, costing £3.

Cricket

England's success in winning back the Ashes, combined with the popularity of shorter Twenty20 matches, has given our domestic cricket scene a boost. Another encouraging development is the return of the game to central London: a major new cricket centre in Regent's Park offers one county-standard and five club-standard pitches, served by a large pavilion, and it will provide a permanent base for Capital Kids Cricket, which was set up in 1991 to encourage school-age children to play. For details, contact Regent's Park on 7486 7905.

There may be a decline in cricket in state schools, but clubs all round the capital have stepped in to develop the game for boys and

Becks' futures

David Beckham first dreamed of becoming a professional footballer when he attended a Bobby Charlton Soccer School as a boy. Now, he has a soccer school all of his own – the David Beckham Academy on Greenwich Peninsula, next to the O2 (Dome). It's an impressive place, with two huge indoor pitches, highly qualified coaches and an impressive array of memorabilia on display from Becks and his Manchester United, Real Madrid and England teammates.

Although the academy is a commercial operation, it is also committed to a school education programme. Ten thousand children each year attend free of charge; their time is spent on team building, tactics, technique and tournaments to complement Key Stage 2 and 3 learning.

However, most kids will experience the Academy through its football camps. These run Monday to Friday during school holidays and follow the same lines as the schools education programme, plus coaching and skills sessions. They seem expensive compared to other football coaching set-ups, but all kids receive a package of Adidas kit, including footwear, plus a healthy lunch and refreshments.

Beckham is often pilloried for the more flamboyant aspects of his lifestyle, but there's no doubting his commitment to sport for young people – the philosophy here is complete inclusion for boys and girls of all abilities – and to the city in which he was born and brought up.

The David Beckham Academy

East Parkside, Greenwich Peninsula, SE10 0JF (8269 4620/www.thedavidbeckham academy.com). North Greenwich tube. **Camps** £175 3 days; £215 4 days; £250 5 days.

Activities

girls aged from six. Many run junior sections, with 11-year-olds and under playing an adapted form of the game called Terrier Cricket, in which everyone gets an equal chance to bat, bowl and field. Safety is to the fore: all under-16s are required to wear a helmet when batting, wicket-keeping or fielding close to the wicket against a hard ball. Most clubs will provide this, along with the other essential protective equipment, until a youngster decides that they want to play regularly and buys their own.

Contact the County Board offices to find a club:
Essex (including East London) *01245 254010/ www.essexcricket.org.uk.*
Hertfordshire *01279 771 551/ www.hertscricket.org.*
Kent *01227 456 886/www.kentsport.org/cricket.cfm.*
Middlesex *7266 1650/www.communigate.co.uk.*
Surrey *7820 5734/www.surreycricket.com.*

For coaching, try the following indoor centres:
Ilford Cricket School *Sussex Close, Beehive Lane, Ilford, Essex IG4 5DR (8550 0041). Gants Hill tube.*
Ken Barrington Cricket Centre *Brit Oval, SE11 5SS (7820 5739). Oval tube.*
MCC Indoor School Lord's Cricket Ground *NW8 8QN (7432 1014/www.mcc.org.uk). St John's Wood tube.*
Middlesex County Cricket Club *East End Road, N3 2TA (8346 8020/wwwmiddlesexccc.com). Finchley Central tube.*

Cycling

In some European countries, as many as 60 per cent of children cycle to school. In Britain, a mere three per cent do. And a UK cyclist is 12 times more likely to be killed or injured than a Danish one, for example. In response to these worrying statistics, Safe Routes to Schools supports projects throughout the country that encourage young people to cycle and walk to school by improving street design, calming traffic and linking with the 8,000-kilometre (5,000-mile) National Cycle Network. Most local authorities include Safe Routes to Schools schemes in their Local Transport Plans.

For more information, see *The Official Guide to the National Cycle Network* by Nick Cotton and John Grimshaw, published by Sustrans at £9.99. Sustrans (www.sustrans.org.uk) is the pressure group working to create a safer environment for cycling. See also www.ridethenet.org.uk.

Cycling England (a body funded by the Department for Transport to promote the growth of cycling in England) also launched a cycling to school initiative in 2006. Parents who aren't aware of a safe cycle route to their child's school or want to find out more about cycle training or Bike to School Week, they can visit www.bikeforall.net for more information.

The best guide to family rides around the capital is *The London Cycle Guide* (Haynes, £8.99), published in association with the **London Cycling Campaign** (7234 9310/www.lcc.org.uk).

Cycle Training UK

7582 3535/www.cycletraining.co.uk.
CTUK's instructors offer individual tuition anywhere in Greater London. Accompanied journeys to school are also available. After attending training, 81% of people said they cycled more often and more confidently.

London Recumbents

8299 6636/www.londonrecumbents.co.uk.
London Recumbents has a large range of cycles for hire.

London School of Cycling

7249 3779/www.londonschoolofcycling.co.uk.
Offering private tuition for all ages and abilities, the London School also runs cycle-maintenance workshops.

Cycle sport

Go-Ride is a British Cycling initiative where under-18s can learn track riding, BMX and mountain biking from qualified coaches. It's delivered through a national network of cycling clubs and includes a skills test designed to challenge even the best riders. Clubs involved include Lee Valley Youth Cycle Club (contact Marc Burden on 8558 1112), Team Economic Energy (contact Leslie Everest on 8989 8429) and Sutton Cycle Club (contact Catherine Mahe 8642 0285, www.suttoncycling.co.uk). The scheme's website (www.go-ride.org.uk) lets you compare test times. The venerable velodrome at Herne Hill (Burbage Road, SE24 9HE, www.hernehillvelodrome.co.uk),

home of track cycling since 1892, reopened in August 2005. Check the website for details of forthcoming events.

Hillingdon Cycle Circuit

Minet Park, Springfield Road, Hayes, Middx UB4 0LF (8737 7797). Hayes & Harlington rail.
This tarmac circuit of almost a mile is popular for road racing and tuition.

Lee Valley Cycle Circuit

Quarter Mile Lane, E10 5PD (8534 6085/www.leevalley park.org/cyclecircuit). Leyton tube.
This 45-acre (18-hectare) site is known as Eastway. It has a tarmac track, a mountain bike and BMX circuit, and Saturday morning sessions for children. Olympic works in Lee Valley mean Eastway's future, however, is uncertain.

Cycle safety

● Always check bikes before setting out, especially the brakes: can your child easily reach the levers? If the gears are slipping, a small turn of the black plastic cap where the gear cable meets the derailleur will usually do the trick.

● Get the right size. Far too many kids are forced to ride a bike that is too big, on the basis that they'll 'grow into it'. Not only is it more dangerous and difficult to control, but it's simply no fun. Many cycle shops offer part-exchange on well-maintained bikes.

● If you're on a road, cycle slightly behind and to the right of your child, looking and listening for other traffic. You can tell your child if a car or lorry is approaching, but don't panic them. Busy roads are not suitable for children under ten, nor are canal towpaths, which can become narrow and slippery. If a road is busy, let your child ride on the pavement while you stick to the road.

● If you're off on an afternoon jaunt, be sure to pack a bicycle pump and a repair kit. If you suffer a puncture, you'll all be deflated.

● When riding off-road, the adult should lead in order to warn about impending obstacles like tree roots and ruts.

● Don't pelt down a hill and think your youngster can do the same. Small wheels are not very stable at high speed, and once a wobble sets in, there's every chance of your child taking a nasty tumble.

Dance

Some children love the formality of ballet, but others prefer more creative contemporary styles, such as the free-spirited **Chantraine Dance of Expression**, for which there are two centres in London. Classes for children aged from four take place in north-west London (contact Patricia Woodall on 7435 4247) and

Activities

Wanstead (contact Kate Green on 8989 8604). These centres put on a summer festival.

Capoeira was created by African slaves as a form of self-defence, and its dynamic leaps, cartwheels and handstands combine agility, flexibility, self-expression and a sense of freedom. Classes run on Saturdays at **The Place** (*see below*). See also *p261* **Martial Arts**.

Dalcroze Eurhythmics is about experiencing music through movement of the whole body and, in some countries, it is a fundamental part of musical education. Contact the **Dalcroze Society** (8870 1986, www.dalcroze.org.uk) for more details.

The **London Dance Network** (www.london dance.com) has a directory of other dance venues and organisations. The following centres all offer classes for kids:

Chisenhale Dance Space *64-84 Chisenhale Road, E3 5QZ (8981 6617/www.chisenhaledancespace.co.uk). Mile End tube.*

Danceworks *16 Balderton Street, W1K 6TN (7629 6183/www.danceworks.co.uk). Bond Street tube.*

Drill Hall *16 Chenies Street, WC1E 7EX (7307 5060/www.drillhall.co.uk). Goodge Street tube.*

East London Dance *Stratford Circus, Theatre Square, E15 1BX (8279 1050/www. eastlondondance.org). Stratford tube/rail.*

Greenwich Dance Agency *Borough Hall, Royal Hill, SE10 8RE (8293 9741/www.greenwichdance.org.uk). Greenwich rail.*

Laban *Creekside, SE8 3DZ (8691 8600/www.laban.org). Deptford rail.*

The Place *17 Duke's Road, WC1H 9PY (7387 7669/ www.theplace.org.uk). Euston tube/rail.*

Ravenscourt Theatre School *8-30 Galena Road, W6 0LT (8741 0707/www.ravenscourt.net). Ravenscourt Park tube.*

Rona Hart School of Dance *Rosslyn Hall, Willoughby Road, NW3 1SB (7435 7073). Hampstead tube.*

Tricycle Theatre *269 Kilburn High Road, NW6 7JR (7328 1000/www.tricycle.co.uk). Kilburn tube.*

Fencing

Modern fencing is more than mere flashing blades. It's physically demanding, very skilful and a cool alternative for kids who don't enjoy team games.

Most sessions comprise warm-up activities to develop co-ordination, flexibility and balance, formal work towards the nine fencing grades, followed by the bit that everyone enjoys best: free fighting. The sport has a strong safety ethic, and no-one is allowed to participate without full protective clothing, a mask and the supervision of a qualified instructor.

For a full list of clubs around London, contact the **British Fencing Association** (8742 3032) or use the search facility at www.britishfencing.com.

The following clubs offer regular junior sessions:

Arena Fencing *County Hall, Kingston-upon-Thames, Penrhyn Road, KT1 2DN (8399 2440/www.fencing courses.pwp.blueyonder.co.uk). Kingston rail.*

Brixton Fencing Club *Brixton Recreation Centre, Station Road, SW9 8QQ (7926 9779). Brixton tube/rail.*

Camden Fencing Club *Ackland Burghley School, 93 Burghley Road, NW5 1UJ (8340 7536/www.camden fencingclub.org.uk). Kentish Town tube.*

Finchley Foil Fencing Club *Copthall School, Pursley Road, NW7 2EP (7485 1498/www.finchleyfoil.co.uk). Mill Hill East tube.*

Haverstock Fencing Club *Haverstock School, Haverstock Hill, NW1 8AS (07811 077 048). Chalk Farm tube.*

King's College School & Wimbledon High School Joint Fencing Club *Southside Common, SW19 4TT (8255 5300/jonmilner@blueyonder.co.uk). Wimbledon tube/rail.*

Kingston Fencing Club *Coombe Boys School, College Gardens, Blakes Lane, New Malden, Surrey KT3 6NU (secretary Joe Shackell 8393 4255/www. kingstonfencing.co.uk). Motspur Park rail.*

Streatham Fencing Club *Dunraven Lower School, Mount Nod Road, SW16 2QB (www.streatham fencing.org/courses@streathamfencing.org). Streatham Hill rail.*

Football

Football dominates the sporting scene in this country. At the top level, it's a billion-pound industry with 13 professional clubs in London (*see p273* **Sports to watch**). Lower down the pyramid, more than 45,000 clubs cater for all standards and ages, and both sexes.

When helping your child find a team, make sure that he or she is of the appropriate standard – beware, in other words, of foisting a child who will never be more than an enthusiast on to a group of athletic high-achievers. Some football clubs will have no hesitation in dropping a child from a team if someone better comes along, so children need to develop a thick skin. That said, football has put in place a number of club development and child welfare programmes, so you should also:

● Ask whether the club holds, or is working towards, the FA Charter Mark.

● Ask whether its coaches hold FA qualifications and have received training in child protection and emergency first aid.

● Watch a session to see how well organised it is.

● Find out the number of children in each age group. Some clubs have large memberships, which may mean only the most talented children get to play regularly.

● Consider the atmosphere and ethos: is this 'sport for all' or is winning the priority?

Activities

● Are parents yelling advice (and abuse) from the touchline, or are they encouraged to lend a hand and offer more constructive support?

To find a girls' team, contact the **Football Association** (7745 4545/www.TheFA.com/women). Clubs with extensive girls' development programmes include **Arsenal** (7704 4140), **Charlton Athletic** (8333 4000), **Fulham** (8336 7578) and **Millwall** (7740 0503).

All the professional clubs in London run Football in the Community coaching courses, fun days and skills clinics. These are suitable for boys and girls aged from about six and are staffed by FA-qualified coaches. Check the club websites below (details are usually listed under the 'Club' or 'Community' headings) for venues and dates:

Arsenal *7704 4140/www.arsenal.com.*
Brentford *8758 9430/www.brentfordfitc.org.uk.*
Charlton Athletic *8850 2866/www.charlton-athletic.co.uk.*
Chelsea *7957 8220/www.chelseafc.com.*
Crystal Palace *8768 6000/www.cpfc.co.uk.*
Fulham *0870 442 5432/www.fulhamfc.com.*
Leyton Orient *8556 5973/www.leytonorient.com.*
Millwall *7740 0503/www.millwallfc.co.uk.*
Queens Park Rangers *8740 2509/www.qpr.co.uk.*
Tottenham Hotspur *0870 420 5000/www.spurs.co.uk.*
Watford *01923 496 256/www.watfordfc.com.*
West Ham United *0870 112 5066/www.whufc.com.*

Similar schemes operate through the County FAs. Contact the following offices for details:

Essex *01245 465271/www.essexfa.com.*
Hertfordshire *01462 677622/www.hertsfa.com.*
Kent *01634 843824/www.kentfa.com.*
London *01959 570183/www.londonfa.com.*
Middlesex *8515 1919/www.middlesexfa.com.*
Surrey *01372 373543/www.surreyfa.co.uk.*

A highly rated scheme is run by former Queens Park Rangers goalkeeper Peter Hucker. Based in Barking and Wanstead, it offers weekly pay-and-play coaching sessions, matchplay and football parties for ages five to 16. Hucker also founded the **East London & Essex Small-Sided Soccer League**, now run by Joe Long (07961 867501, 01375 650 833/www.eleleague.com). Alternatively, **Powerleague** (www.powerleague.co.uk) runs nine centres around London for weekend coaching sessions and leagues for all ages.

There are many commercial football clinics and camps to choose from. An **Ian St John Soccer Camp** (0845 230 0133, www.soccercamps.co.uk) costs £75 for five days (10am-3.45pm) and caters for children aged eight to 15. Other options include **EAC Activity Camps** (0845 113 0022, www.eac-summer-activity-camps.co.uk) and **European Football Camps** (www.footballcamps.co.uk). *See also p254* **Becks' futures**.

Parents of football-crazy ankle-biters can also try the popular **Little Kickers** programme. The classes, developed by a group of FA-qualified coaches and nursery schoolteachers for pre-schoolers (from age two), are a gentle introduction to football. The programme also incorporates a number of early-learning goals and classes operate all over London. For further information and prices, call 01235 833 854 or check the website at www.littlekickers.co.uk.

Golf

Too many golfers still want their clubhouses to be a refuge from kids (and, in some cases, women) for the sport to offer a uniformly warm welcome to would-be juvenile thwackers. However, more is being done to recruit and keep young golfers, and bring those who are interested and able through to competition standard. The English Golf Union has developed Tri-Golf for six- to 12-year-olds and is introducing the game in primary schools, and children can now play golf as part of the Duke of Edinburgh's Award. The **English Golf Union** is a useful contact if you want to get started (01526 354 500, www.englishgolfunion.org).

A driving range is an excellent place to introduce a child to the basics of the game (and the course professional will also offer lessons to help get them into good habits early on). A fun new approach is offered by **TopGolf** (www.topgolf.co.uk) at its centres in Chigwell (8500 2644), Watford (01923 222 045) and Addlestone (01932 858 551). The TopGolf system is based on a point-scoring game using golf balls with a microchip inside them.

Beckenham Place Park
The Mansion, Beckenham Place Park, Beckenham, Kent BR3 5BP (8650 2292). Beckenham Hill rail.
Juniors can use this course after 2pm. Lessons are available on Saturdays at 11am (£3, booking essential). It costs £10 for juniors to play a round at weekends, £8 on weekdays.

Regent's Park Golf & Tennis School
North Gate, Outer Circle, Regent's Park, NW1 4RL (7724 0643/www.rpgts.co.uk). Baker Street tube.
Children who are 'old enough to take instruction' are welcome here. Membership for juniors is £30; the Saturday afternoon clinic for young golfers costs £5 per hour.

Driving ranges
A1 Golf Driving Range *Rowley Lane, Arkley, Herts EN5 3HW (8447 1411). Elstree & Borehamwood rail.*
Chingford Golf Range *Waltham Way, E4 8AQ (8529 2409). Chingford rail.*
Cranfield Golf Academy *Fairways Golf Centre, Southend Road, E4 8TA (8527 7692/www.cga-golf.com). Walthamstow Central tube/rail.*

Croydon Golf Driving Range *175 Long Lane, Addiscombe, Croydon, Surrey CR0 7TE (8656 1690/ www.golfinsurrey.com). East Croydon/Elmers End rail.*

Dukes Meadows Golf Range *Great Chertsey Road, W4 2SH (8995 0537/www.golflessons.co.uk). Hammersmith tube, then 190 bus.*

Ealing Golf Range *Rowdell Road, Northolt, Middx UB5 6AG (8845 4967). Northolt tube.*

Warren Park Golf Centre *Whalebone Lane North, Chadwell Heath, Essex RM6 6SB (8597 1120/www.cga-golf.com). Dagenham Heathway tube.*

World Of Golf *Beverley Way, New Malden, Surrey KT3 4PH (8949 9200/www.worldofgolf-uk.co.uk). New Malden or Raynes Park rail.*

Gymnastics & trampolining

The **British Amateur Gymnastics Association** (01952 820330/www.british-gymnastics.org) has around 100,000 members. Through its clubs and schools, sessions for four year-olds and under are based around soft-play equipment and simple games, leading to a series of proficiency awards. As well as a general scheme for boys and girls, there are separate awards for rhythmic gymnastics and sports acrobatics. The Association is also the governing body for the British Trampoline Federation.

There is an ongoing debate within the sport about the age at which children move from 'recreational gymnastics' – that is, a play-based form of the sport – to the more structured 'Olympic gymnastics', using conventional equipment. In response, Bill Cosgrove, a former national gymnastics coach, created TumbleTots and, later, Gymbabes and Gymbobs. Gymbabes is for babies from six months to the crawling stage, TumbleTots is for walkers, and Gymbobs is for school-aged kids up to seven. For details of centres around the country, call 0121 585 7003 or see www.tumbletots.com. Another useful resource

Let the games begin!

The year 2012 can't come soon enough for a generation of sporty London youngsters. When the Olympic and Paralympic Games hit town, not only will there be an unforgettable six weeks of action to enjoy, but the whole capital will benefit from the legacy left by a staggering £2 billion of investment.

The aims of London 2012 are to transform people's lives, particularly in the poorest and most deprived areas of the city, where the Games will be based; to inspire active sporting activity and achievement; and to foster a healthy and active nation. A few gold medals across the 26 sports won't go amiss, either. The intention is to leave behind world-class sporting facilities at the heart of the community; to drive the regeneration of east London; and to develop a major new urban park, the biggest in Europe for 150 years.

Although the Games are still six years away, preparations are well under way. Work has started on the Aquatic Centre, which will include two 50-metre swimming pools and a diving pool. Also on the main 500-acre Olympic Park site at Stratford will be the 80,000-seat Olympic Stadium, hockey centre, velopark for cycle sports and four multi-sport arenas. In total, nine new venues will be located within easy walking distance of each other, five of which will be retained afterwards. Meanwhile, our much-maligned transport system will be geared up to deliver up to 240,000 people each hour into the Olympic Park.

Once the Games are over, the Olympic Park will be given over to public use. The waterways of the River Lea are to be cleaned and widened, the natural floodplains will be restored as wildlife habitats, and footpaths and cycleways will link the tidal Thames Estuary to the south and the Hertfordshire countryside to the north. The blueprint is for a 'zero-waste Games' by avoiding landfill and using waste as a positive resource for recycling.

Excited? You can get a feel for the enormous scale of the project by walking around the area with the aid of a free 'Walk the Bid' guide produced by Newham Council. There are two circular routes, one starting at Leyton tube station and taking in the sites for the Olympic Village, hockey centre, velopark and multi-sport arenas. The other tour starts and finishes at Stratford station and includes the Olympic Stadium and Aquatic Centre. The guide details a walk through London 2012's 'River Zone', comprising Greenwich, the ExCeL centre and the Dome. To get a copy, either email walkthebid@newham. gov.uk or download a PDF from the official website at www.london2012.org.

The success of the Games will also depend on the volunteers who give up their time to help things run smoothly. The London organising committee will be releasing more details on how to get involved later this year, but you can register now for the Volunteering to Win programme – details, again, are on the website.

And if you're already thinking about whether you and your family would rather watch the hockey or the fencing, the basketball or the wrestling, tickets are expected to go on sale in 2010. A total of 9.6 million tickets will be available, of which six million will be £30 or less (at 2004 prices). Of these, four million will cost £20 or less.

So, it's 27 July to 12 August for the Olympics, 29 August to 9 September for the Paralympics. Put the dates in your diary...

Activities

tumbling this way from over the pond is the Little Gym, an international company whose gym programmes aim to help motor skill development and build confidence. There's a Little Gym franchise in Wandsworth (Compass House, Riverside West, Smugglers Way, Wandsworth Bridge Roundabout, SW18 1DB, 8874 6567, www.thelittlegym.com).

The following clubs offer a range of age-appropriate activities, and most offer trampolining as well. Both sports are also available at many public sports centres. Check that any club you choose displays a current certificate of inspection by BAGA or the **London Gymnastics Federation** (8529 1142, www.longym.freeserve.co.uk):

Avondale Gymnastics Club *Hollyfield Road, Surbiton, Surrey KT5 9AL (8399 3386/www.avondale gymnastics.co.uk). Surbiton rail.*

Camberwell Gymnastics Club *Artichoke Place, SE5 8TS (7252 7353). Denmark Hill rail.*

Charisma Gym Club *Dulwich College PE Centre, College Road, SE21 7LD (8299 3663/www.charisma gymnastics.com). West Dulwich rail.*

East London Gymnastics Club *Frobisher Road, E6 5LW (7511 4488/www.eastlondongym.co.uk). Beckton DLR.*

Heathrow Gymnastics Club *Green Lane, Hounslow, TW4 6DH (8569 5069/www.heathrowgymnastics. org.uk). Hatton Cross or Hounslow West tube/ H23 bus.*

Hillingdon School of Gymnastics *Victoria Road, South Ruislip, Middx HA4 0JE (8841 6666/www.hsg-swallows.co.uk). South Ruislip tube.*

Richmond Gymnastics Centre *Townmead Road, Kew, Surrey TW9 4EL (8878 8682/www.richmond gymnastics.co.uk). Kew Gardens rail.*

Karting & motor sports

Many of the world's top Formula One racers got their taste for speed as kids on a kart circuit. Karting is thrilling stuff for eight-year-olds upwards as the little buggies zip around at speeds exceeding 30 miles per hour, but safety is always uppermost. Drivers receive a full briefing before they get moving, and anyone disobeying the marshals is removed from the track. Modern karts are easy to get the hang of: there are two pedals (stop and go) and no gearbox to confuse the issue. The venues listed below welcome children and can be booked for exciting, if expensive, parties:

Wimbledon Village Stables. See p263.

Brands Hatch

Fawkham, Longfield, Kent DA3 8NG (01474 872 331/ www.motorsportvision.co.uk). Swanley rail, then taxi.
Undoubtedly Britain's most impressive on-track activity venue, Brands Hatch has loads of things to do on two and four wheels, including YoungDrive!, which puts your youngster (aged over 13) in control of a Renault Clio.

Playscape Pro Racing

390 Streatham High Road, SW16 6HX (8677 8677/ www.playscape.co.uk). Streatham rail.
This centre can be booked for children's parties (over-eights only) or for half-hour taster sessions. Those who become addicted can join the Playscape Cadet School, a founder member of the RAC's Association of Racing Kart Schools. The school operates on the first Saturday of each month (8.30am-1pm; £35) and students are put through their paces before gaining an RAC racing licence.

Martial arts

You need only consider how often martial arts are featured in computer games to see their appeal. They're exotic; they require interesting clothes (often supplied by a club as part of the membership fee); many have grading systems

with belts and badges to display, while some offer tournaments and public demonstrations. Most important, all martial arts impart self-confidence, body awareness, assertiveness and resilience.

Most local sports centres will be home to at least one martial arts club; many more are based in church halls and community centres. Look for evidence of a lively but disciplined atmosphere, with well-organised and age-appropriate teaching. Ask instructors about their qualifications – the grading systems used in judo and karate, for example, help to ensure that teachers are of a suitable standard. Note, however, that a black belt is not a teaching qualification. Also ask for proof of insurance cover: martial arts usually involve physical contact, and accidents can happen. What's more, few community facilities extend their insurance to the instructors who rent them.

The following venues offer classes for children in a number of disciplines – call ahead and get the full list before setting off:

Bob Breen Academy

16 Hoxton Square, N1 6NT (7729 5789/www.bob breen.co.uk). Old Street tube/rail.
Children aged seven to 16 can learn kick-boxing skills and effective self-defence techniques at this well-known and highly respected academy.

The Budokwai

4 Gilston Road, SW10 9SL (7370 1000). South Kensington tube, then 14, 345, 414 bus.
This is one of Britain's premier martial arts clubs, offering judo tuition for children aged 4 to 12.

Hwarang Academy

Swiss Cottage Community Centre, 19 Winchester Road, NW3 3NR (07941 081 009/www.taekwondo-london-2012.com). Swiss Cottage tube.
Youngsters aged eight to 18 can learn the Korean martial art of tae kwon do, now an Olympic sport, here.

Jackson's Lane Community Centre

269A Archway Road, N6 5AA (8340 5226/ www.jacksonslane.org.uk). Highgate tube.
Drop-in kung fu classes for children aged six upwards are the speciality at Jackson's Lane.

London School of Capoeira

Unit 1-2, Leeds Place, Tollington Park, N4 3RF (7281 2020/www.londonschoolofcapoeira.co.uk). Finsbury Park tube/rail.
Kids aged six to 16 can learn this ultra-cool Brazilian martial art, in which creative play is a strong element.

Moving East

St Matthias Church Hall, Wordsworth Road, N16 8DD (7503 3101/www.movingeast.co.uk). Dalston Kingsland rail.
Judo and aikido (as well as dance) classes for children are held at this friendly centre devoted to Japanese martial arts.

Activities

Grinding on

Urban sports lovers may not like it, but their passion is moving into the mainstream. Not so long ago skaters and BMXers had a choice of practising on bumpy neglected grounds or risking the wrath of security guards at their favourite public spaces, like the South Bank complex (*see p32*). Until recently, the South Bank tried to dissuade skaters from using its concrete undercroft by blocking off whole sections.

In 2003 there was a radical about-turn in opinion, partly due to the appointment of Michael Lynch as chief executive of the South Bank Centre; Lynch had been a skater in his native Australia. He was joined by an influx of new, young educators, and suddenly the skaters were regarded as creative urban artists instead of messy nuisances – a switch in perception confirmed by the contribution by skaters to Biff! Bang! Pow!, a skateboarding event held in conjunction with the Roy Lichtenstein Exhibition at the Hayward Gallery in 2004. The South Bank Centre also allowed the installation of skateable structures under the Queen Elizabeth Hall, on the understandng that skaters don't invade new areas created by the centre's extensive refurbishment, due for completion in 2007. And the centre has given a commitment that the skaters' turf will not be interfered with before 2010.

Skate and BMX facilities are being upgraded all over London. The popular Stockwell Green site (corner of Stockwell Road and Stockwell Park Walk, stockwellskatepark.com) has been resurfaced, although the skaters complain that bad workmanship failed to produce the perfect smooth surface they require. Regular users have been provided with abrasive blocks to carry out some DIY repairs of their own.

The popular Cantelowes Gardens site beside Camden Road (cantelowesskatepark.co.uk), which is used by BMXers and online skaters as well as skateboarders, is set to reopen in summer this year after a period of closure for redevelopment. The new park has a high-spec design that Camden Council expects will attract skaters Londonwide.

Finsbury Park (finsburypark.org.uk) is another spot to watch. It has received an £80,000 funding injection to produce its own skatepark, planned to be suitable for street and bowl skaters and scheduled to open in spring 2007.

For some, urban sports have become a serious business. The annual Sprite Urban Games (spriteurbangames.com) on Clapham Common has professionals competing for £40,000 prize money and is helping street games gain acceptance as a serious sport. Most of its contests are for adults, but the youth vert (that's a half-pipe to you and me) is for 12-16s, and a replica street course gives novices of all ages the chance to have a go.

School of Japanese Karate (Shotokan International)

Various venues in north London (8368 6249).
Karate is the most popular Japanese martial art in this country. David and Lilian Alleyn run this well-established school and teach children aged six and upwards at venues in Southgate, Arnos Grove, Cockfosters, Whetstone, Edmonton and Enfield.

Shaolin Temple UK

207A Junction Road, N19 5QA (7687 8333/ www.shaolintempleuk.org). Tufnell Park tube.
This rather unlikely location is where 34th-generation fighting monk Shi Yanzi and several other Shaolin masters teach traditional kung fu, Chinese kick-boxing, meditation and tai chi, with weekly classes for children included in the programme.

Orienteering

Orienteering is a great way to make country walks fun for everyone. You navigate your way around a route using a map (and occasionally a compass), collecting points for every station you visit on the way. In addition to competitive events, most of which have a beginners' course (and organisers happy to explain to novices what is involved), there are nine permanent courses in London and more than 40 in the surrounding countryside. The permanent course at Hampstead Heath is particularly enjoyable. Details are online at the **South Eastern Orienteering Association** website (www.post2me.freeserve. co.uk/orienteering). For more information about the sport contact the **British Orienteering Federation** (01629 734 042, www.british orienteering.org.uk).

Riding

Riding lessons and hacks must be booked in advance: ask the stables whether there are 'taster' sessions for newcomers. Riders, whatever their age, must always wear a hard hat (establishments can usually lend one if you don't have your own) and boots with a small heel, rather than trainers or wellies. Some centres run 'own a pony' days and weeks, and offer birthday-party packages. Most stables are also able to cater for riders with disabilities. The rates given below are for children and per hour.

Ealing Riding School

Gunnersbury Avenue, W5 3XD (8992 3808/ www.ealingridingschool.biz). Ealing Common tube. **Lessons** £21/hr (group); £27/hr (individual).
Riders from five upwards can take part in many activities here, including the occasional gymkhana. Lessons are held in an outdoor manège.

Hyde Park & Kensington Stables

Hyde Park Stables, 63 Bathurst Mews, W2 2SB (7723 2813/www.hydeparkstables.com). Lancaster Gate tube. **Lessons** £45/hr (group); £55-£85/hr (individual).
Discounts available for block bookings.
Children aged five upwards can enjoy an hour-long lesson with patient, streetwise ponies in the glamorous surroundings of Hyde Park – not cheap, though.

Lee Valley Riding Centre

Lea Bridge Road, E10 7QL (8556 2629/www.lee valleypark.com). Clapton rail/48, 55, 56 bus. **Lessons** £17.70/hr (group); £12.20/30mins (beginners group; Sat, Sun).
The placid ponies enjoy the open spaces of Walthamstow Marshes and delight a devoted band of regulars.

London Equestrian Centre

Lullington Garth, N12 7BP (8349 1345/www.the londonec.co.uk). Mill Hill East tube. **Lessons** £21 (group); £21-£26 (individual; 30min session, Tue-Sun only).
A busy yard in North Finchley with 30 assorted horses and ponies. There's a junior members' club for regulars, who may be able to take part in informal gymkhanas. Birthday parties can be held here, and the centre can organise pony rides for three- to four-year-olds.

Newham Riding School & Association

Docklands Equestrian Centre, 2 Claps Gate Lane, E6 6JF (7511 3917). Beckton DLR. **Lessons** £15 (group).
This is a much-loved stables, where the 20 horses and ponies have many besotted fans.

Ross Nye's Riding Stables

8 Bathurst Mews, W2 2SB (7262 3791). Lancaster Gate tube. **Lessons** £40/hr (group); £50/hr (individual).
This is the Hyde Park branch of the Pony Club. Membership gives reduced prices for lessons. Clients aged from six learn to ride in Hyde Park.

Trent Park Equestrian Centre

Bramley Road, N14 4XS (8363 9005/www.trent park.com). Oakwood tube. **Lessons** £20-£27/hr (group); £16-£36 (individual).
The leafy acres of Trent Park (£28 per hour for hacking out) and a caring attitude towards young riders (aged from four) make this a justifiably popular place to ride.

Willowtree Riding Establishment

The Stables, Ronver Road, SE12 0NL (8857 6438). Grove Park or Lee rail. **Lessons** from £8 (group); from £16 (individual).
A friendly local venue with more than 40 ponies and horses, some of which are pure-bred Arab.

Wimbledon Village Stables

24A/B High Street, SW19 5DX (8946 8579/www.wv stables.com). Wimbledon tube/rail. **Lessons** £25/ 30mins; £43/hr (individual).
This centre has a small selection of quiet, safe ponies and a popular holiday scheme (£135 for three afternoons). Riding takes place on Wimbledon Common.

Activities

Rugby league

Rugby league is building a profile in the capital. The professional Harlequins RL are drawing bigger crowds to their Super League matches (*see p274*), while the London Skolars are working to introduce the sport in schools around London.

In junior rugby league the emphasis is on running, passing, skills and teamwork rather than crunching tackles and physical contact. And, of course, there's often plenty of mud to wallow in. The Skolars run two junior clubs for kids, and South London Storm run teams for under-nines to under-18s through three junior clubs. And Greenwich Admirals cater for ten- to 15-year-olds in their Junior Admirals set-up. To find out more about the sport in general, contact the Rugby Football League (0113 232 9111, www.rfl.uk.com).

Greenwich Admirals *contact Duncan Smith (07843 634 086/www.greenwichrl.com).*

London Skolars *(8888 8488/www.skolars.com).*

South London Storm *contact Rob Powell (07830 251 529/www.southlondonstorm.co.uk).*

Rugby union

One of the most proactive governing bodies in a sport with well-established programmes for youngsters, the Rugby Football Union (RFU) website has a postcode-based search facility for clubs. Most rugby union clubs cater for boys and girls, with 'minis' for six-year-olds, 'midi rugby' for under-11s, and 'youth rugby' for ages 13 and over. Great emphasis is placed on the fun of handling, passing and running, while the impact arts of tackling, scrummaging and kicking are gradually introduced and carefully controlled. Primary-age children play non-contact 'tag' rugby, using a belt worn around the waist with two 'tags' attached. If an opponent removes a tag, possession switches to the other team. Women's and girls' rugby has made progress in recent years and many clubs are now fully integrated. Contact the RFU for details.

Rugby Football Union

Twickenham Stadium, Whitton Road, Twickenham, Middx TW1 1DS (8892 2000/www.rfu.com). Twickenham rail.

Skateboarding & BMX-ing

See also p262 **Grinding on**.

Baysixty6 Skate Park

Bay 65-66, Acklam Road, W10 5YU (8969 4669/ www.baysixty6.com). Ladbroke Grove tube. **Membership** £10/yr. **Prices** £6 5hrs Mon-Fri, 4hrs Sat, Sun; £3 beginners 10am-noon Sat-Sun.

Sheltered beneath the A40, this enormous park includes the capital's only vert ramp, a medium half-pipe, a mini ramp and many funboxes, grind boxes, ledges and rails. Some skaters mutter that it's a bit much having to pay £6 when it's free to skate everywhere else in London – but the high quality of the ramps here goes some way to making up for it.

Harrow Skatepark

Peel Road (behind the leisure centre), Wealdstone, Middx HA3 5BD (8424 1754). Harrow & Wealdstone tube/rail.
Years of abuse have resulted in the slow deterioration of Harrow's obstacles, but there's still plenty to skate here. There are clover-leaf and kidney bowls, and an unforgiving concrete half-pipe remains a monumental challenge for the fearless.

Meanwhile 3

Meanwhile Gardens, off Great Western Road, W9 (no phone). Westbourne Park tube.
Here are three concrete bowls of varying size and steepness, but no flatland for practising the basics, so it's not for beginners. The bowls are linked together from high ground to low, offering the possibility of long, technical lines as well as limb-threatening transfer attempts.

Skating

On ice

Recent years have seen temporary skating rinks spring up around the city at Christmas time. Session times at London's permanent rinks vary from day to day, but venues are generally open from 10am until 10pm. The prices below include skate hire. For more information, contact the **National Ice Skating Association** (0115 988 8060, www.iceskating.org.uk):

Alexandra Palace Ice Rink

Alexandra Palace Way, N22 7AY (8365 4386/www. alexandrapalace.com). Wood Green tube/Alexandra Palace rail/W3 bus.
Courses for children aged five to 15 run on Saturday mornings and early weekday evenings. Parties are available too.

Broadgate Ice Arena

Broadgate Circle, Eldon Street, EC2M 2QS (Summer 7505 4000/Winter 7505 4068/www.broadgate ice.co.uk). Liverpool Street tube/rail.
This tiny outdoor rink is open from late October to April.

Lee Valley Ice Centre

Lea Bridge Road, E10 7QL (8533 3154/www.leevalley park.org.uk). Clapton rail.
The disco nights are a big hit at this well-maintained and comparatively warm rink. It's never too busy as it's hard to get here by public transport.

Michael Sobell Leisure Centre

Hornsey Road, N7 7NY (7609 2166/www.aquaterra. org). Finsbury Park tube/rail.

Children from four upwards are welcome at this small rink, which runs popular after-school sessions and six-week courses. You can also hold parties here.

Queens

17 Queensway, W2 4QP (7229 0172/www.queens iceandbowl.co.uk). Bayswater or Queensway tube.
The disco nights on Fridays and Saturdays are legendary, but beginners and families are also well looked after at this well-known ice rink.

Somerset House

Strand, WC2R 1LA (7845 4600/www.somerset-house.org.uk). Holborn or Temple tube (closed Sun).
Every winter for a short and extremely popular season, the courtyard here is iced over to become the most attractive rink in London. This year it will be open from 24 November 2006-28 January 2007.

Streatham Ice Arena

386 Streatham High Road, SW16 6HT (8769 7771/ www.streathamicearena.co.uk). Streatham rail.
This popular rink offers six-week courses for all ages. There's even a class for 'toddlers' aged up to four (phone or check the website for details).

On tarmac

Citiskate (7228 3999, www.citiskate.co.uk) teaches hundreds of Londoners how to skate in parks, leisure centres and schools. The instructors all hold qualifications from UKISA (United Kingdom Inline Skating Association); lessons are available seven days a week. Citiskate's weekly Friday Night Skate and Sunday Rollerstroll are popular group skates around the streets starting from Hyde Park. Battersea Park's Easy Peasy skate on Saturday mornings is ideal for families and newcomers.

Skiing & snowboarding

A few practice turns on a dry slope are useful preparation for the real white stuff. Gloves, long sleeves and trousers are compulsory as the surface can deliver a nasty burn should you fall. Also note that, if you're thinking of taking a mixed-ability group out for an open recreational session, perhaps as a birthday party activity, the minimum requirement is to be able to perform a controlled snowplough turn and use the ski lift. For more information, contact the **Ski Club of Great Britain** (8410 2000, www.skiclub.co.uk).

Bromley Ski Centre

Sandy Lane, St Paul's Cray, Orpington, Kent BR5 3HY (01689 876 812/www.c-v-s.co.uk/bromleyski). St Mary Cray rail.
Two lifts serve the 120m (394ft) main slope, and there's also a mogul field and nursery slope. Skiing and snow-boarding taster sessions cost £17. Booking is essential.

Sandown Sports Club

More Lane, Esher, Surrey KT10 8AN (01372 467 132/www.sandownsports.co.uk). Esher rail.
The 120m (394ft) main slope, 80m (262ft) nursery area and 90m (295ft) snowboarding slope are closed during horse-racing meetings. This is a lessons-only venue: tuition is available for seven-year-olds upwards (£39/hr or £80 for three 2hr sessions), although special half-hour classes can be arranged for children as young as four (£21).

Snozone

Xscape, 602 Marlborough Gate, Milton Keynes MK9 3XS (0871 222 5670/www.xscape.co.uk). Milton Keynes Central rail.
This is one of the UK's largest indoor snow domes, with three slopes (in reality they are joined, so they resemble one wide slope): two of 170m (558ft) and one of 135m (443ft), with button lifts running all the way to the top. The place can feel a bit like a big fridge, but beginners couldn't ask for a better environment in which to find their ski legs.

Swimming

Swimming is the most popular participation sport in this country after walking, yet around 1,000 people still drown every year. Being able to swim is more than mere sport – it's a potential life-saver.

Most local authority pools run lessons for children, plus parent-and-baby sessions to develop water confidence from as young as three months. However, these can be oversubscribed and have long waiting lists. Ask at your local pool for details.

Tuition

Contact the **Amateur Swimming Association** (01509 618 700, www.britishswimming.org) for a list of child-friendly swimming clubs in your area.

Dolphin Swimming Club

University of London Pool, Malet Street, WC1E 7HU (8349 1844). Tottenham Court Road tube.
This club teaches aquaphobic children (and adults) to over-come their fear and has turned many quivering wrecks into confident swimmers. A course of 11 individual half-hour lessons costs £225.50.

Leander Swimming Club

Balham Leisure Centre, Elmfield Road, SW17 8AN (www.leanderswimmingclub.org.uk). Balham tube/rail.
Leander runs a programme for children aged seven and above in Balham, Tooting, Crystal Palace and Dulwich. This extends from basic strokes to serious competition. Check website for email contacts.

Little Dippers

0870 758 0302/www.littledippers.co.uk.
Weekly and weekend courses in water confidence for par-ents and babies are offered here. There's a good teacher-pupil ratio: no more than eight babies are in the water at any time, using pools (in Wimbledon, Richmond and London Bridge) chosen for their warm temperature. A six-week course or a weekend costs £69.

Activities

Dip in the briny

The nearest sea may be 50 miles away, but that doesn't stop London kids messing about on the water. Canoes, dinghies or rowing boats can be their vessel of choice, and for the more petrol-headed, there are powerboats down Deptford way.

Children can start **rowing** from the age of 11 and, if they are keen and show ability, progress through the National Junior Rowing Programme. This sport's elitist reputation is somewhat undeserved: some of the country's best oarsmen and women went to landlocked state schools. Most clubs cater for children (contact the Amateur Rowing Association on 8237 6700, www.ara-rowing.org).

Less physically taxing but no less enjoyable is **sailing**. Children start off learning the basics in a one-person dinghy such as a Topper or Laser Pico. Clubs will supply all the necessary kit, from vessel to wetsuit. A beginners' course recognised by the Royal Yachting Association (0845 345 0400/ www.rya.org.uk) can be covered in a weekend.

For children who don't mind falling in and getting wet occasionally, **kayaking** or **canoeing** is great. What's the difference? A canoe is an open boat steered with a one-bladed paddle. A kayak is the one with the closed cockpit, steered by a double-bladed paddle (details from the British Canoe Union on 0115 982 1100, www.bcu.org.uk).

The first few attempts at windsurfing also involve plenty of time in the water or wobbling along in the 'granny position' – back bent, arms tensed. But with practice and a few decent gusts, youngsters will be skimming along (information from the London Windsurf Association on 01895 846 707, www.lwawindsurfing.co.uk).

For speed merchants, the watersport of choice is **waterskiing**, now joined by **wakeboarding**. In this less familiar version, feet are strapped to a single board, wider than a mono-ski and around 1.5m (5ft 4in) long; you're then pulled behind a speedboat generating a 'fat wake'. It's the fastest-growing watersport in the UK. You can practise using cable tows, making learning cheaper and very accessible for kids. For information, check the British Waterski website (www.bwsf.co.uk).

In **dragon-boat racing**, crews paddle large boats with ornate carved heads, while drummers pound out an inspiring rhythm. For information, contact the British Dragon Boat Racing Association (01295 770 734, www.dragonboat.org.uk/bda).

And if all that sounds too much like hard work, try the boating lakes in the parks, listed below.

Ahoy Centre

Borthwick Street, SE8 3JY (8691 7606/ www.ahoy.org.uk). Deptford DLR.
Sailing, rowing and powerboating on the Thames, and in Surrey and Victoria Docks. Members help run the centre, an approach that keeps prices down and fosters a strong community spirit.

Albany Park Canoe & Sailing Centre

Albany Mews, Albany Park Road, Kingston-upon-Thames, Surrey KT2 5SL (8549 3066/www. albanypark.co.uk). Kingston rail.
A lively centre for sailing, kayaking and canoeing. Tuition and taster sessions are available.

BTYC Sailsports

Birchen Grove, NW9 8SA (8731 8083/www.btyc sailsports.org.uk). Neasden or Wembley Park tube.
Club offering dinghy sailing, windsurfing, with basic training and RYA courses held on the Welsh Harp reservoir.

Canalside Activity Centre

Canal Close, W10 5AY (8968 4500). Ladbroke Grove tube/Kensal Rise rail/52, 70, 295 bus.
This centre offers rowing and canoeing, as well as water safety classes.

Dockands Sailing & Watersports Centre

Millwall Dock, 235A Westferry Road, E14 3QS (7537 2626/www.dswc.org). Crossharbour DLR.
Membership youth £20; family £220.
Canoeing, dragon-boat racing, windsurfing and dinghy sailing for over-eights who are confident in the water.

Fairlop Sailing Centre

Forest Road, Hainault, Ilford IG6 3HN (8500 1468/www.fairlop.co.uk). Fairlop tube.
This Royal Yachting Association- and British Canoe Union-approved centre offers windsurfing, dinghy sailing, canoeing and powerboating courses.

Globe Rowing Club

Trafalgar Rowing Centre, Crane Street, SE10 9NP (8859 1078/www.globe.cwc.net). Cutty Sark DLR/Maze Hill rail.
Friendly, Greenwich-based rowing club.

Lea Rowing Club

Spring Hill, E5 9BL (Mark Padfield 07814 408 349/club house 8806 8282/www.learc.org.uk). South Tottenham or Stamford Hill rail.
The club runs rowing and sculling classes and holiday courses for kids aged ten and over who can swim at least 50 metres.

Royal Victoria Dock Watersports Centre

Gate 5, Tidal Basin Road, off Silvertown Way, E16 1AF (7511 2326). Royal Victoria Dock DLR.
Membership junior £53-£75.

The calm waters of Victoria Dock are a great place to master dinghy sailing and tackle an RYA beginners' course. The centre runs the Youth on H$_2$O scholarship scheme, which offers free tuition, and a busy holiday programme.

Shadwell Basin Outdoor Activity Centre

3-4 Shadwell Pierhead, Glamis Road, E1W 3TD (7481 4210/www.shadwell-basin.org.uk). Wapping tube.
Downriver from Tower Bridge, the Shadwell Basin Centre offers fairly priced sailing, canoeing, kayaking and dragon-boating for children aged nine and over.

Surrey Docks Watersports Centre

Greenland Dock, Rope Street, SE16 7SX (7237 4009). Surrey Quays tube.
Sailing, windsurfing and canoeing for over-eights take place in the sheltered dock in school holidays and half-terms. RYA courses are also available.

West Reservoir Centre

Stoke Newington West Reservoir, Green Lanes, N4 2HA (8800 6161). Manor House tube.
This purpose-built environmental education and watersports centre is a good place to learn the basics of dinghy sailing.

Westminster Boating Base

136 Grosvenor Road, SW1V 3JY (7821 7389/www.westminsterboatingbase.co.uk). Pimlico tube.
Canoeing and sailing for over-tens on the tidal Thames. There's no fixed fee for youth membership; instead, the Base asks for a donation according to personal circumstances.

Row, row, row your boat

The following venues for rowing boat hire usually charge by the half hour. Some, like Alexandra Park and The Regent's Park, also have pedaloes. Richmond Bridge can hire out a rowing boat or skiff for a whole day's messing about on a tranquil stretch of the Thames.
Alexandra Park *Alexandra Palace Way, N22 7AY (8889 9089/www.alexandrapalace.com). Alexandra Park Rail/114, W3 bus.*
Battersea Park *SW11 4NJ (8871 7530). Battersea Park rail.*
Finsbury Park *N4 2NQ (7263 5001). Finsbury Park tube/rail.*
Regent's Park *Hanover Gate, NW1 4RL (7724 4069). Baker Street tube.*
Richmond Bridge Rowing Boat Hire *1-3 Bridge Boathouse, Richmond, Surrey TW9 1TH (8948 8270). Richmond tube/rail.*
Serpentine *The Boat House, Serpentine Road, W2 2UH (7298 2100/www.royalparks.gov.uk). Hyde Park Corner tube.*

Activities

Ahoy Centre.

Swimming Nature

0870 900 8002/www.swimmingnature.co.uk.
Since 1992, Swimming Nature has taught thousands of London children to swim using a controlled, progressively hands-on method. Lessons take place in Bayswater, Brondesbury, Victoria, Chelsea, Kensington, Maida Vale, Paddington, Regent's Park and with courses held to coincide with school terms.

Pools

Here's a selection of our favourites. Most pools are open daily; phone for times.

Barnet Copthall Pools *Champions Way, NW4 1PX (8457 9900/www.gll.org). Mill Hill East tube.*
Three pools and a diving area, with coaching and clubs to join if you fancy taking the plunge.

Brentford Fountain Leisure Centre *658 Chiswick High Road, Brentford, Middx TW8 0HJ (0845 456 2935/www.hounslow.gov.uk). Gunnersbury tube.*
Leisure pool with a 40m (131ft) aquaslide, underwater lighting and wave machine alongside a teaching pool.

Crystal Palace National Sports Centre
Ledrington Road, SE19 2BB (8778 0131/www.gll.org). Crystal Palace rail.
One of the capital's two current 50m (164ft) Olympic-size pools which, along with its fine diving facilities, now looks to have a secure future.

Goresbrook Leisure Centre *Ripple Road, Dagenham, Essex RM9 6XW (8593 3570). Becontree tube.*
Fountains, cascades and a 60m (197ft) flume combine here with a small area for length swimming.

Hampton Heated Open Air Pool *High Street, Hampton, Middx, TW12 2ST (8255 1116/www.hamptonpool.co.uk). Hampton rail.*
When the sun's shining, Hampton is hard to beat. It's open all year round, including Christmas Day.

Ironmonger Row Baths *Ironmonger Row, EC1V 3QF (7253 4011). Old Street tube/rail.*
Take a trip back in time at this well-preserved 1930s 30m (98ft) pool and Turkish baths (one of only three remaining in London).

Kingfisher Leisure Centre *Fairfield Road, Kingston, KT1 2PY (8546 1042/www.kingfisher leisurecentre.co.uk). Kingston rail.*
Super-friendly family centre with a teaching pool and a main pool with beach area and wave machine.

Latchmere Leisure Centre *Burns Road, SW11 5AD (7207 8004/www.latchmereleisurecentre.co.uk). Clapham Junction rail.*
Lane-swimming main pool, teaching pool and a beach area to laze about in, with a wave machine and a slide.

Leyton Leisure Lagoon *763 High Road, E10 5AB (8558 8858/www.gll.org). Leyton tube/69, 97 bus.*
A flume, slides, fountains, rapids and cascades liven up and bring a splash of colour to this rather drab slice of north-east London.

Northolt Swimarama *Eastcote Lane North, Northolt, Middx UB5 4AB (8422 1176). Northolt tube.*
Three pools, plus a 60m (197ft) slide and diving boards .

Pavilion Leisure Centre *Kentish Way, Bromley, Kent BR1 3EF (8313 9911/www.bromley.gov.uk). Bromley South rail.*
A large leisure pool with shallows, flumes and a wave machine, lane swimming and a separate toddlers' pool.

Queen Mother Sports Centre *223 Vauxhall Bridge Road, SW1V 1EL (7630 5522/www.courtneys.co.uk). Victoria tube/rail.*
Three excellent pools in this refurbished centre mean it's always popular with schoolkids.

The Spa at Beckenham *24 Beckenham Road, Beckenham, BR3 4PF (8650 0233). Clock House rail.*
An award-winning leisure centre with loads of sports facilities, two swimming pools, the Space Zone soft-play area for children and a crèche.

Tottenham Green Leisure Centre *1 Philip Lane, N15 4JA (8489 5322). Seven Sisters tube/rail.*
Choose between lane swimming and diving in the main pool or splashing amid the waves and slides in the 'beach pool' at this perennially popular leisure centre.

Waterfront Leisure Centre *High Street, SE18 6DL (8317 5000/www.gll.org). Woolwich Arsenal rail/96, 177 bus.*
Four pools, six slides, waves, rapids and a water 'volcano' keep locals happy in Greenwich's flagship centre.

Open-air swimming

When summer arrives and the breeze is warm, all you really want to be doing is having a dip in the great outdoors. For full details of London's outdoor pools (and to join the campaign to reopen those that have closed), visit www.lidos.org.uk.

Brockwell Lido *Brockwell Park, Dulwich Road, SE24 (7274 3088/www.thelido.co.uk). Herne Hill rail.* **Open** July, Aug; check website for details. **Admission** check website for details.
This wonderful listed 1930s lido has received £500,000 from the Heritage Lottery Fund for renovation, so its future seems at last to be secure.

Charlton Lido *Hornfair Park, Shooters Hill Road, Charlton, SE18 4LX (8856 7180/www.gll.org). Charlton or Eltham rail.*
The last lido to be built by London County Council in 1939. Check the Greenwich Leisure website or phone 8317 5000 to confirm opening times and prices.

Finchley Lido *High Road, N12 0AE (8343 9830/ www.gll.org). East Finchley tube.* **Open** check website for times. **Admission** £3.35; £2.05 concession; £1-£2.05 children.
There are two indoor pools here, but it's the outdoor pool and sun terrace that make it such a popular draw for locals during the summer.

Hampstead Heath Swimming Ponds & Parliament Hill Lido *Lido: Parliament Hill Fields, Gordon House Road, NW5 1LP. Hampstead Heath rail. Men & women's ponds: Millfield Lane, N6. Gospel Oak rail. Mixed pond: East Heath Road, NW3. Hampstead Heath rail. Both (7485 4491/www.city oflondon.gov.uk).* **Open** check website for times. **Admission** *Lido* £4.10; £2.50 concession; £12.20 family. *Ponds* £2; £1 concession. Season tickets and early/late entry discounts available.
Children aged between eight to 15 are only allowed in the ponds if under the watchful eyes of an adult.

Oasis Sports Centre *32 Endell Street, WC2H 9AG (7831 1804/www.gll.org). Tottenham Court Road tube.* **Open** 6.30am-9pm Mon-Fri; 9.30am-6pm Sat, Sun. **Admission** £3.45; £1.35 5-16s; free under-5s; £6.75 family.
This 28m (92ft) outdoor pool is open all year round.

Pools on the Park *Old Deer Park, Twickenham Road, Richmond, Surrey TW9 2SF (8940 0561/ www.springhealth.net). Richmond rail.* **Open** 6.30am-10pm Mon-Fri; 8am-9pm Sat, Sun. **Admission** £3.70; £2.90 under-16s; £1.50 concessions; free under-5s.
A 33m (108ft) heated outdoor pool (and one the same size and temperature inside), plus a sunbathing area.

Tooting Bec Lido *Tooting Bec Road, SW16 1RU (8871 7198/www.slsc.org.uk).* **Open** *Late May-Aug* 6am-8pm daily. *Sept* 6am-5pm daily. *Oct-Mar* 7am-2pm daily (club members only). **Admission** phone to check.
At 94m by 25m (308ft by 82ft), this art deco beauty is the second-largest open-air pool in Europe.

Water polo

Aquagoal is a version of this game adapted for kids aged ten and upwards. The aim is to score goals without touching the side or bottom of the pool. Contact the **Amateur Swimming Association** (01509 618 700, www.british swimming.co.uk) for general information. The National Water Polo League website (www.nwpl.co.uk) has useful contacts.

Table tennis

Twenty weekend junior leagues are now running in the capital, and there are several clubs offering coaching for youngsters, such as **London Progress** (London Progress Tournament Centre, Southall Sports Centre, Southall, UB1 1DP; 0780 308 2661, www.londonprogress.com), and a competitive system to feed into. For background information about the sport, contact the **English Table Tennis Association** (01424 722 525, www.englishtabletennis.org.uk).

Tennis

Tennis for Free (TFF) is a campaign to give access without charge to Britain's 33,000 public courts – and encourage a long-overdue change in this country's white, middle-class tennis culture. To find out more, visit www.tennisforfree.com.

The alternative to public courts are private clubs, which require the commitment of an annual fee – anything from £10 to £500-plus per person. But for families who intend to play the game together or want access to qualified instruction, they usually represent good value.

Most London boroughs run holiday tennis courses at Easter and in the summer: contact your local sports development team (details in the phone book or on the council website) or public library for details. The Lawn Tennis Association (7381 7000, www.lta.org.uk) publishes free guides giving contacts for hundreds of private clubs and public courts listed by borough or county, along with contact details for local development officers. Details of tennis holidays are also available.

Clissold Park Junior Tennis Club

Clissold Park Mansion House, Stoke Newington Church Street, N16 9HJ (7254 4235/www.hackneycitytennis clubs.co.uk). Stoke Newington rail/73 bus. **Open** *Apr-Sept* 10am-7.30pm Mon-Thur; 4-8pm Fri; 8.30am-3.30pm Sat; 8.30am-2.30pm Sun. *Oct-Mar* 10am-3pm Mon-Thur; 8.30am-3.30pm Sat; 8.30am-2.30pm Sun. **Court hire** £5.50/hr. Reduced rate available for under-16s, phone to check availability.
The Lawn Tennis Association paid for resurfacing the four hard courts and four mini tennis courts at what was Britain's first City Tennis Centre. Rackets of all sizes and balls are free to borrow. The club is active with squads, coaching, club competitions and teams participating in the Middlesex League. Other City Tennis Centres are at Highbury Fields (contact Rob Achille on 7697 1206), St Mark's Park, Kensington (contact Peter Quek on 8968 2630) and Eltham Park South, Greenwich (contact Jan Wootten on 8921 8088).

David Lloyd Leisure

0870 888 3015/www.davidlloydleisure.co.uk.
There are 11 David Lloyd clubs in the London area, combining tennis with upmarket fitness facilities. All are family-friendly, if not cheap, and the facilities are excellent. Check out the website or phone for your nearest venue.

Islington Tennis Centre

Market Road, N7 9PL (7700 1370/www.aqua terra.org). Caledonian Road tube. **Open** 7am-11pm Mon-Thur; 7am-10pm Fri; 8am-10pm Sat, Sun. **Court hire** *Indoor* £18/hr; £7.30/hr 5-16s. *Outdoor* £8.50/hr; £3.90/hr 5-16s.
Developed under the LTA's Indoor Tennis Initiative, this centre offers subsidised coaching on a membership or 'pay as you play' basis. Tennis courses for youngsters are also available.

Redbridge Sports & Leisure Centre

Forest Road, Barkingside, Essex IG6 3HD (8498 1000/www.rslonline.co.uk). Fairlop tube. **Open** 9am-11pm Mon-Fri; 9am-9pm Sat; 9am-10pm Sun. **Court hire** varies.
Developed over more than three decades by an independent charitable trust, this outstanding multi-sports centre has eight indoor and 18 outdoor courts, which you can use as a member or 'pay as you play'. Holiday activities for six-to 14-year-olds include beginners and improvers courses and 'fun play' sessions. There's also a short tennis club for under-eights and a strong development programme.

Sutton Junior Tennis Centre

Rose Hill Recreation Ground, Rose Hill, Sutton, Surrey SM1 3HH (8641 6611/www.sjtc.org). Morden tube. **Open** 7am-11pm daily. **Court hire** *Indoor* £16.50; £12 5-16s. *Outdoor* £7-£12; £5-£8 5-16s.
Set up more than a decade ago, this is now the top tennis school in Britain, with high-quality performance courses. There are residential courses for full-time players seeking professional status and a scholarship scheme linked with

Activities

Cheam High School. Children can start at three with Tiny Tots classes, move on to mini tennis, join in holiday programmes and book tennis birthday parties. There are six clay, ten acrylic and 11 indoor courts. Membership enables you to book cheaper courts in advance.

Westway Tennis Centre

1 Crowthorne Road, W10 6RP (8969 0992/www. westway.org). Latimer Road tube. **Open** 8am-10pm Mon-Fri; 8am-8pm Sat; 10am-10pm Sun. **Court hire** *Indoor £16-£20; £8-£10 5-16s. Outdoor £8-£9; £5-£7 5-16s.*

Also the product of the LTA's Indoor Tennis Initiative, Westway follows a similar model to Islington (*see p269*) – excellent subsidised coaching, short tennis and transitional tennis. There are eight indoor and four outdoor clay courts – the only ones in London open to the public.

Tenpin bowling

'Bowling is for everyone, from the age of four to 84,' says the British Tenpin Bowling Association. Indeed, a trip to a local centre makes for a great birthday party or family day out. Computerised scoring has made the game less complicated, and the very young can be sure of hitting the target with the aid of ball chutes and bumpers. For youngsters keen to progress towards the magical 'perfect score' of 300, there's a network of regional and national youth tournaments and leagues. For details, contact the British Tenpin Bowling Association on 020 8478 1745.

All the centres listed are open seven days a week, typically 10am to midnight. Admission prices vary according to the time of day but average around £6 per game – which includes the hire of soft-soled bowling shoes. Phone for details of children's parties.

Acton Megabowl *Royal Leisure Park, Western Avenue, W3 0PA (0870 550 1010/www.megabowl. co.uk). Park Royal tube.*

Airport Bowl *Bath Road, Harlington, Middx UB3 5AL (8759 7246/www.airport-bowl.co.uk). Hatton Cross tube.*

AMF Bowling Lewisham *11-29 Belmont Hill, SE13 5AU (0845 658 1272/www.amfbowling.co.uk). Lewisham rail/DLR.*

Bexleyheath Megabowl *Albion Road, Bexleyheath, Kent DA6 7AG (0871 550 1010/www.megabowl.co.uk). Bexleyheath rail.*

Dagenham Bowling *Cook Road, Dagenham, Essex RM9 6XW (8593 2888/www.dagenhambowling.co.uk). Becontree tube.*

Feltham Megabowl *Leisure West Complex, Browells Lane, Feltham, Middx TW13 6EQ (0871 550 1010/ www.megabowl.co.uk). Feltham rail.*

Funland *The Trocadero, 1 Piccadilly Circus, W1D 7DH (7292 3633/www.funland.co.uk). Piccadilly Circus tube.*

Hollywood Bowl *Finchley Leisure Way, High Road, N12 0QZ (8446 6667/www.hollywoodbowl.co.uk). East Finchley tube, then 263 bus.*

Hollywood Surrey Quays *The Mast Leisure Park, Teredo Street, SE16 7LW (7237 3773/www.hollywood bowl.co.uk).*

Queen's Ice Bowl *17 Queensway, W2 4QP (7229 0172/www.queensiceandbowl.co.uk). Bayswater tube.*

Rowans Bowl *10 Stroud Green Road, N4 2DF (8800 1950/www.rowans.co.uk). Finsbury Park tube.*

Streatham Megabowl *142 Streatham Hill, SW2 4RU (8678 6007/www.megabowl.co.uk). Streatham Hill rail.*

Yoga

Yoga is good for children, but you need to enrol your child on an approved and registered course. A splendid arrival on the London scene is the Special Yoga Centre. This registered charity is the UK home for Yoga for the Special Child, a US/Brazil-based programme that offers one-to-one work with infants with a range of special needs, including Down's Syndrome, cerebral palsy, spina bifida, autism, epilepsy and ADD/ADHD.

The therapeutic aspect of yoga is also explored at the Yoga Therapy Centre, which runs weekly sessions for children with asthma. The big stretches of some positions help to unknot the chest muscles and assist with controlled breathing and relaxation. Yoga Bugs, created by Fenella Lindsell for three- to seven-year-olds, has also done much to promote yoga for children. There are now more than 200 trained Yoga Bugs teachers working in nursery, prep and primary schools. Classes also run at venues throughout the capital. Details from www.yogabugs.com.

The following centres offer children's classes:

Holistic Health *64 Broadway Market, E8 4QJ (7275 8434/www.holistic-health-hackney.co.uk). London Fields rail.*

Iyengar Institute *223A Randolph Avenue, W9 1NL (7624 3080/www.iyi.org.uk). Maida Vale tube.*

Sivananda Yoga *Vedanta Centre, 51 Felsham Road, SW15 1AZ (8780 0160). Putney Bridge tube or Putney rail.*

Special Yoga Centre *The Tay Building, 2A Wrentham Avenue, NW10 3HA (8933 5475/www.specialyoga.org.uk). Kensal Rise Rail.*

Triyoga *6 Erskine Road, NW3 3AJ (7483 3344/ www.triyoga.co.uk). Chalk Farm Tube.*

Yoga Junction *Unit 24 City North, Fonthill Road, N4 3HF (7263 3113/www.yogajunction.co.uk). Finsbury Park tube/rail.*

Yoga Therapy Centre *90-92 Pentonville Road, N1 9HS (7689 3040/www.yogatherapy.org). Angel tube.*

Disability sport

The high public profile of Paralympians like Tanni Grey-Thompson is long overdue. However, the broad term 'disability sport' also encompasses

Activities

Hampstead Heath Swimming Ponds. *See p268.*

THE ULTIMATE GUIDES TO LIVING IN LONDON

activities for people with learning disabilities. A number of organisations have responsibilities in this area. The **Inclusive Fitness Initiative** (0114 257 2060, www.inclusivefitness.org) is helping to redevelop public sports and fitness facilities to include accessible equipment.

Footballers can join the National Multi-Disabled Football League; find clubs and junior squads on www.disabilityfootball.co.uk. The **Back-Up Trust** (details on 8875 1805, www.backuptrust.org.uk), a charity working with people paralysed through spinal cord injury, runs multi-activity weeks for kids aged 13 to 17. Canoeing, abseiling, wheelchair basketball and rugby are among the sports offered. More programmes are run by **British Blind Sport** (0870 078 9000, www.britishblindsport.org.uk) and the **British Deaf Sports Council** (www.britishdeaf sportscouncil.org.uk). The former English Sports Association for People with Learning Disability is now run by **Mencap Sport** (01924 239 955).

London Sports Forum for Disabled People

7354 8666/www.londonsportsforum.org.uk.
This is the London wing of the English Federation of Disability Sport (www.efds.co.uk).

Wheelpower

01296 395 995/www.wheelpower.org.uk.
This is the umbrella body for 17 wheelchair sports, from archery to rugby.

Sports to watch

Basketball

London Towers

Crystal Palace National Sports Centre, Ledrington Road, SE19 (8776 7755/www.london-towers.co.uk). **Admission** £8; £6 concessions.
The Towers are one of the leading teams in the British Basketball League, playing home games in front of enthusiastic audiences at Crystal Palace most weekends from October to April.

Cricket

Short, snappy and fast-moving Twenty20 matches have brought a new, younger audience to cricket. The format is ideal for families, with games played at weekends and in the early evenings. Longer county matches are ideal for keen youngsters to while away a day during the summer holidays; tickets for Test matches are more difficult to obtain since England's thrilling victory over Australia in the 2005 Ashes series.

Brit Oval

SE11 5SS (7582 7764/www.surreycricket.com). Oval tube. **Admission** for Surrey matches £10-£15.
Recent developments have turned the Oval into a world-class ground, with fewer airs and graces than Lord's. Home team Surrey are going through a lean spell at the moment.

Lord's Cricket Ground

St John's Wood Road, NW8 8QN (Middlesex 7289 1300/www.middlesexccc.com; MCC 7432 1000/ www.lords.org). St John's Wood tube. **Admission** for Middlesex matches £12-£15 adults; £6-£7 children. Lord's is a magnificent venue to watch a game – any child interested in cricket will be thrilled to attend. Middlesex, whose home ground this is, play in Division 1 of both the County Championship and limited-overs National League.

Football

It has become increasingly difficult for young fans to watch Premiership football live rather than on TV. Top clubs may have two or three times as many members as the capacity of their ground, while discounts are few and far between for children who want to attend only occasionally. In the second-tier Coca-Cola Championship and Coca-Cola League, it's far easier to get into games. Indeed, lower-division clubs positively encourage youngsters and families with cheap tickets and special deals: at Leyton Orient, a kids' season ticket costs just £30, little more than £1 a match.

The season runs from August to May.

Barclays Premiership

Arsenal *Emirates Stadium, Hornsey Road (7704 4040/www.arsenal.com). Arsenal or Holloway Road tube.*
Charlton Athletic *The Valley, Floyd Road, SE7 8BL (0871 226 1905/www.charlton-athletic.co.uk). Charlton rail.*
Chelsea *Stamford Bridge, Fulham Road, SW6 1HS (0870 300 2322/www.chelseafc.com). Fulham Broadway tube.*
Fulham *Craven Cottage, Stevenage Road, SW6 6HH (0870 442 1234/www.fulhamfc.com). Putney Bridge tube.*
Tottenham Hotspur *White Hart Lane, 748 High Road, N17 0AP (0870 420 5000/www.spurs.co.uk). White Hart Lane rail.*
West Ham United *Boleyn Ground, Green Street, E13 9AZ (0870 112 2700/www.whufc.com). Upton Park tube.*

Coca-Cola Championship

Crystal Palace *Selhurst Park, Park Road, SE25 6PU (0871 200 0071/www.cpfc.co.uk). Selhurst rail.*
Millwall *The Den, Zampa Road, SE16 3LN (7231 9999/www.millwallfc.co.uk). South Bermondsey rail.*

Queens Park Rangers *Rangers Stadium, South Africa Road, W12 7PA (0870 112 1967/www.qpr. co.uk). White City tube.*

Watford *Vicarage Road, Watford, WD18 0ER (0870 111 1881/www.watfordfc.com). Watford High Street rail.*

Coca-Cola League

Barnet *Underhill, Barnet Lane, Barnet, EN5 2BE (8441 6932/www.barnetfc.premiumtv.co.uk). High Barnet tube.* Division 2.

Brentford *Griffin Park, Braemar Road, Brentford, Middx TW8 0NT (8847 2511/www.brentfordfc.co.uk). Brentford rail.* Division 1.

Leyton Orient *Matchroom Stadium, Brisbane Road, E10 5NE (8926 1010/www.leytonorient.com). Leyton tube.* Division 2.

Horse racing

All 59 racecourses around Britain offer a warm welcome to children. Admission for under-16s is free at the majority of meetings, and most racecourses stage special 'family days'. Admission prices stated below are for adults attending regular meetings; children go free.

Ascot
High Street, Ascot (0870 727 1234/www.ascot.co.uk). Ascot rail. **Admission** £7-£20.
This refurbished course is best known for the 'Royal' meeting, but there are plenty of lower-key race days as well.

Epsom Downs
Racecourse Paddock, Epsom, Surrey KT18 5LQ (01372 726 311/www.epsomderby.co.uk). Epsom Downs rail. **Admission** £5-£18.
The grassy Lonsdale Enclosure is ideal for a picnic – though probably not on Derby day, when around 150,000 people are attracted to one of the great occasions in Britain's sporting calendar.

Kempton Park
Staines Road East, Sunbury-on-Thames, Middx TW16 5AQ (01932 782 292/www.kempton.co.uk). Kempton Park rail. **Admission** £9-£20.
There's a playground and crèche at this busy course, while the grandstand includes a food hall with the parade ring and winners' enclosure just behind.

Sandown Park
Esher Station Road, Esher, KT10 9AJ (01372 470 047/www.sandown.co.uk). Esher rail. **Admission** £5-£35.
This frequent winner of Racecourse of the Year is attractively sited in a natural amphitheatre. The Park Enclosure is the best place for a family outing.

Windsor
Maidenhead Road, Windsor, Berks SL4 5JJ (0870 220 0024/www.windsor-racecourse.co.uk). Windsor & Eton Riverside rail. **Admission** £6-£20.

One of Britain's most picturesque courses holds two Sunday Fundays each year and a series of popular summer evening meetings. On a fine day, this can be a great place for keeping the kids happy, while managing to place a couple of bets yourself.

Rugby league

Harlequins RL
Twickenham Stoop Stadium, Langhorn Drive, Twickenham, Middx TW2 7SX (8410 6000/ www.quins.co.uk). Twickenham rail. **Admission** £12-£30 adults; £6-£15 5-16s.
The rebranded London Broncos have found a permanent home after years of nomadic wandering around the grounds of the capital. Family-oriented entertainment accompanies the Engage Super League games in a season that runs from March to October, with games on Saturday or Sunday afternoons.

Rugby union

The top London rugby unionn clubs have a slew of internationals in their line-ups, and a trip to a match is an absolute bargain compared to football. The season runs from September to May.

Guinness Premiership

Saracens
Vicarage Road, Watford, Herts WD18 0EP (01923 475 222/www.saracens.com). Watford tube/Watford High Street rail. **Admission** £17-£30 adults; £10-£15 5-16s.

Harlequins
Twickenham Stoop Stadium, Langhorn Drive, Twickenham, Middx TW2 7SX (8410 6000/ www.quins.co.uk). Twickenham rail. **Admission** £10-£30 adults; £5-£15 5-16s. Division 1.
The Harlequins return to take a place in the Premiership again for the 2006-7 season.

National League

London Welsh
Old Deer Park, 187 Kew Road, Richmond, Surrey TW9 2AZ (8940 2368/www.london-welsh.co.uk). Richmond tube/rail. **Admission** £12 adults; £6 concessions; free 5-16s. Division 1.

Stock car & banger racing

Wimbledon Stadium
Plough Lane, SW17 0BL (01252 322 920/www. spedeworth.co.uk). Wimbledon Park tube. **Admission** £11 adults; £5 children.
Sunday night meetings at Wimbledon Stadium are great fun for all ages. It's the element of surprise that's key: anything can happen when the stock cars and bangers get out on the track – and it usually does.

Activities

Days Out

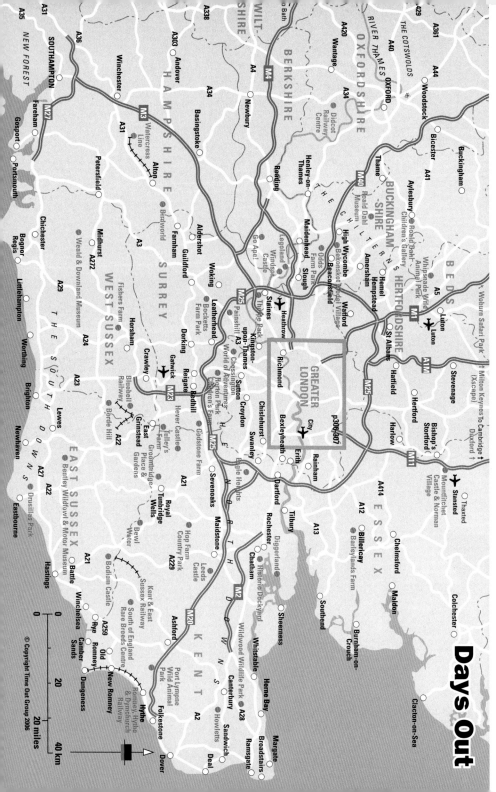

Days Out

Days Out

Go wild in the country – for one day only.

London has everything a family could possibly want, but we'd grudgingly admit that some folk may want more pastoral pleasures. We'd rather you didn't go too far, however, so our selection of top days out only includes places within two hours' journey from the capital. Most are accessible by train (some may necessitate a taxi ride from the station). A list of London's main-line rail stations is on p291. For an online journey planner, try the National Rail Enquiries website – www.nationalrail.co.uk.

Activities

Go Ape!
The Look Out, Nine Mile Ride, Swinley Forest, Bracknell, Berks RG12 7QW (0870 444 5562/ www.goape.co.uk). **Getting there** *By train* Bracknell rail, then bus 158, 159 or taxi. *By car* J10 off M4. **Open** *Mar-Oct* 9am-dusk daily. *Nov* 10am-4pm Sat, Sun. (groups leave every 30mins). *Feb* Berkshire schools half-term; phone for details. **Admission** £21; £17 10-17s. **Credit** MC, V.
There's some really challenging high-wire action in the forest canopy at this adventure course of rope bridges, Tarzan swings and zip slides. All the obstacles are located up to almost 11m (35ft) above the forest floor so you can really make like a primate here. Children must be aged over ten and measure at least 1.4m (4ft 7in) to have a go. Pre-booking is essential. This is a most adrenalin-filled walk in the woods, so tinies can't get involved.
Café. Car park (free). Disabled access: toilets. Nearest picnic place: grounds. Shop.

Bewl Water
Lamberhurst, nr Tunbridge Wells, Kent (01892 890 661/www.bewl.co.uk). **Getting there** *By train* Wadhurst rail, then taxi, or Tunbridge Wells rail. *By car* J5 off M25. **Open** 9am-dusk daily. **Closed** Concert Day (phone for details), 25 Dec. **Admission** (per vehicle) *Apr-Oct* £4 Mon-Fri; £5 Sat, Sun. *Nov-Mar* £2.50 daily. *Concert tickets* phone for details. **Credit** MC, V.
An area of serene beauty, Bewl Water is perhaps most famously a fisherman's paradise and a water-sports fanatic's dream. For those who want to have a bit more of an adrenalin rush on the open water, windsurfing tuition is given by qualified RYA (Royal Yachting Association) instructors: all equipment is provided, and kids with a taste for water sports can then graduate on to rowing and powerboat lessons. You can book on the premises (phone the Outdoor Centre on 01892 890 716).
Café. Car park. Disabled access: toilet. Nappy-changing facilities. Nearest picnic place: grounds. Restaurant. Shop.

Xscape
Milton Keynes MK9 3XS (0871 222 5670/www.xscape. co.uk). **Getting there** *By train* Milton Keynes Central rail. *By car* J14 off M1. **Open** 9am-11pm Mon, Tue, Thur-Sat. **Admission** prices vary according to activity. **Credit** AmEx, MC, V.
Sporty children have the most fantastic time in this huge complex with showdome, skydiving tunnel and tubing (sliding down an ice luge). This man-made mountain has a vast roof has 1,500 tonnes of real snow, with a 175m (575ft) main slope and 135m (443ft) nursery run. If all the activity gets too much, there's après ski in the form of a 16-screen cinema, pool and video games. The Airkix skydiving tunnel is the most expensive activity at £33 per introductory session for children. It all adds up to an expensive day out, but, heck, it's cheaper than a skiing holiday.
Buggy access. Café. Car park. Disabled access. Nappy-changing facilities. Restaurant. Shop.

Diggerland/The Snow Park
Medway Valley Leisure Park, Roman Way, Strood, Kent ME2 2NU (0870 034 4437/www.diggerland.com/ www.thesnowpark.co.uk). **Getting there** *By rail* Strood rail, then taxi. *By car* J2 off M2, then A228, then follow signs towards Strood. **Open** 10am-5pm weekends, bank hols, school hols, half-terms; check website for details. **Admission** £2.50; free under-2s. **Day pass** (includes all rides) £12.50; £6.25 over-65s. **Credit** AmEx, MC, V.
Drivers of all ages can get behind the wheel of heavy plant in this park where the trucks are the stars. Dumper and JCB racing is organised for adults, and themed birthday party packages are available for children. You can even adopt a digger (ie, have your name on it for a year). Other activities include bouncy castles, ride-on toys, a vast sandpit and a land train. During winter (Dec 2006-Easter 2007), snow is shipped in and Diggerland becomes a snow park with a 100m (328ft) tubing run, a 50m (164ft) main slope and – best of all – a large play area for building snowmen and throwing snowballs. An all-day ski/board pass is £7.50 (ski and boot hire £10), ski and board lessons are available from £25 per hour, and toddler ski sessions cost from £12.50 per hour.
Buggy access. Café. Car park (free). Disabled access: toilet. Nappy-changing facilities. Nearest picnic place: grounds. Shop.

Bird sanctuaries

Birdworld
Holt Pound, Farnham, Surrey GU10 4LD (01420 22140/www.birdworld.co.uk). **Getting there** *By rail* Farnham rail, then taxi or 18 bus. *By car* J4 off M3, then A325 & follow signs. **Open** *Feb-Oct* 10am-6pm daily. *Nov-mid Feb* 10am-4.30pm daily. **Admission** £9.95; £8.25 concessions, 3-14s; £32.95 family (2+2); free under-3s. **Credit** MC, V.

The feathered residents of Britain's biggest bird park come from all over the world. They live in aviaries; some, like the ostriches, have enclosures big enough to sprint in. There's also a tropical aquarium, and the on-site Jenny Wren farm sustains rabbits, lambs, horses, donkeys and a variety of poultry. The best way to get an overview of all the residents is on a guided 'safari train'. Penguin-feeding displays take place at 11.30am and 4pm daily; book in advance for a chance to feed them yourself (£14.95). Special events take place throughout the year, including Treasure Island Fun Day (24 Aug 2006), which the parrots are no doubt dreading, and Hallowe'en and festive December specials.
Buggy access. Café. Car park (free). Disabled access: toilet. Nappy-changing facilities. Nearest picnic place: grounds. Restaurant. Shop.

Eagle Heights
Lullingstone Lane, Eynsford, Kent DA4 OJB (01322 866 466/www.eagleheights.co.uk). **Getting there** *By rail* Eynsford rail, then 1.5-mile walk or taxi. *By car* J3 off M25; J1 off M20. **Open** *Mar-Oct* 10.30am-5pm daily. *Jan, Feb, Nov* 11am-4pm Sat, Sun. Closed Dec. *Flying displays* Mar-Oct noon and 3.30pm daily; Nov, Jan, Feb noon and 3pm daily. **Admission** £6.95; £5.95 concessions; £4.95 4-14s; free under-4s. **Credit MC, V.**
Eagle Heights has approximately 150 raptors of more than 50 species, many of which can be seen flying in daily demonstrations. The centre provides sanctuary for wild, injured raptors and regularly releases rehabilitated birds back to the wild. There's also a collection of reptiles and mammals and, new for 2006, an otter enclosure. The views over the beautiful Darent Valley are fine. In a bid to be more 'all weather', the Centre puts on indoor flying displays, but seeing the raptors fly out of doors is much more inspiring.
Buggy access. Cafe. Car park (free). Disabled access: ramps, toilets. Nappy-changing facilities. Nearest picnic place: grounds. Restaurants. Shop.

Castles

Bodiam Castle
Nr Robertsbridge, East Sussex TN32 5UA (01580 830 436/www.nationaltrust.org.uk). **Getting there** *By rail* Wadhurst rail, then 254 bus. *By car* J5 off M25. **Open** *Mid Feb-Oct* 10.30am-6pm or dusk daily. *Nov-mid-Feb* 10.30am-4pm or dusk Sat, Sun. Last entry 1hr before closing. **Tours** groups (min 15 people) by prior arrangement; phone for details. **Admission** (NT) £4.60; £2.30 5-16s; £11.50 family (2+3); free under-5s. **Credit** AmEx, MC, V.
Built in 1385, Bodiam Castle was ransacked during the Civil War and, until the 20th century, its ruins were visited only by just a handful of Romantic artists. There's no roof to speak of, but the towers and turrets still offer sweeping views across the Rother Valley. Family activities take place throughout the school holidays – events are listed on the website (weekly storytelling, armour-trying sessions, evening 'bat watches' and the like).
Buggy access. Café. Car park (£2). Disabled access: toilet. Nappy-changing facilities. Nearest picnic place: castle grounds. Restaurant. Shop.

Hever Castle
Nr Edenbridge, Kent TN8 7NG (01732 865 224/ www.hevercastle.co.uk). **Getting there** *By rail* Edenbridge Town rail, then taxi, or Hever rail, then

1-mile walk. *By car* J5 or J6 off M25. **Open** *Gardens* Mar-Oct 11am-6pm daily (last entry 5pm). Nov 11am-4pm daily (last entry 3pm). *Castle* Mar-Oct noon-6pm daily (last entry 5pm). Nov noon-4pm daily (last entry 3pm). **Tours** groups (min 20 people) by prior arrangement. **Admission** *Castle & gardens* £9.80; £8.20 concessions; £5.30 5-14s; £24.90 family (2+2 or 1+3); free under-5s. *Gardens only* £7.80; £6.70 concessions; £5 5-14s; £20.60 family (2+2 or 1+3); free under-5s. **Credit** MC, V.
The childhood home of Anne Boleyn, this 13th-century castle is tuffed with Tudor furnishings; the interiors display waxwork scenes and weaponry, as well as Anne Boleyn's illuminated *Books of Hours*. The main attraction, though, is the great outdoors: throughout the school holidays various events take place here; jousting and archery are the most popular. There are mazes galore. The water maze (open Apr-Oct) is the children's favourite, a shallow lake with a rocky island. The paths are on legs above the water, but some of the stone slabs you tread on while walking to the island trigger a spray of water.
Buggy access (grounds only). Car park. Disabled access: ramps, toilets (grounds only). Nappy-changing facilities. Restaurants. Shops.

Leeds Castle
Maidstone, Kent ME17 1PL (01622 765 400/ www.leeds-castle.com). **Getting there** *By car* J8 off M20/A20. *By rail* Bearsted rail. **Open** *Castle* Apr-Oct 10.30am-5.30pm daily. Nov-Mar 10.30am-5pm daily. Last entry 3pm. *Gardens & attractions* Nov-Mar 10am-5pm daily. Apr-Oct 10am-7pm daily. **Tours** pre-booked groups only. **Admission** (unlimited re-entry over 1yr except for special events) £13.50; £11 concessions; £8 4-15s; free under-4s. **Credit** MC, V.
Erected soon after the Norman Conquest, lovely Leeds has been immaculately maintained. Inside, magnificent halls and chambers contain historical displays (from the Heraldry Room to the unique Dog Collar Museum), but it's the outdoor wonderland that we love. Leave time to lose yourself in the famous maze. Its castellated hedges have a grotto at the centre, which takes you through an underground passage. The riverside pathways bustle with black swans and peacocks, and more exotic birds can be pondered in the aviaries. Bird walks take place daily (check the website). Daily falconry displays are choreographed to music by castle falconers. The Museum of Kent Life (01622 763 936, www.museum-kentlife.co.uk) is nearby.
Buggy access. Car park. Disabled access: lift, toilet. Nappy-changing facilities. Nearest picnic place: grounds. Restaurant. Shops.

Mountfitchet Castle & Norman Village
Stansted Mountfitchet, Essex CM24 8SP (01279 813 237/www.mountfitchetcastle.com). **Getting there** *By rail* Stansted Mountfitchet rail. *By car* J8 off M11. **Open** *Mar-Nov 2006* 10am-5pm daily. **Admission** £6.50; £5.50 concessions; £5 2-14s; free under-2s. *House on the Hill Toy Museum* £4; £3.50 concessions; £3.30 2-14s; free under-2s. 10% discount if visiting both on same day. **Credit** MC, V.
The 11th-century Mountfitchet Castle today is reduced to isolated piles of rubble, although a 'working' Norman village has been constructed on the original site to give some indication of life more than 900 years ago. Thus the many buildings scattered around the original motte date from the

1980s and are populated by waxwork figures. There's a host of tame animals, including fallow deer, Jacob sheep (an ancient breed kept by the Normans) and poultry. Events take place throughout the school holidays. In summer 2006 Mountfitchet is running a medieval football tournament to complement certain events in Germany. Medieval History Week takes place from Monday 25 September 2006. The adjoining House on the Hill Toy Museum is also great for younger kids, with more than 80,000 exhibits from the Victorian era through to the 1980s. New for 2006 is The Haunted Manor, starring the ghosts of Mountfitchet Castle that have haunted the site for over 1,000 years.
Café (castle). Disabled: ramps, toilet (castle). Nappy-changing facilities. Nearest picnic place: picnic tables in grounds. Shops.

Windsor Castle

Windsor, Berks SL4 1NJ (01753 868 286/www.royal. gov.uk). **Getting there** *By rail* Windsor & Eton Riverside rail. *By car* J6 off M4. **Open** *Mar-Oct* 9.45am-5.15pm daily (last entry 4pm). *Nov-Feb* 9.45am-4.15pm daily (last entry 3pm). **Admission** (LP) £13.50; £12 concessions; £7.50 5-16s; £34.50 family (2+3); free under-5s. **Credit** AmEx, MC, V.
A working royal residence, Windsor Castle is perennially attractive to tourists, so it pays to pre-book to avoid queues. The castle houses a unique collection of art and artefacts, with works by Rembrandt, Gainsborough and Rubens, and a collection of medieval weaponry and armour. The exhibit most likely to appeal to younger kids is the intricate Queen Mary's Dolls' House, created by Sir Edward Lutyens in 1924 on a scale of 1:12. It was intended as an accurate record of contemporary domestic design and it remains perfect, from the working water and electrics to the hand-made wool rugs. The Jubilee Garden has St George's Chapel, which contains the tombs of ten monarchs, including Henry VIII and the Queen Mum.
Buggy access/storage. Disabled access: lift, toilet. Nappy-changing facilities. Nearest picnic place: grounds. Shops.

Country estates

Borde Hill

Balcombe Road, Haywards Heath, West Sussex RH16 1XP (01444 450 326/www.bordehill.co.uk). **Getting there** *By rail* Haywards Heath rail, then taxi. **By car** A272 off A23 off M23. **Open** *Mar-Nov* 10am-6pm or dusk (if earlier) daily. **Admission** £6; £5 concessions; £3.50 3-15s; free under-3s. *Season ticket* £12; £8 3-15s. **Credit** AmEx, MC, V.
Borde Hill is renowned for its champion trees, most of which grow in the Warren Wood, planted in 1905. The rest of the 200 listed acres include parkland and lakes. As well as rare plants from China, Burma and the Himalayas, the Garden of Allah and nearby Azalea Ring – a traditional English rose garden with picturesque woodland walks – there's an extensive adventure playground, the best in the area, with a cowboy fort, pirate ship, swings, slides and an obstacle course. Daily events for children (1-31 Aug 2006) include puppet shows, teddy bears' picnics and soccer schools. A pond is set aside for children's fishing classes at weekends and during school holidays (10am-4pm; £4 per hour including equipment hire). A 'photographic treasure trail' and a woodland trail are both fun to follow.
Buggy access. Café. Disabled access: toilet. Nappy-changing facilities. Nearest picnic place: parkland. Restaurant. Shop.

Groombridge Place Gardens & Enchanted Forest

Groombridge Place, Groombridge, nr Tunbridge Wells, Kent TN3 9QG (01892 861 444/www.groombridge. co.uk). **Getting there** *By rail* Tunbridge Wells rail, then 290, 291 bus or taxi. *By car* B2110 off A264 off A21. **Open** *April-early Nov* 10am-5pm or dusk (if earlier) daily. **Admission** £8.70; £7.20 concessions, 3-12s; £29.50 family (2+2); free under-3s. **Credit** MC, V.
This lovable heritage garden, ancient woodland and all-round children's paradise (look out for the giant rabbits) earned itself the Tourism South East Award for Excellence last year and continues to add to its many attractions. For 2006 they've netted a giant (2m, 6ft 6in) 'Jurassic butterfly' to watch over the dinosaur valley. The beautiful formal gardens are supplemented by the Enchanted Forest, a wonderland of giant swings, the Dark Walk adventure trail, and the Drunken Garden, where asymmetrical topiary leans as if half cut. In the school holidays, kids are treated to a variety of fun and games, including a large-scale sports day, a medieval encampment (16, 17 Sept) and Hallowe'en in the Spooky Forest (27, 28 Oct).
Buggy access (limited). Café. Car park (free). Disabled access (limited). Nappy-changing facilities. Nearest picnic place: grounds. Shop.

Hop Farm Country Park

Beltring, Paddock Wood, Kent TN12 6PY (01622 872 068/www.thehopfarm.co.uk). **Getting there** *By rail* Paddock Wood rail, then (peak times only) shuttle bus. *By car* J5 off M25, then A21 south. **Open** 10am-5pm daily. **Admission** £7.50; £6.50 concessions, 3-15s; £27 family (2+2); free under-3s. Prices vary on event days. **Credit** MC, V.
Kent's largest tourist attraction was once a working hop farm. Now its oast houses store an amusing museum harking back to the glory days of hop-picking, as well as a giddying number of family-fun possibilities – children's playgrounds and play barns, go-karts, crazy golf, petting corners and rides on dray carts pulled by lofty shire horses. Hop Farm's diary remains full all year round, so you're unlikely to visit during any school holiday without becoming embroiled in some sort of special event. Summer holidays in 2006 bring gladiatorial fun and games, extreme mountain biking and sporting events, and Animal Crackers attractions, including falconry displays. Check the website events diary for details.
Buggy access. Car park (free). Café. Disabled access: toilet. Nappy-changing facilities. Nearest picnic place: grounds. Shop.

Painshill Park

Painshill Park Trust, Portsmouth Road, Cobham, Surrey KT11 1JE (01932 868 113/www.painshill. co.uk). **Getting there** *By rail* Cobham or Esher rail. *By car* J10 off M25, then A3, exit A245. Check website or phone (0870 608 2608) for details of the Surrey Parks & Gardens Explorer bus. **Open** *Apr-Oct* 10.30am-6pm daily (last entry 4.30pm). *Nov-Mar* 10.30am-4pm or dusk (if earlier) daily (last entry 3pm). **Admission** £6.60; £5.80 concessions; £3.85 5-16s; £22 family (2+4); free under-5s. **Credit** MC, V.
Painshill consists of 160 acres of subtle and surprising vistas created by Charles Hamilton in the 18th century. The landscapes – which include a vineyard, Chinese bridge, crystal grotto, Turkish tent, a newly restored hermitage and a Gothic tower – are a work of art that influenced the

Bocketts Farm Park.

future of England's countryside. Family events take place on Sundays and bank holidays throughout the year. For information on activities such as mini-beast safaris, summer picnics and 18th-century costume days, as well as August 2006's Battle of Painshill reconstruction, starring Napoleon and his army and Wellington's troop, check the website. Painshill also does brilliant camp-building parties for outdoorsy children.
Buggy access. Café. Car park (free). Disabled access: toilet. Nappy-changing facilities. Nearest picnic place: grounds. Shop.

Farms

Barleylands Farm Centre & Craft Village

Barleylands Road, Billericay, Essex CM11 2UD (01268 532 253/www.barleylands.co.uk). **Getting there** *By rail* Billericay rail. *By car* J29 off M25. **Open** *Farm Centre* 10am-5pm daily. *Craft village* Mar-Oct 10am-5pm Tue-Sun. Nov-Feb 10am-4pm Tue-Sun. **Admission** *Farm Centre* £3; £10 family (2+2). *Craft village* free. **Credit** MC, V.
The nostalgic character of Barleylands is concentrated in the Farm Centre, which has more than 2,000 exhibits of vintage tractors and other ancient pieces of earth-tilling paraphernalia. The Craft Village is where glassblowers, woodturners and blacksmiths show off their skills. Children love the chickens, rabbits and turkeys near the picnic area; larger animals, including ponies, cows and pigs, graze out near the pond. There's also an activity playground and stables, plus tractor rides, a bouncy castle, giant trampolines and an equally vast sandpit. The twice-monthly farmers' markets pull in the ethical shoppers, and many East Londoners and Essex folk make a date to attend

the busy Essex Country Show – a jamboree of steam engines, heavy horses, rural crafts and fun (9, 10 Sept 2006). *Buggy access. Café. Car park. Disabled access: toilet. Nappy-changing facilities. Nearest picnic place: grounds.*

Bocketts Farm Park

Young Street, Fetcham, nr Leatherhead, Surrey KT22 9BS (01372 363 764/www.bockettsfarm.co.uk). **Getting there** *By rail* Leatherhead rail, then taxi. *By car* J9 off M25. **Open** 10am-6pm daily. **Admission** £5.95; £5.40 concessions, 3-17s; £4.25 2s; free under-2s. **Credit** MC, V.
Sitting pretty in a valley in the glorious North Downs, Bocketts is a working farm that goes a bundle on play. Sheepdogs take time out from sheep work to show off their agility, and lambs, chicks and calves stagger about winsomely in the spring. There are plenty of opportunities for small-animal handling, as well as the chance to ride ponies, milk goats and watch pigs race. Other attractions include play barns with astroslides and trampolines, sandpits and a children's birthday party service. The café sits in a handsome 18th-century building, but there are loads of places to enjoy a picnic. Come in autumn for the picturesque pumpkin harvest, or at Christmas for a home-grown tree and the chance to meet Santa.
Buggy access. Café. Car park (free). Disabled access: toilet. Nappy-changing facilities. Nearest picnic place: grounds. Shop.

Fishers Farm

New Pound Lane, Wisborough Green, West Sussex RH14 0EG (01403 700 063/www.fishersfarmpark. co.uk). **Getting there** *By rail* Billingshurst rail, then taxi. *By car* J10 off M25. **Open** 10am-5pm daily; ring for times during special events. **Admission** *Nov-Mar* £7.75; £6.25 concessions; £7.25 3-16s; £4 2s. *Apr-Oct* £9.75; £8.25 concessions; £9.25 3-16s; £6 2s. *Summer hols* £10.75; £9.25 concessions; £10.25 3-16s; £7 2s; £41 family. **Credit** MC, V.

Fishers Farm is a vast family fun area with added animals. The livestock includes poultry, cattles, horses and donkeys, goats, sheep and cuddly alpacas. City folk can learn more about them in the Barn Theatre's daily Meet the Animals events. The theatre also hosts musicals, pantos, marionette and magic shows during the hols. Once all the animals have been met, children can make the most of the playgrounds, trampolines and bouncy castles. There are also pedal tractors and, in summer months, a giant paddling pool with sandy shores. Other child magnets include an adventure golf course and an animated ghost tunnel.
Buggy access. Cafés. Car park (free). Disabled access: toilet. Nappy-changing facilities. Nearest picnic place: grounds. Restaurants. Shops.

Godstone Farm

Tilburstow Hill Road, Godstone, Surrey RH9 8LX (01883 742 546/www.godstonefarm.co.uk). **Getting there** *By rail* Caterham rail, then 409 bus. *By car* J6 off M25. **Open** *Mar-Oct* 10am-6pm daily. *Nov-Feb* 10am-5pm daily. **Admission** £5.80 2-16s (accompanying adult free); free under-2s. **Credit** MC, V.

Always good for the small, cuddly end of the agricultural scene, Godstone is particularly rewarding come spring, when wobbly lambs careen around the paddocks and fluffball chicks bask in the incubators' glow. The pre-schoolers love it. Children with their hearts set on something altogether less profound can chase each other across the adventure playground, the biggest, allegedly, in south-east England, and the little ones lose themselves in the ball pools and on the walkways that make up the play barn. There's also a new slide and a crow's nest to climb on. Godstone has a sister in Epsom, Horton Park (01372 743 984/www.hortonpark.co.uk).
Buggy access. Café. Car park (free). Disabled access: toilet. Nappy-changing facilities. Nearest picnic place: grounds. Shop.

Odds Farm Park

Wooburn Common, nr High Wycombe, Bucks HP10 0LX (01628 520 188/www.oddsfarm.co.uk). **Getting there** *By rail* Beaconsfield rail, then taxi. *By car* J2 off M40 or J7 off M4. **Open** *Early Feb-mid July, early Sept-late Oct* 10am-5.30pm daily. *Mid July-early Sept* 10am-6pm daily. *Late Oct-mid Feb* 10am-4.30pm daily. Closed 18 Dec 2006-2 Jan 2007. **Admission** £6.50; £5.50 concessions, 2-16s; free under-2s. **Credit** MC, V.

Odds Farm was created with small children in mind, so expect plenty of activities that will interest them: feeding the chickens; Rabbit World; farmyard tea-time, and tractor and trailer rides. Some activities are dependent on the time of year (sheep-shearing, for example, is between May and July). Seasonal events – notably Easter egg hunts, Hallowe'en pumpkin carving and an encounter with Father Christmas – take place in the relevant school holidays. Several outdoor play areas form focal points for the many birthday parties held at Odds all year round (phone for more information); they also make a nice spot for kids to amuse themselves while parents linger over a picnic.
Buggy access. Café. Car park (free). Disabled access: toilet. Nappy-changing facilities. Nearest picnic place: grounds. Shop.

South of England Rare Breeds Centre

Highlands Farm, Woodchurch, nr Ashford, Kent TN26 3RJ (01233 861 493/www.rarebreeds.org.uk). **Getting there** *By rail* Ham Street rail, then taxi. *By car* J10 off M20. **Open** *Apr-Sept* 10.30am-5.30pm daily. *Oct-Mar* 10.30am-4.30pm Tue-Sun. **Admission** £6.60; free under-3s. **Credit** MC, V.

Operated by the Canterbury Oast Trust, a charity dedicated to the care of adults with physical and learning difficulties, these 120 woodland acres host a breeding programme for animals once common to the British Isles, but now endangered. There are unusual species of goat, cattle and poultry to spot. The obligatory play barn for wet weather fun and piggy-racing activities add to the interest. Children can play with piglets and small animals in the handling pens, and tear around the Mysterious Marsh Woodland Adventure playground. During school holidays there are activity quiz trails, scavenger hunts and 25-minute tours of the farm on tractors and trailers.
Buggy access. Café. Car park (free). Disabled access: toilet. Nappy-changing facilities. Nearest picnic place: grounds. Shop.

Tulley's Farm

Turners Hill, Crawley, West Sussex RH10 4PE (01342 718472/www.tulleysfarm.com). **Getting there** *By rail* Three Bridges rail, then taxi. *By car* J10 off M23. **Open** *Summer* Shop 9am-6pm daily. Tea room 9.30am-5pm daily. *Winter* Shop 9am-5pm Tea room 9.30am-4.30pm daily. *Maze* (8 July-4 Sep, 9-10 Sep) 10am-6pm daily (last entry 5pm). **Admission** free. Maze £7; £6 4-14s; £22 family (2+2, 1+3); free under-4s. **Credit** AmEx, MC, V.

Fruit and veg is what this farm's all about, but rest assured that Tulley's makes it fun. The fruit is pick-your-own; the fields of berries are ready to plunder from 8 July 2006, and children are entranced by the rabbits, guinea pigs and pot-bellied pigs in the farmyard. The famous maize maze – whose closely planted plants, with their thick, dark-green foliage and sturdy stems, create a series of dead-ends and impenetrable walls – opens the first weekend in July 2006. The maze has a different theme every year and has become the highlight of the increasingly popular Tulley's summer festival, when children can go mad on the farm and eat a load of fresh fruit into the bargain.
Buggy access. Café. Car park (free). Shop

Specialist museums

Bentley Wildfowl & Motor Museum

Halland, nr Lewes, East Sussex BN8 5AF (01825 840 573/www.bentley.org.uk). *By rail* Uckfield or Lewes rail, then taxi. *By car* A22, then follow signs. **Open** *Summer* 10.30am-5.30pm daily. *Winter* 10.30am-4.30pm Sat, Sun. House closed during winter. **Admission** £6.50; £5.50 concessions; £4.50 3-15s; £21 family (2+3); free under-3s. **Credit** AmEx, MC, V.

More than 1,000 swans, geese and ducks from all over the world live alongside a highly polished display of veteran Edwardian and vintage cars and motorcycles. And if neither motor nor fowl interests you, the craftspeople might. They include a glass sculptor, woodcarvers and a jewellery maker. Bentley House, a Palladian-style mansion restored by Raymond Erith, has a gallery with a permanent exhibition by the Sussex artist Philip Rickman. There are also

Days Out

formal gardens, an adventure playground and the beautiful Glyndebourne wood, where there's a new wildlife trail with interactive boards. The Bentley Woodfair (15-17 Sept 2006) is a timber-based extravaganza.
Buggy access. Café. Car park (free). Disabled access: toilet. Nappy-changing facilities. Nearest picnic place: grounds. Shop.

Chatham Historic Dockyard

The Historic Dockyard, Chatham, Kent ME4 4TZ (01634 823 800/www.thedockyard.co.uk). **Getting there** *By rail* Chatham rail. *By car* J1, 3 or 4 off M2. **Open** *14 Feb-31 Oct* 10am-6pm daily (last entry 4pm). *8-30 Nov* 10am-4pm Sat, Sun (last entry 3pm). Closed Dec, Jan. **Admission** (lasts 1yr, not valid on event days) £11.50; £9 concessions; £6.50 5-15s; £29.50 family (2+2 or 1+3; £5 per additional child); free under-5s. **Credit** AmEx, MC, V.
Jewel of the tidal Medway, this ancient maritime centre was famously the starting point of Horatio Nelson's distinguished career in 1771. Many buildings from Nelson's time survive on the site. There are tours around both a 40-year-old submarine, HMS *Ocelot*, the last warship to be built at the dockyard, and a World War II destroyer, HMS *Cavalier*. The working Ropery is a source of fascination, as is Wooden Walls, which evokes the sights, sounds and smells of the dockyard of 1758. Interactive displays include a radio-controlled ship-docking exercise and a mock ship fight. The Dockyard hosts the Medway Maritime Festival and other themed events throughout the year. Trafalgar Night, staged to celebrate the battle's bicentenary, was so succesful in 2005 that another is planned for 2006. There are special Smugglers' Days on 27 and 28 August 2006.
Buggy access. Café. Car park (free). Disabled access: toilet. Nappy-changing facilities. Shop.

Imperial War Museum Duxford

Cambridge CB2 4QR (01223 835 000/www.iwm. org.uk). **Getting there** *By rail* Cambridge rail. *By car* J10 off M11. **Open** *Summer* 10am-6pm daily (last entry 5.15pm). *Winter* 10am-4pm daily (last entry 3.15pm). **Admission** £13; £8 concessions; £7 16-18s; free under-16s. **Credit** MC, V.
Duxford, a huge aviation and military vehicle museum, has four themed hangars of exhibits, as well as the futuristic glass-fronted American Air Museum, designed by Lord Foster, and the Land Warfare Hall, filled with tanks and military vehicles. The complex is so huge that a convenient (and free) 'road train' operates all day, dropping people off at the major attractions. The air shows are superb (there are about four each year), and Action Afternoons (check the website for dates), when military vehicles are demonstrated and historic aircraft perform short displays, take place monthly. Dates for the diary include the Spitfire Anniversay Air Show (2, 3 Sept 2006). For terrestrial activities, learn about the Normandy campaign in the Land Warfare Hall. Here, tanks, military vehicles and artillery pieces are on show in battlefield scenes. Work started in April 2004 to redevelop Hangar 1 into AirSpace, a 10,000sq m (108,000sq ft) exhibition area, whose opening is scheduled for summer 2007. Thirty classic aircraft will be displayed. A new education centre for schoolchildren is also planned. For the time being, Concorde stands gloriously in all its pointy-nosed glory.
Buggy access. Cafés. Car park (free). Disabled access: lift, ramps, toilet. Nappy-changing facilities. Restaurant. Shops.

Roald Dahl Children's Gallery

Buckinghamshire County Museum, Church Street, Aylesbury, Bucks HP20 2QP (01296 331 441/ www.buckscc.gov.uk/museum). **Getting there** *By rail* Aylesbury rail. *By car* J8 off M40. **Open** *Term time* 3-5pm Mon-Fri. *School hols* 10am-5pm Sat; 2-5pm Sun. Phone to confirm times. **Admission** £3.50; free under-3s. **Credit** MC, V.
An extension of the child-friendly County Museum, this gallery is divided into five main areas, decorated with colourful frescoes by Quentin Blake, which introduce different themes based on Roald Dahl's stories. Visitors encounter James and his mini-beast friends inside the Giant Peach, and examine the insect world with the aid of a video microscope. Then there's the Twits' Upside Down Room, a great glass elevator and a chance to discover Willy Wonka's inventions, and Matilda's Library, where you can discover more about Dahl's life and work. The Dahl Gallery only holds 85 people, so it's worth pre-booking in the school holidays. Picnic in the walled garden or snack in the café.
Buggy access. Café. Disabled access: lift, toilet. Nappy-changing facilities. Nearest picnic place: grounds. Shop.

Roald Dahl Museum & Story Centre

81-83 High Street, Great Missenden, Bucks HP16 0AL (01494 892 192/www.roalddahlmuseum.org). **Open** 10am-5pm Tue-Sun. **Admission** £4.95; £3.50 concessions, 5-16s; £16 (2+3); free under-5s. **Credit** AmEx, MC, V.
Opened in 2005, this museum has been designed to explore the craft of storytelling, as well as furnishing inquisitive young readers with all the information they could hope to have on the eponymous Dahl, his life, his methods and his much-loved canon. In the Story Centre, displays and interactive games reveal how contemporary children's authors work; the Centre's writer in residence (Val Rutt, author of *The Race for the Lost Keystone*, is the current incumbent) is also on hand to encourage children to think (and write) creatively. All kinds of workshops (there was a wonderful chocolatey one last Easter), changing Dahl-related exhibitions and storytelling sessions are offered.
Buggy access. Café. Disabled access: lift, ramps, toilet. Nappy-changing facilities. Nearest picnic place: courtyard. Shop.

Weald & Downland Open Air Museum

Singleton, Chichester, West Sussex PO18 0EU (01243 811 348/811 363/www.wealddown.co.uk). **Getting there** *By rail* Chichester rail, then 60 bus. *By car* A3, turn off at Milford, A286 to Midhurst & follow signs. **Open** *Apr-Oct* 10.30am-6pm daily (last entry 5pm). *Nov-21 Dec* 10.30am-4pm daily (last entry 3pm). *26 Dec-1 Jan* 10.30am-4pm Wed, Sat, Sun (last entry 3pm). *4 Jan-mid Feb* 10am-4pm Wed, Sat, Sun (last entry 3pm). *Mid Feb-Mar* 10.30am-4pm daily (last entry 3pm). **Admission** £7.95; £6.95 concessions; £4.25 5-15s; £21.95 family (2+3); free under-5s. **Credit** MC, V.
More than 45 original buildings have been preserved for posterity in this beautiful parkland setting in the South Downs. They've been refurbished to bring to life the homes, farms and workplaces of south-east England over the past 500 years. Visitors can see shire horses at work, visit a medieval farmstead or just picnic by the lake. Children can also find out what life was like for their contemporaries in the Victorian schoolroom. Events include children's Activity Wednesdays from 26 July to 30 August

Days Out (side margin)

PAINSHILL PARK

PORTSMOUTH ROAD, COBHAM
SURREY KT11 1JE

Painshill Park, one of the most important 18th century parks in Europe, hosts a series of Family Fun Days on Sundays, Holidays and School Holidays throughout the year plus a special Christmas Event in the real crystal grotto throughout December.

Painshill Partytime offers outdoor, active parties - a perfect choice for 5 - 11 year olds set in the stunning 18th century landscapes.

For more information please visit
www.painshill.co.uk
or telephone **01932 868113**

BEKONSCOT
MODEL VILLAGE & RAILWAY

**Warwick Road,
Beaconsfield,
Bucks HP9 2PL.
Tel: 01494 672919
www.bekonscot.com**

BE A GIANT IN A MINIATURE WONDERLAND
depicting rural England in the 1930's.
Gauge 1 model railway, moving models, play area, souvenirs, refreshments, children's parties.

OPEN: DAILY UNTIL 29th OCT

Sit-on railway open weekends and school holidays.
'A little piece of History that is forever England'
Family Ticket (2 plus 2) £17.50
Jnct.16 M.25 - Junct.2 M.40.
Rail: Marylebone/Bsfld./B'ham

2006, a gypsy festival and autumn harvest celebrations in September 2006, an ominous sounding Pig to Pork weekend in October, and all manner of rural festivities for a traditional Sussex Christmas in December.
Buggy access. Café. Car park (free). Disabled access: toilets. Nappy-changing facilities. Shop.

Steam trains

Bluebell Railway
Sheffield Park Station, on A275 between Lewes & East Grinstead, Sussex TN22 3QL (01825 723 777/talking timetable 01825 720 825/www.bluebell-railway.co.uk). **Getting there** *By rail* East Grinstead rail, then 473 bus. *By car* J10 off M23. **Open** *Easter-Sept* 11am-4pm daily. Phone for details of additional Sat, Sun, school & bank hol openings. **Admission** £9.50; £4.70 3-15s; £27 family (2+3); free under-3s. **Credit** MC, V.
Bluebell is the UK's first preserved standard-gauge passenger railway. It runs along the Lewes to East Grinstead line, with each station the line passes through restored according to a different era: Victorian, the 1930s and the 1950s. Work is progressing well on the track extension (the train only runs between Sheffield Park and Kingscote, but it will eventually reach East Grinstead). Childish delights include Easter specials, Thomas the Tank specials and Christmas specials, but we like the sound of the popular Fish and Chip specials and the Mother's Day Cream Tea special.
Buggy access. Café. Car park (free). Disabled access: toilet. Nappy-changing facilities. Nearest picnic place: grounds. Shop.

Didcot Railway Centre
Didcot, Oxon OX11 7NJ (01235 817 200/www.didcot railwaycentre.org.uk). **Getting there** *By rail* Didcot Parkway rail. *By car* J13 off M4. **Open** 10am-4pm Mon-Fri; 10am-5pm Sat, Sun (last entry 30mins before closing). Phone to confirm times. **Tours** bank hols (times depend on events; phone for details). **Admission** *Steam days* £6.50; £6 concessions; £5.50 3-16s; £22 family (2+2); free under-3s. *Non-steam days* £4; £3.50 concessions; £3 3-16s; £12 family; free under-3s. *Special event days* £9.50; £8 concessions; £7.50 3-16s; £29 family; free under-3s. **Credit** MC, V.
Regular steam days at Didcot's collection of antique carriages and engines involve steam-age activities like 'turning' locomotives and the chance to ride in an original 1930s carriage. You can have as many rides as you like during your visit. The new Science, Learning & Railways exhibition and learning centre is housed in two railway coaches. Its interactive exhibits are designed to interest and involve visitors in science and engineering.
Buggy access. Café. Car park. Nappy-changing facilities. Shop.

Kent & East Sussex Railway
Tenterden Town Station, Tenterden, Kent TN30 6HE (Tenterden, Northiam & Bodiam stations: 01580 765 155/www.kesr.org.uk). **Getting there** *By rail* Headcorn rail, then bus to Tenterden. *By car* J9 off M20. **Open** *Apr-July, Sept-Oct* 10am-4pm Sat, Sun. *Aug* 10am-4pm daily. *Nov-Mar* times vary; phone for details. **Admission** £10.50; £9.50 concessions; £5.50 3-15s; £27 family (2+3); free under-3s. **Credit** MC, V.
The antique carriages and engines servicing this railway line were scavenged and restored by enthusiasts, which

makes this the most pleasing method of getting from Bodiam (for the castle, *see p278*) to Tenterden.
Buggy access. Café (Tenterden & Northiam stations). Car park (not at Bodiam). Disabled access: carriage (book in advance), toilet. Nappy-changing facilities (Tenterden). Shop.

Romney, Hythe & Dymchurch Railway
New Romney Station, Kent TN28 8PL (01797 362 353/ www.rhdr.org.uk). **Getting there** *By rail* Folkestone Central rail, then 711 bus to Hythe. *By car* J11 off M20. **Open** phone or check website for timetable. **Admission** £10.90; £9.25 concessions; £5.45 3-15s; £31 family (2+2); free under-3s. **Credit** MC, V.
Racing driver Captain Howley built the 'world's smallest public railway' back in 1927. Nowadays, his locomotives, one-third of the scale of the real thing, puff along a similarly downsized track (it covers 22km or 13.5 miles) between the Cinque Port of Hythe and Dungeness, where the RHDR café can do you a fish and chip lunch (there's also a café and a model railway exhibition at New Romney).
Buggy access. Café. Car park (50p/day). Disabled access: carriages, toilet. Nappy-changing facilities. Shop.

Watercress Line
The Railway Station, Alresford, Hants SO24 9JG (01962 733 810/talking timetable 01962 734 866/ www.watercressline.co.uk). **Getting there** *By rail* Alton rail. *By car* A31 off A3 to Alton or A31 off M3 to Alresford. **Open** *May-Sept* Tue-Thur, Sat, Sun. *Oct, Dec, mid Jan-Feb* Sat, Sun. *Easter hols* daily. Phone or check website for timetable. **Admission** £10; £9 concessions; £5 3-16s; £25 family (2+2); free under-3s. Phone for special event prices. **Credit** MC, V.
Beginning in the market town of Alresford, this 16km (ten-mile) railway winds through Home Counties countryside. Londoners can hop on the train at Alton, which has a main-line station for Waterloo. Children love the summer Thomas specials, October's Wizard Week and Santa specials for December.
Buggy access (footbridge at Alton). Café (Alresford). Disabled access: carriages, toilet. Shop (Alresford).

Theme parks

Bekonscot Model Village
Warwick Road, Beaconsfield, Bucks HP9 2PL (01494 672 919/www.bekonscot.com). **Getting there** *By rail* Beaconsfield rail. *By car* J2 off M40. **Open** *Feb-29 Oct 2006* 10am-5pm daily. **Admission** £5.90; £4.20 concessions; £3.80 2-15s; £17.50 family (2+2); free under-2s. **Credit** MC, V.
This is a miniature world, stuck in an idyllic 1930s time warp. The six model villages, in their landscape of farms, fields, woodland, churches, castles and lakes, were created as a hobby by Roland Callingham in 1929. Bekonscot is now a charitable organisation. A busy gauge-one model railway stops at each village, and at Chessnade Zoo, where you can see a chimps' tea party, aviary and elephant rides. The fairground has working mini rides. There's also a playground and a ride-on railway (50p per person; runs at weekends, bank holidays and during local school holidays).
Buggy access. Café. Car park (free). Disabled access: toilets. Kiosk. Nappy-changing facilities. Nearest picnic place: grounds. Shop.

Sea views

Pro-biotic yoghurt drinks come and go, but when it comes to mental and physical well-being, the bracing British sea air never seems to go out of fashion – and it's not as far from the smog of central London as you might think.

Take **Whitstable**, for example (01227 275 482, www.visitwhitstable.co.uk): less than an hour and a half from London Victoria by train, yet more than a million miles aesthetically. Its cluttered harbour, sleepy town centre and shingle beach seem immune to the ravages of passing time. Grown-ups may fancy a local oyster or two at the famous Whitstable Oyster Fishery Company (Horsebridge, 01227 276 856). The coastal path from here, along the grassy **Tankerton** slopes, takes you the 6.5 kilometres (four miles) or so to **Herne Bay** (01227 361 911, www.canterbury.co.uk). Here, Victorian summer gardens, a playground and intriguing World War II defence turrets, currently rusting like abandoned robots 11 kilometres (seven miles) or so out to sea, all add to the singular English seaside atmosphere. Young TV addicts may be more amused by the promenade's regular appearance in the first series of *Little Britain*, but sit them through a screening of *The Dambusters* before heading out and they'll be blown away by a stroll to neighbouring **Reculver**, five kilometres (three miles) or so east of Herne Bay on the old Saxon Shore Way coastal trail. It was here that Barnes Wallace's famous bouncing bombs were first tested in the shadow of ruined St Mary's church, the twin towers of which are still used as a navigational waypoint by passing ships.

More military associations can be found in **Ramsgate**, where the white cliffs once overlooked the launch of 4,200 boats to rescue British soldiers from the beaches of Dunkirk. One of those ships, the *Sundowner* – then commandeered by one CH Lightroller, formerly a senior officer on the *Titanic* – remains moored in Ramsgate's Royal Harbour, and is open to the public.

The ultimate white cliffs experience is at **Dover** (01304 205108, www.whitecliffscountry.org.uk), the chalk walls of which are riddled with medieval tunnels that were expanded during the Napoleonic Wars, later serving as a nerve centre for the Allied campaign in World War II and finally as a defensive bunker during the Cold War-era nuclear panic. The tunnels are maintained by English Heritage and open to the public along with the castle above them. You can trace the Saxon Shore Way atop the cliffs to **St Margaret's Bay**, just over seven kilometres (four miles) away, or all the way to **Deal** (01304 369 576, www.deal.gov.uk), 16 kilometeres (10 miles) away. The coastal path has sweeping clear day views across to France.

Margate (0870 264 6111,www.tourism.thanet. gov.uk) has suffered from the closure of its landmark Dreamland amusement park. Pressure groups are pushing for Dreamland to be reopened but it's slated for redevelopment. Main Sands is a short hop over the tracks from the train station. There are more cultural diversions here, including the indecipherable, possibly ancient mosaics of the enigmatic Shell Grotto (01843 220 008, www.shellgrotto.co.uk).

Brighton (www.visitbrighton.com) is a town that more convincingly melds culture with carefree seaside frolics. Tacky Palace Pier (01273 609 361, www.brightonpier.co.uk), may be all arcades and funfair, but there are less jangling ways to amuse the family, such as the attractive wooden walkway, with its artists' quarter. The Sea Life Centre (01273 604 234, www.sealifeeurope.com), Volk's Railway, Britain's oldest electric railway, running along the promenade (01273 292 718, www.volkselectricrailway.co.uk), and the excellent shops and restaurants, are other draws.

Broadstairs (0870 264 6111, www.tourism. thanet.gov.uk), is home to a Charles Dickens festival every June. The author, who visited

Chessington World of Adventures

Leatherhead Road, Chessington, Surrey KT9 2NE (0870 444 7777/www.chessington.com). **Getting there** *By rail* Chessington South rail, then 71 bus or 10-min walk. *By car* J9 off M25. **Open** Mar-31 Oct 2006. Check website for timetables. **Admission** £29 (accompanying child free), £19.50 additional 4-11s; £14.50-£18 concessions; free under-3s or under 1m (3ft 3in) in height. Check website for advance bookings for fast-track entry. **Credit** AmEx, MC, V.

It's 75 years since Chessington Zoo first opened here in the wilds of Surrey, so Animal Land, as the fauna part of this theme park is now known, has been given a boost with the opening of some new animal adventures. Alongside the gorillas, tigers, sea lions and otters, there is now a walk-through squirrel monkey enclosures and a new Monkey and Bird Garden. Another innovation for 2006 is the introduction of foam into Bubbleworks, the loveable indoor bubble adventure. With most of the attractions now suitable

for the under-12s, Chessington is altogether a jollier option for young families. There's Beanoland with Dennis the Menace shenanigans (check the website for special events), and Land of the Dragons with a soft-play area and slippery slides. Older children can venture into the Forbidden Kingdom to brave the park's most scary ride, Rameses Revenge (height restriction 1.4m, 4ft 6in). A child gets in free with each paying adult, and express tickets promise allotted time slots on the top six rides.

Buggy access. Café. Car park (free). Disabled access: toilets. Nappy-changing facilities. Restaurant. Shops.

Legoland

Winkfield Road, Windsor, Berks SL4 4AY (0870 504 0404/www.legoland.co.uk). **Getting there** *By rail* Windsor & Eton Riverside or Windsor Central rail, then *shuttlebus. By car* J3 off M3 or J6 off M4. **Open** *Mid Mar-late Oct* Times may vary, check website for timetables. **Admission** *One-day ticket* £30; £23

Broadstairs regularly, is also the subject of a museum (2 Victoria Parade, 01843 861 232, www.dickenshouse.co.uk). His clifftop home, now a private residence called Bleak House, was in the news in 2006 when it was partially destroyed by fire.

For something a little closer to home, try **Southend** (01702 215 120, www.southend. gov.uk): bookish it ain't, but it lays claim to the world's largest rock factory as well its longest pier (2.2km, 1.3 miles) with a pleasure railway running from end to end). And with only an hour's train ride between its beaches and central London, this is one summer break that doesn't need to be planned weeks in advance.

concessions, 3-15s; free under-3s. *Two-day ticket* £57: £45 3-15s; free under-3s. *Shuttlebus* £3.50; £2 concessions, 3-15s; free under-3s. **Credit** AmEx, MC, V.
We love Legoland, with its witty brick-built surprises round every corner, its ability to engage all ages and its beautifully landscaped features. Yes, it's expensive, and yes, it attracts crowds and causes traffic jams. Do make an early start (queues for the entrance build up from about 9am) or go in the rain (uncomfortable, but queues are shorter). It is also wise to check the day before that a) the centre is open (we have known the park to close for random days in September for various reasons) and b) the attractions your children are most interested in are open.
Legoland celebrates its tenth season in 2006 with a bunch of new features. Most impressive, for us Londoners, is the hugely expanded London skyline in Miniland, where Canary Wharf, the Gherkin, City Hall and the Millennium Bridge now join the other London landmarks. Our other new favourite is the brilliant live-action show, starring some very plucky gymnasts and a lot of wet play in LEGO City

Harbour. The new JCB challenge has small children operating their own JCBs to scoop balls into bunkers. It's all great fun, especially the old stalwarts like the LEGO driving school and classic rides such as the Dragon Coaster and Pirate Falls. While you're being organised about planning your visit and arriving before gates open, pack a picnic too, because the food is an expensive let-down.
Buggy access. Cafés. Car park (free). Disabled access: toilet. Nappy-changing facilities. Nearest picnic place: grounds. Restaurants. Shops.

Thorpe Park

Staines Road, Chertsey, Surrey KT16 8PN (0870 444 4466/www.thorpepark.com). **Getting there** *By rail* Staines rail, then 950 shuttlebus. *By car* J11 or J13 off M25. **Open** times vary, check website for timetables. Height restrictions vary, depending on rides.
Admission £28.50; £20 concessions, 4-11s; £78-£98 family (2+2 or 2+3); free under-4s or under 1m (3ft 3in) in height. Check the website or phone for advance bookings; allow 24hrs to process advance ticket purchases. **Credit** MC, V.
Europe's fastest rollercoaster, Stealth, rising to a knee weakening 61m (205ft) and launching riders heavenward by achieving 0-80mph in under 2.3 seconds with a gut wrenching vertical lift and drop, has landed at Thorpe. Colossus – the world's first ten-looping rollercoaster – twists through the skies of the Lost City and Nemesis Inferno. After these come the Vortex, which whirls above the lake, Slammer, one of only two sky-swat rides in the world, and Rush, the world's biggest air-powered speed swing. Although Thorpe's more gruesome rides aren't suitable for little ones, there are tamer attractions for them, such as the swinging seashells and happy halibuts, and cuddly experiences await across the lake at Thorpe Farm's petting zoo. The Top Rockers Show is an all-family experience in the Sing Zone, where Sony Singstar lets visitors take part in the fun.
Buggy access. Café. Car park (free-£3). Disabled access: toilets. Nappy-changing facilities. Restaurants. Shops.

Wildlife parks

Drusillas Park

Alfriston, East Sussex BN26 5QS (01323 874 100/ www.drusillas.co.uk). **Getting there** *By rail* Polgate or Berwick rail, then taxi. *By car* M23, then A23, then A27. **Open** *Apr-Oct* 10am-6pm daily. *Nov-Mar* 10am-5pm daily. Last entry 1hr before closing. **Admission** *Off peak days* £10; £9 concessions, 2-12s; £18-£45 family; free under-2s. *Standard days* £11.50; £10.50 concessions, 2-12s; £21-£52.50 family; free under-2s. *Peak days* £12.25; £11.25 concessions, 2-12s; £22.50-£56.25 family; free under-2s. Prices vary depending on date, check website for details. **Credit** MC, V.
A great choice for little children, this zoo focuses on interactive involvement, conservation and fun fact-finding. Its naturalistic animal enclosures, innovative design and low-level viewing (most famously demonstrated in the meerkat mound) let you get nose to nose with nature. Animal residents include lemurs, prairie dogs, otters, marmosets, macaques, penguins and (less cuddly) crocodiles, snakes, bats and insects. There's also a petting farm. Kids are given free animal-spotter books for easy identification, and they can join in activities, such as panning for gold, crazy golf and workshops. There are a number of well-equipped playgrounds. A large paddling pool called Explorers' Lagoon attracts swimsuit-clad children in the summer. Check the

website for details of party packages, animal-adoption schemes and how to be a junior keeper for the day. *Buggy access. Café. Car park (free). Disabled access: toilet. Nappy-changing facilities. Nearest picnic place: grounds. Restaurant. Shops.*

Howletts Wild Animal Park

Bekesbourne, nr Canterbury, Kent CT4 5EL (01227 721 286/www.totallywild.net). **Getting there** *By rail* Bekesbourne rail, then 30-min walk or shuttle bus available in holidays (call or consult website for info); Canterbury East rail, then taxi. *By car* M2, then A2. **Open** *Summer* 10am-6pm daily (last entry 4.30pm). *Winter* 10am-dusk daily (last entry 3pm). **Admission** £13.95; £10.95 4-16s; £42 family (2+2); £49 family (2+3); free under-4s. **Credit** AmEx, MC, V.
The late John Aspinall, who founded this park, and its sister at Port Lympne (*see below*), had a policy of non-containment. There are no cages and the enclosures replicate specific environments as far as is humanly possible. The John Aspinall Foundation runs two gorilla rescue and rehabilitation projects in Africa, as well as caring for the largest breeding group of western lowland gorillas in the world at its wild animal parks. About 50 gorillas live here, as well as African elephants, Siberian tigers and many more. In the Wood in the Park, you can walk alongside and below a free-roaming family of lemurs. Many of the species of wolves, tapirs and antelopes here are endangered species, and this is one of the few zoos in the world to run a programme reintroducing such species into the wild. *Buggy access. Café. Car park (free). Disabled access: toilet. Nappy-changing facilities. Nearest picnic place: grounds. Restaurant. Shop.*

Port Lympne Wild Animal Park

Lympne, nr Hythe, Kent CT21 4PD (0870 7504 647/ www.totallywild.net). **Getting there** *By rail* Ashford rail, then link bus. *By car* J11 off M20. **Open** *Winter* 10am-dusk daily (last entry 3pm). *Summer* 10am-6pm daily (last entry 4.30pm). **Admission** £13.95 ;£10.95 4-16s; £42 family (2+2); £49 family (2+3); free under-4s. **Credit** AmEx, MC, V.
Even larger than sister site Howletts (*see above*), Port Lympne has room for the African Safari Experience, bounded by 3.2km (two miles) of reinforced steel, which now contains two rare black rhinos. The park covers 350 acres of wilderness, where animals coexist in the closest thing this country has to an uninterrupted nature reserve. Indeed, the easiest way to see everything is on a trailer tour, which takes you through communities of wildebeest, zebra and giraffe. Still, expeditions on foot (a round trip of the amphitheatre-shaped park covers roughly five kilometres or three miles) can be far more rewarding. Don't miss Palace of the Apes, the largest family gorilla house in the world. *Buggy access. Café. Car park (free). Disabled access: toilet. Nappy-changing facilities. Nearest picnic place: grounds. Restaurant. Shop.*

Whipsnade Wild Animal Park

Whipsnade, Dunstable, Beds LU6 2LF (01582 872 171/ www.whipsnade.co.uk). **Getting there** *By rail* Hemel Hempstead rail, then 43 bus from coach station. *By car* J21 off M25, then J9 off M1. **Open** *Early Mar-Sep* 10am-6pm daily. *Oct, mid Feb-early Mar* 10am-5pm daily. *Late Oct-early Mar* 10am-4pm daily. Last entry 1hr before closing. Times subject to change, so phone to check. **Tours** free bus around the park; phone for

times. **Admission** £15; £13 concessions; £11.50 3-15s; £48 family (2+2 or 1+3); free under-3s. Cars £12. **Credit** AmEx, MC, V.
The ZSL (Zoological Society of London), the charity that also operates London Zoo (*see p67*), runs this 600-acre site. There's a small herd of elephants, plus giraffes, bears, tigers, rhinos and hippos. Lions of the Serengeti, in the heart of Whipsnade's 'African' region, follows a village trail to the lion viewing shelter. A daily programme of activities keeps family groups busy, and there are frequent special events scheduled for school holidays. At other times, you can learn about long-tailed lemurs in the Acrobat in Action session, or there are birds of prey flying displays, sea lion capers in the Splashzone area, feeding time for the penguins, chimp chats and giraffe encounters. There's also a children's farm with marmosets, goats, alpacas and ponies. The new attraction for 2006 is the Jumbo Express, named after the biggest elephant ever in captivity, who grew up at London Zoo. *Buggy access. Café. Car park (£3.50). Disabled access: toilet. Nappy-changing facilities. Restaurant. Shop.*

Wildwood Wildlife Park

Herne Common, Herne Bay, Kent CT6 7LQ (01227 712 111/www.wildwoodtrust.org). **Getting there** *By rail* Herne Bay rail, then 4 bus. *By car* A2, A299 then A291. **Open** *May-Oct* 10am-6pm daily (last entry 4.30pm). *Nov-Apr* 10am-5pm or dusk daily (last entry 1hr before close). **Admission** *Easter-30 Oct* £8.50; £7.50 concessions; £7 3-15s; £28 family (2+2); free under-3s. *Nov-Easter* £7; £6.50 concessions; £6 3-15s; £24 family (2+2) free under-3s. **Credit** MC, V.
There are about 50 different species of animal and bird in Wildwood's Kentish woodland. The enclosures for wild cats, beavers, badgers, otters, red squirrels, owls, and even wolves and wild boar, are designed to blend into the countryside. During the summer hols children can get involved in workshops based round various Wildwood inhabitants, such as owls and wolves. October half-term's pyjama party has children turning up in their nightwear to learn about the animals settling down for hibernation. There's a restaurant for snacks and hot meals, and an adventure playground for monkeys of all ages and sizes. Check the website for a list of upcoming events; there are plenty. *Buggy access. Café. Car park (free). Disabled access: toilet. Nappy-changing facilities. Shop.*

Woburn Safari Park

Woburn Park, Beds MK17 9QN (01525 290 407/ www.woburnsafari.co.uk). **Getting there** *By car* J13 off M1. **Open** *Late Mar-29 Oct* 10am-6pm daily. *30 Oct-late Mar* 11am-4pm Sat, Sun (last entry 3pm). **Admission** £15-£16.50; £12.50-£14 concessions; £11.50-£13 3-15s; free under-3s. Prices vary during peak season; phone for details. **Credit** MC, V.
Car safaris in the Duke of Bedford's Woburn spread let you see the free-ranging elephants, giraffes, camels, black bears, monkeys, lions (with four new cubs for 2006), tigers and wolves, all from the safety of the family jalopy. You can also stretch your legs on a foot safari, taking in demonstrations of birds of prey and keeper talks on penguins, lemurs and sea lions. At Rainbow Landing (an indoor aviary) you can buy nectar to attract colourful lorikeets to land on your hand to drink (it opens four times a day). The sea lion pool is another must-see. Once you've said hello to the animals, there's fun for human young, with adventure playgrounds. *Buggy access. Café. Car park (free). Disabled access: toilet. Nappy-changing facilities. Restaurant. Shop.*

Directory

Directory

Getting around

Public transport

The prices listed for transport and services were correct at the time of going to press, but bear in mind that some prices (especially those of tube tickets) are subject to a hike each January.

Public transport information

Details can be found online at www.thetube.com and/or www.tfl.gov.uk, or on 7222 1234.

Transport for London (TfL) also runs Travel Information Centres that provide maps and information about the tube, buses, Tramlink, riverboats, Docklands Light Railway (DLR) and national rail services within the London area. You can find them in Heathrow Airport, as well as in Liverpool Street and Victoria stations.

London TravelWatch

6 Middle Street, EC1A 7JA (7505 9000/www.londontravel watch.org.uk). **Open** *Phone enquiries* 9am-5pm Mon-Fri. This is the official, campaigning watchdog monitoring customer satisfaction with transport in London.

Fares, Oyster cards & travelcards

Tube and DLR fares are based on a system of six zones stretching 20 kilometres (12 miles) out from the centre of London. A flat cash fare of £3 per journey applies across the tube for zones 1-4 (£4 for zones 1-5 or 1-6); customers save up to £1.50 with Oyster pay-as-you-go (*see below*). Beware of £20 on-the-spot penalty fares for anyone caught without a ticket.

Children aged under 11 travel free on buses, DLR and most tubes. If you are only using the tube, DLR, buses and trams, using Oyster to pay-as-you-go will always be cheaper than a Day Travelcard (*see below*). If you are using National Rail services, however, the Day Travelcard may best meet your needs (children travelling with you can buy a Day Travelcard for £1). Under-16s travel free on buses.

Travelcards, which can be used on tubes, buses, DLR and rail services, can be the cheapest way of getting around. Travelcards can be bought at stations, London Travel Information Centres or newsagents.

Day Travelcards

Day Travelcards (peak) can be used all day Mondays to Fridays (except public holidays). They cost from £6.20 (£3.10 for under-16s) for zones 1-2, with prices rising to £12.40 (£6.20 for under-16s) for zones 1-6. Most people use the off-peak Day Travelcard, which allows you to travel from 9.30am (Mon-Fri) and all day Saturday, Sunday and public holidays. They cost from £4.90 for zones 1-2, rising to £6.30 for zones 1-6.

Oyster card

The Oyster card is a travel smart-card that can be charged with Pre Pay and/or seven-day, monthly and longer-period (including annual) travelcards and bus passes. Oyster cards are currently available to adults and under-16 photocard holders when buying a ticket. Tickets can be bought from www.oystercard.com, by phone on 0870 849 9999 and at tube station ticket offices, London Travel Information Centres, some National Rail station ticket offices and newsagents. A single tube journey in zone 1 using Oyster to pay-as-you-go costs £1.50 at all times (children under 11 go free).

Children

Under-16s can travel free on buses and trams; under-11s travel free on the tube at off-peak hours and at weekends with an adult with a valid ticket. Children aged 14 or 15 need a child – or 11-15 – photocard to travel at child rate on the tube, DLR and trams. Children who board National Rail services travelling with adult-rate 7-day, monthly or longer travelcard holders can buy a day travelcard for £1. An under-16 Oyster photocard is required by children aged 11-15 years to pay as they go on the Underground or DLR or to buy 7-day, monthly or longer period travelcards.

Three-day travelcards

If you plan to spend a few days charging around town, you can buy 3-Day Travelcards. The peak version can be used for any journey that starts between the ticket start date and 4.30am on the day following the expiry date, and is available for £15.40 (zones 1-2) or £37.20 (zones 1-6). The off-peak travelcard, which can be used from 9.30am costs £18.90 (zones 1-6).

London Underground

The tube in rush hour (8-9.30am and 4.30-7pm Mon-Fri) is not pleasant, so it is best to travel outside these hours with your children if at all possible.

Using the system

Tube tickets can be purchased or Oyster cards topped up from a ticket office or self-service machines. Ticket offices in some stations close early (around 7.30pm), but it's best to keep an Oyster card charged with value. For buying Oyster cards, *see above*.

To enter and exit the tube using an Oyster card, touch it to the yellow reader that will open the gates. Make sure you touch the card when you exit the tube otherwise you may be fined.

There are 12 Underground lines, colour-coded on the tube map for ease of use; we've provided a full map of the London Underground on the back page of this book.

Underground timetable

Tube trains run daily from around 5.30am (except Sunday, when they start later). The only exception is Christmas Day, when there is no service. During peak times the service should run every two or three minutes. Times of last trains vary, but they're usually around 11.30pm-1am daily, and 30 minutes to an hour earlier on Sunday. Debates continue as to whether to run the tube an hour later at weekends. The only all-night public transport is by night bus (*see p291*).

Fares

The single fare for adults within zone 1 is £3 (Oyster fare £1.50). For zones 1-2 it's £3 (Oyster fare £2 or £1.50). The zones 1-6 single fare is £4 (Oyster fare £3.50 or £2). The single fare for 11-15s in zone 1 is £1.50 (Oyster fare 70p), £1.50 for zones 1-2 (Oyster fare £1 or 70p) or £2 for zones 1-6 (Oyster fare £1). Children under 11 travel free at off-peak times.

Docklands Light Railway (DLR)

The DLR (7363 9700, www.dlr.co.uk) runs trains from Bank (Central or Waterloo & City lines) or Tower Gateway, close to Tower Hill tube (Circle and District lines), to Stratford, Beckton and the Isle of Dogs as far as Island Gardens, then south of the river to Greenwich, Deptford and Lewisham. Trains run 5.30am to 12.30am Monday to Saturday and 7am to 11.30pm Sunday.

Fares

The single fare for adults within Zone 1 is £3 (Oyster fare £1.50). For Zones 1-2 it's £3 (Oyster fare £2 or £1.50. The zones 1-6 single fare is £4 (Oyster fare £3.50 or £2). Children under 11 travel free. Children aged 11-15 pay £1.50 (Oyster fare 70p) or £2 for zones 1-6 (Oyster fare £1). One-day 'Rail & River Rover' tickets combine unlimited DLR travel with hop-on, hop off boat travel on City Cruises between Greenwich, Tower, Waterloo and Westminster piers, starting at Tower Gateway. Tickets cost £10.50 for adults, £5.25 for kids and £26 for a family pass); under-5s go free.

Buses

New buses, with low-floors for wheelchair-users and passengers with buggies, have been added to the fleet. 'Bendy buses' with multiple-door entry and the 'pay before you board' schemes have also helped reduce boarding times. Buses in central London require you to have an Oyster card or buy a ticket before boarding. Do so: there are inspectors about. Where you do not already have a ticket, you can buy one (or a bus pass) from pavement ticket machines.

Fares

Using an Oyster card (*see p290*) to pay as you go costs £1 or 80p depending on the time you travel; the most you will pay a day is £3. Paying by cash at the time of travel costs £1.50 for a single trip. A one-day bus pass gives unlimited bus and tram travel at £3.50. Children under 16 travel free on buses.

Night buses

Many night buses run 24 hours a day, seven days a week, and some special night buses with an 'N' prefix to the route number operate from about 11pm to 6am. Most services run every 15 to 30 minutes, but many busier routes have a bus around every ten minutes. Travelcards and Bus Passes can be used on night buses until 4.30am on the day after they expire. Oyster Pre Pay and bus Saver tickets are also valid on night buses.

Green Line buses

Green Line buses (0870 608 7261, www.greenline.co.uk) serve the suburbs and towns within a 40-mile radius of London. Their main departure point is Ecclestone Bridge, SW1 (Colonnades Coach Station, behind Victoria), and they run a 24-hour service.

Coaches

National Express (0870 580 8080) runs routes to most parts of the country; coaches depart from **Victoria Coach Station**, a five-minute walk from Victoria rail and tube stations.

Victoria Coach Station

164 Buckingham Palace Road, SW1W 9TP (7730 3466/ www.tfl.gov.uk/vcs). Victoria tube/rail. **Map** p316 H1. National Express, which travels to the Continent as Eurolines, is based at Victoria Coach Station.

Rail services

Independently run services leave from the main rail stations. Travelcards are valid on services within the right zones. The useful Silverlink line (0845 601 4867, www.silverlink-trains.com) goes through north London from Richmond to North Woolwich, via Kew, Kensal Rise, Gospel Oak, Islington, Stratford and City Airport.

If you've lost property on an overground station or a train, call 0870 000 5151; an operator will connect you to the appropriate station.

Family Railcard

This costs £20 and lasts one year. Valid across Britain, it gives travellers with children one year of discounts from standard rail fares (a third off adult fares, 60 per cent off child fares, £1 minimum fare). Under-fives travel free. Up to two adults can be named as cardholders – and they do not have to be related. The minimum group size is one cardholder and one child aged five to 15; maximum group size is two cardholders, two other adults and four children. To pick up a form for the Family Railcard, visit your local staffed station.

London's mainline stations

Charing Cross *Strand, WC2N 5LR.* **Map** p317 L7. For trains to and from south-east England (including Dover, Folkestone and Ramsgate).
Euston *Euston Road, NW1 2RS.* **Map** p315 K3. For trains to and from north and north-west England and Scotland, and a suburban line north to Watford.
King's Cross *Euston Road, N1 9AP.* **Map** p315 L2. For trains to and from north and north-east England and Scotland, and suburban lines to north London.
Liverpool Street *Liverpool Street, EC2M 7PD.* **Map** p319 R5. For trains to and from the east coast, Stansted airport and East Anglia, and services to east and north-east London.
London Bridge *London Bridge Street, SE1 9SP.* **Map** p319 Q8. For trains to Kent, Sussex, Surrey and south London suburbs.
Paddington *Praed Street, W2 1HB.* **Map** p311 D5. For trains to and from west and south-west England, South Wales and the Midlands.
Victoria *Terminus Place, SW1V 1JU.* **Map** p316 H10. For fast trains to and from the channel ports (Folkestone, Dover, Newhaven); for trains to and from Gatwick Airport, and suburban services to south and south-east London.
Waterloo *York Road, SE1 7ND.* **Map** p319 M9. For fast trains to and from the south and south-west of England (Portsmouth, Southampton, Dorset, Devon), and suburban services to south London.

Tramlink

Trams run between Beckenham, Croydon, Addington and Wimbledon in south London. Travelcards and bus passes taking in zones 3-6 can be used on trams; otherwise, cash single fares cost from £1.50 (Oyster fare £1 or 80p; 50p for 16-to 17-year-old photocard holders). A one-day bus pass gives unlimited tram and bus travel at £3.50 for adults.

Water transport

The times of London's assortment of river services vary, but most operate every 20 minutes to one hour between 10.30am and 5pm. Services may be more frequent and run later in summer. Call the operators listed below for schedules and fares, or see www.tfl.gov.uk. Travelcard holders can expect one-third off scheduled riverboat fares. Thames Clippers (0870 781 5049, www.thamesclippers.com) runs a fast, reliable commuter boat service. Piers to board the Clippers from are: Savoy (near Embankment tube), Blackfriars, Bankside (for the Globe), London Bridge and St Katharine's (Tower Bridge).

The names in bold below are the names of piers.
Embankment–Tower (40mins)–**Greenwich** (30mins); Catamaran Cruises 7987 1185, www.bateauxlondon.com.
Greenland Dock–Canary Wharf (8mins)–**St Katharine's** (7mins)–**London Bridge City** (4mins)–**Bankside** (3mins)–**Blackfriars** (3mins)–**Savoy** (4mins); Collins River Enterprises 7977 6892, www.thamesclippers.com.
Westminster–Festival (5mins)–**London Bridge City** (20mins)–St Katharine's (5mins); Crown River 7936 2033, www.crownriver.com.
Westminster–Greenwich (1hr); Thames River Services 7930 4097, www.westminsterpier.co.uk.
Westminster–Kew (1hr 30mins)–**Richmond** (30mins)–**Hampton Court** (1hr 30mins); Westminster Passenger Service Association 7930 2062, www.wpsa.co.uk.
Westminster–Tower (30mins); City Cruises 7740 0400, www.citycruises.com.

Taxis

Black cabs

Licensed London taxis are known as black cabs – even though they now come in a variety of colours – and are a quintessential feature of London life. Drivers of black cabs must pass a test called the Knowledge to prove they know every street in central London and the shortest route to it.

If a taxi's yellow 'For Hire' sign is switched on, it can be hailed. If a taxi stops, the cabbie must take you to your destination, provided it's within seven miles. Expect to pay slightly higher rates after 8pm on weekdays and all weekend.

You can book black cabs in advance. Both Radio Taxis (7272 0272, credit cards only) and Dial-a-Cab (7253 5000) run 24-hour services for black

cabs (there'll be a booking fee in addition to the regular fare). Enquiries or complaints about black cabs should be made to the Public Carriage Office. (0870 602 7000, www.gov.uk/pco).

Minicabs

Be sure to use only licensed firms and avoid minicab drivers who tout for business on the street, as they'll be unlicensed and uninsured.

There are, happily, plenty of trustworthy and licensed local minicab firms around, including Lady Cabs (7272 3300, www.ladyminicabs.co.uk), which employs only women drivers, and Addison Lee (7387 8888, www.addisonlee.com). Whoever you use, always ask the price when you book and confirm it with the driver when the car arrives.

Driving

Congestion charge

Everyone driving in central London – an area defined as within King's Cross (N), Old Street roundabout (NE), Aldgate (E), Old Kent Road (SE), Elephant & Castle (S), Vauxhall (SW), Hyde Park Corner (W) and Edgware Road tube (NW) – between 7am and 6.30pm Monday to Friday, has to pay an £8 fee. Expect a fine of £50 if you fail to do so (rising to £150 if you delay payment). Passes can be bought from newsagents, garages and NCP car parks; the scheme is enforced by CCTV cameras. You can pay any time during the day of entry, even afterwards, but it's an extra £2 after 10pm. After September 2006 however, payments will be accepted until midnight on the next charging day after a vehicle has entered the zone. For more information, phone 0845 900 1234 or go to www.cclondon.com. The current Congestion Charge zone is marked on the Central London by Area map on p308. Plans to extend the zone westward to Kensington and Chelsea will come into play on 19 February 2007; check the website for more details.

Parking

Central London is scattered with parking meters, but finding a vacant one can take ages and, when you do, it'll cost you up to £1 for every 15 minutes to park there, and you'll be limited to two hours on the meter. Parking on a single or double yellow line, a red line or in residents' parking areas during the day is illegal. In the evening (from 6pm or 7pm in much of central London) and at various times at weekends, parking on single yellow lines is legal and free. If you find a clear spot on a single yellow line during the evening, look for a sign giving the regulations. Meters are also free at certain times during evenings and weekends.

NCP 24-hour car parks (0870 606 7050, www. ncp.co.uk) in and around central London are numerous but expensive. Fees vary, but expect to pay £10-£55 per day. Among the NCP's central car parks are those at Arlington House, Arlington Street, St James's, W1; Upper St Martins Lane, WC2; and 2 Lexington Street, Soho, W1. Most NCPs in central London are underground, and a few are frequented by drug-users. Take care.

Driving out of town

Check out your route for possible roadworks and delays, and, where psossible, avoid the morning and evening rush hours. Try the route-planner service available from the Royal Automobile Association (RAC, www.rac.co.uk).

Cycling

The London Cycle Network (7974 8747, www. londoncyclenetwork.org) and London Cycling Campaign (7234 9310, www.lcc.org.uk) help make London better to pedal in. Free London Cycle Guide maps are available from some tube stations and bike shops, or the Travel Information Line (7222 1234). Children must wear head protection and stick to cycle paths.

Cycle hire

London Bicycle Tour Company
1A Gabriel's Wharf, 56 Upper Ground, South Bank, SE1 9PP (7928 6838/www.londonbicycle.com). Blackfriars, Southwark or Waterloo tube/rail. **Open** 10am-6pm daily. Hire £3/hr; £16/1st day, £8/day thereafter. **Deposit** £1 (or credit card). **Credit** AmEx, DC, MC, V.
Bike, tandem and rickshaw hire, and guided bicycle tours.

Walking

The least stressful way to see London is on foot; it's also the safest way to travel with your head stuck in a map. A selection of street maps covering central London in the back of this book is on pp308-319, but we recommend that you also buy a separate map of the city: both the standard Geographers' *A–Z* and Collins's *London Street Atlas* versions are very easy to use.

A new map, designed by and for children is also on sale. The Guy Fox London Children's Map was launched to put the power of planning fun excursions straight into the hands of young people. The comprehensive map is packed with colourful illustrations of city icons and landmarks; buy it at www.guyfox.co.uk at £2.95 or bookshops and selected tourist attractions.

Resources

Councils

Barnet *8359 2000, www.barnet.gov.uk.*
Brent *8937 1234, www.brent.gov.uk.*
Camden *7278 4444, www.camden.gov.uk*
Corporation of London *7606 3030, www.cityoflondon.gov.uk.*
Ealing *8825 5000, www.ealing.gov.uk.*
Greenwich *8854 8888, www.greenwich.gov.uk.*
Hackney *8356 5000, www.hackney.gov.uk.*
Hammersmith & Fulham *8748 3020, www.lbhf.gov.uk.*
Haringey *8489 0000, www.haringey.gov.uk.*
Hounslow *8583 2000, www.hounslow.gov.uk.*
Islington *7527 2000, www.islington.gov.uk.*
Kensington & Chelsea *7361 3000, www.rbkc.gov.uk.*
Lambeth *7926 1000, www.lambeth.gov.uk.*
Lewisham *8314 6000, www.lewisham.gov.uk.*
Merton *8274 4901, www.merton.gov.uk.*
Newham *8430 2000, www.newham.gov.uk.*
Richmond-upon-Thames *8891 1411, www.richmond.gov.uk.*
Southwark *7525 5000, www.southwark.gov.uk.*
Tower Hamlets *7364 5020, www.towerhamlets.gov.uk.*
Waltham Forest *8496 3000, www.walthamforest.gov.uk.*
Wandsworth *8871 6000, www.wandsworth.gov.uk.*
Westminster *7641 6000, www.westminster.gov.uk.*

Education

Advisory Centre on Education (ACE) *0808 800 5793/exclusion advice line 0808 800 0327/www.ace-ed.org.uk.* **Open** 2-5pm Mon-Fri.
Ring the centre for advice about your child's schooling; the advice line is for parents whose children have been excluded from school, or have been bullied, or have special educational needs. School admission appeals advice is also available.
British Association for Early Childhood Education *136 Cavell Street, E1 2JA (7539 5400/www.early-education.org.uk).* **Open** *By phone* 9am-5pm Mon-Fri.
A charitable organisation that provides information on infant education from birth to eight years. Send an SAE for additional publications.
Gabbitas Educational Consultants *Carrington House, 126-130 Regent Street, W1B 5EE (7734 0161/ www.gabbitas.co.uk).* **Open** 9am-5pm Mon-Fri.
The consultants at Gabbitas give advice on choosing an independent school.
Home Education Advisory Service *PO Box 98, Welwyn Garden City, Herts AL8 6AN (01707 371 854/ www.heas.org.uk).* **Open** *By phone* 9am-5pm Mon-Fri.
Call for information if you want to educate your child at home. An introductory pack costs £2.50, a year's subscription £13.50.
ISC Information Service London & South-east *7798 1560/www.iscis.uk.net.* **Open** By phone 9am-5pm Mon-Fri.
The Independent Schools Council Information Service works to help parents find out about independent schools.
Kid Smart *www.kidsmart.org.uk*
Kidsmart is an internet-safety-awareness programme run by Childnet International and is funded by the DFES and Cable & Wireless. Its guide is available to all primary schools.
National Association for Gifted Children *Suite 14, Challenge House, Sherwood Drive, Bletchley, Milton Keynes, Bucks MK3 6DP (0870 770 3217/www.nagcbritain.org.uk).* **Open** *By phone* 9.15am-4pm Mon, Wed-Fri.
Support and advice on education for parents of the gifted.
Parenting UK *Unit 431, Highgate Studios, 53-79 Highgate Road, NW5 1TL (7284 8389/www.parenting-forum.org.uk).* **Open** *By phone* 10am-5pm Mon-Fri.
Information about parenting classes and support for parents.
Pre-School Learning Alliance Units 213-216, 30 Great Guildford Street, SE1 0HS (7620 0550/www.pre-school.org.uk). **Open** *By phone* 9am-5pm Mon-Fri.
The PSLA is a leading educational charity specialising in the early years. It runs courses and workshops in pre-schools around the country for parents of children under the age of five.

Directory

Fun & games

Activity camps

Barracudas *Young World Leisure Group Ltd, Bridge House, Bridge Street, St Ives, Cambs PE27 5EH (0845 123 5299/www.barracudas.co.uk).*
School holiday camps based in country schools in outlying countryside. Children aged 5-16 welcome.
Cross Keys *48 Fitzalan Road, Finchley, London N3 3PE (8371 9686/www.xkeys.co.uk/www.miniminors.co.uk).*
Day camps in Finchley for kids aged 12 or under and rural week-long camps in Norfolk, for children aged up to 17.
eac Activity Camps *Ltd 45 Frederick Street, Edinburgh, EH2 1EP (0131 477 7574/www.eacworld.com).*
Day and residential camps for children aged five to 16 in countryside sites across the land.
PGL Travel Ltd *Alton Court, Penyard Lane, Ross-on-Wye HR9 5GL (0870 050 7507/www.pgl.co.uk).*
Sport and activity camps for children aged up to 16 in the United Kingdom and Europe.
Wickedly Wonderful *Russett Cottage, Itchenor, PO20 7DD (0794 123 1168/www.wickedlywonderful.com).*
A holiday company that runs weekly buses from London down to the beach in the summer holidays.

Indoor play

Crêchendo *www.crechendo.com.*
Active play classes for babies and pre-school children.
Gymboree Play & Music *0800 092 0911/ www.gymboreePlayUK.com.*
A parent-and-child play organisation for children aged 16 months to four and a half years.
National Association of Toy & Leisure Libraries (NATLL) *68 Churchway, NW1 1LT (7255 4600/helpline 7255 4616/www.natll.org.uk).* **Open** *Helpline 9am-5pm Mon-Fri.*
For information on more than 1,000 toy libraries.
Toys Re-united *www.toys-reunited.co.uk.*
Check the website to see if a missing plaything might have been found.
TumbleTots *0121 585 7003/www.tumbletots.com.* **Open** *By phone 9am-5.30pm Mon-Fri.*
Phone to find out about TumbleTot play centres in your area.

Health

Asthma UK *Helpline 0845 701 0203/www.asthma.org.uk.* **Open** *9am-5pm Mon-Fri.*
Advice and help if you or your child has asthma.
Contact-A-Family *7608 8700/helpline 0808 808 3555/ www.cafamily.org.uk.* **Open** *Helpline 10am-4pm, 5.30-7.30pm Mon; 10am-4pm Tue-Fri.*
Support for parents of children with disabilities.
NHS Direct *Helpline 0845 4647/www.nhsdirect.nhs.uk.* **Open** *24hrs daily.*
Confidential information and health advice.

Help & support

Bestbear *0870 720 1277/www.bestbear.co.uk.* **Open** *9am-6pm Mon-Fri; 24hr answerphone other times.*
Information about childcare agencies.
Childcare Link *0800 096 0296/www.childcarelink.gov.uk.* **Open** *By phone 8am-8pm Mon-Fri; 9am-noon Sat.*
Provides a list of childcare organisations in their area.
ChildLine *0800 1111/www.childline.org.uk.*
Confidental 24-hour helpline for young people in the UK.
Daycare Trust *21 St George's Road, SE1 6ES (7840 3350/ www.daycaretrust.org.uk).* **Open** *9.30am-5.30pm Mon-Fri.*
A national charity that works to promote high-quality, affordable childcare.
4Children *7512 2112/info line 7512 2100/www.4children.org.uk.* **Open** *By phone 9am-5pm Mon-Fri.*
Information on after-school clubs, children's and family services.

Nannytax *PO Box 988, Brighton, East Sussex BN1 3NT (0845 226 2203/www.nannytax.co.uk).* **Open** *By phone 9am-5pm Mon-Fri.*
For £260 a year, Nannytax registers your nanny with the Inland Revenue, organises National Insurance payments and offers advice.
National Family & Parenting Institute *430 Highgate Studios, 53-79 Highgate Road, NW5 1TL (7424 3460/ www.nfpi.org). Kentish Town tube/rail.* **Open** *By phone 9.30am-5.30pm Mon-Fri; 24hr answerphone other times.*
A resource centre that produces fact sheets covering all aspects of parenting.
Night Nannies *7731 6168/www.nightnannies.com.*
Night Nannies provides a list of qualified carers who may be able to provide respite from sleepless nights.
The Parent Company *6 Jacob's Well Mews, W1U 3DY (7935 9635/www.theparentcompany.co.uk).* **Open** *booking line 9am-2.30pm Mon-Fri.*
Runs seminars on diverse subjects, from time-management to discipline issues, costing from £45 per session per person.
Parent Courses *Holy Trinity Brompton, Brompton Road, SW7 1JA (7581 8255/www.htb.org.uk). South Kensington tube.* **Open** *9.30am-5.30pm Mon, Wed-Fri; 10.30am-5.30pm Tue.*
Runs the Parenting Course for parents with children under the age of 12 and Parenting Teenagers, for parents of children aged 13-18. Each course costs £30.
Parentline Plus *Helpline 0808 800 2222/www.parentline plus.org.uk.* **Open** *24hrs.*
Organises nationwide courses on how to cope with being a parent. For more details, phone the free helpline.
Parents for Inclusion *Helpline 0800 652 3145/www.parents forinclusion.org.* **Open** *10am-noon, 1-3pm Mon, Tue, Thur.*
Organises a series of workshops for parents of disabled children.
Parent Support Group *72 Blackheath Road, SE10 8DA (helpline 8469 0205/www.psg.org.uk).* **Open** *Helpline 10am-7pm Mon-Fri; 24hr answerphone other times.*
As well as the helpline, staff run one-to-one support sessions and offer courses on parenting skills to the parents and carers of adolescents who are acting in an antisocial or criminal manner.
Simply Childcare *16 Bushey Hill Road, SE5 8QJ (7701 6111/www.simplychildcare.com).* **Open** *By phone 9am-5.30pm Mon-Fri.*
If you are seeking a nanny, you can pay £30 to advertise the job in three issues of this listings magazine, or £40 for five issues. No fee for prospective nannies.
Sitters *0800 389 0038/www.sitters.co.uk.* **Open** *By phone 8am-7pm Mon-Fri; 9am-1pm Sat.*
A babysitting agency with locally based nurses, teachers and nannies on its books.

Tourist information

Visit London (7234 5800, www.visitlondon.com) is the city's official tourist information company. There are also tourist offices in Greenwich, Leicester Square and next to St Paul's Cathedral.

Britain & London Visitor Centre
1 Lower Regent Street, Piccadilly Circus, SW1Y 4XT (8846 9000/www.visitbritain.com). Piccadilly Circus tube. **Open** *Oct-May 9.30am-6.30pm Mon; 9am-6.30pm Tue-Fri; 10am-4pm Sat, Sun. June-Sept 9.30am-6.30pm Mon; 9am-6.30pm Tue-Fri; 9am-5pm Sat; 10am-4pm Sun.*

London Information Centre
Leicester Square, WC2H 7BP (7292 2333/www.london town.com). Leicester Square tube. **Open** *By phone 8am-midnight Mon-Fri; 9am-10pm Sat, Sun. In person 8am-11pm Mon-Fri; 10am-6pm Sat, Sun.*

London Visitor Centre
Arrivals Hall, Waterloo International Terminal, SE1 7LT. **Open** *8.30am-10.30pm Mon-Sat; 9.30am-10.30pm Sun.*

Further reference

Books

Joan Aitken *Black Hearts in Battersea*
Simon comes to London to learn painting with his old friend
Dr Field only for to find the doctor has dissapeared under
mysterious circumstances.
Bernard Ashley *Little Soldier*
The 1999 Carnegie Medal-winning story of Kaminda, a refugee
from an African war brought by aid workers to England, where
he finds a different kind of warfare on London's streets.
JM Barrie *Peter Pan* (play), *Peter & Wendy* (novel)
Three children in Edwardian Kensington Gardens meet
the boy who never grew up.
Ludwig Bemelmans *Madeline in London*
A classic picture book with beautiful illustrations.
Michael Bond *A Bear Called Paddington*
From darkest Peru to 32 Windsor Gardens, the bear
wears it well in this and subsequent adventures in London
and abroad.
Charles Dickens *Oliver Twist; David Copperfield;*
A Christmas Carol
These three of the master's London-based novels are the best
suited to children, but there are plenty more.
Berlie Doherty *Street Child*
A modern classic based on the true story of an orphan who
prompted Dr Barnardo to begin his life's work of providing
care for homeless children.
Travis Elborough *The Bus We Loved*
A celebration of the late lamented Routemaster bus.
Michelle Magorian *A Spoonful of Jam*
A dramatic tale for teenagers set in 1947. A poor London
girl goes to a posh grammar school.
Beverley Naidoo *The Other Side of Truth*
The 2001 Carnegie Medal winner, this is the story of two
children smuggled to London after the death of their mother.
E Nesbit *The Story of the Amulet*
Robert, Anthea, Cyril and Jane are reunited with the Psammead
in a London pet store, and he tells them of the amulet.
Philip Pullman *The Sally Lockhart Trilogy*
A classic adventure set in the Victorian London underworld.
Gregory Rogers *The Boy, the Bear, the Baron, the Bard*
A pictures-only story set in Shakespeare's London with an
intrepid little boy, a captive bear and the Bard himself.
Anna Sewell *Black Beauty*
The passages that exposed the cruelties done to cab horses are
set in London. Indeed poor Ginger, Black Beauty's friend, meets
her end in harness in the mean streets of the capital.
Jonathan Stroud *The Amulet of Samarkand*
Nathaniel, a magician's apprentice, summons up the *djinni*
Bartimaeus in modern-day London.
GP Taylor *Wormwood*
A Gothic tale of sorcery and treachery in 18th-century London.
Jean Ure *Plague*
Three teenagers survive a plague that has killed their parents
and left London as a ghost town.

Films

101 Dalmatians (U; 1961)
Disney's masterpiece included that most fabulous of all screen
baddies, Cruella de Vil, animated by Marc Davis. It's based on
the Dodie Smith story, about two spotted dogs that have an
embarrassment of puppies out Regent's Park way.
A Fish Called Wanda (15) dir Charles Crichton (1988)
This madcap smash hit about a London-based plot to commit
armed robbery stars John Cleese and Jamie Lee Curtis.
Agent Cody Banks 2 – Destination London (PG)
Dir Kevin Allen (2004)
Parents will loathe having to sit through this lame film about a
teenage CIA agent on a mission in London, but there are some
great London scenes, and ex-S-clubber Hannah Spearitt as Emily
gives it child appeal.
Bedknobs and Broomsticks (U) dir Robert Stevenson (1971)
An apprentice witch, three kids and a conman search for the
component to a spell. Look out for a youngish Bruce Forsyth
as a surprisingly good gangster.

Finding Neverland (PG) dir Marc Forster 2004
Johnny Depp stars in a tale of magic and fantasy inspired
by the life of *Peter Pan* author James Barrie.
Harry Potter and the Sorcerer's Stone dir Chris Columbus
(2001); **Harry Potter and the Chamber of Secrets** dir Chris
Columbus (2002); **Harry Potter and the Prisoner of
Azkaban** dir Alfonso Cuarón (2004) all PG
The boy wizard passes through Kings Cross Station, Borough
Market and other London landmarks on his way to Hogwarts.
Mary Poppins (U) dir Robert Stevenson (1964)
The supercalifragilisticexpialidocious magic nanny brings
joy to an unhappy London family.
My Fair Lady (U) dir George Cukor (1964)
Audrey Hepburn is a luminous Eliza Doolittle in this
blockbuster adaptation of George Bernard Shaw's Pygmalion.
Notting Hill (PG) dir Roger Michell (1999)
A starry romance blossoms in west London.
Oliver! (U) dir Carol Reed (1968)
A musical adaptation of the story by Charles Dickens.
One of Our Dinosaurs is Missing (U) dir Robert
Stevenson (1975)
Toffs, Chinese spies and feisty nannies run off with a large
exhibit from the Natural History Museum.
Peter Pan (PG) dir PJ Hogan (2003)
An enjoyable family film, creating an impressive fairy-tale world
representing Barrie's 'original vision'.
Passport to Pimlico (U) dir Henry Cornelius (1949)
Residents of a part of London declare independence when they
discover an old treaty.
Scrooge (U) dir Brian Desmond Hurst (1951)
The atmospheric screen version of Charles Dickens's story
stars Alastair Sim as the mean London miser.
Shaun of the Dead (15) dir Edgar Wright (2004)
This romantic comedy with zombies set in north London is one
for teens only – gruesome comic violence is the reason.
Wimbledon (12A) dir Richard Loncraine (2004)
Paul Bettany and Kirsten Dunst play a love match on grass.

Websites

BBC London *www.bbc.co.uk/london.*
Blue Plaque Project *www.blueplaqueproject.org.*
Locator site for places associated with historical figures –
marked with a blue plaque.
Children First *www.childrenfirst.nhs.uk.*
Run by Great Ormond Street Hospital and children's charity
WellChild, this website has age-appropriate information on
all aspects of healthy living, with special sections about going
into hospital
Classic cafés *www.classiccafes.co.uk.*
London's 1950s and 1960s caffs.
Department for Education and Skills
www.parentscentre.gov.uk.
The DfES website gives parents advice on schools and
other aspects of children's education.
London Active Map *www.uktravel.com.*
Click on a tube station and find out which attractions are nearby.
London Parks & Gardens Trust *www.ParkExplorer.org.uk.*
A website aimed at Key Stage 2 children and their teachers,
designed to help them learn more about the parks, gardens and
open spaces of London.
London Town *www.londontown.com.*
The official tourist-board website is full of information and offers.
London Underground Online *www.thetube.com.*
Meteorological Office *www.met-office.gov.uk.*
The most accurate source of weather forecasts.
Place names *www.krysstal.com/londname.html.*
The River Thames Guide *www.riverthames.co.uk.*
Street Map *www.streetmap.co.uk.*
Time Out *www.timeout.com.*
An essential source, of course, with online city guides and the
best eating and drinking reviews.
Transport for London *www.tfl.gov.uk.*
The official website for travel information about buses, DLR
and river services.
Yellow Pages Online *www.yell.com.*
The best online resource for numbers and addresses.

Advertisers' Index

Please refer to relevant sections for addresses/telephone numbers

Advertisers' Index

Index

Index

Index

Index

Index

Index

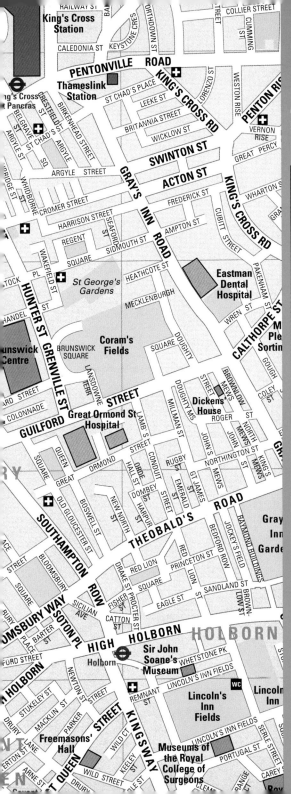

Maps

Place of interest and/or entertainment . . .
Hospital or college . . . .
Railway station . . . .
Park . . . .
River . . . .
Motorway . . . .
Main road . . . .
Main road tunnel . . . .
Pedestrian road . . . .
Airport . . . . ✈
Church . . . . ✚
Synagogue . . . . ✡
Congestion charge zone . . . . Ⓒ
Underground station . . . . ⊖
Area name . . . . SOHO

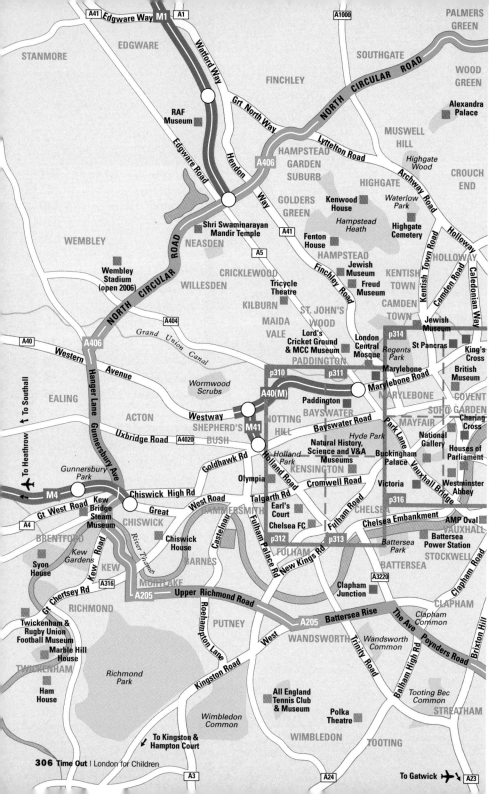

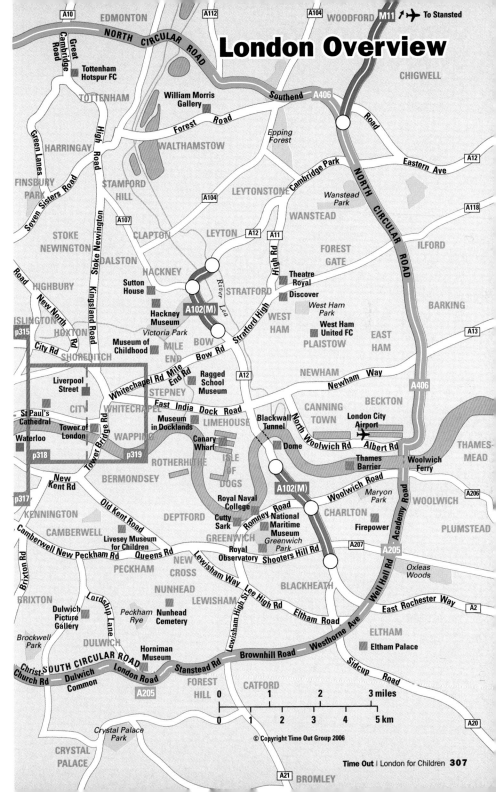

London Overview

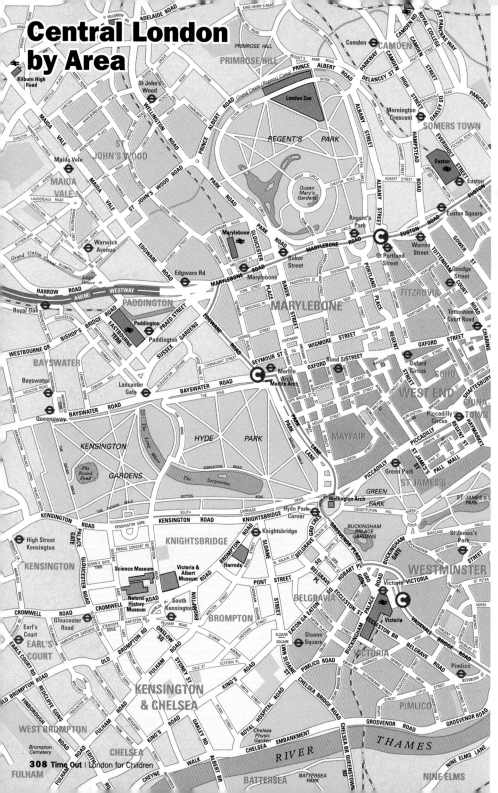

Central London
by Area

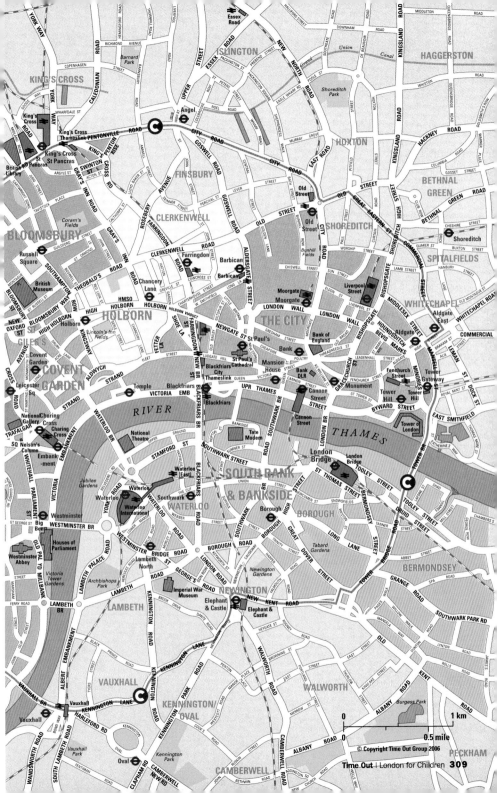

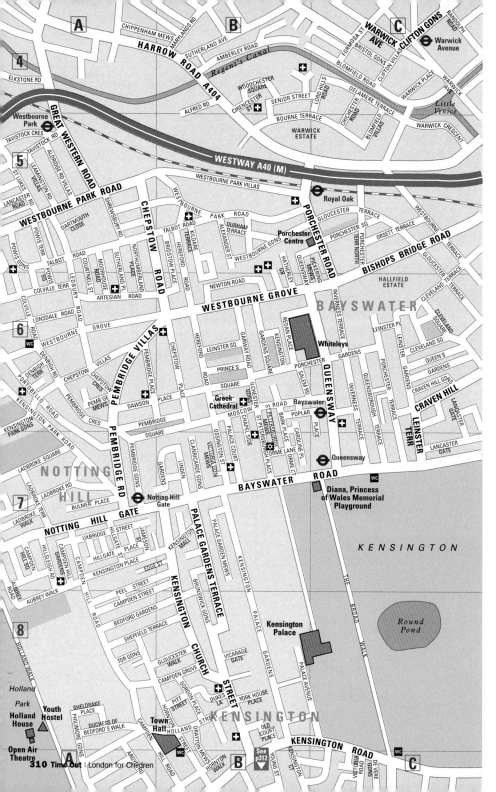

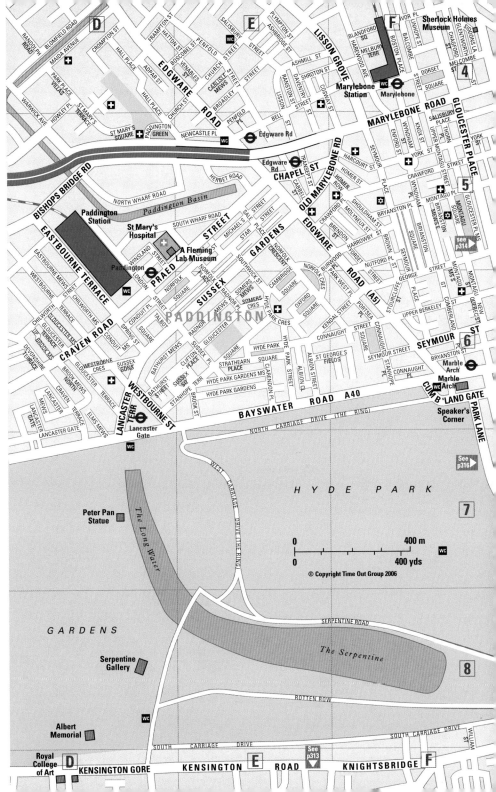

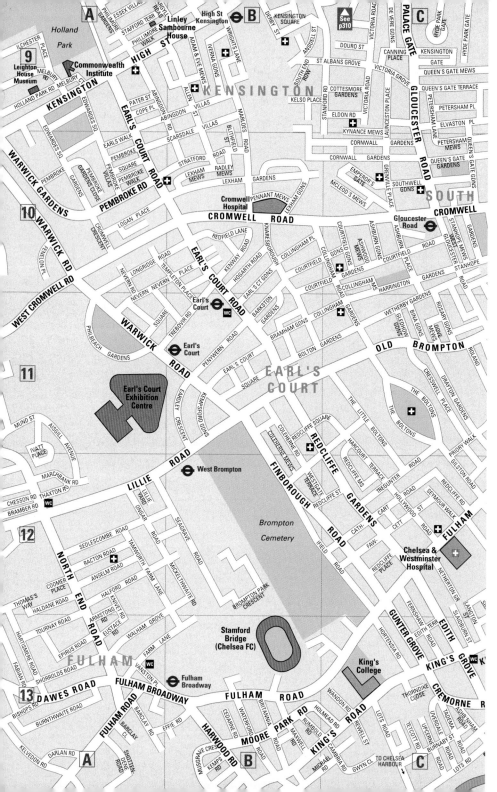

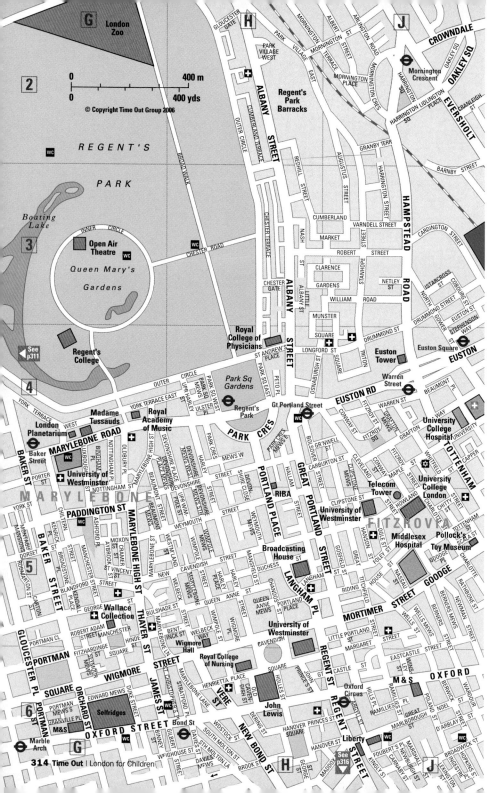

G London Zoo

2

0 _____ 400 m
0 _____ 400 yds

© Copyright Time Out Group 2006

WC

REGENT'S

PARK

Boating Lake

3

INNER CIRCLE
Open Air Theatre

Queen Mary's Gardens

BROAD WALK

CHESTER ROAD

WC

See p311

Regent's College

4

OUTER   CIRCLE

YORK   TERRACE

YORK TERRACE WEST

London Planetarium

Madame Tussauds

Royal Academy of Music

Baker Street

MARYLEBONE ROAD

WC

UXBRIDGE PL

University of Westminster

York St

NOTTINGHAM PL

NOTTINGHAM ST

BINGHAM PL

OLDBURY PL

PADDINGTON ST

DEVONSHIRE PL

DEVONSHIRE PLACE MEWS

DEVONSHIRE MEWS WEST

DEVONSHIRE STREET

BEAUMONT MEWS

BEAUMONT ST

UPR WIM. ST.

POLE ST

DEVONSHIRE

WEYMOUTH   STREET

WIMPOLE MEWS

WEYMOUTH MEWS

WIMPOLE   STREET

HARLEY   STREET

M A R Y L E B O N E

ASHFORD ST

MARYLEBONE HIGH ST

MOXON ST

AYBROOK ST

CRAMER

ST VINCENT ST

NEW

CAVENDISH

WELBECK   STREET

WC

BAKER   STREET

PORTER ST

KENRICK

CHILTERN

MONTAGU MANSIONS

DORSET

RODMARTON ST

BLANDFORD ST

MANCHESTER STREET

BROADSTONE PL

GEORGE STREET

5

SEYMOUR PL

BICKENHALL ST

GLENTWORTH ST

BROADSTONE PL

ST

ROBERT ADAM STREET

FITZHARDINGE ST

MANCHESTER SQUARE

Wallace Collection

HINDE ST

BULSTRODE ST

MARYLEBONE LN

THAYER   ST

BENT-INCK ST

Wigmore Hall

WELBECK WAY

MARYLEBONE

QUEEN ANNE

Wigmore Hall

QUEEN ANNE

WIGMORE PL

Royal College of Nursing

HENRIETTA PLACE

OLD CAVEN-DISH ST

PORTMAN CL

GLOUCESTER PL

PORTMAN

SQUARE

Selfridges

M&S

Marble Arch

6

MONTAGU PL

PORTMAN MEWS S

GRANVILLE PL

EDWARD MEWS

ORCHARD STREET

DUKE ST

JAMES   STREET

ST CHRISTOPHER'S PL

STRATFORD PL

VERE ST

HENRIETTA PLACE

OXFORD   STREET

Bond St

G

Time Out | London for Children

BINNEY ST

GILBERT ST

BALDERTON ST

DAVIES ST

SOUTH MOLTON ST

BLENHEIM

DAVIES MEWS

WFIGHOUSE ST

H

GLOUCESTER GATE

PARK VILLAGE EAST

PARK VILLAGE WEST

ALBANY   STREET

CUMBERLAND TERRACE

OUTER   CIRCLE

CHESTER TERRACE

CHESTER GATE

CHESTER ROAD

WC

St ANDREW'S PLACE

Royal College of Physicians

PARK SQ WEST

PARK SQ EAST

UPR HARLEY ST

ULSTER ST

Park Sq Gardens

Regent's Park

PETO PL

PARK   CRES

PARK CRES MEWS W

PARK CRES MEWS E

MEWS W

CARBURTON ST

DEVONSHIRE STREET

Redhill St

Augustus St

NASH

Park Village West

MORNINGTON TERRACE

GRANBY TERR

CUMBERLAND

MARKET

ROBERT

CLARENCE GARDENS

MUNSTER

SQUARE

WILLIAM   Road

OSNABURGH ST

LONGFORD ST

St

Little Albany St

CHESTER

ALBANY   STREET

MORNINGTON

ALBERT ST

ARLINGTON RD

MORNINGTON ST

MORNINGTON PLACE

MORNINGTON CRES

HARRINGTON SQ

HARRINGTON STREET

HARRINGTON SQ

VARNDELL STREET

STANHOPE

STREET

NETLEY ST

TRITON

Euston Tower

Warren Street

EUSTON RD

HAMPSTEAD   ROAD

LIDLINGTON PL

CROWNDALE

OAKLEY SQ

EVERSHOLT

CRANLEIGH

BARNBY STREET

CARDINGTON STREET

ISTABCROSS ST

COBOURG ST

NORTH GOWER STREET

DRUMMOND STREET

EUSTON ST

STEPHENSON WAY

Euston Square

EUSTON

Drummond St

MELTON ST

BEAUMONT PL

WAY

Gt Portland Street

WC

Great Portland Street

CONWAY ST

FITZROY ST

WARREN ST

GROSVENOR

FITZROY SQ

GRAFTON

MAPLE

BOLSOVER ST

GT TITCHFIELD ST

NWELL ST

CLEVELAND ST

CLIPSTONE MEWS

CLIPSTONE ST

University of Westminster

Telecom Tower

HANSON ST

GREAT   PORTLAND   STREET

PORTLAND PLACE

HALLAM   ST

RIBA

DEVON. ST

SHIRE CLOSE

WESTMORLAND

WESTMORELAND

MANSFIELD MEWS

CHANDOS ST

DUCHESS ST

Broadcasting House

LANGHAM PL

Langham St

PORTLAND PLACE

QUEEN ANNE MEWS

MARGARET   STREET

University of Westminster

CAVENDISH

SQUARE

John Lewis

HOLLES ST

PRINCE'S ST

GT CASTLE ST

MARKET

Oxford Circus

REGENT ST

ARGYLL ST

RAMILLIES ST

HANOVER   SQUARE

PRINCES ST

HANOVER ST

NEW   BOND   STREET

BROOK ST

MADDOX

GEORGE ST

See p316

H

University College Hospital

TOTTENHAM

HOWLAND

CHITTY ST

University College London

CHARLOTTE STREET

FITZROVIA

Pollock's Toy Museum

Middlesex Hospital

FOLEY ST

RIDING HOUSE

NASSAU ST

TITCHFIELD

GOODGE   STREET

GOODGE

MORTIMER   STREET

LITTLE PORTLAND ST

WELLS ST

BERNERS MEWS

NEWMAN

RATHBONE PL

EASTCASTLE   STREET

BERWICK

WARDOUR

BERNERS STREET

CHARLOTTE

WELLS MEWS

OXFORD

POLAND ST

NOEL

GREAT   MARLBOROUGH ST

D'ARBLAY

M&S

Liberty

FOUBERT'S PL

WC

KINGLY ST

CARNABY ST

LEXINGTON ST

BEAK ST

MARSHALL

GANTON ST

NEWBURGH ST

BROADWICK ST

HOPKINS ST

INDUSTRIAL

J

CROWNDALE

OAKLEY SQ

EVERSHOLT

314

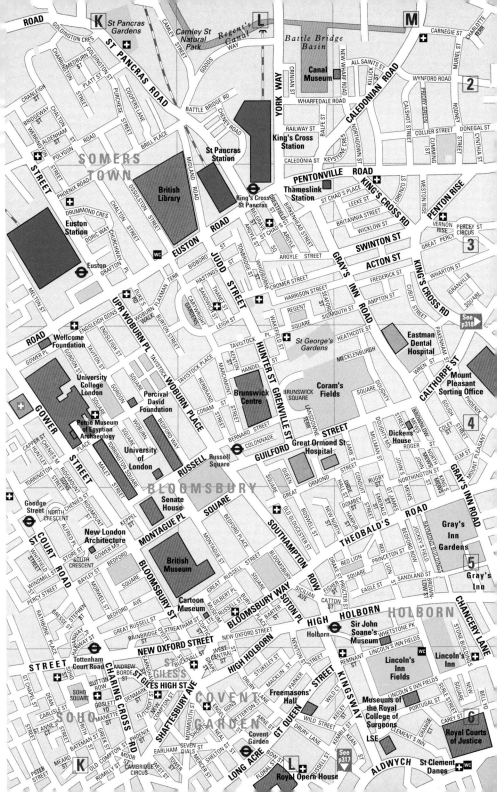

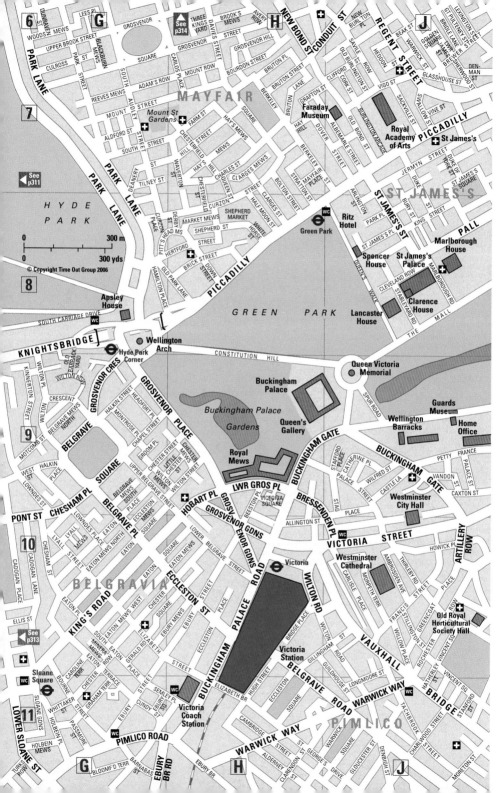

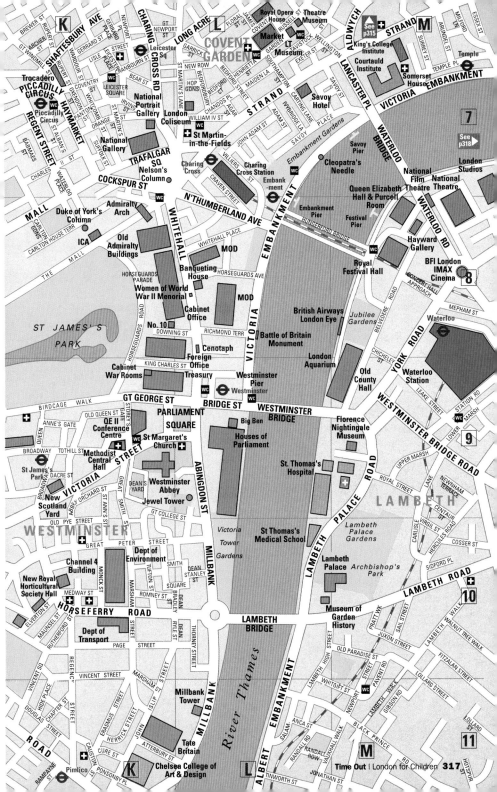

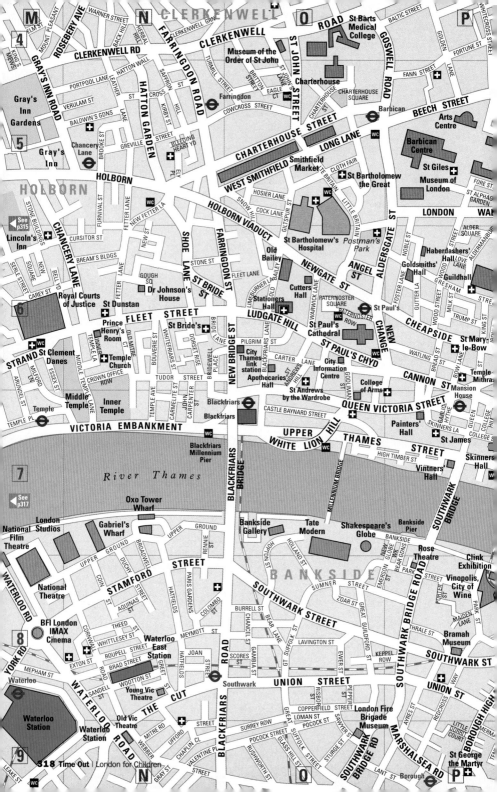

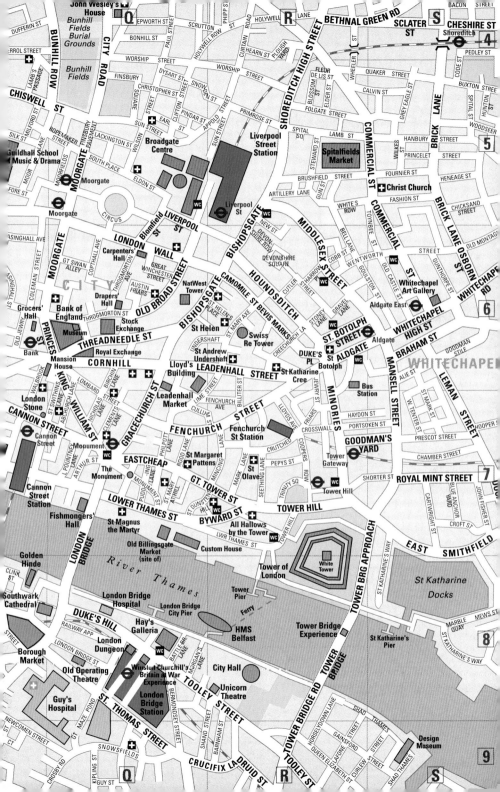

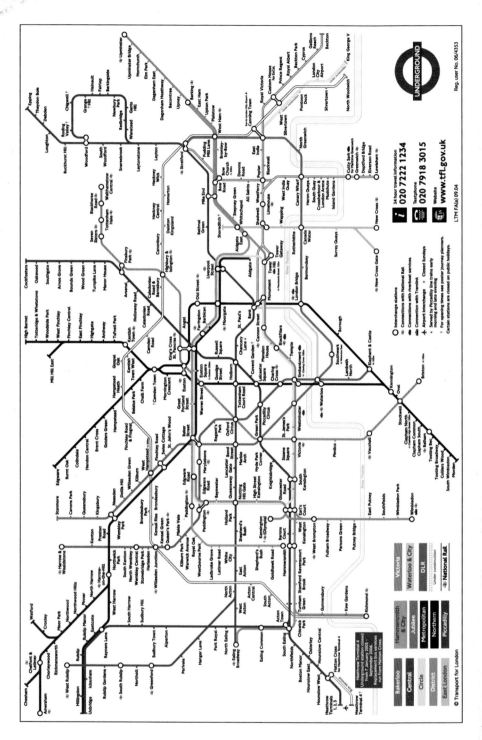